EUROPEAN MONOGRAPHS

Mandating Identity

Citizenship, Kinship Laws and Plural Nationality in the European Union

Enikő Horváth

ISBN 9789041126627

Published by:
Kluwer Law International
P.O. Box 316
2400 AH Alphen aan den Rijn
The Netherlands
E-mail: sales@kluwerlaw.com
Website: http://www.kluwerlaw.com

Sold and distributed in North, Central and South America by:
Aspen Publishers, Inc.
7201 Mc Kinney Circle
Frederick, MD 21704
United States of America

Sold and distributed in all other countries by:
Turpin Distribution Services Ltd.
Stratton Business Park
Pegasus Drive, Biggleswade
Bedfordshire SG18 8TQ
United Kingdom

This text is up to date as of 1 October 2007.

© 2008 Kluwer Law International BV, The Netherlands

All rights reserved. No part of this publication may be reproduced, stored in a retrieval system, or transmitted in any form or by any means, mechanical, photocopying, recording or otherwise, without prior written permission of the publishers.

Permission to use this content must be obtained from the copyright owner. Please apply to: Permissions Department, Wolters Kluwer Legal, 76 Ninth Avenue, 7th floor, New York, NY 10011, United States of America. E-mail: Permissions@kluwerlaw.com.

Továbbra is, szüleimnek

Table of Contents

Acknowledgments		xi
Introduction		xiii

Chapter I
Basic Concepts 1
A. Nationality 3
   1. The Functions of Nationality 6
      a. As the Individual's Link to International Law 6
      b. As an Expression of Attachment 7
      c. The Role of Path Dependency 10
   2. Evaluating Attachment to the National Community 12
      a. The Role of State Interests 12
      b. The Role of Individual Interests 15
   3. Nationality in International Law 18
      a. The Right to Nationality 18
      b. Diplomatic Protection and the Right to Admission ... 20
B. Citizenship 26
   1. The Functions of Citizenship 26
      a. The Emergence of Modern Citizenship 27
      b. Challenges to Modern Citizenship in the Name of Identity ... 29
   2. Citizenship as Practice 33
      a. Post-National Citizenship and its Discontents 35
      b. The Importance of National Frames of Reference ... 39
C. Individual and Collective Identities, as Concept and as Right 41
   1. The Construction (and Re-Construction) of Identity 41
   2. The Particularities of National Identity 46

	3.	Boundaries of Belonging	52
	4.	A Right to Cultural Identity	55
		a. Cultural Identity in International Law	57
		b. Cultural Identity Matters before the European Court of Human Rights	60

Chapter II
European Union Citizenship   67

A.	The Idea of European Identity	69
B.	The Role of Culture in the European Union	74
	1. Article 151 and its Effects	74
	2. 'Sensitive' National Interests before the European Court of Justice	78
	3. Cultural Policy in Practice	83
	a. Programmes under the Aegis of Article 151	83
	b. A More Than Complimentary Use of Cultural Policy	85
C.	European Citizenship, or the Question of Instrumentality	90
	1. Appearance and Appraisal of a New Legal Status	90
	a. A Self-Foundational Status?	92
	b. The Interaction of European Citizenship and Member State Nationality	95
	2. Fleshing Out the Status of European Union Citizen	98
	a. The Rights of Free Movement	99
	b. The Right to Equal Treatment	100
	c. The Citizens Directive	104
	d. Questioning Developments in the Area of Freedom, Security and Justice	107
	e. A Newly Symbolic Role for the Union Citizen	113
	f. The Missing Link of Cultural Rights	116
	3. Citizenship and Identity	121
	a. The Rise of a European Value Community?	122
	b. The Practical Realities of Identification with Europe	125
D.	Final Considerations	128
	a. At the Junction of European Citizenship, Culture and Identity	129
	b. Inherent Challenges to Current Developments in European Citizenship	132

Chapter III
Kinship Laws   137

A.	Emergence of a New Phenomenon	139
	1. Constitut(ionaliz)ing the Nation	139
	a. The Complexities of Promoting a 'Cultural' Nation	142
	b. Political Strategies of Trans-Sovereign Nationalism	145
	2. Kinship and Status Benefits	148

B.	The Hungarian Status Law	156
	1. Adoption and Content	157
	2. Reactions and Counter-Reactions	164
	a. The Venice Commission	168
	i. Pacta Sunt Servanda	169
	ii. Friendly Relations	169
	iii. Territorial Sovereignty	171
	a. International Practice and Bilateral Treaties on Granting Extra-Territorial Benefits	172
	b. Procedures Determining Eligibility	176
	iv. Discrimination	178
	b. Political Compromises	183
	i. The Revised Status Law	185
	ii. The After-Effects of the Law	187
C.	The Evolution of a Concept	191
	1. General Questions	192
	a. Interference	193
	b. Perceptions and Loyalties	195
	c. The Nation as Legal Entity	198
	2. The Possibilities of Resolution through Existing Statuses	204
	a. European Citizenship	204
	b. Plural Nationality	207

Chapter IV
Plural Nationality   213

A.	The Traditional Approach and Recent Legal Evolution	215
	1. Balancing State and Individual Interests	215
	2. Changing Views in Europe	218
	3. The Question of Immigration	224
	a. Expulsion Measures before the European Court of Human Rights	225
	b. The Importance of Individual Choice	228
	4. Managing the Side-Effects of Plural Nationality	232
	a. The Factor of European Citizenship	234
	b. Applicable Law and Respect for 'Cultural Identity'	236
	5. Revising Approaches in Domestic Legislation	239
B.	Transformation in Germany	242
	1. Legal Stasis and Initial Steps toward Reform	242
	2. New Provisions on Plural Nationality	250
	3. The Question of Integration	258
	a. Identifying the Elusive 'German'	259
	b. The *Spätaussiedler* v. Other Immigrants	261
	c. Further Revision of German Nationality Law	265
C.	Variations on the Theme of Adaptation	268
	1. Integration, Assimilation, Acculturation and Other Responses to Migration	268

	2.	An Individual Rights Approach to Nationality	274
	3.	The Consequences of Transnationalism	279
		a. Transnational and Local Ties	280
		b. Diaspora Policies	282
		c. The Political Issues Raised by Diaspora Ties	284
		d. The Legal Issues Raised by Diaspora Ties	286
D.	Tendencies Of Development		289
	1.	The Trend Toward Plural Nationality, with Strings Attached	290
	2.	Nationality as Confirmation of Identity	296

Conclusion — 301

References — 317
E. Primary Materials — 317
   1. Legal Instruments — 317
      a. International (Conventions, Treaties, Recommendations and Resolutions) — 317
         i. Bilateral Conventions and Treaties — 317
         ii. Multilateral Instruments — 319
      b. European Union — 322
      c. National — 325
   2. Proposals/Reports/Declarations/Drafts/Etc. — 331
      a. International and Non-Governmental Organizations — 331
      b. European Union — 334
      c. National — 337
   3. Commentaries/Speeches/Additional Sources — 339
   4. Press — 341
F. Cases — 342
   1. International Courts — 342
      a. European Court of Human Rights — 342
      b. Inter-American Court/Commission of Human Rights — 344
      c. International Court of Justice/Permanent Court of International Justice — 344
      d. Permanent Court of Arbitration — 344
      e. United Nations Human Rights Committee — 345
      f. Other Courts and Tribunals — 345
   2. European Court of Justice/Court of First Instance — 345
   3. National Courts — 348
      a. Courts and Tribunals in Germany — 348
      b. Courts and Tribunals in Hungary — 349
      c. Courts in the United States — 349
      d. Other Courts and Tribunals — 350
G. Literature — 350

Index — 383

Acknowledgments

This book owes its existence to the members of the examining panel for my Ph.D. at the European University Institute. It was their generous encouragement that prompted a hesitant author to take a chance on her doctoral thesis. Although the work has been updated, supplemented and slightly revised, it is essentially the same thesis presented before the panel in November 2006. I thank them wholeheartedly for their support.

I am also grateful to Kluwer Law International for shepherding this work through the publication process, and to my place of employment, which granted a new associate time to work on a personal project.

Finally, all the thank-yous offered in the thesis continue to apply, and especially those to my supervisor, who has continued to give his advice on any and all issues, not to mention on general musings completely unrelated to work.

Needless to say, I remain wholly responsible for all flaws, mistakes, possible mis-translations and other shortcomings.

On a personal note, I still owe a huge, huge (huge!) thank you to family and friends for their love, faith and support. They're proof that some things thankfully never change, no matter where in the world one happens to be.

Finalement, à C: pour toutes les 'jolies, jolies' choses ... merci.

New York, September 2007

Introduction

> *I'd root out bureaucracy once and for ever.*
> *I have no respect for formalities.*
> *May every paper go to the devil*
> *But for this ...*
> *This little thing, so dear to me ...*
> *Read it and envy me: I happen to be*
> *A citizen of the Soviet Union.*

Vladimir Mayakovsky, Poem of the Soviet Passport, 1929

Imagine a (fairly neurotic) personal ad: 'Short, blond, green-eyed, vegetarian, atheist, German-speaking engineer, descended from Hungarian and unknown Slavic ancestors, with Italian passport, looking for swing dance and in-line skating partner. London and environs only. Call Giulia at ...' While Giulia may feel that she belongs to a number of groups, cultural and otherwise, only one of her social identities (and the one a hopeful Romeo is least likely to note) will be of interest to the authorities in London – her Italian nationality. Her nationality will determine her status as a European citizen, with attendant rights, and allow her to forgo the visa and other requirements of the person in the line next to her at passport control. On entry, it will determine the conditions (and length) of her stay, as well as her treatment by authorities and the private sector. Should she decide to move back to Bolzano, Italian authorities will be interested in another element of her identity – specifically her identity as a German speaker and hence a member of a linguistic minority – but this interest will be conditioned on establishing, in the first instance, her Italian nationality. In turn, should she decide that her Hungarian and Slavic roots are important to her, she could rely on them in applying for cultural and other benefits in a number of Central European states. The success of her application would, however, depend in large part on the nationality she holds, as well as those her ancestors carried. Franck is thus right when he claims that 'the state has been the alpha and omega of personal identity'.[1]

It has assumed this role through a monopoly on establishing, maintaining and monitoring the legal personality of individuals. In essence, an individual does not (legally) exist until recognized by the state: registered at birth, endowed with characteristics like name and sex retained throughout her life, and given a status, as a national (and generally also as a citizen). The effect of legal personalities on individual identities – and vice versa – is a matter of some debate. To the extent that individual legal personality remains fixed, even as the individual changes – so that each of us has an abstract counterpart, with an ever-expanding set of characteristics monitored by the state – the former provides a sense of continuity; its very constancy renders it an inaccurate reflection of the real individual, however.

For most matters, approximate resemblance between the individual and her legal counterpart is enough – hence the sometimes unfamiliar photos of our (much) younger selves in our national identity cards. In certain cases, however, legal personality, including legal status, can interfere with some element of individual identity. Hence the determination of the European Court of Human Rights (hereinafter, ECtHR) that a refusal to change the gender noted on the birth registration of a post-operative transsexual by state authorities constitutes a violation of the right to respect for private life under Article 8 of the European Convention on Human Rights (hereinafter, ECHR).[2] As the Court noted:

> [T]he stress and alienation arising from a discordance between the position in society assumed by a post-operative transsexual and the status imposed by law which refuses to recognise the change of gender cannot, in the Court's view, be regarded as a minor inconvenience arising from a formality. A conflict between social reality and law arises which places the transsexual in an anomalous position, in which he or she may experience feelings of vulnerability, humiliation and anxiety.[3]

Such a conflict may arise in the context of any number of social signifiers, however, and helps account for the ever-expanding bases of demands for legal recognition in modern democratic states.[4]

While a number of elements of our legal personality – including gender, name or marital status – may be of import to us, only one is also regularly associated with a collective identity actively and overtly constructed, even manipulated, by the state: nationality. This dualistic nature of nationality – both legal status and source (or confirmation) of collective identity – renders it a singular component of individual identity, conferred unilaterally. It would thus be more precise, in terms of the temporal dimension, to say: the legal status comes first – when one is born, in most cases – and is complemented by the state's efforts to make it

---

1. Franck (1996), p. 360.
2. *Christine Goodwin v. the United Kingdom* (Grand Chamber), ECtHR (2002).
3. *Ibid.*, at para. 77.
4. Compare Taylor (1992), p. 25.

meaningful to the individual. This is not to say that other elements of identity may not find legal or administrative expression. The proliferation of communities and entities that require proof of both identity and membership seems endless (as anyone with a wallet knows). Even the state dispenses other statuses – permanent resident, for example. But none have the identity function of nationality. As Cassuto recognizes, 'nationality ... goes beyond the individual and refers to a community and hence to identification, to the feeling of belonging to that community'.[5] As such, state power to include or exclude – to grant nationality or refuse it – is simultaneously a matter of resource distribution (of rights and benefits) and of symbolism.

Proof for the continuing relevance of this identity, at least from the state's point of view, can be gleaned from a number of sources. Most obviously, this is the case for government statements in the context of naturalization, articulating that nationality should be either the end-result of integration or an element of it.[6] As the French Commission on Nationality, constituted in 1987 to examine all aspects of nationality before a major overhaul of the country's laws, noted:

> [T]he Code of Nationality is simultaneously conceived as *a tool of ... integration* and a *reference point for national identity*. It should organize, together, the right to integration of the foreigners concerned, acknowledging their individual choice, and, if the need arises, a capacity to verify the degree of this integration. National identity effectively expresses itself through nationality.[7]

This identity function is embedded primarily in domestic regulation of nationality, as one would expect, but can also be glimpsed in international norms, as courts examine the existence of attachment in decisions on the recognition of state attribution of nationality.

Yet, a number of writers describe the disappearance of nationality's identity function – from post-nationalists to theorists of citizenship.[8] Is it then really true

---

5. Cassuto (2001), p. 45. *See also* Comments of Council of Europe Deputy Secretary General Krüger on the occasion of the 1st European Conference on Nationality, Proceedings (1999). This has especially been true for state of emigration, such as Italy, Spain, Greece or Ireland in the past. *See* Pastore (2001), p. 110; Moreno Fuentes (2001), p. 124; Rozakis (2001), p. 173 and p. 178; and Symmons (2001), p. 275 *et seq.*
6. *See Fünftes Bericht über die Lage der Ausländer in der Bundesrepublik Deutschland* 53 (2002); remarks of United Kingdom Home Secretary David Blunkett on the occasion of the first citizenship ceremony performed in February 2004, in accordance with the requirements of the Nationality, Immigration and Asylum Act (2002). For the views of some of the participants, *see* <www.indymedia.org.uk/en/regions/london/2004/02/285998.html>. *See also* Bousakla (2004).
7. '*Le Code de la Nationalité est conçu à la fois comme* un instrument d[']intégration ... *et* un point de référence pour l'identité nationale. *Il doit organizer, ensemble, le droit à l'intégration des étrangers concernés, la prise en compte de leur choix individuel et une capacité à verifier, le cas échéant, le degré de cette intégration. L'identité nationale trouve en effet à s'exprimer à travers la nationalité*' Rapport Long, Tome II (1988), p. 87 (emphasis in original). *See also* pp. 25–26 and p. 28. *All translations in the text are by the author, unless otherwise noted.*
8. *See* discussion at Sec. I.B.

that 'passports ... tell us little about loyalties or habitus, but they tell us a great deal about the relative likelihood of their holders being permitted to seek jobs in Milan or Copenhagen', and, as such, are 'counterfeit in the sense that they are less and less attestations of citizenship, let alone loyalty to a protective nation state?'[9] Individuals certainly seem to attribute continuing relevance to their nationality. Specifically – and as would be expected from theories of social psychology – individuals socialized into a national identity do so. This does not stop them (why should it?) from acquiring other nationalities for reasons of practicality, of course; but many immigrants are reluctant to give up their original nationality, which is viewed as a sign of belonging to the community.[10] In a comparable manner, numerous national minorities in East-Central and Eastern Europe have demanded the nationality of their kin-state, as a means to *nemzetegyesítés*.[11] In their case, nationality serves as *de facto* recognition of belonging to a larger cultural (in this case national) community.

Concurrent with increased interest in such questions of identity, national and international norms of nationality have been undergoing a series of transformations; a notable development, given the emergence of the latter, for the most part, in the 19th century and their relative stagnation from the 1950s onwards. (Only the entrance of human rights considerations brought some development). On the national level, more activity could be observed during this period, mainly in the form of facilitated access to nationality through *jus domicilii*, but no large-scale change. The 1990s, however, brought a sudden burst of activity – European citizenship, growing acceptance of plural nationality and, finally, kinship laws – with the potential for upheaval.

Despite their varied geneses, then, each development challenges existing practice (and norms believed to be accepted) in matters of nationality, as well as (on a more conceptual level) the rights/duties and identity functions of the concept. The appearance of European citizenship in 1992 and its development since that time fundamentally re-fashions approaches to a status that grants rights in the state of nationality only, while simultaneously attempting to mobilize the power of national identity (if not its form) on a supra-national level. The rise of plural nationality, on the other hand, questions the assumption of a necessary link to one state only, and leaves states scrambling to regulate the contours of multiple membership not only as a legal matter but, in determined efforts at management of

---

9. Anderson (1994), p. 323.
10. '[R]espondents ... mentioned in the interviews that they were afraid that the acquisition of Dutch nationality would go at the cost of contacts within the [sic] own community'. Netherlands (van den Bedem, 1993), pp. 4–5. This Summary provides a good overview of other considerations for and against naturalization (including limited knowledge of its advantages, pragmatic concerns and integration requirements). *Also see ibid.* for a discussion of motives for naturalization in the Dutch context.
11. 'Union or unification of the nation'. From *Délvidéki Levél Gyurcsány Ferenchez* (Letter from Vojvodina to [the Hungarian Prime Minister]).

Introduction xvii

a perceived threat to societal security,[12] as one of identity. Finally, kinship laws and especially the subset of status laws-break with the idea that individuals can be linked to a state only through the status of nationality; at the same time, such laws introduce the nation as an entity with a claim to recognition in a manner not heretofore considered.

In contrast to earlier periods of state self-reflection on national identity (or navel-gazing, if you will), individuals are consciously considering whether to play along. If individuals have always picked and chosen from among the groups around them those that would constitute elements of their social identity, they are doing so today in the context of 'a world in which self-determination evolves from a plural to a singular entitlement, from a right of peoples to that of *persons*'.[13] In fact, if individuals have been moulded in the past to be Frenchmen, rather than peasants[14] (or more likely, subjects of King XYZ), they are now the ones demanding, from states, recognition of their identity, as composed, in light of a claimed right to that identity. This development is clearest in the case of the growing acceptance of (the former 'evil' of) plural nationality; but is also present in the appearance (and proliferation) of kinship laws. In the case of European citizenship, the turned tables are harder to spot, but are nonetheless present in individuals' measured reactions to Commission-developed definitions of what it means to be 'European'.

Still, we have not quite arrived at the point of treating nationality, especially a particular nationality, as a personal right. This would mean a complete inversion of the idea of nationality, as something state-focused, into either an active implementation of personal identity ('I feel Brazilian and should accordingly have that nationality') or a matter of convenience ('A United States passport allows me to travel without visa restrictions, so I should hold it'). While some may welcome such rights-based development, it is hard to imagine how a system of this kind would function in practice – not only for reasons of administrative (in)convenience, but also because of conflicting approaches to what nationality signifies. How would those who consider nationality an implementation of identity view those who regard it as a matter of convenience, for example? In addition, to the extent that nationality is not only a link to a state, but also (hopefully, from the point of view of the state) to a group with a given collective identity with which one shares a sense of belonging, any transformation of nationality is also mediated by developments in citizenship.

The gradual transformation (or erosion) of the ideal of national citizenship, as citizenship rights are extended to non-nationals, allows for the appearance of community membership on other bases. One possibility is a community of those residing in the territory of a given state. In this approach, it is geographical proximity and the traditional principle of state sovereignty within its territory that provide the basis for membership. Another possibility, however, is the radiation of diaspora identities – centred either on the state that institutionalizes a particular

---

12. *See* Theiler (2003).
13. Franck (1996), p. 359.
14. Weber (1976).

collective identity or on the territory inhabited by a nation, or possibly not focused on any geographical place. In this view, a community is constituted by individuals with shared (linguistic, national, religious or other) cultural identities wherever they may find themselves. Still another possibility is the cosmopolitan or postnational model, whereby individuals belong to communities of norms and beliefs (without a necessarily shared national identity). Though this form of community is also not perforce linked to a territorially delimited state, it does rely on some entity to organize the development and maintenance of the norms that form the basis of commonality.

How these developments may be accommodated by changes in laws of membership remains to be seen. The three processes discussed in this book are, in any case, steps toward reconciling new forms of membership with the framework of nationality, with greater or lesser efficacy. Policies combining the acceptance of plural nationality with more stringent requirements of integration are an example of the territorial approach. Kinship laws (and diaspora programmes) are instances of overt reliance on shared cultural identity; while European citizenship is, at least officially, an attempt to mobilize of shared norms and beliefs across state boundaries.

As even this brief introduction to our subject has illustrated, any discussion of particular legal statuses with claims to anchoring cultural identities requires taking into account a multiplicity of factors (and actors). In the name of clarity, then, we must set out the assumptions on which this work proceeds. In the first place, it is assumed that an examination of the legal developments presented here through the prism of as amorphous a concept as 'cultural identity' is, in fact, worth the effort. (Certainly, some may find that it is too imprecise to form the basis for any comparison.) This is not to say that other approaches are not valid or useful; this same project could have been undertaken from the starting point of resource distribution, for example. Nor is it to say that the legal statuses discussed here are all 'about' culture. Rather, we accept that understandings of cultural identity both inform and are influenced by legal norms of membership, and attempt to understand this dynamic in three particular instances. In a related point, it is also considered that legal developments in functionally dissimilar legal systems are comparable. In particular, it is assumed that the emergence of European citizenship in a *sui generis* entity like the European Union is comparable to a legal development in the regulation of membership in (member) states, despite the divergent foundations of the legal orders in which the they have originated.

Third, we assume that nationality cannot be understood purely as a legal phenomenon. Any proper discussion of the concept must also take into account the manner in which it fulfils its secondary role of circumscribing the national community, too. (To understand the perceived need for improvement or the consequences of particular amendments, for example, we must look not just at the content of the laws in question, but also at how these laws are embedded in particular political and social frameworks.) Legal approaches don't offer sufficient tools for such a discussion; the disciplines of sociology, social psychology and political theory, on the other hand, do. To give but one example, law doesn't even know what to make of the concept of 'cultural identity', fundamental to our discussion. For this reason, our discussion of nationality is necessarily multi-disciplinary.

A fourth assumption underlying this work is that 'nationality' and 'citizenship' do not signify the same legal status or legal relationship. Although the distinction made here is often blurred both in theory and legislation, it remains a crucial one. In short, the two serve different functions: nationality has heretofore been the sole individual-state link recognized for the purposes of international law. It has traditionally been the primary legal status for both rights purposes – as the basis for claims of diplomatic protection, for example – and for that of identity. In the domestic realm, nationality has served as a gateway to citizenship rights; the ensemble of these rights, in turn, has been termed 'citizenship'. The rights and identity functions of citizenship have thus traditionally functioned in the domestic realm only. Granted, the two statuses were fused to create the predominant (ideal) form of legal membership in the 20th century – national citizenship – but this fusion is neither necessary nor absolute.

Finally, this work does not consider that facile conclusions can be drawn regarding the legal developments presented. While the secondary effects alluded to above do allow us to identify certain consequences for regional and general international law then, the very novelty and even controversiality of the statuses, not to mention the considerable role of unforeseeable political and sociological processes in questions of legal membership, mean that any claim to prediction would amount to mere guesswork.

Instead, this work has four modest aims. In the first place, it aims to draw attention to a phenomenon: to show how states and entities (like the EU) in Europe have in recent years devised legal statuses supplementary to that of nationality to anchor cultural identities. We propose that three processes of legal evolution – European citizenship, kinship laws and the acceptance of plural nationality – may be identified, each aiming to harness and manipulate a particular type of cultural identity. It is hoped that our discussion will clarify the manner in which the corresponding legal statuses have emerged since the early 1990s.

Our second aim is to compare the three processes. It is proposed that these developments, each in its own way, deconstruct the unified individual-state link created by an ideal national citizenship and reconstruct it on the basis of new (or re-tooled) statuses, in the process revealing the variety of ways in which the union of nationality and citizenship can come undone. It is also suggested that these three sites of contention undermine the identity and rights functions of both nationality and citizenship; and present new scenarios in the ongoing contest between personal and territorial conceptions of community.

Our third aim is to point out the ways in which the three processes of evolution, each with different roots, have influenced one another, in both public discussion and legal effects. To the extent the European Union can be considered a singular legal space, with multiple levels of criss-crossing legal orders, each separate legal development presented here interacts with the others, intensifying or constricting their respective endemic effects.

Our final aim is to expose the tensions inherent in any linkage of cultural identity and legal status and, more generally, of identity-formation and maintenance and law. Identity matters necessarily constitute a unique challenge to a discipline as sluggish as law, since the very stability that lends any legal categorization force may also prevent it from reflecting ongoing evolution. In the face of individual demands for respect of varied identities, the developments presented here demonstrate the challenges and advantages of particular legal responses.

In proceeding toward our goal, each topical chapter hopes to demonstrate the following: In the first place, it seeks to show how each process of legal evolution has unfolded in a given context, providing descriptions of both background and legal content. Second, it seeks to explain why each development has occurred in the manner that it has, with special emphasis on non-legal approaches. Third, it seeks to present both the legal and political or sociological issues raised by the particular development, where necessary through comparison with the other developments.

Our examination begins in the customary manner, with the status quo. In the chapter titled 'Basic Concepts', the concepts of 'nationality' and 'citizenship' are distinguished, their meanings, background and relationship discussed, and their traditional place in international and domestic law presented. Our primary focus here is on legal materials and commentary, though some references are also made to political theory. Given that all three of our examined processes are unfolding in the (claimed) name of 'identity', specifically individual and collective cultural identity, this is the final concept to be examined, mainly from the perspective of social psychology, but with due consideration for its place in international law.

The second chapter, on 'European Union Citizenship', presents our first case study. We begin with a brief historical survey of the emergence of scattered identity policies – and the idea of a 'European identity' – before 1992. After a look at legal and policy developments in the area of identity/culture before, and especially since, the Maastricht Treaty, the seemingly distinct idea of European citizenship – as legal status and as the foundation for an emerging European identity – will be presented. The existing, practical link between identity/culture and citizenship in recent policy, even if separate in official discourse, will then be set out, along with some considerations for future development.

In the third chapter, on 'Kinship Laws', legislation targeted at non-nationals with claimed kinship (usually linguistic, ethnic or broad cultural) ties to a given state are examined. Various kinds of kinship legislation, including their scope and the benefits they confer both inside and outside the territory of the legislating state, will be discussed before the Hungarian status law of 2001 – one of the most controversial – is delineated in greater detail. The history of this law, its content, international and domestic reactions, and subsequent amendments will be presented in turn. Finally, the significance of this and other similar laws will be considered, in light of their reliance on a novel legal role for the nation and a new understanding of minority protection.

The fourth chapter, on 'Plural Nationality', starts with a presentation of the traditionally hostile state approach to multiple membership – as well as its neutral treatment in international law – before moving on to recent claims for acceptance. The context of the wholesale transformation of nationality regulation in Germany in the late 1990s will then serve as an example of possible reaction to such claims, as well as of the manner in which laws on various kinds of membership can interact in public discourse to re-frame a common approach to national identity. A discussion of the general considerations of membership and belonging that underlie any public discourse on this issue follows. The chapter finishes with a look at the tendencies of development in Europe.

The final chapter of this work brings together the three developments and presents their commonalities. As part of this discussion, the general interaction of law and identity is considered. It is argued that the boundary-maintenance necessary to all groups is externalized – and legalized – in ever more diverse ways by states in Europe. The diffusion of claims for recognition across state borders and the parallel process of entrenching national identities, in turn, threaten to undo the established, albeit tenuous balance between community belonging (as social concept) and membership (as officially recognized by legal status). More generally, the proliferation of legal statuses with claims to expressing or re-enforcing identity encompasses new conceptions of the interaction between individual and group, national and state, and domestic (or regional) and general international law, presented in turn.

Chapter I
Basic Concepts

> *Wandelt sich rasch auch die Welt*
> *wie Wolkengestalten,*
> *alles Vollendete fällt*
> *heim zum Uralten.*
>
> R.M. Rilke, XIX Sonett, 1922

Our first chapter serves as a building block for the legal developments presented in the following three, as we identify and characterize the basic concepts necessary for discussion. Our aim in this chapter is accordingly not only to present the concepts concerned in their full socio-legal context, but also to foreshadow some of the themes in our work going forward. In the first place, we distinguish between the concepts of 'nationality' and 'citizenship', discussing their meanings and historical background and presenting their traditional place in international and domestic law. Our primary focus here is on legal materials and commentary, though some references are also made to political philosophy.

In short, 'nationality' is considered the principal legal status of individuals for the purposes of international law. As such, it is primarily a means to determine membership in a state-centred community. However, recognized membership in a particular state begets not only legal privileges – like diplomatic protection – but also assumptions of some form of attachment to that state. These two functions – termed the 'rights' and 'identity' function, respectively – are presented in some detail in the first part of our discussion. In addition, the role of path dependency in determining access to nationality is also analysed. The second part of our discussion presents the many factors involved in any assessment of nationality's 'identity' function. In particular, the role of state and individual interests in evaluating attachment to the national community is examined. Our presentation of this legal status ends with a detailed exploration of its 'rights' function, particularly in light of recent developments in international law.

'Citizenship', our second basic concept, determines the content of the bond between state and individual for domestic purposes by circumscribing the scope and quality of rights/duties within a given territory. The development of this concept – from a social status to a legal one – with corresponding evolution in its 'rights' function is presented in the first part of our discussion, as is the eventual interconnection of its 'identity' function with that of nationality. It will be argued that although the two concepts intertwine for the purpose of the ideal of 'national citizenship', they are increasingly disaggregated in practice, in part as a response to new claims made in the name of cultural identity. The second part of our discussion takes a distinctly non-legal approach, preferring to rely on political theory in presenting conceptions of 'citizenship' as a practice. In particular, the most far-reaching reworking of the concept – post-national citizenship – is presented with all its consequences for the 'rights' and 'identity' functions of citizenship, while its claim regarding the declining importance of the state is evaluated.

Given that all three of our examined processes are unfolding in the (claimed) name of identity – and in a general context of identity politics[1] – the notion of 'identity', specifically individual and collective 'cultural identity', is the final concept to be examined, mainly from the perspective of social psychology, but with due consideration for its place in international law. The first part of our discussion focuses on social identity theory, particularly its insight into the role of comparison and categorization in identity/formation and maintenance. The second part of our discussion applies what we have learned about processes of identity formation and maintenance to state-focused (i.e., national) groups and argues that the traditional theoretical distinction between 'civic' and 'ethnic' nations disregards the actual identity processes involved. It is suggested that national identity of all kinds is really a cultural identity like any other. The third part of our discussion draws attention to another conflict, that between the fixed categories of membership established by states – e.g., through nationality – and the sociological reality of shifting boundaries in all cultural identities, including national ones. In particular, it is argued that the sociological process of 'belonging' is effectively irreconcilable with the categories of 'membership' established by states. A short look at ongoing attempts to account for 'cultural identity' in international and regional instruments and in the case-law of the E.Ct.H.R. serves to underline the nature of the problem.

Having presented and characterized our use of the terms – 'nationality', 'citizenship' and 'cultural identity', as well as 'membership' and 'belonging' – central to our discussion, we then proceed to the first of our legal developments attempting to refashion state-centred membership with variations on the theme of identity.

---

1. As one author has noted, in present-day discussions the 'issue is [often] not who should be included within an already recognised identity; it is rather which identities or descriptions or categories should receive recognition [in the first place]'. In this sense, identity politics frames discourse in a manner that is qualitatively different from earlier demands for recognition, which generally involved inclusion in existing categories. Jones, at 132 (2006).

A. NATIONALITY

The concept of 'nationality' is chameleon-like, changing meaning in the context of discipline, language and legal system. The terminological disarray is especially prevalent in the social sciences and law, where 'nationality' may refer to kinship ties,[2] to ethnic origin,[3] to a collective group with lesser rights to self-determination than a nation[4] or to citizenship.[5] This last usage has become increasingly widespread in legal parlance, as certain academic pieces (and even laws) do not differentiate between the individual's legal status in the domestic and international contexts, using the terms for each interchangeably.[6] Hence, clarification is in order. For our purposes, nationality denotes an ongoing legal tie between a natural person and a state – encompassing state control and protection – recognized by the international community. It is thus primarily a legal status (e.g., when used as a link to international law), but also an ongoing legal relationship (e.g., when establishing jurisdiction).[7] Nationality is thus 'contrasted with occasional particular exercises of competence under varying principles of jurisdiction',[8] such as long-arm statutes in the United States.

The concept must also be clearly distinguished from that of citizenship, discussed below. The tendency to use 'citizenship' and 'nationality' interchangeably in English is widespread and, in states where the two groups are identical, not technically wrong, however, incongruous.[9] But other languages, like German, make a clear distinction even in every-day usage: '*Staatsangehörigkeit*' (nationality) and '*Staatsbürgerschaft*' (citizenship) thus function in different contexts. Even the existence of only one commonly-used word, such as *állampolgárság* (in Hungarian) or *cittadinanza* (in Italian), does not mean that the individual's

---

2. See, inter alia, Linke (2004), p. 206 Balibar (1991), p. 96.
3. See entries on 'Nationality' and 'Passports' in Encyclopedia of Soviet Law (Feldbrugge et al,. eds, 2nd ed. 1985).
4. See the discussion of Arts 2 and 11 of the 1978 Spanish Constitution in Conversi (2002), p. 227 et seq.
5. See, e.g., Neff (1998), p. 105; Heater (1999), p. 80; Hansen and Weil (2001), p. 1; and Weissbrodt and Collins (2006), n. 4, p. 246.
6. See Council of Europe, Report Giving an Opinion on the Draft European Convention on Nationality (1997), paras 40–42; Council of Europe, Parliamentary Recommendation 1410 on Links between Europeans living abroad and their countries of origin (1999). See also discussion in Kondo (2001), pp. 2–3 for the distinctions made (and not made) in domestic laws, as well as by a significant portion of the authors discussed here.
7. The ongoing discussion of whether nationality constitutes a status or a relationship – I believe it constitutes both, depending on context – will not be touched on here. See Grawert (1973), pp. 230–231 for an overview; see also Panzera (1984), p. 26 et seq.
8. McDougal, Lasswell and Chen (1974), p. 901.
9. Sometimes we do encounter problems with such usage, however. For example, the US Department of State states on its web-site that '[t]he concept of dual nationality means that a person is a citizen of two countries at the same time'. Any number of US nationals who also hold the nationality of certain Latin American states – and who have no voting rights in these states while resident in the US – could inform the State Department that this is not quite the case.

domestic and international legal status, expressed respectively through 'citizenship' and 'nationality' in English, cannot be differentiated, however, or that the de-coupling of citizenship rights and nationality has not occurred as elsewhere.

Despite the direct link between the two concepts – since today, the group of 'nationals' and that of 'citizens' is generally identical – they do not mean the same thing. The former is simply a mechanism devised by the international community to assign individuals to given states, or, to put it more cynically, a 'global protection racket run by states'.[10] It has little to do with rights accorded directly to individuals, though on an international level, individuals do gain advantages, like diplomatic protection. Citizenship, on the other hand, is determined by the scope and quality of the rights it entails within a given territory. Thus, while 'nationality' is used to define the bond between an individual and a state on the international level, 'citizenship' determines the internal content of that bond.[11] Or, to paraphrase Chief Justice Warren (himself echoing Hannah Arendt),[12] if nationality is indeed the 'right to have rights',[13] then citizenship establishes what those rights encompass within the state.

This distinction is important to make since the two needn't necessarily be co-extensive. Some states continue to differentiate among nationals in the citizenship rights accorded them,[14] while others have strengthened explicit distinctions between nationality and citizenship,[15] often in the context of plural membership.[16]

---

10. Blackman (1998), pp. 1150–1151.
11. *See* Gargas (1928), p. 6.
12. *See* Arendt (1979) [1951], p. 226.
13. *Perez v. Brownell*, US (1958), p. 64.
14. *See*, in the context of the United States, 7 F.A.M. 1111 (Basic Terms and Distinctions). For example, a US national of Puerto Rico has no right to vote in national elections as long as she remains resident on the island and pays no federal income tax. For the purposes of international law, however, she is no different from any other US national. *See* Declet (2001), p. 19, n. 1

    For a historical example, *see* the British Commonwealth Immigrants Act (1962), which severed the link between nationality and citizenship. Only those whose passports were issued under London's authority (i.e., citizens of the United Kingdom and its colonies) were entitled to entry into the UK, though they possessed the civic rights of citizenship.

    This authority-based regulation was abolished with the British Nationality Act (1981), when British citizenship was introduced. The new regulation, with two additional kinds of citizenship (British overseas citizenship [BOC] and British dependent territories citizenship) – for a total of three – created a new legal anomaly, however. BOCs were British citizens (of some sort), but could be considered stateless for the purposes of international law if the state of residence refused its nationality. *See* discussion in Hansen (2001), p. 78 *et seq.*
15. *See, inter alia*, Secs I (*Nacionalidad*) and II (*Ciudadania*) of Title III of the Constitution of the Dominican Republic (2002); Chaps II (*De los Mexicanos*) and IV (*De los Ciudadanos Mexicanos*) of Title I of the Constitution of the United Mexican States (1917, as amended).
16. Especially in the context of migration, then, the 'distinction between nationality and citizenship in Mexico has important implications for patrimonial and job-related rights. The basic assumption behind it is that nationality is part of a heritage an individual cannot erase even if he or she wants to. In this sense it is like the parents one had, the colour of one's skin, language first spoken, religion, etc. Citizenship, in contrast, derives from fundamental rights of any individual

Still others, particularly in Europe, have extended certain citizenship rights to non-nationals, in a reversal of the traditional dichotomy.[17] In light of the historic plurality of legal statuses – besides 'citizen', 'national' and 'alien', 'subject', *indigénat*, *ressortissant*, and *sociétaire d'Etat*, to name but a few – with specific rights and duties in a particular time and place, the monopoly of the nationality/citizenship duo in recent decades is a curious anomaly. The adage that 'every citizen is a national, but not every national is a citizen'[18] is thus increasingly a (telling) leftover of an earlier era.

The muddle around the two concepts has also led some theorists to argue that nationality is an empty concept, a 'formal frame' without any legal consequences.[19] Others, like Weis, argue that nationality is, by its very nature, a 'relationship ... conferring mutual rights and duties'.[20] While the former view is simply not true – a number of rights stem directly from nationality even if they are not directly granted to individuals[21] – the latter is also problematic, since it blurs the distinction between nationality and citizenship already discussed. This distinction is crucial, however, not only in the terminological sense, but also because international law has traditionally considered differences in the substance of citizenship rights irrelevant.[22] In other words, the fact that African-Americans were not considered citizens for domestic-law purposes in the wake of the United States Supreme Court's decision in *Dred Scott*,[23] did not make them any less nationals of the United States for the purposes of international law.[24] At the

---

to wilfully select one's allegiance to a nation and government in association to the residence one wants to have on a permanent basis'. Bustamante *et al.* (1998), pp. 697–698. *See also* discussion of the nationality and citizenship reforms in Mexico, p. 154 and p. 247 *et seq.*, below.

17. The most famous example is perhaps that introduced by the Convention of Brasilia (1971) between Portugal and Brazil. On the basis of this agreement, all nationals of one state residing in the other have equal civic rights with the nationals of the host state (but no right to permanent residence), while their equivalent rights in the country of origin are temporarily suspended.
18. Weis (1979, 2nd ed.), pp. 5–6.
19. *See* Koessler (1946), p. 70.
20. Weis (1979), p. 29 Compare discussion in the International Law Commission's (hereinafter, ILC) Survey of the Problem of Multiple Nationality (1954), p. 58–59. *See also* Feldblum (1999), p. 1 and von Gierke (1961) [1883], p. 36 *et seq.*, but *see* Makarov (1962, 2nd ed.), p. 28.
21. *See* discussion at Sec. I.A.3.
22. *See* Oppenheim's International Law (1992, 9th ed.), p. 850. That said, the creation of a class of nationals deprived of certain rights considered basic human rights would not be acceptable under international law. Thus, the revocation of all political and civil rights of Jewish nationals by Nazi Germany – including, in 1941, their nationality, if resident abroad – was never recognized by the international community.
23. *Dred Scott v. Sandford*, US (1857).
24. The discrimination between male and female citizens in most states was, on the other hand, mirrored in the differing regimes on attribution and withdrawal of nationality, as well as the transmission of nationality under domestic laws until the recent past, despite a number of international instruments declaring sex-discrimination unacceptable. *See, inter alia*, Arts 2 and 7 of the Universal Declaration of Human Rights (hereinafter, UDHR) (1948); Art. 26 of the UN International Covenant on Civil and Political Rights (hereinafter, ICCPR) (1966); ECHR Art. 14; Art. 1 of the OAS (Montevideo) Convention on the Nationality of Women (1933); Arts 1–3 of the UN Convention on the Nationality of Married Women (1957); Art. 5

same time, nationality has been considered something equal on the international plane, regardless of the granting state,[25] and has resulted in the same nationality-linked privileges (such as diplomatic protection) under international law. (That the quality of those rights may have differed by nationality was again not of international concern.)

1. THE FUNCTIONS OF NATIONALITY

a. **As the Individual's Link to International Law**

But what of the functions of nationality? What does it serve to do, exactly? In the first place, nationality has served as the individual's link to international law, since approximately the mid-19th century.[26] One observer has even gone so far as to state that 'without legal allegiance (or without nationality, if one prefers), this person isn't [a person], since she lacks legal personality. She doesn't exist and can't exist legally but through her attachment to a law, whether state legislation or international law'.[27] This link was and remains necessary since classical writers' understanding of the individual as the ultimate subject of all law,[28] including international, has been superseded by the emergence of the state as the primary actor of the international system. Accordingly, 'private persons may derive their international rights only by means of an agreement of states endowing individuals with their own limited international personality'.[29] International agreements can only be concluded by states to the benefit of a particular, legally delimited group of individuals, however: its nationals. In the Westphalian system, then, the individual has access to international law only through the intermediary of nationality.

---

of the Declaration on the Elimination of Discrimination Against Women (1967); and Art. 9 of the Convention on the Elimination of All Forms of Discrimination against Women (1979).

Thus, women were (and in some states continue to be) treated as not only lesser citizens, but also lesser nationals. *See* International Law Association (2000); and Knop and Chinkin (2001). For one example of reform, *see* Papi (2005). For a general critique of international law from a feminist perspective, *see* Charlesworth and Chinkin (2000).

25. I.e., under international law, a French and Chilean national are equal, just as their states are. This complies with the principle of a system of equal sovereign states as the foundation for the Westphalian international system. *See also* Art. 2(1) of the UN Charter (1945).
26. Although the concept of 'nationality' entered domestic legal systems earlier, it did not have a role to play in private international law until the mid-1800s. *See* discussion in Verwilghen (1999), p. 63–64.
27. '[S]ans allégeance juridique (ou si l'on préfère, sans nationalité), cette personne n'en est pas une, puisqu'elle est dépourvue de personnalité juridique. Elle n'existe et ne peut juridiquement exister que par son rattachement à un droit, soit une législation étatique, soit le droit international', *ibid.*, p. 39.
28. *See* discussion of works by Grotius, Pufendorf, Hobbes and Vattel in St. Korowicz (1956), p. 534 *et seq.* and Donner (1983), p. 40.
29. St. Korowicz, (1956), *ibid.*, p. 536.

Basic Concepts

Oppenheim's stated this most clearly when it characterized nationality as 'the principal link between individuals and the benefits of the Law of Nations'.[30]

This link was, until very recently, limited to state claims on behalf of the individual, generally through diplomatic protection, or to particular international agreements. While the individual now has standing to bring claims before certain international and regional tribunals on her own behalf – exactly on the basis of such agreements[31] – and despite the emergence of individual (criminal) liability, natural persons still cannot be said to have a complete, independent legal personality for international law purposes,[32] nor can the rights granted to individuals on the basis of particular treaties be considered inherent to them.

International instruments in the second half of the 20th century have maintained the traditional approach by relying on the relationship between individual and state in conferring of rights. The arrival of international (and regional) human rights law in the mid-20th century has thus not done away with the state as primary actor. There has been some development, however, in that individuals 'under the jurisdiction' of a given state or, in certain cases, only nationals, have gained internationally recognized (human) rights against states.[33] In fact, under the present system – whereby a given state guarantees individuals' rights stemming both from domestic and international law – the distinction between citizenship rights and fundamental political, social or economic rights as defined in international instruments has become increasingly blurry.[34] That said, the extension by certain states of political and social rights, once granted only to nationals, to long-term residents has resulted primarily from changes in domestic or supra-national, not international, law.[35]

b. As an Expression of Attachment

The second role of nationality, after that of a link to international law, is more intangible: the expression of attachment between an individual and a specific

---

30. Oppenheim's International Law (1992, 9th ed.), p. 857. For more recent commentary along the same lines, see Blackman (1998), p. 1150.
31. See e.g., Optional Protocol to the ICCPR (which entered into force in 1976); ECHR Art. 34; Art. 44 of the American Convention on Human Rights (hereinafter, ACHR) (1969), but see Art. 61 of the latter Convention.
32. Orakhelashvili (2001); Hofmann (1998), p. 11–12. See also Oppenheim's International Law (1992, 9th ed.), p. 846–849; Patsch (2000); and the Seventh UN Report on Diplomatic Protection (2006), p. 4.
33. See ECHR Art. 1; ACHR Art. 1; ICCPR Art. 2. Compare Art. 6 of the Declaration on the Elimination of All Forms of Racial Discrimination (1963).
34. '[A] view of human rights norms backed by legal sanctions and judicial enforcement [exists]. This conception of rights also derive[s] from a largely unspoken analogue of international human rights to constitutional rights on the domestic plane and to rights protection in an age of constitutional democracy'. Teitel (1997), p. 306.
35. See Arts 17–20 of the Treaty Establishing the European Community (Consolidated) (hereinafter, ECT). The rights granted to European Union citizens, as well as the basis for these rights – a supra-state citizenship based on nationality in a Member State – show, simultaneously, the tenacity of the link between nationality and citizenship and the reconfiguration of what this link entails.

state.[36] In particular, the assumption has been that nationality includes cultural, social and political considerations.[37] The presence of these considerations is clearest in domestic laws on nationality – historical experiences, beliefs about what distinguishes the (national) community, as well as a number of cultural and social particularities influence and in turn can be gleaned from such laws.[38] For example, the development of nationality regulation in Germany – long the *bête noire* of theorists – cannot be understood outside the context of German unification or the post-World War II division of that state.[39]

However, the attachment goes further: States, and many societies, attribute cultural and social *functions* to the concept.[40] This is perhaps un-surprising, since nationality is in the first instance a means to determine membership in a given (state-centred) community.[41] As McDougal, Lasswell and Chen discuss, despite increased international movement, 'people remain an important base of power for each of the different territorially organized communities of the world'.[42] The nature of a given state is thus closely related to the quality and number of its members;[43] and the question of who is to be a member of the given political (and national) community has shifted, with time, from the question of citizenship to that of nationality.

---

36. For example, the United States Immigration and Nationality Act (hereinafter, INA) (1952) defines a 'national' as '(a) a citizen of the United States, or (b) a person who, though not a citizen of the United States, owes *permanent allegiance* to the United States', United States Code (hereinafter, U.S.C.) Title 8, sec. 1101a, para. 22 (emphasis added).

    Within the framework of the European Union, the European Court of Justice (hereinafter, E.C.J.) has noted the 'special relationship of allegiance to the state and reciprocity of rights and duties which form the foundation of the bond of nationality'. Case 149/79 *Commission v. Belgium* (No. 1), E.C.J. (1980), para. 10.
37. *See*, e.g., Weis (1979), p. 249; de Groot (1989), pp. 10–11 and p. 16; and the authors discussed below. Extreme forms of the approach have had unacceptable results in theory and practice; for example, wholly ethnic conceptions of nationality would demand that only kin who can trace their roots back to a specified time (and only they) have the right to a particular nationality. *See* Art. 2(a) of the European Convention on Nationality (1997) for a clear rejection of this extreme approach. *See also* discussion in Pérez Vera (1996), p. 277.
38. *See also* Kojanec (2000), p. 47; and Autem (2000), p. 26.
39. For a comparison of the interaction between national identity and nationality regulation in France and Germany, *see* Brubaker (2002). *See also* discussion on the amendments to German nationality law in the 1990s at Sec. IV.B.
40. *See* Council of Europe Recommendation 1410; also, the generally contentious debates on immigration in many countries. However, certain states buck the trend: the Caribbean islands of St. Kitts/Nevis (since 1984) and Dominica (since 1991) offer 'economic citizenship' or 'citizenship by investment' (sic) without any requirement of enduring attachment. In other words, a second nationality is granted in exchange for 'suitable economic contribution to the country'. *See*, e.g., St. Kitts/Nevis Citizenship Act Sec. 3(5). Belize, Grenada and Ireland also had similar programs until 2002, 2001, and 1998, respectively.
41. 'Nationality always connotes ... membership of some kind in the society of a state or nation'. Harvard Draft on Nationality (1929).
42. McDougal, Lasswell and Chen (1974), p. 904.
43. *See* e.g., Aleinikoff and Klusmeyer (2002), p. 3. While this is certainly the case at a given point in time 'citizenship [nationality] also denotes the members of an intergenerational project, who are committed to honouring a past and promoting a better future for generations to follow'.

Basic Concepts

The two principles governing attribution of nationality at birth – *jus soli* and *jus sanguinis* – clearly reflect the importance of attachment.[44] They are premised, respectively, on the idea that an individual born in the territory of a given state or to a parent with the nationality of that state is in some manner more closely connected to that state than others. That this is no longer necessarily the case does not negate the fact that when these principles developed the assumption was generally valid. In fact, in the context of mass emigration from many European states in the late 19th and early 20th centuries, one of the main advantages of *jus sanguinis* was its inclusiveness, allowing the foreign-born children of nationals to maintain ties with the state of origin and leaving the option of return open[45] – something that remains true for states of emigration today. However, in the context of mass immigration, this same regime serves as a mechanism to exclude new arrivals, undermining the democratic legitimacy of the state in question.[46] Thus, the (moral, human rights, etc.) acceptability of nationality regulation – from theorists' point of view, at least – depends almost wholly on demographic context.[47] This was no less true in the past than today, since even the roots of *jus sanguinis* and *jus soli* are to be found in considerations of the ties that (should) bind individuals to the state.

In particular, the decision by France in 1791 to rely (in part) on *jus sanguinis*[48] was a conscious rejection of feudal *jus soli* – stipulating that all individuals born within the dominions of the sovereign (or other noblemen) were his subjects – on the basis that the latter was both outdated and too insubstantial a tie to link individuals to the state.[49] The Civil Code of 1804 went on to establish *jus sanguinis* as the main principle governing birthright nationality. Other European states quickly followed suit, with only Great Britain and Portugal continuing to adhere to *jus soli*, as well as (in the case of the former) to the principle of perpetual allegiance.[50] However, *jus soli* took on new life with the increasingly popular belief that the *demos*, or political community, should be conflated with the geographical boundary of the state, so that all those residing within its borders were to be national citizens. We know that this aspiration was limited in scope, as female and/or non-Caucasian nationals were systematically excluded from the rights of citizenship[51] –

---

44. McDougal, Lasswell and Chen (1974), p. 904.
45. For example, return-migration to Germany from the United States in the 19th century ranged between 4.7 per cent (1857) and 49.4 per cent (1875) by one estimation. Moltmann (1980), p. 383.
46. *See* discussion in Koslowski (2000), p. 73.
47. *Ibid.* p. 84.
48. France, Constitution (1791), Title II, Art. 2.
49. Brubaker (2002), p. 171. *See also* Grawert (1973), pp. 159–161.
50. This principle (*nomo potest exuere patria, jus originis nemo mutare est*), whereby allegiance to the sovereign was indefensible, played an important role in British common law until 1870 (*see* Sec. 6, Act of 5 May 1870). In fact, the War of 1812 broke out partially because Great Britain persisted in forcing naturalized Americans born in Great Britain into military service, despite protests from the United States.
51. Examples could be cited at considerable length, but lack of space constrains us to only a few. In the context of the United States, the Fourteenth Amendment explicitly excluded Native

but the logic of state ties remains. Already in 1851, France introduced the principle of double *jus soli* – whereby the second generation born in France automatically received nationality – due to concerns about equality, state security and assimilation.[52] With the reforms of 1889, *jus soli* (linked to past residence, rather than feudal allegiance) assumed a central place in French nationality regulation. It was with the ratification of the Fourteenth Amendment in the United States (in 1868), however, that the tide had begun to turn, as *jus soli* was adopted by an increasing number of states of immigration.[53]

c. **The Role of Path Dependency**

It was thus a mixture of traditions inherited from common or Roman law, the circumstances of state formation, and the balance of migration at decisive periods that determined which principles of nationality at birth would become dominant in a given European state.[54] For example, the decision at the drafting of the Constitution of the *Norddeutscher Bund* (1867) to opt for the *kleindeutsch* solution to unification (and for the definitive exclusion of Austrians from the possibility of '*Indigenat*' status, in accordance with Article 3 of the Constitution) led directly to post-Bismarckian Germany's decision in 1913 to extend nationality only to the descendants of those living in the *Deutsches Reich*.[55] The choice made in 1791 or 1913 between, or among, constellations of *jus sanguinis* and *jus soli* as the basis for nationality at birth – in light of a particular historical moment and reflecting the concerns of that moment – set the standard for changes at a later point in time, however.[56] An obvious matter perhaps, but one important to note, given the force of status quo as an (ostensible) outcome of past consensus. Thus, historical traditions of membership draw the normative and legislative outlines of future development: a clear instance of path-dependency. This is not to say that shifts are impossible, just that a radical departure from existing policies is improbable given nationality's social functions. A state having chosen pure *jus sanguinis* as the main rule is thus unlikely to change to a pure *jus soli* regime, social upheavals

---

Americans (*see Elk v. Wilkins*, US (1884)); in the context of France, Algerian Muslims were excluded from citizenship until 1947 despite the incorporation of Algeria into France in 1848. With regard to women, full citizenship rights were not granted in any state until the 20th century (and in some states still have not been). In Europe, the right to both vote and stand in elections was first granted by Finland, in 1906; the last state to grant these rights was Liechtenstein, in 1984.

52. *See* Weil, pp. 55–56 (Hansen and Weil, eds, 2001).
53. There were earlier precedents of *jus soli*, as in Mexico's Apatzingán Constitution (1814), but the principle was either not dominant for long or the state making the decision was not an independent one.
54. Koslowski (2000), p. 81.
55. Germany (*Deutsches Reich*), Constitution, Art. 3 (1891).
56. For example, the factor of migration was important in determining whether *jus sanguinis* or *jus soli* should become the basis for nationality at birth.

notwithstanding.[57] An incremental introduction of new elements is considerably more likely. As Lagarde has noted in the context of modifications to French nationality law, '[I]t is not that the legislator wished to modify his understanding of the French nation each time. It is rather [that] this law no longer permitted him to confront an urgent problem he had to solve'.[58]

The same observation can be made for decisions about naturalization, in a slightly different context. *Jus domicilii*, or the acquisition of nationality by naturalization after a period of residence, is generally affected by the underlying philosophy behind birthright nationality; a state focused on the creation (and maintenance) of a homogenous national community is likely to make naturalization difficult, for example. Or, in a more direct link, individuals from a particular territory, of a particular linguistic, religious or ethnic group or of particular ancestry (e.g., the children of former nationals) have facilitated access to nationality in many states. Thus, changes to *jus domicilii* are conditioned by broader re-interpretations of the national community, just as birthright nationality is. Since *jus domicilii* has generally been seen in Europe as a secondary mechanism of nationality-ascription, after that of birth,[59] it has seen greater experimentation. Fine-tuning has been constant in requirements of residence and assimilation (or integration), as ascertained by relinquishment of former ties (i.e., nationality), linguistic ability, adherence to constitutional traditions, etc. However, rapid turn-around is unlikely here, too, so that an assimilationist policy will not morph unto a pluralist one overnight.

That said, the wave of multiculturalist-inspired regulation that swept much of Western Europe from the 1970s to the late 1990s constituted significant policy change in many states. According to Hansen and Weil, for example, parallel changes to nationality laws in the old Member States of the European Union could be observed: in particular, entitlement to national citizenship for second-generation immigrants; a trend toward liberalization (in Northern Europe) and restriction (in Southern Europe) of naturalization requirements for first-generation immigrants; and conscious (albeit contradictory) responses to plural nationality.[60] Despite the claim to convergence,[61] however, 'factors influencing the evolution of nationality law have been almost entirely domestic'[62] – hence the varied answers to similar questions raised by immigration and integration in each state. (The requirement in Article 6 of the European Convention on Nationality [1997] that states

---

57. A number of states significantly changed their nationality regulation after the collapse of the Soviet bloc, for example.
58. '[C]e n'est pas ... que le législateur ait voulu chaque fois modifier l'idée qu'il se faisait de la nation française. C'est bien plutôt parce que ce droit ne lui permettait plus de faire face à un problème pressant qu'il avait à résoudre'. Lagarde (1993), p. 536.
59. *See*, e.g., Grawert (1973), pp. 184–185.
60. Hansen and Weil (2001), p. 10.
61. *Ibid.*, pp. 2–3. *See also* discussion in Shachar (2003), pp. 350–356 and 359; Weil (Aleinikoff and Klusmeyer eds, 2001), p. 20; McDougal, Lasswell and Chen (1974), p. 919.
62. *Ibid.*, p. 11.

limit residence requirements to a maximum of 10 years, at the most, is a rare example of an international legal factor.)

2. EVALUATING ATTACHMENT TO THE NATIONAL COMMUNITY

One should not assume, however, that a given constellation of *jus sanguinis* or *jus soli* is a clear signifier of a particular kind of national community. In particular, the distinction made by many social scientists between 'ethno-cultural' nations (with *jus sanguinis*) and 'civic' nations (with *jus soli*) – with distinct opinions as to which is retrogressive or progressive – is highly problematic. Though recent writings have introduced a further axis, differentiating between assimilationist and pluralist states,[63] a number of assumptions are thereby made with regard to 'the role of *jus sanguinis* in constructing ethno-national identity',[64] that both over-estimate the deterministic quality of any law in relation to identity and under-estimate the role of education and other policies, as well as social developments.

In reality, even states with predominantly *jus soli* regimes retain elements of *jus sanguinis* (and vice versa), both in order to avoid statelessness and because of a recognition that pure regimes could result in unwelcome outcomes. For this reason, to the extent that *all* European states today maintain elements of both *jus soli* and *jus sanguinis* in their regulation of nationality, albeit to differing degrees, the correlation between type of national identity and choice for one of the two means of ascribing birthright nationality is quite low. The importance of attachment has not gone out the window in either case, as requirements of residence can be attached to both kinds of regimes. Thus, since 1998, a child born in France to two foreign-born parents is a French national if she lives in France at the age of majority and has done so for five (non-continuous) years since the age of 11.[65] Conversely, a child born abroad with one US national parent will only receive US nationality if that parent can prove a certain number of years of residence in the United States.[66]

a. The Role of State Interests

The traditional discouragement of plural nationality – the result of a combination of varied nationality regimes and migration – also relies on the existence of a singular attachment. 'As a corollary of this identification of the citizen with the State it was permissible for an individual to have one, and only one, nationality. This has also been explained as the impossibility for an individual to owe allegiance to two sovereigns at once'.[67] Accordingly, until a few years ago, plural nationality was a phenomenon to be avoided: at the national level through legislation, making

---
63. Castles and Miller (1993), Chapters 2 and 8; Koopmans and Statham (2003), pp. 208–209.
64. Koslowski (2000), p. 87. *See* also, Balibar (1991), p. 100; and Linke (2004), p. 209.
65. Art. 21-7 of the *Code Civil*, as amended by Art. 2 of *La loi relative à la nationalité (loi no. 98-170)* (1998).
66. INA, Title III, Chap. 1, Sec. 301(g); *see also* paras (c) to (e).
67. Donner (1983), p. 34.

naturalization conditional upon loss of previous nationality, or requiring the withdrawal of nationality from any national acquiring another. At the international level, numerous international instruments – most notably the 1963 European Convention on the Reduction of Cases of Multiple Nationality – attempted to create conditions for its avoidance. Though recent legislative changes in a number of states have since allowed for some form of plural nationality, and despite the 1997 European Convention on Nationality, which is neutral on the issue, many states continue to forbid any national from holding another nationality as a matter of principle, in particular out of concern for singular loyalty.[68]

The identity function of nationality also finds expression in the notion of 'effective link' in the context of international law. Or, as the International Court of Justice (hereinafter, ICJ) stated in the (in)famous *Nottebohm* case, nationality has 'as its basis a social fact of attachment, a genuine connection of existence, interest and sentiments, together with the existence of reciprocal rights and duties'.[69] Though the Court here examined the bond between a state and an individual in the context of the diplomatic protection of a naturalized national (and determined that a genuine connection must exist between the two for other states to recognize such protection) some writers have extended this notion to nationality as a concept.[70] Similarly, Article 1(a) of the 1929 Harvard Draft Convention on Nationality (hereinafter, Harvard Convention) defined the national of a state as 'a natural person attached to that State by the tie of allegiance'.[71] By the 1930s, a theorist could state that 'as international jurisprudence perfects itself, it takes account of all of its subjects' behaviour; and signs revealing more intense social attachment multiply: domicile, residence, links of public service, the exercise of public functions, declarations of will, family relations, etc.'.[72] In fact, the possible bases of attachment have likely multiplied even further since that time. Certain states (e.g., Romania) even grant nationality on the basis of a *jus sanguinis* delimited by territory; one's ancestor needs to have been the national of the predecessor state only.[73]

---

68. *See* further discussion in Sec. IV.A.1, below.
69. *Liechtenstein v. Guatemala* (Judgment, Second Phase), ICJ (1955), p. 23.
70. *See* Blackman (1998), pp. 1155–1156; and Aleinikoff (1999), p. 15, but *see* Art. 4 of the ILC Draft Articles on Diplomatic Protection (2006), which seems to abandon the principle altogether.
71. For a discussion of the idea of allegiance in common law systems, as well as their after-effects, *see* Verwilghen (1999), pp. 55–56.
72. 'Man mano che la giurisprudenza internazionale si perfeziona, essa tiene conto di tutto il contegno dei soggetti ed i segni rilevatori dell'attacco sociale più intenso si moltiplicano: domicilio, residenza, rapporti di servizio pubblico, esercizio di pubbliche funzioni, dichiarazioni di volontà, rapporti di famiglia, ecc'. Quadri, quoted in Panzera (1984), p. 108.
73. In particular, Moldovans whose ancestors were Romanian nationals when the country formed part of Romania (before 1940) may apply for Romanian nationality. This practice can be distinguished from general cases of state succession both because many decades have passed since the two states separated and because Moldova (then part of the U.S.S.R.) extended its own nationality to the inhabitants of the territory in question. The focus on territory and the attachment of individuals to a geographical place is shared, however.

On the other hand, even significant attachment is sometimes not enough under international law to protect a person without the nationality of a given country. For example, the UN Human Rights Committee has found that an individual who lawfully entered a country that facilitated the acquisition of nationality but who refrained from getting that nationality cannot consider the state her 'own country' pursuant to Article 12(4) of the ICCPR, even if she has never lived elsewhere.[74] Thus, nationality is the only legal nexus to a state fully recognized under international law: granted on the basis of some attachment and a declaration of its existence in the eyes of both domestic and international actors.

Given the functions of nationality, it should come as no surprise that the determination of who has the requisite attachment to hold its nationality remains for the state to decide (and other states to recognize).[75] But the central role of states in granting or withdrawing nationality is not just due to the importance of nationality in drawing the outlines of the individual-state relationship for the purpose of international law, or in cohering national identity in the domestic sphere. It is also linked to questions of control. A state could not exercise personal supremacy without being able to determine who its nationals are and what the content of their rights and duties is.[76] In the final instance, then, nationality leads us to the *éminence grise* of the international system: sovereignty. As Oppenheim's bluntly put it, 'the right of a State to determine who are, and who are not, its nationals is an

---

74. *Stewart v. Canada*, UN H.R. Comm. (1996). In this context, *see also The New York Times Magazine*, 'In a Homeland Far From Home' (16 November 2003), discussing US practice in deporting permanent legal residents with criminal convictions.

    In this respect, there is a difference between rights granted in the United States and in the states of the Council of Europe. As the E.Ct.H.R. has repeatedly held, non-nationals have a right to respect for family and private life under ECHR Art. 8; if deportation would endanger this right, it is acceptable only if it has a legitimate objective and the interference is proportionate to achieving that objective. *See Berrehab v. Netherlands*, E.Ct.H.R. (1988). Thus, the right of the individual under Art. 8 is balanced against the state interest in maintaining public order. *See Boultif v. Switzerland*, E.Ct.H.R. (2001).

    In contrast, while the United States Supreme Court has repeatedly held that permanent residents continuously present in the country are entitled to a fair hearing when threatened with deportation (*see* e.g., *United States ex rel. Tisi v. Tod*, US [1924], pp. 133–134) and to due process rights (*see* e.g., *United States ex rel. Vajtauer v. Commissioner of Immigration*, US [1927], p. 106), the Illegal Immigration Reform and Immigration Responsibility Act (1996) and the Antiterrorism and Effective Death Penalty Act (1996) made relief from deportation impossible for aggravated felons. *See Maria v. McElroy*, E.D.N.Y. (1999). In 1997, the bar for exemption from deportation was raised for all individuals. *See* U.S.C., Title 8, Sec. 1227. Finally, the USA Patriot Act (Uniting and Strengthening America by Providing Appropriate Tools Required to Intercept and Obstruct Terrorism Act, 2001) has further enlarged the grounds on which non-nationals may be removed from the United States. In such circumstances, there is no balancing or consideration of attachment to the United States.

75. For an overview of writers on the exclusive competence of states to regulate nationality, as well as the limits of this competence, *see* the ILC Survey, *supra* note I.20, p. 59 *et seq*.

76. One prominent 19th century theorist even called nationality an '*organisches Gewaltverhältnis*' (organic relationship of force). Gerber, *Über Öffentliche Rechte* 47 (1968) [1852] as quoted in Grawert (1973), p. 228. *See also* Panzera (1984), p. 114 *et seq*.

essential element of its sovereignty'.[77] Hence the discretion of states in such questions.[78] This element of sovereignty remains intact for the most part, even within the European Union – an entity to which many other sovereign functions have been ceded – as Member States remain free to attribute nationality to whomever they want, without the possibility of being second-guessed.[79]

Sovereignty has never been the exclusive principle determinative of international norms on nationality, however. At first the interests of other states, which could be affected by unilateral action, imposed some small limits. Or, as the Permanent Court of International Justice (hereinafter, PCIJ) stated in its advisory opinion in the case concerning *Nationality Decrees Issued in Tunis and Morocco*: '[Although] nationality, is not, in principle, regulated by international law, the right of a State to use its discretion is nevertheless restricted by obligations which it may have undertaken towards other States. In such a case, jurisdiction ... is limited by rules of international law'.[80] In other words, questions of nationality were matters for domestic law, unless a state had bound itself in some manner toward another state. This view, supported by theorists of international law at the time of the decision,[81] seems to have been confirmed by the International Law Commission in 1999,[82] which added that the PCIJ here 'emphasized that the question whether a matter was solely within the jurisdiction of a State was essentially a relative question'.

b. The Role of Individual Interests

This 'relativity' had, in fact, been further broadened by 1930, when the Hague Convention on Certain Questions Relating to the Conflict of Nationality Laws (hereinafter, Hague Nationality Convention) declared that the nationality law of a given state must be accepted by the international community only 'insofar as it is

---

77. Weis (1979), p. 65. *See also* Guerrero, the Rapporteur of the First Committee at the Hague Conference for the Codification of International Law, as quoted in Weis, p. 67. This same principle explains why a state cannot grant nationality to an individual not in its territory at the relevant time. *See* McDougal, Lasswell and Chen (1974), p. 925.

    'Sovereignty' is defined here as 'the supreme and independent authority of States over all persons and things in their territory; [with] independence and territorial and personal supremacy ... [its] elements'. Oppenheim (1955), p. 186. *See also* the *Island of Las Palmas Arbitration (United States v. The Netherlands)*, Perm. Ct. Arbit. (1928).
78. Similarly, if nationals are in some sense always under the jurisdiction of their state, a lack of respect for the rights of these individuals implies lack of respect for the state of nationality.
79. *See* discussion of E.C.J. Case C-200/02 *Zhu and Chen* at Sec. II.C.2.a.
80. *Nationality Decrees Issued in Tunis and Morocco*, PCIJ (1923). *See also* Garner (1926) for a discussion of the Arbitral Opinion following the opinion in the case *Acquisition of Polish Nationality*, PCIJ (1923).
81. *See* Oppenheim's International Law (1955), p. 643; and Lauterpacht (1933), p. 300.
82. Commentary (3) to Preamble of Draft Articles on Nationality of Natural Persons in Relation to the Succession of States (1999) (hereinafter, ILC Draft Articles on Nationality at State Succession) in the Report of the International Law Commission On the Work of Its Fifty-First Session (1999), p. 24.

consistent with international conventions, international custom and the principles of law generally recognized with regard to nationality'.[83] Thus, questions of nationality have increasingly included a balancing of the interests of specific states with those of the international community. With the development of the international human rights system, moreover, the interests of individuals have also gained in prominence.[84] As one international court recently stated, the power of states in questions of nationality is 'also circumscribed by their obligations to ensure the full protection of human rights'.[85] Some have gone so far as to insist that 'only the development of international human rights law has placed any new restraints whatsoever on traditional state sovereignty over nationality matters'.[86]

The nature of these restraints has been two-fold. First, certain basic international principles have emerged, setting outer limits on state practice, as will be discussed. Second, a number of tribunals have examined the application – if not the content – of specific regulatory systems. The E.Ct.H.R., for example, has repeatedly stated that neither the Convention nor any of its Protocols guarantee a right to a particular nationality.[87] However, the Court has examined the nature of particular decisions on the attribution of nationality for arbitrariness. In a decision on the admissibility of a case brought by an individual claiming 'that the compounded effect of the refusal of citizenship, together with the overall situation of the [...] family, constitutes a violation of Articles 8 and 14 of the Convention' and emphasizing 'the allegedly arbitrary nature of the refusal to recognise the applicant as a citizen',[88] for example, the Court examined the actions of Finnish authorities in light of the particular circumstances of the individual; but determined that the application was manifestly ill-founded, despite the fact that the individual was thereby essentially left stateless.

---

83. Art. 1 of the Hague Nationality Convention. *See also* Art. 2 of the Harvard Convention.
84. On a theoretical note: the development of nationality law in the 19th century had moved the individual-state relationship further and further away from theories of law based on the free will of the individual, whether in natural law or approaches focused on the contractual nature of society. *See* Locke (1690), Chap. XIII, Secs 96 and 116–122, where he argued for the necessity of individual consent to membership in a political community and against the principle of perpetual allegiance. *See also* discussion in Grawert (1973), p. 86 *et seq.* and p. 225.
85. *See* para. 32 of *Proposed Amendments to the Naturalization Provisions of the Constitution of Costa Rica*, Inter-Am. Ct. H.R. (1984). *See also* para. 4 of the Preamble of the European Convention on Nationality; and Commentary 5 to the Preamble of the ILC Draft Articles on Nationality at State Succession, *supra* note I.82, p. 24: 'the Commission finds it appropriate to affirm that, in matters concerning nationality, the legitimate interests of both States and individuals should be taken into account'.
86. *See* Report of the International Law Commission On the Work of Its Forty-Seventh Session (1995), para. 188. *See also* Mikulka (1996), p. 9, n. 26.
87. *See*, e.g., *Family K and W v. the Netherlands*, E.Ct.H.R. (1985) and *Kafkalsi v. Turkey*, E.Ct.H.R. (1997). *See also X v. Germany*, E.Comm.H.R. (1970), where the Commission examined the possible relationship between a refusal to grant nationality and an order of expulsion.
88. *Karassev v. Finland* (Admissibility), E.Ct.H.R. (1999).

Consideration of the interests of individuals – not just their states – would seem prudent given how crucial the possession of a nationality is to individuals and how minor a say they have traditionally had in its attribution and withdrawal.[89] However, while the Hague Convention provision quoted above is likely a rule of customary international law[90] – and while the introduction of human rights principles into conventions on nationality[91] has made human rights an important consideration in evaluating state practice – no significant protection actually exists for individuals under international law, for three reasons. First, there is a relative lack of customary international law regarding nationality.[92] Second, there is no enforceable right to nationality recognized under international law. Thus, whatever benefits may accrue from having a nationality are not available to all persons. Third, there aren't many actual limitations on states' prerogative over questions of nationality in practice. Accordingly, while there is no paucity of multilateral (and bilateral) conventions in the field of nationality,[93] these have not generally been ratified by many states, so that their effects have been rather indirect and political than strictly legal. As Weis discusses, it is difficult to find 'general principles' recognized by states with regard to nationality.[94] What principles do exist – such as the prohibition on discriminatory denationalization – are of a negative character and derivative of general principles of international human rights law (such as non-

---

89. The practice of stripping individuals of their nationality – including those who had been banned from the territory of the state for political reasons – after a period of residence abroad was, for example, widespread among European states into the 20th century. In context of Hungary, *see* Art. 31 of the Nationality Law of 1879 (in force, with amendments, until 1949). *See also* discussion in Kisteleki (2000).
90. *See* Randelzhofer (2000). With regard to determining what customary international law is, *see* Art. 38(1)(a) of the Statute of the International Court of Justice (1945). For a summary of both traditional and modern approaches to customary international law, as well as the problematics of determining custom, *see* Roberts (2001). *See also* Schindler (2000).
91. *See, inter alia,* Art. 9 of the UN Convention on the Reduction of Statelessness (1961) (hereinafter, Statelessness Reduction Convention); Art. 5 of the European Convention on Nationality.
92. *'Dans la domaine de la nationalité on a vu que les principes généraux du droit des gens et les règles coutumières ne sont pas en grand nombre'.* Rezek (1986), p. 385.
93. *See* 1906 Rio de Janeiro Convention on the Status of Naturalised Citizens; 1930 Hague Convention on Certain Questions Relating to the Conflict of Nationality Laws; 1930 Protocol Relating to Military Obligations in Certain Cases of Double Nationality; 1930 Special Protocol Concerning Statelessness; 1933 Montevideo Convention on Nationality; 1933 Montevideo Convention on Nationality of Women; 1954 Convention Relating to Status of Stateless Persons; 1954 Convention on Nationality Between the Members of the Arab League; 1957 United Nations' Convention on the Nationality of Married Women; 1963 European Convention on Reduction of Cases of Multiple Nationality and Military Obligations in Cases of Multiple Nationality; 1973 Convention for the Reduction of the Number of Cases of Statelessness; 1977 Protocol to the European Convention on Reduction of cases of Multiple Nationality and Military Obligations in Cases of Multiple Nationality; 1977 Additional Protocol to the European Convention on Reduction of Cases of Multiple Nationality and Military Obligations in Cases of Multiple Nationality; 1997 European Convention on Nationality. Quoted in Rubenstein and Adler, at p. 525 no. 32 (2000), as compiled by Bar-Yaacov (1961) and Weis (1979).
94. Weis (1979), p. 246.

discrimination).[95] It would be difficult to argue that they constitute rules binding on all states, as discussed below.[96] But let us examine some of the possible rights relating to nationality in turn, beginning with whether individuals have a right to have one in the first place.

3. NATIONALITY IN INTERNATIONAL LAW

a. **The Right to Nationality**

Article 15 of the UDHR declares that 'everyone has a right to a nationality'.[97] What this statement means in practice is unclear, however. Is it a general statement on the part of the signatory states or an enforceable right for individuals? The latter is unlikely, given the non-binding nature of the Declaration. But, assuming the possibility of an individual right, who is to enforce the right? Against which state? It is perhaps no wonder that commentators have reservations about the actual existence of this right in international law.[98] In practice, there seems to be a difference between not granting a nationality and withdrawing an existing one. While there is little pressure on states to grant nationality (except in the context of state succession),[99] withdrawal is more difficult in practice, particularly if this act would render the individual stateless.[100] Thus, statelessness, while not looked upon favourably, is still not inadmissible.[101] With regard to the conditions of granting or withdrawing nationality, certain minimum standards can be viewed as emerging international norms – for example, a state may not impose nationality

---

95. See Art. 3 of the UN Convention Relating to the Status of Stateless Persons (1954) (hereinafter, Stateless Persons Convention); and Art. 5 of the European Nationality Convention. See also Art. 15(1) of the UDHR, in conjunction with Art. 7.
96. Clearly, the norm of non-discrimination is binding on the vast majority of states, as they have signed and ratified the ICCPR. (See Art. 26). However, the implications of adherence to this norm in the context of attribution and withdrawal of nationality are, egregious violations aside, unclear.
97. See also, among others, ICCPR Art. 24(3) or ACHR Art. 20 for a similar right.
98. See Chan (1991); Rezek (1986), p. 354 (arguing in particular that there is no addressee to such an obligation); Weis (1979), p. 125 (in the context of denationalization) and 248 (no basis in customary international law); Randelzhofer (2000), p. 508; but see the Inter-American Court's Costa Rica Opinion, at para. 35 (which states that the 'right of every human being to a nationality has been recognized as such by international law').
99. See ILC Draft Articles on Nationality at State Succession, at Art. 1 and Commentaries (1) and (2), supra note I.82, pp. 23–24. See also the Council of Europe Convention on the Avoidance of Statelessness in Relation to State Succession (2006); and ICCPR Art. 2(1) in conjunction with Art. 24(3). See discussion in Donner (1983), p. 215, but see Blackman (1998), p. 1163; Hoffmann (1998), p. 10.
100. See Art. 15(2) of the UDHR; and Art. 5–10 of the Statelessness Reduction Convention; McDougal, Lasswell and Chen (1974), p. 949 et seq.; and Gelazis (2000).
101. While numerous international instruments deal with the problem of statelessness, they are binding only on a small number of states. See the Stateless Persons Convention (22 signatories, 54 parties); the Statelessness Reduction Convention (1961); and the Convention for the Reduction of Cases of Statelessness (1973, not in force).

against the will of an individual[102] or denationalize individuals or groups on an arbitrary basis (e.g., race, ethnicity or religion).[103] On the other hand, as Grawert discusses, there is no right to be freed from a particular nationality.[104] In the 19th century, the Bancroft Treaties (1868) were a first attempt by the United States to co-ordinate the legal status of immigrants with their states of origin, since many refused to free their nationals from (the obligations of) citizenship. Even today, certain states refuse to allow individuals to give up the particular nationality (or do so only after the fulfilment of onerous requirements).

Even with some recent developments, however, from a human rights perspective the lack of a right to nationality under customary international law is doubly damning. First, the stateless individual has no access to some rights guaranteed under international conventions,[105] since these must be granted by states only to their nationals (e.g., the right to vote). Other rights, while guaranteed in theory, are unlikely to be respected in practice (e.g., right to free movement within the territory of the given state). In fact, the container in which the rights of equality discussed above, as well as most others, were to be guaranteed at the time the UDHR was drafted was fixed by the boundaries of the given state. In other words, equality is to be guaranteed by the state to its nationals, as well as individuals under its jurisdiction. But, given that differentiated treatment of nationals and non-nationals is in certain circumstances accepted under international law,[106] and considering the lack of citizenship rights in any given state,[107] a stateless person is restricted by her very statelessness in numerous fundamental rights.

Second, should the rights of a stateless person be infringed upon, she may not have access to either national or international courts in which to seek redress. Some writers have gone so far as to state that 'the individual human being is almost completely dependent on a state of nationality for securing a hearing upon the merits upon injuries done to him by other states'.[108] This is certainly a misleading view when applied to Europe, where Article 1 of the ECHR requires that states grant enumerated rights and freedoms – including the right to turn to the E.Ct.H.R. – to everyone within their jurisdiction. It nonetheless remains true

---

102. But *see* Weis (1979), p. 110 *et seq.* for a discussion of some inconsistencies.
103. *See* Art. 9 of the Statelessness Reduction Convention, and Arts 4(c) and 5(1) of the European Nationality Convention. According to some authors, however, denationalization must be coupled with expulsion to be an international delict; otherwise, the matter remains a domestic one. *See* Donner (1983), p. 178.
104. Grawert (1973), pp. 234–235. (In the case of states with strong *jus sanguinis*, the imposition of a nationality and its forced maintenance may go hand in hand.)
105. *See, inter alia*, Arts 12 and 25 of the ICCPR.
106. As Lillich discusses, there is likely an 'international minimum standard' of non-discriminatory treatment to be afforded to non-nationals, subsumed into the general body of international human rights law. Lillich (1984), pp. 49–56. However, the 'sartorial tastes of the State involved' still determine the extent of actual protection. *Ibid.*, p. 122. *See also* Bernsdorff (1986), p. 81 *et seq.*; and Fletcher (2004) for a discussion of recent US Supreme Court decisions on the rights of non-national detainees at Guantánamo Bay.
107. *See* discussion of citizenship below at Sec. I.B.1.
108. McDougal, Lasswell and Chen (1974), p. 918.

that in most regions of the world, including Europe, states place limitations on access to national courts or have different standards for non-nationals.[109] And since access to certain international courts is limited to countries that have agreed to be bound by the decisions of the given court (whether the International Criminal Court or the E.Ct.H.R.), a stateless person may in many places still find no court to hear her case. What court could a Moroccan national turn to, for example, if her consulate in Madrid refused to renew her passport? Certainly not Spanish, since that state has nothing to do with Morocco's passport regime. Likely also not Moroccan, since she could not even re-enter her country without proof of nationality. International courts would clearly also be out of the question, whether for questions of jurisdiction *ratione personae* or *ratione materiae*.[110]

In addition, diplomatic protection has traditionally depended on proof of nationality,[111] so that it was unavailable to stateless persons. Were an individual's rights infringed on by a given state, no other state could come to her aid.[112] As Article 8 of the ILC Draft Articles on Diplomatic Protection makes clear, international opinion is changing. In an instance of progressive development, the article drafted by the Commission allows for diplomatic protection in respect of stateless persons and refugees 'lawfully and habitually resident' in the given state. Though there is some disagreement among states regarding the level of attachment necessary – could 'lawfully staying' in the state be enough or should permanent residence be required? – the general principle itself now seems to be widely accepted.[113]

b.   Diplomatic Protection and the Right to Admission

Despite such development, the right of a state to exercise diplomatic protection on behalf of its nationals remains one of the – traditionally most important – consequences of nationality.[114] Such protection generally takes the form of intervention (by means of judicial proceedings, negotiation or official protest) on behalf of a national in a claim against another state responsible for an internationally wrongful act, once local remedies have been exhausted.[115] In theory, diplomatic

---

109. *See* Arts 14 and 15 of the French *Code Civil*; but compare Arts 9, 32, and 37 of the Italian *Legge 31 maggio 1995, n. 218 (Riforma del sistema italiano di diritto internazionale privato)*. *See also* Final Report on the Rights of Non-Citizens (2003), paras 6 and 17 *et seq.*
110. In this context, *see Sophie Vidal Martins v. Uruguay*, UN H.R. Comm. (1982); and *Juan Raul Ferreira v. Uruguay*, Inter-Am. Comm. H.R. (1983).
111. '[I]t is the bond of nationality between the State and the individual which alone confers upon the State the right to diplomatic protection'. *Panevezys-Saldutiskis Railway* (Judgment), PCIJ (1939). For a discussion of questions regarding proof of nationality and timing, *see* Verwilghen (1999), pp. 93–95.
112. As per UN General Assembly Resolution 3274 (XXIX) (1974), the UN High Commissioner for Refugees may exercise this function. This protection was qualitatively different from that which could be given by a state, however. *See also* ECHR Art. 24.
113. *See* para. 50 of the Seventh UN Report on Diplomatic Protection (2006) (hereinafter, Report on Diplomatic Protection).
114. *See* Leigh, Nationality and Diplomatic Protection (1971) for a general discussion.
115. On the last requirement, *see* paras 69 *et seq.* of the Report on Diplomatic Protection.

protection may extend to the use of all legal means available.[116] It is important to make a distinction here between such protection and consular assistance, which generally involves only immediate assistance to individuals in the pursuit of lawful activities or specific rights in a given domestic jurisdiction.[117] Though both kinds of action involve state action on behalf of a national, only the former also involves state interests.[118]

In this context, the problematic nature of diplomatic protection should be noted. For the individual, it is 'an extraordinary legal remedy', not a right under international law.[119] However, it *is* a right of the state – perhaps even its prerogative, since an individual's renunciation of her claim may not necessarily extinguish the international claim to protection.[120] As the PCIJ stated in the *Mavrommatis Palestine Concessions Case*:

> [B]y taking up the case of its subjects and by resorting to diplomatic action or international proceedings on his behalf, a State is in reality asserting its own rights – its right to ensure, in the person of its subjects, respect for the rules of international law … in the eyes of the latter the State is sole claimant.[121]

---

116. *See Barcelona Traction Case* (Judgment), ICJ (1970), p. 44. '[W]ithin the limits of international law, a State may exercise diplomatic protection by whatever means and to whatever extent it thinks fit'. Despite the breadth of this statement, the means allowed likely do not include the use of force. *See* Arts 2(3), 2(4), 39, and 51 of the UN Charter (1945) and Art. 1 of the ILC Draft Articles on Diplomatic Protection, *supra* note I.70.
117. The difference is not always so clear in either legal texts or practice, however. Compare Art. 3(1)(b) if the Vienna Convention on Diplomatic Relations (1961) with Arts 5(a) and (e) if the Vienna Convention on Consular Relations (1963); but *see* paras 75–77 of the *La Grand Case* (Judgment), I.C.J. (2001) for a discussion elucidating, simultaneously, a clear distinction and the link between the two.
118. Numerous other structural differences also exist, including timing (consular assistance is largely preventive, not remedial in nature), level of representation (the consul, rather than the diplomatic branch is responsible) and the role of the individual (individual consent is required for consular protection). *See* discussion in the Report on Diplomatic Protection, para. 15 *et seq. See also* Künzli (2006).
119. Weis (1979), p. 34. If the right does not belong to the individual, she has no access to remedies. Further, state rights with an effect on individuals, as opposed to individual rights, may garner more respect. Henkin (1981), p. 273.
120. Weil, *ibid.,* p. 38. *See also* Borchard (1915) (arguing that an individual cannot renounce the right of her state to intervene on her behalf).
    On the flip side, no state has a duty of diplomatic protection under international law. (For a recent confirmation, *see* Art. 2 of the ILC Draft Articles on Diplomatic Protection, *supra* note I.70.) Any duty of this kind comes from domestic law. *See Abbasi and Another v. Secretary of State for Foreign and Commonwealth Affairs and Secretary of State for the Home Department*, UK Ct. Appeal (2002), para. 80 *et seq.* (and paras 104–106 in particular); and *Al Rawi and Others v. Secretary of State for Foreign and Commonwealth Affairs and Secretary of State for the Home Department*, UK High Ct. (2006), paras 56 *et seq.* (finding that no such duty exists under domestic law). *See also* BVerfG, BVerfGE 55, 349 (1980); and *Kaunda & Others v. the President of the RSA and Others*, Const. Ct. South Africa (2004).
121. *Mavrommatis Palestine Concessions Judgment* (Judgment), PCIJ (1924), p. 12. *See also* the *Panevezys-Saldutiskis Case*, p. 16.

Thus, when defending a national, a state is in fact acting on its own behalf. Though this traditional approach has been strongly criticized in recent literature – which views diplomatic protection as a procedure for the protection of individual human rights – the Draft Articles on Diplomatic Protection, first considered by the International Law Commission in 2000 and continuously revised through 2006, continue to rely on the premise that it is sound. The I.C.J.'s recent decision in the *La Grand Case* has, in any case, confirmed that lack of notification of a right to consular assistance is a violation of both the right of the individual concerned and of the state of nationality.[122] Though the Court did not consider Germany's contention that the individual right to be informed without delay of a right to consular assistance now assumes the character of a human right – and keeping in mind the difference between diplomatic protection and consular assistance – it is clear that human rights considerations are slowly creeping into legal debates on state action on behalf of nationals, as a corollary to the parallel debate on the international legal personality of individuals.[123]

It should also be noted that certain human rights claims (those with the status of *jus cogens* or *erga omnes* obligations) are exempt from any links to nationality. States may (and increasingly must) protect, by protest, negotiation and even judicial proceedings, all individuals in the context of violations of such norms.[124] The separate opinion of Judge Simma in the *Case Concerning Armed Activities on the Territory of the Congo*, in which he argued for state standing before the I.C.J. on the basis of international humanitarian and human rights law regardless of the nationality of the individual victims at issue, set out an alternate scenario: the creation of 'open black holes in the law in which human beings may be disappeared and deprived of any legal protection whatsoever'[125] if the current trend of hair-splitting legal statuses to avoid international obligations continues.[126]

---

122. *See* paras 38 and 65–77 of *La Grand*; but compare the *Avena and Other Nationals* Case (Judgment), I.C.J. (2004), para. 40.
123. *See* paras 238 and 241 of the Report of the Fifty-Seventh Session of the ILC (2005). The ongoing discussion in the context of the ILC Draft Articles on Diplomatic Protection on whether to recognize the right of an injured national to receive compensation also reflects the growing influence of human rights considerations. *See* discussion in Report on Diplomatic Protection, para. 93 *et seq.*
124. *See* Arts 40, 41, and 48 of the ILC Draft Articles on the Responsibility of States for Internationally Wrongful Acts (2001); and the Commentaries thereto, in the ILC Report on the Work of the Fifty-Third Session, p. 277 *et seq.*, for Arts 40–41, and p. 318, for Art. 48.
125. Case concerning *Armed Activities on the Territory of the Congo*, I.C.J. (2005), Separate Opinion of Judge Simma, para. 41. For the general argument, *see* paras 17–41.
126. The practice of the United States in labelling individuals 'enemy combatants' in the context of the so-called 'war on terror' to avoid obligations undertaken under the Geneva Conventions (1949) and attendant Protocols (1977) would be a prime example of this phenomenon. In light of our discussion of post-national citizenship below, it is worth highlighting that limited relief for the individuals concerned came from the US Supreme Court, which applied domestic law and precedent with reference to the Geneva Conventions in determining that the military commissions set up by the US government violated both the Uniform Code of Miltiary Justice and the laws of war. *See Hamdan v. Rumsfeld*, US (2006).

Basic Concepts

In most circumstances, however, the *Nottebohm* principle – in which the connection between a state extending protection and the national it is acting on behalf of can be examined by the international community for effectiveness – remains valid.[127] The result of that particular decision, while possibly laudable for piercing the exclusivity of domestic jurisdiction over nationality matters, is perverse. On the basis of 'regard to the concept of nationality in international relations'[128] or, according to one of the dissenting judges, on the basis of 'doctrine of abuse of right'[129] incorrectly applied, an individual is deprived of the protection of a state willing to support her claim, as well as a hearing on the merits. As Judge Guggenheim pointed out in the decision, the protection of the individual under international law is severely curtailed, since no other state is in a position to exercise protection.[130] Furthermore, the consequences of finding a nationality granted and accepted under domestic law invalid for international purposes are unclear. To what extent does such invalidity extend to other areas?[131]

In the case of plural nationals, the problem is similar albeit on a different plane, since one state of nationality cannot traditionally defend the individual against another.[132] The individual is again left without state protection under international law, here due to the principle of the sovereign equality of states.[133] Though recent practice seems to point to an extension of the principle of effectivity to this context, the right of one state of nationality to defend an individual against another is not yet firmly accepted.[134]

---

127. *Nottebohm*, p. 23.
128. *Ibid.*, p. 26.
129. *Ibid.*, p. 37.
130. *Ibid.*, p. 63.
131. Were the *Nottebohm* rule generally applied, the question of discrimination between naturalized and born nationals for purposes of citizenship rights would also be an issue, for example.
132. *See, inter alia*, Art. 4 of the Hague Nationality Convention; *Reparation for Injuries Suffered in the Service of the United Nations* (Advisory Opinion), I.C.J. (1949), p. 186.
133. *See Mergé Claim (United States v. Italy)*, US-Italian Conciliation Comm. (1955), p. 455. In theory, the plural national is to be treated like all other nationals, so that protection by another state of nationality should be unnecessary. This is often not the case, however.

    For example, in the wake of the killing of Theo van Gogh, the Netherlands announced that 'terror suspects' who were dual nationals could be deported to their other state of nationality. *See* BBC News Online, 'Dutch Pledge Islamist Crackdown' (5 November 2004). The UK, in turn, had considered stripping a Muslim cleric of his British nationality and deporting him for claimed terrorist activities. *See The Guardian*, 'Once a Citizen, Always a Citizen' (25 February 2003); by 2006, however, there was instead talk of extradition once his sentence in the UK had been served. *See The Guardian*, 'Hamza to Face US Extradition' (7 February 2006).
134. *See, e.g., Decision in Case No. A/18 Concerning the Question of Jurisdiction Over Claims of Persons With Dual Nationality*, Iran-US Claims Trib. (1984); *Nasser Esphahanian and Bank Tejarat*, Case 157, Iran-US Claims Trib. (1983). Individuals had standing before this tribunal on the basis of the Claims Settlement Declaration of the Democratic and Popular Republic of Algeria concerning the Settlement of Claims by the Government of the United States and the Government of the Islamic Republic of Iran (1981). Thus, the tribunal functioned within a very specific context. *See* discussion in Verwilghen (1999), pp. 464–465; but *see* Art. 7 of the ILC Draft Articles on Diplomatic Protection, *supra* note I.70.

Even the underlying practice for which the international nationality regime developed – namely, the movement of individuals between states – is not a right directly related to nationality. With regard to entry rights, UDHR Article 13(2), as well as ICCPR Article 12(4) and Article 3(2) of Protocol No. 4 to the ECHR, among others, all mention the individual right to enter (and reside in) the state of nationality, as do many constitutions.[135] However, the individual likely does not yet have this right under customary international law.[136] First, because nationality needn't necessarily be the sole criterion for entry into a state;[137] second, and more importantly, because under international law we more correctly speak of a state duty to admit under the principle of territoriality. (Should one state refuse entrance to its own nationals, another state would be forced to retain these individuals within its territory, without its consent to do so. The second state's territorial sovereignty would thereby be infringed upon). Some writers have gone so far as to state that the duty to admit 'is considered so important a consequence of nationality that it is almost equated with it'.[138] Whether this is actually the case is questionable, since the duty to admit doesn't necessarily give a corresponding right to individuals. The individual is thus in an ambiguous situation: While her state has the duty to admit her under international law and while she may also have an entry right under domestic law, she may not be in the position to claim this right internationally. (The difficult position of a stateless person, whose freedom of movement is already severely restricted, is all the more evident since she has no right to enter or remain in any country, nor does any state have a duty to admit her).

On the flip side, individuals (theoretically) have a right to leave their country of nationality.[139] This right is often not respected by states in practice, however.[140] Generally, limitations come not through an outright ban on international travel, but through a refusal to grant a passport or exit visa.[141] As

---

135. *See*, e.g., Art. 69(2) of the Constitution of the Republic of Hungary (1949); Art. 16 of the Constitution of the Republic of Italy (1947); Art. 23 of the Constitution of the Republic of Turkey (1982); Art. 51 of the Arab Republic of Egypt (1980); Sec. 14 of the Constitution of the Republic of Argentina (1853). *See also In re Martonelli*, C.C.S.D.N.Y. (1894) where the court held that a national has the constitutional right to enter his own country.
136. Randelzhofer (2000), p. 507; Torpey (2000), p. 164; but *see* Hofmann (1998), p. 14 for a claim that such a right exists even in the absence of customary international law to regulate applicable restriction clauses.
137. In this regard, *see* Hannum, at 20 (1987) for a distinction between the right of nationals and non-nationals; for the latter, we deal with a right to travel.
138. Van Panhuys (1959), p. 56.
139. Hannum (1987), p. 139, Appendix B.
140. *See* Dowty (1987). Among other states, Cuba, South Africa, North Korea, Somalia, Mongolia, Vietnam, Myanmar, China, Laos, Israel, Saudi Arabia, the United States, many Central and South American states, and the entire former socialist bloc have, at some time in the last 60 years, restricted their nationals' right to depart.
141. *See* discussion in Turack (1972), pp. 1–2 and p. 33. As Weis discusses, there is also no necessary link between diplomatic protection and the possession of a passport. Weis (1979), p. 226; but *see United States v. Laub*, US (1967), p. 481 (one of the functions of a passport is to designate individuals who may receive diplomatic protection from the issuing state); *Kent v. Dulles*, US (1958), p. 129 (act of issuing a passport implies an intent to extend

Torpey discusses, 'because states and the state system have monopolized the power to regulate international movement, persons must possess a passport'.[142] Accordingly, they 'have come to be more or less universally required for admission to a foreign territory'.[143] Even where the right to depart is recognized, states may place certain limits on individuals' right to leave, as Article 2(3) of Protocol No. 4 to the ECHR makes clear. In *Napijalo v. Croatia*, for example, the E.Ct.H.R. determined that the state had violated Article 2 when its authorities seized an individual's passport for two years, because it was not 'necessary in a democratic society proportionate to the aims pursued'.[144] While the outcome of the case was in this instance favourable to the individual, the vagueness of the provision examined leaves states a significant amount of wiggle room – it is conceivable that the confiscation of a passport could be deemed both necessary and proportionate in some circumstances.[145] Under international law then, an individual's right to enter and leave her state of nationality is precarious at best. In sum, international norms have made some, albeit limited, inroads into questions of nationality. Pressure from the international community to respect these minimal norms can go a long way, however, as could be seen in the Latvian case in the mid 1990s.[146]

Domestic law generally gives some additional protection to individuals, since the attribution or withdrawal of nationality (like that of any other legal status) is an administrative decision subject to judicial review. In fact, the constitutional principles of most states can be used to protect individual interests. Thus, the United States Supreme Court has determined that depriving an individual of his nationality on the basis of a court-martial conviction is 'cruel and unusual punishment' in violation of the Eighth Amendment of the Constitution.[147] In another example, it was the *Bundesverfassungsgericht* (German Constitutional Court) that determined in 1974 that the state interest in restricting plural nationality could not override a child's interest in holding the nationality of both parents[148] – despite repeating the official view that plural-nationality is an 'evil' (the *Übel*-Doctrine).[149] In other words, the balancing of individual and state interests already discussed occurs on the basis of domestic law too. Another notable example is the Slovenian Constitutional Court's decision declaring the removal of former Yugoslav nationals from the Slovenian population registry in 1992 unconstitutional (because it constituted a violation of the principle of equality and in situations where the individuals concerned had to leave Slovenia, gave rise to a violation of their rights

---

diplomatic protection to the bearer). Thus, domestic law determines what a passport is and what its functions are.
142. Torpey (2000), p. 162.
143. *Ibid.*, p. 163.
144. *Napijalo v. Croatia*, E.Ct.H.R. (2003), para. 82. *See also* Art. 12(3) of the ICCPR; UN Human Rights Committee, General Comment 27, Freedom of movement (Art. 12) (1999).
145. *See* discussion in Torpey (2000), p. 131.
146. Kalvaitis (1998).
147. *Trop v. Dulles*, US (1958).
148. BVerfG, BVerfGE 37, 239, para. 116 *et seq.* (1974).
149. *Ibid.*, para. 117.

to a family life and to freedom of movement).[150] Though the removal of the individuals in question was based on their cultural and ethnic affiliation (they were not Slovenian), the court determined that they had an equal right to Slovenian nationality as members of the majority. Besides the question of legal status for the purposes of international law, the Court also established that their rights as citizens had been violated.

It is to the nature of such citizenship rights that we now turn.

B. CITIZENSHIP

As a concept, citizenship exists since the appearance of participatory political communities. A Greek *polis* had 'citizens' just as the Florentine city-state of the Renaissance, Hobbes' England or the pre-World War I Austro-Hungarian Empire did. However, the content of citizenship rights has differed markedly through time and location, so that it would be more correct to speak of citizenships in the plural. One commonality, however, has been the existence of two constitutive elements – rights/duties and identity. In other words, all citizenships are 'intimately linked to the ideas of individual entitlement on the one hand and of attachment to a particular community on the other'.[151] Accordingly, citizenship, like nationality, has clear rights functions, as well as intangible cultural and political aspects.[152] Let us take a look at both.

1. THE FUNCTIONS OF CITIZENSHIP

The rights function of citizenship centres around the duties an individual owes to and the rights she holds against (and in modern times through) the state.[153] Traditionally, this function has been linked to a given territory. This territorial understanding has resulted in a number of characteristics: 1. The citizens of the political community within the given territory, and only these individuals, enjoyed certain rights; 2. Rights could be exercised only within the territory of the political community; and 3. Citizens determined the content of rights (on the basis of the principle of popular sovereignty).

---

150. *Case U-I-284/94*, Const. Ct. Slovenia (1999), as discussed in Amnesty International's Briefing to the UN Committee on Economic, Social and Cultural Rights (2005). *See also* para. 10 of the Human Rights Committee Report on Slovenia (2005).
151. Kymlicka and Norman (1995), p. 283.
152. For a three-fold breakdown of the dimensions of citizenship, *see* Carens (2000), Chapter 7. Carens argues that there are legal, psychological and political dimensions of citizenship. I would, however, argue that what he defines as 'political' dimensions are either the wider context or result of the other two.
153. The most obvious example of a right against the state is that of participation in all its forms (through voting, forming parties, expressing one's opinion); rights through the state include all the trappings of the modern welfare state and, until recently, many human rights. Duties to the state include paying taxes, military service and respect for the law.

a. The Emergence of Modern Citizenship

Who the citizens of a given political community are has depended on the nature of the polity. With time, this group has increased in size through the abolishment of requirements for property ownership, age, ancestry, race and gender. Thus, T.H. Marshall saw (English) citizenship as the outcome of step-by-step advancement toward *full membership* in the community with equal rights and duties.[154] The concept has always implied exclusiveness, however. Through the Middle Ages and into the 19th century, towns, in particular, set high barriers to membership, in order to forestall the arrival of 'unwanted' persons, like the old, sick or poor.

As Preuß states, 'citizenship circumscribes a status of not just physical, but social belonging. It...therefore...set[s] boundaries between "ins" and "outs"'.[155] This function of social boundary-maintenance plays out through the organization and re-organization of both bases of distinction and their content, as broad categories of persons are designated, with a particular set of relations to the state.[156] Differences in emphasis on what 'membership' in the form of citizenship (or nationality) entails, though seemingly insignificant, are at the heart of contemporary debates, as will be discussed below.

In the case of pre-modern citizenships (i.e., those before the American and French revolutions), there were very few 'ins'. These citizenships can be best understood as an elite status, 'a matter of active participation and belonging in a community', whereby 'the status of being a citizen was a function of the community's recognition of one's belonging'.[157] Citizenship, generally limited to cities or city-states, thus allowed one to take part in community decision-making, in contrast to subject status – the lot of the vast majority – which generally implied allegiance to and control by a sovereign. This allegiance was directly tied to territory – if the sovereign of the territory changed, so did one's allegiance – so that individuals were born into subjecthood and had little influence over their fate.

The concept of national citizenship that emerged in the wake of the American and French revolutions extended citizenship status to all (male and Caucasian) nationals, however, thereby transforming it from the privilege of few to the right of all.[158] The group of 'ins' now constituted the whole (male and Caucasian)

---
154. T.H. Marshall (1998), p. 102 (emphasis added).
155. Preuß (1995), p. 269. *See also* Thomas (2002) (distinguishing between five ways of understanding belonging to a political polity – descent, culture, belief, contract and monetized contract).
156. Compare Tilly (2005), esp. Chapter 11.
157. Koslowski (2000), p. 64 (2000). *See also* Grawert (1973), p. 71 *et seq.* for a discussion of how traditions of membership in German towns influenced the development of later laws on nationality.
158. The (then) Austrian Empire's parallel (and earlier) conception of national-citizen is all but ignored in literature, perhaps due to the limited rights available to individuals. Nonetheless, it should be noted that the notion whereby '*die bürgerlichen Gesetze verbinden alle Staatsbürger*' (Sec. 4 AGBG of 1812) and the concept of an '*allgemeines österreichisches Staatsbürgerrecht*' (Sec. 23 *Reichsverfassung* of 1849) – i.e., a general and abstract status

community, as bounded by the borders of the state, on the basis that the people themselves truly constituted the sovereign state. Accordingly, all (male and Caucasian) nationals were to have equal rights and duties and an equal stake in decisions regarding matters of the state. In this manner, however, the question of who was a citizen (and who was not) also defined what the state was (and was not).

Hence the intangible cultural and political aspects of citizenship. While citizenship had previously implied social status within society – since very few members of the given society were citizens – the rise of the modern nation state gave citizenship a symbolic function, through a link to nationality. Specifically, the borrowing of 'nationality', a status that served as an international ordering mechanism, as the basis for the *demos*-to-be allowed for a near parallel of international and domestic law: the (male and Caucasian) nationals of the state were simultaneously its citizens and vice versa. Once this pairing occurred, however, the exclusive character of citizenship became equated with nationality: the nationals of a state – now the nation state[159] – became a distinct community, with a supposedly singular national identity. As Schnapper stated, 'nationality law, which defines the legal bond between individual and State, is effectively the translation of the conception of the nation into the order of concrete realities'.[160] The borders of the nation state, in turn, marked the geographical boundary of the sovereign political community.

The notion of equal citizenship within the sovereign territory of the nation state has with time encompassed an ever-greater number of rights. In Marshall's conception, for example, the scope of this extension can be traced through civil, political and social rights.[161] This last group of rights – including public education, health care and pensions – is the hallmark of the welfare state. 'By guaranteeing these rights to all, a welfare state ensures that every member of society can feel like a full member'.[162] According to some authors common national identity is a prerequisite for such an extended scope of rights, however.[163] Otherwise, 'there is nothing to hold citizens together, no reason for extending the role to just these people and not to others'.[164] Thus, while policies linked to the increasing convergence of nationality and citizenship resulted in a common national identity and the rise of the nation state, this identity has been a prerequisite for the gradual increase in the scope of citizenship

---

    of membership to all within the territory of the state – has its origins in a *Denkschrift* from 1753. See Grawert (1973), p. 146 *et seq.* for an extended discussion.

159. For a discussion of the concept of 'nation' *see* Sec. I.C.2. (Suffice to note for now that in the context of the 'nationstate' we can only speak of an ideal; few states, if any, were ever nation-states).

160. '[L]e droit de la nationalité, qui définit le lien juridique entre l'individu et l'État ... est en effet la traduction, dans l'ordre des réalités concrètes, de la conception de la nation', Schnapper (1991), p. 51.

161. Marshall (1998), p. 94.

162. Lehning (2001), p. 242.

163. *See* Oldfield (1998), p. 80. *See also* Koslowski (2000) on the importance of 'closed membership', p. 91; but *see* Engelen (2003) for a discussion of differentiated inclusion in citizenship rights.

164. Miller (1992), p. 94.

rights. The centrality of a shared identity helps explain why states[165] have attempted through a variety of means, including nationality policies, education systems and citizenship practices, to create a sense of uniqueness as the basis for solidarity. As Kymlicka argues, 'a shared conception of justice throughout a political community does not necessarily generate a shared identity, let alone a shared civic identity'.[166] A commonality of history and language or culture, however, seems to have done so to some extent, at least in the context of the nation state.[167]

b. Challenges to Modern Citizenship in the Name of Identity

Traditionally citizenship and nationality are thus inextricably linked, their identity function intertwined as a building-bloc of national identity. This is particularly true for states – the United States foremost – that have relied on a given, supposedly civic, ideal as the focal point for national identity. This explains why the real legal divide in the US has (until recently) been between nationals and legal permanent residents on the one hand and all others ('aliens' in US legal parlance) on the other – in contrast to the national/non-national distinction prevailing in other states. The latter don't belong to the national community in any manner, while the former groups are either already practicing their citizenship (as national citizens) or on their way to doing so (as green-card holders).[168] (Incidentally, the appearance and development of European citizenship has created a similar dynamic in Member States, as the nationals of all Member States share a number of rights and duties, while third-country nationals remain outsiders). To the extent one speaks of patriotism as the basis for solidarity in such a context – rather than nationalism – one is referring to loyalty focused on the identity of the state, rather than of the nation.[169] All those loyal to the state – all those part of the *demos* – are welcome for membership; since membership is claimed to be a matter of civic idea(l)s, however, citizenship becomes central not just in its rights/duties function, but also in that of identity.[170]

---

165. The conceptual separation of the 'state' and 'society' is in some ways problematic in the context of national identities (and many others). Behind the former is, after all, not some Wizard of Oz, but many individuals frantically pulling levers and pushing buttons. The construction and maintenance of national identity cannot succeed without the (tacit or public) agreement and participation of at least part of the population. Herzfeld's point of the mutual dependence of nationalism and cultural intimacy is thus well taken. Herzfeld (1997), pp. 5–6.
166. Kymlicka (1998), p. 181.
167. *Ibid.*
168. Ongoing US debates on granting citizenship rights (and legal status) to illegal aliens centres on exactly the continuing validity of this distinction. *See The New York Times*, 'The Immigration Debate: The Overview; Immigrants Rally in Scores of Cities for Legal Status (11 April 2006); BBC News Online, 'US Immigration Bill Impasse Eases' (12 May 2006).
169. *See* Connor (2002). As will be discussed, patriotism is more correctly deemed a subset of nationalism than something apart from it. *See* discussion at Sec. I.C.2.
170. This fact goes far in helping to explain why the US government's shamefully inadequate response to Hurricane Katrina led not just to discussion of responsibility and race, but also the meaning of American citizenship. As one commentator recalled, '[w]hen government

Though citizenship would at present be a difficult basis for maintaining national identity in many European states, certain citizenship rights have in recent years been extended to non-nationals in numerous countries, in a manner comparable to the United States. Sweden granted voting rights in local and regional elections to those who had been resident in the state for three years in 1975. Other states have followed suit, and have added certain social and civil rights; very few, however, have granted general voting rights in national elections to non-nationals. In fact, only two European states have even granted this right to foreigners with a particular nationality, reciprocally, in a very specific context.[171] The aura of the national community thus remains, despite the assertions of some authors that the extension of citizenship rights to non-nationals devalues the former[172] – an idea particularly central to the post-nationalists, discussed below.

Simultaneously, the presence of immigrant minorities has brought to prominence the actual social and cultural plurality of European societies, and has buried any claims to unified national identity. In fact, the much-vaunted unity had never become reality – though arguably there was a high degree of convergence and agreement – as other identities, including religious, regional, ethnic, linguistic and cultural ones, interfered with the national project to a greater or lesser extent. The constant and increasingly vocal calls for 'group differentiated' citizenship by autochthonous minorities (now joined by immigrant minorities) are one clear sign of the unfinished national project.[173] The proponents of such differentiation argue that equal treatment of citizens does not result in actual equality, due to the varied needs and expectations of specific social groups. Hence, there should be public recognition and various sets of rights accorded to minority cultural groups in society.[174] A differentiated set of citizenship rights may, under certain circumstances, do away with the ideal of equal national citizenship,[175] however, and risks becoming enmeshed in arguments of what constitutes discrimination (or distinction).

---

failed so dismally in New Orleans, the betrayal was of the same order [as the outcome of the Rodney King trial]: it was no longer possible to believe in the contract that binds Americans together'. Accordingly, '[m]illions of acts of common decency and bureaucratic courage will be necessary before all Americans, and not just the storm victims, feel that they live, once again, in a political community and not in a savage and lawless swamp'. Michael Ignatieff in *The New York Times Magazine,* 'The Broken Contract' (25 September 2005).

171. Irish nationals have voting rights in Great Britain since 1949; while British nationals have the right to vote in national elections in Ireland since 1984. In addition, the nationals of states of the British Commonwealth have voting rights in national elections in the UK under certain circumstances. (The system is a remnant of colonialism.)
172. *See* discussion in Schuck (1989); Soysal (1994), p. 163–164; and Jacobson (1996), pp. 8–10.
173. *See* Kymlicka (1995), p. 107 *et seq.* and Sajó (1995), p. 177 *et seq.*
174. Kymlicka (1995); Young (1989); and *Ibid.* (1990).
175. The most obvious example would be acceptance of the 'cultural defence' in criminal law, in circumstances in which victims have not (or could not have) consented to their treatment or in which lasting harm results; e.g., sexual molestation or rape. *See* Dundes Renteln (2004) for a discussion. *See also* Offe (1998) for a critique of such 'identity group' rights, due to lack of agreement on what the rights should entail and which groups are entitled to them.

The idea of such a regime is not new, of course. Santi Romano suggested the possibility of a plurality of legal orders within one state order in the early 20th century.[176] There have even been administrative systems based on legal plurality in the not-so-distant past. The Ottoman Empire's *millet* system, for example, allowed for separate courts to religious minorities in matters of personal law within the territory of the empire; but only Muslims (members of the *Umma*) enjoyed citizenship rights.[177] Today, the legal systems influenced by Islam maintain vestiges of a distinction between Muslims and non-Muslims (as set out in the *Quran*), but these are limited in the vast majority of states to the areas of family and personal law. In a further example, all Israeli nationals must have their marriage and divorce matters adjudicated by the courts of their respective religious communities.[178] (The multicultural practice in Canada and Australia also bears some resemblance to such plurality, but is not as wide in scope.)[179] The theoretical and practical implications of such systems are too vast to discuss here, but it should be noted that the E.Ct.H.R. has determined, in the *Refah* case, that the proposal of the applicant party (banned by the Turkish government) requesting:

> that there should be a plurality of legal systems would introduce into all legal relationships a distinction between individuals grounded on religion, would categorize everyone according to his religious beliefs and would allow him rights and freedoms not as an individual but according to his allegiance to a religious movement.
>
> The Court takes the view that such a societal model cannot be considered compatible with the Convention system, for two reasons.
>
> Firstly, it would do away with the State's role as the guarantor of individual rights and freedoms and the impartial organizer of the practice of the various beliefs and religions in a democratic society, since it would oblige individuals to obey, not rules laid down by the State in the exercise of its above-mentioned functions, but static rules of law imposed by the religion concerned. But the State has a positive obligation to ensure that everyone

---

176. Romano (1975) [1915], p. 88. *See also* Karl Renner, who imagined a two-pronged nationality: one a sign of membership in the (Austro-Hungarian) state, the other a personal attribute – to be chosen by the individual as a matter of right – expressing membership in a cultural nation. Renner (1965) [1904].
177. Ottoman Law on Nationality (1869), as quoted by Kiliç (2002), p. 33.
178. *See* discussion in Schachar (1998), p. 291.
179. The systems have recently come under strain as a result of claims raised by new immigrant groups. In the context of Canada, significant (international and domestic) public opposition to government plans to introduce *shari'a* into the existing system eventually led to a decision to ban the use of all religious law. *See* BBC News, 'Sharia law move quashed in Canada' (12 September 2005); and Aslam (2006) for a proposal to introduce judicial review of decisions handed down by religious arbitration tribunals. *See also* the Report of Attorney General Marion Boyd, Dispute Resolution in Family Law (2004), pp. 78–87 for a discussion, as well as p. 138 *et seq.* for a suggestion that the use of religious law continue to be allowed in matters of personal law in the province of Ontario.

within its jurisdiction enjoys in full, and without being able to waive them, the rights and freedoms guaranteed by the Convention...

Secondly, such a system would undeniably infringe the principle of non-discrimination between individuals as regards their enjoyment of public freedoms, which is one of the fundamental principles of democracy. A difference in treatment between individuals in all fields of public and private law according to their religion or beliefs manifestly cannot be justified under the Convention, and more particularly Article 14 thereof, which prohibits discrimination.[180]

On the basis of this decision, it is highly unlikely that any European state would publicly introduce a system of plural jurisdictions. In most states they already exist to some degree, however, on the basis of nationality. Given that many European states continue to adhere to the exclusive link of nationality for the purposes of legal jurisdiction in matters of family and personal law and in light of the high ratio of non-nationals in the general population judges often apply (and interpret) the laws of other states, including legal systems based on the principles of Islam.[181]

For permanent residents without the nationality of the state of residence, possible affinity to (the society and legal system of) more than one state is thereby disregarded. The question of whether this practice means that 'a significant part of the cultural identity of a bicultural [individual], at any rate, is cut off'[182] is not considered. (This is equally true for the growing reliance by European states on residence as a link to the law of the state in the context of family and private law.)[183] Though such biculturalism is officially recognized in the case of plural nationals, the practice whereby a state ignores any additional nationalities its national may hold[184] means that questions of identity don't enter into decisions on the law to be applied in this context either. Given that identity doesn't necessarily run parallel to nationality, however – or at least not the cultural identity considered important by the individual – this is not perforce a bad thing.[185]

---

180. *Case of Refah Partisi (The Welfare Party) and Others v. Turkey* (Third Section), E.Ct.H.R. (2001), para. 70. *See also* paras 119 *et seq.* of the judgment of the Grand Chamber (2003), confirming the outcome.
181. Developments in private international law (specifically judicial co-operation in civil and criminal law matters) within the European Union may also lead to the recognition and application of foreign judgments in Member States, but rely on an entirely different logic; *see* discussion at Sec. I.C.2.d. Furthermore, the Regulations applicable in this area of law rely equally on nationality and 'habitual residence' for the purposes of establishing jurisdiction. *See* Article 3(1) of Council Regulation 2201/2003 of 27 November 2003 concerning jurisdiction and the recognition and enforcement of judgments in matrimonial matters and the matters of parental responsibility, repealing Regulation 1347/2000.
182. '*Dem Bikulturellen jedenfalls ein ... wesentliche[s] Teil seiner kultureller Identität ab[ge]schn[itten] [wird]*'. Mankowski (2004), p. 285.
183. Mansel (2003), p. 129.
184. *See* discussion at Sec. IV.A.4.
185. In other words, most other sentiments of belonging don't find recognition in internationally recognized forms of membership, as discussed above.

Basic Concepts

In any case, choice of law issues, especially the use of *lex fori* or of permanent residence as the basis for a link to a particular legal system, have become increasingly culture-laden as a result of large-scale immigration and concurrent demands – for official recognition of diverse cultural practices within the state.[186] Moreover, in the context of ongoing legal ties to multiple states, the question of membership in one particular state goes beyond consideration of the state-individual relationship generally discussed in scholarship. (Which rights will a state grant? To whom? How are they to be institutionalized?) Instead, we are dealing with the issue of official recognition of not only specific ties, but of the kinds of identities that should be publicly recognized within the state. If official discourse has thus far been focused on the existence and maintenance of the nation state, it must now also consider cultural, linguistic, religious and other groups (with or without state ties) that demand legal recognition of their particularities within and across state borders.

This growing disconnection of legal statuses has meant that citizenship is increasingly only a secondary source of identity – possibly even after education policies – as its identity function is subsumed by that of nationality. To put it bluntly, being a national is a sign of membership; having (limited) voting rights in a state or paying taxes is not. We thus face an unusual discrepancy with regard to identity and national citizenship. On the one hand, writers speak of a 'functionally differentiated network of affiliations and loyalties' or a 'disconnection of ...: nationality, citizenship, [and] national identity',[187] and point to the increased legal acknowledgement of differentiated personal identities as a sign that national citizenship is increasingly irrelevant. At the same time, nationality, heretofore only a legal category, has emerged as a respectable foundation for collective and, as will be shown, personal identity. Otherwise, legal documents could not speak of 'preserving the diversity of the ... national identities of Member States'[188] – whatever the core of such national identities may be – while said states could not so openly rely on the identity function of nationality, especially in the context of integration, to help maintain their much-vaunted 'identity' in the first place. The carefully constructed national identity of the so-called nation state – with all its cultural and institutional specificities – has thus, paradoxically, gained acceptance, while the duality of citizenship-nationality, from which it was born and which it maintained, is slowly dismantled.

2. CITIZENSHIP AS PRACTICE

In discussions on modern citizenship, citizenship is more than just a link between the individual and the state. Social science literature, in particular,

---

186. In this context, *see* Asad's articulation of the need for states to create circumstances in which 'multiple ways of life and not merely multiple identities [can] flourish'. Asad (2002), p. 227.
187. Preuß (1995), p. 280.
188. Preamble, Charter of Fundamental Rights of the European Union (2000) (hereinafter, 'Charter of Fundamental Rights').

endows citizenship with many more facets than are present (or even possible) in legal discourse. Since the content of citizenship in the legal sense is, however, affected by broader of conceptions of what citizenship is (and what it could be), we must look at these broader perspectives. As Schöpflin defines it, citizenship is 'the package of overt legal, political, institutional, economic and other analogous relationships that bind society and the individual to the state and which govern political relationships within society'.[189] Hence, citizenship in the wider sense is a commonality in the understanding of the basic principles underlying the given political community. This commonality is most clearly expressed in activist understandings of citizenship, whereby citizenship entails an engagement with other individuals and groups in society. In this understanding, citizenship is not only a status but also a process. It is 'about acknowledging the community's goals as one's own, choosing them, and committing oneself to them'.[190]

In traditional approaches, the most important community was (hoped to be) the national one, composed of the nationals of the nation state; the basis of identification, in turn, was the unique character of the national community.[191] In a modern twist on the pre-requisites for such uniqueness, Habermas has argued for a 'constitutional patriotism', deriving from 'the *praxis* of citizens who actively exercise their civil rights'.[192] According to Habermas, citizenship is not conceptually linked to a national identity, but results from the political socialization of individuals. For this reason, acculturation to the ethno-cultural characteristics of the given community is not necessary. Loyalty to a political community can be based only on the underlying constitutional principles of the given community,[193] while agreement on and recognition of a shared practice of citizenship – public participation, deliberation and law-making – is seen as strong enough a bond to maintain the national community. Others have criticized this view, arguing that a shared political culture is not a deep enough basis for a common identity, and that no system can function without some integration of individuals.[194]

Some authors have gone even further in deconstructing the traditional approach by arguing that even a territorial component is superfluous to understandings of citizenship. One can be the citizen of a virtual community[195] or of

---

189. Schöpflin (2000), p. 42.
190. Oldfield (1998), p. 81.
191. For a discussion of such identification *see* Sec. I.C.2, below.
192. Habermas (English, 1990), p. 259. *See also* Fine and Smith (2003); and Beiner (1995), p. 8 and pp. 19–20.
193. *See also* Tassin (1992); and Delanty (1995), p. 163.
194. *See* Schlesinger (1992); and Kraus (2000), p. 206. *See also* the result of surveys carried out in ten cities (in six states) in 2002, where, despite large differences by state and region, 'being integrated in a country's society in terms of work, language and acceptance of institutions [wa]s obviously the basic precondition for nationality and full citizenship'. Fuss (2003), p. 9.
195. Vandenberg (2000), p. 299 *et seq.*

the global commons.[196] In the same vein, some writers speak of 'global' or 'cosmopolitan' citizenship[197] – for traditional theory, a contradiction in terms. The proponents of such non-territorial citizenship argue, however, that the increasing interdependence of states and societies, the emergence of international organizations and the changed moral relevance of the national community all point to a need for re-evaluation.[198] In other words, traditional understandings of citizenship no longer suffice, due to changed circumstances.

a.   **Post-National Citizenship and its Discontents**

The most widely discussed version of such deterritorialized conceptions has been developed by proponents of 'post-national citizenship'. Soysal, for example, has argued that 'national citizenship is losing ground to a more universal model of membership, anchored in deterritorialized notions of person's rights'.[199] In particular, citizenship rights and privileges once due only to nationals are supposedly now extended to non-members on the basis of personhood, derived from international human rights norms and structures. Specifically, the civil and social rights granted to former guest workers in Western European states[200] and the claims-making of immigrant groups on the basis of universal human rights is pointed to. Migration is thus claimed to have played an important role in this re-conceptualization, as the presence of non-members has shifted the basis of state legitimacy from that of popular (national) will to that of state respect for international human rights norms.[201] The result of these developments is contended to be a 'deterritorialized' membership, reflected in a shifting of personal identity[202] from one focused on singular belonging to one composed of multi-level transnational and supra-national memberships. As Heater argues, 'it is necessary to accept as perfectly feasible the notion that an individual can have multiple civic identities and feel multiple loyalties'.[203]

Proponents of post-national identity hence articulate not only 'the emergence of membership that is multiple in the sense of spanning local, regional, and global identities', but also an accommodation by such multi-level identity of 'intersecting complexes of rights, duties and loyalties'.[204] Citizenship thus seems to retain its

---

196. Newby (1996); and van Steenbergen (1994).
197. Habermas (English, 1990), p. 279; Carter (2001). The two writers most associated with the idea are David Held and Richard Falk. *See*, respectively, Held, *Democracy and the Global Order: From the Modern State to Cosmopolitan Governance* (1995) and Falk, *The Making of Global Citizenship* (1994), p. 131 *et seq*. For a good critique of the approach, *see* Calhoun (2004).
198. *See* Linklater (1999), p. 47 *et seq*.; and Held, *ibid*.
199. Soysal (1994), p. 12. *See also* Jacobson (1996), pp. 2–3 for another proponent of this view.
200. *See* Bauböck (1994).
201. *See* discussion in Jacobson (1996).
202. *See below* at Sec. I.C.1 for a discussion of theories of identity.
203. Heater (1990), p. 320.
204. Soysal (1994), p. 166.

identity function, but is an increasingly irrelevant source of rights. Elsewhere, however, Soysal states that the 'ties that bind' manifest themselves through participation in and by 'vertical connection' to common, universalistic discourses that transcend the very ethnic idiom of community'.[205] Overlooking the mis-use of terms (why is a community necessarily ethnic?) it seems that the changed rights function of citizenship actually does have an effect on identity, as the community is re-interpreted as a community of human rights.

So let us look at both propositions in turn. A conjecture of new developments in identity, namely that of the possibility of multiple ones, is not too problematic, though somewhat late – social and individual identity theories have been discussing the nuances of its existence for decades, after all.[206] As for its increasingly transnational and deterritorialized (or more correctly, non state-focused) nature, however, it is a doubtful one. One of the prime examples referred to – the recently created European citizen – is hardly deterritorialized or post-national, as will be shown in the next Chapter. In fact, the rights and privileges that accompany this status rely on the existence of special ties between the Member States of an entity (the European Union) that guards its borders jealously. And while it is true that rights-discourse in the European Union is increasingly focused on jurisdiction rather than on nationality *qua* membership – so that resident third-country nationals gain ever more rights in Member States – this transformation is premised on solidarity within the 'European' community, not the global one.

As for claims for the existence of transnational identities in the context of migration, a number of studies have in fact shown the pertinacity of identities developed in the context of the nation state and (re-)articulated in that context, no matter where the individual may be.[207] In such instances, we deal with either long-distance nationalism (identification with a nation despite geographical distance from its territory) or dual-nationalism (identification with two separate nations).[208] To the extent that individuals in the former group live in diasporas, they are not acting transnationally (or post-nationally)[209]– they have merely crossed state borders, while remaining within their nation in cultural terms. It is only the second group that can be considered truly transnational, since it belongs to multiple national groups; the groups remain *national*, however. No group is post-national, in the sense of giving up on national membership as an important element of identity. Thus, first-generation immigrants tend to continue identifying with elements of the national cultures of their state of emigration,

---

205. Soysal (2000), p. 11.
206. *See* discussion at Sec. I.C.1.
207. *See* discussion at Sec. IV.C.3.a.
208. *See* Fitzgerald (2004).
209. Given the conflation of the borders of cultures, nations and states in much of the transnationalism literature (e.g., Basch *et al.*, 1994), transnationalism is used by some authors as the equivalent of post-nationalism, or the 'supercession of nationalism in legitimating universal rights of citizenship'. *Ibid.*, p. 229. For an example of such equivalence, *see* Bauböck (1994).

while possibly forming an attachment to their (local) place of residence. Individuals from the second-generation, in turn, have been shown to re-interpret emigrant national identity in light of the social conditions in their immigrant state. In particular, studies of acculturation strategies[210] have shown integration and separation to be the models most preferred by second-generation immigrants (as opposed to assimilation and marginalization). But preferences vary by age, gender and minority group, as well as in reaction to the identity politics of the state of residence.[211] Acculturation can result in either 'caught between two cultures' adaptation[212] or 'feet in both worlds' integration[213] with trans-state involvement.[214]

That global cultural flows have an effect on individual and collective identity formation should also not come as a surprise – and does not change the reality that they are filtered through societies bounded by the state.[215] Is there any identity not affected by such cultural flows? Those who negate the possibility of evolving diaspora identities rooted in national (or other cultural) identities and who instead argue for purely transnational or global ones do so with the same static view of culture and identity they attack elsewhere – or, worse, make a general phenomenon appear singular to only certain groups.[216]

It is with the second contention – that of superseding national citizenship – that we run into real trouble, however.[217] In the first instance, the quality of such post-national rights is distinctly fuzzy. Certainly, non-nationals have a limited number of rights under international law, beyond those basic human rights laid down in relevant human rights treaties (*inter alia*, UDHR, ICCPR).[218] But in Europe, at least, the three main sources of rights for non-nationals have been (likely in this order) the constitutional principles and domestic legislation of states,[219]

---

210. Berry *et al.* (1989).
211. *See* Neto (2002); Morawska (2003), p. 160; and Koopmans and Statham (2003), p. 216 *et seq.*
212. *See* Anwar (1976). *See also* Brah (1996), p. 41 *et seq.*
213. *See* Morawska (2003); and Levitt (2003).
214. Morawska (2003), p. 158. *See also* Guarnizo *et al.* (2003).
215. *See* discussion in Soysal (2000), pp. 10–11.
216. *See* Oksenberg-Rorty (1994) for a discussion of the difficulty of identifying cultural groups (since the very things that should unite members, such as tradition or heritage, are often the most important points of contention).
217. The emergence of a common, 'international citizenship among the states of the world' (p. 314), with residence as a more modern conception of membership than nationality was debated in legal scholarship as far back as 1918, then on the basis of the 'weakening of the traditional relation between sovereign and subject' (p. 306) and increased global mobility, *see* McMurray (1918).
218. For a good overview of the interaction between citizenship and human rights, *see* Shafir (2004).
219. *See* Aleinikoff (2003), p. 111. At the same time, certain rights remain limited to nationals only. In Germany, for example, these include: freedom of assembly (GG Art. 8(1)); freedom of association (GG Art. 9(1)); freedom of movement in the territory of the state (GG Art. 11); right to choose an occupation (GG Art. 12); prohibition of extradition (GG Art. 16(2)(1)); right to vote (GG Art. 20(2)(2)); the right to resist (GG Art. 20(4)); and equal political status in all federal states, including access to public office (GG Art. 33). Some of these rights have been extended to European citizens, however.

the fundamental freedoms and rights of European citizenship developed in the European Union and the negative rights (more correctly protections) of the E.C.H.R. In all three cases, we can speak of regional or supra-national norms at best, certainly not universally enforceable ones.[220] This brings us to the second difficulty, which is that all three sources of rights rely on states directly or indirectly; and what the state gives, it can take away.[221] Third, the evolution of supranational entities has, in some cases, resulted in lessened rights for non-nationals – in the European Union, for example, certain elements of the Tampere Agenda, as well as developments post-September 11 have arguably decreased the scope of rights to third country nationals.[222] Finally, the link between multiple identities and corresponding intersecting complexes of rights is problematic. As Koopmans and Statham have shown, the claims-making of migrant groups in Western Europe depend, at least in part, on 'conceptions of citizenship and national identity in a particular setting'.[223] In other words, the citizenship policies and political/ social structure of the state of residence, as well as the political, social and cultural influence of the state of origin condition not only the identities of migrants, but also the rights they claim, and get.[224] For

---

220. For a discussion of citizenship as a political tool in the context of post 9/11 US practice, *see* Falk (2004). For an example of restrictions of social rights, *see* US developments in the late 1990s, as discussed in Schuck (1998), p. 206 *et seq.*; and Martin (2003). For a study of the consequent rush to naturalize *see* Singer and Gilbertson (2002).

    See also, in the context of France, the announcement of then-Minister of the Interior Sarkozy that all non-nationals found guilty of involvement in the riots of October-November 2005 were to be expelled, regardless of residence status. Le Monde, *M. Sarkozy demande l'expulsion des étrangers impliqués dans les violences urbaines* (9 November 2005); Le Figaro, *Banlieues: dix émeutiers étrangers menacés d'expulsion* (16 November 2005); and *ibid.*, *Expulsions: trente étrangers dans le collimateur du ministre de l'Intérieur* (15 November 2005). (Compare also Arts 36–38 of *Loi No. 2003-1119 du 26 novembre 2003 relative à la maîtrise de l'immigration, au séjour des étrangers en France et à la nationalité* (2003), making the expulsion of certain groups of permanent residents practically impossible). The first expulsion took place in February 2006. *See* BBC News, 'France deports African "rioter"' (3 February 2006).
221. That the E.C.H.R mirrors many of the rights and takes the jurisdictional approach of the UN Covenants does not mean that the latter provide the same protection to individuals as the Council of Europe system does - while the rights of the UN Covenants set minimum standards of protection, they are barely enforced and are certainly not adjudicable.
222. *See* Amnesty International's Human Rights Assessment of the Tampere Agenda (2004). *See also* the E.C.J. order in Case C-45/03 *Prefetto della Provincia di Catania c. Oxana Dem'Yanenko*, E.C.J. [2004], finding that the Court has no jurisdiction to examine the expulsion procedures of Member States relating to third-country nationals not covered by Council Directive 64/221/EEC of 25 February 1964 on the coordination of special measures concerning the movement and residence of foreign nationals which are justified on grounds of public policy, public security or public health (Repealed by Council and Parliament Directive 2004/58/EC of 29 April 2004 on the right of citizens of the Union and their family members to move and reside freely within the territory of the Member States) or by E.C.T Art. 68(1).
223. Koopmans and Statham (2003), p. 199.
224. In an unusual example of the identity-rights duality, explicable by the particular history of the states in question, the Russian-speaking minorities of the Baltic countries are entitled to 'social

this reason, at least one study of immigration has claimed that adopting the identity categories of the state – and making claims on that basis – is the 'most profound form of assimilation' for migrants.[225]

b. The Importance of National Frames of Reference

In reality, the very categories used in public discussion are state-specific and 'entrenched in governmental and other organizational routines of social counting and accounting'.[226] In other words, even the construction of official categories (e.g., in the census) is an attempt at moulding collective identity.[227] The discussion of integration that has accompanied amendments to the regulation of legal status in a number of European states, discussed below, has revealed such differences of approach. Even the determination of who was to be integrated, let alone the degree of integration expected was determined largely by prevailing frames of reference, as shown by a comparison of two major surveys on immigrants prepared in the early 1990s in France and Great Britain. In France, the National Institute of Demographic Studies prepared a study titled *'De l'immigration à l'assimilation: une enquête sur les immigrés et leurs enfants'*, or 'From Immigration to Assimilation: A Survey of Immigrants and their Children' in 1992.[228] (Even the title of the study is unusually candid, given that the body responsible for immigrant matters is the *Haute Conseil à l'Intégration*, or the High Council on Integration). The equivalent study prepared in Britain by the Policy Studies Institute was 'Ethnic Minorities in Britain: Diversity and Disadvantage' prepared in 1994.[229]

The French study ordered persons by *origine ethnique* (ethnic origin, on the basis of ancestors' nationality) and *appartenance ethnique* (ethnic belonging, on the basis of first language spoken). The former results in a lack of differentiation between those born in France or elsewhere and, more speciously, equates nationality with ethnicity; while the latter, an attempt at more precise differentiation, relies on a static and one-sided view of belonging: if one was born a Berber-speaker, apparently, one is Berber for life. The British study, in turn, took

---

citizenship' (on the basis of non-citizen passports), which entails social security and residence permits – different from that of newer immigrants – but which do not include political participation, *see* van Meurs (2003). For a general look at institutional factors, *see also* Guiraudon (2003), p. 297.
225. Kasinitz *et al.* (2002), p. 117.
226. Brubaker (2004), p. 62.
227. *See* Kertzer and Arel (2002). The most extreme example of using classification for political purposes in the recent past was the apartheid regime of South Africa, in which an individual's racial category defined the bounds of her rights – and in which administration boards and courts regularly adjudicated cases on reclassification, on the basis of criteria such as 'appearance and general acceptance and repute'. *See* Bowker and Leigh Star (1999), p. 206 *et seq*.
228. Tribalat (1995).
229. Madood *et al.* (1997).

the opposite approach, and classified by a shockingly loose conceptualization of 'ethnicity'. As the report states, 'the most common expression of ethnicity is not what people do but what people say or believe about themselves – it is possible for people to have a sense, even a strong one, of an associational minority identity without participation in many distinctive cultural practices'.[230] While self-description is an important element of group adherence, this approach not only conflated culture and ethnic origin, it also treated ethnicity as 'a sort of in-dwelling psychological determinant looking for ways to express itself'.[231] (Assumedly, I would be laughed at if, in light of the claimed provenance of *magyar* from a nomadic group in Asia, I were to suddenly discover my Mongolian ethnicity). In fact, the ethnic minorities identified by the study (Caribbean, Indian, Pakistani, Bangladeshi and Chinese but no Irish, the largest minority in the country) hint at a clear preoccupation with visible (or racial) minorities; apparently all those who are Caucasian are part of the majority. It would have been more honest on the part of the government to admit that the particular categorization used is a function of historical development, rather than a universal truth.

If even the language used to speak of groups within a given state is specific to that state – as are the social structures that rely on (and perpetuate) the particular approach – then the context-specificity of claims-making should come as no surprise. As Aleinikoff argues, 'rather than witnessing the dawn of a postnational era, we are likely to see ... a thickening of relations between domestic and foreign populations ... that will occur *within* the regime of nationstates'.[232] For individuals, the outcome can be a fragmented identity, with a sense of vacillating belonging, or one rooted firmly in several communities. For societies, it could mean a blurring of the lines between insiders and outsiders, leading to radical re-assertions of 'traditional' national identity or a diversified community with new and continuously re-interpreted bases of cohesion. For states, it may lead to a new focus on territoriality, in the form of equal rights granted to all those present in the given territory for a set period (while those absent would lose such rights) combined with or in opposition to increased de-territoriality, with a focus on those individuals who are no longer in the state, but who nonetheless belong to its community. What form such thickening takes will differ from one context (and state) to another, but will lead to increased tension under all circumstances, as different states and communities evolve in variegated ways, with concomitant legal regimes to deal with the new reality. The proliferation and transformation of the legal statuses discussed here is thus only one element of change, though arguably one of the most important.

Before turning to the legal changes, however, let us take a short look at the nature of personal identity, as well as the national identity we have been referring to.

---

230. *Ibid.*, p. 332.
231. Banton (2001), p. 154.
232. Aleinikoff (2003), p. 122.

C. INDIVIDUAL AND COLLECTIVE IDENTITIES,
AS CONCEPT AND AS RIGHT

On the most basic level, 'identity is such a rudimentary notion that it would be futile and furthermore impossible to attempt to define it'[233] – we identify other people, places and things on a daily basis, after all. We also have no difficulty recognizing ourselves – 'I am me' – even if the constitution of that self remains a puzzle well past the self-conscious years of adolescence. On further thought, however, an individual's identity becomes chimerical: Do I, like Descartes' wax, remain the same, despite not being able to recognize my younger self? Do I remain the same, previously Yugoslav, now Croat? And does it matter what I think, rather than how others define me? Can I even be defined without the context of others?

> Shouldn't we reverse the usual categories and say that what is truly real is not at all the person – a person without historical identity, that is to say without a past or roots – but the community that has shaped his being and without the work of which the person is but an abstraction and even a fiction?[234]

Surely not, but the approach is not far off the mark.

1. THE CONSTRUCTION (AND RE-CONSTRUCTION) OF IDENTITY

Individual identity – however complex – is in all cases constructed, at least in part, through and in response to 'meanings imparted by a structured society'.[235] In other words, whether through a process of self-categorization (in social identity theory) or identification (in identity theory), the individual places herself in relation to the relevant social categories or classifications of her society.[236] As social identity theory views it, for example, through a process of social comparison individuals who are perceived as like oneself on the basis of a pertinent factor (e.g., language, religion, race, nationality, gender, sexuality or membership in the 'Real Madrid' fan club) are categorized as part of one's in-group, different from those who remain outside. Identity theory, in turn, focuses not on group belonging, but on individual

---

233. '[L]'identité est une notion si primitive qu'il serait vain et de plus impossible de tenter de la définir'. Guenancia (1995), p. 563. If one needed a general definition, however, the one in the Oxford English Dictionary (2nd ed., 1989) would be acceptable.
234. 'Ne faut-il pas renverser le catégories ordinaires et dire que ce qui est vraiment réel, ce n'est nullement la personne, une personne sans identité historique c'est-à-dire sans passé ni racines, mais la communauté qui a façonné son être et sans l'œuvre de laquelle la personne n'est qu'une abstraction et même une fiction?' Guenancia, ibid., pp. 610–611.
235. Stets and Burke (2000), p. 226.
236. Though both social identity and identity theory have much to tell about the self in relation to society, they two branches of social psychology focus on different aspects of the individual; the former approaches the person in relation to her surroundings, the latter through the general development of that individual's identity.

'roles' – mother, wife or professor – that are relatively stable components of social structure.

As Stets and Burke recognize, the focus on social identity and role corresponds to Durkheim's distinction between organic and mechanical forms of social integration[237] – 'people are tied organically *to* their groups through social identities; they are tied mechanically through their role identities *within* groups'.[238] Of course, a particular aspect of identity can at once be a role and a social identity, and operate simultaneously as such, so that the two are separated with difficulty. With regard to approach, however, and to the extent that identity theory disregards master statuses[239] – such as religion, race or nationality – that in certain contexts over-ride all other characteristics, the former is not as relevant to our discussion as social identity theory. So let us take a closer look at social identities.

Tajfel defined social identity early on, as 'that part of an individual's self-concept which derives from [her] knowledge of [her] membership in a social group (or groups) together with the value and emotional significance attached to that membership'.[240] As this definition shows, there are multiple dimensions to the structure of social identity: in-group ties (or perception of belonging), centrality (or commitment to/ importance of belonging), as well as self-esteem (or the emotions associated with belonging).[241] To the extent that any of the three factors above may differ from social identity to social identity, in specific contexts and at various times, one social identity (e.g., religion) may generally mean more to a person than another (e.g., nationality), or may matter more in a certain situation (e.g., when at a referendum on abortion) or at a given point in life. In fact, many identities (including national identity) may become socially significant in only certain situations and lie dormant in everyday interactions.[242] In addition, since the balance of factors for a given social identity will differ from person to person, the same social identity ('New Yorker') may matter more to Jack than to Jill,[243] or be understood in a different manner.[244] It is this, the unique and constantly evolving combination of social identities that makes each person's self-concept singular. Exactly because of changing contexts, however, the self is a fluid concept. Moreover, to the extent that the self-concept may differ from society to society, cultural background plays a role in the salience of group membership, generally speaking,[245] as well as in normative orientation and in the individual's perception of the self as a distinct entity. It may also affect the relation between self and environment, and what is

---

237. Durkheim (1997) [1893].
238. Stets and Burke (2000), p. 228 (emphasis added).
239. Stryker (1987).
240. Tajfel (1978), p. 63. *See also* Bauman (1999), p. xxxi.
241. Cameron (2004), p. 240.
242. *See* Kiely *et al.* (2001), p. 34.
243. *See* Krosnick (1988) for a distinction between identity salience and identity solidity.
244. For example, aspects of identity attribution may be resisted by individuals despite their acceptance of belonging to a social group. *See* Widdicombe and Wooffitt (1995).
245. *See inter alia*, Dhawan *et al.* (1995).

constitutive of identity (e.g., which memories are salient);[246] while historical and social factors may cause differentiated development in the context of immigration.[247] Regardless of such variation, belonging (or the process of social identification) has been suggested as a fundamental human motivation, a need for all individuals.[248]

As Hogg and Abrams showed, however, the social categories to which individuals belong exist only in relation to other, contrasting categories.[249] In other words, one could not conceive of oneself of as 'white' in American race discourse if there were no 'black'. Such duality (or plurality) is necessary both to the process of social identity formation and to its maintenance. With respect to the identity formation process, the element of self-categorization already discussed is complemented by that of social comparison, whereby the individual's self esteem becomes intertwined with her view of the group. A person's self-esteem is accordingly enhanced by viewing the in-group and out-groups on the basis of dimensions favourable to the in-group.[250] Thus, social identities are not just descriptive (or prescriptive) but also evaluative – in a given context (e.g., when watching the Olympics or World Cup), 'self-perception and conduct become in-group stereotypical and normative, perceptions of relevant out-group members become out-group stereotypical, and intergroup behaviour acquires competitive and discriminatory properties to varying degrees depending on the nature of the relations between the groups'.[251] In a more literary vein, Esterházy's description of a reaction to a swimming gold for Hungary at the 1988 Olympics is exemplary of this process:

> [T]hen we watch Darnyi again, for the third time. And for the third time, again, though we knew every second by heart, tears sprang to my eyes. And his too. 'Why does this happen?' he asks, sniffling, 'have we gotten old? Is that why?' 'Noho, Maaaaarty', I answer, snivelling, 'it's because weheee're a smaall cohooountry, and still, lohoook, what beautifuuul suhhuceeess ...' 'Crazy', [my wife] said ... proudly and made ... some food.[252]

---

246. Cross and Gore (2003), p. 537.
247. *See* e.g., Driedger (1976) and discussion of the 'bicultural self' in Cross and Gore (2003), p. 554 *et seq*.
248. Baumeister and Leary (1995).
249. Hogg and Abrams (1998), p. 19 *et seq*.
250. In an eloquent recognition of this process, the Supreme Court of Canada has noted that a 'person's sense of human dignity and belonging to the community at large is closely linked to the concern and respect accorded the groups to which he or she belongs. The derision, hostility and abuse encouraged by hate propaganda therefore have a severely negative impact on the individual's sense of self-worth and acceptance'. *R. v. Keegstra* (Supr. Ct. Can.) (1990).
251. Hogg, Terry and White (1995), p. 260.
252. '*[A]kkor harmadszor is megnézzük a Darnyit. És harmadszor is, pedig már másodpercre tudtunk fejből mindent, könny szökött a szemembe. Meg az övébe is. Mért van ez? kérdi szipogva, megöregedtünk, és azért? Nehem, Mahacihika, válaszolom hüppögve, hanem mert kihis ohország vagyunk, azt látod, mégis milyen széhép sihekereket ... Hibbantak, mondta büszkén a kis fekete eszmei mondanivaló, és csinált ... valami ennivalót*'. Esterházy (1991), p. 127.

The explosion of national colours on every piece of clothing imaginable during the 2006 World Cup would be another, more conspicuous example of in-group stereotypical conduct.

The cognitive process underlying such reactions – in fact all group phenomena from co-operation and altruism through cohesiveness to ethnocentrism – is depersonalization. Through depersonalization, the individual acts (in the specific situation) like the perceived prototype of the in-group member, rather than as a unique individual; this does not mean a loss of her personal identity, however, just that the contextual level of salience has changed. In this manner, socially defined shared meanings become incorporated into one's own identity standard, so that '[c]ulturally patterned practices, customs, situations, and languages act as a continual priming effect'.[253] To put it crudely, individuals want to act in the manner they are expected to act, and derive personal gratification from such action – whether decorating a Christmas tree or voting in a national election. Furthermore, such culturally configured models become the 'norm' against which others are measured. This process comes in handy for the constructors of collective identities, and is often handily exploited by them. The tendency to highlight this process primarily in the context of national communities – as if it were somehow unique – is hence deceptive. Yes, states have special capacities in exploiting processes of social identification – and in mobilizing individuals for their purposes – but they are not singular in doing so. For this reason, when writers refer to an 'imagined community'[254] or state that 'nationalism is directly predicated on resemblance'[255] – they could be referring to any kind of collective identity.

Moreover, the in-group serves not only as a supplier of categories, but also as a feedback mechanism. Group recognition of belonging may thus play a role in heightened self-esteem;[256] leading to the enhancement of behaviour viewed as appropriate by the group. If I view myself as a punk, for example, I will likely wear clothing viewed as appropriate by the group – the (hopefully) positive reaction of other punks to my attire will, in turn, lead to heightened self-esteem on my part; I will, in reaction, attempt to behave and look more punk. Because group prototypes are constructed in the context of both (maximized) inter-group differences and (minimized) intra-group differences, however, the relevant out-group (and society at large) influences the nature of the prototype. Whether I define myself as Catholic in opposition to Protestant, Muslim or atheist matters. Since prototypes are thus 'context dependent and are particularly influenced by

---

253. Cross and Gore (2003), p. 542.
254. Anderson (1983), pp. 6–7.
255. Herzfeld (1997), p. 27. In fact, Max Weber's status model of group relations had already recognized the importance of maintaining inter-group difference, while enforcing homogeneity within the group, at the turn of the century. *See* Weber (1948) [posthumous].
256. *See* Ellison (1993).

which out-group is contextually salient',[257] they are dynamic. As Nagel discusses in the context of Arab immigrants, for example, 'Arabness' is re-constructed in relation to 'the English' and other minorities, rather than being carried over and sustained from the states of immigration.[258] Immediate social context thus influences the individual as group member, while being influenced by the individual in turn, as she attempts to bring reality into line with her perceptions of the group (and her role within it).

In fact, it is more correct in this context to speak of a 'prototypicality gradient'[259] than of a particular prototype. As a function of who is compared in given situations, some will be considered more prototypical than others; evaluation by the in-group (and out-groups) will thus result in either acceptance or marginalization. The attempts of individuals to be accepted as e.g., 'black' or 'white' in societies where these racial identities have social or political implications rely on exactly this process, for example.[260] Since the individual – and her positive self-image – is so intertwined with her group(s), a constantly changing social dynamic results with linked re-making of self, in-group and out-groups. The dynamic is repeated in the wider realm of society, as groups vie for status, power and prestige.[261] Such competition may not result in many waves if the two groups at issue are local chapters of the *Pokémonu* fan club, but the potential for trouble is obvious if we are dealing with religious or national groups. The process of self-categorization also becomes more problematic than may first appear in the case of individuals belonging to national minorities or immigrant groups. Yes, individuals may need a clear sense of identification with the culture and heritage of their perceived in-group for wellbeing (the alternative being self-hatred and in-group denial), but the identification of a particular in-group and the degree of identification with that group is not a clear-cut matter. As a member of the German minority in Hungary, am I Hungarian or German? Both? Also, what if society or other out-groups disallow some expression of the culture one identifies with?[262]

---

257. Hogg (2003), p. 469.
258. Nagel (2002), p. 271 *See also* Campani (1993), p. 186.
259. Hogg (2003), p. 471.
260. A timely example of the process would be the view of some African-Americans that presidential hopeful Barack Obama is not 'black enough' – not because of his mixed race heritage, but because of his personal background. *See The Guardian*, 'Is Obama black enough?' (1 March 2007).
261. As a form of self-enhancement, in-group bias is thus necessary for the maintenance of positive distinctiveness. *See* discussion in Hogg, (2003) pp. 466–467. Moreover, '[s]ubjective belief structures influence the specific behaviours that group members adopt in pursuit of self-enhancement through positive social identity' (at 467). How the situation of the group is perceived by group members – particularly the stability and legitimacy of intergroup status relations – as well as the possibility of social mobility thus influences action.
262. Cameron *et al.* (2005), pp. 73–74 *et seq.*

2. THE PARTICULARITIES OF NATIONAL IDENTITY

Such questions bring us to a consideration of the in-group most closely linked to the state: the nation. As both Brubaker and Tishkov have argued,[263] the concept of 'nation' is best approached in scholarship as a metaphorical heading – a way of organizing social space – rather than an actual category of analysis. It serves as the foundation for a series of assumptions and actions; it is as a symbol around which to rally. Because it is both a source of legitimacy and a focus for loyalty, however, 'the nation' is not generally considered a discursive practice by individuals in daily life. It is rather a powerful, and for many politicians crucial, sociological category.[264]

On this basis, model membership in the nation state is 'egalitarian, sacred, national, democratic, unique, and socially consequential'.[265] It is the 'national' and 'unique' element of this membership that is relevant to us here; aspirants must be recognized as 'of' the given nation, and traditionally no other, to be full members of the political community. The idea of 'membership in a nation' highlights the incongruence between possible bases of membership and belonging, however. While the former is a more-or-less clear-cut question – either one is a member of a given entity or one is not – the other is a much more complex notion, with psychological connotations. Belonging cannot be divided into simple categories of 'in' and 'out' in the manner of memberships. When the two conceptions of group collide – such as when nationality, a form of membership, is given an identity function – the impossibility of fitting fluctuating boundaries into clear borders becomes obvious.

In the context of national identity, many social scientists distinguish between civic and ethnic nations[266] – the former relying on shared civic norms, the latter on a belief in common descent as the basis of membership – as well as respective processes of 'patriotism' and 'nationalism'.[267] While the United States, Australia and France are usually held up as examples of the former, specimens of the latter are generally the likes of Germany, Japan or Serbia (in fact all of the satellite states of former 'Eastern' Europe).[268] The general (implicit or explicit) preference for a

---

263. Tishkov (2000); and Brubaker (1996), p. 7.
264. The concept of 'nation' is thus a community that claims singularity on the basis of a number of shared and unique criteria that may include myths and symbols, history, religion, language and/or descent and that aspires to control of a given territory.

    For the sake of clarity – and given the propensity to confusion in English – affiliation with a nation will *not* be referred to as 'nationality' (which is limited to the legal status already discussed), but as 'kinship'.
265. Brubaker (1998), p. 132.
266. Ethnicity is thus defined as a '*subjective[s] Glauben an eine Abstammungsgemeinsamkeit*' Weber (5th ed., 1972), p. 237.
267. For a discussion of the questionable difference between the two, *see* Canovan (2000).
268. Hans Kohn laid the seeds for this division in the context of Europe with *The Idea of Nationalism* (1945). His legacy was taken up by Anthony Smith, who distinguished between (Western) civic and (Eastern) ethnic national identities. *See ibid.* (1991) and (1994). *See also* Williams (2003), p. 210 *et seq.*

'civic nation' relies on the claim that such a nation rests on shared commitment to certain civic principles – and is therefore open to everyone. In contrast, ethnic nations are closed to newcomers because of their reliance on descent. To give an example: a Namibian emigrating to the United States can become both an American in identity terms and a national of the United States; the same person emigrating to Germany could never be German in identity terms, even if she acquired German nationality, because she could not trace her provenance from a German ancestor – or so the story goes.

Frankly, this approach is deceptive and out-dated. The same social identity processes occur in all collective groups, including nations, and result in the same suspicion of individuals deemed different, whether on the basis of skin colour, religion or language spoken. The approach also misses – or perhaps ignores – the common reliance of all nations on culture, defined as shared customary beliefs, symbols, attitudes, values and social forms passed on from one generation to the next.[269] As Conversi discusses, there is a tendency to see culture as intrinsically linked to ethnicity (as in the much-used term 'ethno-cultural'),[270] so that 'political conflicts are first reified as being fundamentally ethnic, then as being cultural'.[271] In other words, culture is equated with ethnicity as something intrinsically closed, therefore unacceptable, and contrasted with the 'civic', somehow separate from culture. Since both rely on inter-generational continuity, culture and ethnicity are to some extent attached, but should be distinguished at least in scholarly discussion.[272] Otherwise, there is a danger that 'no conflict can be resolved without extirpating the troublesome "culture" identified as the "cause" of the conflict'.[273] (In fact, cultural identity allows for development and overlap, while ethnicity does not).[274]

The concept of nation – by the very fact that it is a collective identity – cannot be separated from a reliance on culture. This reliance is clearest in the case of overt

---

      Recently, theorists have attacked this viewpoint – Kürti going so far as to label it a product of colonial Western thinking, *see* Kürti (1997). For data showing little difference between the two *see* Hjerm (2003).
269. As discussed by a number of authors, 'culture' is a contested concept. *See*, e.g., Jenks (1993) for a survey of views from the perspectives of sociology, anthropology and cultural studies; and Stavenhagen (2001), pp. 86–91 for a look at understandings of culture in legal and social science discourse. Unless otherwise stated – e.g., when specific definitions used by given entities and instruments – the meaning attributed above will be used here.
270. *See, inter alia*, Fenton (2003), p. 20 *et seq.*
271. Conversi (2004), p. 819. *See also* Brubaker (2004), p. 53 *et seq.* and esp. p. 60.
272. *See also* Introduction in Barth (1994) [1969].
273. *Ibid.* Social science literature in particular has a tendency of 'culturalizing' conflicts that may be better explained by socioeconomic or racial factors. *See* discussion in Barry (2001), p. 305 *et seq. See also* Swidler (1986) for an early distinction between structural and cultural factors that shape behaviour; and Dhamoon (2006) for a call for a normative approach to culture in political and legal discussion.
274. 'Ethnic identification, then, is possible any time, any place, whatever one's emic culture may be, as long as a common link of biological filiation can be claimed [...so that] cultures and cultural differences change and evolve in almost total independence from ethnicity and ethnic relations'. Roosens (1995), p. 32.

nation states, where the state publicly supports and propagates a national culture that forms the basis for national identity. It is less clear-cut in the case of states that claim to be multicultural, but is nonetheless present to the extent that no state is actually culture-neutral. Each has (a) national language(s) (whether set out in law or not), a social and organizational culture and certain myths of foundation. The etymological origin of the word 'nation' (from the Latin word *nasci*, 'to be born'), implying common origin, is thus accurate for all states.

The example of the United States, supposedly a civic state, is instructive. The teaching of American history (at least as experienced by this writer in the late 1980s and early 1990s) begins with references to the Mayflower and the Pilgrims (while Native Americans make a short appearance at Thanksgiving dinner), continues to the Founding Fathers and Lincoln, through the great wave of immigration in the early 1900s to the civil rights movement. Throughout, emphasis is laid on the 'chosen' nature of the country,[275] as one imbued with a special quality that makes it singular in the world: the only place where anyone, of any background, can succeed (a.k.a. the 'American Dream'). As Conversi notes, this myth can be easily passed on to new arrivals and new generations, but is nonetheless 'a rhetorical device based largely on a "necessary" myth of political citizenship: the parallel fiction of shared descent, even if solely ideological, can be discerned through regular references to the first colonists and common 'ancestors''.[276] The fabrication of history is not, of course, limited to one state, but constitutes a necessary element of the creation and preservation of all national identities.[277]

The distinction between 'civic' and 'ethnic' nations is thus not as functional as it may initially appear – it would be more correct to speak of cultural nations, with varying emphases on shared features, ranging from values and norms through language and history to descent. For this reason, one should also speak of cultural nationalism – whereby 'nationalism' is understood as an ideology and/or political movement geared toward constituting and/or maintaining the nation.[278] As Nielsen

---

275. For more a more objective look at what was a subjective impression, *see* Longley (2003). For a general discussion of the role of public education in socialization, *see* Piaget and Weil (1951); and in constructing and maintaining power relations in society, *see* Callan (1997); Feinberg (1998), pp. 47–48; and Collins and Blot (2003), Chapters 4–5.
276. Conversi (2004), p. 823. *See also* Salins (1997). For a less academic approach, *see* Yezierska, *Bread Givers* (1925) or Zangwill, *The Melting-Pot: Drama in Four Acts* (1908). In the context of France, *see* Weber (1976) and Chapter 5 in Brubaker (1992).
277. As Renan noted, 'Forgetting, I would even go so far as to say historical error, is a crucial factor in the creation of a nation, which is why progress in historical studies often constitutes a danger for nationality. [T]he essence of a nation is that all individuals have many things in common, and also that they have forgotten many things'. Renan, at 11 (1990). In the context of the fabrication of tradition, *see* Lowenthal (1998).
278. Accordingly, both nationalism and the 'nation' are continuously constructed through cycles of action and reaction, shaped by both elites and common people. The process of nationalism is not necessarily linked to a state, then in many cases (Kurds in Turkey, Basques in Spain) nationalism may even pit the nationals of a state against the state itself.

    Through the process of interaction with other nationalisms, communities (e.g., Armenians and Turks) may even find themselves in conflict with another over the important

bluntly puts it: [A]*ll nationalisms are cultural nationalisms of one kind of another*.[279] Even if a given national community is 'constituted by political unity, it is centrally *expressed* in the striving for cultural unity'.[280] To this end, the state maintains certain educational and cultural policies and monitors membership through nationality laws in the manner already referred to.[281] Through these means, a shared symbolic universe is created (i.e., collective memory, 'national' literature, monuments, anthem, flag); this universe, in turn, helps 'establish the cultural autonomy of [the] population, [and] becom[es] the basis of a unique conceptual community'.[282] The multicultural claim of a lack of dominant culture in modern democracies is thus not only false, but directly misleading: 'the refusal to accept oneself as anthropologically dominant results, in practice, in *hiding* the rules of the game of society from immigrants: [even] if this [society] accepts small differences more than others, it does not accept a right to difference at its innermost depths'.[283] No surprise, perhaps, since state policies help create a 'symbiotic relationship between the [aspiring] nation and the symbolic nation',[284] of which individuals are simultaneously members. In this manner, the nation state can lay claim to a sense of continuity – near-eternity – while simultaneously adapting collective identity to the needs of the historical moment.

Ideally, the individual develops an attachment to the symbolic nation, as well as the actual community. The direction of attachment-formation can go in either direction. It may begin with a sense of emotional connection with the symbolic nation, for example, leading to a feeling of belonging to its present incarnation in the population of the nation state. Or, the sense of security or belonging provided by the actual community – as well as the elements of the social structure it provides – may lead to identification with the symbolic nation. As discussed above, the individual's sense of self, and of self-esteem, becomes entwined with her evaluation of the community in the process of such identification – in our case the national

---

elements of identity they use to define themselves; history, territory, language and symbols are often the most explosive of these elements. In such cases, as Bibó so succinctly puts it, 'Fear for survival tends to cull out representatives of sober rationality from the participants so that there will come a time when efforts to have minority children learn the folk songs of the majority appears as underhanded and dangerous attempts to force the use of the majority language, while agitation opposing these efforts and stressing the singing of folk songs in their native language is depicted as dangerous anti-state activity'. Bibó (1991) [1946], p. 50

279. Nielsen (1996–1997), p. 50 (emphasis in original).
280. Brubaker (1998), p. 139 (emphasis in original).
281. For discussions of the importance of schooling in this context, *see* Dewey (1996) [1916], p. 22; Dornbusch, Glasgow and Lin (1996); Gellner (1983), p. 35 *et seq*.; Yoshino (1992), p. 64 *et seq*. In the context of modern Germany, *see* Brötel (1999).
282. Anthony Giddens, as quoted in Cerulo (1995), p. 15.
283. *'Le refus de s'assumer comme anthropologiquement dominant aboutit en pratique à cacher aux immigrés les règles du jeu de la societé ... : si celle-ci accepte, plus que d'autres, de petites différences, elle ne reconnaît dans ses tréfonds aucun droit à la différence'*. Todd (1994), p. 382 (emphasis in original).
284. Cerulo (1995), p. 23.

one.[285] Loyalty to group then develops and becomes a source of cohesion within the group itself. It also allows the individual to order her environment with help from the values, norms and customs of the national group. Shared views and cohesion, in turn, help the evolution of the collective norms the nation state relies on for its continued existence.

However, the ideal of identity-formation just described holds true for all kinds of collective identities – not just the one advanced by the state. This, obviously, is a problem for the nation state. As Kovács argues, 'we do not "discover" our identities, but construct and portray them in competing cultural discourses'.[286] In other words, a number of identities compete with the national one for relevance to the individual: gender, culture, class, religion and region among others. In most cases the competing collective identities can co-exist, since individual identity is fluid. Depending on the context, people define themselves and are defined by others in various ways: as a Catholic, a woman, a Hungarian national, a European. However, some identities are irreconcilable.

Given the exclusivity called for by the ideal of membership in the nation state, as well as the complexity of the symbolic universe it aims to create, national identity has the potential to conflict with a number of other identities. The very process of collective identity formation and maintenance requires an (or numerous) other(s), in relation to whom the group's own identity can be distinguished, as discussed. For this reason, it was difficult until recently for an individual to be accepted as both French and German, due to fundamental differences in collective memory. Some national identities in Europe are still difficult to accommodate with other national or regional identities. In certain cases, this is also true for religious or other cultural identities.

In fact, national identity is *itself* a cultural identity, if we understand the latter as 'a sense of a shared *continuity* on the part of successive generations of a given unit of population, ... shared *memories* of earlier periods, events and personages in the history of the unit and ... a collective belief in a common *destiny* of that unit and its culture'.[287] In this sense, cultural identities are particular kinds of collective identities and encompass the likes of religious, linguistic and national identity. Of course, the given group is also likely to have the shared customary beliefs, symbols, attitudes, values and social forms that constitute culture in the classic sense. The pattern of these elements, while persistent, is not fixed; its importance and content may change over time without the cultural identity of the group having been altered. Hence, it is not the elements of the given culture that constitute the substance of a cultural identity, including the national, but the group's collective memories and sense of continuity/destiny.

---

285. Druckman (1994).
286. *'Identitásunkat nem "felfedezzük", hanem konstruáljuk, versengő kulturális diskurzusokban jelenítjük meg'*. Kovács (2003), p. 44; but *see* Fitzgerald (2004), p. 243 for a claim that members of minorities may adhere to the 'container' version of distinct natural cultures despite their sociological inaccuracy.
287. Smith (1992), p. 58.

Still, the two facets of cultural identity – its temporal substance and pattern of elements – interact, so that change in one can cause a transformation in the other. For example, a minority[288] may, as a result of continuous interference with their right to use a language – an element of their culture – change its conception of destiny and continuity, or the temporal substance of their cultural identity.[289] This phenomenon both explains why states can develop and maintain a national identity through educational and cultural policies and why they may attempt to interfere with collective identities deemed to be undesirable.

Questions pertaining to the accommodation of multiple cultural identities are now raised mainly in the context of immigration, although the constantly changing borders of European states have required some policy on the matter for millennia. The traditional state approach to competing cultural identities has been quite consistent, in any case: assimilation. Immigrants were historically expected to assimilate in clear terms, national minorities in a more covert manner – both by relinquishing their cultural norms, beliefs and customs, and adopting the characteristics of the dominant culture.[290] By the 1970s, reconsideration of, and later a strong backlash against, this mode of dealing with cultural minorities resulted in theories of multiculturalism, put into practice in the Netherlands, the United Kingdom and Sweden, among others. In particular, Berry's identification of four possible forms of acculturation (assimilation, integration, separation and marginalization)[291] opened the door to more nuanced study of multicultural societies. Theorists since that time have identified differences in minority and majority attitudes to cultural maintenance and adaptation,[292] differentiated acculturation in varied spheres of life, and varied strategies by generation. Recently, even assimilation has been re-invented, in a new form: namely, as a conscious assertion of sameness by immigrants in public spheres of life.[293] That said, no state today admits to processes of assimilation; the more innocuous 'integration' is preferred.

---

288. Deschênes' definition of 'minority' (intended to refine Capotorti's widely used definition) as found in para. 181 of the UN Proposal Concerning a Definition of the Term 'Minority' (1985) will be the one used here.
289. For example, the presence of dual-language signs designating geographic names, as well as the maintenance of monuments has been a matter of contention between many Central European states and their minorities. A minority's sense of continuity and destiny is obviously affected when such signs are removed, or monuments altered.
    One concrete example of the symbolism behind such gestures is a controversy that centred on the placement, by members of the Hungarian minority in Romania, of a sign stating '*Székelyföld*' (Land of the *Székely*, who are a regional group of Hungarians) at the border of a particular county in Transylvania, as a sign of their demand for autonomy. The sign was promptly removed by the police. See Népszabadság, 'Táblaháború a Székelyföldön' (24 November 2004); erdely.ma, *Rendőrségi Eljárás Indul a 'Székelyföld'-tábla Elhelyezői Ellen* (25 November 2004).
290. For the classic enumeration in the context of the United States, *see* Gordon (1964).
291. Berry (1980), p. 9.
292. *See*, e.g., Verkuyten and Thijs (2002).
293. *See* Nagel (2002), p. 271 *et seq.*

3. BOUNDARIES OF BELONGING

In this context, the interaction of the individual and the group becomes crucial. As Mannens notes, 'culture as a process ... forms the interactive link between the individual and the community'.[294] In other words, a culture cannot continue to exist without individuals continuing to identify with it. In turn, if the culture ceases to exist, the cultural identity of the given group is also threatened with extinction, hence, so is the group, as such. Naturally, the link functions in both directions: a group can be created through an ever-increasing identification by individuals with the given cultural identity, as nationstates well know. The much discussed concept of 'European identity' also relies on this process.

The European project is but one example of the move away from state-centred cultural identities in Europe. Others include the rise (or return) of regional identities ('Scandinavian', *toscano*'), cross-border cultural identities ('Basque', 'Hungarian'), religious identities ('Sunni Muslim') and mixed cultural identities ('Asian-British', 'Turkish-German') among others. As Mannens puts it:

> The claims that are made nowadays by individuals and groups do not correspond any more with the 'theoretical boundaries' of the classic nation state ... As the direct link between the character of the nation state and the individual's identity seem to dwindle, a revision of the morality of States seems appropriate.[295]

The 'clash of seemingly archaic legal structures with new socio-political notions of culture-based identities'[296] is now real. To some extent, states are reacting, both by reconsidering existing legal regulation and creating new frameworks, as we will soon see. But the problem goes deeper. As Crowley discusses, the nation state offers a normative framework in which the overlap of territory, cultural and political community is coveted and has to some extent been attained.[297] Because of the lack of neat boundaries – or their actual, inherent messiness – the question of belonging become central, however. Separating the two elements of the nation state, for example, means asking who belongs to the state and who to the nation. With regard to the former, we can give a simple answer: all those within its territory, since they are subject to its laws. The latter, however, presents difficulties. The nation is simultaneously an expression of the *demos* (in the civic sense) and the nation ('the historical permanence of which the people ... is the manifestation').[298] The two are intertwined, but not identical, since there is a difference between formal membership and substantive belonging. In the context of European states, for example, questions of membership may be solved by changing the regulation of nationality; but belonging is a more complex matter. Thus, it is

---

294. Mannens (1999), p. 34, n. 25.
295. *Ibid.*, p. 62.
296. *Ibid.*
297. Crowley (1999), p. 30.
298. *Ibid.*, p. 34.

Basic Concepts

'impossible to formulate admission to the nation solely in terms of legal procedures, which may not be socially recognized of they conflict too sharply with the underlying cultural basis of nationhood'.[299] Extending nationality to an ever-wider group of individuals will thus not necessarily solve problems of multiculturalism, even if may solve nagging problems of democratic legitimacy.

As Bleich describes it, the sociological boundary of belonging can only be surmounted if the national community is 're-imagined' not only in legal terms, but also in substance (e.g., through education policies).[300] In fact, any understanding of belonging as a clear-cut question of 'in' or 'out' ignores the existence of social group prototypes already discussed. If a prototype the exists, however, we more correctly speak of hierarchical structures of belonging – some will be considered more 'Hungarian' or 'German' than others, in light of the prototype. The heated debate preceding the referendum in Hungary on dual nationality for Hungarian minorities in neighbouring states (in December 2004), for example, involved a debate about what a 'Hungarian' is – interestingly, not in the context of the minorities, but that of Hungarian nationals. Some leading politicians, as well as certain members of the minorities declared that those who voted against the proposal were not 'real' Hungarians[301] – in other words they did not fit the(ir) prototype. Given extant divisions in Hungarian society, the attempt at forcing a prototype not shared by all nationals on everyone failed, but not by much.[302]

The struggle over which groups gain the upper hand in determining 'Hungarianness', 'Germanness', etc. and the very inability to agree on who can be considered to possess this quality shows not only the inadequacy of labels like 'ethnic', 'civic', 'transnational' or 'post-national' but also the lack of a hegemonic prototype.[303] Self-conscious reflection on national identity – what constitutes it and how much it matters – may or may not lead to a re-imagination of the nation (toward a more or less inclusive understanding), but in any case highlights, through the ongoing process, the shifting boundaries of belonging.

If there are shifting boundaries of belonging, however, we face a dilemma, since law does not – by nature – allow for such nuances. Nationality is, after all, a distinctly 'in' or 'out' affair, based on categorical thinking. Although the emergence of the alternative legal statuses and approaches to nationality discussed here

---

299. *Ibid.*
300. Bleich (1999), p. 62. The author argues that, while Britain has re-made its educational policies to allow for an encompassing view of Britishness, French policies have reaffirmed the dominant cultural view of Frenchness.
301. The most controversial remark was perhaps that of the (then) vice-president of the MKP (Hungarian Coalition Party) in Slovakia, Miklós Duray, who stated *'végre élvált a szar a víztől'* ('finally the shit has separated from the water'), in reference to the refusal of the socialists and the liberals to sign the closing statement of the MÁÉRT (Hungarian Standing Conference) meeting (12 November 2004), supporting a 'yes' vote in the December referendum. Interview with Miklós Duray, Magyar Rádió, 'Határok Nélkül' (15 November 2004).
302. *See* discussion at Sec. III.B.2.b.ii.
303. *See also* Tsoukala (1999), pp. 120–121; Levy (1999), pp. 104–105; and Münz and Ohlinger (1998), p. 173 *et seq.* for discussions of similar self-reflection in other European states.

is a sign of greater flexibility, such identity-focused statuses necessarily remain legal categories with clear borders. (To some extent, the group-differentiated rights already mentioned are also a recognition that not all nationals fit the prototype).[304] The cleavage of citizenship rights from nationality, or the separation of nationality's identity function from the actual legal status (as in status laws), are both attempts at creating legal gradations of belonging, but have been problematic in light of existing international norms. Whether such innovations are a positive development is a consideration for later. Suffice it to say for now that the context of the nation state makes any non-categorical thinking both legally and politically difficult.

In particular, we should not forget two more features of the nation state when considering the formal membership-substantive belonging duality. First, that the individuals seeking admission (e.g., migrants) themselves belong to cultural communities (whether religious, national, linguistic or other) and have 'baggage' of their own – traditions, histories, mythologies – to be preserved. Hence, boundary maintenance turns on the question acculturation, as already mentioned. Crowley even goes so far as to state that 'even taking the long view, the nation state principle can cope with migration [and national minorities] only by cultural assimilation'.[305] While this statement is perhaps no longer true, at least in the case of Western European states, the problem of competing cultural identities remains a relevant point. The second important feature to remember is that 'boundary maintenance is of vital importance to people because it commands not just symbolic self-definition but tangible resources'.[306] In other words, membership has clear social and economic advantages for individuals, particularly in the context of European welfare states. As we will see in our discussion of European Union citizenship and kinship laws, the consequences of particular decisions on resource distribution can in turn shape political and legal responses to issues of membership.

The problems presented by the membership-belonging duality are not limited to the nation state, however. While post-nationalists (cosmopolitans, etc.) may be correct in attacking the nation state as incoherent, its disappearance would not solve the dilemma sketched above.[307] We are in essence dealing with the underlying issue of the link between social identity and law. As we saw in our discussion of social identity theory, any grouping of individuals will, as a result of psychological and sociological processes, establish benchmarks of belonging: an in-group with a prototype member, as well as relational out-groups. Assuming this grouping

---

304. Thus, a decision of the Israeli Supreme Court has upheld measures limiting the right of some Israeli nationals – in effect Arab-Israelis – to family reunification. (Only women over the age of 25 and men over 35 from the West Bank are eligible to join their families in Israel and eventually to apply for nationality). *See* BBC News, 'Court upholds Israeli spouse ban' (15 May 2006).
305. Crowley (1999), p. 34.
306. *Ibid.*, p. 38.
307. *Ibid.*, p. 20.

is to form a political community – with set rules for interaction and participation in society – questions of legitimacy arise as a matter of course. In other words, individuals in the community will accept only those norms and rules as legitimate that they recognize as their own: expressive of the community's values, beliefs, customs, etc. Accordingly, the legitimacy of norms and rules will be tested continuously as collective identity develops. Assuming the community is a democracy – in fact, the only kind of political community where such questions arise publicly – the 'people', or the community itself, will be both the source and the judge of norms and rules. In such a context, however, informal benchmarks of belonging – the essence of 'us' – will require translation into formal membership. Otherwise, there will be no way to determine who has the right to participate in judging the legitimacy of the norms and rules that regulate life in the community. Formal membership will, in turn, impose categories of inclusion and exclusion on individuals that may not coincide with their sense of belonging. In this setting, Barthes' claim that 'all language is a classification; and all classification is oppressive'[308] assumes concrete form in the filing of individuals, by entities, into groups of 'insiders' and 'outsiders'.

In the case of states, such boundary drawing has increasingly assumed new forms since the 1990s. Accordingly, each of the legal statuses discussed here draws its boundaries in a different and, from the point of view of the traditional 'national-citizen'/ 'non-national' dichotomy, novel manner. All rely on and negotiate the identity function of the 'national-citizen' as a central component of their particular legal development, however. Plural nationality and kinship laws do so outright, in the name of protection of a claimed individual (and group) right to cultural identity. But does such a right even exist?

4.   A Right to Cultural Identity

As a general matter, despite Türk's contention that 'without affording full guarantees for ... cultural rights, including the right not to assimilate and the right to cultural autonomy, the protection offered ... by other rights can become practically meaningless',[309] the substance – and possibly even the idea – of such rights remains problematic. In the first place, there seems to be no one internationally accepted enumeration of what cultural rights are. The recent UNESCO Universal Declaration on Cultural Diversity (2001) (hereinafter, UDCD) does attempt to specify a bundle of rights to which this tag can be attached, but does so on the

---

308. *'Toute langue est un classement, et. ... tout classement est oppressif'*. Barthes (1978), p. 12.
309. United Nations Final Report of the Special Rapporteur of the Sub-Commission on Prevention of Discrimination and Protection of Minorities on the Realization of Economic, Social and Cultural Rights (1992), para. 198. *See also* Eide (2001), p. 289 (who refers to cultural rights as a 'remnant category'); and Meyer-Bisch (1991).

basis of an existing, rather scattered framework. Article 5, in particular, is worth quoting at full length:

> Cultural rights are an integral part of human rights, which are universal, indivisible and interdependent. The flourishing of creative diversity requires the full implementation of cultural rights as defined in Article 27 of the Universal Declaration of Human Rights and in Articles 13 and 15 of the International Covenant on Economic, Social and Cultural Rights. All persons have therefore the right to express themselves and to create and disseminate their work in the language of their choice, and particularly in their mother tongue; all persons are entitled to quality education and training that fully respect their cultural identity; and all persons have the right to participate in the cultural life of their choice and conduct their own cultural practices, subject to respect for human rights and fundamental freedoms.

The basic definition of 'cultural rights' thus seems to be that enunciated in the foundational international human rights instruments,[310] and centres on two central concerns: participation and distinctness.

The first reference to 'culture' in an international human rights instrument was in the ADHR,[311] which referred to the right of every person to 'take part in the cultural life of the community'. The reference in the UDHR to an individual right 'freely to participate in the cultural life of the community, to enjoy the arts and to share in scientific advancement and its benefits'[312] came approximately six months later. The International Covenant on Economic, Social and Cultural Rights (hereinafter, ICESCR) (1966) echoed this formulation and added an obligation for states to 'achieve the full realization' of this right.[313] Cultural rights are thus understood here as a right of *participation* in a *general* culture; and, in light of similar provisions in state constitutions,[314] can be conceived of as an extension of the right to education.[315] To the extent that the ICESCR left the implementation of cultural

---

310. That said, international instruments have 'various, distinct conceptions of culture which are not always clearly spelled out in the texts, and which are in fact often used rather loosely in general discourse'. Stavenhagen (2001), p. 87.
311. ADHR Rec. 5 and Art. 13.
312. UDHR Art. 27(1). *See also* Art. 22. As Art. 27(2) of the UDHR shows, cultural rights in a wider sense include intellectual property rights, which will not be touched on here. For a discussion of all aspects of cultural rights, *see* Eide (2001).
    Besides the narrow approach to 'cultural rights' taken here, in which we consider only the provisions of international instruments that include the word 'culture', we could also consider these rights in the broadest sense, as a bundle of provisions that contributes to the maintenance of (or has an effect on) culture. The latter would include practically all modern individual human rights, however, even if some – like the right to education, the right to free expression (including the use of a chosen language), the right to religion and the right to equal treatment – are more directly linked to the maintenance of culture than others.
313. ICESCR Arts 15(1)(a) and 15(2), respectively.
314. *See* Rec. 13 of the *Préambule* of the French Constitution of 1946; Art. 70/F of the Hungarian Constitution of 1949.
315. *See* UDHR Art. 26(1).

rights in the hands of a particular state, however, the *'State's cultural monopoly* has been consolidated'.[316] This should not be surprising, in light of our discussion of the manner in which states have generally seen cultural assimilation as an element of full national citizenship.

a.   **Cultural Identity in International Law**

The general, participatory approach to cultural rights has continued to play an important role,[317] but has been complemented by one focused on specific cultures. The UNESCO Declaration of Principles of International Cultural Co-operation (1966), in particular, declared that 'every people has the right and the duty to develop its culture'.[318] This more particularistic approach to cultural rights has developed rapidly since that time, and has taken two directions. One, a focus on the protection of the objective elements (or output) of a specific culture – cultural heritage[319] – has emerged, although it has not (yet) been framed in the language of rights.[320] Two, cultural diversity has become a matter of concern, most clearly in the right to (a specific) cultural identity – as can be seen in UDCD Article 5, above.[321] This concept is difficult to grasp, at least if we try to understand it as a right. As Donders discusses, rights, generally speaking, include a three-term relationship of object, subject and addressee.[322] A given individual is thus entitled to the right to vote, guaranteed by her state. In the context of cultural identity, however, the three-term relationship breaks down. What legal rights flow from a social concept like cultural identity? Different identities may require different sets of rights, thereby undermining the principles of universality and equality that are a cornerstone of the modern human rights system. Moreover, given the relationship between the pattern of elements (or the culture) and the temporal substance of

---

316. Szabó (1974), p. 48 (emphasis in original).
317. *See* Art. 14 of the Additional Protocol to the American Convention on Human Rights in the Area of Economic, Social and Cultural Rights (1988); but *see* Art. 17(2) of the African Charter of Human and Peoples' Rights (1981) (where the reference is to 'his' culture, i.e., a particular one).
318. In Art. 1(2). *See also* Arts 2(1) and 4(2) of the UN Declaration on the Rights of Persons Belonging to National or Ethnic, Religious and Linguistic Minorities (1992) (hereinafter, UNDRM); *See also* Art. 4 of the UNESCO Recommendation on Participation by the People at Large in Cultural Life and their Contribution to it (1976).
319. The determination of what constitutes cultural heritage is still open to debate. The definition found in Art. 1 of the UNESCO Convention Concerning the Protection of the World Cultural and Natural Heritage (1972) (hereinafter, CCPCH) is no longer exhaustive; *see* Art. 2(1) and (2) of the UNESCO Convention for the Safeguarding of the Intangible Cultural Heritage (2003).
320. *See* the UDCD above, as well as the CCPCH; *see also*, in the context of Europe, Arts 1 and 5 of the Council of Europe European Cultural Convention (1954); Arts 1 and 2 of the Council of Europe European Declaration on Cultural Objectives (1984).
321. *See* also, *inter alia*, Council of Europe Declaration of the Committee of Ministers on Cultural Diversity (2000).
322. Donders (1999), p. 69 *et seq.*

cultural identity already discussed, shouldn't the protection of a right to culture suffice?[323]

Despite these (and other) theoretical problems, a right to cultural identity has been included in Articles 1(3) and 5(1) of the UNESCO Declaration on Race and Racial Prejudice (1978), Article 1 of the UN Declaration on the Rights of Persons Belonging to National or Ethnic, Religious or Linguistic Minorities (1992) and Articles 4, 8 and 12 of the UN Draft Declaration on the Rights of Indigenous Peoples (1994).[324] However, none of these instruments are legally binding. Moreover, their treatment of cultural identity is somewhat sloppy: sometimes groups, at other times individuals are referred to, while there is not always a clear addressee. The attempt to move from a general focus on culture to a consideration of its most socially intangible realm – identity – is thus fraught with obstacles. The UNESCO Project Concerning a Declaration of Cultural Rights, which attempted a legal definition of cultural identity, highlights the absurdity of the approach. Cultural identity is defined there as:

> all the cultural references through which individuals or groups define and express themselves and by which they wish to be recognized; cultural identity embraces the liberties inherent to human dignity and brings together, in a permanent process, cultural diversity, the particular and the universal, memory and aspiration.[325]

---

323. Many other questions could be added to the list: Who is the addressee of the right? Who is to be responsible for the enforcement of a right to cultural identity? The group's state? What about the fact that it is simply not in the state's interest to protect certain cultural identities (namely, whichever ones it deems most threatening to national identity)? Would the obligation to protect extend only to non-interference or also positive measures? Would interference by another state (or states) in support of the group be acceptable? Finally, what about the rights of individuals against their groups? Elements of certain cultures are in tension with other human rights. Who would determine whether a certain practice is in fact central to a given cultural identity?
    Finally, who is entitled to the right – the individual or the group? Despite the centrality of the individual in maintaining a collective cultural identity, the identity itself still remains a collective one. In other words, the individual exercise of the right is conditional on it being practiced in a collective setting. As we saw in the context of identity-formation, the individual relies to a significant extent on the in-group in both developing and maintaining her social identity. Thus, it is the individual as a member of the cultural group who should be the subject of a right to cultural identity, at least conceptually. But no such subject exists. (An exception is to be found in ICCPR Art. 27, which provides for the right to 'enjoy' one's culture 'in community with' the members of the minority group.) Is it then enough to protect an individual's right to speak a language, if the group as a whole cannot use the language in public discourse?
324. ILO Convention No. 169 concerning Indigenous and Tribal Peoples in Independent Countries (1991) also includes references to culture in a number of provisions, most clearly in Art. 2(2) (respect for cultural identity) and Art. 5(a) (recognition and protection of cultural values). The Convention, with 18 signatories (as of March 2007) is the only binding legal instrument in the realm of cultural rights, but is limited to a very distinct type of group. *See* Art. 1(a) and (b).
325. Art. 1(b) of Draft Declaration on Cultural Rights prepared by the UNESCO Project Concerning a Declaration of Cultural Rights (11th version, 1996).

Basic Concepts

The drafters of this definition seem to have gotten lost in prose. As a legal definition, it is simply useless.

The Council of Europe(CoE) in its Framework Convention for the Protection of National Minorities (1995) (hereinafter, CEFCM or Framework Convention) – the first international instrument to deal seriously with a right to cultural identity – does not even attempt a definition. Instead, the 'essential elements' of this identity are mentioned, and are named as 'religion, language, traditions and cultural heritage'.[326] Given the difficulty of definition, a list of fundamental elements is not a bad approach; its exhaustive nature is, however, unfortunate.[327] It is also worth noticing that the language of the relevant sections of the Convention is not formulated in terms of a specific right to a cultural identity;[328] rather, it is formulated in the language of obligations. Thus, CEFCM Article 5(1) requires that states 'undertake to promote the conditions necessary' for members of national minorities to preserve their culture and identity. In other words, the preservation of cultural identity can only be considered the eventual aim of the state obligation to 'promote' beneficial policies, not the 'object' of a right as such. The general formulation also leaves states with a wide degree of latitude in determining what is 'necessary' in a given circumstance, albeit checked by the reports of the CEFCM Advisory Committee.[329] In certain articles,[330] moreover, the state obligated to act is not named – a fact not left unnoticed by the kin-states of particular minorities. Still, at least we do find an addressee in the state, as well as, for once, a subject in the 'person belonging to a national minority'.[331]

The Convention thus presents a way forward for the idea of cultural identity in (regional) international law. It should be noted, however, that a number of Council of Europe Member States with minority issues have refused to (sign and) ratify the treaty;[332] moreover, the CEFCM system does not provide for judicial remedies, despite extensive monitoring.[333]

---

326. CEFCM, Art. 5(1).
327. A working group discussed the possible addition of a protocol to the ECHR on the right to cultural identity, but eventually decided against its preparation, due to concerns about the vagueness of the concept and uncertain consequences. *See* Council of Europe Committee for the Protection of National Minorities, Draft Articles and Alternative Versions for Possible Inclusion in a Protocol Complementing the ECHR in the Cultural Field (1995).
328. CEFCM, Preamble and Art. 5.
329. That said, the Advisory Committee has focused mainly on the importance of consultation, participation and financial support, rather than specific measures. *See* discussion in Gilbert (2005).
330. *See* CEFCM Art. 4, as compared with Art. 12.
331. But *see* Arts 1 and 12(1), where the 'minority' is recognized as the bearer of distinctive traits. Despite such references, the rights extended in the Convention are not collective, as Art. 1 makes clear. Moreover, the rights of the Convention extend only to members of national minorities, not other groups. *See* Council of Europe, Explanatory Report on the Framework Convention for the Protection of National Minorities, paras 11 and 29, 20(2) NJCM Bulletin 199 (1995).
332. As of March 2007, these states include Belgium, France, Greece, and Turkey. (Latvia and the Netherlands, as well as Georgia, ratified in the course of 2005.)
333. As the Explanatory Report noted, the aim of the instrument is (only) to set out 'legal principles' rather than to provide enforceable individual rights (para. 10). Still, some national courts have

b. Cultural Identity Matters before the European Court of Human Rights

Besides the theoretical difficulties of definition discussed above, this lack of complete concensus perhaps helps explain why the Framework Convention has played a nearly non-existent role in recent case law at the E.Ct.H.R., dealing with questions of cultural identity.[334] In a series of submissions, groups have claimed a cultural identity their states either refuse to acknowledge the existence of[335] or which they refuse to give legal recognition to. In essence, these cases force the question of the relationship between a cultural identity and a (domestic) legal status.

The Court has used existing provisions to manage such submissions and has gone out of its way to 'abstain ... from formulating any opinion on the issue of identity itself'.[336] It has instead tried to ensure that 'individuals are free to define themselves in the way they wish, to express attachment to a certain community, and to associate in order to promote a culture or defend a group they consider to belong to, even if their views do not fit with the dominant conception of national culture and history'.[337] In one case, however, the Court has determined, in line with the generally accepted approach, that objective substantiation may be required by a state when individuals – as opposed to groups – claim a particular minority cultural identity as the basis for a special right. Thus, '[w]hile the notion of the State sitting in judgment on the state of a citizen's inner and personal beliefs is abhorrent and may smack unhappily of past infamous persecutions', when a:

> claim to a privilege or exemption to which [an individual is] not entitled unless he [is] a member of the faith concerned and in circumstances which arguably gave rise to doubts as his entitlement ... it [is] not unreasonable or disproportionate to require [that individual] to show some level of substantiation of his claim.[338]

While state courts may take decisions on identity matters then, the E.Ct.H.R. continues to refrain from doing so. As will be discussed, the Court has been

---

      been using the Framework Convention as a parameter (or even a standard) in adjudicating cases on minority rights. *See also* the contributions in Weller (2005) for discussions of the role of the Advisory Committee.

334. That said, the Court has made reference to the Convention on at least one occasion (but does not seem to have read it, in light of the outcome in the case). *See Chapman v. United Kingdom*, E.Ct.H.R. (2001), paras 93–94. *See also* discussion of minority protection through the articles of the ECHR in Gilbert (2002).
335. 'The existence of a minority within the territory of a given state is, in fact, a matter of objective criteria'. *See* Art. 5(2) of United Nations Human Rights Committee General Comment No. 23(50) (1994). Legal recognition is a different matter, however, left to state discretion.
336. Ringelheim (2002) (electronic journal).
337. *Ibid.*
338. *Kosteski v. (FYRO) Macedonia*, E.Ct.H.R. (2006), paras 39 and 46, respectively. Applicant had argued that the requirement of proof by organs of the state of his Muslim faith (incidentally found to be lacking by all domestic courts) amounted to violation of ECHR Arts 9 and 14.

less shy about ruling on the identity claims of individuals in the context of immigration matters; the courts of particular states in Europe, in turn, are not shy in making such decisions in either context.

In the first of the minority recognition cases, *Ahmet Sadik v. Greece*[339] – centred on the use of the designation 'Turk' (i.e., a cultural/ ethnic category) in an electoral campaign by a minority politician, when the government considers the group a religious minority only – the Court refused to examine the merits of the case; however, the partly dissenting opinion of Judge Martens[340] pointed the way toward the Court's later judgments. Specifically, in the *Sidiropoulos* case,[341] arising from the refusal of Greek authorities to allow the registration of an association aiming to promote Macedonian culture and identity – the existence of which Greece viewed as threat to 'the maintenance of national security, the prevention of disorder and the upholding of Greece's cultural traditions and historical and cultural symbols'[342] – the Court found a violation under ECHR Article 11. It argued that:

> [t]erritorial integrity, national security and public order were not threatened by the activities of an association whose aim was to promote a region's culture, even supposing that it also aimed partly to promote the culture of a minority; the existence of minorities and different cultures in a country was a historical fact that a 'democratic society' had to tolerate and even protect and support according to the principles of international law.[343]

The *Stankov* case,[344] decided three years later, confirmed the right of groups to claim a cultural identity. In fact, the Court extended protection to the political views of that group, as long as these are not to be reached through violent means.[345] Thus, the refusal by Bulgarian authorities of registration, and later ban of an association claiming the recognition and unity of the Macedonian minority was found to be in violation of ECHR Article 11. Moreover,

> [t]he fact that what was at issue touched on national symbols and national identity cannot be seen in itself – contrary to the Government's view – as calling for a wider margin of appreciation to be left to the authorities. The national authorities must display particular vigilance to ensure that national

---

339. *Ahmet Sadik v. Greece*, E.Ct.H.R. (1996).
340. *See* para. 19 ('When criminal provisions purporting to prevent disturbance of public peace are relied on against a politician who is not only an opponent and a critic of the Government but also a member of a minority, the European Court of Human Rights should apply its highest standards of scrutiny in order to ascertain whether these provisions have been abused, as they easily may be and often are. There is all the more reason for extreme vigilance because the criticism concerned the Government's attitude towards the minority in question and more especially their policy of denying that the minority is not only a religious but also an ethnic one'.)
341. *Sidiropoulos and Others v. Greece*, E.Ct.H.R. (1998).
342. Para. 37.
343. Para. 41.
344. *Stankov and the United Macedonian Organisation Ilinden v. Bulgaria*, E.Ct.H.R. (2001).
345. *See* para. 97.

public opinion is not protected at the expense of the assertion of minority views, no matter how unpopular they may be.[346]

The Court has also denied state claims of necessity on grounds of national security and territorial integrity – both possible defences to state action which may otherwise be deemed in violation of the Convention – in cases dealing with religious minorities. In the *Metropolitan Church* case,[347] in particular, the Court determined a Violation of ECHR Article 9, in conjunction with Articles 6 and 11, in the context of a refusal by Moldova to recognize a church. In fact:

> the State's duty of neutrality and impartiality ... is incompatible with any power on the State's part to assess the legitimacy of religious beliefs, and requires the State to ensure that conflicting groups tolerate each other, even where they originated in the same group. In the present case ... by taking the view that the applicant Church was not a new denomination ... the State failed to discharge its duty of neutrality and impartiality.[348]

Thus, the state has no greater a role in determining the acceptability of a religious identity than of another cultural one.

In a series of cases dealing with the Turkish Constitutional Court's dissolution of certain political parties – owing to a refusal to recognize the existence of a Kurdish nation[349] – the Court even upheld the right of a cultural group to claim legal status (even if this was prohibited by the Constitution).[350] Thus, Turkey's view that 'the proposals ... covering support for non-Turkish languages and cultures were intended to create minorities, to the detriment of the unity of the Turkish nation' – although 'national unity was achieved through the integration of communities and individuals who, irrespective of their ethnic origin and on an equal footing, formed the nation and founded the State' – was essentially rejected.[351] The Court has also found in a number of cases that questioning the current principles and structures of the state cannot be grounds for the dissolution of political parties, so long as the means used are legal and democratic, and the change proposed is itself compatible with fundamental democratic principles.[352]

---

346. Para. 107.
347. *Metropolitan Church of Bessarabia and Others v. Moldova*, E.Ct.H.R. (2001). *See also Biserica Adevárat Ortodoxá din Moldova and Others v. Moldova*, E.Ct.H.R. (2007), para. 34.
348. Para. 123.
349. *Inter alia, Unified Communist Party of Turkey and Others (TBKP) v. Turkey*, E.Ct.H.R. (1998); *Socialist Party of Turkey and Others v. Turkey*, E.Ct.H.R. (1998); *Party of Freedom and Democracy (ÖZDEP) v. Turkey*, E.Ct.H.R. (1999); *Affaire Dicle pour le Partie de la Democratie (DEP) c. Turquie*, E.Ct.H.R. (2002); *Affaire Parti Socialiste de Turquie (STP) et Autres c. Turquie*, E.Ct.H.R. (2003).
350. *Ibid. TBKP*, paras 56–57.
351. *Ibid.*, para. 10 (paraphrasing the Turkish Constitutional Court); *see also Socialist Party*, para. 15, *ÖZDEP*, para. 14.
352. *See, inter alia, Socialist Party*, para. 47 and *ÖZDEP*, para. 41. *See also* discussion in *Selim Sadak and Others v. Turkey*, E.Ct.H.R. (2002); paras 97 and 98 of *Ždanoka c. Lettonie*, E.Ct.H.R. (2004) and *Affaire Linkov c. République Tchèque*, E.Ct.H.R. (2006).

Basic Concepts

In fact, there has only been one case dealing with the issue of cultural identity in which the Court has not found a violation: *Gorzelik*, where applicants' claims were there twice rejected.[353] The issue raised in the case was whether the refusal by Polish authorities to register an association of the 'Silesian national minority' – since the state considered the group an ethnic minority only – constituted an infringement of Article 11. While the Fourth Section judgment focused on applicants' refusal to make certain changes to the name of their association and its memorandum's provisions – and touched on the question of what a national minority is only in passing[354] – the second judgment devoted considerable space to this issue.

The Grand Chamber approached this question by stating that '[i]t is not for the Court to express a view on the appropriateness of methods chosen by the legislature of a respondent State to regulate a given field' and that, accordingly 'practice regarding official recognition by States of national, ethnic or other minorities within their population ... must, by the nature of things, be left largely to the State concerned, as it will depend on particular national circumstances'.[355] The Court made much of the lack of agreement on the term 'national minority' in international law, as well as the various meanings given to the term in domestic systems;[356] and eventually found that the lack of an express definition in Polish law does not constitute a lack of legal precision infringing ECHR Article 11(2).

The Court's general reference to 'official recognition' is misleading, however. A distinction needs to be made between legal recognition for the purposes of minority protection, in which recognition comes with particular benefits, and legal recognition for the purposes of freedom of association. The line of cases presented above falls into the second camp, since no particular benefits accrue to the cultural minority legally recognized as such. The Polish law, with its linkage of 'official recognition' as a national minority to special benefits would, rather, be an instance of the former. Granted, the difference may be minor in many instances. More importantly, however, the consequences of legal recognition should not determine whether recognition takes place. To the extent that the Court seems to leave Poland with near-unfettered discretion in determining which groups can legally constitute a national minority – with all the rights that may attach to that status – we enter dangerous waters. Even if a definition is 'difficult to formulate',[357] the lack of practically all oversight, despite a reference to conformity with the Convention, is hard to explain. Specifically, it is difficult to reconcile the outcome of this case with those in *Stankov* or *Sidiropoulos* – as even the Joint Concurring Opinion acknowledged. Though the Grand Chamber agreed with the Fourth Section that the particular facts of this case – specifically appellants'

---

353. *Gorzelik and Others v. Poland* (Fourth Section), E.Ct.H.R. (2001) and *Gorzelik and Others v. Poland* (Grand Chamber), E.Ct.H.R. (2004).
354. *Gorzelik* (Fourth Section), para. 62.
355. Para. 67.
356. Paras 67–68.
357. Para. 67.

refusal to make the modifications requested by the state – make the difference, the underlying reason for the outcome seems to be another.

While in the former cases, the states refused registration on the basis of dubious public security arguments (and defended non-recognition on this basis), Poland relied on the existing legal category of 'national minority' as the basis for its refusal. Thus, Polish courts repeatedly stated that Silesians were not a national minority, because there was no such thing as a Silesian nation;[358] a Silesian nation, in turn, did not exist because it was missing 'national awareness established on the basis of the existing culture by a society residing on a specific territory'.[359] The Grand Chamber did not really examine the reasoning behind these opinions (though it discussed them),[360] since its task is confined to examining whether the methods used and their effects are in conformity with the Convention. Given the existence of law considered precise enough, its *content* is not for the Court to judge. Reliance on a domestic legal category, however vague, thus seems like a good strategy for a defending state, especially given the inability of the Court to interpret domestic law, while reliance on terms in the Convention – which may be interpreted by the Court – is riskier. Though the group in this particular case was not claiming the rights attached to national minority status explicitly, the Court, in effect, came close to deciding the question of identity here.[361]

It is with the Court's reasoning on the question of what constitutes a 'pressing social need' for refusing recognition to the association that there are real difficulties, however. First, the Court acknowledged the importance of political parties and associations to democracy, generally speaking, and even recognized that 'freedom of association is particularly important for persons belonging to minorities, including national and ethnic minorities, and that ... [i]ndeed, forming an association in order to express and promote its identity may be instrumental in helping a minority to preserve and uphold its rights'.[362] However, it then found that 'the appropriate time for countering the risk of the perceived mischief, ensuring that the rights of other persons or entities participating in parliamentary elections would not be actually infringed, was at the moment of registration of the association and not later'.[363] Considering that the refusal to register constituted a *de facto* ban on the activities of the association, as well as the lack of any stated intention by the association to run in elections, the finding of a pressing social need, in the name of the protection of the rights of others – or a seeming balance of interests – seems a dubious approach, at best.

---

358. *Inter alia*, para. 36 (quoting the Polish Constitutional Court).
359. Para. 32 (quoting the Katowice Court of Appeal).
360. Para. 71.
361. This, despite its claim that such a finding is not for the Court to make. See *Gorzelik* (Fourth Section), para. 55.
362. Para. 93.
363. Para. 103 (emphasis added).

As if assuring itself that it was the minority's refusal of flexibility that led to the difficulties, the Court then stated:

> [i]n the instant case the refusal was not a comprehensive, unconditional one, directed against the cultural and practical objectives that the association wished to pursue, but was based solely on the mention, in the memorandum of association, of a specific appellation for the association ... It by no means amounted to a denial of the distinctive ethnic and cultural identity of Silesians or to disregard for the association's primary aim, which was to 'awaken and strengthen the national consciousness of Silesians' ... On the contrary, in all their decisions the authorities consistently recognised the existence of a Silesian ethnic minority and their right to associate with one another to pursue common objectives.[364]

To the extent, however, that the group in question considers itself a national minority and not an ethnic one, as repeatedly declared in its programme – in contravention of the definition of national minority in Polish law – the Court (purposefully?) misconstrued the problem.

The ECHR doesn't include any right to a minority cultural identity – except for religious – so that any question of group belonging is likely to be funnelled through Article 11, whether recognition comes with particular benefits or not. In other words, questions of the social and legal existence of cultural minorities – and of the possible risk they pose to the majority – will arrive in the guise of freedom of association. The Court even seemed to recognize this when it noted that:

> [T]he disputed restriction on the establishment of the association was essentially concerned with the label which the association could use in law – with whether it could call itself a 'national minority' – rather than with its ability 'to act collectively in a field of mutual interest'. As such, it did not go to the 'core or essence of freedom of association'.[365]

True. That is why it was so easy for the Court to focus on the supposed intentions of the minority to contravene electoral laws, and gloss over 'labels'. But are questions of designation so unimportant?

Whatever answers one may come up with, it is perhaps possible to claim that cultural rights and the proper bounds of respect for cultural identity are at the centre of public debate in Europe in a manner not seen before. The legal developments presented here are thus but one track of discussion. The claim of one author that 'the universal right to "one's own culture" has gained increasing legitimacy [and that] collective identity has been redefined as a category of human rights'[366] is perhaps too optimistic, however. The debate on cultural identity is still constrained by the structural *status quo* of international human rights law. Among other consequences, this means that the idea (1) of a right to culture necessarily assumes

---

364. Para. 105.
365. *Ibid.*
366. Soysal (2000), p. 6.

involvement by the state. As the recently adopted UNESCO Convention on the Protection and Promotion of the Diversity of Cultural Expressions (2005) clearly demonstrated,[367] the legitimacy of this role is increasingly accepted, so that disputes centre rather on its scope. The trend of the recent past has been toward a hands-off approach. As Rigobello comments, 'on the one hand, one asks the State to guarantee cultural activity with operative spaces and adequate financial subsidies; on the other, one wants the State to abstain from imparting cultural directives, from entering into the merits of out-and-out cultural questions'.[368] How realistic this expectation is in light of the importance of the national identity project to states – in fact, the assumed necessity of such a project in an era of linked citizenship-nationality – is open to debate. At a time when cultural identity issues are increasingly legal battlegrounds, it is a safe to say that the aspiration is less and less realistic, in any case.

Let us turn then to our three developments, each with its own response to this issue. The emergence of European citizenship and concurrent discussions about European identity will be our first case, primarily because the European Union provides an important frame for all other developments within its borders.

---

367. *See* Art. 2(2) of the Convention.
368. '*Da un lato si chiede allo Stato di garantire con spazi di operatività e adeguati sussidi finanziari l'attività culturale, dall'altro si vuole che lo Stato si astenga dall'impartire direttive culturali, di entrare nel merito delle questioni culturali vere e proprie*'. Rigobello (1986), p. 60.

Chapter II
European Union Citizenship

A Dunának, mely múlt, jelen s jövendő,
egymást ölelik lágy hullámai.
A harcot, amelyet őseink vívtak,
békévé oldja az emlékezés
s rendezni végre közös dolgainkat,
ez a mi munkánk; és nem is
kevés

Attila József, A Dunánál, 1936[1]

The pomp and circumstance surrounding the signing of the Treaty Establishing a Constitution for Europe (hereinafter, Constitutional Treaty)[2] constituted the finale of years of deliberation on what the European Union (hereinafter, EU or Union) is and what it should be – as the Laeken Declaration put it, at stake was the 'future of the Union'.[3] In particular, 'the work of the Convention ha[d] been closely related to an attempt to express a European identity'.[4] At the signing ceremony, speech-makers avoided this exact phrase, speaking instead of a *fraternité Européenne*,

---

1. 'The soft waves of the Danube,/ itself past, present and future, embrace./ The battle our ancestors fought,/ memory melts into peace/ and orders, finally, our common things/ This is our work, and it is not scarce'. (Incidentally, the reference in the poem is to the necessity of making peace with the past, as well as social justice.)
2. The Constitutional Treaty was signed on 29 October 2004 by all (then) 25 Member States, as well the three candidate countries of the time. As of March 2007, 18 out of 27 Member States have ratified it; two (the Netherlands and France) have rejected it in public referenda.
3. The Future of the European Union – Laeken Declaration (2001). The Laeken Declaration's query of whether the Convention, 'might not lead in the long run to the adoption of a constitutional text in the Union' seems quizzical in hindsight.
4. Mayer and Palmowski (2004), p. 583; de Búrca (2004).

of a *solidarité Européenne*[5] and of the 'values' of Europe[6] – all of which assume identification, without declaring its existence outright. The information booklet on the 'Constitution for Europe' – meant for the general public – was more candid, however. When introducing the 'symbols of the European Union', it stated that they are 'important, since they enable Europeans to identify more with Europe' – the flag, in particular, was proclaimed a symbol of 'Europe's unity and identity'.[7] In hindsight, the unity professed in 2004 has proven illusory, though the goal of proclaiming a common vision remains. But what constitutes the European identity so often relied on? What kind of identity is it anyway? And why is it necessary?

This Chapter will show how 'European identity' has emerged as a refrain in two distinct, but distinctly inter-related policy areas of the European Union: the emergence and reinforcement of European Union citizenship, with attendant rights, and the appearance of an explicit cultural policy that aims to strengthen not only the collective identity it claims provenance from, but also the citizenship it emerged in parallel to. The nexus of culture, identity and citizenship at the European level is thus the focus of our discussion here.

Scattered identity policies have been part and parcel of the European project (almost) since its inception. As we will see in first section of this chapter, discussion of what is 'European', and the manner in which it is so, have informed not only specific policy areas, but also the general development of the entity that is now the European Union. It was only in 1992, however, that possible focal points for such efforts emerged: Article 151 on cultural policy and European Union citizenship, two of the many innovations introduced by the Maastricht Treaty. The second section of this chapter will present the content of this cultural policy, beginning with the general legal implications of the cultural clause newly introduced with Maastricht. We will then take a brief look at the practice of the European Court of Justice, where cultural considerations have been taken into account by the Court since the 1970s in the context of 'sensitive' national issues, and have not been much affected by the new clause. As the third part of our discussion of cultural policy will show, its practical effects have been considerable, however. In fact, it seemed for a time that any concrete identity policies would fasten onto this policy area rather than on European Union citizenship. Section three of this Chapter will show how initial squeamishness regarding the new status of European citizen has been replaced by (recent) attempts to link citizenship and identity (and even cultural) policies, in general discussion, legislation and, in an instance of the E.C.J. in activist mode, case law. We begin here with a general presentation of what European Union citizenship entails, and how it has been viewed by commentators. In the second part of this section, we show how an eager Court and a (somewhat) more reluctant Commission have, in essence, taken this now 'fundamental status' and run with it, using attendant rights of free movement and equal treatment to expand the reach of EU law despite increasing national opposition, as well as

---

5. José Manuel Barroso, Speech 04/478 (29 October 2004).
6. Romano Prodi, Speech 04/479 (29 October 2004).
7. A Constitution for Europe 11 (2004).

fundamental rights concerns in the context of the Third Pillar. The increasingly central role of the European citizen for the process of integration will also be presented, in the context of provisions in the Constitutional Treaty (as the imagined blueprint for further integration). Finally, the missing link of cultural rights will be discussed. Part three will show how European Union citizenship has been used to anchor discussion of European identity in official documents and commentary, as well review what European identity actually means to individuals and Member States in practice.

The last section of this chapter will draw out the latent interlinkages between European citizenship, culture and identity and will attempt to point out the challenges inherent in any linkage of the three by the European Union in official policy.

A. THE IDEA OF EUROPEAN IDENTITY

One should generally be careful to distinguish between possible types of European identity – historical, cultural, constitutional, legal and institutional, in one typology – when assessing the effects of European integration.[8] In practice, few academics actually differentiate in this manner, perhaps because European identity is so 'obviously' a collective identity comparable to or distinguishable from national identity[9] – and a conglomeration of the types of identity discussed above. In fact, until a critical turn in the early 1990s, there seems to have been a general understanding whereby 'European identity, European values, European culture and the like were depicted as self-evident facts, merely in need of being "rediscovered" or "strengthened" rather than constructed or invented'.[10] Remnants of this approach are still present in both Commission documents and commentary to varying degrees, despite references to 'evolving' identity. The main point of contention seems rather to be content.

In fact, the European Union and its entities seem themselves unable to determine what they mean when they refer to European identity. The Maastricht Treaty[11] (hereinafter, TEU) (1992), for example, saw the forceful appearance of the concept of identity in a European treaty. Rec. 9 of the Preamble speaks of 'reinforcing European identity', but does so in the context of a common defence policy. Are we then dealing with an institutional identity here? Meanwhile, Article 2 refers to a European Union identity, again in the context of an eventual defence policy. Are the two the same? Finally, Article 6(3) states that the Union will respect 'the national identities of its Member States'. There is, unsurprisingly, no mention

---

8. *Ibid.*, p. 575.
9. For a look at the development of the idea of 'Europe' in tandem with or against nation states, *see* (especially essays two and three in) *The History of the Idea of Europe* (Wilson and van der Dussen, eds, 1993). *See also* Chaps 1 and 2 in Part I and Chap 1 in Part II of Chabot (2005) for a look at intellectual currents (most prominently the movement 'Paneuropa') in support of a united Europe in the first half of the 20th century.
10. Theiler (2005), p. 56.
11. The Treaty on European Union. The Treaty entered into force in 1993.

of Europe here. Well and good, but is a European identity only for external show then? And is the reference to 'national' identity one to collective identity or political autonomy? The now-defunct Constitutional Treaty, in turn, seems at first sight to skirt the issue of European identity. The word 'identity' appears often, generally in the context of national identities (and histories) in Rec. 3, as well as Article I-5(1), but the 'European' aspect is missing.[12] Instead, we find a reference to a 'common destiny'. Nonetheless, European identity is implied throughout the Treaty as the basis for its very existence. In other words, there is *something* that joins the states of the European Union (and their populations) in a common enterprise – at the very least, the values and objectives listed in the Constitutional Treaty. Rec. 4, for example, declares, 'thus "United in diversity", Europe offers them [the peoples of Europe] the best chance of pursuing ... the great venture which makes of it a special area of human hope'.

Granted, the passage just cited raises more questions than it answers. Since when does Europe equal the European Union? Or is Europe something that goes beyond the entity of the Union? Is the European Union the basis for the unity referred to? Or is there a deeper unity beyond the institutional? These are in many ways novel questions, since the European Community (hereinafter, Community), as an essentially economy-focused entity, initially paid no attention to identity or culture. Besides a mention of possible 'ever closer union among the peoples of Europe',[13] no thought was even given to cultural interaction, let alone identity-issues. By the early 1970s, however, as integration spread beyond the economic sector, interest in culture as a sphere of Community interest had emerged. On the one hand, the 'cultural sector', as a distinct area of Community competence, developed. On the other, discussion of the idea of culture as linked to identity began.

The first strand of Community action was relatively practical: culture in commercial terms. In 1977 the European Commission (hereinafter, Commission) submitted to the Council a communication titled 'Community action in the cultural sector', which dealt with the application of the Rome Treaty to the cultural sector, as well as 'other measures'.[14] The 'cultural sector' in this document was defined as 'the socio-economic framework of persons and undertakings producing and distributing cultural goods'.[15] Given this definition, the sphere of action was wide-ranging; free trade in cultural goods, copyright issues, cultural exchanges, taxation, vocational training of individuals in the cultural sector and the maintenance of architectural monuments were all discussed. From these beginnings, the

---

12. In fact, the sloppy use of the concept of 'national identity' in the Constitutional Treaty is worth noting – and is emblematic of general approaches to identity in official EU documents. In the Preamble, the reference seems to be to collective identity, possibly in the sense used in Maastricht; in Art. I-5(1) the reference is clearly to political autonomy.
13. The Treaty Establishing the European Economic Community (hereinafter, Treaty of Rome), Preamble (1957).
14. Commission Communication 'Community action in the cultural sector' (1977), p. 20.
15. *Ibid.*, p. 5.

Community and later the European Union developed a wide-ranging regulation of the commercial aspects of cultural policy.[16]

The second strand of Community action – and the strand we are concerned with here – had a much slower start. Parallel to the growing interest in commercial cultural policy, it was recognized that, while 'consciousness of citizenship was a prerequisite for the formation of a European Community, a deficit of European identity on the part of the citizens of Europe'[17] was, instead, characteristic. Thus, a European identity was necessary to further integration. Despite this recognition, the first mention of a 'European identity' in a Community document, in the 1973 Copenhagen Declaration on European Identity, was in the context of external relations: 'the moment has come to draw up a document on European identity, allowing notably for better definition of [our] relations with other countries'.[18] The declaration characterizes European identity as the sum of: a variety of cultures in the frame of a shared civilization, attachment to shared values and principles, similarity of conceptions of life, consciousness of common specific interests and a determination to participate in the construction of Europe.[19] The contrast with later conceptions of a European culture, or symbolic culture when linked to citizenship, is notable.

Also conspicuous in the Declaration is an approach to European identity oriented toward the international community – both as addressee and as that in the context of which a European identity can be distinguished. Thus, European identity is declared in order to better define relations with non-European states. This approach, though increasingly overshadowed by a focus on defining 'European' from within, remains omnipresent, particularly in the area of a common security and defence policy. As Stråth argues in general terms, 'Europe acquires distinction and salience when pitted against the Other'.[20] Who this 'Other' is remains fuzzy – historically, Islam and the Eastern reaches of the continent have both had the distinction – but the necessity of its existence is, in light of what we have learned of social identity theory, likely certain.

In fact, a number of approaches to what constitute 'Europe' openly rely on the 'Other', defined in varied spheres and different ways.[21] But an understanding of

---

16. For a thorough look, *see* the contributions in Craufurd Smith (2004a).
17. '[E]in Bürgerbewusstsein ... Voraussetzung [war], um eine Europäische Gemeinschaft zu bilden, [ein] Defizit an europäischer Identität der Bürger Europas'. Schwencke (2001), p. 162.
18. '*Le moment [est] venu de rédiger un document sur l'identité européenne permettant notament de mieux définir [des] relations avec les autres pays*'. Preamble, Copenhagen Declaration on European Identity (1973).
19. *Ibid.*, Art. 22a.
20. Stråth (2002), p. 388.
21. *See* Hutton (2002) (where the 'Other' is the United States, in the context of a European social/economic model); Asad (2002) (where the 'Other' is Islam, in the context of a European culture); and af Malmborg and Stråth (2002) (where the 'Other' is Europe itself, in the context of nation state discourse). *See also* the booklet on the Constitution discussed above, *supra* note II.7, in which the first two elements of the 'area of freedom, security and justice' are the lack of 'checks' at internal borders and 'intensified checks' at external borders; and de Búrca (2004).

Europe rooted in a lacuna – or what is not European – cannot result in stable, long-term identification, exactly because of a lack of content. Hence the increased focus by the European Union on filling the idea of 'Europe' with meaning – any meaning, it seems. That this question should arise – repeatedly, and in recent years increasingly insistently – in the context of quickened integration should not come as a surprise, since it goes to the heart of conceptions of the Union, for two reasons. One, because if we consider Europeanization, or the increasing scope and depth of the European Union, as an ongoing process rather than a concrete entity, then one's concept of 'Europe' will determine the future path of development.[22] This path is obviously of some concern to all actors involved, from the Member States to the Commission. Two, because the general recognition of a need for legitimacy for the European project has focused interest on existing tools of legitimization on the model of nation states – a shared collective identity (a 'European' one) would seem to be a good means to the end envisaged.

This symbolic, identity-linked element of culture appeared for the first time in the Community context only in 1983, as part of the Stuttgart Solemn Declaration. '[C]loser co-operation in cultural matters, to affirm consciousness of a common cultural heritage as an element of European identity'[23] is a stated objective of the inter-governmental Declaration. In the months after Stuttgart, a number of committees were set up to examine aspects of further integration. One of these committees, under the leadership of Pietro Adonnino, dealt with the concept of a common European identity, as well as how such an identity could be developed. The Adonnino Report[24] made specific recommendations with regard to rights that are now considered fundamental to European citizenship – including freedom of movement, right of establishment, right of residence – as well as to citizens' participation. It also recommended action in the spheres of education and commercial culture 'which is essential to European identity and the Community's image in the minds of its people',[25] focusing on television and science. Thus, by the mid-80s the concept of European identity had been linked to citizenship, as well as to a wider Community role in symbolic cultural policy.

This wider role can clearly be seen in some of the most important suggestions of the Report. In a number of areas a concern with developing and strengthening European identity appears. The suggestions made by the Report in fact mirror efforts made in the past by nation states to develop national identity – from a flag and emblem to an anthem, money, stamps ('which commemorate particularly

---

(arguing that it is the Union's external identity that is most likely to generate a sense of internal commonality)

22. In this context, *see* Eriksen and Fossum (2004) (identifying three possibilities for future development, namely as a problem-solving entity, as a value-based community or as a post-national union).
23. '*Coopération plus étroite en matière culturelle, pour affirmer la conscience d'un héritage culturel commun en tant qu'élément de l'identité européenne*'. Stuttgart Solemn Declaration (1983), para. 1.4.3.
24. Also referred to by the title 'A People's Europe' (1985).
25. *Ibid.*, p. 21.

important events in Community history'[26]) and 'Europe Day'.[27] In addition, a wider dispersal of European driving licenses and a European passport are proposed. Finally, school materials and institutions 'appropriate' for presenting 'European achievements, and the common heritage'[28] as well as 'the originality of European civilization in all its wealth and diversity'[29] are suggested.[30] This last idea, of common education and a focus on 'originality', reads not unlike the recipe – a dash of memories and sense of continuity, a pinch of exclusivity – for the nourishment of a traditional cultural identity already discussed.[31] In fact, some theorists at the time argued that such policies heralded the emergence of a 'super-nation state founded on European chauvinism'.[32] At the same time, the Adonnino Report was careful not to hurt national interests. Any common emblem is 'without of course prejudice to the use of national flags'[33] for example. Still, all of these suggestions, and the symbolic Europe they hoped to create, were much more emotional than the stale version of European identity presented by the 1973 Declaration. The difference, obviously, comes down to audience: the authors of the Report to the Council were trying to create a 'European citizen'[34] in more than name only.[35]

A concern with the European citizen could, in fact, already be seen in the 1975 Tindemans Report.[36] There, two specific courses of action were suggested in the sphere of citizenship: one, an increase in and protection of fundamental rights and two, external signs of solidarity.[37] The second path is the one further developed by the Adonnino report ten years later through its suggestions on European identity. The big breakthrough came in 1992, however, with the inclusion of Articles 151 (on culture) and 17 (on citizenship) through the Maastricht Treaty. This breakthrough also brought a clear decision to disconnect cultural identity and citizenship; the fact that there are two separate articles shows as much. This determination was but momentary, it seems, and is present only in the text of the Treaty itself, since the link of culture and citizenship seems to have become more central again in recent years.

We will take a look at the two, seemingly distinct policy areas in turn.

---

26. *Ibid.*, p. 29.
27. This latter was to be introduced officially in CT Art. I-8, though it has been celebrated on 9 June (the day the Schuman declaration was presented) for a while now.
28. Adonnino Report, *supra* note II.24, p. 24.
29. *Ibid.*, p. 22.
30. Some of the other suggestions, such as Community sports teams or a 'Euro-lottery', were never developed further.
31. For a similar view *see* de Witte (1987), p. 137.
32. Nairn (1977), p. 16. *See also* Connerton (1989).
33. Adonnino Report, *supra* note II.24, p. 30.
34. *Ibid.*, p. 18. *See also* Commission Communication 'A Fresh Boost for Culture in the European Community' (1987).
35. The ultimately unsuccessful (and embarrassing) Commission projects for 'Europa TV' and a common European history textbook, both from the mid/late 1980s, were more practical expressions of this wish. *See* Theiler, p. 92 *et seq.* and p. 122 *et seq.*, respectively.
36. Also referred to by the title 'European Union'.
37. *Ibid.*, p. 26.

B.　　　　THE ROLE OF CULTURE IN THE EUROPEAN UNION

1.　　　　ARTICLE 151 AND ITS EFFECTS

The Maastricht Treaty, which established the ground rules for the transformation of the European Community into the European Union, also extended the realm of Community competence to include culture (ECT Article 151(1), CT Article III-280(1))[38] as well as education (ECT Article 149(1), CT Article III-282(1)). The appearance of these new competences can be understood as an acknowledgment of extant functional spillover, to the extent that EC law (the fundamental freedoms like competition law) has had a growing impact on the cultural (and to a lesser extent educational) sector of Member States. As this was the case, it was considered better for the Community to have the power to act directly.[39] An additional reason is certainly to be found in the effect of these policy areas on the emergence of a European identity, in light of the aims of the Adonnino Report. Both developments were, in any case, potentially far-reaching. As Colette Flesch[40] (cryptically) stated at the time with regard to the new cultural competence of the Community: 'Culture has something to do with identity. Identity has something to do with sovereignty'.[41] Through these articles, the Member States could have handed over to the Community important elements of traditional state sovereignty – ones that go to the heart of national identity projects.

But a closer look at the articles in question shows that we are dealing rather with a reconfiguration of competence than with a transfer of powers. Article 151(1) states that the:

> The Community shall contribute to the flowering of the cultures of the Member States, while respecting their national and regional diversity and at the same time bringing the common cultural heritage to the fore.

Exactly how the Community is to aid in such a botanical enterprise is left unsaid here, although the reference to '[a]ction by the Community' in Article 151(2) confirms that any role will be a functional one. Moreover, despite constant references, the concept of 'culture' is not defined for the purposes of the ECT, or in fact anywhere in Community law – perhaps an understandable state of affairs in light of the general terminological difficulties already noted in the previous chapter. Instead, focus is always on concrete elements, so that 'culture' seems to be something mystical and whole, in need of protection but strong enough, in its incarnation as heritage, to be the basis for the 'unity' expressed in the Union's motto of 'unity

---

38. All references in this paper will be to the numbering system in effect since the Amsterdam Treaty, i.e., to the consolidated version of the EC Treaty, unless otherwise noted. The numbering of the Constitutional Treaty is included in parentheses.
39. Nic Shuibhne (2002), p. 115. Compare Theiler (2005), p. 148 *et seq.*
40. Ms. Flesch was Director-General at the European Commission for Information, Communication, Culture and Audiovisual Media 1990–1997 and 1997–1999.
41. '*Kultur hat etwas mit Identität zu tun. Identität hat etwas mit Souveränität zu tun*'. As quoted in Schwencke (2001), p. 232.

in diversity'. Culture does not seem to be understood as a process expressed in the way of life of a community, however. The lack of a dynamic approach is all the more striking, given the Community's view of 'European identity', discussed below. In any case, the Community now has a basis on which to act in purely cultural matters – something it didn't possess before.[42]

However, the reference in Article 151 to respect for 'national and regional diversity' shows that any action will not undermine Member State policies on culture as related to collective identity.[43] The equivalent passage regarding education also clearly states that any Community action will 'contribute ... by encouraging ... supporting and supplementing [Member State] action' (Article 149(1)) – hardly a recipe for cultural revolution. This supplementary language reappears in Article 151(2), in the areas of 'improvement of the knowledge and dissemination of the culture and history of the European peoples' and 'conservation and safeguarding of cultural heritage of European significance'. Thus, the Community leaves primary responsibility for the European identity project in the hands of the Member States – seemingly a step back from the days of Council considerations of an anthem and flag.[44] That said, the singular reference to *a* culture of European peoples and *one* cultural heritage should make any reader take note: it is commonality that is to be highlighted, not difference.

A number of structural elements also serve to protect Member State sensibilities. In theory, another newcomer to the European legal landscape, subsidiarity (Article 5), could serve to 'protect' Member State policies.[45] In fact, the language of Articles 149-151 is itself restrictive enough to make subsidiarity superfluous here. As per Article 151(5), as well as 149(4), the Council is limited to adopting 'incentive measures', excluding any action that may be harmonizing in nature; moreover, any action by the Council under the Article 251 co-decision procedure must, unusually, be unanimous in the case of action in the realm of culture (though not education).[46] Also, Article 87(3)(d) (CT Article III-167(3)(d)) specifically allows for state aid 'to promote culture and heritage conservation where such aid does not affect trading conditions and competition in the Community to an extent that is contrary to the common interest', so that Member States may, to a

---

42. Article 151 differentiates between purely cultural Community action (paras 1 and 2) and action in another area with effects on the cultural sphere (para. 3). This difference is important not only because of the varied bases on which any Community action will rely, but also because of possible procedural differences. *See* discussion below; and Schmahl (1996), p. 199–200.
43. The formulation also recalls the Preamble of the Maastricht Treaty, where a stated objective is to 'deepen the solidarity between [Member States'] peoples while respecting their history, their culture and their traditions'. *See also* TEU Art. 6(3).
44. *See* McMahon (1995), p. 169 and p. 172 for a similar conclusion. However, given the language of Art. 151(3), the Community may have gained treaty-making powers in the area of culture. Since such power is not exclusive, pursuant to the wording of the article, mixed-agreements would be most likely. *See* discussion in Loman *et al* (1992)., p. 198–201.
45. The Community clearly does not have exclusive competence in the field of culture, so that the principle of subsidiarity can be applied.
46. The Constitutional Treaty would have removed the unanimity requirement, pursuant to CT Art. III-280(5).

significant extent, continue funding national culture even in the commercial context.[47]

This does not mean, however, that the articles on culture and education aim to safeguard the competence of Member States[48] in all aspects of culture and education, nor even merely the identity-linked aspects of it. As the E.C.J. found in the *Erasmus* case,[49] before the inclusion of an article on culture, the construction of a 'people's Europe'[50] can be included among the objectives of the Community. In a general manner, the general cultural objectives of the Community were thereby accepted by the Court. The judgment also amounted to a tardy acknowledgement of what was already reality, given that the commercial aspects of culture were already regulated by the Community in the 70s, while identity-linked Community action could be observed in the 1980s, as mentioned above.

Even if the exclusion of Community competence in matters of culture had been a goal, it would have been an impracticable one given the bleeding of culture into questions of fundamental rights and economy in Community law. What the articles on culture in fact signify is that in individual cases cultural interests may prevail over a planned Community action. Such cultural considerations, to be examined by all Community institutions in all actions according to Article 151(4), were given a boost by the Amsterdam Treaty amendment of that paragraph. As the article now reads, cultural matters must be taken into account in order to 'respect and ... promote the diversity of [the Community's] cultures'.[51] This doesn't necessarily mean national cultures, so that Member States may not be the beneficiaries in all cases.

It is thus correct to say that European competence in cultural matters is complementary to that of Member States: 'European cultural policy can and will not replace national cultural policy; but will simply lend it an additional European dimension'.[52] In other words, Member States are free to continue their own national identity politics,[53] but the Community will continue to prod them to inject European elements into their respective collective identities. This approach is reminiscent of the approach of the Council of Europe, where cultural

---

47. *See* Psychogiopoulou (2006) for a recent, positive evaluation.
48. In this regard, *see* Niedobitek (1997), p. 195–196.
49. Case 242/87 *Commission v. Council (Erasmus)* E.C.J. [1989].
50. *Ibid.*, paras 28–29.
51. But *see* Cunningham (2001), p. 153–158 for an argument that the Community continues to give priority to economic considerations over diversity and has thereby not made use of available possibilities.
52. '[D]ie ... europäische Kulturpolitik kann und will nationale Kulturpolitik nicht ersetzen, sondern ihr nur eine zusätzliche europäische Dimension verleihen'. Schwencke (2001), p. 236. *See also* Commission Communication, 'New Prospects for Community Cultural Action' (1992), p. 8. ('The role of the Community in contributing to the flowering of our cultures must be subsidiary to that of the Member States'.)
53. The backlash against integration from the mid 1980s onwards – as 'Brussels' increasingly emerged as a threat to all things national in the public spheres of many Member States – is clearly also a significant factor in the retreat from a unified conception to culture. *See* Theiler (2005), p. 110 *et seq.*

policies – including those aimed at fostering identity – have a significant history. As Pickard notes, '[t]he Council of Europe's cultural policy, of which the cultural heritage forms part, has been aimed at developing a European cultural identity'.[54] This identity is, in turn, to be the basis for 'Europe's unity and the diversity of its cultural identities', as the Helsinki Declaration has noted.[55] Echoes of this approach in the equivalent EU policy area are obvious, as will be shown.[56]

The increased focus on a shared cultural identity – whatever it may be – seems initially to be reflected in the text of the Constitutional Treaty, which also added that one of the objectives of the Union was to be 'respect [for] its rich cultural and linguistic diversity'.[57] The general references to protection of 'cultural', 'national' and other identities and diversities in the Constitutional Treaty are also noteworthy – frankly, almost neurotic. In addition to the Preamble and Article I-3(3), cited above, we find such a reference in Article I-5(1), Part II (Rec.and Article II-82), as well as part III (Article III-280). Looking at the language of the articles, however, something is wrong. In the first instance, 'diversity' is not a founding value of the Union (as are the values listed in Article I-2), but an objective without any active undertaking. In other words, 'respect' implies passive maintenance of the status quo, in contrast to the promises to 'work for', 'combat' and 'promote' other objectives. Given that we are dealing with identity – which is inherently mutable – the onlooker status is all the more jarring. Considering that the same language is repeated in the section on fundamental rights, one gets the feeling that we are dealing with a non-right (or at least none that may be relied on in any way before a court). As for the reference to 'diversity' in Article III-280, it is not even clear whether the focus is on institutional structure or identity.[58]

'Culture' also appears constantly in the Constitutional Treaty, as a source of shared values (Rec. 1), as something Europe wishes to stay open to (Rec. 2), in the guise of 'cultural heritage' to be 'safeguarded and enhanced' (Article I-3(3)), even as something the elderly have a right to be involved in (Article II-85), as well as the target for continued 'incentive measures' through European laws or framework laws (these being one of the few, cosmetic innovations the Constitutional Treaty would have introduced).[59] On the other hand, 'culture' is listed as an area of competence in which the Union is to have only 'supporting, coordinating or

---

54. Pickard (2002), p. 11.
55. *See* Sec. 2 of the Helsinki Declaration on the Political Dimension of Cultural Heritage Conservation in Europe (1996), adopted at the 4th European Conference of Ministers Responsible for the Cultural Heritage. *See also* Resolution No. 1, The Cultural Heritage as a Factor in Building Europe, adopted at the same conference – and note the reference to 'Europe's citizens'; and the Conclusions of the Fifth European Conference of Ministers Responsible for the Cultural Heritage (2001).
56. In fact, the European Heritage Network, established in 1999, is a common project of the Council of Europe and the European Union.
57. CT Art. I-3(3).
58. One positive sign for diversity, however, is the enhanced role of the Committee of the Regions, as per CT Arts III-388 and III-365(3).
59. CT Art. III-280(5).

complementary action'.[60] There seems to be some tension here in the actual competence of the Union, as expressed in the two articles – 'ensuring' the maintenance of cultural heritage, for example, would seem to imply a positive obligation going past the complementary.

As we will see in the next two sections, E.C.J. decisions and cultural policy in practice have indeed done more than complement national efforts.

2. 'SENSITIVE' NATIONAL INTERESTS BEFORE THE EUROPEAN COURT OF JUSTICE

In considering the role of culture in the European Union, some E.C.J. judgments from both before and after the Maastricht Treaty are relevant to the extent they impact on and may even direct the national projects of Member States: in particular, decisions that touch on issues considered 'sensitive' in the given state – whether the role of religion, fundamental rights, minority protection, public defence, education or even football. In short, the Court has had a tendency to seek loopholes in Community law when it recognizes a sensitive national interest, most obviously in the contest of constitutional principles. The indirect effects of regulation in an ever-expanding number of areas have in fact resulted in numerous cases with cultural undertones before the Court,[61] so that cultural considerations have become an increasingly central preoccupation in matters ranging from sports through food labelling to telecommunications.

Already in 1974, in the case of *Walrave and Koch*,[62] the Court rendered a near-incomprehensible judgment in its effort to maintain the acceptability of national sports teams. It found that the general prohibition on discrimination on the basis of nationality present in European law (most clearly in ECT Article 12) 'does not affect the composition of sports teams, in particular national teams, the formation of which is a question of purely sporting interest'. One wonders how 'sporting' – and increasingly even economic – interest[63] in a national team is different from a local team, unless, as Niedobitek states 'the actual criterion ... is not the existence of a "sporting interest" ... but the fact that the team is made up exclusively of *nationals*. ... It is not a question of serving purely sporting purposes by focusing on a sportsman's nationality, but, conversely, of using sport for nationality purposes'.[64] The pre-eminence of national as opposed to local or club teams was

---

60. CT Art. I-17.
61. *Inter alia*, Case 7/68 *Commission v. Italy*, E.C.J. [1968]; Cases 60 and 61/84 *Cinéthèque SA v. Fédération Nationale des Cinémas Français*, E.C.J. [1985].
62. Case 36/74 *Walrave and L.J.N. Koch v. Association Union Cycliste Internationale, Koninklijke Nederlandsche Wielren Unie and Federación Española Ciclismo*, E.C.J. [1974], 1418 *et seq*. See also Case 13/76 *Donà v. Mantero*, E.C.J. [1976].
63. See Case T-313/02 *David Meca-Medina and Igor Majcen v. Commission*, C.F.I. [2004], para. 44.
64. Niedobitek (1997), p. 170.

indirectly confirmed in *Union Royale Belge v. Bosman*, where the Court found measures limiting the number of non-nationals in a club team in violation of ECT Article 39.[65]

The strategy of removing given national provisions from the scope of Community law in cases in which justification of the wished-for result would be difficult has been adopted by the Court in other areas also. In the *Dory* decision, for example, the Court determined that '[t]he decision of the Federal Republic of Germany to ensure its defence in part by compulsory military service is the expression of ... a choice of military organization to which Community law is ... not applicable'.[66] The Court could easily have decided to frame the matter in a less restrictive manner, especially in light of previous case law that arguably also touched on matters of military organization.[67] Had the Court taken this route, it could not have avoided the conclusion that compulsory military service only for males, is sexually discriminative under Article 2 of Directive 76/207,[68] however, with significant effects on a national policy area that remains uniquely sensitive.[69] The Court's decision in *Grogan*[70] – holding that the Irish student groups challenging a prohibition on the distribution of information about abortion clinics in the UK as an obstruction to the free flow of services were not qualified to do so, not having been linked to the UK provider – can also be construed as a familiar tactic of avoidance.[71] In the end, the question of the ban's compatibility with European Community law was never addressed, and the injunction against the student groups remained. Had the Court addressed the actual issue, it would with high probability have had to find the ban on information on services closely enough linked to a restriction on the freedom to supply services to constitute a violation of ECT Article 49. Since the ban was directly related to the Eighth Amendment of the Irish Constitution, the Court was in dangerous waters not only for legal reasons (would the Constitution prevail?) but also because of questions of national identity.[72]

In recent years, the Court has become less shy with Community scrutiny of sensitive constitutional rights and principles, however. In *Schmidberger*, freedom

---

65. Case C-415/93 *Union Royale Belge des Sociétés de Football Association and Others v. Bosman and Others*, E.C.J. [1995]. *See also* Cases C-51/96 and C-191/97 *Deliège v. LFJ et Disciplines ASBL*, E.C.J. [2000], para. 43 *et seq.*
66. Case C-186/01 *Alexander Dory v. Federal Republic of Germany*, E.C.J. [2003], para. 39.
67. *See* Case C-285/98, *Tanja Kreil v. Germany*, E.C.J. [2000].
68. Council Directive 76/207/EEC of 9 February 1976 on the implementation of the principle of equal treatment for men and women as regards access to employment, vocational training and promotion, and working conditions.
69. In fact, the court clearly recognized the consequences of finding that a violation had occurred. *See* paras 40–42 of Case C-186/01 *Dory*.
70. Case C-159/90 *Society for the Protection of Unborn Children Ireland v. Grogan*, E.C.J. [1991].
71. *Ibid.*, paras 26–27.
72. For other cases touching on 'sensitive' national matters, *see* Case 34/79 *Regina v. Henn and Darby*, E.C.J. [1980]; Case C-145/88 *Torfaen Borough Council v. B&Q*, E.C.J. [1989]; Cases 60 and 61/84 *Cinéthèque*; Case C-288/89 *Stichting Collective Antennevoorziening Gouda and others v. Commissariaat vor de Media*, E.C.J. [1993], especially para. 23; and Case C-154/89 *Commission v. France (Tour Guides)*, E.C.J. [1991].

of assembly, as guaranteed by the Austrian Constitution and the ECHR, was balanced against the free movement of goods. After a thorough analysis, including the length of the demonstration at issue, its geographic scale, the 'intrinsic seriousness of the disruption' and the conduct of the authorities, the restrictions placed upon intra-Community trade were deemed proportionate in the light of the legitimate objective pursued, namely, the protection of fundamental rights.[73] To the extent the right in question is not only crucial to any functioning democracy, but expressly protected in all the constitutions of Member States and the ECHR, any other outcome would have been incongruous, to say the least.

The discussion in *Omega*, a judgment from 2004, was more explicit in its reasoning.[74] In determining whether the prohibition of an economic activity (here the marketing of a laser game in which players shoot each other) for reasons arising from the protection of fundamental values laid down by a Member State constitution (here human dignity), is compatible with Community law, the Court clearly re-stated that any reference to a national constitutional right or principle as an exception to a fundamental freedom (here public policy in the context of freedom to provide services and free movement of goods) would be examined for compatibility with Community law, and would be allowed only if 'there is a genuine and sufficiently serious threat to a fundamental interest of society'.[75] In other words, though the decision noted that 'the specific circumstances which may justify recourse to the concept of public policy may vary from one country to another and from one era to another'[76] – so that the ability of Member States to restrict fundamental freedoms is not necessarily conditioned on a legal conception common to all Member States – it is nonetheless true that constitutional values (even that of human dignity) may, in principle, lose out to common market freedoms.[77]

Still, a number of cases besides *Omega* and *Schmidberger* could be cited as evidence of Court deference to national culture in sensitive areas, even in the context of fundamental freedoms. In *Groener*, for example, the Court determined that a Member State may 'adopt a policy for the protection and promotion of a national and first official language' despite the indirect discrimination this may result in, so long as any action is proportional to the aim.[78] Some authors have gone

---

73. *See* Case C-112/00 *Eugen Schmidberger, Internationale Transporte und Planzüge v. Republic of Austria*, E.C.J. [2003], para. 69 *et seq.*
74. Case C-36/02 *Omega Spielhallen- und Automatenaufstellungs-GmbH v. Oberbürgermeisterin der Bundesstadt Bonn*, E.C.J. [2004].
75. *Ibid.*, para. 30 (referring to para. 17 of Case C-54/99 *Association Église de Scientologie*, E.C.J. [2000]).
76. *Ibid.*, para. 31.
77. Though a discussion of the consequences of this approach is outside the scope of our discussion, it is perhaps worth noting that balancing fundamental rights against market freedoms (even when they function as derogations to Community law) – as well as their re-framing as a 'public policy' issue – clearly trivializes the former. *See also* para. 53 *et seq.* of the Opinion of Advocate General Stix-Hackl in Case C-36/02 (18 March 2004).
78. Case C-379/87 *Groener v. Minister for Education*, E.C.J. [1989], para. 19. Compare Case C-473/93 *Commission v. Luxemburg (Public Sector Posts)*, E.C.J. [1996] (finding that maintaining

so far as to say that, in addition to the express derogations found in the ECT, policies promoting cultural diversity and national identity can be seen as an implied limitation to the free movement of workers, so long as the ensuing discrimination is indirect.[79] In the case of free movement of goods, Shuibhne also identifies the protection of cultural heritage as a 'mandatory requirement'[80] that may justify indirect discrimination.[81]

The reason for deference to delicate matters of national identity should not be hard to find. It is, after all, the Member States that have built and continue to guide the Community. Given the perceived lack of Community legitimacy in many Member States, certain E.C.J. decisions would be political suicide.[82] The exceptions to all manner of Community (including core) requirements on grounds of 'public policy' in Articles 30, 39, 46, 58 and 186,[83] as well as the 'national treasures' exception to free movement of goods under Article 30,[84] are more obvious structural expressions of caution. The introduction of ECT Article 151(4) could also have resulted in greater deference to cultural considerations, but has not lived up to its potential in practice.[85] (In fact, it seems to have been disregarded completely.)

Varying degrees of deference notwithstanding, state attempts to restrict the scope of Community action, usually on the basis of said public policy exceptions, 'require Member States to articulate more clearly the basis for their own cultural policies',[86] as well as for actions in other policy areas. Thus, policies that would otherwise have been formulated in the vacuum of the nation state are now inspected by an entity with limited sympathy for purely national concerns. The many cases in which the Court has determined that exceptions do not apply show that the Community wields a significant amount of power in determining which elements of national identity are 'sensitive' enough to be left alone.[87] In a

---

    nationality requirements for primary school teachers and other posts in the public services with the aim of preserving national identity are contrary to the principle of freedom of movement for workers because they are directly discriminatory).

79. Shaw (1991), p. 37.
80. On such mandatory requirements *see* Case 120/78 *Rewe-Zentrale v. Bundesmonopolverwaltung für Branntwein (Cassis de Dijon)*, E.C.J. [1979]; Case 302/86 *Commission v. Denmark (Containers)*, E.C.J. [1988] (environmental protection); and Case C-368/95 *Vereinigte Familia Press v. Heinrich Bauer Verlag*, E.C.J. [1997] (press diversity).
81. Nic Shuibhne (2002), p. 98–99; but *see* Case C-17/92 *Federacíon de Distribuidores Cinematográficos (Fedicine) v. Spanish State*, E.C.J. [1993], para. 20 (for a seeming limitation on cultural policy as an exception to the free movement of services).
82. *See also* McMahon, who comments that the Court has 'studiously avoided commenting on the role of cultural policy within the framework of the Treaty'. McMahon (1995), p. 163.
83. CT Arts III-154, III-133, III-140, III-158 and III-290, respectively.
84. CT Art. III-154.
85. *See* Council Resolution of 21 January 2002 on the Role of Culture in the Development of the European Union, Sec. B. For a similar conclusion in the context of the case law of the E.C.J., *see* Craufurd Smith (2004b), p. 55 *et seq.*
86. Craufurd Smith (2004c), p. 11.
87. *See* discussion of interaction between the four freedoms and cultural policy in Chapter 2 of Loman *et al.* (1992).

comparable manner, European legislation – especially in cases such as the prohibition of unequal treatment on the basis of nationality – leads to 'tension with national identities, because it greatly constrains the legal accompaniment of national processes of group-forming differentiation'.[88] In effect, the Community is increasingly drawing the outlines of the areas in which national identity may continue to matter.

A series of cases in which the Court has taken a stand (generally for the principle of non-discrimination), without much consideration for the effects of the judgment, only prove the point. In the Dutch media case above, for example, the confirmation that cultural policy may justify a restriction on freedom to provide services did not save the broadcasting policy in question. The Court found no connection between cultural policy and the cable retransmission rules at issue.[89] More recently, the Court found an instance of indirect discrimination (on the basis of nationality) in an Austrian provision requiring that students who have obtained their secondary education in another Member State and have applied for higher education in Austria provide proof of having fulfilled the conditions of access to higher education in the Member State in question (e.g., entrance examination), as well as their diploma (whereas only the latter is required of students who have studied in Austria.)[90] The outcome is not only puzzling – given the difference in education systems in Member States, it can be reasonably argued that Austria required only proof of aptitude for university studies in the given education system[91] – but also has important secondary effects on the entirety of the Austrian education system even though the Community supposedly 'fully respect[s] the responsibility of the Member States for ... the organization of education systems'.[92]

---

88. '*Spannungsverhältnis zu nationalen Identitäten, weil [es] die rechtliche Begleitung von nationalen gruppenbildenden Differenzierungsprozessen massiv beschränkt*'. von Bogdandy (2002), p. 185.
89. Case C-288/89 *Stichting Collective*, para. 24.
90. C-147/03 *Commission v. Austria*, E.C.J. [2005]. *See also* Case C-65/03 *Commission v. Belgium*, E.C.J. [2004].
91. This is in fact what Austria had argued, as noted by the Court in para. 40. One could further question the reasoning of the E.C.J. in this case, for example its reference to differential treatment not only between students who have studied in or outside Austria, but also within the latter group (in para. 43). It is difficult to see how different tests of aptitude among individuals from highly varied education systems, as judged by their own systems, could be a sign of discriminatory treatment on the basis of nationality, unless the (unsaid) wish is for uniformity. (This is not to say that the provision could not be attacked as an instance of failure to recognize diplomas from other Member States.)

  Uniformity does, in fact, seem to be the goal judging by the Court's understanding of which circumstances amount to the 'same situation' (para. 45): general instances of application to university. One could argue that it is not individuals applying for university studies in Austria who are in the same boat, but individuals with diplomas from a particular Member State, to the extent that a high school diploma is generally the culmination of a process of secondary education and not necessarily a ticket to university studies.
92. ECT Art. 149(1). *See also* Hilpold (2005) for a strong critique of the judgment. In light of the E.C.J. ruling – and the subsequent influx of German students especially into faculties of

3.   CULTURAL POLICY IN PRACTICE

The point of indirect impact wider than generally acknowledged is also a valid one for Community cultural activity in general. At present, such activity, in the widest sense, can be grouped into three areas. The first, most general area, encompasses regulatory activity with primary or secondary effects on culture, as already discussed. The basis for action in this context can obviously be any number of Treaty articles. The second, more limited area is more correctly one of inactivity, and comprises direct and indirect checks on Community action by Member States that more often than not rely primarily on general exceptions to the four freedoms (such as public policy), as discussed above. The third consists of funding and co-ordination initiatives based directly on Article 151. It is only this last group that constitutes the core of a cultural policy, properly understood.

a.   **Programmes under the Aegis of Article 151**

When looking at the actual effects of Article 151, we do, in fact, find that the quality of Community action in the cultural area has changed. A 1992 Commission communication on culture, for example, acknowledged a 'new era' and planned action on three fronts: contributing to a growth in culture, in general; bringing greater prominence to the common cultural heritage; and increased co-operation with non-Member States and international organizations. It is the last two points that are most interesting for our purposes. The goal of bringing to the fore the common cultural heritage focused on the commercial aspects of culture: books, cultural heritage and the audio-visual sector in particular. The role of the Community in this regard consisted of planning/choosing and funding programmes in these sectors. The era of obvious symbolic, identity-building Community action would, on this basis at least, seem to have been over.[93] As for the goal of reaching out to non-Member States, the focus was mainly on Central and Eastern Europe, or the states who were then most likely to join and the Council of Europe.

The Council endorsed the Commission's plans as set forth in the communication[94] (while the Parliament criticized them for not going far enough).[95] On this basis, the Commission developed a number of pilot programmes through the mid-90s. Among the most important were: Kaléidoscope (1996–1999), which aimed to

---

medicine – Austria (like Belgium before it) has introduced a quota system for students with Austrian secondary diplomas (75 per cent of students), as part of a new federal law regulating university admission. It is unlikely that this quota will be upheld as a proportionate measure if the Austrian admission system is again scrutinised by the Court, however.

93. Given that only 38 per cent of the citizens of the 15 Member States believe that a 'shared European cultural identity' exists, the idea of a unified, top-down identity does not seem to have had much success, in any case. *See How Europeans See Themselves* 12 (2001).
94. Conclusions of the Ministers of Culture meeting within the Council of 12 November 1992 on guidelines for Community cultural action (1992).
95. Parliament Resolution on the Commission communication entitled 'New Prospects for Community cultural action' (1992).

encourage artistic/cultural creation and co-operation with a European dimension; Ariane (1997–1999), which supported the field of books and reading, including translation, and; Raphaël (1997–1999), the goal of which was to complement Member States' policies in the area of cultural heritage of European significance. Aside from problems caused by delayed adoption, all three projects were criticized for their piecemeal approach.[96]

In an acknowledgment of such critique, the joint Parliament and Council decision on the establishment of the Culture 2000 programme created a general cultural fund, extended the scope of such programmes to encompass more sectors and increased their geographic range to cover all associate and European Economic Area states.[97] Thus, the cultural programme for the years 2000–2004[98] extended both the geographical reach and the scope of Community cultural policy, leading to a remarkably broad cultural mandate. (Article 1 of the Decision set out no less than nine objectives, not only cultural but also economic and social.) Despite wide-ranging goals, the entire programme initially received only 167 million euros (EUR) in funding, however. (As a general matter, the amount allocated in the Commission budget for such matters is, as yet, only a fraction of what Member States spend on their own policies.[99]) The evaluation of activity for the first year of the programme nonetheless determined that 'the Programme is succeeding in creating European added value in terms of creating new transnational co-operation and new partnerships that appear to be sustainable'.[100] However one may view this opinion, European identity supporting measures continued throughout the duration of the programme, especially by means of funding and co-ordination of cultural activity. The Culture 2000 decision was, in fact, itself noteworthy for its constant references to the 'peoples of Europe', 'European society' and the 'European peoples',[101] as well as the recognition that '[i]f citizens give their full support to, and participate fully in, European integration, greater emphasis should be

---

96. *See*, e.g., Opinion of the Committee of the Regions 'On Culture and Cultural Differences and their Significance for the Future of Europe' (1998).
97. Decision 508/2000/EC of the European Parliament and of the Council of 14 February 2000 on establishing the Culture 2000 programme.
98. Extended to 31 December 2006 by Art. 1(1) of Decision 626/2004/EC of the European Parliament and of the Council of 31 March 2004 amending Decision No. 508/2000/EC establishing the Culture 2000 programme, with a commensurate rise in budget.
99. In the 2004 Budget, for example, the amount allocated by the Commission for 'Culture and Education' was EUR 804 770 054, of which only EUR 38 708 000 was intended for 'Culture and Language'. (*See* Final adoption of the general budget of the European Union for the financial year 2004.) It should be noted, however, that significant additional resources are available through Structural Funds. See Craufurd Smith (2007), pp. 66–68 for a discussion.

    In comparison, the budget of the French Ministry for Culture and Communication in 2004 was EUR 263 billion, an amount supplemented through regional and local funds. *See Projet de loi de finances pour 2004, adopté par l'Assemblée nationale, Tome I, Culture, La Progression des Dotations.*
100. Commission Report 'On the implementation of the "Culture 2000" programme in the years 2000 and 2001' (2003), p. 4; but *see* Craufurd Smith (2007), pp. 61–62 for a more critical view.
101. *Ibid.*, Preamble Recs. 6, 4 and Art. 1, respectively.

placed on their common cultural values and roots as a key element of their identity'.[102]

The new Culture 2007 programme is noticeably more focused in its general aims than its predecessor. Only three goals are set out, while funding has more than doubled to EUR 400 million. The Decision establishing the new programme identifies as its general objective to make 'common cultural area for the peoples of Europe a reality'[103] through financial support, structural intervention in favour of co-operation and information activities. In particular, increased mobility of individuals active in the cultural sector, increased circulation of works of art and cultural products, and increased intercultural dialogue are the objectives any projects or actions must meet in order to gain Community support.[104] The additional criterion of a 'real European added value' (e.g., in Rec. 12) is a more nebulous requirement for any project to fulfil. In particular, it seems the programme cannot decide whether all culture in Europe with a trans-national dimension is 'European' or something more is necessary to assume the mantle.[105] In a similar vein, the text of the decision repeatedly refers to the 'diversity' of 'European cultures', but simultaneously – and in line with a decision from 2004[106] – relies on the existence of a 'European culture' in the singular in the external context.[107] The exact quality of the European cultural area being constructed thus remains amorphous, to say the least.

b. A More than Complimentary Use of Cultural Policy

Despite this vagueness, we do not encounter a totemistic use of both 'diversity' and 'Europe', as 'value[s], attached to everything valuable or in need of valorisation'[108] – and a role for the Community in encouraging such valorization, providing its framework and, more problematically, drawing the outlines of what is 'European' or 'diverse' enough to merit attention. This role, presently focused on the creation of networks and programmes to stimulate interaction between the nationals of Member States, is not necessarily (just) supportive or

---

102. *Ibid.*, Preamble Rec. 5.
103. Decision No. 1855/2006/EC of the European Parliament and of the Council of 12 December 2006 establishing the Culture Programme (2007 to 2013) (hereinafter, Decision on Culture 2007), Rec. 10. The Commission Proposal for a 'Decision of the European Parliament and of the Council establishing the Culture 2007 programme (2007–2013)' (2004) originally referred to the 'achievement of a common cultural area'. *See* Rec. 11, and p. 4.
104. Decision on Culture 2007, Art. 3(2).
105. Compare Annex, Secs 1.1 (where the participation of operators from between six different countries is required) and 2 (where a 'real European dimension', e.g., 'potential influence at the European Union level' is preferred).
106. *See* Decision No. 792/2004/EC of the European Parliament and of the Council of 21 April 2004 establishing a Community action programme to promote bodies active at the European level in the field of culture.
107. *See, inter alia*, Rec. 14 of the Decision on Culture 2007.
108. Sassatelli (2002), p. 445.

complementary, however, and may go hand-in-hand with instrumentalization. Thus, a Council Resolution from 2002 called on the Commission and Member States to 'regard culture as an essential component of European integration'.[109]

The strategy has, in fact, been outlined in a 2004 communication, where the Commission states that the Community's main goal is now 'to contribute to the flourishing of shared European cultural values on the basis of cultural cooperation'.[110] A 'bottom-up development of a dynamic European identity' is the expected outcome of such 'intercultural dialogue', due to an increased 'awareness of the diversity and richness of European cultures'.[111] The Community supposedly expects only to increase the 'opportunities to create networks'[112] between individuals and organizations by 'fostering mobility'.[113]

However, the reader becomes slightly suspicious on reading that 'promoting European culture and diversity contributes to making European citizenship a reality through encouraging direct involvement of European citizens in the integration process'.[114] As if the instrumental promotion of culture were not clearly enough stated we find that the Commission has identified 'the need to make citizenship a reality by *fostering European culture and diversity*'.[115] In other words, cultural policy is to be a tool to advance the concept of European citizenship. The Decision on Culture 2007 already discussed states matters most clearly: 'For citizens to give their full support to, and participate fully in, European integration, greater emphasis should be placed on their common cultural values and roots as a key element of their identity'.[116]

In turn, the decision establishing the new MEDIA 2007 programme, which replaces more piecemeal audiovisual measures, refers in its Preamble not only to Article 151 – and the need for a common cultural space – but also to the 'role' the audiovisual sector has to play in 'the emergence of European citizenship' as one of the 'principal vectors for conveying the Union's common and shared fundamental social and cultural values'.[117] Accordingly, the global objectives of the programme include 'preserv[ing] and enhance[ing] European cultural and linguistic

---

109. Sec. C. of the Council Resolution on the Role of Culture in the Development of the European Union (2002).
110. Commission Communication, 'Making Citizenship Work: Fostering European Culture and Diversity Through Programmes for Youth, Culture, Audiovisual and Civic Participation' (2004), p. 9.
111. *Ibid.*, pp. 9–10. *See also* Eder (2001), p. 231 (foreseeing 'social integration through communication').
112. Commission Communication, 'Making Citizenship Work', *supra* note II.110, p. 12.
113. *Ibid.*, p. 2.
114. *Ibid.*, p. 3. *See also* José Manuel Barroso, Speech 04/495 (26 November 2004) ('I have already stressed the *links between culture, identity, and citizenship*') (emphasis in original).
115. *Ibid.*, p. 3 (emphasis in original).
116. Rec. 3 of the Decision on Culture 2007. *See also* Art. 3(1).
117. Decision No. 1718/2006/EC of the European Parliament and of the Council of 15 November 2006 concerning the implementation of a programme of support for the European audiovisual sector (MEDIA 2007), Rec. 1. *See also* Art. 1(2).

diversity'[118] through practical provisions aimed at the enhancement of the 'European audiovisual sector'.

In a final example, a recent Decision on promoting active European citizenship lists as one of its aims: 'developing a sense of European identity, based on recognized common values, history and culture'.[119] This newly overhauled programme (whose precursor ended in 2006) is noteworthy not only for its general aims, including 'fostering action, debate and reflection related to European citizenship and democracy, shared values, common history and culture',[120] but also for its legal basis. In addition to ECT Article 308, Article 151 is also relied on. In other words, Community action to enhance citizenship – to the tune of EUR 215 million – has been marshalled on the basis of the Community's limited competence in cultural matters.

On the basis of such developments and corresponding statements[121] – and leaving aside, for now, the question of how one affects the other – the role of the Community in cultural matters is unlikely to emerge as quite the supplementary one theorists could have envisaged, given the limitations of ECT Article 151 (or CT Article III-280). This seems to have been recognized in the relevant circles, since the Decisions referred to above take pains to explain the supportive and 'transnational' character of the proposed activities.[122] The Commission Proposal for the Decision on promoting active European citizenship even claimed that 'proposing a specific and ambitious programme' that includes financial support for town-twinning, citizens' projects, conferences, opinion polls, the preservation of historical sites, as well as structural support for civil society organizations, and involves individuals, towns, organizations of civil society and think tanks, is merely 'complementary'.[123]

In the international arena, the role of the European Community has already emerged as more than co-coordinative. In accordance with a Commission Recommendation,[124] the Community represented its Member States in the

---

118. *Ibid.*, Art. 1(2)(a).
119. Decision No. 1904/2006/EC of the European Parliament and of the Council of 12 December 2006 establishing for the period 2007 to 2013 the programme Europe for Citizens to promote active European citizenship (hereinafter, Decision on promoting active European citizenship), Art. 1(3). The Commission Proposal for this Programme (2005) was a bit more forthright and spoke simply of 'forging a European identity' (Art. 1[3]).
120. Decision on promoting active European citizenship, *Ibid.*, Art. 2(b).
121. *See* Viviane Reding, Speech 04/322 (18 June 2004); and Concluding Remarks on the Intellectual, Spiritual and Cultural Dimension of Europe (2004), Sec. 6 (declaring that a new source of 'political cohesion' 'must be looked for and found in Europe's common culture'.)
122. *See, inter alia,* Recs. 10 and 30 and Art. 3(2) of the Decision on Culture 2007; and Recs. 7, 10, and 11 and Art. 2 of the Decision on promoting active European citizenship.
123. *See* Commission Proposal on promoting active European citizenship, at 7 and Art. 2; and .Art. 3, respectively.
124. Recommendation from the Commission to the Council to authorize the Commission to participate, on behalf of the Community, in the negotiations within UNESCO on the convention

negotiations toward a UNESCO Convention on the Protection and Promotion of the Diversity of Cultural Expressions[125] to ensure, *inter alia*, that the provisions of the convention are consistent with relevant Community legislation, as well as the *acquis*, that the primacy of Community law in the European Union is ensured and that the convention contains a provision enabling the Community to become a contracting party to it.[126] Obviously, these goals go beyond specific Member State interests and represent the beginnings of an external Community cultural policy[127] – a novel development perhaps, but not in itself problematic, unless the Community wishes to become a signatory to the Convention. Since it does, questions of competence arise.

Granted, the goal of promoting and protecting the diversity of cultural expressions fits squarely into Article 151, but this article (and especially paragraph two) nowhere considers a Community interest amounting to a separate agenda. In turn, the fact that Article 151(3) makes reference to a Community role in fostering 'co-operation' with third states[128] and international organizations does not necessarily imply treaty-making powers. Finally, the reference in Article 151(4) to taking cultural aspects into account in action under other provisions of the Treaty clearly requires a legitimate basis for action under another ECT article. It seems, then, that the legal effects of external cultural policy are to emerge under the banner of other policy areas. (For example, a role for the Community in international negotiations is foreseen in the area of trade in cultural goods as an element of the common commercial policy.[129] But this provision would certainly not cover the scope of the Convention and disregards the fact that the place of trade in and in relation to the Convention is a matter of considerable controversy.)[130]

---

on the protection of the diversity of cultural contents and artistic expressions (2004). The Recommendation was formally adopted by the Council in November 2004. (Press Release 261, Sixth Council Meeting, Education, Youth and Culture (15–16 November 2004)).

125. *See* Convention on the Protection and Promotion of the Diversity of Cultural Expressions (2005). The Convention was adopted in October 2005 by a large majority at the 33rd General Assembly of the Organization.

126. Thus, while the Convention repeatedly underlines the principle of state sovereignty in cultural policy (*see* Arts 2(1) and 5(1)) it also makes express provision for treaty accession by 'regional economic integration organizations' (in Art. 27(3)); in essence, this is an EU clause.

127. Rather, this is a concrete manifestation of what is increasingly a wide-ranging (albeit still amorphous) preoccupation with cultural matters in both bilateral relations (particularly as an element of development policy) and multilateral ones (especially in the framework of WTO trade negotiations on the liberalization of services).

128. *See also* CT Art. III-286(2), in the context of association.

129. Unanimity is required, however. *See* ECT Art. 133(6).

130. In fact, the Council Decision on the conclusion of the Convention on the Protection and Promotion of the Diversity of Cultural Expressions relied not only on ECT Art. 151, but also exactly on Art. 133 (common commercial policy) and, in light of certain Convention provisions, ECT articles on developmental co-operation (181 and 181(a)), in conjunction with Art. 300. *See* Proposal for a Council Decision on the conclusion of the UNESCO Convention on the Protection and Promotion of the Diversity of Cultural Expressions (2005) (hereinafter, UNESCO Convention on the Diversity of Cultural Expressions), as adopted, with minor changes, on 18 May 2006.

In a related matter, the E.C.J. seems to have interpreted Article 151 rather narrowly, allowing the Community to adopt internal measures with significant impact in the sphere of culture on the basis of other articles. As the Advocate General in *Parliament v. Council (Linguistic Diversity)*[131] stated, a measure based on Article 151 'must directly and specifically have as its "subject-matter" the cultural actions to which that provision of the Treaty relates'.[132] On this basis, the Court in the given case determined that the Council did not need to rely on Article 151 as the basis for a programme on linguistic diversity in information technology.[133] Given that, as de Witte has argued, legislative measures dealing with or impacting on culture 'cannot be enacted primarily for the sake of promoting cultural diversity, but only as an integral part of laws whose central aim is defined otherwise'[134] such programmes, with only 'indirect or incidental'[135] effects on culture, have the potential for significant effects on European identity in the medium and long term.[136]

In light of this status quo, the reliance of the new 'Citizens for Europe' programme on Article 151 is especially puzzling – if linguistic diversity cannot be subsumed into the rubric of 'cultural' subject matter, how can 'the development of … European identity' be accommodated? Although Article 151(2) allows for action to improve 'the knowledge and dissemination of the culture and history of the European peoples', citizenship-boosting measures have little, if anything, to do with this aim. (Granted, ECT Article 22 does not admit of much flexibility with regard to measures to strengthen EU citizenship, so that another legal basis had to be located, but why doesn't Article 308 (continue to) suffice?) The Commission seems to have made a decision to couple citizenship and culture not only in rhetorical, but also legal terms here. One wonders, however, whether promoting the unifying strand of European identity is sufficiently different from the promotion of cultural diversity – especially in light of the constant linkage of the two in policies – to warrant legitimate reliance on Article 151 for this particular programme. It would be incongruous, to say the least, if initiatives aimed at maintaining cultural diversity could not piggyback on Article 151, while programmes to boost European identity could instrumentalize the same article.

Similar questions of instrumentality arise with respect to European Union citizenship, the focus of our next section.

---

131. Case C-42/97 *European Parliament v. Council of the European Union*, E.C.J. [1999].
132. Opinion of Advocate General La Pergola in Case C-42/97 (5 May 1998).
133. Council Decision 96/664/EC of 2 November 1996 on the adoption of a multiannual programme to promote the linguistic diversity of the Community in the information society.
134. De Witte (2003).
135. Case C-42/97 *Linguistic Diversity*, para. 63.
136. For an argument that Community efforts to highlight the 'European' dimension have had an effect, *see* Streek (1999). *See also* Lepsius (2001), p. 208–209 ('Europe has become a concrete object of reference for a collective identity').

C. EUROPEAN CITIZENSHIP, OR THE QUESTION OF INSTRUMENTALITY

1. APPEARANCE AND APPRAISAL OF A NEW LEGAL STATUS

The concept of European citizenship, though sporadically present in Community discourse since 1969,[137] assumed a legal character only through the introduction, through Maastricht, of ECT Articles 17–22 (CT Article I-10).[138] As a practical matter, the new status bestowed few new rights, but did serve as a useful new classificatory device. Three elements in particular were considered important in its creation: freedom of movement, political rights and 'identification with Europe'.[139] The first two of these aims are, in fact, reflected in the ECT articles: freedom of movement is guaranteed in Article 18(1); the right to vote in municipal and European Parliament elections in Articles 19(1), 190(4) and 19(2) respectively;[140] the right to information regarding Union institutions in one of the (now 23) official languages of the Union in Article 21 and a related right to access to documents in Article 255; and the right to petition an ombudsman or the European Parliament in Articles 21, 194 and 195. The right to protection by the diplomatic or consular authorities of any Member State in countries without representation by one's own state is included in Article 20.[141] However, the rights of Union citizens reach farther than those enumerated in these articles. Pursuant to Article 17(2), European citizens enjoy all rights 'conferred by the Treaty' – i.e., all rights through secondary law issued on the basis of the Treaty, or all those available under Union law, including those found in the (still legally non-binding)

---

137. *See* Sec. F of the Parliament Resolution and Sec. 6 of the Commission Memorandum included in Third General Report on the Activities of the European Union: 1969 (1970), p. 482 and p. 84 respectively. *See* also, *inter alia*, Sec. 11 of the Communiqué for the Conference of Heads of Government (1974); and Art. 3 of the Draft Treaty Establishing the European Union (also known as the Spinelli Treaty) approved by Parliament in 1984.
138. The idea of a 'European citizenship' was first suggested by Spain in the course of an inter-governmental conference called to reform existing treaties in 1990. Two distinct understandings – that of the Commission (EU Bulletin Suppl. 2/91, pp. 85–88) and an alternative suggested by Spain (*see* Proposal of the Spanish Delegation at the Inter-Governmental Conference on Political Union, on European Citizenship (1991)) – emerged during general discussion. It is the approach of the Commission that is reflected in the Maastricht Treaty, although the Spanish position was the more novel, foreseeing a stronger, direct link between the Union and the citizen than in fact emerged.
139. Kadelbach (2003), p. 9. *See also* the Tindemans Report already discussed, p. 72.
140. *See* Connolly, Day and Shaw (2006) for a recent evaluation of the effects of this right.
141. *See also* Decision of the Representatives of the Governments of the Member States meeting within the Council of 19 December 1995 regarding protection for citizens of the European Union by diplomatic and consular representations (1995). In light of recent activity by the Commission, there seems to be growing interest in rendering this right a meaningful one in the future. It should be noted, however, that the right may be highly problematic in practice, not only because it blurs the diplomatic protection/consular assistance distinction already discussed, but also because it requires the co-operation of third states.

European Charter,[142] as well as 'fundamental rights, as guaranteed by the [ECHR] and as they result from the constitutional traditions common to the Member States'.[143]

On the other hand, European citizenship is not a prerequisite for fundamental rights.[144] A European citizen is an individual who holds the nationality of a Member State.[145] But, as Kadelbach discusses, 'holders of fundamental freedoms are all those upon whom the Community legal order has conferred such rights'.[146] For example, the right to free movement may be extended to nationals of third countries[147] and denied European citizens;[148] the right to petition the European Parliament or the Ombudsman extends to all legal residents.[149] In the context of human rights more generally, instruments such as the European Charter and the ECHR extend rights to all individuals under the jurisdiction of the given state (except where otherwise stated). Thus, whatever human rights (as distinct from some citizenship rights) are afforded European citizens are extended to third-country nationals both through the Community framework[150] and through regional

---

142. The Charter constituted Part II of the Constitution. Thus, it would have become legally binding if the Constitution had come into effect; But *see* para. 48 of Case T-54/99 *Maxmobil v. Commission* C.F.I. [2002], where the Court of First Instance already referred to the Charter as a source of fundamental rights. The E.C.J. itself relied (to a limited extent) on the Charter for the first time in a recent decision. See Case C-540/03 *Parliament v. Council (Family Life)*, E.C.J. [2006], at para. 38. ('The Charter was solemnly proclaimed by the Parliament, the Council and the Commission ... While the Charter is not a legally binding instrument, the Community legislature did, however, acknowledge its importance.... Furthermore, the principal aim of the Charter, as is apparent from its preamble, is to reaffirm rights as they result, in particular, from the constitutional traditions and international obligations common to the Member States, the Treaty on European Union, the Community Treaties, the [ECHR], the Social Charters adopted by the Community and by the Council of Europe and the case-law of the Court... and of the European Court of Human Rights').
143. TEU Art. 6(2).
144. For a discussion of the typology of rights, *see* Hilson (2004).
145. ECT Art. 17(1).
146. Kadelbach (2003), p. 7.
147. *See* Arts 28, 31, and 36 of the EEA Treaty for the conditions that apply to EFTA Member States; and Case C-262/96 *Sema Sürül v. Bundesanstalt für Arbeit*, E.C.J. [1999] for a discussion of the conditions that apply to Turkish nationals. *See* the Agreement between the European Community and its Member States and the Swiss Confederation for the conditions applicable to Swiss nationals.
148. E.g., the 2+3+2 year restriction on the nationals of the new Central European and Baltic Member States. For discussions and critique, *see* Reich (2005), p. 684 *et seq.*; and Carrera (2005), p. 706 *et seq.*
149. Curiously, a number of rights not exclusive to European citizens – right to good administration under Art. II-101, right to access documents under Art. II-102, right to petition the Ombudsman under Art. II-103 and right to petition the European Parliament under Art. II-104 – were kept under the heading of 'Citizens' Rights' in Part II, Title V the Constitutional Treaty (in line with the original Charter of Fundamental Rights) and were mixed in among rights truly limited to European citizens.
150. E.g., Council Directive 2000/43/EC of 29 June 2000 implementing the principle of equal treatment between persons irrespective of racial or ethnic origin (hereinafter, Race Equality Directive); and Council Directive 2000/78/EC of 27 November 2000 establishing a general

and international instruments.[151] The Amsterdam Treaty, for example, has created a number of rights based on criteria other than European citizenship.[152]

Commentary on all elements of European citizenship, from the idea to its content and significance has covered a wide range, but can generally be grouped into two approaches: the first looks at the rights and duties that accompany it (and is accordingly purely legal); the second at its identity function (with consideration for its symbolic, social and legal implications). A parallel line of scholarship has also focused on the *concept* of European citizenship itself, from the point of view of political theory. Despite differences in discipline and focus, all have assessed European citizenship in the context of some pre-existing notion of citizenship, one based, often unconsciously, on that of nation states, as either a positive or negative template. The general view has accordingly been that European citizenship does not go far enough – an increased scope of rights to an expanded group of persons is urged.[153]

Commentary from political theorists, in particular, has two recurring strands: one arguing that European citizenship should become a self-foundational status; the second concerned with a delinkage of European citizenship from Member State nationality. Given that the rights of European citizenship, Member State nationality and human rights instruments – the main avenues of guaranteeing rights to individuals in the European Union – interact on multiple levels to produce varying matrixes of rights, the call for a simplification of European citizenship into what would essentially be a version of national citizenship is an outcome of somewhat limited thinking – one based on existing prototypes, not on possibilities of development.

Let us take a look at both suggestions regarding the concept of European citizenship before turning to the rights and identity functions of the status.

a.   A Self-Foundational Status?

With regard to the call for a European citizenship that is completely self-foundational,[154] it is one based on a fundamental misunderstanding of what nationality

---

framework for equal treatment in employment and occupation (hereinafter, Employment Directive).
151. E.g., the UDHR, ICCPR, ICESCR, to name a few of many.
152. See Arts 141, 153, 255, and 286.
153. *See,* e.g.,, Bhabha (1998), p. 605; O'Leary (1996), p. 89 *et seq.*; Mouton (1996), p. 18 *et seq.*; Staples (1999), p. 335 *et seq. See also* discussion of the thread of literature on the emergence of a 'market citizen', without political and social overtones in Shore (2000), p. 84–85; and Schönberger (2005) for a nuanced comparison with the development of federal citizenships in Germany, Switzerland and the United States.
154. *See* e.g., Castro Oliveira, who seems to base his argument for a direct attribution of European citizenship to third-country nationals on placing such individuals on the same footing as the nationals of Member States in the European context. Castro Oliveira (1998), p. 196. *See also* Marias (1994), p. 15 and European Parliament Report of the Committee of Institutional Affairs on Union Citizenship (1991), p. 10. Compare CT. Art. III-265(2), which foresees a right to travel for third-country nationals, independent of European citizenship.

and citizenship signify. In the case of those who advocate the replacement of Member State nationality with European citizenship, in particular, the ideal seems to be some European super-state. It is otherwise difficult to comprehend how a legal status that exists only and wholly within the jurisdiction of the European Union could replace nationality, a status that still remains a mechanism of ordering individuals to states for international law purposes. In reality, a transformation of this kind would mean only a transfer of competence on the attribution and withdrawal of nationality to the European level, with a concurrent (faulty) change of terminology.

As a practical matter, this is exactly what is happening since the development of the Schengen area in the context of 'common policy on asylum, immigration and external border control'.[155] As Favell and Hansen have recognized, the nascent common EU migration policy has 'transform[ed] the channels by which ... migrants can legitimately move into, around and through Europe'.[156] Guild, in turn, has argued that the power to control the right of residence, itself at the core of 'control of identity', is divided not only between the Union and its Member States, but shared also with the Council of Europe – and that the 'right to define identity' is accordingly also divided among these entities.[157] As we will later see when reviewing E.Ct.H.R case-law on immigration matters, he is quite correct in this contention. In fact, the emergence of a fully-fledged Community migration policy is but a matter of time.[158]

In the shorter term, its latest envisaged incarnation in the Constitutional Treaty mentioned the absence of any internal border controls and made reference to common visas and short-stay residence permits.[159] In other words, the power of a state to determine who enters and exits its territory (a fundamental element of territorial sovereignty under international law) was to be officially removed from Member State competence. In fact, this has already occurred bit by bit, even without the provisions of the Constitutional Treaty.[160] The Commission

---

155. ECT Art. 63(3) (CT Art. III-257(2)).
156. Favell and Hansen (2002), p. 582. The authors, in a rare refutation of the 'fortress Europe' account, argue that migration in Europe is increasingly market-driven, with states incapable of controlling the process. Public perception aside, if the account of state impotence is true, migration is no longer a political phenomenon but an economic one.
157. Guild (2004), p. 17.
158. *See* discussion in the European Commission Green Paper on an EU approach to managing economic migration (2005); the Policy Plan on Legal Migration (adopted by the Commission in December 2005); as well as Commission Communication, 'The Global Approach to Migration one year on: Towards a comprehensive European migration policy' (2006).
159. CT Art. III-265(1) and CT Art. III-265(2)(a), respectively.
160. *See* Regulation (EC) No. 562/2006 of the European Parliament and of the Council of 15 March 2006 establishing a Community Code on the rules governing the movement of persons across borders (Schengen Borders Code) (2006).
    In fact, all aspects of the arrival and residence of third country nationals are now discussed at the level of the European Union. Aside from provisions related to the common European asylum system, the following legal provisions (in addition to those mentioned above) have been accepted or discussed in the last five years: Council Directive 2003/109/EC of

has already presented a view on immigrant naturalization,[161] while the European Council has accepted common norms on the integration of legal migrants, as well as accepted qualified majority voting and the co-decision procedure for decisions in most areas of immigration (and asylum).[162] The call for a European nationality – that, in essence, is what replacement means – would only remove a further competence, that of determining membership in constituent political communities to the European level. (In the alternate, the matter could be framed as determining membership in a nascent European political community.) One would thereby eliminate the diversity of laws on nationality existing within the Union, fundamentally changing the 'national identity' of Member States as they are conceived of at the present time.[163] Despite increasing convergence, states have given regimes on nationality because of specific historical and social developments;

---

25 November 2003 concerning the status of third-country nationals who are long-term residents (applicable as of 26 January 2006); Council Directive 2003/86/EC of 22 September 2003 on the right to family reunification (applicable as of 3 October 2005); Council Regulation (EC) No. 859/2003 of 14 May 2003 extending the provisions of Regulation (EEC) No. 1408/71 and Regulation (EEC) No. 574/72 to nationals of third countries who are not already covered by those provisions solely on the ground of their nationality; Proposal for a Council Directive on the conditions of admission of third-country nationals for the purpose of studies, pupil exchange, unremunerated training or voluntary service (political agreement reached in March 2004); Proposal for a Council Directive on a specific admission procedure for third country researchers (2004) (no agreement reached); Proposal for a Council Directive on the conditions of entry and residence of third-country nationals for the purpose of paid employment and self-employed economic activities (2001) (no agreement reached).

In addition, *see* (Second) Annual Report on Migration and Integration (2006); Commission Communication, 'Implementing the Hague Programme: the Way Forward' (2006); Commission Communication, 'Policy Priorities in the Fight against Illegal Immigration of Third Country Nationals' (2006); Commission Communication, 'Study on the Links between Legal and Illegal Immigration' (2004); First Annual Report on Migration and Integration (2004); Commission Communication, 'On Immigration, Integration and Employment' (2003); and Commission Communication, 'On Integrating Migration Issues in the EU's relations with Third Countries' (2002).

161. Commission Communication, 'On immigration', *Ibid.* Obviously, the Community has come a long way since Cases C-281, 283, 284, 285, and 287/85 *Federal Republic of Germany and Others v. Commission*, E.C.J. [1987], in which the Court declared that integration and migration policy in general are linked to Community matters only in a very tenuous manner (*see* paras 22–24).
162. Press Release 14615/04 (Presse 321), 2618th Council Meeting, Justice and Home Affairs (19 November 2004). *See also* Brussels European Council Conclusions (4–5 November 2004), p. 19 *et seq.*; and Council Decision of 22 December 2004 providing for certain areas covered by Title IV of Part Three of the Treaty establishing the European Community to be governed by the procedure laid down in Article 251 of that Treaty. *See also* Peers (2005) for a discussion of the significance of this move.
163. This is not to say that in the future their role may not change. United States citizenship was derivative of and dependent on state citizenship until well after the Declaration of Independence, for example. *See Colgate v. Harvey*, US (1935), p. 426 *et seq.* for a discussion of the changing relationship of the two.

the legal singularities of such diverse developments, arguably covered under the Union's motto, should not be effaced without deliberation.[164]

b. The Interaction of European Citizenship and Member State Nationality

Turning now to calls for a de-linkage of European citizenship from Member State nationality for internal purposes – i.e., one would not need to be a Member State national to be a European citizen but rather a legal resident, for example[165] – the problem is more one of effects.[166] In the first place, delinkage would have unforeseen legal, administrative and sociological effects. What would the right to diplomatic or consular protection by any Member State, for example, signify when the individual is not the national of a Member State – in other words, when European citizenship is an inexistent status in international law? In the realm of the EU, would 'European' identity cards be issued to all citizens to discourage official differentiation between 'Member State' and 'third-country' nationals? Administrative and related difficulties aside, there is certainly the danger of first and second-tier citizens under such a scenario. On a sociological plane, assuming that the status of 'European citizen' connotes more than the sum of its most popular rights – free movement and non-discrimination – how would 'European identity' evolve in light of less exclusive citizenship?

If we consider the effects of such delinkage from the point of view of Member State regimes on nationality, the problems are compounded. In short, the interaction of Member State nationality and European citizenship at this point in time begets a situation in which delinkage could well undermine the former. On a practical level, would time spent in Tallinn count toward Spanish nationality for a Brazilian national (Ronaldo) who, after X years of residence in Spain is now a European citizen, has decided to move to Estonia, but has also applied for Spanish nationality? If he is granted Spanish nationality, would other states recognize it, in light of the principle of effectivity? Would Ronaldo even have an incentive to apply – i.e., wouldn't the effort to have immigrants apply for nationality in many European states be undermined?[167]

---

164. For a discussion of the cultural dimension of legal systems and an argument that '*kulturell verwurzelte Rechtsregeln*' are to be considered a part of the 'national identity' of Member States under TEU Art. 6(3), *see* Jayme (2003a), p. 214. *See also ibid.* (2003b), p. 12–13.
165. *See*, e.g., Art. 14(v) of Council of Europe Parliamentary Resolution 1314 (Contribution of the Council of Europe to the constitution-making process of the European Union) (2003); and the Opinion of the European Economic and Social Committee on 'Access to European Union citizenship' (2003). (The latter, in particular, echoes the idea of 'civic citizenship' first introduced by the Commission in 2000. *See* COM (2000) 757 final.)
166. The possibility of European integration engendering indirect effects on established principles of nationality law was noted quite early on. *See* Evans (1991).
167. *See also* Pérez Vera (1996), p. 337 (for a view that a self-standing European citizenship '*se traduiraient nécessairement par une profonde modification des nationalités étatiques*').

On a theoretical plane, we would need to consider issues of popular sovereignty. To the extent that the Constitutional Treaty was to have reiterated the importance of Member States[168] and given that we continue to deal with multiple political communities rather than one unified one, the extension of certain European citizenship rights, like the right to vote in European elections, to individuals not members of the constituting political entities, is problematic from the point of view of democratic legitimacy.[169]

Given that third-country nationals already hold (limited) rights of European citizenship – and to the extent these rights are likely to be extended – it is probably not European citizenship, as such, that should be granted to third-country nationals, but certain of the rights conferred by it. In fact, a number of authors have viewed the protection provided by ECT Article 13 and by the Race Equality Directive as an element of social citizenship, extending a number of social rights to nationals and non-nationals alike, regardless even of the prior exercise of the right to free movement.[170] Along with other rights already discussed, we are essentially dealing with an evolving, 'intermediate body of rights – a form of quasi-citizenship'.[171]

In a step in this direction, a 2006 E.C.J. decision effectively unhinged, at least legally, a further right of European citizenship from Member State nationality. In a case that stemmed directly from the efforts of the UK to comply with the judgment of the E.Ct.H.R. in the *Matthews* case[172] – which had concluded that the UK had breached Article 3 of Protocol 1 to the ECHR in failing to organize European parliamentary elections – the E.C.J. determined the following:

> [T]he definition of the persons entitled to vote and to stand as a candidate in elections to the European Parliament falls within the competence of each Member State in compliance with Community law, and ... Articles 189 EC, 190 EC and 19 EC do not preclude Member States from granting that right to vote and to stand as candidate to certain persons who have close links to them, other than their own nationals or citizens of the Union resident in their territory.[173]

In other words, although European citizenship, *qua* status, is a corollary of Member State nationality, Member States may expand the pool of individuals to whom the

---

168. One could even argue that the CT would have reinforced their importance, e.g., through the new monitoring functions of national parliaments in Arts 4–8 of CT Second Protocol on the Application of the Principles of Subsidiarity and Proportionality.
169. Naturally, if a Union with lesser focus on Member States were to emerge, this would no longer be the case. It should also be noted that local and municipal voting rights are on different footing and are, in any case, extended by domestic law in many Member States.
170. *See* Barnard (1997), p. 70 *et seq.* and Bell (2002), p. 82 *et seq.*, respectively.
171. Bell, *ibid.*, p. 195.
172. *Matthews v. the United Kingdom*, E.Ct.H.R. 24833/94 (1999).
173. *Case C-145/04 Spain v. the United Kingdom*, E.C.J. [2006], para. 78. *See also* the Opinion of Advocate General Tizzano in Cases C-145/04 and C-300/04 (6 April 2006), in which he argued that 'it is not possible to dispute a Member State's right to define its own electorate for European elections, if necessary even extending (or ... restricting), by reference to the circle of its own citizens and having regard to the particular features of its own legal order, the range of persons entitled to vote' (para. 101).

rights of the status of European citizen, particularly voting in European elections, may be granted. These individuals must have 'close links' to the Member State in question. Conversely, as a case decided on the same day noted, 'the criterion of residence in the territory in which the elections are held' may be a factor in defining who may vote, but the principle of equal treatment prevents differential treatment of nationals who are in comparable situations, unless that difference in treatment is objectively justified.[174] On this basis, the pool of European voters can conceivably exclude some nationals of Member States.[175]

Given the proliferation of legal statuses in Europe – among others, (Member State) national, dual national, European citizen, third-country national, resident, permanent resident – traditional notions of citizenship are simply not the correct standard against which to measure the actual context of European citizenship.[176] The authors asserting that European citizenship does not go far enough seem to forget that the European Union is not a nation state – nor even an entity with official legal personality for the moment – but 'something' near the confluence of international, regional and domestic law. In terms of international law on nationality, the fact that Member States must provide diplomatic or consular protection to each others' nationals is already an anomaly – despite the lack of guarantees for this right to individuals.[177] That Member States must mutually recognize decisions on the attribution or withdrawal of nationality[178] and that Community law may interfere in such matters[179] is even more unusual. Since nationality has not only been an important function of sovereignty, but also a sign of the national identity politics of the given nation state, as discussed, states generally guard their right to its near-unfettered attribution and withdrawal jealously.[180]

In fact, considering that most citizenship rights are traditionally, and in accordance with international law, restricted to nationals,[181] the development of

---

174. Case C-300/04 *Eman and. Sevinger v. College van burgemeester en wethouders van Den Haag*, E.C.J. [2006], para. 61.
175. On this basis, Bulgaria has already announced that only nationals resident in Bulgaria or another Member State will be allowed to vote in the first European Parliamentary elections held in the country. The move seems to be targeted mainly at members of the Turkish minority, over 40 000 of whom are now resident in Turkey. See Népszabadság, *Bulgária korlátozza az EP-választásokon szavazásra jogosultak körét* (14 February 2007).
176. See (Third) Report from the Commission on Citizenship of the Union (2001), p. 7.
177. See Kadelbach (2003), p. 28 *et seq.*
178. See Case 369/90 *Mario Vicente Micheletti and others v. Delegación del Gobierno en Cantabria*, E.C.J. [1992]; and Case C-200/02 *Zhu and Chen v. Secretary of State for the Home Department*, E.C.J. [2004]. *See also* Declaration No. 2 on Nationality of a Member State, annexed to the Final Act of Maastricht (1992). The extension of the nationality by the Federal Republic of Germany to former East-German nationals is a concrete example.
179. See Case C-192/99 *The Queen v. Secretary of State for the Home Department, ex parte Manjit Kaur*, E.C.J. [2001], para. 19. *See also* Hall (1999), p. 598 *et seq.* and *ibid.* (2001).
180. See *Liechtenstein v. Guatemala* (Judgment, Second Phase), ICJ (1955), p. 23.
181. As Lillich discusses, there is likely an 'international minimum standard' of non-discriminatory treatment that must be afforded to non-nationals subsumed into the general body of international human rights law. Lillich, p. 49–56 (1984). However, the 'sartorial tastes of the State involved' still determine the extent of non-national protection. *Ibid.*, p. 122.

European citizenship has been spirited, and atypical of international practice. None of the three traditional elements of citizenship identified previously[182] apply, for example. The political community – circumscribed by state borders – is no longer linked to the territory in which rights may be exercised. Instead, the territory of rights spreads far beyond the territory of the community. Thus, Member State nationals enjoy a number of citizenship rights (free movement and residence, non-discrimination, etc.) throughout the Union that used to be limited to the nation state, in contrast with the second characteristic of traditional understandings. As a corollary, in contrast with the first assumed characteristic, it is not only nationals who enjoy certain rights in the territory of the Member State, but a much larger group, including European citizens and extending, through the Long-Term Residence Directive,[183] to third-country nationals legally residing in a Member State.[184] The citizenship-nationality link that formed the basis of the nation state has thus been broken. Because of this development, in contrast to the third traditional characteristic – and in a nod of good-bye to sovereignty – it is not the members of the given political community who determine the content of applicable rights, but a supra-state entity, namely, the European Union.

2. FLESHING OUT THE STATUS OF EUROPEAN UNION CITIZEN

The fact of citizenship rights, as such, with an extended geographical reach beyond the nation state is thus distinctly new. Moreover, despite early pessimism,[185] the legal effects of European citizenship have not been so insignificant. Recent scholarship has actually rung alarm bells in light of the decidedly activist jurisprudence of the E.C.J., which has harnessed Union citizenship – especially the right to free movement in Article 18(1) and the closely-related non-discrimination principle enunciated in Article 12 – as a tool for the extension of rights into areas Member States likely never intended.[186]

See also, Arts 4, 5(2), and 8 of the Declaration on the Human Rights of Individuals Who are Not Nationals of the Country in which They Live (1985), which refer to a whole series of rights afforded non-nationals that may be restricted due to 'customs and traditions' as well as 'national security, public safety, public order, public health or morals or the rights and freedoms of others'.

182. *See* above, Sec. I B.1.
183. Council Directive 2003/109/EC of 25 November 2003 concerning the status of third-country nationals who are long-term residents.
184. As Reich discusses, a whole thread of literature on European citizenship focuses on its possible development as a means to grant citizenship rights through residence in the Member States, rather than nationality. *See* Reich (2001), p. 15 *et seq.*
185. Within the vast literature, *see* d'Oliveira (1995), p. 147; and Barnard (1999).
186. *See, inter alia,* Hailbronner (2004) and (2005); and Hilpold (2005). For a more positive evaluation *see* Kostakopoulou (2005).

a. The Rights of Free Movement

As regards free movement, the Court first determined in *Martínez Sala*[187] that 'a national of a Member State lawfully residing in the territory of another Member State ... comes within the scope *ratione personae* of the provisions of the Treaty on European citizenship'.[188] In other words, the mere (legal) presence of a European citizen in another Member State is enough for Community law to apply to them. Later, in *D'Hoop*, the Court determined that reverse discrimination – i.e., discrimination against the nationals of a given Member State in that state – is also prohibited when it results from the right of a Union citizen to practice her right to free movement.[189] Clearly the scope of national legislation in which Community law principles may enter has been expanded significantly.[190]

The recent *Tas-Hagen* judgment, in turn, concluded that exercising the free movement rights of European citizenship may also expand the scope of EC law *ratione materiae*. If a 'right recognised by the Community legal order has had an impact on [claimants'] right to receive a benefit under national legislation, such a situation cannot be considered to be a purely internal matter with no link to Community law'.[191] Thus, even national provisions (like compensation to civilian war victims) that fall within the competence of the Member States may be examined for compatibility with EC law if the rights of European citizenship (particularly free movement) have been exercised by individuals to whom these provisions apply. In the *Schempp* case, the court also relied on the free movement right of Article 18 to restrict the scope of internal situations, without a link to Community law. There, the tax deduction of a maintenance grant awarded to a former spouse now resident in another Member State was not assimilated to an internal situation, because 'the exercise ... of a right conferred by the Community legal order [by the former spouse] had an effect on [applicant's] right to deduct in his Member State of residence'.[192]

In a number of decisions, moreover, the E.C.J. has given the free movement principle a generous interpretation.[193] For example, in the *Zhu and Chen* case, the

---

187. Case C-85/96 *Martínez Sala v. Freistaat Bayern*, E.C.J. [1998].
188. *Ibid.*, para. 61.
189. Case C-224/98 *Marie-Nathalie D'Hoop v. Office National d'Emploi*, E.C.J. [2002], para. 28 *et seq.* (finding that a national exercising her right to free movement to pursue education had been placed at a disadvantage when compared to other nationals).
190. *See also* Case C-413/99 *Baumbast and R. v. Secretary of State for the Home Department*, E.C.J. [2001], para. 81 ('since ... Union citizenship has been introduced into the EC Treaty ... Article 18(1) EC has conferred a right, for every citizen, to move and reside freely within the territory of the Member States').
191. Case C-192/05 *K. Tas-Hagen and R.A. Tas v. Raadskamer WUBO van de Pensioen- en Uitkeringsraad*, E.C.J. [2006], para. 28.
192. Case C-403/03 *Egon Schempp v. Finanzamt München*, E.C.J. [2005], para. 25.
193. *See* Case C-348/96 *Criminal Proceedings against Donatella Calfa*, E.C.J. [2000]; and Case C-413/99 *Baumbast*. *See also* Opinion of Advocate General Jacobs in Case C-224/02 (20 November 2003), para. 22 ('subject to the limits set out in Article 18 itself, no unjustified

Court determined that a the (third-country national) mother of a minor child holding the nationality of Ireland – born in the Member State exactly so both could reside in the UK – had a right to residence in the UK, on the basis of the child's right to free movement and to residence under Article 18, in conjunction with Council Directive 90/364.[194] The case is noteworthy not only because of the extended chain of entitlements, but also because the child's right to residence in the UK is clearly based only on Article 18.[195] It is worth considering that there are no other regions in the world where a comparable right to free movement beyond and between state borders (or the right to equal treatment with nationals of other states, as will be discussed) exists.[196] But its significance extends beyond this as we just saw: the free movement right of Union citizenship is increasingly used by the Court to extend the reach of Community law.

b.   The Right to Equal Treatment

With regard to equal treatment, the *Martínez Sala* decision above also served to forge a link between citizenship and non-discrimination (on the basis of Article 12). In turn, this connection has been the mechanism by which the court has not only fleshed out the concept of Union citizenship,[197] but also imagined novel rights for the holders of this status. In *Bickel and Franz*[198] the Court determined that the right of minority individuals in a given state to use their language in criminal proceedings must be extended to non-nationals speaking the same language, on the basis of the principles of free movement and non-discrimination. It is the opinion of Advocate General Jacobs in that case that makes the root of the decision clear: '[T]he notion of citizenship of the Union implies a commonality of rights and obligations uniting Union citizens by a common bond transcending Member State nationality'.[199]

---

burden may be imposed on any citizen of the European Union seeking to exercise the right to freedom of movement or residence'); but *see* Case C-378/97 *Criminal Proceedings against Wijsenbeek*, E.C.J. [1999].
194. Case C-200/02 *Zhu and Chen*, E.C.J. [2004].
195. *See ibid.,* paras 26 and 27.
196. The freedom of movement was not, however, complete, given applicable limitations and conditions, as well as the exceptions that may be instituted through Arts 39(3), 46(1), and 55. *See also* Council Directive 90/364/EEC of 28 June 1990 on the right of residence; Council Directive 90/365/EEC of 28 June 1990 on the right of residence for employees and self-employed persons who have ceased their occupational activity; and Council Directive 93/96/EEC of 29 October 1993 on the right of residence for students. (All have been repealed by the Citizens Directive discussed below.) *See also* Carrera (2005) for a discussion of limitations and challenges in practice.
197. *See* Reich (2005), p. 683. *See also* Case C-281/98 *Angonese v. Cassa di Risparmio di Bolzano SpA*, E.C.J. [2000] (extending the prohibition of discrimination on the basis of nationality to private actors).
198. Case C-274/96 *Criminal Proceedings against Bickel and Franz*, E.C.J. [1998].
199. Opinion of Advocate General Jacobs in Case C-274/96 (19 March 1998), para. 23 (emphasis added). The Advocate General also distinguished the case from Case 137/84 *Ministère Public v.*

This supposed bond has, in turn, served to extend the principle of equal treatment to social rights, including in the area of education.[200] Specifically, in the *Grzelczyk* case[201] the Court determined that a Member State could not refuse student benefits to a student who is a national of another Member State solely on this basis, since such action constitutes discrimination under Article 12. The decision is especially interesting because the Court specifically stated that the introduction of European citizenship made the outcome possible:[202] in other words, a conscious choice was made here to expand on the concept of European citizenship.[203] (In fact, the Court gave a somewhat tortured interpretation of Directive 93/96 in its attempt to explain away the articles of a Directive that would make the given outcome impossible).[204]

The *Bidar* case[205] is also worth noting, since the Court there essentially overturned its earlier judgments when determining that even student maintenance grants fall within the scope of Community law, again on the basis of the introduction of European citizenship, as well as of ECT Article 149 on education.[206] Moreover, the Court determined that while a certain period of residence could be required as proof of integration into the society of the Member State, no requirement of being 'settled' in the host-state could be added,[207] since this would amount to nationality discrimination.[208] This reliance on some degree of 'integration' is actually but further clarification of the idea of a 'genuine link' already articulated in the *Collins* case;[209] in which the UK's requirement of 'habitual residence' for grants of a job-seekers' allowance was found to be a form of indirect nationality discrimination.[210] As these cases show, the social rights of European citizenship have developed quickly in the last few years.

Robert Heinrich Maria Mutsch, E.C.J. [1985], where the right to use a given language in court proceedings emanated from a specific Regulation.

200. National healthcare systems have also been subject to considerable E.C.J. scrutiny in recent years, albeit generally on the basis of consistency with ECT Arts 49 and 50. *See, inter alia*, Dawes (2006), discussing not only jurisprudence, but also commentary on the issue.
201. Case 184/99 *Rudy Grzelczyk v. le Centre public d'aide sociale d'Ottignies-Louvain-la-Neuve*, E.C.J. [2001].
202. *Ibid.*, paras 34–36.
203. *See also* discussion of case law on citizenship in Jacqueson (2002), p. 268 *et seq.* A comparison with Advocate General Alber's opinion in the case at issue, in which he attempted to subsume Mr. Grzelczyk into the category of 'workers' and relied only hesitantly on Art. 17 rights shows the more traditional route the Court could have taken.
204. Case 184/99 *Grzelczyk*, at paras 39–45.
205. Case C-209/03 *The Queen on the application of Dany Bidar v. London Borough of Ealing*, E.C.J. [2005].
206. *Ibid.*, paras 39–42.
207. *Ibid.*, paras 61–62.
208. Compare also Case C-258/04 *Office national de l'emploi v. Ioannis Ioannidis*, E.C.J. [2005], esp. para. 26 *et seq.* (finding an instance of indirect discrimination contravening ECT Art. 39 in a requirement that applicants for a tideover allowance have completed their secondary education in Belgium).
209. Case C-138/02 *Brian Francis Collins v. Secretary of State for Work and Pensions*, E.C.J. [2004], paras 69–70.
210. *See also* Case C-346/05 *Monique Chateignier v. Office national de l'emploi (ONEM)*, E.C.J. [2004] (finding that Regulation No. 1408/71 on the application of social security schemes, as

Two (joined) cases now before the Court reverse the basic fact patterns dealt with thus far: Cases C-11/06 and C-12/06[211] ask whether a Member State (Germany) may condition education or training grants awarded to nationals for a full course of study in another Member State on attendance at a German education or training establishment for at least a year. In a second question, the Court must also determine whether 'permanent residence' in a given region of a Member State may be required for grants to be awarded to a cross-border commuter for study in another Member State, if the individual has relocated to the border region only for education or training purposes. In other words, these cases consider whether states of origin – not, as heretofore, states of residence – must extend certain social (educational) benefits to all individuals who wish to study in a Member State other than their 'own'.

A personal connection – or 'genuine link' – between the claimants and their states of origin can thus be assumed in these cases (because they are nationals); what is at issue is rather whether educational benefits usually granted to nationals only in the territory of the Member State – or in exceptional circumstances outside it, if the course of study represents a continuation of studies begun in the Member State – must also be conferred in other Member States. As things stand now, a link with the educational system of the Member State of nationality – not just the legal status of national – is necessary to receive educational and training grants. On the basis of the line of case law discussed above (as well as the judgment in *ITC*), it is likely that the Court (and the Advocate General) will find the conditions set out by Germany to be disproportionate to any aim of, for example, protecting its budget or the integrity of the national educational system, with serious consequences for existing practice on public funding for university studies abroad.

Considering that the extension of provisions to *nationals* only, generally exclusively in the territory of the state, has been both a founding element of the modern welfare state and a reason behind the link of citizenship-nationality, these are significant developments. They are also curious in light of secondary Community law, which places clear (financial) conditions on the right to free movement. In fact, one commentator has attacked the recent string of judgments referred to above as an instance of 'far-reaching disregard for case law precedent, wording and intention in secondary Community law' in an effort at rendering European citizenship the functional equivalent of Member State citizenship.[212]

---

       amended, precludes national legislation denying unemployment benefits to the national of another Member State on the ground that the individual has not completed a specified period of employment, if no such requirement applies to nationals of the Member State in question).

       See also Case C-406/04 *Gérald De Cuyper v. Office national de l'emploi*, E.C.J. [2006] (finding that Art. 18 does not preclude a residence clause for an individual exempt from having to prove that he is available for work, as a condition for the retention of entitlement to unemployment benefit).

211. Cases C-11/06 and C-12/06 *Rhiannon Morgan v. Bezirksregierung Köln / Iris Bucher v. Landrat des Kreises Düren*, lodged before the E.C.J. on 11 January 2006.
212. '*Weitgehender Ignorierung von Entscheidungsgeschichte, Wortlaut und Zweck des sekundären Gemeinschaftsrechts*'. Hailbronner (2004), p. 2185. *See* Hailbronner (2005); Martin (2002),

It is true that the reference to European citizenship as a 'fundamental status' has resulted in what is essentially a disregard of existing secondary legislation;[213] to the extent that this is done in reliance on what the Court sees as overriding (and subsequent) basic principles, as discussed below, this is not so unusual. It is rather the scope granted to the new fundamental status that is likely to raise some doubts. As Hailbronner notes, there have not heretofore been signs that the status of European citizenship 'like nationality, also comprises standing by each other without regard for origin, residence ... and income in an expression of solidarity'.[214] Yet this is exactly what the Court is increasingly insisting on, most clearly in its reference in *Grzelczyk* to 'financial solidarity' between the nationals of various Member States.[215]

This same assumption underlay the judgment in *ITC*, in which the Court found that national legislation conditioning payment to a private recruitment agency for job placement on the job found being subject to compulsory social security contributions in the Member State is contrary to Articles 39, 49 and 50 (as well as 18, which 'finds specific expression' in the first two articles).[216] Neither the argument that the limitation is part of a new national employment policy, nor that its purpose is to protect the national security system was given particular credence by the Court. (This last argument, in particular – in fact, any reference to considerations of a budgetary or economic character – is regularly dismissed by the Court in social rights cases.) An argument that relied on a causal link between the integrity of the national labour market and social security system was also passed over by the Court. Instead the E.C.J. focused on the individual in the context of the European labour market.[217]

The Court reiterated that 'the broad margin of discretion which the Member States enjoy in matters of social policy may not have the effect of undermining the rights granted to individuals by the Treaty provisions'.[218] Rather than considering the rights and duties of the individual as a member of the national community, or even the possible interests of the national community itself, the E.C.J. thus focuses on the individual exercising her rights at the European level. A number of commentators have criticized recent E.C.J. jurisprudence on social rights – including education, welfare and health benefits – for exactly this individualist approach. As one

---

p. 139 *et seq.*; and para. 66 *et seq.* of the Opinion of Advocate General Ruiz-Jarabo Colomer in Case C-138/02 (10 July 2003).
213. This development also raises issues related to the competence of the Community legislature, as a number of E.C.J. decisions effectively reverse its regulatory choices. *See* Dougan (2006).
214. '*Ahnlich der Staatsangehörigkeit – auch das solidarische Füreinandereinstehen ohne Rücksicht auf Herkunft, Wohnsitz ... und Einkommen beinhaltet*'. Hailbronner (2004), p. 2188.
215. Case 184/99 *Grzelczyk*, at para. 44 (on the basis of a highly questionable reading of Directive 93/96).
216. Case C-208/05 *ITC Innovative Technology Center GmbH v. Bundesagentur für Arbeit*, E.C.J. [2007].
217. *See,* e.g., *Ibid.*, at para. 43 ('the departure of a worker to another Member State may be counterbalanced by the arrival of a worker from another Member State').
218. *Ibid.*, at para. 40.

author wrote in the context of health care, '[t]hese developments may be intended to promote European "citizenship", but they may corrode the sense of social solidarity essential to any fair-minded [national social policy] system'.[219]

Incongruously, it seems that this trans-national solidarity is to develop at the expense of even local ones. A decision from 2003 has accordingly seen local residence conditions as an indirect form of nationality discrimination.[220] This approach is perplexing not only because such conditions are attempts at establishing membership on a basis other than nationality, not only because the Court makes only superficial efforts to understand the real economic costs of sweeping statements on the universality of fundamental freedoms, and not even because the argumentation used is reflective of a shaky grasp of structural governmental realities. It is baffling for what it reveals about the Court's understanding of community. As Davies well argues: '[T]he question of whether a given local authority service falls within what may be legitimately provided to residents, or whether it is the sort of service that must be provided universally if it not to be discrimination, then becomes a question of whether that service falls within the scope of acceptable and reasonable local community solidarity'.[221] While this balance is regularly drawn on the national level in accordance with Community principles, one may question its application at the local level, especially in light of its affect on the future viability of benefits provided by local authorities to residents, from subsidized transport for pensioners to discounted student rates at the local beach. The outcome of this case is also puzzling in light of the constant references to multiple identities (and conceptions of community) in Community documents, and near-incomprehensible in light of the emergence of residence as the new reference point for membership in Community law.

c.   The Citizens Directive

In fact, the possibility that nationality will give way 'to the residence principle in relation to Union citizens' is already present.[222] In a significant step in this direction, a 2004 Directive on the right of citizens of the Union and their family members to move and reside freely within the territory of the Member States,[223] first suggested by the Commission's Third Report on Citizenship of the Union,

---

219. Newdick (2006), p. 1646. For general overviews of effects, both positive and negative, *see* the contributions in Spaventa and Dougan (eds), (2005).
220. *See* Case C-388/01 *Commission v. Italy (Museum Entry)*, E.C.J. [2003], where the Court determined that advantageous entry rates for local residents are discriminatory toward nationals of other Member States. (The case is also worth noting because the Court did not rely on European citizenship to bring the matter within the scope of Community law; instead, it used the free movement principle).
221. Davies (2005), p. 48–49.
222. Kadelbach (2003), p. 33.
223. Directive 2004/38/EC of the European Parliament and of the Council of 29 April 2004 on the right of citizens of the Union and their family members to move and reside freely within the territory of the Member States (hereinafter, Citizens Directive).

clarifies and adds to the rights of European citizens with regard to residence in another Member State. As Rec.1 states, 'citizenship of the Union confers on every citizen of the Union the primary and individual right to move and reside freely within the territory of the Member States'. This right – encompassed by one of the fundamental freedoms – has nonetheless been conditioned on a number of limitations, financial, administrative and legal, and differentiated by categories, such as 'worker' or 'student'.[224] Under the terms of the Citizens Directive, however, European citizens, as such, have the clear right to exit their Member State and enter another with valid identity cards only.[225] The right, while not new, is now clearly affixed to European citizens and their family members in a piece of legislation. Alas, it is still not absolute, since possible restrictions on the grounds of public-policy, security and health remain;[226] however, the potential scope of such restrictions have been considerably curtailed, while a number of procedural safeguards (including redress procedures) have been added.[227] The Hague Programme, adopted in November 2004, even foresees a possibility 'for allowing citizens to move within the European Union on similar terms to nationals of a Member State moving around or changing their place of residence in their own country'[228] – i.e., a right to free movement without any conditions.

According to Articles 6 and 7 of the Directive, moreover, individuals have the right to residence in other Member States, without any conditions, for a period of three months and on the basis of strictly limited conditions (and administrative formalities)[229] for periods extending beyond three months. The financial requirements of earlier Directives remain, but have been circumscribed in greater detail than heretofore.[230] The actual restrictions still placed on the right of residence have been framed in fuzzy terms, without exact criteria, however – most clearly in the requirement that individuals not become an 'unreasonable burden' on the social assistance system of the host Member State – so that states continue to have significant leeway. Still, individuals are now entitled to permanent residence in any Member State in which they have legally resided for 'a continuous period of five years'.[231] As the Preamble states, this right 'would strengthen the feeling of Union citizenship and is a key element in promoting social cohesion'.[232] In other words,

---

224. Family members (as defined in Art. 2(2)), whether European citizens or not, also enjoy the rights enumerated. In fact, the right of family members, once acquired indirectly through a European citizen, are in many cases retained even after family ties have been broken (*see* Art. 12). (The status of family members has been the subject of a number of E.C.J. decisions, most notably Case C-413/99 *Baumbast*.)
225. Citizens Directive, *supra* note II.223, Arts 4 and 5, respectively.
226. *Ibid.*, Arts 27–29.
227. *Ibid.*, Arts 30–33.
228. Presidency Conclusions, Annex I, The Hague Programme, Sec. III/1.1. (4–5 November 2004).
229. Citizens Directive, *supra* note II.223, Art. 8.
230. *Ibid.*, Arts 7(1) and 8, respectively.
231. *Ibid.*, Art. 16(1), but *see* shorter period, as per Art. 17.
232. *Ibid.*, Rec. 17.

permanent residence is a means to the end of identification with European citizenship and the development of solidarity among European citizens.

The nod to 'integration' into host Member State society[233] as the basis for protection against expulsion, in turn, reflects a new concern with identification. Pursuant to Article 28(1) of the Directive, any expulsion decision must take into account not just length of residence, state of health, economic and family ties, but also 'social and cultural integration into the host Member State and the extent of his/her links with the country of origin'.[234] It seems that the possibility of attachment by European citizens to more than one Member State (culture and society) is acknowledged, though not concretized. The Commission's Fourth Report on Citizenship takes this final step, discussing the possibility of a right to participate in national and regional elections[235] – and thereby reconstituting, at the most fundamental level, not only one of the few remaining rights of national citizenship but also the meaning of the *demos* in Member States.

The remaining exceptions to the right to equal treatment for European citizens have also been clearly defined in the new Directive,[236] in an effort at setting boundaries. Before the Directive came into effect, however, one of its explicitly noted exceptions to equal treatment (in the context of student maintenance grants) had been found by the E.C.J. to be unacceptable in principle.[237] This situation only highlights the growing tension between matters considered by states to be outside the scope of Community law (most obviously financial and other conditions necessary for residence) and those same matters, framed as social rights, considered by the Court to fall within its scope and treated as restrictions subject to examination for proportionality. In effect, one's understanding of a given benefit may hinge on whether it is viewed through the lens of equal protection (Article 12) or that of free movement (Article 18(1)) – an admittedly difficult distinction in some contexts.

On the one hand, if equal protection is chosen, we deal with a principle to which there can be (almost) no limitations, as the Court reaffirmed in the *Bidar* case. On the other, if a given benefit is framed as a condition of free movement, one would need to determine whether the (financial) conditions for the right to free movement are met in the first place. As Hailbronner notes, '[C]onditions, unlike

---

233. *Ibid. See* Preamble Recs. 23 and 24.
234. The echo of E.Ct.H.R. jurisprudence in the context of expulsion procedures is perhaps no coincidence; otherwise, third-country nationals would have more protection from expulsion under regional human rights law than European citizens through EU law. *See also* paras 58–60 of Case C-109/01 *Secretary of State for the Home Department v. Hacene Akrich*, E.C.J. [2003].
235. Commission (Fourth) Report on Citizenship of the Union, pp. 8–9, and p. 11.
236. Citizens Directive, *supra* note II.223, Art. 24.
237. *See* the Court's judgment in the *Bidar* case, which found that a genuine link with the educational system of a given Member State – but not permanent residence – may be required for the purposes of establishing eligibility for such grants. Although the decision was based on earlier Directives on residence, the Court was well aware of the provisions of the Citizens Directive, going so far as to refer to them (para. 43). *See* Case C-209/03, *Bidar. See also* Opinion of Advocate General Geelhoed in this case (11 November 2004).

restrictions, are constitutive requirements for bringing a right into existence'.[238] The E.C.J. is increasingly blurring this distinction by regarding free movement, post-Maastricht, as a principle subject to restrictions, but no longer to (real and substantive) pre-conditions, whatever secondary legislation may say. In fact, it looks as if ECT Articles 12 and 18 are utilized in combination to mark the foundation for a citizenship without boundaries. As the *Austria* case already discussed has clearly shown, such an expansive understanding of Union citizenship has the potential to intrude on areas central to the 'national identity' of Member States – like education – not, as yet, considered ripe for integration by the Member States themselves.

d. Questioning Developments in the Area of Freedom, Security and Justice

In a less tangible development, European citizenship has also played an increasingly central – in any case rhetorical – role in the emergence of the 'Area of Freedom, Security and Justice' tentatively introduced by the Maastricht Treaty[239] as part of the Third Pillar, and more substantively developed by the Amsterdam Treaty.[240] In particular, one of the objectives expressed in TEU Article 2 – to strengthen the protection of the rights and interests of the nationals of its Member States through the introduction of a citizenship of the Union – has been understood to extend to procedural matters. The argument has been that the creation of a European judicial space is fostered by citizenship, i.e., that the latter in some form necessitates the former,[241] and that the practical effects of such a common space will, in turn, help to make citizenship more relevant.[242] Besides the commonly raised criticism regarding the absence of fundamental rights concerns in many elements of this 'Area' (discussed below), the reference to the needs of citizens is out of place here, inter alia, because of the growing reliance of international and European procedural law on 'habitual residence' rather than nationality in establishing jurisdiction; it is thus the residents of the European Union that are affected by such measures, not its citizens.[243] As in the context of culture already discussed, concern with the 'citizen' is here rather instrumental, and serves to give a broad policy objective a more human face. (Whether the particular measures will actually contribute to making European citizenship

---

238. Hailbronner (2005), p. 1263.
239. *See* Citizens Directive, *supra* note II.223, Art. 29 *et seq.*
240. Title IV. *See also* ECT Art. 65.
241. *See* Szyszczak (1996); paras 2, 15 and 16 of the 'Action plan of the Council and the Commission on how best to implement the provisions of the Treaty of Amsterdam on an area of freedom, security and justice' (1999).
242. *See* Sec. 1(2) of Commission Communication, 'A Project for the European Union' (2002).
243. *See* Arts 2–4 of Council Regulation 44/2001 of 22 December 2000 on jurisdiction and the recognition and enforcement of judgments in civil and commercial matters; and Art. 8 of Council Regulation 2201/2003, *supra* note I.181.

more relevant, as the Commission hopes, is a slightly different matter; based on the example of previous policy areas, the answer is likely to be 'not necessarily'.)

And what about obligations? Strictly speaking, we still cannot speak of the direct obligations of European citizens[244] – but the development of Member State obligations under the Third Pillar has had consequences for individuals, suggesting that European citizenship may soon come with duties.[245] One example of this phenomenon is that, as a result of the European arrest warrant (hereinafter, EAW) introduced in 2002,[246] the principle of international law whereby states may refuse the extradition of their own nationals (enshrined in a number of Constitutions, e.g., Article 16 of the *Grundgesetz*) has been invalidated in the context of the European Union. European citizens must now be surrendered to another Member State for any of the offences covered by the Framework Decision with only few exceptions. (Though a number of conventions relating to extradition had been in place among Member States,[247] the new practice (as of 1 January 2004), based on the principle of 'mutual recognition',[248] has limited the grounds for refusal of surrender to the grounds listed in Articles 3 and 4 of the Framework Decision.) All grounds are administrative or judicial in nature, and are independent of traditional sovereignty concerns. In fact, only Preamble Rec. 12 makes any reference to the application of the 'constitutional rules' of Member States, but curtails these to a very limited area.[249]

Unsurprisingly, courts initially proved quite creative in finding reasons to refuse surrender;[250] while constitutional and supreme courts in many Member

---

244. During the inter-governmental conference called to draft the Maastricht Treaty, both the Commission and the Spanish delegation had suggested the inclusion of some basic civic obligations, without success. See Art. 1(2) of the Proposal of the Spanish Delegation, *supra* note II.138 (1991).
245. For a discussion of the rights-duties duality in the European context, *see* Reich (2001), p. 20 *et seq.* Though most authors argue that European citizenship does not come with duties, it would be more precise to state that they exist only in indirect form (e.g., a portion of our taxes go to the community; we obey Community legislation).
246. Council Framework Decision 2002/584/JHA of 13 June 2002 on the European arrest warrant and the surrender procedures between Member States (hereinafter, EAW Framework Decision).
247. In particular, the European Convention on Extradition (1957) and subsequent Protocols; the Convention of 10 March 1995 on simplified extradition procedure between the Member States of the European Union; and the Convention of 27 September 1996 relating to extradition between the Member States of the European Union. For a look at the emergence of the EAW *see* Plachta and van Ballegooij (2005).
248. *See* Art. 1(1) of the EAW Framework Decision, *supra* note II.246.
249. With regard to the fundamental rights considerations in Recs. 12, and 13, as well as Art. 1(3), one would do well to be suspicious. For a look at some of the possible problems, *see* Alegre and Leaf (2004). *See also* Commission Proposal for a Framework Decision on certain procedural rights in criminal proceedings throughout the European Union (2004).
250. *See*, i.e., Le Monde, *Le tribunal de Pau émet une interprétation restrictive du mandat d'arrêt européen* (2 June 2004). *See also* Report from the Commission based on Art. 34 of the Council framework decision of 13 June 2002 on the European arrest warrant and the surrender procedures between Member States (2005) for an initial evaluation.

States examined the legality of the EAW in light of domestic law.[251] The decisions of the Czech, Polish and German Constitutional Courts, in particular, confirmed the validity of the EAW, *qua* practice, despite the existence of constitutional prohibitions on extradition, noted above. In two of the cases, it was the inadequacy of domestic (constitutional or implementing secondary) law that resulted in a finding of unconstitutionality, not the conflict of a constitutional norm and European law. The Czech court, in turn, found the law in conformity with the Constitution. Specific outcome aside, the decisions of the Polish and German courts are especially interesting, since they formulated a re-contextualization of Member State nationality in light of European citizenship.

In Poland, the Court reiterated that the constitutional prohibition on extraditing Polish citizens (nationals) is absolute, so that the personal right thereto may generally not be curtailed.[252] However, it also determined that the concept of Polish citizenship had been transformed through the superimposition of the rights of European citizenship, as a consequence of which the citizens of one Member State are not regarded as 'aliens' in the territory of another Member State.[253] Though this development is not, in itself, sufficient to warrant derogation from the prohibition on extradition – since doing so would weaken the role of Polish citizenship as the 'essential criterion for the assessment of the legal status of the individual'[254] – the existence of (international) legal obligations assumed through EU membership and the existence of a shared 'community of principles' was considered to constitute a circumstance requiring amendment of the Polish Constitution.[255] In effect, the Court thereby circumvented the real issue of the *Manner* of transformation and grounded its argument on the (admittedly crucial) technicality of the necessity of respect for international obligations instead.[256]

The German *Bundesverfassungsgericht*, in turn, embarked on a thorough discussion of the nature of citizenship in its EAW decision, rendered a few weeks after the Polish one. As an initial presumption, the Court noted citizens' 'special bond with the free legal order established by them'[257] and underlined that 'nationality is

---

251. The Constitutional courts of Poland, Germany, Belgium, Portugal, and the Czech Republic, as well as the Supreme Courts of France, Hungary, Finland, Cyprus, Greece, Poland, and Portugal all examined the EAW.
252. Case P 1/05 (*Application of the European Arrest Warrant to Polish Citizens*), Polish Constitutional Court (2005), at Sec. 4.2.
253. *Ibid.*, at Sec. 4.3.
254. *Ibid.*
255. *Ibid.*, at Sec. 5, particularly 5.2.
256. The 18-month layover period granted for amendment – during which the unconstitutional provision was to be applied in order to comply with international obligations – and the various arguments presented in support of the decision (*see* Sec. 5.6 *et seq.*) only underline the unusual dilemma the Court found itself in.
257. BVerfG, 2 BvR 2236/04 (2005), para. 66 (*besondere Verbindung der Bürger zu der von ihnen getragenen freiheitlichen Rechtsordnung*).

the legal prerequisite for equal citizenship status'.[258] In fact, the 'civic rights and duties that are, for every individual, connected with the possession of nationality at the same time form the constituent bases of the entire community',[259] and are accordingly a source for the legitimacy of public authority. This constitutionally sanctified connection may be limited on the basis of (recently introduced) Article 16(2) of the Constitution – which allows for extradition to other EU Member States or international courts – but only to the extent that it does not result in *'Entstaatlichung'*, or a loss of the core elements of statehood. This is not the case as regards application of the EAW, since it neither devalues citizenship[260] nor is 'tantamount to the waiver of a state task that is essential in its own right'.[261]

As regards individual rights, the *Grundgesetz* sets legal limits on the restriction of any fundamental right, including the prohibition of extradition, in the context of which compliance with the general principles of law must be guaranteed. In the case of other Member States, the principles set out in TEU Article 6(3) allow for basis for mutual trust as regards the rule of law. However:

> The mere existence of [homogenous Member State structures, in line with TEU Art. 6], of a sanctioning mechanism to secure the structural principles [TEU Art. 7] and of an all-European standard of human rights protection established by the [ECHR] do not, however, justify the assumption that the rule-of-law structures of Member States of the European Union are materially synchronised and that a corresponding case-by-case examination at the national level is therefore superfluous. In this respect, putting into effect a strict principle of mutual recognition, and the extensive statement of mutual state confidence that is connected with it, cannot restrict the constitutional guarantee of the fundamental rights.[262]

---

258. *Ibid.* (*'Die Staatsangehörigkeit ist die rechtliche Voraussetzung für den gleichen staatsbürgerlichen Status'*).
259. *Ibid.* (*'Die staatsbürgerlichen Rechte und Pflichten, die für jeden Einzelnen mit dem Besitz der Staatsangehörigkeit verbunden sind, bilden zugleich konstituierende Grundlagen des gesamten Gemeinwesens'*).
260. *Ibid.*, para. 74.
261. *Ibid.*, para. 75 (*'es handelt sich ... nicht um den Verzicht auf eine bereits für sich genommen essentielle Staatsaufgabe'*).
262. *Ibid.*, para. 118 (*'Die bloße Existenz dieser Vorschrift, eines die Strukturprinzipien absichernden Sanktionsmechanismus (Art. 7 EU), und eines gesamteuropäischen Standards des Menschenrechtsschutzes durch die Europäische Konvention zum Schutze der Menschenrechte und Grundfreiheiten rechtfertigen aber nicht die Annahme, dass die rechtsstaatlichen Strukturen unter den Mitgliedstaaten der Europäischen Union materiell synchronisiert sind und eine entsprechende nationale Einzelfallprüfung deshalb überflüssig ist. Insoweit kann durch das Inkraftsetzen eines strikten Grundsatzes der gegenseitigen Anerkennung und der damit verbundenen weitgehenden gegenseitigen Vertrauensbekundung der Staaten untereinander die verfassungsrechtliche Gewährleistung der Grundrechte nicht eingeschränkt werden'*) (translation from the web-site of the Constitutional Court).

Accordingly – in light of possible cultural differences, linguistic difficulties and procedural hindrances, as well as the fact that the individual would be judged on the basis of substantive criminal law she had no means to shape (or even know) through the democratic process[263] – the German legislation implementing the Framework Directive was considered unconstitutional (since its outcome was not proportional in all circumstances). According to the Court, it had to be reformulated.[264] In the meantime, German nationals could not be subject to EAWs. (Clearly, this Constitutional Court took an approach exactly opposite to its counterpart in Poland on this point.[265])

The Czech Constitutional Court, in turn, determined that the substance of its respective ban on extraditing nationals left room for criminal prosecution in states that meet the standard of fair trial before a Czech court, which the other Member States certainly do.[266] In this decision it diverged both from the Polish court – which had determined that the essence of its ban was that individuals be tried in Polish courts – and the German one, which did not express the same degree of trust in the judicial systems of fellow Member States. The Czech court's decision nonetheless left open the possibility of refusing surrender if execution of an EAW would result in a violation of the Czech Constitution.

The Opinion of Advocate General Colomer in Case C-303/05 – a request from the Belgian Constitutional Court for a preliminary ruling on the compatibility of the Framework Decision with the TEU – painted a very different picture of European integration from that presented by either the Polish or German constitutional courts, and aligned itself with the finding of the Czech court. The entire Opinion of the Advocate General – from the distinction made between 'extradition' and the EAW to its consideration from a fundamental rights perspective – relied in large part on the actuality of a 'high level of confidence', 'mutual trust' and a 'common interest' among Member States. In the words of the Opinion:

> [T]he aim is to provide assistance to someone with whom one shares principles, values and objectives, through the creation of an institutional framework with its own special sources of law which vary in force but which ultimately are binding and which seek to prevent and combat crime in a single area of freedom, security and justice.[267]

The existence of shared principles, values and objectives does not displace the basic fundamental rights question addressed by the constitutional courts of the Member States, however. In other words, while a clear Third Pillar objective

---

263. *Ibid., see* para. 85.
264. An amended version of the German law, now deemed constitutional, was adopted by the Bundestag in May 2006.
265. In fact, this aspect of the judgment has been subject to much criticism from dissenting judges and academics alike. *See, inter alia,* Vogel (2005); Böhm (2005); Mölders (2006); and Hinarejos Parga (2006).
266. Case Pl. ÚS 66/04 *(European Arrest Warrant Decision)*, Czech Constitutional Court (2006).
267. Opinion of Advocate General Colomer in Case C-303/05 (12 September 2006), para. 44.

may exist and be furthered by the existence of the EAW, from the perspective of the individual, this circumstance does not justify a distinction between extradition and the EAW surrender. While '[t]he move from extradition to the European arrest warrant constitutes a complete change of direction'[268] for procedural purposes, its outcome is exactly the same from the point of view of the person handed over, as the Opinion itself admits.[269] To the extent the Community (and the Union) remains a community of peoples – and not a single people – with separate (albeit increasingly convergent) institutional and legal systems that function with popular oversight, the relinquishment of the fundamental right not to be ousted (even temporarily) from a particular community does not follow automatically from a change of procedure.[270] Moreover, despite the contention that this right 'remains on the fringes of the common constitutional traditions'[271] – one wonders in this regard whether the Advocate General has taken note of the *Omega* decision, in which it was found 'immaterial' that a general objective was deemed an independent fundamental right in only one Member State – the majority of Member States have until recently given the right constitutional status. (The principle is even recognized in international human rights law, as discussed above, and can also be subsumed under ECHR Article 8.) Finally, the fact that the legislatures of Member States have amended their constitutions in consideration of the Framework Decision does not diminish the importance of the basic principle: it was a deliberate decision by the custodian of popular sovereignty that determined to modify constitutional rules and constituted a fundamental re-constitution of membership. The transformation should not be dismissed as a mere question of judicial procedure.

The unusual jurisdictional consequence of the EAW is also worth noticing. As personal jurisdiction over nationals is given up in one area,[272] and while internal market principles require the importation of foreign law into the domestic framework, territory becomes increasingly important as one of the few bases on which to exert sovereignty. The European arrest warrant is thus an example of legislation that strengthens the importance of territorial jurisdictions, while weakening that of a personal one. (Since the question of extradition is no longer a *political* one, but hinges rather on the place in which the crime was committed, any consideration of protecting 'our' nationals is displaced.) It is also a perfect example of a little-noticed phenomenon: concurrent to increased openness toward 'foreigners' – their near-equal treatment – the idea of a special bond between national and state is being eroded.

---

268. *Ibid.*, para. 41.
269. *Ibid.*, paras 41 and 48.
270. It is for this reason that the Advocate General's comparison of surrender procedures between the federal *Länder* in Germany or between the autonomous communities of Catalonia and Andalusia with action under the EAW are misleading. *See* footnote 40 of the Opinion.
271. *See* footnote 75 of the Opinion.
272. *See,* e.g., *Arrêt no. 7071 du 14 décembre 2004*, French *Cour de Cassation (Chambre criminelle)* (2004) (where even the ongoing proceedings against defendant in France were not enough to reject a request from Belgian authorities).

When residence emerges as the central factor in rights matters, while the heretofore sacred correlatives of nationality (like that of unquestioned presence in the 'home' state) are de-constructed, less and less remains of the attachment that has traditionally been one of the functions of nationality on the international (and national) plane. This, in turn, raises the possibility that there is increasingly no legal bond by birthright that serves as the foundation for a meaningful notion of national community in Europe. If there are ever fewer differences in legal rights that ground the political communities of the European Union, however, it may easily be more ascriptive differences, like language or common history, that serve to highlight uniqueness and condition solidarity. The consequences of such a development may be minor for Union citizenship, since rights are no longer linked to nationality; but a cultural turn would likely impact on the nationality (and kinship) laws of Member States, as well as the future development of the concept of European identity.

In the alternate, the disappearance of a meaningful concept of nationality – and, seemingly, the increasingly suspect one of residence – may mean that solidarity, as expressed by rights granted to identifiable members is unacceptable on any level but the European one. This should not be an acceptable outcome; and is in any case unlikely in light of the identity theories already discussed. A final possibility, foreshadowed by the concepts of 'genuine link' to and 'integration' into host Member States already floating around in Community law is that of a gradual accumulation of rights for new residents.[273] This is the least clear-cut of the three possibilities, but is also the one that most respects existing 'national identities'. If nationality is an increasingly meaningless source of rights in Europe, then – though still a marker of identity – and if residence is to replace it, we effectively see a return to citizenship as social status. Thus, five years of residence would make a European citizen a 'full' member (or citizen) of the given society, with attendant rights, while shorter periods would suffice for welfare or other benefits.[274] Publicly, Union citizenship would not be overtly central to such an activist turn, however, since the Member State would still remain the democratic container. Given that boosting the relevance of citizenship, particularly active citizenship, is an increasingly central concern for the Commission, linked to the legitimacy of the entire EU project, this would be a particular problem.

e. A Newly Symbolic Role for the Union Citizen

The newly central role of European citizenship as a linchpin in the process of integration could be observed in the Constitutional Treaty, which referred to citizenship in almost mantra-like fashion.[275] Article I-1(a) set out why this was the

---

273. Davies (2005), p. 55.
274. Echoes of this approach can already be seen in current discussions of a European migration law. *See* Sec. 2.6 of the Green Paper on an EU approach to managing economic migration (2005).
275. Among others in Arts I-1, I-3(2), I-10, I-45-I-47, all of Title V of Part II and all of Title II of Part III of the Constitutional Treaty.

case. The Constitution was, after all, meant to be a document in the name of the people of the political entity in question, [r]eflecting the will of the citizens and States of Europe (That in the case of the European Union the document also expressed the will of the Member States did not mean diminished importance in this respect). The consciously consolidated place of the citizen in the European project could be glimpsed most clearly in the CT articles declaring the Union a 'representative' and 'participatory' democracy.[276] Though the process of citizenship – like the identity-linked function of the status – had been the focus of considerable concern from its introduction into European law in 1992, the Constitution thus articulated a change of angle.

ECT Article 191 had already opened up the possibility of a European politico-legal space – and the eventual emergence of a European *demos* – through the reference to 'political parties at European level'. The activist turn referred to above was present in language declaring that such parties contribute to 'expressing the political will of the citizens of the Union', while an identity function was present in their conceived role in 'forming a European awareness'. Still, not much happened until the Nice Treaty came into force in 2003, when a new provision allowed for the drafting of regulations governing such parties. The requisite regulation was quickly adopted,[277] but has not resulted in significant advancement for such parties. As Day and Shaw discuss, 'they continue to suffer from a series of "deficit-gaps" which make it abundantly clear that formal-legal developments ... need to be paralleled by forms of structural and psycho-emotional linkage with European citizens'.[278]

The Constitutional Treaty attempted to make a few of these linkages, however small. One, the accentuation of the Union's participatory – not only representative – character announced a more direct link between itself and individuals. The best example for this is the only new citizenship right to have been introduced, under Article I-47(4): the right to initiate Commission law-preparation, through the procedure of a 'citizens' initiative'. The other paragraphs of that article generally suggest a more inclusive approach, with references to 'dialogue' with 'civil society' and 'representative associations'; these do not have the legal rights underpinning that the citizens' initiative does, however. Another change was the repeated emphasis placed in Article I-46 on the ways in which the Union is not only 'representative', but also 'accountable', as well as on the newly added 'right to participate' listed in Paragraph three.[279] Thus, political parties were now to be only one means of participation, not the means to 'integration' – in fact, they were now a means to 'European political awareness', not 'European awareness', generally

---

276. *Ibid.*, Arts I-46 and I-47, respectively.
277. Regulation 2004/2003 of the European Parliament and of the Council of 4 November 2003 on the regulations governing political parties at European level and the rules regarding their funding.
278. Day and Shaw (2006), p. 113.
279. Compare Art. II-72, which includes no such right. In fact, the placement of the right in Part III and its omission among the 'fundamental rights' is striking. (The active and passive voting rights included in Arts II-99 and II-100 cover slightly more limited ground).

speaking.[280] One can, of course, read these modifications as a downgrading of the role of political parties. In light of the stellar symbolic rise of the European citizen – now one of the two pillars of the European constitutional enterprise – however, they are better read as normalization. In other words, European political parties were (hoped to be) no longer the anomalies they were upon their introduction.

Given the prominent role of the European citizen in the Constitutional Treaty as well as in the recent Berlin Declaration[281] and, more generally, in the Union framework,[282] it is striking that her rights and obligations have seen no significant change in the more recent treaties. That said, our discussion of recent E.C.J. judgments demonstrated how the Court is in the process of attaching meaningful social rights to the status of European citizen. The Citizens Directive, in turn, has set new guidelines on remaining restrictions to the free movement and other rights associated with the status. Clearly, the status of European citizenship continues to evolve.

Aside from the actual content of Community and Union instruments, however, it is also worth considering the broader political and legal consequences of European citizenship. In this context, the symbolism of European citizenship has had a major impact, leading to greater acceptance of European citizens in the communities of Member States other than their own. For example, European citizenship has had indirect legal effects on the Member State level. Germany now allows nationals of other Member States to keep their original nationality at naturalization on the condition of reciprocity, while third-country nationals must give theirs up (special circumstances notwithstanding), in line with Article 12(2) of the German law on nationality.[283] In Italy (as well as a number of other Member States) European citizens have access to nationality after a shorter period of residence (four years) than third-country nationals (ten years), on the

---

280. The addition of the adjective 'political' here speaks volumes about the changed approach to identity on the part of 'Brussels', as discussed below.
281. Declaration on the occasion of the 50th anniversary of the signature of the Treaty of Rome (2007). The Declaration specifically states: 'We, the citizens of the European Union, have united for the better'. The text was signed, for the first time, only by the Presidents of the European Parliament, the Commission and the Council.

    But, in a perfect example of the paradoxes of European integration, the text above is an example of (likely politically motivated) mis-translation. The original German states, *'Wir Bürgerinnen und Bürger der Europäischen Union sind zu unserem Glück vereint'*, which should be rendered 'We, the citizens of the European Union, have united in our fortune/ happiness'. The Hungarian text, in turn, speaks only of how the 'unification of Europe fills us, the citizens of the European Union, with happiness'.
282. *See also* Commission Proposal on promoting active European citizenship, p. 2, which states 'citizens should ... become actively involved in the process of European integration, developing a sense of belonging and a European identity'.
283. *See also Staatsangehörigkeitsgesetz* (hereinafter, StAG) Arts 4(1), 4(3), and 29 in conjunction with StAG Art. 12, whereby German-Member State dual nationals may keep both nationalities, while German-third country dual nationals must renounce one of the two on reaching the age of majority, with proof of loss to be provided by the age of 23.

basis of a law from 1992.[284] Mayer and Palmowski are thus right when they state that 'EU nationalities are less exclusive in relation to each other than they are to outside nationalities'[285] – on the basis of both European and domestic law. The legal effects spread beyond laws regulating nationality, however. In Hungary, for example, the proposed Minority Rights Act submitted to Parliament in March 2004 (amending and revising the 1993 Act),[286] was to extend personal application to European citizens, among others.[287]

f. The Missing Link of Cultural Rights

Development is thus foreseeable in the realm of numerous categories of rights, from civic to political, through social and economic. One group of rights is conspicuously missing, however: cultural rights. As Nic Shuibhne argues in the context of extended language rights, '[t]o fulfil the idea of citizenship in real terms, the expansion of associated rights must reflect the integrity of various identity-forming characteristics'.[288] Thus far, European citizenship has not taken this step.

In light of the decidedly activist approach of the E.C.J. in the realm of social rights, it is striking that the Court has thus far refused to interpret European citizenship as a 'whole' concept, its rights capable of reflecting and protecting existing identities. The Court has, in fact, delivered a number of decisions protecting some element of individual identity, but always indirectly. In the *García Avello* case,[289] for example, it determined that a Member State could not refuse an application to change the surnames of resident dual Member State nationals 'in the case where the purpose of that application is to enable those children to bear the surname to which they are entitled according to the law and tradition of the second Member State'.[290] The reasoning of the Court was based on a reaffirmation that 'citizenship of the Union is destined to be the fundamental status of nationals of the Member States'.[291] Through this status, nationals of the Member States in the same situation may, within the scope *ratione materiae* of the EC Treaty, enjoy the same treatment in law irrespective of their nationality.[292]

---

284. *Legge 5 febbraio 1992, no. 91*, Art. 9(1)(d). The common practice in Italy of sub-dividing foreigners into *comunitari* and *extracomunitari* (generally on the basis of skin colour and/or accent, rather than nationality) is a less obvious example of indirect effects. Compare also provisions in Austria since 1999.
285. Mayer and Palmowksi (2004), p. 591.
286. *1993. évi LXXVII. törvény a nemzeti és etnikai kisebbségek jogairól* (1993).
287. *T/9126 számú törvényjavaslat a kisebbségi önkormányzati képviselők választásáról, valamint a nemzeti és etnikai kisebbségekre vonatkozó egyes törvények módosításáról*, Art. 28. This provision was removed from the draft legislation at the last minute. *See* discussion in Horváth (2006), p. 292 *et seq.*
288. Nic Shuibhne (2002), p. 45.
289. Case C-148/02 *Carlos García Avello v. État Belge*, E.C.J. [2003].
290. *Ibid.*, para. 45.
291. *Ibid.*, para. 22.
292. *Ibid.*, para. 23.

On this basis, the Court could have found that the principle of non-discrimination required dual-nationals to be treated in accordance with the law of the state in which they reside, instead of determining that the law of another Member State could be imported into the state of residence. (In this manner, it would also have stimulated respect for the conflict of laws rules of the given jurisdiction.) However, the Court decided that the situation of a dual-national was different from that of a national, due to possible administrative difficulties.[293] In this sense, the judgment presents a novelty: an endorsement of a pluralistic conception of equality in which persons must occasionally be treated differently in order to be equal not just as a formal matter, but also in practice.[294] The final result, then, is a boost for individual cultural identity, albeit on the basis of bureaucracy, not respect for that identity, as such.[295] But what if the Court had gone a different route? What if, as Advocate General Jacobs argued back in 1993,[296] the Court had decided that an inability to use one's name, in accordance with one's own tradition, in another Member State constituted a loss of 'dignity, moral integrity and sense of personal identity'[297] – and that such treatment, in itself, constituted discrimination when compared to the nationals of the given Member State, whose names (and identities) were respected? Or, that such treatment could be a hindrance to freedom of movement, since individuals presumably do not enjoy markers of their identity being tampered with, and may consider such a possibility when deciding whether to exercise this particular freedom?

These considerations, whether viewed as issues of dignity, integrity or identity bring the inadequacies of rights protection at the Community level to the fore.[298] In the first place, there is the issue of time. Despite the E.C.J.'s announcement of a role for human rights in Community jurisprudence as far back as 1974,[299] it took twenty-six more years for a Charter of Fundamental Rights to be drawn up. Second, there is the issue of legal force. Even if the Charter had been given legal force as part of the Constitutional treaty[300] – and despite the foreseen accession of the

---

293. *Ibid.*, paras 36–37.
294. *See also* discussion of effective equality as opposed to equality at law, Sec. III.B.2.a.iv.
295. *See also* Case 168/91 *Christos Konstantinidis v. Stadt Altensteig Standesamt*, E.C.J. [1993] (finding that the individual in question was entitled to a given transliteration of his name on the basis of the 'inconvenience' diverse spellings may cause and the effect they may have on freedom of establishment).
296. *See also* the decision *Burghartz v. Switzerland*, E.Ct.H.R. (1994), para. 24; and ICCPR Art. 24(2).
297. Para. 39 of Advocate General Jacobs' opinion in Case 168/91 (9 December 1992).
298. For a (now somewhat dated but still good) discussion, *see* O'Leary (1995), p. 544 *et seq.*
299. Case 4/73 *Nold v. Commission*, E.C.J. [1974] (identifying 'international treaties for the protection of human rights on which the Member States have collaborated or of which they are signatories' and the common constitutional traditions of Member States – whatever these may be – as the source of fundamental rights principles; para.13).
300. It remains to be seen whether the creation of a European Union Agency for Fundamental Rights will bring significant development. *See* Arts 2–4 of Council Regulation (EC) No. 168/2007 of 15 February 2007 establishing a European Union Agency for Fundamental Rights (2007) for details on the objectives, scope and tasks of the Agency.

European Union to the ECHR[301] – problems would have remained, particularly in the area of cultural rights and in the closely related real of minority rights.

In the context of the former, for example, Community law has little relevance, despite the abundance of general references to 'Union [...] respect' for 'cultural, religious and linguistic diversity' and the 'national identities' of Member States (as embodied in institutional structures).[302] No Community instrument refers to a right to a cultural (or other) identity, in any context. On the other hand, there are allusions to language rights – generally an important element of cultural identity – in Community law.[303] In fact, this is the only front on which some development is presently foreseeable, given the existing legal toehold. All in all, one could perhaps forgive the Union for not dealing with a right that is generally so problematic – as discussed – if it were not for its constant pre-occupation with and instrumentalization of all kinds of identity.

As for minority rights, the story of how the recent rounds of enlargement resulted in mainstream EU engagement with internal and external minority issues has been told numerous times.[304] The extent of actual commitment to minority issues – as opposed to the security-threat based view represented by the OSCE – remains to be seen, however. The signs are not encouraging, in any case, due to both political sensitivities and questions of competence. During the first stage of the Inter-Governmental Conference negotiations for the Constitutional Treaty, the only states to actively support the Hungarian proposal for a reference to the protection of minorities in the Preamble were Austria and Italy, for example. The reference to respect for 'the rights of persons belonging to minorities' did, finally, find a place among the values of the Union (in CT Article I-2), but was not followed up on later in the treaty. (Even this placement was an attempt at neutralization, considering the questionable justiciability of the article, unless as a guiding or meta-value in the German tradition).

More correctly, the reference was followed up in bits and parts only. For example, Article II-81 included a long list of the prohibited grounds of discrimination, including that of membership in a national minority, but the list of grounds that may become the object of protective European legislation in Article III-124 did not cover the same prohibited grounds – language and membership in a national minority, among others, were conspicuously missing. Or, to take another example, while regions were to have a constitutionally protected place in the European Union

---

301. See CT Art. I-7, in conjunction with Opinion 2/94 *European Convention*, E.C.J. [1996]. See also *Bosphorus Hava Yollari Turizm v. Ireland*, E.Ct.H.R. (2005) for elaboration of the doctrine of 'equivalent protection' in the context of E.Ct.H.R. oversight of EU Member State action.
302. CT Art. II-82. *See also* Arts I-3(3) and III-280.
303. *See*, e.g., Case 137/84 *Mutsch*; and ECT Art. 21.
304. *See* Pentassuglia (2001) for an early evaluation; and de Witte and Horváth (forthcoming) for a recent one. *See also* the contributions in Minority Protection and the Enlarged European Union: The Way Forward (Gabriel N. Toggenburg, ed. 2004) for a thorough examination of the constitutional, political and social questions surrounding European Union action in the area of minority protection.

system,[305] as well as a place in its structure through the Committee for the Regions, minorities had no such protection under the Constitutional Treaty.[306] This lacuna is all the more striking since Community law may have considerable secondary (and even negative) effects on existing minority protection regimes. In case of a direct conflict, for example, it is difficult to imagine that a Member State minority rule would be upheld by the Court, despite a recognition that 'protection of [...] a minority may constitute a legitimate aim'[307] for a state. In practice then, the EU may function as a 'means to rebalance systems of minority protection',[308] but only to the extent they already exist – monitoring is to be a one way street, allowing for inspection, but not for new development. As such, the metaphorical burden of proof is on those who would argue for new minority protection systems, qua minority protection systems, to show that the policies are in conformity with European law.

But why should the Community care? Do such rights even have a place in the Community legal framework? If the constant references to respect for cultural diversity are more than platitudes, they should. For one thing, few Member States recognise the right to cultural identity of even their national minorities (when the existence of such groups is acknowledged). How is 'diversity' within Member States then to be protected? At best, the international human rights framework provides spotty guidance in this regard, so that groups and individuals are generally left to manage as best they can. This situation could, arguably, be acceptable in a system of fully sovereign states. But in an entity that, at the same time, increasingly affects the cultural, educational and other 'sensitive' policies of its Member States and develops its own cultural policy with an eye to increased cross-cultural interaction[309] – while considering 'diversity' a value and an objective – a disregard for such questions is out of place. As a political matter, no extension of extant cultural competence is probable; and a newly recognized role is even less likely. But even the present framework offers possibilities for a more dynamic approach.

The Commission and Parliament have already been active in the areas of cultural and minority rights, without much result.[310] During the preparation of the text on Union citizenship in 1992, for example, the Commission proposed a TEU article stating that '[e]very Union citizen shall have the right to cultural expression and the obligation to respect cultural expression in others'.[311] The

---

305. *See* CT Art. I-5(1).
306. In fact, a proposal for a Committee of National and Ethnic Minorities was distinctly rejected during the Convention process. *See* CONV 580/03 (Contribution of József Szájer, 26 February 2003).
307. Case C-274/96 *Bickel and Franz*, at para. 29.
308. Toggenburg (2004), p. 31.
309. *See* discussion in Secs II.B.2 and II.B.3 respectively.
310. *See* also: 'Call for proposals for European Commission backing involving actions in favour of promoting and safeguarding regional or minority languages and cultures' (1995); and 'Call for proposals for support from the European Commission for measures to promote and safeguard regional and minority languages and cultures' (2000). For an example of a measure by the Parliament, *see* Resolution on Linguistic and Cultural Minorities in the European Community (1994).
311. EC Bulletin Suppl. 2/91, p. 86.

necessity of such an article was explained with reference to the principle of dignity and the diversity of individuals; and was regarded as a corollary of Community competence in cultural matters.

In other words, the Commission linked a right to cultural expression both to European citizenship and to the Community's newly gained cultural functions.[312] It seems to have noticed the possibility of using the many references in treaties to maintaining diversity as a basis for granting individuals cultural rights. After all, 'national' and 'regional' identities cannot be respected if the rights of individuals are not. In a similar manner, the European Bureau for Lesser Used Languages called for the inclusion of the following clause during preparation of the European Charter: 'European citizens have the right to maintain and develop their own language and culture, in community with the other members of their group, as an expression of the cultural and linguistic diversity that is a common heritage of Europe'.[313] Granted, this clause could have been read as either an extension of the existing Union commitment to respect the diversity and national identities of Member States – although focus would finally have shifted to individuals – or as a provision for the protection of minorities, in which case it would have been quite revolutionary. In any case, the provision that was adopted instead, as Article 22, falls far short of even being couched in the language of rights.

Given the likely intransigence of Member States in such matters, only the E.C.J. – through a return to the judicial activism of *Stauder*,[314] *International Handelsgesellschaft*[315] and *Nold*[316] – is a possible source of development. Obviously, a first step would be to take a stand for the value of cultural identity, *in lieu* of relying on administrative inconvenience in the next *García Avello* or *Konstantinitis* to come the Court's way. Lenaerts' recognition that 'the central protection of fundamental rights in a composite legal order should shield citizens not only in their relationship with the institutions of that legal order itself, but also in their relationship with its component identitied'[317] is also worth remembering here. It is no coincidence that he identified exactly social and cultural rights as the foremost among such possible 'aspirational' fundamental rights.[318] The first has already been taken up by the E.C.J. with mixed results, as we saw in the decisions discussed above; the second waits in the wings, for now.

---

312. In fact, the Commission continues to hold this view. *See* Commission Communication, 'Proposal for a European Parliament and Council Decision establishing a single financing and programming instrument for cultural co-operation (Culture 2000 programme)' (1998), p. 10 ('each European citizen must have the right to access to culture and to express his creativity. The recognition of cultural rights is an important objective'.)
313. Charter 4237/00, Contrib. 110 (18 April 2000).
314. Case 29/69 *Stauder v. City of Ulm*, E.C.J. [1969], para. 6 (referring to the 'fundamental human rights enshrined in the general principles of Community law and protected by the Court').
315. Case 11/70 *International Handelsgesellschaft*, E.C.J. [1970], para. 4 (confirming that 'respect for fundamental rights forms an integral part of the general principles of law protected by the Court').
316. Case 4/73 *Nold*.
317. Lenaerts (1991), p. 368.
318. *Ibid.*, 376. *See also* Kadelbach (2003), p. 41–42.

3. CITIZENSHIP AND IDENTITY

We are thus back to the question of identity – the second function of European citizenship. As noted above, the last aim of the European citizenship project, after freedom of movement and political rights, has been 'identification with Europe': the symbolic aspect of citizenship already identified by the Tindemans Report. Though there is no reference to this aim in the actual articles of any treaty – is it any wonder? – the concern is certainly behind many Community acts.[319] As Prodi stated a few years ago:

> We have created a customs union ... We have built an economic and monetary union ... We have laid the foundations of a political union ... What we need now is a union of hearts and minds, underpinned by a strong shared sentiment of a common destiny – a sense of common European citizenship. We come from different countries. We speak different languages. We have different historical and cultural traditions. And we must preserve them. But we are seeking a shared identity – a new European soul.[320]

This statement fits well with the view, expressed in ECT Article 17(2), that European citizenship is a process rather than a thing ready-made.[321] Whatever its contents then, European citizenship is a concept oriented toward a sometime, future conception of 'common destiny'. This was also reiterated in Rec. 3 of the Constitutional Treaty. But a sense of common destiny is an element of any collective identity, as discussed in our previous chapter. How can it also be the basis for it? The underlying reasoning is a tad circular: 'while identification with a "European" consciousness can be said to derive from some sort of shared loyalty, this affinity is equally necessary for its continued fabrication'.[322] This is something the Commission also seems to have recognized. In the 2004 Communication on cultural and educational policies discussed above – which suspiciously abounds with references to European citizenship[323] – a strengthened sense of 'shared European cultural values'[324] is the hoped-for basis for a '*developing* European identity',[325] which could, in turn, provide a deeper basis for citizenship than exists at present. It is thus hoped that the discovery of existing commonalities, coupled with a sense of participation in the European project will be enough to

---

319. *See* Chap. 1 of O'Leary (1996) for a survey of the considerations taken into account during the preparation of the TEU articles on citizenship. *See also* the link drawn between culture and citizenship in the context of the Kaléidoscope programme, Decision No. 716/96/EC of the European Parliament and of the Council of 29 March 1996 establishing a programme to support artistic and cultural activities having a European dimension.
320. Romano Prodi, President of the Commission, addressing the European Parliament on 14 September 1999. EU Bulletin 9/1999, para. 2.2.1.
321. *See also* Commission Communication, 'Making Citizenship Work', *supra* note II.110, p. 2.
322. Nic Shuibhne (2002), p. 130.
323. Commission Communication, 'Making Citizenship Work', *supra* note II.110, p. 2–7.
324. *Ibid.*, p. 9.
325. *Ibid.*, p. 5 (emphasis in original).

make European citizenship matter. In turn, the claimed representative and participatory nature of the Union is to help the formation of *'political* awareness', in part through political parties at the European level – which could affect the European identity that informs citizenship. Seemingly a two-pronged attack on perceived indifference to the European project, then – but what if the cycle never takes off?

a. The Rise of a European Value Community?

Unsurprisingly, the symbolic element of European citizenship (especially its activist incarnation) has also captured the imagination of many commentators – who seem to agree that politics can be a means to creating identification – and constitutes the second main line of commentary on this status.[326] As in discussions of its rights function, the example of the nation state is not far in the background,[327] though the commentators in question generally assume they are going past the national in grounding the collective identity to be developed on core values rather than a common culture or identity.[328] This approach is clearest in the arguments of those who viewed the text of the Constitutional Treaty as an 'aid of the identification and the construction of political community'.[329] Values were thereby seen as a means to link past and future in a more neutral and less exclusive way than by relying on culture or on a unified 'European identity'. This assumption is dubious on a number of levels, however.

It assumes that values are somehow less 'problematic' than identity, not to mention culture, despite the fact that values themselves result from some shared understanding of heritage or tradition: they are essentially an expression of a community's deepest consensus on what it stands for.[330] As such, they are as much an element of collective identity as a means to its creation. For this reason, a reliance on 'values' only displaces many of the identity-related questions already discussed to a less obvious level. Sure, few would argue with 'respect for human dignity, freedom, democracy, equality, the rule of law and respect for human rights, including the rights of persons belonging to minorities'.[331] Similarly,

---

326. *See* Habermas (1995) [1990], p. 255; MacCormick (1997), p. 342; Weiler (1999), p. 244; and Lehning (2001). *See also* Gamberale (1997).
327. In some cases the connection is clearly stated: 'the concept of liberal democratic citizenship developed for a nation state, should be extended'. Lehning, *ibid.*, p. 257. *See also* Pagden (2002), p. 24.
328. E.g., Habermas (1995) [1990]; Curtin (1997); Chryssostalis (forthcoming).
329. Walker (forthcoming). *See also* discussion in von Bogdandy (2002), pp. 187–188.
330. In the Durkheimian tradition, it could be called the objective documentation of social norms. To the extent these are reflected in law, '*[p]arce que le droit se présente comme neutre et universel, les produits du travail juridique – normes, langages, codes – peuvent jouer ainsi un rôle central dans la conservation et la consolidation de ... l'ordre social*'. Roussel (2004), p. 44.
331. CT Art. I-2. Compare TEU Art. 6(1), where many of these 'values' were already named, but were referred to as 'principles'. All others were added by the Constitutional Convention, with the exception of the reference to minorities, which found its way into the document during the Inter-Governmental Conference.

few would have problems with societies where 'pluralism, non-discrimination, tolerance, justice, solidarity and equality between men and women prevail'. But here comes the crunch: the reference in Article I-2 was to a singular 'society', mirrored in the constant references to 'the Union' in the other articles of Title I. Thus, there seems to be some assumption that agreement exists not only on support for these values, but also an what they constitute.[332]

The 'idea of a European normative order based on European values'[333] is just as much a construction as, for example, European identity on any basis is, however. (In fact, many of the 'values' and understandings articulated are intrinsically Western[334] European). Even the concept of 'European values' is intrinsically cultural – and one that may be an obvious example to follow in the Anglo-Saxon or German tradition, but is wholly foreign to other parts of Europe. In this context, the increasingly popular references in Community documents to 'cultural values' – as opposed to, for example, 'religious values', 'political values' or even just 'values' – are somewhat befuddling. Use of the term seems to be an attempt at having it both ways: simultaneously camouflaging, through the reference to 'values', that the allusion is in fact to a politically troublesome common foundation, and leaving the option of a recourse to a 'cultural' connection open.[335]

In practice, reliance on a 'European value community' may be even more problematic than looking to a 'European identity' since the very legalization of the former – for example, through incorporation in the Constitutional Treaty – begs questions of interpretation[336] that an open reliance on identity, constantly evolving and acceptably diverse in meaning, may avoid. Not only are there problems of interpretation, even the presence of the values listed – and only these – can be a tool of exclusivity. What would have become of the elements of national constitutions not reflected in the Constitutional Treaty, for example? Are those not European? The pick-and-choose approach, as well as the necessity for some degree of fixed meaning – for legal purposes – holds as much potential for discord as unity. These dilemmas, though they crop up in all societies, are exacerbated at the European level by fragmentation and the existence of multiple histories, as the acrimonious debate over the place of 'Christianity' in the Preamble of the Constitutional Treaty (and the recent Berlin Declaration) showed.[337]

---

332. As the results of a recently released study demonstrate, this may not be the case. The authors of the study specifically noted that the 'most important conclusion of the European Values Study may be that Europe is not a homogenous part of the world in terms of its values'. Halman, Liujkx and van Zundert (2005), p. 128.
333. Stråth (forthcoming).
334. *See also* Pagden (2002), p. 12. As Derrida has argued, no cultural identity is 'identical with itself' by the very nature of culture. In this approach, it would be unusual if there were no plurality of opinions as to European values. *See* Derrida (1991), pp. 16–17.
335. *See* Commission Communication, 'Making Citizenship Work', *supra* note II.110, p. 9. For a more recent use of the 'cultural values' formula, *see* Rec. 1 of the Decision on Culture 2007.
336. In this context, *see* Sadurski (forthcoming).
337. The debate over which (if any) totalitarian symbols to include in a proposed Framework Decision on racism and xenophobia – if one was to be adopted at all – was also good example

Moreover, an 'overlapping consensus that results in a political conception of justice, shared through a political community'[338] doesn't necessarily create a 'common future', as the failure of the Constitutional Treaty project at public referenda, amid much finger-pointing and accompanied by references to 'common values', showed. For one thing, there is not yet a European political community – despite elections to the European parliament, European political parties and European citizenship, few EU citizens see themselves as joined in a shared political space;[339] the Member State remains the container instead.[340] Even if such a political community existed, however, no institutional identity can, at present, compete with (more obvious) cultural identities: the former does not inspire the emotive connection of the latter. The ability to order individuals' perceptions of reality through values, beliefs and traditions just does not extend in the case of a political identity through a wide-enough area to encompass all that cultural identity does. My identity as a citizen may thus be important when voting in elections, but irrelevant when deciding which book to buy, what to eat or what colour to wear at a wedding without causing offence.[341] In case of a conflict between the various levels of values in such a 'concentric circles'[342] approach then, it is not clear that the Community would win out over the Member State. Even if it could, why would the attachment to this particular family of values be stronger than to another? In other words, why the European Union and not Greenpeace?

Even the assumption that public participation is not tinged with cultural particularity is problematic, to the extent that the former is not 'separate from the processes through which culture is produced and reproduced in modern societies; it is integral to them, and likewise part of the process by which individual and collective identities are made and remade'.[343] Culture is not just a matter of heritage, after all, but daily reality: it is a process that re-constitutes and renegotiates itself. Thus, all political decisions and all forms of participation – including those

---

of diverse histories seeping into 'European' values. Though the plan for such a Decision is now back on track, the perceived difference in the Commission's attitude toward communist and fascist symbols – one less 'European' than the other, some claimed – led to cries of 'double standards' during the first attempt at drafting. See BBC News, 'EU ban urged on Communist symbols' (3 February 2005); and BBC News, 'EU rejects Communist symbol ban' (8 February 2005). In this context, see also Tony Judt in 52(15) The New York Review of Books, 'From the Home of the Dead: On Modern European Memory' (6 October 2005), discussing the problematics of a collective European memory.

338. See Lehning (2001), p. 250.
339. In other words, there is no European *demos* yet. See ibid., p. 275; Preuß (1995), p. 214; Weiler (1999), pp. 346–347; and Eriksen (2005). See also BVerfG, 2 BvR 2134/92 (*Maastricht-Urteil*) (1993). The reference in CT Art. I-46 to the 'formation of European political awareness' is perhaps a sign that even 'Brussels' recognizes its present non-existence.
340. See, e.g., Rumford (2003), p. 33, arguing that European civil society is only 'in-the-making'. See also Habermas and Derrida (2003) for a view that the anti-war demonstrations that took place in Europe on 15 February 2003 were 'a sign of the birth of a European public sphere'.
341. See also Smith (1992), p. 62 in the context of national identification.
342. Weiler (1998), p. 17.
343. Calhoun (2002), p. 157.

on what is public and open to discussion – are particular to given societies. This is why the 'public sphere is a crucial site for the production and transformation of politically salient identities and solidarities',[344] including on questions of membership and belonging. In short, values – even political ones, whatever they may be – are an innate part of cultural identity; they are not to be separated from either the process of culture or identity-formation and maintenance.

Finally – moving from the realm of theory to that of reality – a social contract-based European polity is no longer possible. The founding documents of the Community (and the Union) have not been voted on by the majority of European citizens. Even the Constitutional Convention was far from a participatory process, or one that created any (real) public discussion. In turn, the referendums that took place in some Member States *post factum* did not replace the missing discussion, since the terms had already been set. A continuous top-down determination of what shared political and social values are to be simply does not (necessarily) resonate with individuals, however, as the clear 'no' in both France and the Netherlands showed. In that sense, the Constitutional Treaty project was a sign of more of the same, despite the changes of Articles I-46 and 47. There was not even the possibility of Habermasian constitutional patriotism, unless one could identify with the process of late night bargaining that has emerged as essentially European. As a general matter, 'public consultation' in its many guises simply does not substitute for real public participation, in which individuals or even communities can affect both the process and the outcome of decision-making.[345] This is especially true if the touted values seem to be guided (and even trumped) by pseudo-economic considerations. For the nationals of the new Member States, for example, the Community's references to the principles of equality and dignity sound false in light of (many) old Member States' free movement policies, not to mention the unequal system of subsidies and aid that apply to old and new states (however temporarily).

b. The Practical Realities of Identification with Europe

For these reasons, Prodi's reliance only on 'the core values we all share: peace and stability; freedom and democracy; tolerance and respect for human rights; and solidarity and social justice'[346] as the basis for the 'soul' the Community is searching for is likely insufficient. In fact, any attempt at manufacturing one shared feeling of belonging to a single European entity on any basis is likely to fail when faced with the 'axiomatically integrated' identities of most individuals today.[347] Simply put, if a monolithic collective (especially national) identity

---

344. *Ibid.*, p. 163.
345. A presentation of the issues surrounding the EU's much-touted democratic deficit is outside the scope of our discussion. For two recent, insightful evaluations, *see* Bellamy (2006) and Shore (2006).
346. *Ibid.*, Enlargement Weekly (11 February 2002).
347. Soysal (2001), p. 169.

was difficult to create in the 19th century, the technologies that have emerged since that time would make such a project near impossible today. A shared consciousness between different communities, peoples and groups could nonetheless emerge from geographical proximity, collective history and experiences, ambitions and, yes, certain common values. Given a stable economic basis, identification with the European project may accordingly be promoted, through co-operation, education, cultural and social ties – something the Commission seems to have realized and acted upon in its cultural policy since 1992.[348] In this sense, the Community is not only re-interpreting the function of nationality through the extension of citizenship rights beyond the nation state community, but also transforming the role of a political entity in creating and guiding the relevant cultural identity; traditional national identity creating policies can no longer be the model. But will the outcome of this unorthodox approach correspond to what is hoped for?

One manner in which European citizenship has, perhaps, fulfilled the hope for identification envisaged is that outlined by Mayer and Palmowski. Namely, it allows European citizens to live in any other Member State, as equals with the nationals of those states. As such, European citizenship – the 'fundamental status of nationals of Member States'[349] – goes a long way in giving concrete form to the myriad ways in which integration has affected the lives of individuals. In other words, Franz or Antonella can now say it is because they are European citizens that they can take an Easyjet or SkyEurope flight to Budapest to look for a job or just sit around coffee houses, rather than because Directive XXXX/ZZ/EC says so. European citizenship is, as the authors above state, the *'sine qua non* for a meaningful European identity'.[350] Whether identification as a European citizen will actually result in a sense of European identity is another question, however.

Some sense of a European identity does in fact seem to have emerged among individuals, but its content and relation to other collective identities has only of late become the subject of in-depth empirical study.[351] As regards quantitative research, Eurobarometer surveys, for example, regularly ask respondents about Europeanness: in 2003, 57 per cent of those asked in the old Member States felt to some degree European (three per cent felt exclusively European, seven per cent first European then their own nationality, 47 per cent first their nationality then European).[352] In the new Member States, the run down was almost the same:

---

348. According to a recent study, student exchange programs (like Erasmus) come fourth (behind peace, free movement and the Euro) as 'the most positive result of European unification' among the European citizens interviewed – a striking result, considering the relative youth of the program. In any case, at least this element of the 'meet and greet' approach seems to exhibit untapped potential. The Future of Europe (2006), p. 31. But *see* discussion in Sec. II.D.
349. Rec. 3 of the Citizens Directive, *supra* note II.223.
350. Mayer and Palmowski (2004), p. 592.
351. Theoretical approaches to this question have a longer history, however. For good (recent) socio-political discussions *see*, *inter alia*, Bruter (2005) and Risse (2004).
352. Standard Eurobarometer 60, p. 27 (Autumn 2003). (The generally recognized inadequacy of Eurobarometer surveys for the purposes of drawing general conclusions is duly noted; they are, at present, the only empirical results with a temporal dimension, however.)

58 per cent felt European to some degree (three per cent felt exclusively European, eight per cent felt European first then their own nationality, 47 per cent first their own nationality then European).[353] Comparison with earlier surveys has shown that the trend is toward greater attachment to Europe in all Member States (but one).[354] The 2004 research project 'Orientation of Young Men and Women Toward Citizenship and European Identity', concluded under the auspices of the Fifth Framework Programme of the Commission, was one of the first to examine in greater depth the matrix of European citizenship, Member State nationality and identity discussed here. On the basis of surveys in ten cities (in six states), attitudes toward European identity were seen as compatible with national and regional identities and were 'associated to state-related identity'.[355] In other words, 'nation and Europe serve as complementing rather than competing sources'[356] for collective identity. Some multi-level identity, recognized by an increasing number of theorists as the way forward, may thus be in the making.[357]

But the quality of this identity may not correspond to the hopes expressed by either Prodi or theorists. A series of studies have shown that both civic and cultural aspects are present in its composition – and that there are significant differences by Member State, region, level of education and gender.[358] The presence of both 'civic' and 'cultural' aspects should not be surprising if, as Bruter has claimed in a recent, informative study on European identity, 'the European Union has constantly need[ed] to produce both [cultural and civic] symbols, which most certainly means that it has been looking for both cultural – one could say almost 'national' – and civic or institutional legitimacy'.[359] The claim of a need (and certainly wish) for both cultural and institutional legitimacy rings quite true, even if a clear distinction between the symbols of one or the other is perhaps not as easily to make as the author claims. In any case, the official symbolism constructed by the Commission has certainly had some effect, not only as seen by the general salience of European identity, but also in its particulars. Individuals tend to associate the European flag, anthem and passport, as well as the Euro with 'values of peace, harmony, co-operation', at the same time as perceiving the European project as 'non-national'.[360] That said, some have noted that it is the

---

353. Candidate Countries Eurobarometer (Autumn 2003), pp. 71–72.
354. Citrin and Sides (2004), p. 169.
355. Ros et al. (2004), p. 4. See also Meyer (2004), p. 46.
356. Fuss (2003), p. 13. See Citrin and Sides (2004), p. 171–172 for empirical confirmation.
357. See, e.g., Bauböck (1997); O'Keeffe and Bavasso (1998), p. 264–265; and Preuß (1995).
358. Bruter (2004), p. 36. See also the survey quoted above, in which association with Europe emerged through: an automatic mechanism ('the country is in Europe', nationals 'have EU passport'), identification based on pride (particularly 'in a common European culture' or 'shared political attitudes') and/or personal experience (travel, family, etc.). Ros et al. (2004), p. 3.
359. Bruter (2005), p. 86.
360. Bruter (2004), p. 30. See also ibid. (2005), pp. 128–129, where he argues that European Union symbols affect the cultural component of European identity more than its civic one.

very invisibility of the EU – the lack of 'perception of the EU as a real entity'[361] when it comes to identifying the source of policies – that hinders further (or deeper) identification. Also worth noting, in light of our previous discussion of the role of the 'Other' in both social identity theory and earlier Commission documents, is the fact that European-ness is seen through the lens of the disappearance of borders (both literal and symbolic) within Europe and their increased salience toward the rest of the world.[362] The 'Other' thus remains relevant for identity-formation even in the European context.

D.   FINAL CONSIDERATIONS

On closer examination, an approximation between the development of European citizenship and the evolution of the Community's role in cultural matters, formerly quite distinct, can be easily glimpsed. In fact, recent Commission documents and E.C.J. case law seem to point to attempts at linking the two in a bid at giving more sense to both strands of policy. In particular, as discussed, the cultural role of the Community post-Maastricht consists of helping to preserve Member State identities (national, mainly) and simultaneously highlighting the 'European' in the hope of the emergence of a European identity. Similarly, while European citizenship serves to guarantee a given, constantly accumulating number of shared and equal rights to the nationals of Member States – increasingly on the foundation of some conception of solidarity – it also serves as a means to ensure the maintenance of national identities, albeit in altered form. That EU citizenship is the result of 27 nationality policies is but one sign of this dualistic nature.

The evolution of these two policy areas demonstrates the emergence of a multi-level understanding of both citizenship rights and cultural identity. Accordingly, both processes present new developments in the context of theory. European citizenship has extended the reach of a number of citizenship rights beyond the nation state, while the concept of a European identity, in whatever form, is an effort at supporting the development of a supra-national identity for an emerging political community.[363] Moreover, the identity being developed is not the homogenous one of the nation state, but one that relies on cultural diversity.[364]

---

361. Castano (2004), p. 55.
362. Bruter (2004), p. 33.
363. Although a number of new legal statuses emerged in the context of colonialism – most famously that of British subject (later Commonwealth citizen) – with attendant supra-state rights and duties, they were not accompanied by significant attempts at identity construction. *See* Verwilghen (1999), p. 225 *et seq.*
364. *See* de Witte (2003) for a discussion of the place of the principle of cultural diversity in Community law.

a. **At the Junction of European Citizenship, Culture and Identity**

So far, so good – but is there a further bond between the two? Certainly, there seems to have been a recognition – albeit unsaid – that the extension of ever-more rights to an ever-larger group of people is not enough to engender the loyalty hoped for. As Weiler confirms, 'citizenship is as much a state of consciousness and self-understanding and only in smallish part is translatable to positive law'.[365] In fact, rights and identity may, in the case of European citizenship, be at odds. As Shore has noted, 'the identity-endowing element of citizenship derives precisely from the legal and political benefits, rights and duties that citizenship confers upon its members'.[366] In other words, if the (increasing) rights of European citizenship are extended to an ever-larger group and are thereby rendered less and less exclusive, the border between 'ins' and 'outs' – a boundary necessary in some form or another to any concept of citizenship – becomes increasingly blurry. European citizenship then becomes a framework for certain rights in the spirit of international human rights and loses its link to a given political (as well as social and cultural) community. This may be a positive outcome from the view of rights: but one needs to recognize that their basis in a European citizenship that individuals identify with may be lost.

As already discussed, the Commission has in fact come to see some developing European cultural identity as a prerequisite for a European citizenship that means more to individuals than it does at present. The instrumental development of a European culture that would 'challenge or even displace'[367] national identities – something the Commission aimed for a time – has been abandoned, however. Still, as Shore shows, 'culture building' as a 'political objective' has not gone away in Community discourse.[368] In fact, attempts at using the banner of culture to 'galvanize and mould public opinion'[369] in times of increased scepticism about the European project continue – and have, it seems, received a new lease on life in attempts to combat post-constitutional referenda blues – since 'political leaders recognize [that] the credibility of the European Union hinges on the development of a more tangible and coherent sense of shared identity among the peoples of Europe whose interests the Union aims to serve'.[370] However, the methods used have changed, to the diversity-embracing, bottom-up formula we increasingly find post-Maastricht. The cornerstones of the new policies are thus (vaguely defined) cultural networks, to surface on the basis of common interests (beyond the financial, it is hoped). The quality of this bottom-up identity, emerging through growing

---

365. Weiler (1998), p. 4.
366. Shore (2004), p. 29.
367. Shore (2000), p. 21.
368. Ibid., pp. 15–26.
369. Ibid., p. 222.
370. Ibid.

interaction among individuals and groups and relying, in its very existence, on diversity is something wholly new, as is the laid-back role of the entity that aims to harness it. Support for town-twinning, Erasmus student exchange (and its descendants), as well as Culture 2000 and 2007 networks thus exists not only to allow individuals to meet and get to know each other – and, it is hoped, like each other – but also to discover that they have more in common with each other than with fellow non-Europeans.

It is easy to imagine the ideal outcome of this new approach. As Smith discusses, a number of shared legal and political traditions/experiences, as well as cultural and religious heritages, exist across Europe. 'Not all Europeans share in all of them; some share in particular traditions and heritages only minimally. But at one time or another all Europe's communities have participated in at least *some* ... to some degree'.[371] These partially shared traditions/experiences and heritages include humanism, romanticism and classicism in the arts; empiricism and rationalism in philosophy and the sciences; democracy, fascism and communism in politics; as well as Roman law and Judeo-Christian ethics.[372] Such 'boundary-transcending political traditions and cultural heritages ... make up what we may call the European experience and the European family of cultures'.[373] In a mundane example of this common experience: a visitor from Paris would supposedly feel more at home in the cityscape of Ljubljana or Riga than in Mumbai.

Commonality in all forms is likely exactly what the Commission hopes individuals will discover, in anticipation of a meaningful sense of community belonging, rather than just a perception of being part of the same institutional construction. Along with the shared political values advanced by some commentators, we could easily be looking at the basis for a European identity that respected existing cultural (including national) identities, while leaving open the possibility of emerging new ones.[374] In this sense, cultural identity would be regarded as the process it really is. A stronger civic basis for identification with the Union may emerge than exists presently. Perfect, no? Sure, if one is trying to re-create a more tolerant form of the national identity that came with the pairing of nationality and citizenship. But the European Union is not a nation state; and we are not in 1830.

An acceptance that citizenship – and accordingly European citizenship – can be multi-layered and unhinged from the nation state would serve commentators, as well as politicians, well. Calls for, or accusations of, an 'overarching' European identity, somehow serving to cover other cultural identities,[375] assume that the

---

371. Smith (1992), p. 70.
372. Certainly some of these, especially national collective memories of shared history, could serve as much to divide as to unite. Ask an Austrian, French, Hungarian, and Romanian about the Versailles Peace Treaties of 1919–1920, for example, and it's best to flee. As many theorists have discussed, however, history is mainly a matter of interpretation and presentation. For the role of history in the public education system, *see* Citron (1988).
373. Smith (1992), pp. 70–71.
374. *See also* Bauböck (1997), p. 5.4.
375. Shore (2000), p. 225. *See also* García and Wallace (1993), p. 172.

former will be like national identities – necessarily linked to a political community, partaking of the same characteristics and covering the same ground.[376] A European identity based on diversity is not 'intellectual gymnastics',[377] however, but a recognition that no other basis for European identity can exist.[378]

As Waldron has discussed, cultures merge into each other; there is no clear boundary.[379] This is as true in temporal terms as in geographic ones. Thus, it is not some 'past' set in stone that provides the basis for any identity, but current interpretations of it as they function for the present and future.[380] How individuals view their heritages today is what determines how they feel about a given cultural identity, not the elements of the common culture. Thus, individuals may well decide that only some of the elements of the 'European experience', or perhaps none at all, matter to them, or, that they have a great deal in common with neighbouring countries and very little with those farthest from them. The 'European experience' is unlikely to be unified, but rather one influenced by existing identities and interpretations of the past. Accordingly, what or who is European for one may not be European for another. This means that it is not only those with a 'European background',[381] whatever that is, who may or may not develop a sense of European identity. But it also means that some groups will have a more inclusive view of the European than others, in accordance with the prototypicality gradient introduced in our previous Chapter.

The cross-cutting identities discussed above, along with the multi-level identification discussed by the theorists of cosmopolitan citizenship will thus be an element of any European identity. However, it is more likely that national, European, as well as a multitude of other cultural identities will (continue to) co-exist – and at times clash – than that one homogenous and over-arching identity will encompass others. Some dimensions of national and regional self-understanding will accordingly become more 'European', others less. The disappearance of national currencies has not, for example, made the Member States concerned less national, but has certainly given a more European dimension to their economies. In other words, not only is any European identity unlikely to be homogenous geographically, it is also likely to vary in intensity depending on which element of cultural identity one examines. For these reasons, any emerging European identity will be less exclusive than traditional cultural identities or the homogenous European identity the Commission flirted with for a period; and it is unlikely to be similar to existing national identities.

---

376. *See*, e.g., Barber, who argues that '[t]he boundaries of Europe and its relationship with its putative citizens is shaped by the past' and that the Community is accordingly involved in an 'attempt to stimulate nationalist sentiment at a European level'. Barber (2002), pp. 256–257.
377. Shore (2000), p. 126.
378. In this regard, compare the suggested *'identité européene 'en réseau'* ('European network identity') set out in Haenel and Sicard (2003), pp. 41–42 and p. 55 *et seq*. For social psychological confirmation, *see* Mummendey and Waldzus (2004), p. 70 *et seq*.
379. Waldron (1992), pp. 777–778.
380. *See* Sec. I.C.2. *See also* The Observer, 'Vikings? Such Friendly Folk, Say Textbooks' (13 April 2003) for what can go wrong when new interpretations are introduced.
381. Barber (2002), p. 258.

b. Inherent Challenges to Current Developments in European Citizenship

Given this, the nature of the membership to be defined by European citizenship needs to be given greater thought than heretofore. To the extent that there is no prototype 'European', fuzzy conceptions of belonging do not enter into debates on European identity in the same manner as for national identity. When they do make an appearance, they do so during discussion of possible membership for aspiring Member States, not individuals. In other words, it is the given nation state, *qua* nation state, whose 'European' credentials are inspected, not those of individuals. In addition, it is exactly the foundation of European citizenship on Member State nationality that may make diffuse boundaries of belonging irrelevant at the European level; though they do not make these boundaries any less problematic on the Member State level. This does not mean that the identity functions of citizenship or identity can be wholly disregarded, however. The view of European citizenship as a problem-solving mechanism,[382] present to varying degrees in activist conceptions of (Union) citizenship, for example, neglects reality beyond the daily: what happens when some degree of solidarity is necessary?[383] What community is to be pointed to as its basis?

In light of the growing reliance of both the E.C.J. and the Commission on the supposed identity function of European citizenship – for the former as solidarity among Union citizens, for the latter as shared norms, traditions and heritage – it is worth remembering that 'European identity' (or rather, identities) may not even serve the legitimating function hoped for. In the first place, exchanges and cultural networks will not necessarily result in the kind of malleable collective identity that can be mobilized, if need be. In other words, the diversity that underlies understandings of Europeanness hinders the utilization of a singular conception to justify policy-making in the traditional manner of the nation state. Second, the new (or retro) return to European values, rather than culture, as the basis for a useful conception of citizenship is, as discussed, flawed from its inception.

In this context, Bruter's distinction between the 'cultural' and 'civic' nature of European identity – the former expressing belonging to a particular community, the latter identification with a political structure (the European Union) – is crucial.[384] For the nationals of the new Member States, for example, membership in the European Union did not mean a sudden discovery of being European because they were now European citizens; instead, it was an institutional confirmation of

---

382. *See* d'Oliveira (1994), pp. 147–148. ('Member States have to a large extent become multicultural and multilingual societies which may be bound together not by a set of common values, but the development of a competence to deal with their differences. It is this competence to deal with differences which may be the nucleus of active modern citizenship, and European citizenship may be useful as a laboratory'.)
383. There were many references to 'solidarity' among Member States during negotiations for the European Union's 2007–2013 budget in the course of 2005, for example, yet little sign of it in practice.
384. Bruter (2004), p. 22.

something many had felt all along. Individuals can thus feel 'European' without having any view of the European Union. In fact, those asked generally do express much stronger attachment to the idea of 'Europe' than to the European Union, as institution.[385]

That said, even as theorists discuss the possible existence and quality of European identity, Member States have certainly determined that there is some commonality among Union citizens. No Member State has attempted, for example, to assimilate the nationals of other Member States. Certainly, there are enough non-national European citizens resident in certain regions of Member States to have a potential effect on identities. Unsaid though it remains, there seems to be a presumption that other European citizens are enough like 'us' not to be a threat to 'our' national identity.[386] (The contrast with the integration requirements for third-country nationals only confirms this point). But each state frames 'Europeanness' in a different manner, consonant with re-constructions of national identity: German 'Europeanness' is thus different from the Hungarian one, and certainly the British one. And who is to say that such bottom-up conceptions of European identity will mesh with the one the Community could utilize to gain legitimacy for its policies? Individuals may develop a (version of) European identity and still determine that certain matters should not be governed by 'Brussels'. For example, one can feel European without agreeing that other European citizens should have equal placement on organ donation lists as co-nationals – indeed the case under Community law.

The danger then, from the Community's point of view at least, is that, along with the reconfiguration of citizenship rights and the citizenship-nationality link that has occurred, the identity function of citizenship will also come undone, leaving the European political community in a vacuum between two non-existent pillars. If that were to happen, European citizenship would be a still-born status, not-much cared about by the individuals it guarantees rights to and, accordingly, an illegitimate reference point for further integration. On the other hand, a return to the pre-Maastricht attempt to emulate nation-building from an earlier time[387] is also not an answer. Forcing on individuals the idea that there are commonalities to be discovered and that these latter are justification enough for given policies – a kind of cultural consciousness-spreading exercise – is unlikely to have positive

---

385. In the same 2003 survey quoted above, only 44 per cent of respondents had a 'very' (eight per cent) or 'fairly' (36 per cent) positive image of the European Union. (32 per cent were neutral, while 19 per cent had a 'very' or 'fairly' negative one.) Eurobarometer 60, *supra* note II.352, p. 35. In 2006, support was at 50 per cent. Eurobarometer 65 (Spring 2006) p. 15 and p. 54. However, on average 58 per cent of respondents (in 2000) felt an attachment to 'Europe'. Eurobarometer 54 (Autumn 2000), p. 12; but *see* Bruter, *ibid.*, p. 37.
386. In at least one Member State (Germany) there is now a specially designated law in force (since January 2005) applicable only to EU citizens. *See Gesetz über die allgemeine Freizügigkeit von Unionsbürgern (Freizügigkeitsgesetz/EU)*, contained in *Gesetz zur Steuerung und Begrenzung der Zuwanderung und zur Regelung des Aufenthalts und der Integration von Unionsbürgern und Ausländern (Zuwanderungsgesetz)* (hereinafter, ZuWG).
387. According to certain theorists, this period continues. *See* Shore (2000).

results.[388] The Community thus walks a fine line between instrumentalizing culture for its own purposes and supporting it in the hopes that individuals will find meaningful commonalities.[389]

The shades of nuance are especially pronounced when integration is perceived rather as a danger to the rights of national citizenship, or even cultural diversity, than as an enhancement. The manner in which the E.C.J. dismissed language as an 'instrument of economic activity'[390] in the *Linguistic Diversity* case, for example, made appeals to respect for diversity ring farcical. In a comparable manner, the domination of certain languages – and the clear lack of cultural parity among Member States – tarnishes claims for (equal) respect for Member State cultures.[391] As for citizenship, it is perhaps difficult for German nationals to appreciate European citizenship as the new foundation for a collective identity when it is the lightning rod for policies – like the EAW – that are perceived as undermining the democratic legitimacy of the (still) primary political community to which they belong. Similarly, when welfare rights that go to the heart of the national project – in some Member States, like France or Denmark, they are arguably a crucial element of the very *quality* of national identity – are disassembled by the E.C.J. in the name of a nebulous European citizenship, the latter may well become a symbol of all that is undemocratic in or wrong with the EU. Finally, when the assumed requirements of this same citizenship act on minority protection regimes so as to result in (arguably) lesser rights[392] the claimed concern with both participation and diversity may well be greeted with scepticism.

This brings us to a second danger. While particular E.C.J. judgments may represent a victory for individuals, the sense of cohesion that (still) provides a basic substructure for national communities in Europe should not be sloughed off, *ad hoc*, on the basis of principles – like the four freedoms – that were never cultivated with public policy concerns in mind.[393] Doing so risks not only the legitimacy of the EC (and EU) but also of its Member States. No political community, however, can function without legitimacy in the eyes of the individuals who belong to it.

---

388. For plans along these lines, *see* Commission Communication, 'A People's Europe' (1988).
389. The language of the Commission Communication 'Making Citizenship Work', *supra* note II.110, offers hints of both approaches.
390. Case 42/97 *Linguistic Diversity*, para. 53, especially in conjunction with para. 50 ('As regards marginalization of the languages that remain excluded from the information society, mentioned in the twelfth recital, it is not a risk of a specifically cultural nature. Marginalization of languages may be understood as the loss of an element of cultural heritage, but also as the cause of a difference of treatment between economic operators in the Community, who enjoy greater or lesser advantages depending on whether or not the language they use is widespread'.)
391. *See* Case T-120/99 *Christina Kik v. Office for Harmonization in the Internal Market (Trade Marks and Designs)*, C.F.I. [2001]; and Case C-361/01 P *Christina Kik v. Office for Harmonization in the Internal Market (Trade Marks and Designs)*, E.C.J. [2003], paras 81 *et seq.* The fact that regional and minority languages are not treated as equal to national ones by the Community language regime is a further sign of inconsistency.
392. *See* discussion in Horváth (2006).
393. For an excellent discussion of the effects of free movement and competition law on European welfare states, *see* Davies (2006).

Indeed, though European citizenship needs to develop in both the area of rights and that of identity, its maturation now risks maiming the very bases it draws on. An emerging European identity – the multi-layered, fluctuating one already described – may help make European citizenship 'matter', but it cannot substitute for missing political allegiance at any level.

It has been argued here that the rights of European citizenship are quite unusual in the context of international law. In addition, the status already has a progressive role in re-interpreting the citizenship-nationality link;[394] a number of supra-state and trans-state rights are already elements of it, for example. But further development is necessary. Why not strengthen rights of consumer and environmental protection for all? And why not grant certain European citizenship rights to long-term residents (such as voting in European elections) while extending (and reserving) others for those who are European citizens through the nationality of a Member State? For example, why not express the Community's supposed respect for diversity in the language of rights? More pragmatically, why not fill the right to consular protection with actual content? Finally, why not clarify the social consequences of European Union citizenship in updated legislation, in which public policy principles may be taken into account, rather than allowing for piecemeal deconstruction and reconstruction on the basis of the four freedoms?

Whatever its course of development, the overlapping nature of any emerging European identity will frame the evolution of other collective identities in Europe, including the national. Possibly, the change will be toward a less exclusive national identity than has existed in the past, as the shared memories that help form its basis are re-interpreted. On the other hand, the ongoing fragmentation of national citizenship could also result in both increased alienation and renewed reliance on overtly ethnic conceptions of belonging for members of European political communities, at all levels. The rise of plural nationality and kinship laws, discussed next, in fact show that the questions of culture and citizenship struggled with on a Community level are also matters of contention on the Member State level. The answers given, however, are in their own way just as unusual as the processes to be found in the context of Europe.

---

394. *See also* d'Oliveira (1994), pp. 147–148 for a similar view, albeit on the basis of reasoning that has proven wrong in hindsight.

Chapter III
Kinship Laws

> *Tietek vagyok, mindegy most már,*
> *Hogy nem kellek, vagy kellek-e*
> *Egy a Napunk gyönyörű égen.*
>
> Endre Ady, Küldöm a Frigy-ládát, 1909[1]

Following the collapse of the socialist bloc, issues arising from the existence of minorities re-emerged, to differing extents, in all the states of East-Central Europe.[2] While the tragic results of an inability to co-exist in some of these cases needs no introduction, other communities have gone the legal route, attempting to use and develop frameworks to suit their specific circumstances. Matters have been complicated by the fact that, besides the Roma, recognized minorities in the region are not only national minorities[3] in their home-states, but also the

---

1. 'I am yours, it doesn't matter now/ if you don't need me, or do./Our sun is one in a beautiful sky'.
2. Unless otherwise stated, discussion in this Chapter is limited to national minorities only. Immigrant communities are considered qualitatively different in many respects, including, often: a voluntary decision on the part of individuals to emigrate; greater willingness to integrate/assimilate in the adopted country; greater geographical distance between home- and kin-state; a significantly shorter history in the territory of the home-state; and a lack of ongoing discussion/conflict over minority affairs between the kin and home-states. Granted, the distinction can become nebulous in certain contexts – what are Russian-speakers in the Baltics? – but does hold in most cases.
   In a related point, the theories and suggestions discussed here apply only to national minorities in Europe and migrants within the EU; immigrant communities from elsewhere stand on different footing for a number of reasons. *See also* Kymlicka (2001a), p. 55 for differences between the two groups.
3. Defined here as 'a group of persons in a state who: (a) reside on the territory of that state and are citizens thereof; (b) maintain longstanding, firm and lasting ties with that State; (c) display distinctive ethnic, cultural, religions or linguistic characteristics; (d) are sufficiently representative, although smaller in number than the rest of the population of that state or of a

kin-minorities of states in close proximity.[4] As Brubaker has recognized, the existence of a kin-state significantly changes the relationship between minority and home-state, since the former frames and modifies what may otherwise be a closed system circumscribed by borders, albeit affected by the international community.[5] In fact, a 'triadic nexus' emerges, in which all three actors (as well as the international community) interact on an on-going basis.[6] Accordingly, even if the home-states (attempt to) control their nationals – *qua* nationals – in the manner already discussed, kin-states also attempt to exert some influence by relying on kinship ties.

This Chapter will consider the scope and quality of such influence, particularly in the guise of kinship laws. As we will see in the first section, many states in Europe have enacted constitutional provisions that ensure rights and benefits to specific categories of individuals outside their borders, whether expatriates or kin-minority individuals. In dispensing these advantages, some of the states concerned rely openly on culture to function as an adhesive to connect the state to kin-individuals. The first part of this section explains how the co-existence of numerous political strategies of nationalism in Europe renders the assertion of such ties problematic; while part two presents the political strategy of nationalism – 'trans-sovereign nationalism' – that best explains why such constitutional clauses and attendant kinship legislation are enacted in the first place. In section two of this Chapter, we turn to a presentation of the wide range of kinship laws in force today. It will be argued that we can identify four distinct models of kinship regulation in Europe, each with a particular target group and strategy; in addition, one breed of kinship laws – status laws – is distinguished from the others on the basis of its characteristic content and reach.

The model of kinship regulation developed by Hungary and most concretely implemented in its status law from 2001 has been particularly controversial, and will be presented in the first part of section three; in the process, its history, context and content will be detailed. Part two will focus on reactions and counter-reactions to the law, including the Report of the European Commission for Democracy

---

region of the state; (e) are motivated by a concern to preserve together that which constitutes their common identity, including their culture, their tradition, their religion or their language'. *See* Council of Europe, Parliamentary Recommendation 1201 on an Additional Protocol on the Rights of Minorities to the European Convention on Human Rights (hereinafter, Recommendation 1201) (1993), Art.1.

4. While there is no settled terminology used in reference to the actors in such situations, I have adopted the terms used by the Venice Commission in its Report on the Preferential Treatment of National Minorities by their Kin-state (hereinafter, Venice Report) (2001).
5. *See also* Culic (2001). 'The "civic" identity of the Hungarians in Romania is substantially influenced by the positions taken by the Romanian state in devising and implementing legislation with respect to national minorities, local administration, and education; by the positions taken by the Hungarian state expressed in the degree and form of responsibility assumed for the ethnonational kin abroad; and by the relations between the two states'. *Ibid.*, p. 232.
6. *See* Brubaker (1996), Chapter 3 and *ibid.* (2000), 4–6.

through Law (hereinafter, the Venice Commission), the only comprehensive examination of the legal questions surrounding kinship laws. Developments in Hungary since 2001, including the eventual amendment of the status law in 2003, will also be examined. Section three will draw on the example of the Hungarian status law to present some of the general legal and political questions raised by the introduction and evolution of legal statuses premised on kinship, including interference in the affairs of other states, the role of perception and loyalty and a conception of the 'nation' as legal entity. It is argued that these issues are not unique to kinship laws, but spring from the tension inherent in the co-existence of cultural and political communities. Finally, we will examine whether existing legal statuses and policies, particularly European citizenship and plural nationality, could provide alternative solutions to the dilemma of status laws in Europe.

A.   EMERGENCE OF A NEW PHENOMENON

1.   CONSTITUT(IONALIZ)ING THE NATION

Almost all the states in East-Central Europe have recognized, in their Constitutions, a responsibility toward individuals belonging to the given cultural or ethnic nation and resident outside the given state. It is perhaps Article 10 of the Croatian Constitution that states things most clearly: '[p]arts of the Croatian nation in other states are guaranteed special concern and protection by the Republic'. In many cases, however, the language of the relevant clause obscures the scope of the provisions in question. Article 6(2) of the Polish Constitution, for example, states that '[t]he Republic of Poland shall provide assistance to Poles living abroad to maintain their links with the national cultural heritage'. Are we dealing with nationals here? Or non-nationals? Similarly, Article 6(3) of the Hungarian Constitution states that 'the Republic of Hungary bears a sense of responsibility for the fate of Hungarians living outside its borders and shall promote and foster their relations with Hungary'. Based on the language of the clause, one would perhaps assume that we are dealing with nationals. But in the Hungarian context, the words *határon túli magyarok* ('Hungarians beyond the border') are used almost exclusively in the context of non-nationals, and generally in reference to Hungarian minorities in the neighbouring states. Moreover, given the existence of a separate clause (Article 69(3)) that deals with the protection of Hungarian nationals, a reference to these individuals in Article 6(3) would be redundant.[7]

---

7. Separate clauses or references also exist in the Constitutions of Albania, Croatia, Greece, Poland, Portugal, Romania, and Ukraine.

The Romanian Constitution, in turn, states in Article 7 that the 'State supports the strengthening of links with Romanians outside the country's borders and works for the preservation, development and expression of their ethnic, cultural, linguistic, and religious identity *by respecting the legislation of the State of which they are citizens* [nationals]' (emphasis added). Here, at least, we know we are not talking about nationals (though dual nationals are covered). But then what is the role of Romania in preserving and developing any collective identity? Similarly, Article 49 of the Constitution of the FYRO Macedonia stipulates that '[t]he Republic cares for the status and rights of those persons belonging to the Macedonian people in neighbouring countries, as well as Macedonian expatriates, assists their cultural development and promotes links with them'. This clause applies to nationals and non-nationals alike, without distinction in the kind of links promoted.

Still other provisions provide both geographic and personal limitation, as expressed in Article 5 of the Slovenian Constitution: 'Slovenia shall maintain concern for the autochthonous Slovene national minorities in neighbouring countries and shall foster their contacts with the homeland.... Slovenes not holding Slovene citizenship [nationality] may enjoy special rights and privileges in Slovenia'. The clause thus refers to nationals and non-nationals, so long as they form part of a national minority in a neighbouring state. The reference to a Slovene 'homeland' is particularly noteworthy, since it hints at the reasoning behind all such constitutional provisions. In a similar manner, the Slovak Constitution provides support for the 'national consciousness and cultural identity of Slovaks living abroad, supports their institutions for the attainment of this purpose as well as their relations with the motherland' (Article 7(a)).

A number of other Constitutions in Europe also make special provisions for non-nationals on the basis of kinship, as the table below shows. In other cases, the divide between the rights granted to nationals and non-nationals is not so clear, especially in the context of cultural and other ties to the kin-state. Still other states accommodate only nationals but grant nationality to those with ethnic or cultural ties through special procedures (e.g., Bulgaria, Germany, and Spain). Moreover, given the rise of plural nationality, many of the constitutional provisions applicable to nationals – whether assuming general responsibility or granting the right to vote in elections while resident abroad – raise the same general questions as provisions for non-nationals. As Brubaker has recognized in a specific context, 'an expansive politics of citizenship [nationality] enables Russia to combine the traditional (and from the point of view of international law more legitimate) rhetoric of protecting citizens [nationals] in other states with homeland nationalist claims to protect non-citizen [non-national] co-[kin]'[8] – the difference can be small indeed.

---

8. Brubaker (2000), p. 17.

Table 1. Constitutional Provisions in Europe on the Role of the State with Regard to Individuals Outside its Territory

	Nationals	Non-Nationals
General Responsibility	FYRO Macedonia, Art. 49 (including culture) Greece, Art. 108(1) (including education) Slovenia, Art. 5 (including ties) Turkey, Art. 62 (including ties and return)	Croatia, Art. 10 Greece, Art. 108(1) (including ties) Hungary, Art. 6(3) (including ties) Slovenia, Art. 5 (including ties)
Cultural and other ties to homeland	Albania, Art. 8(3) (may also apply to non-nationals) Armenia, Art. 11(1) (may also apply to non-nationals) Switzerland, Art. 40(1)	FYRO Macedonia, Art. 49 (also protection) Ireland, Art. 2 Poland, Art. 6(2) (see also 6(1) which may apply to nationals) Portugal, Art. 74(2)(i) (see also (d)) Romania, Art. 7 Serbia, Art. 72 (may also apply to nationals) Slovakia, Art. 7a Ukraine, Art. 12
Protection	Albania, Art. 8(2) Armenia, Art. 11(3) Belarus, Art. 10(1) Bosnia-Herzegovina, Art. 7(e) Bulgaria, Art. 25(5) Croatia, Art. 10 (also ties) Georgia, Art. 13(1) and 30(3) (labour rights) Hungary, Art. 69(3) Poland, Art. 36 Portugal, Arts 14 and 59(2)(e) Romania, Art. 17	Albania, Art. 8(1)

Table 1. (Continued)

	Nationals	Non-Nationals
	Spain, Art. 42 (and return) Ukraine, Art. 25	
Right to exercise right to vote abroad	Croatia, Art. 45 Italy, Arts 48, 51, 56 and 58 Norway, Art. 50 Portugal, Arts 121(1), 121(2), 115(12) and 397 Switzerland, Art. 40(2) Turkey, Art. 67	
Other	Turkey, Art. 90 (protection of property)	
Kinship preference in according nationality or residence		Bulgaria, Art. 25(2) Germany, Art. 116 Poland, Art. 52(5) Slovenia, Art. 5 Spain, Art. 11(3) (also allows dual nationality)
Provisions allowing for dual nationality	Armenia, Art. 11(3) Malta, Art. 22(2) Russia, Art. 62(1)	

Let us return to the provisions of the Constitutions just quoted to understand the assumptions that underlie them. Their reasoning, at least, is clear: individuals who form part of the 'nation', whether nationals or not, are to consider the kin-state their 'motherland'. Accordingly, they may expect various measures, ranging from the promotion of 'contacts' and 'links' with the kin-state to 'special rights and privileges' in its territory, to assistance in general 'cultural development' and support for the specific 'institutions' involved in such activities in their home-state. Behind this reasoning is an openly cultural, and sometimes ethnic, approach to the concept of 'nation'.

a.   The Complexities of Promoting a 'Cultural' Nation

As discussed in Chapter II, all nations are cultural on some level, with varying emphasis on shared attributes, including language, norms and/or descent. The constitutional provisions above make the reliance of these particular states on culture (and sometimes ethnicity) as the glue holding the nation together explicit, however. This understanding of the nation leads to an especially close connection between loyalty to the nation and loyalty to a particular state, since one state generally presents itself as the natural 'home' of the culture in question. Thus, Budapest is to be the cultural centre of Hungarians, regardless of where they reside, just like Rome is to be a focal point for Italians. The assumption, then, is that individuals will have a special link to this one state, regardless of their actual nationality. In one manner, state sovereignty is to be superseded, since borders serve as a means to divide the purportedly unified community. Since each state-centred society constructs its own cultural discourse, however, sovereignty remains crucial in another. While Poland may aim to maintain 'ties' or support 'cultural development' wherever Poles may find themselves, France, Brazil and the UK simultaneously aim to integrate the targeted individuals into their own national discourse. Individuals, in turn, are free to accept or reject the myriad policies directed at them. In some cases, however, they may feel threatened by action hindering the expression of some element of their identity, whether national or religious. The preservation of identity is in all circumstances conditioned by the policies of both the state of residence and the 'cultural home' state (if the two do not coincide). In this manner, states constrain cultural nations irrespective of whether their policies support or undermine the given cultural community.

This state of affairs would not be particularly disruptive if the concept of 'nation' were really only a discursive practice in the manner already discussed. Individuals could then be both Dutch and Moroccan (or Muslim) and live each identity freely, without any friction. In particular, if the 'cultural' and 'civic' strands of the 'nation' really could be separated for the purposes of national identity, nationals who have close ties to another culture – whether national or any other – would not be perceived as suspect. But state-centred societies rarely take such a tolerant view of belonging and membership, exactly because the two strands are intertwined in all national identities in Europe. For example, an individual may posit that he, as a national of Romania, is a member of the Romanian political nation, while also belonging to the Hungarian cultural nation. Romania, however, needn't necessarily recognize the possibility of such a division – in other words the division between a national and a member of the nation – since it claims that all nationals are members of the 'civic' Romanian nation. (This supposed 'civic' understanding is at present dubitable, as Articles 1(1) and 4(1) of the Romanian Constitution show.[9]) Particular circumstances aside, however, this difference of approach may lead to tension between the state and certain nationals. Thus:

---

9. 'Romania is a national state, sovereign and independent, unitary and indivisible', and, since the 2003 amendment, 'The State foundation is laid on the unity of the Romanian people and the solidarity of their citizens' respectively. *See also* Art. 2(1). (The recent amendment of the Constitution did not include a relevant change to these provisions, although it did add a provision on the right to identity of national minority individuals).

On the one hand [Gheorghe] Funar [then mayor of Cluj-Napoca and former leader of the Romanian National Unity Party] has it announced that there aren't even Hungarians in Romania, only Hungarian-speaking Romanians; at the same time his followers angrily shout 'Out of the country with the Hungarians'! This is what leads to conflicts and may make us question our attachment to the political nation.[10]

In reality, it is often not so easy to determine where to draw the line between the 'civic' and 'cultural' nation. The former does not end with state-linked entities, but encompasses all elements of civil society, including NGOs and a variety of clubs, associations and organizations – many of which may not care about the neatness of borders (or theories, for that matter). Where does a Hungarian minority organization committed to cultural exchanges with Hungary belong, for example? Is it 'civic' or 'cultural'? Are Hungarian-minority individuals who demand the recognition of the minority as a separate group entitled to autonomy within the state functioning as part of the Romanian political nation? Are those who look to Hungary to help push for these goals doing so? Can measures that come from a kin-state ever have an effect on only the 'cultural' nation, without secondary effects on the 'civic' one?

To be more precise, it is useful to differentiate between nationalism as a political strategy, used by the state to further its goals, and nationalism as a social process defining and redefining the 'nation'. The two rely on each other – nationalism as a political strategy uses the domestic and international arena to push for the goals of nationalism as an expression of the 'nation' – but are not identical. The former may change from government to government, while the latter evolves slowly. In the case of Hungary, for example, the concept of 'nation' is primarily cultural, with a reliance on common language, history, traditions and self-identification; in turn, the strategy of nationalism is, at present, aimed at uniting this 'nation', regardless of where its members are in geographical terms, but especially if they are in the Carpathian basin.[11]

Aside from the validity of purely 'civic' conceptions of the nation, then, the real question is how the political strategy of nationalism is expressed through state policies and laws. It is these policies and laws that have the greatest effect on individual lives, not the ponderous evolution of conceptions of the 'nation'. This is why even a supposedly civic nation like France can produce a law that alienates a large number of its nationals, since they perceive it as an attack on some element of their cultural identity.[12]

---

10. Romániai Magyar Szó (László Fey), *Politikai nemzet és kultúrnemzet* (22 June 2001). (*'Egyrészt Funar kinyilatkoztatja, hogy Romániában nincsenek is magyarok, legfeljebb magyarul beszélő románok, másrészt az ő hívei üvöltik dühödten, hogy Afară, afară/cu ungurii din țară! (Ki a magyarokkal az országból). Ez az, ami konfliktusokhoz vezet, és kérdésessé teheti a politikai nemzethez való kötődésünket'.*)
11. The above-mentioned traditional distinction between 'civic' and 'ethnic' nationalism is thus tricky not only when looking at concepts of the 'nation', but also when examining national identity-building measures.
12. *See*, e.g., France, *'La loi encadrant, en application du principe de laïcité, le port de signes ou de tenues manifestant une appartenance religieuse dans les écoles, collèges et lycées publics' (loi n° 2004-228)* (2004). For a critical look at the issues raised, *see* Balibar (2004).

Laws on nationality and other legal statuses with identity functions are influenced by and reflective of both nationalism as social process and nationalism as short-term political strategy. It is the latter, however, that explains frequent amendment to provisions in nationality laws, as well as the general context in which such changes are perceived. Different nationalist strategies – and the laws that result from them – are, however, constrained by external and internal factors, such as international law or demographic trends. In this manner, the possible range of variation is considerably curtailed. Accepted conceptions of the nation, which evolve at a much slower pace, also hinder any radical transformation of nationality law, due the identity function of the latter. The (indirect) link between conceptions of the 'nation' and nationality laws is, in turn, mediated by the dual-pronged process of nationalism, presented above.

The interaction of nation, nationalism and law can thus be pictured in the following manner:

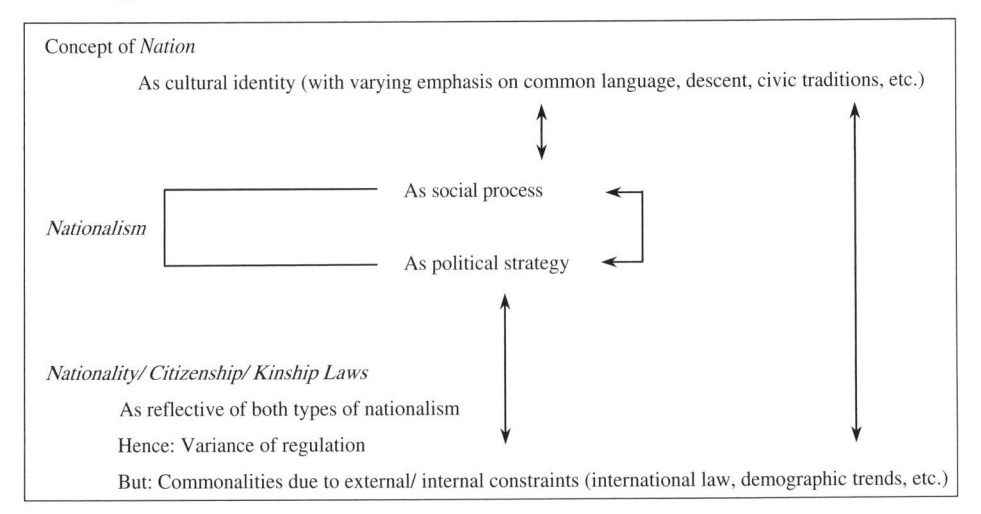

Concept of *Nation*
    As cultural identity (with varying emphasis on common language, descent, civic traditions, etc.)

Nationalism
    As social process
    As political strategy

Nationality/ Citizenship/ Kinship Laws
    As reflective of both types of nationalism
    Hence: Variance of regulation
    But: Commonalities due to external/ internal constraints (international law, demographic trends, etc.)

---

b. **Political Strategies of Trans-Sovereign Nationalism**

A closer look at political strategies of nationalism is thus necessary to understand the genesis of kinship laws. As Csergő and Goldgeier argue, four strategies of nationalism can be discerned in contemporary Europe: traditional nationalism, aimed at the creation of a 'territorially sovereign, culturally homogenous nation-state'[13] (e.g., Estonia, Latvia, Romania, Croatia, Slovakia); sub-state nationalism, or the aspiration of national minorities 'to maintain political representation and institutions that guarantee the continued reproduction of the community'[14] (e.g.,

---

13. Csergő and Goldgeier (2002). Much the same run-down has been suggested by Brubaker. *See* Brubaker (2001), p. 120 *et seq.*
14. Csergő and Goldgeier, *ibid.*, p. 5.

Scotland, Bavaria, Catalonia, Flanders); protectionist nationalism, whose 'fundamental goal is preserving the established national culture in the face of immigration and rapid social change'[15] (e.g., France, Belgium, Austria, Germany); and trans-sovereign nationalism, which 'creates institutions that maintain and reproduce the nation across existing state borders'[16] (e.g., Hungary). No state exhibits only one of these strategies, though a dominant one can usually be discerned.

It is trans-sovereign nationalism that is most interesting for our purposes, since the constitutional clauses discussed are an element of this approach. In its clearest form, this strategy can be summarized as the virtualization of state borders. For this purpose, a 'strong trans-sovereign ... institutional network' is developed, to 'provide financial and other kinds of support in education, political organization, cultural activities, media, economic projects, health care and science'.[17] Such institutional autonomy 'relies heavily on concepts largely accepted in [W]estern Europe, such as regionalism, devolution, and subsidiarity'.[18] However, the hoped-for result of multiple loyalties and centres of the power – in the Hungarian context, 'Hungarians abroad should be able to claim Budapest as their national cultural centre, Bratislava, Bucharest or Belgrade their state capital, Cluj-Napoca, Novi Sad, and other cities as their regional centres'[19] – is not likely to be one that many states in Europe will be comfortable with. Still, almost all states in the East-Central European region are experimenting with some form of trans-national nationalism.

The support of kin-minorities or nationals abroad, as the case may be, is a prerequisite for such strategies to succeed. Thus far, Hungarian minorities have been quite open to the trans-national project; Slovak minorities, however, have been less enthusiastic about the efforts of their respective kin-state. Whatever the reactions of individuals and particular minority communities to kin-state policies,[20] however, all kin-minorities are effectively caught in the middle between competing political strategies of nationalism and possibly even competing understandings of the concept of 'nation'. On a theoretical level, the rights/duties and identity functions of nationality also do not cohere in their case and may even be antagonistic. In this context, requests for dual nationality as well as kinship laws are an expression of the split: individuals hope for symbolic recognition of belonging to the cultural nation through a (legal) link to the kin-state, as well as through

---

15. *Ibid.*, p. 13.
16. *Ibid.*, p. 6.
17. *Ibid.*, p. 9. As Sata shows, elements of trans-nationalism were already present in Hungarian political discourse in the period between World Wars I and II. Sata, at 52 (2001).
18. *Ibid.*, p. 10.
19. *Ibid.*, p. 9.
20. *See* Gál, Jarábik and Lamacková, at 320 (2002). No studies have been done to account for such differences. In the Hungarian/Slovak case, some explanation may be sought in the fact that the ancestors of Hungarian kin-minorities were involved in the nation-building of an existing state in the 19th century. Slovakia, on the other hand, did not exist as an independent state before 1993, so that the emergence of Slovak identity predated the establishment of a kin-state; the minorities were never as closely linked to the Slovak state as Hungarians had been to the Hungarian one.

the tangible benefits such licensed belonging may bring. As one commentator discussed in a rather overheated piece about the Hungarian law, it 'is of extraordinary significance in the legal codification of the oneness – of the belonging to one nation – of kin-Hungarians'.[21] Such laws, grounded as they are in an acknowledgement of kin-minorities' special status, may also lead to some formal recognition of the groups in a manner not usually possible in international law.

The discussion between Romania and Hungary during the drafting of a bilateral treaty on good-neighbourliness in 1994–1996 shows the dilemma clearly. Hungary argued that:

> [T]he Hungarian government cannot formally represent the nationals of other states belonging to the Hungarian national minority, but considers it a substantive demand that the representatives of the affected minorities be able to express their opinions during the process, as well as with regard to the agreements[22]

Romania, on the other hand, considered that:

> [I]ndividuals belonging to the national minority are the nationals of Romania, and their relation to the Romanian state is resolved like that of all other nationals. The rights of the Hungarian minority in Romania are not guaranteed by the Romanian-Hungarian treaty, but by the Constitution of Romania, by the laws of the country and by the international agreements signed by Romania.[23]

From the point of view of the kin-state, however, an integral element of transnationalism – or kin-minority protection, depending on one's point of view – is legislation that includes some or all the measures mentioned in the constitutional clauses above. Kin-states thus do have a role to play in ensuring rights to members of kin-minorities. Hungary's Orbán government was most forthcoming with this logic in the context of enlargement:

> The Government's policy on ... Hungarian [kin-] minorities in neighbouring countries aims to build and develop political, cultural and economic ties. In order to achieve this, the bonds between ... Hungarian [kin-] minorities and Hungary must be settled within a framework of legislation and government, so as to preserve the organic ties of Hungarian communities to Hungary, even after its accession to the European Union.[24]

---

21. Csapó (2002), p. 327.
22. Concluding Document of the Inaugural Conference for a Pact on Stability in Europe (Interpretive Statement of Hungary), point 1(5), as quoted in Iordachi (2002), p. 106.
23. Traian Chebeleu, spokesman to the Romanian president (27 May 1997), as quoted in Iordachi, ibid., p. 106. ('A magyar kisebbséghez tartozó személyek Románia állampolgárai, és a román állammal való kapcsolatuk hasonlóképpen nyer megoldást, mint az összes többi állampolgár kapcsolata. A romániai magyar kisebbség jogait nem a román-magyar szerződés garantálja, hanem Románia alkotmánya, az ország törvényei és a Románia által aláírt nemzetközi egyezmények'.)
24. Government Program: For a Civic Hungary on the Eve of a New Millenium (1998), as quoted in Kántor (2001), p. 262.

Giving the substance of the constitutional clauses legal expression in special legislation is thus a means to render the presumed or hoped for links more official.

2. KINSHIP AND STATUS BENEFITS

Laws granting preferential treatment to individuals in the home- or kin-state on the basis of cultural and/or ethnic affiliation with the 'nation' (i.e., kinship) have been adopted in a number of states in the region: Slovenia (1996), Slovakia (1997), Romania (1998, 2004),[25] Russia (1999), Bulgaria (2000), Hungary (2001, revised in 2003), and Ukraine (2004).[26] Others have flirted with various drafts of such laws (e.g., Poland) or are only at the theoretical stage of consideration (e.g., Croatia). Still others have discussed laws based specifically on the Hungarian one (Romania and Slovenia).[27] Based on the diverse histories, politics, priorities and financial resource of the given countries,[28] the range of legislation is quite wide.[29] Some limit their benefits to the kin-state (Slovakia); others aim to give support in the home-states also (Slovenia, Hungary). Some wish to ensure that minorities maintain their identity in the home-state (Hungary), while others focus on the maintenance of links with the kin-state wherever the minority individual may live (Slovakia, Russia and Romania). Accordingly, some consider the establishment of a link with the kin-state a possible first step to nationality (Slovakia), while others hope it can substitute for it (Hungary). Some combine support of kin-minorities with the maintenance of ties with diasporas[30] (Slovakia and

---

25. *See* Venice Commission Opinion on the Draft Law Concerning the Support to Romanians Living Abroad (2004) for a discussion of the modifications to be made to the 1998 law. *See also* Szabadság, *Törvény készül a határon túli románok támogatásáról* (10 August 2004).
26. *Inter alia*, Slovenia, Resolution on the position of autochthonous Slovene minorities in neighboring countries and the related tasks of state and other institutions in the Republic of Slovenia (1996); Slovakia, Law 70/1997 on expatriate Slovaks and changing and complementing some laws (1997); Romania, Law regarding the support granted to the Romanian communities from all over the world (1998); Russia, Federal Law on the State policy of the Russian Federation in respect of the compatriots abroad (1999), Bulgaria, Law for the Bulgarians living outside the Republic of Bulgaria (2000).
27. *See* Népszabadság, *Leszavazták a szlovén státustörvényt* (8 May 2004) for Slovenia; and Népszabadság, *Romániigazolvány* (12 August 2003) and *ibid.*, *Románia státustörvényt alkot magyar mintára* (9 August 2003) for Romania.
28. For example, while both Hungary and Slovakia have the (limited) financial means to support significant minority groups, Slovakia has no large, relatively compact kin-group in neighbouring states; instead, Slovak minorities are fragmented and scattered. A law such as Hungary's would make little sense in this context.
29. For an in-depth comparison of the (first) Hungarian and the Slovak status laws, *see* Gál, Jarábik and Lamacková (2002).
30. A 'diaspora' is defined here as a group of individuals with a consciousness of belonging to a larger community possessing a specific collective (ethnic or national, linguistic, religious or other cultural) identity, with a corresponding sense of solidarity toward the, generally geographically distant, community's institutions (e.g., a state) or the community itself. *See also* discussion in Sheffer (2003), pp. 25–26.

Romania), while others make a clear distinction between the two (Hungary). This last point is especially significant, since the laws with application to diasporas shade into comparable legislation in Western Europe.[31]

The connection is perhaps not clear at first sight. After all, when considered from the point of view of international (and EU) law, the most obvious distinction to make is between kinship laws applicable to nationals and those applicable to non-nationals. Accordingly, there are laws applicable to nationals resident abroad (e.g., Slovenia's) and non-nationals (e.g., Hungary's). The former are acceptable under almost all circumstances, regardless of the effect they may have on the nation-building strategy of another state; the latter are to be examined for possible discrimination along ethnic, racial or national lines, as well as irredentist purpose. Alternately, a distinction may be made between those granting benefits only in the kin-state and those providing some support in the home-state. While the latter have extraterritorial application and may for that reason be unacceptable, the former present no difficulties: within its borders, the state is (almost) sovereign. However, kinship laws cut across such divisions, so that there are no clearly defined categories.

Iordachi draws out the parallels clearly in the context of East-Central Europe in a piece comparing the (first) Hungarian status law and Romania's policy of dual nationality with Moldova. He places both within a framework of the 're-birth of ethno-national politics' in the wake of the fall of communism[32] and argues that both are state-centric, since they target the descendants of former nationals, while making reference to the forced renunciation of nationality.[33] In this context, it is worth noting that political strategies to tinker with legal status have a long and undistinguished history in the region. The re-regulation of nationality (particularly dual nationality) was considered by certain legal theorists between the World Wars as a first step toward the institutional integration of states forbidden by the Versailles Treaties, for example.[34] Austria, in particular, considered the mutual

---

31. See Portugal, *Lei no. 48/96 de Setembro com a redacção que lhe foi dada pela Lei no. 21/2002 de Agosto* (1996) on the establishment of a Council of Portugese Communities; Portugal, *Ministério dos Negócios Estrangeiros, Regulamento de atribuição de apoio pela Direcção-Geral dos Assuntos Consulares e Comunidades Portuguesas (Despacho no. 6162/99)* (1999); Italy, *Legge 27 ottobre 1988, no. 470/88, sull'iscrizione all'AIRE (Anagrafe Italiana Residenti all'Estero)* (1988) (as amended); Italy, *Legge 6 novembre 1989, no. 368, Istitutiva del CGIE (Consiglio Generale degli Italiani all'Estero)*, as amended by *Legge 18 guignio 1998, no. 198* and *Regolamento emanato con D.P.R. 14 settembre 1998, no. 329* (1998); and Italy, *Legge 23 ottobre 2003, no. 286, Norme relative alla disciplina dei Comitati degli italiani all'estero* (2003), which abrogated *Legge 8 maggio 1985, no. 205, istitutiva dei COMITES*, as amended by *Legge del 5 luglio 1990, no. 172* and by *Legge del 31 dicembre 1996, no. 668)* (1996).
32. Iordachi (2002), p. 91.
33. *Ibid.*, pp. 115–116.
34. The attempted use of a common nationality to strengthen political ties also has more amicable precedents. For example, Chancellor Adenauer suggested a joint French-German nationality in 1954 (*see* Frankfurter Allgemeine Zeitung of 2 March 1954), the idea of which was recently revived by (then) Chancellor Schröder and (then) President Chirac. There was once even discussion of a joint British-French nationality, suggested by Churchill in 1940 as part of the common war effort.

establishment of a dual nationality regime with Germany in 1926, as the first step to the unification of the two states.[35]

However, the more significant parallel, shared with diaspora laws in the rest of Europe, is that all such policies assume the existence of a (clearly conceived) cultural nation, whose hub is to be found in one given state. In some form or another, extant kinship ties are thought to require legal expression through laws linking individuals to the 'motherland'.

Table 2. Kinship Laws in Europe

Laws applicable to non-resident: with benefits in:	Nationals	Both nationals/ non-nationals	Non-nationals Kin-minorities	Non-nationals Diaspora
Kin-State	–	–	– Greek law (1998) – Austrian law (1979)	– Slovak law (1997) – Romanian law (1998)
Home-State	– All laws allowing for voting rights for kin-state elections	– None known	– Italian law (1991, 2001) – Austrian grants (ongoing since 1955) – Danish grants – (ongoing since 1955)	– Facilitated access to nationality (e.g., Bulgaria, Germany, Greece, Ireland, Italy, Portugal, Spain) and repatriation (e.g., Estonia, Finland, Germany, Poland) – Former-national status (Turkey since 1995)

In an example with deeper historical foundations, the idea of a Nordic nationality (between Denmark, Norway, Finland and Sweden) has been raised repeatedly since the late 19th century; though it has yet to come into existence, the laws of the named states grant the nationals of other Nordic states a special status.

35. *See* discussion in Grawert (1973), p. 242.

Table 2. (Continued)

Laws applicable to non-resident: with benefits in:	Nationals	Both nationals/ non-nationals	Non-nationals Kin-minorities	Diaspora
Both states	– Portuguese law on Council of Portuguese Communities (1996) – Italian laws on AIRE and CGIE (1988, 1989) – All other laws establishing Councils abroad (i.e., Switzerland, France, Spain, Turkey)	– All laws establishing institutional representation (Switzerland, Greece) – Italian law on COMITES (1985, 2003) (diaspora)[36] – Latvian Regulation (2004) (diaspora) – Portuguese Regulation (1999) (diaspora) – Russian law (1999) (diaspora and kin-minorities) – Slovene Regulation (2002) (diaspora)	– Hungarian law (2001, 2003) – draft Romanian law (2004) – German regulation of Volksdeustche (ongoing) – Slovene law (1996)	– None known

*Given that practically *all* states in Europe have some kind of policy for kin abroad, the table above is not exhaustive.

Lest the phenomenon of kinship laws be dismissed as an East-Central European phenomenon, it should be noted that the first EU states to enact legislation granting

---

36. *See* Catani (1993) for a presentation of the Italian regulations.

preferential treatment or a special status to non-national individuals on the basis of kinship were Germany, Austria, Greece and Italy.

For example, the German regulation of nationality[37] (still) recognizes a category of *Statusdeutsche* (German by status), also called *Spätaussiedler* (late re-settler), comprising those who are *deutscher Volkszugehöriger* (members of the German *Volk*) pursuant to Article 6 of the *Bundesvertriebenen und Flüchtlingsgesetz* (Federal Law on Expelees and Refugees; hereinafter, BVFG) (1953, as amended).[38] *Statusdeutsche* are treated like German nationals in most respects, though the do not hold that status. Between 1953 and 1993, these individuals could apply for a right to settle in Germany (formerly West-Germany) with financial aid from the state and, through a separate process but near-automatically, be granted nationality. Since the 1999 overhaul of German nationality law, discussed in Chapter IV, the fact of immigration to Germany entitles *Statusdeutsche* to the acquisition of nationality; but the right to immigrate is now tied to a quota.

The assumption behind this practice has been that cultural/ethnic Germans in Europe were persecuted in the wake of World War II;[39] on this basis, they had a right to immigrate to Germany. For those born after 1923, a successful claim required descent from a German national or *Volk*-German, so that an element of *jus sanguinis* was, indirectly, part and parcel of any grant of German nationality to such individuals. Though there have been certain changes and a major overhaul of regulations pertaining to them (in 1990, 1993, 1996, and 1999 respectively), the *Statusdeutsche* continue to exist as a separate category of possible German national pursuant to Article 116(1) of the German Constitution,[40] in spite of Article 3(3) of the *Grundgesetz*.[41]

In addition, for individuals no longer considered *Spätaussiedler*, but only *Volksdeustche* – i.e., those considered German but without the right to

---

37. For a thorough discussion, *see* Gyertyánfy (2000). *See also* Singbartl (2003) for a (somewhat emotional) look at the circumstances surrounding the genesis of the regulations, as well as their development since 1990.
38. A finding of this status is also contingent on showing that the individual had claimed to belong to the German nation in her home-state and that such belonging can be supported by an objective factor (use of language, descent, culture, education). *See* BVFG Art. 6(1).
39. *See* BVFG Arts 1(1) and 1(2)(3).
40. *See also, inter alia*, Art. 25(2) of the Bulgarian Constitution for a reference to preferential treatment of ethnic Bulgarians ('Persons of Bulgarian origin acquire Bulgarian citizenship through a simplified procedure'); Arts 6(2)–6(4), 7(2)(a), and 27 of the Irish Nationality and Citizenship Act (1956 to 2001), in essence allowing for nationality through descent without limits, so long as individuals were in the Foreign Births Register; Arts 5, 6(1) and (2), 12, and 13 of the Greek Nationality Code in conjunction with Law 2130/1993 on the supporting documents required for the acquisition of Greek nationality by aliens of Greek origin; Arts 22(1), 22(2)(f), 23(b), and 24(1) of the Spanish *Código Civil: Libro 1, Título 1*; and, in Portugal, Arts 1(b), 6(1)(b), 6(2), 15, 21, and 27 of the *Lei da Nacionalidade* (as amended).
41. '*Niemand darf wegen seines Geschlechtes, seiner Abstammung, seiner Rasse, seiner Sprache, seiner Heimat und Herkunft, seines Glaubens, seiner religiösen oder politischen Anschauungen benachteiligt oder bevorzugt werden. Niemand darf wegen seiner Behinderung benachteiligt werden*'.

immigrate[42] – a series of educational, cultural, social and financial benefits, as well as special entry conditions into Germany were arranged for through bilateral treaties with numerous Central and Eastern European states in the early 1990s (and through the laws adopted giving effect to the agreements).[43] The stated aim of the German state in this context is to preserve the identities and heritage of the communities in their homelands.[44] It is worth noting that this regime has not aroused the ire of the international community in the manner of the Hungarian status law, discussed below, despite the fact that the benefits in question are comparable. The crucial difference would seem to be that the German policies are couched in bilateral agreements – unlike the initial Hungarian law – so that they are not perceived as threatening to the international system.

In further examples, pursuant to a law from 1979, individuals who have 'declared themselves part of the German or Ladin language group'[45] in the province of Bolzano, Italy, are entitled to special treatment in Austria in the areas of education and do not require a visa for their stay in the kin-state. Though the consequences of the law are today practically nil, having been surpassed by developments in the European Community,[46] this was the first legislation in Europe to grant non-nationals special status and rights in a given country on the basis of cultural/ethnic affiliation. In 1991, Greece granted special identity cards ('*homogeneis* cards') to Albanian nationals of Greek origin (and their close family) and allowed individuals with such cards to remain and work in the country without any further requirements.[47] The card is granted, in Greece, essentially on the basis of documents proving Greek descent.[48] Italy, in turn, began providing its kin-minorities

---

42. This is the case for the states of Central Europe, from which individuals acquire the right to immigrate only on a special showing of discrimination, or its after-effects, on the basis of their German identity. *See* Art. 4 of *Gesetz zur Bereinigung von Kriegsfolgengesetzen* (hereinafter, KfbG) (1992).
43. Wolff (2000); and Heintze (2000), p. 206.
44. The range and amount of the benefits involved shows considerable variation. In 1993, for example, Germany spent DM 13.4 million on community support, DM 5.2 million on social aid, DM 3.9 million on health support, DM 2.1 million on occupational support, DM 0.24 million on travel support, and approximately DM 3 million in support of the German language (through grants to educational and cultural facilities). As quoted in Vogel (2002), p. 14.
45. *See* Austria, Arts 1(1) and (2) of the *Bundesgesetz über die Gleichstellung von Südtirolern mit österreichischen Staatsbürgern auf bestimmten Verwaltungsgebieten* (1979).
46. *See also* Secs 3 and 5 of the *Verordnung des Bundesministers für Wissenschaft und Verkehr über die Festlegung von Personengruppen bei der Zulassung zu ordentlichen Studien* (1997).
47. Greece, Law 1975/1991, Art. 17. *See also Décision ministérielle commune No. 4000/3/10/e sur les conditions, la durée et la procédure d'octroi de la carte d'idntité spéciale aux ressortissants albanais d'origine grecque* (1998).
48. *Décision ministérielle commune No. 4000/3/10/e, Ibid.*
    Apparently, negotiations are underway between the two states to allow for dual nationality. In the case of Greeks from territories in the former U.S.S.R. ('Pontian Greeks') the grant of special status cards in Greece pursuant to Art. 1(11) of Law 2790/2000 (and Law 2910/2001) has already been superseded by the right of nationality. Such 'repatriating ethnic Greeks' (*palinnostountes*) are entitled to nationality on application (Citizenship Code Art. 15 (in force since November 2004)); *see also* Arts 59(1)(b) and 76(6) of Law 2910/2001.

in (then) Yugoslavia with funding for economic activities in the home-state, as well as with measures to develop contacts with their kin-state in 1991.[49] In 2001, as an extension of this law, the kin-minorities in Slovenia and Croatia were granted funding for 'measures and activities in the fields of education, culture, information, as well as up to 20 per cent of the annual budget, in the socio-economic field'.[50]

The underlying ideas of the East-Central European laws discussed here are thus not so unusual after all. In fact, we can identify four basic strategies of kinship regulation in Europe today:

(1) The German model: focused on kin-minorities; a mixture of repatriation and/or bilateral treaties (depending on home-state) providing for support and protection in a wide range of policy areas for culture, identity and heritage maintenance in the home-state;

(2) The Hungarian model: focused on kin-minorities; bilateral treaties and (sometimes unilateral) support in the areas of culture, language and education (widely interpreted) in home and kin-state, combined with high international profile and public support for minority goals in the home-state; aimed at union above borders and the preservation of minorities in the home-state;

* Austria's provisions are closest to the Hungarian model.

(3) The Russian/Romanian model: focused primarily (but not only) on kin-minorities; dual nationality provisions and benefits in kin-state; aimed at culture and identity maintenance and increased political clout in the home-state;[51]

(4) Diaspora model (Estonia, Latvia, Poland, Portugal, Ireland, Israel, Turkey): aimed at diasporas; facilitated repatriation combined with special rights (like equivalent treatment with nationals in the kin-state); often, cultural and educational support in the home-states; aimed at culture and identity maintenance.

* The policies of many developing states (most overtly Mexico, India, China, and the Philippines) can also be grouped here, although official emphasis in these contexts is often placed directly on financial benefits – e.g., remittances as a form of patriotism – rather than on the maintenance of identity highlighted in Europe.

---

49. Italy, *Legge 9 gennaio 1991, no. 19, Norme per lo sviluppo delle attività economiche e della cooperazione internazionale della regione Friuli-Venezia Giulia, della provincia di Belluno e delle aree limitrofe* (1991).
50. Italy, *Legge 8 aprile 1998, n. 89, Proroga dell'efficacia di disposizioni riguardanti il Ministero degli affari esteri* (1998) Art. 3; and *Legge 21 marzo 2001, n. 73, Interventi a favore della minoranza italiana in Slovenia e in Croazia* (2001).
51. As Flynn shows, the Russian government has increasingly removed itself from involvement in the repatriation of Russians abroad, so that no real institutional structures are in place to assist Russians migrating to Russia from the 'near-abroad'. Flynn (2003), p. 174 *et seq.*

A number of states (Slovenia, Slovakia, Italy, Croatia, Greece and Bulgaria) have mixed models, aimed at both kin-minorities and diasporas, with provisions for culture and identity maintenance that combine elements of all of the models above.

It is the policy encompassed by the Hungarian model that has proven the most controversial of the four, mainly because of its recent reliance on status laws. Such laws can be distinguished within the spectrum of kinship laws on the basis of the following shared characteristics: with regard to a constitutional clause expressing the existence of a cultural and/or ethnic nation extending beyond the given state, they grant non-nationals special treatment in the kin-state (ranging from special entry rights to cultural, educational and social benefits), usually on the basis of a special identity card; and sometimes give varied (financial, cultural, educational) support within the home-state in the name of maintaining the given collective identity.[52] As such, these laws and regulations challenge the very notion that the boundary between 'ins' and 'outs' may be determined through nationality or that the specific 'community' a given state may interact with is bounded territorially by its borders and personally by the distribution of its nationals in the world. Instead, a line is drawn between the cultural and political community, the members of which may not necessarily overlap and whose rights, stemming from the state but not restricted to its territory, may differ. But let us take a closer look at the emergence and content of the Hungarian law to get a better grasp of what we are dealing with. Having examined this particular policy, we will move on to a general discussion of the legal and political questions raised by status laws in general.

---

52. Laws that fulfil these criteria will be referred to here as 'status laws', despite considerable variation in official names and designations.
53. The Treaty of Trianon (1920) reduced Hungary's territory to one-third its pre-Treaty size; as a consequence, 33 per cent of Hungarians (about 3.3 million individuals) found themselves in the states bordering Hungary. Already at the time, nationality was a controversial question. Although Arts 63 and 64 of the Treaty allowed individuals to choose their nationality among the states that replaced the Austro-Hungarian Monarchy, choosing a state other than the state of residence meant expulsion and, in reality if not according to the Treaty, the loss of all land and immovable property. Thus, many individuals in the former Monarchy were faced with a choice between losing their possessions and choosing the nationality of the state they felt they belonged to. Only the residents of one town, Sopron (now Hungary), had the option of voting on which state to be in.

    The displacement caused by similar provisions in other Treaties required most states to enact special legal measures for the benefit of individuals who applied for nationality. In the context of Hungary, *see* discussion in Kisteleki (2000), pp. 67–70.

    The Trianon Treaty was the focus of irredentist claims by all Hungarian governments until 1945. At the end of the Second World War, through Arts 3 and 4 of the Helsinki Final Act (1975), and in all bilateral treaties with neighbouring countries since 1991, Hungary has declared the inviolability of borders.
54. To avoid confusion, the terms 'Hungarian national' or 'Hungarian minority individual' will be used when referring to the legal status of individuals; the term 'Hungarian' will be reserved to denote kinship ties. For the definition of 'nation' used, *see supra* note I.264.

B. THE HUNGARIAN STATUS LAW

While in the 1970s Hungary began, for the first time since 1945,[53] to show interest in the Hungarian minorities[54] in neighbouring countries, it was not until 1987 that the country declared that minority affairs were not the internal matters of a state.[55] By 1988, the official view stated outright that Hungarian minorities outside the borders of Hungary were considered part of the Hungarian nation, and could rightfully expect Hungary to feel responsibility for their welfare.[56] Since that time Hungary has promoted the interests of Hungarian minorities in international fora.

It has also attempted to negotiate certain minimum and mutual standards of cooperation with neighbouring states, as set out in bilateral treaties concluded with Ukraine (1991), Slovenia (1992), Croatia (1992, 1995), Slovakia (1995), Romania (1996) and (then) Serbia-Montenegro (2003). Since the mid-1990s, bilateral treaties have been increasingly well regarded internationally, as a specific and direct means to regulate possible tensions.[57] Treaties of this kind usually contain declarations of an intent to respect international norms on minority protection and thereby provide for certain widely accepted minority rights (e.g., language and education rights); they also incorporate some soft law provisions, giving them binding effect in the relations between the two countries.[58] However, bilateral treaties also have inherent drawbacks. In the first place, they tend to be framework treaties that require implementing legislation, which, in turn, can stumble on questions of interpretation and accusations of failure to respect the norms agreed to in the treaties themselves.[59] Second, given that the size of the respective kin-minorities involved often differs significantly, reciprocity is not a restraining influence. These difficulties are compounded by the fact that no legal mechanism of control is provided for; the same parties who disagree on implementation and who are meant to police it in the first place.[60] In fact, in the Hungarian context, both

---

55. This became an internationally accepted norm at the 1991 CSCE Meeting of Experts on National Minorities in Geneva. *See also* CEFCM Art. 1.
56. Arday (1990), p. 11.
57. *See* European Union, Concluding Document of the Inaugural Conference for a Pact on Stability in Europe (1994) and the Final Declaration signed by 52 States and adopted in 1995; United Nations, Resolution of the Human Rights Commission of 22 February 1995 (1995); and European Union, Stability Pact for South Eastern Europe (1999).
58. *Inter alia*, Helsinki Final Act (1975), Council of Europe, Recommendation 1201 and Document of the Copenhagen Meeting of the Conference of the Human Dimension of the CSCE (hereinafter, Copenhagen Document) (1990).
59. *See* United Nations (Gál), The Role of Bilateral Treaties in the Protection of National Minorities in Central and Eastern Europe (1998) for a discussion of such difficulties in the context of the bilateral treaties mentioned.
60. Since the treaties with Slovakia and Romania were concluded under the auspices of the Stability Pact, the possibility of turning to the International Conciliation and Arbitration Court or the OSCE High Commissioner of National Minorities in cases of disagreement does exist. (*See* Arts 15 and 16 of the Final Declaration of the Pact on Stability, respectively). These solutions have not been attempted, however. Domestic remedies also exist in theory, but are likely to stay in that realm due to political considerations.

groups within Hungary and the minorities themselves have felt that the treaties are insufficient.

It is against this background that debate on the status law unfolded.

1.   ADOPTION AND CONTENT

The possibility of a status law was first raised in 1994 by the World Federation of Hungarians (*Magyarok Világszövetsége*).[61] At the time, all moderate Hungarian parties rejected the proposal as too radical; similarly, public opinion in Hungary did not seem too keen on the idea. However, once suggested, the idea never truly disappeared. Instead, it co-existed within the minority groups with cultural and social demands, plans for various degrees of autonomy, and the possibility of dual nationality.[62] In contrast, successive Hungarian governments considered some form of status law a possible way out of granting dual nationality, and a means of stemming the flow of Hungarian minority individuals into Hungary.[63] The crucial step occurred in 1999, with the Closing Document of the Second Meeting of the Hungarian Standing Conference (MÁÉRT),[64] which requested the government to examine the 'possibility of regulating the issue of Hungarian

---

61. This organization, founded in 1938, was meant to serve as a forum allowing Hungarians from around the world to share their views on social, political and cultural issues; in fact, meetings have often been controversial, with radical nationalist overtones. Incidentally, the Federation moved on to demanding dual nationality by 1997. In this demand, it came late, since the possibility had been raised in December 1992 by individuals close to the government, and quickly discarded.
62. For example, in a survey conducted in Slovakia, Serbia, Romania, and Ukraine in early 1999, between 59 per cent (Slovakia) and 83 per cent (Ukraine) of those questioned supported dual nationality. HVG, *Remények és Igények* (14 August 1999).
63. According to some estimates, half a million Hungarian minority individuals left their homelands in the last 13 years; some emigrated to Western Europe or the United States, others to Hungary. Between 1993 and 2002, 54,100 Romanian, 12,149 Yugoslav, 962 Slovak and 6,950 (formerly-) Ukrainian nationals received Hungarian nationality. Others have applied for residence permits. In 2002 alone, 6,093 requests were received from Romania, 1,577 from the former Yugoslavia, 388 from the Ukraine. In that year, an additional 37,996 Romanian nationals already possessed residence permits. The numbers add up to over 120,000 individuals and do not include the large-scale immigration directly after 1989, nor a number of other groups. This despite the outlay of HUF 49,130,000,000 (or approximately EUR 230 million) to support the Hungarian minorities in neighbouring states between 1992 and 2003. The trend of emigration does not seem to have changed as a result of the status law. See Népszabadság (József Szabó), *Átjönni, elmenni vagy maradni?* (30 October 2003).
64. This consultative organization, founded in 1999, consisted of the elected representatives of Hungarian minorities in neighbouring countries, the members of parties represented in the Hungarian parliament, the government, as well as individuals from Western Hungarian diasporas. It was generally regarded as an official forum in which to discuss political issues concerning the 'Hungarian nation' and was influential in matters of policy.

It was replaced in 2006 by the Hungarian-Hungarian Government Consultation (MKK), consisting of members of the government and an expanded array of minority organizations and diaspora representatives.

minorities living abroad by law'. Behind the request was a widespread and growing fear that with Hungary's entrance into the EU (and the Schengen zone), the Hungarian minorities would be cut off from Hungary.[65]

Finally, after years of lingering on the outskirts of Hungarian minority politics, the status law made a grand entrance under the Orbán government. In 2000, in a matter of months, a draft law was prepared by the Hungarian Standing Conference, in co-operation with expert committees and various government offices. After further discussion at MÁÉRT's third meeting, this draft was presented to parliament in April 2001. Despite the fact that the Conference – formed mainly of non-nationals – had significant input in the law,[66] officially it was a government (and Parliament) product. On 19 June, the *2001. évi LXII. törvény a szomszédos államokban élő magyarokról* (Law LXII of 2001 Concerning the Hungarians Living in Neighbouring States) (hereinafter, SL or 'Act') was passed by 92.4 per cent of the votes cast in Parliament.

Two particular legal bases were relied on in drafting and enacting the status law. As declared in the Preamble of the Act, its framers looked in the first place to Article 6(3) of the Hungarian Constitution, which states that Hungary feels responsible for Hungarian minorities and 'shall promote and foster their relations with Hungary'. This last section is what was pointed to as proof that active support for the preservation of the minorities' Hungarian identity, and hence the status law, was constitutionally required. However, as Veress discusses, it is unclear how 'from the point of view of constitutional law, a feeling of responsibility and an assumption of responsibility relate to each other'.[67] In other words, there was (and has been) no discussion of what the legal implications of 'responsibility' should be in the context of international law. As discussed, a number of states in the region have comparable 'responsibility' clauses and have interpreted these clauses to buttress kinship laws – but this logic is far from obvious.

---

65. *See*, e.g., MÁÉRT 1999 and MÁÉRT 2000. Pursuant to *2001. évi XXXIX. törvény a külföldiek beutazásáról és tartózkodásáról* (Law XXXIX of 2001 on the Entry and Stay of Foreigners), Schengen visa restrictions have been extended to Hungary. Accordingly, the existing framework of visa waiver- (*vízummentességi-*) and small-border agreements (*kishatár-egyezmények*) left over from socialist times required an overhaul. Furthermore, as per Council Regulation 539/2001/EC of 15 March 2001 listing the third countries whose nationals must be in possession of visas when crossing the external borders and those whose nationals are exempt from that requirement, nationals of the Ukraine and (now) Serbia require visas to enter Hungary; but *see* discussion in Sec. III.C.2.b.

    As Gyertyánfy discusses, there are loopholes in the Schengen system: a number of old Member States, including Greece (for its kin-minority in Albania) and Spain (for Sephardic Jewish individuals) distinguish among non-nationals in the context of entry rights (and attendant rights to remain and work) on the basis of ethnic criteria; others, such as Portugal, make such distinctions using cultural criteria (for individuals from Portuguese-speaking countries). *See* Gyertyánfy (2002), pp. 126–127.
66. The Act itself refers to the role of the Standing Conference in the Preamble.
67. Veress (2002), p. 127 (*'alkotmányjogi szempontból miként viszonyul egymáshoz a felelősségérzet és a felelősségvállalás'*). *See* also Beszélő (János Kis) (2002/3), *Státustörvény: Magyarország válaszúton*.

Even if the logic behind the law was similar to that found elsewhere, however, the rights contained in the Hungarian status law were, in their entirety, more encompassing than those provided by other countries to their kin-minorities. While all existing status laws create rights for individuals on the basis of kinship ties formulated in various ways – some of which amount to less-than citizenship rights in the territory of the kin-state – they differ considerably in other respects. In particular, other status laws (Slovak, Romanian) do not limit their legislation to only certain countries/areas (in contrast to Hungary, but also Italy and Slovenia); also, the institutional requirements of the other status laws mean that individuals deal only with organizations in the kin-state (in contrast to Hungary, but also Greece until recently) and gain benefits only in the kin-state (again, in contrast to Hungary, as well as Romania); finally, there is no requirement in other status laws that individuals stay resident in their home-states.

In addition, Hungary also pointed to international norms granting minorities the right to interaction with kin groups (including in the bilateral treaties with neighbouring countries) to justify the status law.[68] In fact, the Preamble and Article 2(2) of the law specifically state that it conforms to, and is to be applied consistently with, Hungary's obligations as spelled out in international agreements.[69] This was not exactly the case, however.

The stated goal of the law – as opposed to the unstated aims already discussed – was simultaneously cultural, political and economic: cultural/political, in that it aimed to ensure the coherence of the 'Hungarian nation as a whole' in allowing minorities to preserve their 'awareness of national identity within their home country'[70] through the maintenance of 'permanent contacts',[71] including 'undisturbed cultural, economic, and family relations' and the 'free flow of ideas';[72] economic, in that it attempted to give tangible benefits to minority individuals.[73] Considering that the legislation was proclaimed an instrument of minority-protection, it is worth noting that the word 'minority' appears only once in the text, in the context of a reference to principles of minority-protection.[74] Instead, mention is made of 'Hungarians beyond the border' (*határon túli magyarok*), individuals 'of Hungarian kinship' (*magyar nemzetiség*), as well as the 'Hungarian national community' (*magyar nemzeti közösség*). In other words, while the

---

68. *See, inter alia*, UNDRM Art. 2; and Art. 17 of the Framework Convention.
69. *See also* the Statements issued by (then) Foreign Minister János Martonyi on 20 June 2001 and 22 June 2001.
70. SL Preamble. (All citations of the (original and revised) Act are to the official English Translation.)
71. *Ibid.*, Art. 3(a).
72. Art. 3(c) and 3(d).
73. I thus disagree with Stewart's threefold distinction between political, cultural and economic goals. *See* Stewart (2002), p. 14. Although Hungarian nationalism has in recent years been cultural, the aim of preserving the cultural identity of the minorities, as an element of the unification of the Hungarian nation, took on a clear political hue in the language of the law (*see* Preamble); also, culture cannot be de-linked from Hungarian politics in the context of minority questions. *See* Horváth (2000), p. 13 *et seq.*
74. SL Rec. 2.

legislation was clearly aimed at Hungarian minority individuals, this factor of their situation was not even addressed in it; in essence, the law attempted to remove a crucial element of reality from consideration, while claiming to remedy it.

The cultural/political goal of the Act was clearly given form in the provision allowing for Hungarian minority scientists to become members of the Hungarian Academy of Sciences[75] and declaring them eligible to receive distinctions from the Republic of Hungary, as well as prizes, titles and honorary diplomas.[76] In effect, the cultural ties of individuals were given political form here through state honours. The provisions on education were more practical in nature. In Hungary, Hungarian minority individuals were (and are) entitled to the same opportunities for post-secondary education as Hungarian nationals, and, along with any individual studying in Hungarian in the home-states, received the same student discounts.[77] Entry into public cultural institutions (including museums and monuments) was (and is) also ensured on an equal basis to that of Hungarian nationals,[78] while entry and use of public libraries was (and remains) free of charge,[79] something not available to all Hungarian nationals.

The Act also included support for public service media to 'transmit information' that would enhance the 'preservation of cultural identity', spread 'Hungarian and universal spiritual and cultural values' and help form 'an unbiased picture of the world, of Hungary and of the Hungarian nation'.[80] Organizations with goals ranging from cultural and educational development, through the restoration of 'monuments belonging to the Hungarian cultural heritage', to 'the establishment and improvement of conditions of infrastructure for maintaining contacts with … Hungary' were also eligible for funding.[81]

In a more economic vein, Hungarian minority individuals had the right to work for three months of the year in Hungary,[82] during which time they were to pay taxes, health insurance and pension contributions according to the social security legislation in Hungary; in return, they received benefits equivalent to other workers.[83] In some areas, such as long-distance public transport, Hungarian minority individuals got (and still get) more benefits than most nationals did (do): e.g., 90 per cent discounts.[84]

In addition to the benefits available in Hungary, the Act also provided for grants in the home-states to ensure the 'preservation of the mother tongue, culture and national identity' of Hungarian minorities.[85] These grants included financial

---

75. *Ibid.*, Art. 5.
76. Art. 6.
77. Arts 9 and 10.
78. Art. 4(1).
79. Art. 4(2).
80. SL Art. 17.
81. *Ibid.*, Art. 18(2)(a) through 18(2)(f).
82. Art. 17.
83. Art. 7(1).
84. Art. 8.
85. Art. 13.

aid to Hungarian language institutions; funds for the creation of home-state affiliates of universities in Hungary;[86] as well as stipends for individual teachers (for training in Hungary)[87] and 'educational' and 'school supplies' assistance to parents who sent their children to Hungarian-language schools.[88] (For some reason – possibly as some wacky attempt at influencing birth-rates or on the assumption that one-child families could already afford Hungarian language schooling – this provision only applied to two-child households). Requests for all such grants could be made at 'foreign public benefit organizations' operating in the host countries,[89] although applications were evaluated in Hungary.

The relevant benefits and grants accrued to individuals only if they had the requisite 'Hungarian Certificate' from a central public administrative body in Hungary. Individuals 'declaring themselves to be of Hungarian [kinship]'[90] were eligible for the Certificates if they:

(1) were not Hungarian nationals and did not possess a resident card in Hungary;
(2) had lost their Hungarian nationality other than by renunciation;[91]
(3) resided in one of the named states (all surrounding states except Austria); and
(4) had a clean criminal record in Hungary, and were not on the list of individuals prohibited from entering or staying in Hungary, nor on the list to be expelled from its territory.

An administrative body in Hungary issued the Certificate automatically upon recommendation from a minority 'evaluating authority', including Hungarian minority churches and parties.[92] In turn, recommendations were made by such organizations upon individual application. Thus, the criteria determining who was to get the Certificate were, to a large extent, based on the principle of self-identification, i.e., on the principle that the state had no role in questioning an individual's claim to a particular identity.[93] Still, a determination of belonging included intangibles; since the minority evaluating organizations were meant to, in

---

86. *Ibid.*
87. Arts 11 and 12.
88. Art. 14.
89. Art. 25(1).
90. Art. 1(1). In the English version of the text, 'nationality' is used here, in the sense of membership in an ethno-cultural community; in the English text after the 2003 revision 'ethnic origin' is utilized. In the Hungarian original, the word used in both versions is *'nemzetiség'*.
91. The implied reference here was to individuals who had surrendered their Hungarian nationality as a result of the Trianon Treaty, although the legislator neglected to include mention of their descendants. The 2003 revision of the Act added the missing language and also made reference to the *Csángó*, who have never been Hungarian nationals but many of whom speak a medieval dialect of Hungarian.
92. Arts 19 and 20.
93. However, an individual could still institute proceedings in a court in Hungary to contest the denial or withdrawal of a Certificate (Art. 22(2)).

effect, verify that the individual was, as she claimed, Hungarian. The decision on who belonged was thereby transferred to the community itself, but without any objective criteria.

In addition, the close family members of individuals could apply for a 'Dependant Certificate' if they:

(1) met the requirements above, regardless of kinship (i.e., the individual did not need to be Hungarian) and;
(2) were the spouse or child of a 'Hungarian Certificate' holder, living in the same household.

An individual with a Dependant Certificate was entitled to the same rights as the Hungarian Certificate holder. Though this provision was meant to be a sign of support for family unity, it was greeted by Slovakia and Romania as a tool of creeping 'Hungarian assimilation' and was later explicitly prohibited in the Agreement with Romania allowing for implementation of the (revised) Act. The fact that both the Hungarian and the Dependant Certificates included (and continue to include) a photo and personal information and, not coincidentally, resemble Hungarian passports, likely did not help the evident dismay of some of the home-states.

A few remarks about the most unusual features of the criteria for eligibility – namely, the importance of self-identification, the role of the recommending authorities and the absence of Austria among the countries listed – are worth making here. The prominence of self-identification can be explained by the nature of Hungarian nationalism as a sociological process. Before 1920, two strains, one of civic, the other of cultural nationalism, co-existed in historic Hungary. The Trianon Treaty led to a prolonged crisis of identity in both Hungary and the newly created minority groups; but today the minorities clearly see 'Hungarianness' in cultural terms,[94] while within Hungary, the two types of nationalism continue to co-exist. In a number of surveys both within Hungary and among the minorities, speaking the language, knowing Hungarian culture, 'feeling' Hungarian, and 'being born' Hungarian (identified as such by self and others) have been the main factors determining Hungarianness.[95] This situation is further complicated by the fact that – despite some populist attempts to make it seem otherwise – there is no unified Hungarian identity; instead, it is a conglomeration of regional and other identities. One can be Transylvanian-Hungarian (*erdélyi magyar*), Jewish-Hungarian or

---

94. *See* Culic (2001), p. 237 and pp. 238–240.
95. This is not to say that there are no ethnic tensions among Hungarian nationals or within Hungarian minority communities. The Roma, for example, while nationals of Hungary and (mostly) native speakers of the language, are consistently considered less Hungarian than integrated (or assimilated) non-Roma (e.g., Germans, Greeks, etc.). Also, Hungarian-speaking Roma outside the country are often not considered Hungarian minority individuals, because they are seen as too culturally dissimilar to Hungarians. It is this same cultural distance, significant economic and educational disadvantages, as well as racism that make Roma distinct among Hungarian nationals. *See* discussion in Horváth (200), p. 19 *et seq.*

returned *émigré* Hungarian, depending on the situation.[96] In light of this reality, the Act's requirement of self-identification was consistent with contemporary Hungarian nationalism, and incidentally mirrored the minority legislation in force in Hungary at the time.[97]

With regard to the function of the recommending authorities, despite the fact that the procedure was ultimately short-lived, the relaying of applications through a Hungarian minority organization, and especially the absence of any objective criteria, raised all kinds of uncomfortable possibilities. How would such a Hungarianness-examining panel function? What if the applicant was an atheist and ignored politics? Who would vouch for her Hungarian identity? Who had the right to even judge the claimed identity? One possibility with echoes of the past:

> The president of the tribunal glances glumly at her assessors – the decision is difficult. The written exam has proven successful, but the environmental-survey reveals that the ratio of those representing the majority nation in the social circle of the candidate is higher than expected. Moreover, he does not intend to send his kindergarten-age child to a Hungarian school in three years time. The tribunal finally determines that it cannot grant the recommendation necessary for the candidate to obtain the special license.[98]

In a related question, what if the individual – found Hungarian enough – were more interested in moving to Hungary than in receiving support for staying in her home-state? The granting of the Hungarian Certificate was (and is) closely linked to a showing – or at least an affirmation – that the individual does not wish to settle in Hungary (or presumably elsewhere than her home-state), since one of the stated aims of the law was (and continues to be) to help the minorities stay 'within their home country'.[99] But why? Is the aim of the law only to maintain Hungarian populations in areas that were once Hungary (a kind of reverse-*Lebensraum* theory)[100] or primarily the enhancement of individual welfare? The two are

---

96. However, in all these cases one assumedly speaks Hungarian, knows and appreciates Hungarian culture and history, feels Hungarian and (admittedly to various extents) is seen as Hungarian by other Hungarians. *See* Fox (2003) for an analysis of developing differentiation within the cultural nation. But *see* Sata (2001) for a discussion of such differentiation in the 1920s.
97. *See* Art. 1(1) of *1993. évi LXXVII. törvény a nemzeti és etnikai kisebbségek jogairól* (Law LXXVII of 1993 on the rights of national and ethnic minorities); also, *inter alia*, ÉS (Erika Törzsök), 'Státus' (17 March 2000); and Magyar Hírlap (Ottó Neumann), *Ki a magyar és mennyit ér ha az?* (18 January 2000).
98. 'Komoran tekint ülnökeire az itélőszéki elnök – nehéz a döntés. Az írásbeli nyelvvizsga sikeresnek bizonyult, ám a környezettanulmányból kiderül, hogy a jelölt baráti körében a többségi nemzetet képviselők aránya az elvártnál magasabb mértékű. Sőt, óvodás gyermekét három év múlva nem magyar iskolába készül beíratni. Az itélőszék végül úgy határoz, hogy nem adhatja meg az ajánlást, amely a különleges igazolvány megszerzéséhez kellene a jelöltnek'. Magyar Hírlap (Ottó Neumann), *Magyarságot igazoló hivatal* (11 July 2000).
99. *See* the Preambles of both versions of the Act.
100. *See also* Borbély (2000), p. 34, who seems to suggest some legal reconstruction of historical Hungary in speaking of legislation supplemental to the status law: a 'separate law that would deal with the status of the non-Hungarian population living in the territory of historical

obviously linked – the former has a lot to do with some elements of the latter, for example – but the place of emphasis makes a significant difference. If the latter – and this is the only acceptable answer – then it is unclear whether the law can help overcome the manifold challenges of being a minority in the region. In fact, whether the Act achieves its aim or, conversely, makes immigration to Hungary more likely, has been a matter of some debate.[101]

As to the absence of Austria among the states of application, there are two explanations. On the one hand, it has been claimed that, since 1989, Hungary has consistently treated Hungarians from Western Europe and the rest of the world as a distinct category, separate from the minorities in countries that were once part of historic Hungary; this is in fact true.[102] However, the decision not to include Austria likely had more to do with the European Union than with continuing differentiated treatment of kin-minorities; in short, it was suspected that the law would be unacceptable within the Union, given ECT Article 12.[103] By not including Austria, the drafters of the law likely hoped to escape scrutiny by Union officials – unsuccessfully, as we will see.

2. REACTIONS AND COUNTER-REACTIONS

Once Parliament passed the status law, reactions from all corners were immediate.[104] Domestically, the law was met mainly with perplexity. In the first place,

---

Hungary. This could state that the non-Hungarian population born and living within the Hungarian boundaries [established by] the 1867 Agreement enjoys a special status in Hungary, separate from the other peoples of the world'. (*'külön törvény, amely ... a történelmi Magyarország területén élő nem-magyar lakosság magyarországi státusával foglalkozna. Ez kimondhatná, hogy ... a kiegyezés (1867) utáni magyar határokon belül született és elő, nem-magyar lakosság, Magyarországon külön státust élvez, a földkerekség egyébb népeivel szemben'*).

101. See Csaba Tabajdi and István Szent-Iványi's comments in Népszabadság, *Az ellenzéki pártok a bizottságokban bírálják a kormány tervezetét* (12 April 2001); Romániai Magyar Szó (Attila Varga), *Státustörvény vagy vándorbot* (16, 17, and 18 May 2001); and Korhecz (2000). *See also* Dobos and Apró (2000), p. 40 for a 1999 poll showing that a (then planned) status law would reduce the per centage of those planning to emigrate.
102. This differentiation is due both to the different histories of the two groups and to the fact that individuals from the diaspora (as the 'Western Hungarians' are generally called), or at least their ancestors, gave up their Hungarian citizenship voluntarily. Accordingly, different rules apply to the two groups with respect to naturalisation. *See* Arts 4(3), 5, and 5/A of the *1993. évi LV. törvény a magyar állampolgárságról* (Law LV of 1993 on Hungarian Nationality). This also serves to explain why Hungarian governments have seen the status law as an alternative to dual nationality. *See also* Liebich (2000) for a survey of nationality laws in the region as they relate to the question of plural nationality and a general discussion in Sec. V.A.
103. Art. 27(2) of the Act even stipulates that its provisions shall be applied in accordance with EU law.
104. As Weber discusses, this may not be a coincidence. Though many of the benefits contained in the law could have been guaranteed through other channels, the message of the law to the minorities, their home-states, Hungarian nationals and possibly the international community, would not have been as clear. *See* Weber (2002a).

assessments by scholars were mixed. Certainly it was a framework,[105] so that much of the real regulation was to be completed through secondary legislation. But was it only an attempt at co-ordinating the over 150 existing laws that referred to Hungarian minorities[106] or a means to create something radically new?[107] Was the Act here to stay or were there so many legal problems – sloppy language,[108] possible violation of (definitions used in) existing laws and the Constitution,[109] reversal of the legal hierarchy of laws and regulations – that it would soon need to be revised?[110] Legal matters aside, in contrast to the (seemingly) overwhelming consensus among political actors, the Hungarian public was less than enthusiastic; in a poll from February 2002, only 33 per cent agreed that the law was necessary.[111] Media in Hungary, in turn, raised additional issues, including the cost of the undertaking, the claimed 'real' motivation behind the law, and its effect on minorities in Hungary with respect to their feeling of acceptance.[112]

As for those targeted by the law, responses varied considerably. Some minority individuals argued that it did not go far enough, or that it was an attempt to appropriate their decision of whether to remain in or leave their home-states.[113] Others noted that the idea of needing a license (and a recommendation from either the church or Hungarian minority parties) to prove their identity as Hungarians was

---

105. *See* SL Arts 8(4), 10(2), 11(3), 12(3), 15, 16(2), 22(3), 28, and 29.
106. Kántor (2002); Majtényi (2002); and Tóth (1999). *See also* Bárdi (2003) for an excellent overview of the actual (financial and other) support policies in place; as well as the Document on the 2002/2003–2004 budget of Hungary, pp. 80–82 of the same journal.
107. Kántor, *ibid.*; Kis in Beszélő, *supra* note III.67.
108. Majtényi (2002); and Küpper (2001), p. 420.
109. Majtényi, *ibid.*; Kis in Beszélő *supra* note III.67.
110. ÉS (Boldizsár Nagy), *A szándék-buborék* (25 January 2002).
111. *See,* Magyar Hírlap, *Csak az emberek egyharmada helyesli a státustörvényt és kedvezményeit* (29 July 2002). It is interesting to note that this poll was only released publicly in July 2002, five months after it was taken. In August 2000, however, 60.7 per cent of those polled had supported some kind of law granting preferential treatment to Hungarian minorities. Dobos and Apró (2000), p. 30. In an April 2001 poll, 61 per cent of those asked agreed with such a law, while here was near-unanimity on cultural and educational benefits in the home-states. *See* Editors (2001), pp. 100–101. The precipitous drop in support can likely be explained by the actual provisions of the law, as well as the acrimonious debates that surrounded it.
112. Some authors (*inter alia*) Szabadság (Zoltán Tibori Szabó), *Státus – egy magyarországi választási kampánytól a másikig* (24 April 2001); Mozgó Világ (Judit Tóth), *Státusmagyarság* (April 2001); Magyar Narancs (Mihály Dobrovits), *Létszámellenőrzés a magyarelosztóban: státustörvény és nemzeteszme* (4 January 2001) argued that the status law was in fact an issue of internal politics in Hungary. *See also* Kis in Beszélő, *supra* note III.67, for an argument that the law was a showdown between liberal and nationalist traditions. For other issues raised, *see* Népszabadság (Tamás Bauer), *A hazátlanság tartósítása* (10 January 2001); Szabadság (Tamás Gáspár Miklós), *A magyar külpolitika csődje* (30 June 2001); and Magyar Hírlap (Rudolf Ungváry), *A státustörvény homálya* (8 February 2001). It is worth noting, however, that there were no claims of lack of accountability – considering that individuals not elected by Hungarian nationals had such a significant role in drafting the law, this would not have been an unfair charge.
113. Beszélő (Zoltán Surányi), *Ki a magyar most?* (2001/5); and *ibid.* (Zoltán Tibori Szabó), *Státuskampány* (2001/5).

offensive.[114] Still others saw the law as an attempt to usurp the idea of the 'Hungarian nation' in the name of a particular political agenda – and thus a possible source of division within the minorities.[115]

The law's symbolic significance was for the most part welcomed, however. Many individuals viewed it as recognition of their sense of belonging.[116] The hoped-for effect of silencing discussion on dual nationality did not materialize, however, as controversies around the status law drew more attention to the possibility and led to heated discussion of its perceived advantages.[117] In particular, the World Federation of Hungarians began a campaign in August 2003 for a referendum on the question of whether individuals who can certify their Hungarian kinship in the proper manner (i.e., through Hungarian Certificates) should be entitled to Hungarian nationality through privileged naturalization.[118] As we will discuss below, the campaign eventually proved successful and a referendum was held.

With regard to the number of actual applications for Hungarian Certificates, as of October 2004, over 820,000 Certificates had been issued.[119] The rate of application fluctuated significantly: in Romania, for example, slightly over 20 per cent of the Hungarian minority had applied by September 2002;[120] by March 2005, 500,185 (or about 35 per cent of the population) had picked up a Certificate, in addition to nearly 40,000 student cards and 8,000 teacher cards.[121] The initial rush

---

114. See Magyar Hírlap (Éva Máthé), Ki a magyar? (27 December 2000).
115. Magyar Narancs (Mihály Dobrovits), Magyarfelvétel igényeseknek: Státustörvény és nemzetkép (10 January 2002); and ÉS (Nándor László Magyari), Státusmagyarkodók (1 March 2002).
116. See MÁÉRT (2002a); MÁÉRT (2001b); and ÉS (Sándor N. Szilágyi), Módosító javaslat a státustörvényhez (23 November 2001); but see Magyari in ÉS, ibid. See also the study done by the Inter-Ethnic Research Center of Babes-Bolyai University. To the question, 'why did you get the Hungarian Certificate?', 23.2 per cent answered, 'all Hungarians need to have them', 19.3 per cent stated, 'it is proof of belonging to the Hungarian nation', 19.3 per cent stated, 'it may be of use in the future', 13.7 per cent answered, 'because in it it is written: I am Hungarian'. See Népszabadság, Erdélyi magyarság: önkép és gyorsfénykép (22 January 2004).
117. See, e.g., Borbély (2000); Kovács (2000), p. 69 et seq.; Duna TV, Heti Hírmondó, Stúdóbeszélgetés a kettős állampolgárság kérdéséről (3 August 2003); Népszabadság, Állampolgárság: nincs kivétel (19 December 2003); Népszabadság, Vajdasági lapnak nyilatkozott Kovács a kettős állampolgárságról (9 March 2004).
118. See also 168 Óra (Endre Barcs), Ki lehet magyar? (14 August 2003); Népszabadság, Határon túli dilemmák (6 December 2003) for discussions of the views of some Hungarian minority parties.
119. 58.6 per cent of these had been issued to individuals in Romania; 11.7 per cent in Slovakia; 13.7 per cent in Serbia, 15 per cent in Ukraine, and 1 per cent in Croatia and Slovenia. Table prepared by László Szarka for The Status Law Syndrome: Post-Communist Nation-Building or Post-Modern Citizenship? Conference in Budapest (14–16 October 2004).
120. See Népszabadság, A jogosultak ötöde igényelt magyarigazolványt (24 September 2002). Administrative offices in Hungary initially had to be expanded to deal with the high number of applications; 70,000 Certificates had been issued as of August 1. Magyar Hírlap, Hetvenezer kiállított, de fel nem vett magyarigazolvány várja gazdáját (1 August 2002).
121. Népszabadság, Ötszázezernél többen kértek Romániában magyarigazolványt (14 March 2005).

has thus been replaced by a steady, significantly lower rate of application. As of 31 March 2007, 885,587 Certificates had been granted.[122]

As Stewart discusses, initially it was mainly intellectuals, certain groups of young people, the poor and the elderly who applied; many were deterred for fear of losing the possibility of continuing to work illegally in Hungary for periods longer than three months.[123] The growing furor around the Certificates in certain home-states surely also played a role in dampening interest. Moreover, when the amendments introduced in 2003 disconnected most benefits from possession of the Certificate, the actual practicality of the documents became nil. In this context, the relatively high ratio of holders – of the 2.7 million estimated Hungarian minority individuals in the Carpathian basin, every third has one – is rather surprising and is, in any case, a clear sign that Hungary is a significant focal point for minority individuals.

International reactions were also quick to appear. The Council of Europe rapporteur called for delaying implementation (scheduled for 1 January 2002) pending the completion of his report.[124] The Act also caught the attention of the OSCE High Commissioner for Minorities – who was no fan – as well as the European Union, which seemed puzzled.[125] Meanwhile, a significant share of international media attention was negative.[126] Some neighbouring countries, in turn, lost no time in condemning the law outright.[127] Their main points of criticism were that:

(1) Existing bi-lateral cooperation agreements had not been utilized.
(2) The concept of 'nation' in the preamble of the law was too broad.
(3) The fact that only Hungarians in neighbouring states were eligible suggested underlying motives of territorial aggrandizement by the kin-state.
(4) Spouses and children of members of the kin-minority who were not of Hungarian kinship were included.
(5) Privileges in the social and economic field (especially work permits and social security benefits) within Hungary were discriminatory toward the majority populations of home-states.

---

122. Népszabadság, *Módosul a státustörvény* (9 May 2007).
123. *See* Stewart (2002), pp. 20–24.
124. BBC Monitoring, 'Hungary rejects European rapporteur's request to delay status law introduction' (1 November 2001). The report was eventually presented to the Parliamentary Assembly in May 2003.
125. *See* Statement issued by Rolf Ekeus, OSCE High Commissioner on National Minorities (26 October 2001); and European Parliament, Resolution of 5 September 2001.
126. *See, inter alia*, The Economist, 'Ethnic Pitch' (7 April 2001).
127. *See* Declaration of the Government of Romania with regard to the adoption of the Law concerning the Hungarians living in Neighbouring Countries (2001); and Official Position of the Romanian Government on the Law on Hungarians Living in Neighbouring Countries, submitted to the Venice Commission (2001). In the media, *see*, BBC Monitoring, 'Slovak, Romanian Speakers concerned over Hungary's status law' (9 October 2001); BBC Monitoring, 'Romania to continue drive against disputed Hungarian law' (23 October 2001); *The New York Times*, 'Hungary's Neighbors See Bias in a Law to Aid its Diaspora' (11 December 2001).

(6) Kin-minority organizations were involved in the procedure for granting the Certificates, giving an unacceptable extra-territorial element to the law.[128]

As the Council of Europe noted, however, the main objection of relevant home-states concerned the unilateral nature of the law.[129] In other words, the lack of consultation with governments in neighbouring countries during drafting played an important role in negative international reactions. Given the significant input of minority organizations in its preparation, the lack of effort in seeking home-country input was all the more striking.[130] In fact, Romania (later joined by Slovakia and Serbia) turned to the Venice Commission to examine whether the Act was compatible with 'European standards and the norms and principles of contemporary public international law'.

a. **The Venice Commission**

The report of the Venice Commission stands out from other reactions, since it is the most thorough overview of the legal issues raised not only by the Hungarian law, but by all status laws with respect to principles of international law. In essence, the Commission concluded that states may enact unilateral policies with regard to the protection of their kin-minorities only on condition that any such measure respects the principles of:

(1) *pacta sunt servanda*;
(2) friendly relations amongst states;
(3) the territorial sovereignty of the host state; and
(4) respect for human rights, especially as regards the prohibition of discrimination.

While the principles set out by the Commission validated the opinion that a state's interest in its kin-minorities may extend to legal action, when applied to the Hungarian status law they also suggested that many of the provisions of the law were objectionable.[131] So let us take a look at the Venice Commission's report with the terms of the Hungarian law in mind.

---

128. Para. 15 of Council of Europe, Parliamentary Assembly Committee on Legal Affairs and Human Rights, Report on Preferential Treatment of National Minorities by the Kin-State: the Case of the Hungarian Law of 19 June 2001 on Hungarians Living in Neighbouring Countries ('Magyars') (2003) (hereinafter, CoE Report on the Hungarian law).
129. *Ibid.*, Sec. II.C.a. *See also* para. 11 of Council of Europe Parliamentary Resolution 1335 on the Preferential treatment of national minorities by the kin-state: the case of the Hungarian Law on Hungarians Living in Neighbouring Countries ('Magyars') (2003).
130. In fact, the lack of consultation likely had alot to do with domestic considerations – the Orbán government had considered the law an internal matter and had made its passage (as early before the elections as possible) a matter of prestige.
131. This is also true for provisions in other status laws. However, given that the report was, in large part, prompted by reactions to the Hungarian status law, the opinion of the Venice Commission will be discussed primarily with regard to Hungary.

i.   Pacta Sunt Servanda

Article 26 of the Vienna Convention on the Law of Treaties (1969) codifies the well-established customary rule that treaties must be respected and performed in good faith (*pacta sunt servanda*). The Commission found that with regard to bilateral (minority) treaties, states have a duty to pursue bilateral talks before any modification of the rights granted to the respective minorities of either state. Further, if there are difficulties in holding negotiations, a state may not act unilaterally before exhausting all possible procedures for settling the dispute.

Hungary thus violated its treaty obligations when it did not involve any of the neighbouring states in the preparatory work of the status law, since much of the subject matter was arguably pre-empted by the bilateral treaties in force between Hungary and the respective states.[132] The Commission went no further in its analysis of this point; in particular, it did not go on to consider exactly who was involved in drafting the particular law, although this was one of the novelties of the legislation. As noted above, the Hungarian state and the Standing Conference of Hungarians, which included representatives of the minorities themselves, worked together to draw up the status law. Preparatory work thus involved a group not usually granted legal status to negotiate internationally; as we will see, this has important implications.

ii.   Friendly Relations

The principle of friendly neighbourly relations is recognized in both the bilateral treaties concluded between Hungary and the neighbouring countries, and in Article 2 of the Framework Convention, of which all the countries in question are signatories. The Commission found that unilateral measures have the potential of endangering such good relations. In particular, it focused on the documents used to identify individuals as a sensitive point of status laws in the region, including

---

132. *See* Secs 6, 16 and 17 of the Declaration on the principles of co-operation between the Republic of Hungary and the Ukrainian Soviet Socialist Republic in guaranteeing the rights of national minorities (1991) (later joined by Croatia and Slovenia); Secs 8 and 21 of the Convention on good-neighborliness and the bases of co-operation between the Republic of Hungary and Ukraine (1991); Art. 15 of the Convention on providing special rights for the Slovenian minority living in the Republic of Hungary and for the Hungarian minority living in the Republic of Slovenia (1992); Arts 7 and 21 of the Convention on friendship and co-operation between the Republic of Hungary and the Republic of Slovenia (1992); Arts 8 and 22 of the Convention between the Republic of Hungary and the Republic of Croatia on friendly relations and co-operation (1992); Art. 16 of the Convention between the Republic of Hungary and the Republic of Croatia on the protection of the Hungarian minority in the republic of Croatia and the Croatian minority in the Republic of Hungary (1995); Arts 5(1), 5(3), 15(6), and 21 of the Treaty on Good-neighbourly Relations and Friendly Co-operation between the Republic of Hungary and the Slovak Republic (1995); and Arts 5(1), 5(3), 15(10), and 21(1) of the Treaty between the Republic of Hungary and Romania on Understanding, Co-operation and Good Neighborhood (1996).

the Hungarian one. An ID of this kind, with personal data and a photograph, 'creates [in the Commission's opinion] a political bond between these foreigners and their kin-state' and may be used for the purposes of identification even in home-states. To prevent this practice, the Commission advises that such documents include only the information necessary to prove entitlement.

It is difficult to square the Commission's concern here with the specific implications of unilateral action with its recognition of a possible kin-state role in support of minorities when, as in the case of cultural nationalism, identity in the cultural sense is entwined with the trans-national political strategies that emanate from states.[133] Can a 'climate of co-operation',[134] for example, really be considered to exist when a home-state refuses to negotiate about a matter a kin-state believes or knows is crucial to a kin-minority? It would seem that unilateral non-action is acceptable in this context, in light of the international standard by which home-states have the primary – some would say near-exclusive – responsibility for the minorities resident in their territory.[135] Regardless of how one views this standard, it should nevertheless be recognized that non-action by the home-state can be as damaging to friendly relations as unilateral measures taken by the kin-state. In any case, given the sensitive nature of this issue, some clarification by the Commission of the duties of both kin-state and home-state would have been welcome. However, the Venice Report does not include mention of even Article 18(1) of the Framework Convention[136] in this regard – although it can be considered on point especially in conjunction with Article 17(1) – let alone a deeper analysis of the workings of friendly relations in practice.

As for the matter of documents, it is more than likely that any Certificate granted by the kin-state will be seen as an affront by the home-state, regardless of its format; the very existence of a document giving official expression to ethno-cultural ties galls. Likewise, the very fact that kin-states enact laws that entitle minority individuals to benefits within their boundaries may be interpreted as, and in some cases may in fact be, an attempt to create a political bond – in some countries, like Slovakia and Greece, such entitlements and cards can be the first step to nationality, for example. This situation in itself strains good relations, regardless of the content of specific licenses. In fact, if the real concern were for limiting ties to 'genuine linguistic and cultural links' without the shadow of a political bond, it would make more sense for the kin-states to

---

133. This is true not only for Hungary, but also other culturally nationalist states, as well as for most (if not all) states that attempt to influence the politics of home-states by drawing on kin-minorities. *See* Basch et al. (1994) and Heisler (1999) [1985] on the role of states of origin in the case of diasporas.
134. Venice Report, Sec. D(c).
135. *See* Art. 1 of the Framework Convention and para. 30 of the Explanatory Report thereto.
136. 'The Parties shall endeavour to conclude, where necessary, bilateral and multilateral agreements with other States, in particular neighbouring States, in order to ensure the protection of persons belonging to the national minorities concerned'. *See also* paras 85–86 of the Explanatory Report; and Jackson-Preece (2005) for a discussion of the 'aspirational' nature of this clause.

provide support and encouragement for minorities to maintain their culture within the home-states only; this could easily entail benefits within the territory of the home-states.[137]

iii. Territorial Sovereignty

Such entitlements could, however, be in violation of the principle of territorial sovereignty. This principle implies the jurisdiction of states over, among other things, persons within their borders.[138] In the context of minority protection, in particular, the rule questions whether benefits may ever be given to kin-minorities by kin-states. From the point of view of individuals, the question is better framed as: 'does a minority have the right to freely accept [such] benefits[?] In other words, may the governments of neighbouring states prohibit the Hungarian (or any other kin-)minorities from resorting to and accepting them?'[139] The Commission's opinion states that unilateral legislation concerning foreign nationals is acceptable so long as the effects of the legislation accrue within the boundaries of the legislating state; however, as soon as a state attempts to exercise its powers outside its borders, it is in violation of both international custom and treaties. The fields of education and culture are an exception to this rule, it says, but only insofar as international custom and treaties allow.

The Commission's finding in effect means that any benefits granted to individuals within Hungary would be acceptable despite the fact that they accrue to non-nationals; however, those granted in the home-states are acceptable only within the parameters of international practice and existing bilateral treaties. In the case of Hungary and its neighbours, the Framework Convention, bilateral treaties and the European Cultural Convention are most pertinent in this regard, as will be discussed below.[140]

---

137. As we will see, this is exactly the direction of the 2003 revision.
138. See the *Corfu Channel Case (UK v. Albania)*, ICJ (1949), p. 43 for a discussion of the principle. But *see* Secretary-General Kofi Annan's annual speech to the UN General Assembly (20 September 1999) for thoughts on the evolution of the concept. Certain theorists, Louis Henkin most prominently, have gone so far as to say that sovereignty is not a normative principle of international law. See Henkin (1993). In light of actions in specific circumstances (such as recent international interventions in Serbia and Afghanistan), as well as certain general practices (e.g., the extraterritorial effects of US securities laws), this principle is certainly less absolute than it once was. *See also* E.Ct.H.R. case law, which has recently dismissed numerous arguments resting on principles of sovereignty and territoriality, and has upheld the rights of minority individuals instead. See *Incal v. Turkey*, E.Ct.H.R. (1998), paras 56–59; *Association Ekin v. France*, E.Ct.H.R. (2001), paras 62–63; *Cyprus v. Turkey*, E.Ct.H.R. (2001), paras 250–252.
139. de Varennes (Hungarian) (2002), p. 51) (*'jogában áll-e a kisebbségnek szabadon elfogadni ... kedvezményeket[?] Vagyis a szomszédos országok kormányai megtilthatják-e a magyar kisebbségnek, hogy ezekért a kedvezményekért folyamodjon és elfogadja őket'*.)
140. The Helsinki Final Act, though it discussed Co-operation and Exchange in the areas of both Culture and Education (*see* parts 4 and 5 of the section on Co-operation in Humanitarian and Other Fields), did not include references of any real pertinence to the issue at hand.

a. International Practice and Bilateral Treaties
on Granting Extra-Territorial Benefits

With regard to international practice, the picture is mixed. Let us look first to general cultural policy abroad. While a number of states have established wide-ranging cultural networks outside their borders – most notably France[141] – and despite the central role of state organs in the development and management of such infrastructure, action has not targeted specific individuals or groups. Instead, the networks have been open to anyone with an interest in the respective language and culture. Moreover, particular cultural organizations – the *Alliance Française*, the *Goethe Institut*, etc. – have been established on the basis of either bilateral agreements between the states in question or, where given institutions are independent of the state, specialized agreements. As such, existing custom on this basis is only of limited relevance to status laws.

More interesting for our purposes are diaspora programmes, which are unilateral in nature and target specific individuals or groups on the basis of cultural, linguistic or even ethnic affinity. However, relevant policies – whether regulating the release of sovereign diaspora bonds, structuring diaspora investment or allowing for participation of one kind or another in the cultural, ethnic and sometimes even political community[142] – rarely have effects outside the territory of the home-state. This helps explain why diaspora programmes have generally not elicited protest, despite the fact that many of the individuals addressed may be non-nationals. One exception creating political tension, however, is the increasingly overt assistance furnished by Mexico to migrants – mainly nationals – to the United States through economic, social and political programmes. An uproar from 2005 centred on the publication by the Mexican state of a pamphlet offering safety and health advice for those crossing the border to the United States illegally – including how to get around US Border Patrol[143] – perhaps shows how fine the line between interference with and respect for sovereignty is; the pamphlet was, after all, issued in Mexico and handed out to Mexican nationals, but no one would argue that its effects (if any) will be felt in the United States.

The most comprehensive existing programmes in this area are those provided to the Jewish diaspora. However, the existing system radiates only partly from Israel[144] and is, in that capacity, concerned with facilitating the practical

---

141. *See* Lombard (2003) for a thorough overview of historical development and future prospects, as well as comparisons with other (primarily German, British, Italian, Spanish, Japanese and American) models. As the author states in explaining the importance of such activities, '*Les relations culturelles internationales sont ainsi mises au service de la grandeur de l'Etat considéré. Un lien direct est établi entre le rang d'une nation et le rayonnement de sa culture dans le monde*'. *Ibid.*, pp. 43–44. *See also* p. 208.
142. *See* further discussion of diaspora policies at Sec. IV.C.3.b.
143. *See* James C. McKinley Jr. 'Word for Word/Border Crossing: A Guide for the Illegal Migrant'. *The New York Times.* 9 January 2005.
144. Organizations like the World Jewish Congress and the Joint Distribution Committee (and even the World Zionist Organization) are to a significant degree or wholly independent of the Israeli

application of the Law of Return.[145] The status of *oleh* (Jew immigrating to Israel) is available to all individuals born of a Jewish mother and to those who have converted to Judaism while renouncing any other religion. Eligibility for *oleh* status is thus predicated on overtly ethnic and/or religious criteria for the purposes of the law, raising obvious questions of discrimination.[146] Additional organizations active in this area – such as the Jewish Agency for Israel and the World Zionist Organization – operate for the most part outside Israel and partake of activities that may well infringe on the personal, executive or judicial sovereignty of the states in question.[147] However, no protest has been forthcoming in the past decades of activity, so that tacit consent can be assumed.

Finally, a quick look at the policies of states in Europe toward kin-minorities is warranted, as these practices are most pertinent to the Hungarian Act. In addition to the case of Germany, discussed above, the policies of Austria with regard to *Südtirol* (South Tyrol) merit a closer look. The law granting members of the German and Ladin-speaking minorities special rights in Austria has been mentioned, and is supplementary to ongoing cultural, educational, municipal and parliamentary programmes on the regional level (namely *Tirol* province in Austria), as well as to a series of federal legal regulations on facilitating contacts.[148] In fact, the *Tiroler Landesordnung* (1989) – the province's constitution – speaks in its Preamble of the 'spiritual and cultural unity of the whole *Land*',[149] including the portion of *Tirol* located in Italy. In case the reference was not clear enough, a decision of the provincial parliament clarified in 1994 that '*ganzes Land*' (whole land) is to be understood as encompassing North, South and East Tyrol.[150] Such references to unity are generally explained not only on the basis of a common *Tiroler* identity, but also in reliance on a claimed *Recht auf Heimat* (Right to Homeland). The crux of this claimed right – also a central theme in discussions

---

      state in financial terms and, at times, even goal-orientation, so that the line between Israeli and Jewish diaspora policies is hazy.
145. Law of Return (1950) and subsequent amendments (1954 and 1970).
146. *Ibid.*, Art. 4(b). The determination of who is 'Jewish' – and in which manner – has been an issue of ongoing debate. *See* Emmons (1997), p. 352 *et seq.* and *The Economist*, 'Second Thoughts About the Promised Land' (13 January 2007).
147. For a description of ongoing activities in Ethiopia, *see* Greg Myre. 'Israel to Speed immigration for Jews in Ethiopia'. *The New York Times,* 1 February 2005.
148. Common action has become increasingly frequent since Austria's accession to the European Union in 1995 and includes: yearly common sessions of the regional parliaments (the *Zweierlandtag*), later joined by the province of *Trento*; meetings of the regional governments (since 1995); and common representation on the European level through the creation of a Euroregion (*Tirol-Südtirol/Alto Adige-Trentino*).
149. '*Geistige ... und kulturelle ... Einheit des ganzen Landes*'. In the context of the preparation of a new constitution for Austria – the *Verfassungskonvent* – a petition requesting that reference be made to Austria's protective status (in an additional paragraph to Art. 2) was prepared by former Justice Minister Klecatsky. *See Petition zur Verankerung einer Südtirol-Bestimmung* (14 January 2004).
150. *Entschliessung des Tiroler Tandtages vom 23. November 1994* (1994).

of compensation for Germans expelled from their home-states in Central Europe in the wake of World War II (the *Heimatvertriebene*)[151] – is self-determination in the historical homeland of the community. In other words, in the context of *Tirol*, interaction across borders is claimed as a right because of the historical unity of the community in a given geographic space. This circumstance certainly does not create a right recognized under international law, however, so that it cannot serve as the basis for any status law. Moreover, Austria's (and within it *Tirol*'s) role is unusual in that the state has been recognized in an international treaty as a *Schutzmacht* (protector power) of the minority in Italy[152] – an anomaly that makes all the difference.

The relationship between Romania and Moldova provides a good counter-example. Although Romania's kin policies are wide-ranging, if not consistently funded, the vast majority of its measures are aimed at Moldova (and to a lesser extent Ukraine). In addition to cultural, educational, social and economic programmes,[153] Romania has also adopted certain visa and especially nationality policies that are perceived in Moldova as clear instances of political interference, since they effectively undermine the state's nation-building efforts. This, considering that many Moldovan nationals are also Russian, Ukrainian and Israeli nationals. As Iordachi discusses, a 1991 amendment to the regulation of nationality in Romania – allowing for plural nationality and naturalization even without immigration – prompted especially strong objections from Moldova (and Ukraine) on the basis of its perceived quality as an instrument of nationalism.[154] Moldova retaliated by linking the acceptance of plural nationality to international agreements in its Constitution, well aware that no such agreement had been

---

151. This particular question has been a sensitive one not only in foreign policy – e.g., during discussions with Poland, Slovakia and the Czech Republic on the eve of accession – but also in domestic circles, as shown by debates surrounding the proper place for a *Zentrum gegen Vertreibungen* in 2003. See Deutsche Welle, '*Wohin mit dem "Zentrum gegen Vertreibungen?"*' (3 September 2003).
152. As per the Paris Agreement (or Gruber-Degasperi Agreement) (1946) and the South Tyrol Package (1969) Austria has been granted a mandate to protect the Austrian and Ladin minorities of the region *vis-à-vis* Italy. In 1960, after unsuccessful diplomatic attempts aimed at agreement on the steps to be taken with regard to the minorities, Austria turned to the UN, which proceeded to adopt two resolutions calling on the parties to engage in negotiations. (*See* UN General Assembly Resolutions 1497 and 1661). In 1969, the South Tyrol Package, containing the measures Italy was to take for the benefit of the minority groups, as well as the timetable for implementation was agreed upon. Only in 1992 was the package implemented to the satisfaction of all parties, including the minority parties and the Austrian federal government; accordingly, the Austrian parliament agreed to the settlement of the dispute with Italy in 1992. Austria still remains the protective power of the minorities in the region, however, and continues, in this capacity, to monitor the ongoing implementation of the autonomy agreement.

    In 2001, a major overhaul of existing regulation (effective since 1972) on the special status of the region of *Südtirol* took place in Italy, and resulted in more power for its constituent provinces (e.g., pursuant to the new official designation, which is now *Trentino-Alto Adige* or *Trentino-Südtirol*). See *Verfassungsgesetz Nr. 2 vom 31. January 2001* (2001).
153. For a detailed analysis of Romanian kin-policies, *see* Kiss (2005).
154. Iordachi (Hungarian)(2002), p. 95.

concluded with Romania.[155] Despite negotiation on a possible bilateral treaty, the 2000 law on Moldovan nationality not only kept the restriction on plural nationality in force, but also required that plural nationals register and possibly relinquish their Moldovan nationality. The restrictions were never really put into effect, however, and Moldova eventually relented: plural nationality is once again permitted since 2003. (Incidentally, Romania was also forced to change its provisions in the same year, as public administration could not handle the high number of applications for naturalization.) The issue continues to generate tension, especially in the context of repeated suggestions by Romanian public officials that 'unification' of the two countries in the European Union would be a good idea.[156]

With regard to custom then, one can say that a wide array of state policies exist not only for educational and cultural programmes, but also for economic, social and political ones in the territory of other states. But it should be noted that these policies either flow from an international agreement or occur with the presumed agreement of the affected states. As such, the decisions of particular states are imbued with political considerations – while some may agree to bilateral agreements on particular policies, others will not. Should another state act unilaterally, some will protest the perceived interference, others will not.

Given the raucous protest of two of the states affected by the Hungarian status law, then, the only practical basis for applying the law in those states are existing treaties, namely the Framework Convention and bilateral treaties. While no specific clause allowing unilateral action needs to be present in any treaties, it must also be established that the subject matter of such action has not been preempted by existing agreements.[157] As regards the Framework Convention, reference is made to non-interference with the right of minority individuals to maintain 'free and peaceful contacts' with persons who share their ethnic, cultural, linguistic or other identity and to participate in the activities of NGOs.[158] It is unlikely that unilateral policies that originate in another state – even if they facilitate both of these ends – can be subsumed under this heading. Conversely, the Convention does not necessarily limit such action, in light of its specification that national-minority related questions are 'international' ones.[159]

---

155. Iordachi (Hungarian), pp. 98–101. *See also* Kiss (2005), p. 341.
156. The most recent flare-up occurred in March 2007 in the wake of repeated public declarations by President Basescu of Romania regarding the number of Moldovan applicants for Romanian citizenship. *See Eurasia Daily Monitor*, 'Moldova Refuses Mass Conferral of Romanian Citizenship' (9 March 2007); and BBC News, 'Moldova scraps Romania consulates' (15 March 2007).
157. Obviously, important questions of interpretation arise in this context. Pursuant to Art. 31(1) of the Vienna Convention, a treaty is to be interpreted 'in accordance with the ordinary meaning to be given' to its terms in light of 'its object and purpose'. In any case, a treaty may not be interpreted so as to restrict, unduly, the rights to be protected by it, nor so as to presume limitations on the sovereignty of the parties. *See* discussion in Shaw (5th ed., 2003), pp. 838–844. To the extent that no effective authorities are named in the case of the bilateral treaties, and in light of disagreements between state parties, the scope for disagreement is wide.
158. CEFCM Art. 17.
159. *Ibid.*, Art. 1. Also compare Art. 5(1) in conjunction with Art. 18(2), which can be read to foresee a role for the kin-state.

With regard to the bilateral treaties, these vary in content. Since such variation extends to passages on cultural and minority matters, sections of the Hungarian Act – and the unilateral nature of the Act itself – may be acceptable in certain states, but not in others. For example, in light of Article 15 of the Hungarian-Ukrainian treaty on friendship and Article 6 of the Hungarian-Ukrainian minority declaration, the funding of minority organizations and the extension of financial assistance for cultural and educational purposes by Hungary may (after co-ordination with the home-state) be explicitly accepted.[160] The Slovak-Hungarian treaty, in turn, cannot necessarily be read to allow for such funding and likely pre-empts unilateral action of any kind, in light of the establishment of an inter-governmental joint commission and the 'mutual co-operation' on minority matters foreseen in Article 15(6).

A final question remains. Is the Commission right in its determination? De Varennes, for example, has argued that '[t]he suggestion that minorities in neighbouring countries cannot accept scholarships or benefits from the government in Hungary ... unless approved by their state of citizenship [nationality] is quite simply unsupported from the point of international law and international practice';[161] another observer agreed, adding that the law hurt no one's interests, while helping many.[162] It is true that the principle of teritorial sovereignity cannot be utilized to prohibit support on the basis that such individuals are the nationals of another state – i.e., general cultural benefits would be acceptable – but geography still matters, even when the scope of the benefits is limited to the spheres of culture and education. In other words, the fact that grants were awarded to individuals only in the home-states on the basis of a requisite document issued by Hungary – even if all decisions were made in the latter – certainly raises issues of extraterritoriality.

b.   Procedures Determining Eligibility

The Commission identified a further issue with regard to territorial sovereignty in the procedures determining eligibility for benefits. In the first place, it examined exactly where eligibility is established. The Commission noted that the granting of 'administrative or quasi-official functions to non-governmental associations registered in another country constitutes an indirect form of state power';[163] i.e., it is an infringement of executive jurisdiction. Only embassies and consulates may perform official acts within the territory of another country, in conformity with the norms of international law on this subject.[164] In other words, a kin-state may not out-source any part of the procedure determining eligibility for or even administration of the benefits it grants to kin-minority individuals to non-governmental organizations. With reference to the Hungarian case, the implication

---

160. In fact, Ukraine announced that it had no objections to the Hungarian Act. *See* Joint Declaration of the Prime-Ministers of Hungary and Ukraine (2001).
161. de Varennes (English) (2004), p. 413. *See also* pp. 414–416.
162. Matúš Petrík, as quoted in Szarka (2004), p. 133.
163. Venice Report, Sec. D(a)(ii).
164. E.g., Art. 5 of the Vienna Convention on Consular Relations.

of the Commission's determination was that minority associations in the home-state could only give non-binding informal recommendations, as opposed to compulsory ones.

Second, the Commission declared that exact criteria of eligibility should be spelled out in any law that grants benefits to kin-minority individuals.[165] Despite the centrality of the principle of free choice in minority affiliation, as reiterated by Article 3(1) of the Framework Convention, the Commission thus determined that states may require the fulfilment of certain criteria in granting privileges to persons belonging to minorities. This view was recently reinforced by the E.Ct.H.R. in the *Kosteski* case, as already discussed. With regard to the Hungarian law, this meant that 'self-identification' could not be the only or even the main standard used in assessing 'Hungarianness'. In other words, the provision of Article 1 of the Hungarian law, whereby individuals only had to declare themselves Hungarian to qualify for a recommendation, was not acceptable.[166] This was also true for the recommendations then granted by the minority associations, since they were meant to be binding on the public administrative entity that would grant the Certificate in Hungary.[167]

In fact, the two points identified by the Commission regarding eligibility are closely connected. Presumably, since the minority associations could decide not to grant a recommendation, it was not actually just self-declaration that determined who got the Certificates; but this same discretion is what made the role of the recommending authorities suspect for the purposes of executive jurisdiction. Even reactions to the status law within the minorities show the connection of the two points, since many individuals believed that one had to prove one's affiliation with certain 'traditionally' Hungarian minority organizations before one could get a recommendation – self-identification was thus vetted by the organizations in lieu of the Hungarian state.[168] On a purely legal level, however, it is true that no exact criteria of eligibility were prescribed.

The reasoning of the Commission on this issue is not as sound as it may seem, however. For example, it is unclear how far the Framework Convention, cited by the Commission, applies to the kin-state/kin-minority individual relationship. The Convention refers only to action by the home-state of the minority, in light of signatories' promise to 'protect within their respective territories the existence of

---

165. Venice Report, Sec. D(a)(ii).
166. Irony of ironies: Hungarian commentators pointed to both the tradition of self-identification in Hungarian nationalism (and law, as per Art. 1(1) of the 1993 Law on the rights of national and ethnic minorities) and provisions in international law, including Art. 3(1) of the Framework Convention, Art. 32 of the Copenhagen Declaration and Art. 2(1) of the Protocol proposed in Recommendation 1201, as reasons why any other requirement would be unacceptable. *See*, e.g., Szilágyi in ÉS, *supra* note III.116.
167. For an opinion that the actions of such organizations do not infringe territorial sovereignty because the organizations do not exercise any state functions (even if they may be applying Hungarian law), see de Varennes (Hungarian) (2002), p. 57.
168. *See* Stewart (2002), p. 22.

national minorities'; it is thus to privileges granted by the home-state that the requirement of fulfilling set criteria attaches. Since the Convention does not concern itself with the role of kin-states, no such requirement attaches to any benefits they may grant to individuals. In turn, so long as the kin-state is in compliance with the criteria set out in the Commission's opinion in granting privileges – i.e., they are privileges that accrue in the kin-state and are limited to cultural and educational matters – the possible requirement of the home-state that minority individuals fulfil certain criteria to access these benefits in practice may give undue influence to that state. In other words, what say should Romania have in determining who is Hungarian, for the purposes of a law with effects in Hungary?[169]

Finally, the procedure involved in obtaining Hungarian Certificates could, conversely, have been seen as an attempt to *not* interfere in the matters of another state, since it was not the Hungarian government, but minority individuals and their organizations that were meant to decide who is one of them. The very elements of the procedure that can be viewed as infringements on sovereignty in theory may thus be viewed as attempts to respect it in practice. Given the degree of influence Hungary actually had in distributing the Certificates, this point is perhaps academic; it is nonetheless worth making, since it relates closely to the question of discrimination and respect for human rights.

iv.   *Discrimination*

Countless treaties prohibit discrimination of all kinds.[170] ICCPR Article 26, for example, states that 'the law shall prohibit any discrimination and guarantee to all persons equal and effective protection against discrimination on any ground such as race, colour, sex, language, religion, political or other opinion, national or social origin'. The ECHR, in turn, declares that states will be held accountable for ensuring the non-discriminatory[171] enjoyment of the rights and freedoms enshrined in the Convention to 'everyone within their jurisdiction'.[172] As the Commission notes, a state is held accountable for the extraterritorial effects of its acts, so that any individuals affected, both nationals and foreigners, may fall within the jurisdiction of a state for the purposes of a specific act. The determination of what

---

169. In a related point, Pap argues that in the context of discrimination it is the majority that determines who is a member of the minority. It is only when minority identity and status are linked to material gains that the question of free determination of identity appears and comprehends the possibility of abuse. *See* ÉS (László András Pap), *Státus és identitás* (1 June 2001).
170. *See also* Art. 7 of the UDHR, Arts 1 and 14 of the ECHR, and the Twelfth Protocol thereto (in force since April 2004), as well as Art. 4 of the Framework Convention.
171. *See also* ECHR Art. 14, which more directly prohibits discrimination, but only with regard to the rights enumerated elsewhere in the Convention. Now that the Twelfth Protocol to the ECHR has come into effect, non-discrimination is a free-standing right in the (minority of) states that have ratified it.
172. ECHR Art. 1.

constitutes discrimination is a matter of context, however. As the ECHR stated in the *Belgian Linguistics Case*:

> [T]he principle of equality of treatment is violated if [a] distinction has no objective and reasonable justification. The existence of such a justification must be assessed in relation to the aim and effects of the measure under consideration, regard being had to the principles which normally prevail in democratic societies.[173]

Thus, differential treatment of individuals in similar situations is acceptable under certain circumstances. Besides a determination of whether such a justification may exist, there must be a reasonable relation of proportionality between the aim pursued and the means used to achieve it.[174]

In the context of the kinship laws discussed by the Venice Commission – and understood as intervention in favour of kin-minorities[175] or, more positively, as 'new and original forms of minority protection, particularly by the kin-States'[176] – benefits granted in relation to education and culture, where 'genuinely linked with the culture of the state, and proportionate'[177] were deemed acceptable. Thus, less favourable treatment by a state of individuals outside its territory on the basis of not belonging to a specific ethnic or cultural group is 'not, in itself, discriminatory, nor contrary to the principles of international law'.[178] With regard to the status law then, one could conclude that the provisions relating to education and culture were acceptable, while those that related to work and social benefits were not.

While the result at first sight seems sound – given that the kin-states are linked with kin-minorities on the basis of culture – when seen in conjunction with other elements of the Commission's decision, difficulties emerge, at least in the case of the Hungarian status law.

In the first place, putting 'ethnic' and 'cultural' criteria on the same footing in the context of status or any other kinship laws is disputable. Laws with clear ethnic criteria (e.g., Greece, Slovakia or Israel) provide clearly demarcated, but arbitrary, boundaries based on descent in a manner that policies based on culture do not. In other words, if the underlying assumption of status laws is that the given individuals have a 'link' to the culture of the state – and this reasoning is accepted – then differentiating among individuals who have actual ties to the given culture that state promotes is reasonable; differentiating among individuals because their ancestors were 'Greek' or 'Slovak' on the assumption that this guarantees links, without any further proof of ties required, is not. In the context of the Hungarian status law, for example, the state was arguably not directly discriminating along

---

173. Case *'Relating to certain aspects of the laws on the use of languages in education in Belgium'* (Merits), E.Ct.H.R. (1968), para. 10; *Sidiropoulos v. Greece*, E.Ct.H.R. (1998), paras 40–47; *Petrovic v. Austria*, E.Ct.H.R. (1998), para. 30; *Larkos v. Cyprus*, E.Ct.H.R. (1999), para. 29.
174. See also paras 55–57 of the *Costa Rica* Opinion of the Inter-American Court.
175. Venice Report, Sec. A.
176. *Ibid.*, Sec. D.
177. *Ibid.*, Sec. D(d).
178. *Ibid.*

ethnic lines, since no requirements of ethnicity were set out in the law; the only criteria named were self-identification and non-voluntary relinquishment of Hungarian nationality.[179] Admittedly, the state could nonetheless have spurred discrimination indirectly, since a Roma individual declaring herself to be Hungarian may have been less likely to get the necessary recommendation than a non-Roma.[180]

Assuming that the two can be treated as comparable instances of differentiation, however, we find that determining who exactly is in a 'similar position' for the purposes of differential treatment is less than straightforward. (Hungarian and non-Hungarian) nationals of Hungary and individuals from the Hungarian minority certainly were not, since there would not have been a status law to begin with if they were. Individuals from the minority and non-nationals in Hungary also were not, since the latter tend not to identify as Hungarians. (While non-nationals residing in Hungary thus have the same social rights as granted in the status law, they are in a very different position as regards cultural and educational matters). Finally, Hungarian minority individuals and the co-nationals of the home-states are not in a similar position, since they do not share the (supposed) wish to have close ties with Hungary and the Hungarian 'nation', and are unlikely to be interested in any of the cultural and educational benefits of the status law; the one exception, i.e., the family members of Hungarian minority individuals regardless of kinship, was recognized in the law. In reality, one needs to differentiate among the benefits of the status law: certain provisions may be discriminatory, others justifiable instances of differential treatment. But what about the supposed interrelation of some of the provisions? Can travel benefits, for example, be closely enough linked to cultural matters (and minority protection more generally) to be deemed non-discriminatory despite differentiation by kinship?

This brings us to a third difficulty: the Commission reiterates that the aims, as well as the proportionality of the aims to the content of a law, must be looked at to determine whether the measures introduced by it are, in fact, discriminatory. However, if the aim of the Hungarian status law is accepted – including the aim of 'undisturbed cultural, economic, and family relations' – then it can plausibly be argued that many (all?) of the provisions of the status law are proportional to its aims, since they foresee and encourage repeat cross-border interaction in all of the fields above. It is more likely that the aim of such laws should have been more closely examined and circumscribed, but that is not something the Commission was willing to do, in light of its acceptance of the general principle that kin-states have a role to play 'in the preservation and protection of kin-minorities'. While this declaration does recognize the fact of a kin-state role, it ignores the real source of contention then: the exact scope of this protective role. It was thus the quality of the

---

179. How far this went back was unclear – presumably Hungary at the moment of the Trianon Treaty. If so, the state at the time was certainly multi-ethnic.
180. This is a serious charge, but still does not involve the state in ethnic differentiation in the manner certain other status laws do – e.g., those laws where the acquisition of a Certificate hinges on proving kin ancestry. *See* Slovak law, Secs 2(2), (3), (4) and (5).

kin-state role that was really behind the status law controversy; and this was something the Venice Report did not address.

Alas, the reasoning behind the Commission's determination of what constitutes preservation/protection is also somewhat wobbly. In particular, the limitation of acceptable benefits to the areas of education and culture only seems to be the result of an overly restrictive approach, given both international practice (discussed above) and the recognition of the Framework Convention that measures 'in all areas of economic, social, political and cultural life'[181] may be necessary in order to place members of a minority on equal footing with the majority.

It is likely this broader approach that lead de Varennes to state that 'the aim pursued by the [status] law is just and in line with the requirements and standards of European treaties; the benefits guaranteed by the law are related to the stated aim'.[182] He relied in his argument on the reasoning found in the *Minority Schools in Albania Case*.[183] The case is worth quoting at length, as one of the first examples of a legal argument for differential treatment of minority populations:

> The idea is to secure for certain elements incorporated in a State, the population of which differs from them in race, language or religion, the possibility of living peaceably alongside that population and co-operating amicably with it, while at the same time preserving the characteristics which distinguish them from the majority, and satisfying the ensuing needs.
>
> In order to attain this object, two things were regarded as particularly necessary ... The first is to ensure that nationals belonging to racial, religious or linguistic minorities shall be placed in every respect on equal footing of perfect equality with the other nationals of the State. The second is to ensure for the minority elements suitable means for the preservation of their traditions and their national characteristics. The two requirements are indeed closely interlocked, for there would be no true equality between the majority and a minority if the latter were deprived of its own institutions, and were consequently compelled to renounce that which constitutes the very essence of its being as a minority.[184]

In order to attain the two goals, a difference must be made between 'effective, genuine equality' and 'equality in law'.[185] While the latter 'precludes discrimination of any kind; equality in fact may involve the necessity of different treatment in order to attain a result which establishes the equilibrium between different situations'.[186] Accordingly, in the context of cultural benefits in the home-state, de

---

181. CEFCM Art. 4(2).
182. de Varennes (Hungarian), at 67 (2002) (*'a cél, amelyet a törvény követ, jogos és összhangban van az európai egyezmények kötelezettségeivel és standardjaival; a törvény által garantált kedvezmények kapcsolódnak a leszögezett célhoz'*.) *See also* Pan (2003), pp. 8–9.
183. *Minority Schools in Albania* (Advisory Opinion), P.C.I.J. (1935), p. 4.
184. *Ibid.*, p. 17.
185. *See also Case of the German settlers in Poland* (Advisory Opinion), P.C.I.J. (1923).
186. *Minority Schools in Albania*, p. 19.

Varennes claimed 'one cannot seriously argue that Hungary is pursuing illegal aims when it provides benefits in the interests of the preservation of the identity of Hungarian minorities'.[187] In other words, if the Act helps Hungarian minority individuals to be genuinely equal to the majority population, it should not be considered discriminatory. In fact the Hungarian government's argument ran along these lines.

As the (then) Political State Secretary at the Hungarian Foreign Ministry (Zsolt Németh) stated, '[Hungarian minority individuals] do not get the benefits because they are Hungarians, but because they have problems, stemming from their Hungarianness, to which they expect solutions from the Hungarian state'.[188] The distinction is elusive, but crucial: Hungary is supposedly giving the benefits to individuals because they, as individuals, are disadvantaged in their home-states by being Hungarian. As such, they need these benefits to be able to function as full members of the Hungarian nation, to which they want to belong, as well as genuinely equal nationals of their home-state. In fact, it is argued that, in a climate where Hungarianness is supposedly denigrated – where Hungarian minorities are ostensibly systematically discriminated against while the host-state proves unwilling or unable to remedy the situation – a compensation of sorts is necessary.[189] Thus, it is only through special provisions that individuals can be reinforced in their group identity. Supposedly only Hungary, as the kin-state, can provide solutions to this problem;[190] the home-state can provide solutions to others. In fact, even if there were complete harmony between majority and minority in the home-states, a status law would still be necessary: Németh went so far as to say that a model home-state would actually encourage such a law, since it would recognize that there must be a law regulating Hungarian-Hungarian relations.

These statements may be questioned on a number of points – for example, why Németh was speaking in the name of the minorities in the first place, why a status law should be necessary in all circumstances if the supposed reason is to remedy discrimination not dealt with by the home-state or even why all of this was not stated in the law itself.[191] However, if this view is accepted – and no one doubts that the minorities pushed for such legislation most forcefully[192] – then present legal theory, and practice, provides no answer besides admonishing all parties involved

---

187. de Varennes (Hungarian), p. 66 (*'nem lehet komolyan érvelni amellett, hogy Magyarország jogellenes célt követne akkor, amikor kedvezményeket biztosít a magyar kisebbségek identitásának megtartása érdekében'*). *See also* Weber (2002b) for a similar opinion as regards the benefits granted in Hungary.
188. Németh (2002) (*'De a kedvezményeket nem azért kapják, mert magyarok, hanem azért, mert olyan problémáik vannak, amelyek magyarságukból erednek, és amelyek megoldását a magyar államtól várják'.*)
189. *See* Nagy (2004), p. 225; Németh, *ibid.*; Kántor (2002); Szabó, as quoted in Kántor, *ibid.*; and Beszélő (Miklós Duray), '*Sosemvolt törvényünk lesz'*! (2001/5).
190. *See*, e.g., Szabó as quoted in Kántor, *ibid.*
191. *See also* Magyar Hírlap (Rudolf Ungváry), *A státustörvény homálya* (8 February 2001) arguing that both the discrimination-remedying function of the law and its temporary nature should have been clearly stated.
192. *See also* Sec. 1 of the MÁÉRT Declaration made shortly after the law was passed by Parliament (2001a).

for not playing by the accepted rules of the 'home-state as container' game. It is true that a number of international instruments have stated that differentiated treatment of minorities is acceptable.[193] The question, however, turns on who may give such individuals preferential treatment.

Though de Varennes pointed to a number of instruments allowing for unimpeded contacts with a kin-state[194] as the basis for his argument that kin-states may be the source of such preferences,[195] his interpretation falls short; it is one thing to speak of 'free and peaceful contacts' generally, but quite another to speak of such contacts – or legal links – with another state. Simply stated, there is no precedent for such a situation in any of the major international instruments or courts.[196] What case law does exist, at least at the E.Ct.H.R., provides 'little scope for the pillar of minority protection, which pursues substantive equality through rights that contribute to the preservation and promotion of the distinctive identity of minorities'.[197] The Strasbourg court does not really deal in identity-protection matters, as discussed above.[198] Nor has international custom developed to deal with such situations. As Kymlicka and Opalski have noted, 'proposals [for minority protection] typically involve codifying Western models as universal standards'[199] – but the question of kin-minorities did not come up with much frequency at the time the basic pillars of minority-protection system developed.[200] The same holds true for the development of today's relevant fundamental rights provisions in the European Union, developed with the needs of immigrant minorities in mind.[201] Though the lack of clear guidance in international law could theoretically allow for experimentation, the actual result, given political realities, is that all the cards are held by the home-state.

b. Political Compromises

The Venice Commission report, while shedding some light on the legal issues surrounding status laws, still left room for considerable confusion; more to the

---

193. *See, inter alia*, Art. 4(2) of the Framework Convention; and Art. 5 of the UNDRM in conjunction with Art. 8(3). *See also Beard v. United Kingdom*, E.Ct.H.R. (2001), para. 104.
194. *See* Art. 17(1) and 17(2) of the Framework Convention; para. 32(4) of the Copenhagen Document; and Art. 2(5) of the UNDRM.
195. de Varennes (Hungarian) (2002), pp. 64–66.
196. In fact, existing international instruments are somewhat unclear on who is to pursue 'full and effective equality' for minority individuals. Hungary pointed out that Art. 4(2) of the Framework Convention does not exclude parties other than the minority home-states from doing so, while Romania pointed to the same Convention (likely the Preamble) when arguing that the language commits states to protect minorities *within* their borders. *See* Fowler (2002) (emphasis added).
197. Henrard (2000), pp. 125–128 and pp. 142–143. *See also* Gilbert (2002) for how piece-meal the existing standards really are.
198. *See* Sec. I.C.4.6.
199. Kymlicka and Opalski (eds) (2001), p. 4.
200. The only real exception in Europe is the case of *Süd-Tirol*, discussed above.
201. *See* discussion in Horváth (2006); and, in the context of the Race Equality Directive (which emerged from anti-racism policies), Bell (2002), pp. 63–87 and pp. 191–198, for an example of near exclusive focus on immigrant groups.

point, it was not binding on the parties. Still, the controversy garnered by the law sufficed to force the Orbán government to introduce provisional changes to the application of the law in consultation with MÁÉRT. The Memorandum of Understanding signed shortly thereafter between Romania and Hungary (2001) set out that all Romanian nationals could apply for work permits in Hungary (i.e., this benefit was no longer limited only to Hungarian minority individuals); that the entire procedure of granting the Hungarian Certificates would take place in Hungary (and would be funnelled through consulates); that the Certificates would not include any reference to 'ethnic origin/identity'; that Hungarian representative organizations would not issue recommendations regarding 'ethnic origin and other criteria'; and that the basis for granting the Certificates would also have supplementary objective criteria (including knowledge of Hungarian and any one of the following: a declaration in the state of nationality of Hungarian identity, membership in a Hungarian church or membership in a Hungarian minority organization). The additional criteria used in granting the Certificates were, again, suggested by MÁÉRT.[202]

While Romania now found the law acceptable, reactions in Hungary ranged from negative to scathing;[203] accusations of having betrayed both Hungarian workers and Hungarian national interest were the most common charge. In fact, certain elements of the Memorandum were so irreconcilable with the stated goal of the law that they can only be explained by the wish of the Orbán government to have the system up and running before upcoming parliamentary elections. This strategy was a bad miscalculation, however, as government approval plummeted, and FIDESZ, Orbán's party, lost the elections a few months later.[204] The new, Medgyessy-led government that won the April 2002 elections found itself in quite a quandary; not only was it left with a law to overhaul in a manner pleasing to all parties involved, but it had to do so in light of, now definite, EU accession.[205]

In July, MÁÉRT agreed to suggested amendments to the law;[206] when a new draft was made public in the autumn of 2002,[207] a new meeting of the organization was called together and the draft approved.[208] Further changes were made by December of that year, but it was not until 23 June 2003 that the revisions were

---

202. See MÁÉRT (2001b).
203. See, inter alia, Népszabadság, *Az SZDSZ és a MIÉP a munkavállalásról* (22 December 2001); and Magyar Hírlap, *Az ész féltekéje* (28 December 2001).
204. For polls and the results of the elections, see Népszabadság, *Újra az MSZP vezet* (22 January 2002); and Népszabadság, *Nyertek a kormányváltó erők* (22 April 2002).
205. See HVG, *Zavarok a státustörvény körül: lassuló idő* (10 August 2002); and MÁÉRT 2002a.
206. See MÁÉRT, ibid.
207. See Népszabadság, *Státusvita az ET-vel* (24 October 2002). See also Népszabadság, *Tartalmi változások a státustörvényben* (29 October 2002) for a discussion of the changes proposed.
208. MÁÉRT 2002b.

passed by Parliament (in a close vote).[209] A number of significant modifications were introduced.

i.   The Revised Status Law

In the Preamble, the reference to the need to 'ensure that Hungarians living in neighbouring countries form part of the Hungarian nation as a whole' was removed. Instead, the law now mentions 'their Hungarian identity and their links to the Hungarian cultural heritage as expression of their belonging to the Hungarian nation' as well as 'ties to Hungary'. In other words, a clear line was drawn between belonging to the Hungarian cultural nation and possible organizational, institutional or other ties to the kin-state; one does not equal the other. Accordingly, the goals of 'undisturbed cultural, economic and family relations', as well as 'permanent contacts', 'free movement of persons and free flow of ideas' in Article 3 of the original were replaced, in Article 2 of the new version (hereinafter, Revised Status Law or RSL), with a wish to contribute 'to the well-being and prosperity of Hungarians living in neighbouring states and to the preservation of their cultural and linguistic identity'.[210] The law thus no longer means to announce the union of the Hungarian nation in all senses – personal, economic, cultural, spiritual and political – but aims only to ensure the protection of the cultural identity of kin-minorities in their home-states. A look at the changed provisions of RSL Article 18 confirms this: home-state organizations whose goals are 'the establishment and improvement of conditions of infrastructure for maintaining contacts' or 'the enhancement of the capacity to improve [Hungarian kin-communities'] ability to preserve their population and to develop rural tourism' need no longer apply for grants from the Hungarian state, since these activities are not deemed closely enough linked to culture.[211]

The change of focus can also be detected in adjustments to the support system, the criteria used in establishing 'Hungarianness' and the procedure for granting

---

209. *2003. évi LVII. törvény a szomszédos államokban élő magyarokról szóló 2001. évi LXII. törvény módosításáról* (Law LVII of 2003 on the Amendment of Law LXII of 2001 Concerning the Hungarians Living in Neighbouring States) (hereinafter, RSL or Revised Act). 195 deputies voted for, 173 against the revisions. The contrast with the near-unanimous support the original law received is worth noting. The reaction of Hungarian minority media was also less than enthusiastic. See Romániai Magyar Szó, *További módosításra nincs szükség* (7 July 2003).
210. The official English translation unfortunately modifies the emphasis of this section. In the original, focus is on well-being and prosperity while remaining in the home-state, rather than on who the law applies to: '*A szülőföldön való megmaradást és gyarapodást, továbbá a kulturális és nyelvi azonosságtudat megőrzését a Magyar Köztársaság kívánja elősegíteni*'.
211. But see Romániai Magyar Szó, *A Magyar Állandó Értekezlet VII. üléséről* (27 May 2003), where the Head of the (recently disbanded) Office for Hungarian Minorities Abroad (HTMH) noted that this does not rule out economic and infrastructural support. Instead 'their possibilities and details will not be fixed through the Law on Hungarians Living in Neighbouring States' ('*ezek lehetőségét és részleteit nem a szomszédos államokban élő magyarokról szóló törvény fogja rögzíteni*').

Hungarian Certificates, as well as their function. The law now makes a clearer distinction between 'benefits', to be granted in Hungary on the basis of possession of a Hungarian Certificate,[212] and 'grants' to be distributed in the home-states on the basis of request only.[213] With regard to the former, there are no longer references to 'rights identical to those of Hungarian citizens [nationals]',[214] though all the provisions related to culture, education and travel benefits in which these references could be found remain unchanged.[215] This is also true for the possibility of being a member of the Hungarian Academy of Sciences[216] and receiving state distinctions and scholarships 'in recognition of outstanding and exemplary activities in the service of all Hungarians and in enriching Hungarian and universal human values'.[217] The link of the Hungarian cultural nation to the Hungarian state – and its politicization – thus remains. On the other hand, the social security and health services benefits and the employment opportunities provided by the original status law were abrogated in line with the refocused goal of the law.[218] With regard to the grants available in home-states, these remain much the same, though the educational grants available under Article 14(1) are now due to all minor children studying Hungarian culture or in Hungarian, not their parents; also, the two-child household restriction has been lifted. Moreover, pursuant to RSL Article 27(3), the grants may be extended to all students in the neighbouring states studying Hungarian culture or in Hungarian on the basis of international agreements; through bilateral agreement, parents' and teachers' associations may also apply for the grants.[219]

The rules of procedure for the granting of Hungarian Certificates have been completely overhauled. A Hungarian state agency now grants the cards on the basis of self-identification[220] and:

(1) proficiency in Hungarian; or

---

212. *See* RSL Arts 3(1), 3(2), 4(4), 8(5), 10, and 12.
213. *Ibid.*, Arts 3(1) and 3(2). As per Art. 27(5) of the Revised Act, a government ordinance details the rules on awarding grants. *See* Government Ordinance 31/2004 on the Regulation of the Support Granted on the Basis of Law LXII on Hungarians Living in Neighbouring States (2004). The funds are channelled through civic organizations (Art. 1(3)), overseen by the HTMH (Arts 2 and 3). The requirements to be fulfilled by both organizations and individuals is set out in treaties between the given civic organization and the HTMH (Arts 3(1) and 4(1)).
214. *See* RSL Arts 4(1), 10(1), and 12(2).
215. *Ibid.*, Arts 4, 5, 6, 8, 9, 10, 11, and 12. The ordinances that set out the precise rules have, however, been amended or added to. *See, inter alia*, Ordinance 18/2003 of the Minister of National Cultural Heritage on the Benefits Due to Individuals Covered by Law LXII on Hungarians Living in Neighbouring States (2003); and Ordinance 36/2003 of the Minister for Education on the Amendment of Ordinance 47/2001 on the Implementation of the Provisions on Education set forth in Law LXII on Hungarians Living in Neighbouring States (2003).
216. SL/RSL Art. 5.
217. RSL Art. 6.
218. *See ibid.*, Arts 7 and 16; but *see* Art. 15, which allows for derogation from the general rules governing employment in Hungary on the basis of treaties.
219. *Ibid.*, Arts 14(2) and 27(4).
220. *Ibid.*, Art. 19(2)(a).

(2) registered status in the state of residence as a person declaring herself to be Hungarian; or
(3) registration by a Hungarian church as Hungarian; or
(4) membership in a Hungarian organization or association in the state of residence.

The scope of those who can apply is thus very wide: anyone who feels herself to be Hungarian and who can give some evidence of attachment to this identity. It is worth noting that there is still no ethnic element – i.e., requirement of descent – to 'Hungarianness' in the law.[221] Moreover, recommending authorities are no longer involved in the decision on issuance; anyone who fulfils one of the objective criteria automatically receives the Certificate.

The changes made to the law were – and were presented as – a response to the intense round of criticism set off by the first version. In particular, the newly inserted reference in RSL Article 2(2) to the 'generally recognized rules of international law', specifically the four identified by the Venice Commission, as well as to the 'obligations of the Republic of Hungary assumed under treaties', was a response to opinions that the legislation contravened international law. Assurances that the provisions not directly related to culture or education – e.g., travel benefits – are nonetheless 'in accordance with the purpose of this Act and strengthen [the minorities'] attachment to the Hungarian culture'[222] serve a similar purpose, underlining the cultural function of the law.

ii. The After-Effects of the Law

A few days after passage of the new law, the Assembly of the Council of Europe noted that, although the amendments made were satisfactory, the revision nonetheless did not result from bilateral efforts.[223] This is an overly legal response to what was, in part, a political problem: how could Hungary have begun consultations with neighbouring states at the re-drafting stage when the intention of the (revised) law was, on the one hand, the enhancement of Hungarian-Hungarian ties disapproved of by the home-states and, on the other, the granting of support the kin-minorities felt their home-state refused to give? In fact, within days, the Slovak government announced it refused even the possibility of negotiation with Hungary about the status law;[224] Romania simply stated that the revised law was not in accordance with 'European norms' and therefore unacceptable.[225] The newly

---

221. *See also* Nagy (2004), p. 259.
222. RSL Art. 8(1).
223. *See* para. 13 of the CoE Report on the Hungarian law. *See also* Statement issued by Rolf Ekeus, OSCE High Commissioner on National Minorities (24 June 2003).
224. *See* Romániai Magyar Szó (7 July 2003), *supra* note III.209; Népszabadság, *Poszony tárgyalni sem hajlandó* (27 June 2003); and Népszabadság, *Pozsony mégis hajlandó tárgyalni* (3 July 2003). There were even rumours of a counter-law, making acceptance of the grant provided by the Hungarian law illegal in Slovakia. *See* Népszabadság, *Elkészült a szlovák ellentörvény?* (30 June 2003); and Népszabadság, *Ekeus Pozsonyban puhatolódzott* (2 July 2003).
225. *See* Romániai Magyar Szó (7 July 2003), *supra* note III.209.

added language of the Preamble regarding 'bilateral treaties with neighbouring countries to maintain good neighbourly relations and co-operation, and to guarantee the rights of minorities', as well as international pressure, made bilateral talks a prerequisite to the application of the law abroad, however.

After months of negotiations, agreements were finally reached with both Romania and Slovakia.[226] The agreements reflect the specific concerns of the home-states. For example, the Romanian agreement (whose original language of drafting was, strangely, English) states that 'non-ethnic Hungarians' will be unable to receive Hungarian Certificates or the benefits of the law;[227] what this means in practice is difficult to know. Will the Romanian state monitor whether those who claim the Certificates are ethnically Hungarian?[228] Or, in a related question – given that there is no requirement that the recipients of the educational grants be Hungarian, only that they study in Hungarian or Hungarian culture – has the agreement hereby added an overtly ethnic element to the application of the law? Other provisions seem concerned with the sovereignty of Romania,[229] as well as with leaving open the possibility of similar benefits for Romanians in Hungary.[230]

The Slovak Agreement, in contrast, is organized around the principle of reciprocity and provides for the same rights to both kin-minorities, despite the non-existence (at least at present) of comparable benefits to the Slovak minority in Hungary; however, there are no provisions relating to territorial sovereignty. Instead, the focus is on who may receive educational grants. In Article 2(3), the Agreement states that Hungary may provide financial support for educational activity that takes place in institutions providing Hungarian language or Hungarian culture focused education.[231] This does not necessarily equal grants to individuals, in line with Articles 14(1) (and possibly 27(3)) of the revised Hungarian law, however. In fact, in the context of Article 2(4) of the Agreement, specifically providing for such funding to university students, it seems likely that educational grants to primary and secondary education students are expressly not allowed. The Agreements thus contravene or limit the scope of the revised law they were meant to provide agreement on. No agreements were concluded with Croatia, Slovenia, (then) Serbia-Montenegro or Ukraine – the other

---

226. Agreement between the Government of Romania and the Government of the Republic of Hungary on Implementation of the Amended Benefit Law in Romania (2003); and Agreement between the Government of the Republic of Hungary and the Government of the Slovak Republic on Mutual Educational and Cultural Support of National Minorities (2003).
227. *Ibid.*, Agreement with Romania, Art. 1.
228. The result does not seem to be an instance of faulty drafting, since the Hungarian translation also includes the words '*etnikai hovatartozás*' – not the word *nemzetiségű* used in the Hungarian Act itself.
229. Agreement with Romania, *supra* note III.226, Arts 2, 3, and 7.
230. *Ibid.*, Art. 9.
231. In February 2004, the Pázmány Péter Foundation was registered in Slovakia as the organization through which funds are to be channelled, so that the structure providing for the grants is now in place in both states. *See* Népszabadság, *Oktatási forintok koronában* (13 February 2004).

home-states involved – since they did not express disagreement with the status law.[232]

Given that Slovenia, Slovakia and Romania, not to mention Hungary, are now members of the European Union, SL/RSL Article 27(2), stating that its provisions 'shall be applied in accordance with the *acquis communautaire*' also becomes significant.[233] In particular, one legal question regarding the revised status law remains outstanding: namely, its compatibility with ECT Article 12, prohibiting discrimination among Union citizens on the basis of nationality. In light of the broad notion of 'social advantage' developed by the E.C.J. for Article 12 purposes,[234] the Hungarian grants could certainly be considered such an advantage – and a problematic one to boot, since the law benefits only individuals residing in the named states.[235] Thus, individuals residing in Slovakia, Slovenia or Romania enjoy certain rights not available to individuals in Austria: a possible instance of indirect discrimination.[236] In a recent ruling on nationality discrimination – in the context of student maintenance grants to those 'settled' in the Member State – the E.C.J. effectively summarized its policy when saying that 'a difference in treatment can be justified only if it is based on objective considerations independent of the nationality of the persons concerned and is proportionate to the legitimate aim of the national provisions'.[237] That the grants of the revised Hungarian law extend to the *residents* – as opposed to the nationals – of the given states, so that there is no overt discrimination, may not be enough to establish a lack of indirect discrimination, since the provisions in question may in practice lead to the same result. On the other hand, both culture and minority matters (not to mention nationality) are areas of primary state action – and these are the bases on which any argument for differentiated treatment on the basis of a public policy or other exception would rely. The clearly sensitive nature of minority issues, not to mention the necessity of analyzing policy areas outside the scope of Community law, may also make the E.C.J. hesitant to intervene, so that this may be one of the cases in which the Court sidesteps the underlying question.

Still, the assessment of the Venice Commission on status laws seems more lenient than that of the European Union is likely to be: the former does not require that the nationals of state A be entitled to the same rights in state C as those of state

---

232. On 27 June 2003 the Hungarian Ministry of Foreign Affairs sent a notice to the Embassies of all relevant states, suggesting the creation of committees to discuss the (implementation of the) Revised Act.
233. Thus, ECT Arts 6(1), 6(2), 7, 12, and 13 should be considered. If the Charter of Fundamental Rights (2000) ever becomes binding, Art. 21(1) would also be relevant.
234. *See* discussion at Sec. II.C.2.b.
235. The grants would certainly come under the ambit of EU law, since cross-border action is necessary to take advantage of them.
236. For discussion of residence as an indirect form of discrimination, *see* discussion at Sec. II.C.2.b. *See also* para. 14 of Case C-224/97 *Ciola v. Land Vorarlberg*, E.C.J. [1999]; and para. 29 of Case C-350/96 *Clean Car Autoservice v. Landeshauptmann von Wien*, E.C.J. [1998].
237. Case 209/03 *Bidar*, para. 54.

B, while Community law requires the equal treatment of nationals of all three states in most areas. The possibility of inconsistent approaches between the Council of Europe and the Union is thus certainly present, especially in light of ECT Articles 6(1) and 6(2). (With regard to Hungary, the ECT Article 307(1) subordination clause must also be taken into account in the context of bilateral treaties on good neighbourliness or minority rights with third states, since they entered into force before Hungary's date of entry into the Union.[239]) On the other hand – an overly broad interpretation of the phrase 'ethnic origin' aside – the Race Equality and Employment Directives[238] should not pose a problem unless the specific status law relies on ancestry or race to determine eligibility.

Finally, the interaction of status laws with the Union's scant minority policies[240] and its increasing focus on a European identity based on diversity should be recalled here. First, given the near-absence of the European Union in the circus surrounding the status law, its contradictory role in regional minority protection re-appears. Since minority protection does not feature in any of the founding instruments of the Union, conditioning entry of the East-Central European states on 'respect for and protection of national minorities'[241] was an unusual step, leading to a much-discussed 'double standard'. But the problem is not just one of discrepant treatment of new and old Member States. The lack of clear benchmarks,[242] specifically the factual lack of the 'international standards' the Union (as well as other organizations, like the OSCE) kept and keep on referring to, has led to a status quo in which all parties toss around references to 'European standards' as and when it suits them. The standards that do exist are thus diluted and become ineffectual in particular contexts. In addition, there is a tendency to view these same standards as a ceiling rather than a floor, so that minorities (or kin-states) claiming anything beyond the rights guaranteed in the star instruments (especially the Framework Convention) are labelled 'radicals'.[243] This does not bode well for the post-accession period.

We thus veer back to the question of how the much-touted European diversity already discussed is to be maintained without recognized norms of minority protection in Europe[244] – unless, of course, the Union aims to protect the diversity of

---

238. Directives 2000/43/EC and 2000/78/EC respectively, *supra* note II.150. As a general matter, little guidance exists on the meaning of 'racial and ethnic origin': the Directives give no indication, nor have the C.I.F. or E.C.J. presented opinions. The context out of which the Directives emerged (namely immigration) would point to a concern with visible minorities; to the extent cultural, linguistic or other, similar traits were considered 'ethnic', however, we would be entering dangerous waters, enforcing, in legal terms, a creeping equation of culture with ethnicity in the social sciences. *See also* discussion Sec. I.C.2.
239. *See* Manzini (2001) for a look at case law and the problems of interpreting this article.
240. *See* de Witte and Horváth (forthcoming) for a recent evaluation.
241. *See* the criteria enumerated at the Copenhagen European Council (1993).
242. For a good overview of the problematic role of the Union in minority rights matters during the accession process, *see* Sasse (2004).
243. *See* the excellent discussion in Kymlicka (2004).
244. *See,* e.g., Sec. 10 of Council of Europe, Parliamentary Recommendation 1492 on the Rights of National Minorities (2000).

national identities only.[245] Even assuming that respect for diversity is to pierce the veil of the member-nation-states – a big 'if' – respect 'does not translate easily into concrete minority protection standards',[246] as noted above.

C. THE EVOLUTION OF A CONCEPT

The Hungarian status law as it stands today, though stretching international norms, falls within their scope. For the most part, then, the controversy around it has died down, only to be replaced by debates on dual nationality, as will be discussed. The law has, however, focused attention on a number of issues not heretofore present in either theoretical discourse or policies on minority protection. What, exactly, is the role of kin-states in relation to kin-minorities? What does nationality mean when one of its important functions – that of creating a community – is taken over by, or at least is made ancillary to, another legal category of belonging? What remains of the role of states in regulating the identity of individuals? Can the nation be an international actor, on any basis? Given that more and more countries find themselves with (both national and non-national) residents who identify themselves with cultures other than the majority cultures of the state they are resident in, the controversy around the Hungarian status law may be only a preview of what is to come.

The larger question can thus be framed in the following terms: if an individual or a minority group as a whole feels that its home-state has neither the wish nor the capacity to provide the conditions necessary for the maintenance of a given identity, should a path to seeking support elsewhere be available? Status laws rely on the assumption that it should, for the reasons presented above. In turn, those who believe that home-states should have an exclusive role in such matters generally rely on two arguments. One, because the individuals are the nationals of a given state and thus under its jurisdiction. In other words, while the premise of state sovereignty remains an ordering principle of international law, other states may not establish legal or other relationships with these individuals without the consent of the state of nationality. Two, because states are relatively free, barring extreme circumstances, to apply their chosen policies for the maintenance of national identity within their sovereign territory. Is either of these answers convincing? Despite the pull of tradition, recent legal and political developments weaken any unequivocal affirmation.

---

245. Some authors go so far as to say that international norms of minority protection are 'alien' to the European Union. Gyertyánfy (2002), p. 118; but *see* Görömbei (2001) who argues that norms of minority protection will seep into European Union law through ECT Art. 6(2), given that many Member States (especially the new ones) have signed and ratified, among others, the Framework Convention and its Protocols, so that these may be considered part of the 'constitutional tradition' of the Union. (One should remember that some Member States have not done so, however.)
246. *See* discussion in de Witte (2004); *see also* Toggenburg (2004), for a discussion of existing competence, as well as possibilities for development.

1. GENERAL QUESTIONS

So let us take a closer look at some of the more general questions. As discussed, though the category of 'status laws' is here limited to legislation that applies to non-nationals and (primarily) kin-minorities on the basis of an ethno-cultural understanding of nationhood, their appearance cannot be detached from the proliferation of diaspora policies and plural nationality.[247] On the most general level, they all reconstitute the manner in which one state may create legal ties with individuals in another state in the name of a cultural identity. While the fact of plural nationality and some diaspora policies simply dismiss the idea that membership in a political community or even a nation-state must be unique, allowing for the possibility that an individual may have multiple cultural and political loyalties, status laws (claim to) focus only on the cultural aspect. Though the legal effect of such attention may actually be weaker than that of plural nationality, for example, its political and emotional ramifications may nonetheless be much more revolutionary (and destabilizing): one, because a strange new legal status is created and two, because the split between political and cultural community may not be so clear as it is assumed to be.

In fact, as Fowler has noted, the (first) Hungarian status law went farther than the notions of either vertical (European) or horizontal (plural) citizenship/nationality in undermining traditional ideas about what these concepts mean.[248] In particular, she spoke of an 'alternative to the territorial state and its citizenry as the only means of organizing political space',[249] apparently seeing no problem with overlapping nations. Unfortunately, she took at face value the statements of the Orbán government regarding the status law as a model for a future Europe of communities instead of states[250] and painted a rather rosy picture of a 'postmodern' reality of deterritorialized nationality.[251]

In this vision she echoes theorists of transnationalism (and the craftsmen of diaspora policies), who see the emergence of a future in which 'the nation's people may live anywhere in the world and still not live outside the state'.[252] These theories, whereby individuals have social relations and thus strong attachments to more than one state[253] in the context of migration are applicable to kin-minorities[254] only insofar as they describe the existence of ties across borders.[255] Aside from the existence of multitudinous legal and social ties, however, there are few underlying similarities, since it is exactly because minority individuals

---

247. *See* the chapter on 'Plural Nationality' below.
248. Fowler (2002), p. 10.
249. *Ibid.*, p. 58.
250. *See* Népszabadság, *A státustörvény Európa jövője* (28 June 2001).
251. Fowler (2002), pp. 46–47.
252. Basch, *et al* (1994)., p. 269.
253. *Ibid.*, p. 5 and pp. 7–8; Faist (2001); and Vertovec and Cohen (eds) (1999), pp. xx–xxv.
254. Stewart (2000). *See also* Brubaker (2000), pp. 1–2.
255. As Cohen makes clear, 'societies bleeding into each other create new complex and other intermediate identities, not diasporas'. Cohen (1997), p. 190. *See also* Clifford (1994), p. 307.

have clung to 'traditional' identities in their homelands that difficulties exist. If the borders had not shifted, there would be no question of discontinuities of identity. Despite some common legal issues then, diaspora policies are in most cases a different category of kinship laws for the simple reason of geographical proximity, not to mention the ratio of individuals involved in the entirety of the state population.

In a more sceptical vein, another commentator has noted that the status law is a 'deeply ideological and largely fantastical rejection of the world as it is'.[256] This may be true. However, the author missed the point in concluding that, because individuals live their daily lives in their home-states, the 'post-modernist fantasy of belonging to a deterritorialized nation offers ... no more than a mirage'.[257] In fact, it is no mirage: the status law redefines the actors involved in the politics of Hungarian – and other kin – minorities, changes incentives, and transforms the perceptions of those involved. Andreescu pointed to exactly this reconfiguration of the state container when he asked: 'What happens ... when the very ability to define who the ethnopolitical actors are within a state's internal frontiers is disappearing?'[258] What indeed?

a. **Interference**

On a practical level, the most obvious question is one of interference. First, interference by the kin-state in minority affairs. It is claimed that Hungary, for example, influences significant elements of minority politics, including education policies, family decisions, and the legitimacy of the organizations claiming to represent the minority through its status law.[259] In fact, Hungary's policy thus far has been aimed at the minorities as groups, so that only organizations were supported. Increased focus on supporting the individual may actually result in less direct influence on the actions of the minority as a group, to the extent that there is less (political or financial) meddling in the affairs of organizations. However, the status law may certainly shift incentives for individuals. On the one hand, economic incentives may influence the perceived value of given identities, since a cultural identity with perceived rewards is likely to gain in the popularity race. On the other hand, in the context of minorities, a positive interference with the pattern of elements of a cultural identity (e.g., better equipped schools, more opportunities to use a language) may, as discussed,[260] lead to a positive change in the temporal substance of

---

256. Stewart (2000), p. 29.
257. *Ibid.*
258. Andreescu (2002).
259. *Ibid.* In fact, Hungary has influenced minority organizations for a good while. In 1994, a scandal involving funds from Hungary given to certain minority organizations in Serbia led to a split in the Hungarian minority party there. Horváth (2000), p. 48 and p. 114. Following an overhaul of the system granting financial support, successive governments have vowed not to favour certain groups within the minorities over others; it is difficult to tell how this promise bears out in practice.
260. *See* Secs I.C.1 and I.C.2.

that identity. The conception of a destiny for the group, in particular, may ameliorate. In the medium or long-term, such developments could have significant effects on the decisions of a minority group in their home-state.

Accordingly, the second question revolves around interference by a kin-state in the internal politics of home-states. Certainly, the possibilities of reaching acceptable minority-majority accommodation in the home-state are affected by the existence of kin-states. For one thing, the multicultural solutions advocated by liberal critics like Kymlicka become impossible, since those theorists envisage vacuum states.[261] In reality, not only do kin-states play an active role in framing and influencing the interactions of the minorities and their home-states, they change the existing dynamic of the 'triadic nexus' by means of legislation. Not, however, as Andreescu claims in the Hungarian context, because the 'minority will ... no longer negotiate with the majority as a well-delimited group, but as part of the ethnic nation to which it belongs'. That argument is faulty for a number of reasons; first, because the minorities have separate and well-defined identities within the Hungarian nation. They are under no illusions that they act in their own name, not that of Budapest. The very existence of the status law proves this, since the minorities first suggested it and kept it on the agenda. Second, because if Hungary could influence minority identity to the extent Andreescu assumes, the effect of the status laws would have been manifest by now; in fact, this influence would have been an element of politics since 1989. But the Hungarian-minority parties have been enthusiastic actors in their home-states since entering politics and continue in that role now. (Neither the minority party in Slovakia nor in Romania has lost significant support in national elections since passage of the status law.[262]) Finally, because individuals decide of their own accord whether to apply for the Certificates. In this respect, it is not the existence of the status law that matters, but how it is received: if the risks of getting a

---

261. *See* Kymlicka (2000), p. 201. In discussing the difference between 'Western' and 'Eastern' nationalisms, the author notes that the 'danger of irredentism' is a reason why the 'liberal' nationalism of Western Europe is much more difficult to achieve in East-Central Europe. (In the process, he repeats the old argument that East-Central European minorities are more 'dangerous' to the state than those in Western Europe). *See also* Vertovec (2001), pp. 5, 9, and 15.
262. In the 2002 Slovak elections, the MKP (Hungarian Coalition Party) received 11.16 per cent of the votes; in 2006, 11.68 per cent. This exceeds, slightly, the per centage of self-declared Hungarian minority individuals in the country (9.7 per cent in the 2001 census) and is a significant gain from the 1998 elections when they received 9.12 per cent of the votes cast; participation did not change. Thus, either non-minority individuals had to have voted for the party, presumably based at least partly on their involvement in the last government coalition; or thousands more had to have considered themselves 'Hungarian', and thus supporters of the Hungarian minority party, than in any elections since 1990. In either case, the problems of the status law seem to have done no long-term political damage to the party.

Similarly, in the 2004 Romanian elections, the Hungarian Democratic Alliance in Romania (RMDSz) received 6.2 per cent of the votes cast in both the Lower House and the Senate, as opposed to 6.8 per cent (6.9 per cent in the Senate) in 2000. In light of the defection of the radical wing of the RMDSz in the course of that year and the disqualification of their newly-formed party from the elections, some had feared a significant drop in support.

Certificate outweigh its benefits or if it is simply deemed irrelevant, few will apply.[263] Thus, any change of dynamics hinges on perception, or the question of loyalty.

b.   Perceptions and Loyalties

The Hungarian Certificates are a physical manifestation of what hitherto may only have had symbolic relevance to both minority and majority individuals: belonging to the Hungarian (cultural) nation. In theory, there should be nothing to argue with the fact of such belonging, since individuals have the right to freely determine which cultures (and communities) they wish to belong to; however, in the prevailing political climate of the region, choices of this kind are never without consequences. More threatening still, the Certificates also seem to imply loyalty to Hungary. Whether this is a function of the actual provisions of the status law or the nature of any such law, since it comes from the kin-state, is debatable. In either case, the Certificates may leave the majority feeling that the minority – likely already suspicious – does not even wish to try to 'belong' to the home-state. This perception makes the 'treason of identity' all the more galling, with political consequences.[264] In this manner, any (claimed) multicultural project in the home-state is derailed not only by the fact of external interference, but also by the perception of what interference in the form of a status law (or other kinship law) means.

Aside from changing perceptions, status laws also adjust understandings of the underlying principles of citizenship. As noted, traditional citizenship theory emphasized the rights and duties that individuals have as members of bounded sovereign communities.[265] However, like European citizenship, status laws redefine the functions of citizenship. Besides the primary political community, whose members, and only they, possess rights in the territory of the state, we now deal with a parallel cultural community, whose members – neither nationals nor citizens of the state – have rights inside and outside the territory of the state on the basis of the cultural (or ethnic) affinity. Thus, the first and second characteristics of the traditional understanding of citizenship – that only members of the political community enjoy rights and that these rights may only be exercised within the territory of the political community – no longer hold true. In fact, neither does the third feature – that members of the political community define the content of their

---

263. Kis argues a similar, and very lucid, point when he states that the status law could, given the poisoned atmosphere surrounding its inception, produce a larger and now concrete split within the minorities – between those who apply, and whose identity it confirms, and those who do not, since they are put off by the possible confrontation with the majority the Certificate would entail. Kis in Beszélő, *supra* note III.67.
264. For example, a study done in Romania in July 2001 revealed that 51 per cent of the Romanian-Romanian nationals polled believed that the law would have negative effects on the interaction between the Hungarian minority and the majority. See Népszabadság, *Románia: romlik a megítélésünk* (10 July 2001).
265. *See also* Linklater (1998), p. 23.

rights – since it is not necessarily citizens who designate the rights in question. Other actors, including members of the diaspora or the kin-minority, may have a say in determining the content of status laws or of referenda on kin-minority issues, as the case may be. From the angle of active or participatory citizenship, it is obvious that individuals who are subject to laws should have a say in their content – but in the context of status laws the individuals affected are generally not nationals. The citizen-national link is thus clearly broken, despite the continued importance of sovereignty in all its forms, as the ruckus surrounding the Hungarian law highlighted. In place of the traditional link, the conception of citizenship behind status laws assumes the existence of new communities with 'citizens'. The political community of the state is no longer singular, but challenged by cultural and other identities as legitimate bases of membership.

Unlike plural nationality, however, which proclaims that individuals belong to two political and cultural communities – as evinced by their two nationalities – status laws consider a possible division of the two: the individual may be a member of one political community (that of the home-state) and one cultural community (that of the cultural nation). But what about the mixed nature of these so-called cultural communities? Perhaps the multiple loyalties of plural nationality or transnationalism can be applied in this context too? Not necessarily.

So long as the 'sacred' element of nationality – particularly the attribution of a moral function to the idea of loyalty – also remains an element of citizenship, individuals are necessarily considered, in some form, the 'property' of the state.[266] They are not only citizens, with rights and duties in the territory of the state, and nationals, with the right to expect protection by their state when outside its borders, but also breathing placards for state sovereignty. (This philosophy was traditionally most apparent in the requirement of expatriation permits for nationals before naturalization could occur elsewhere, as well as in the earlier principle of perpetual allegiance. Remnants of the approach survive in the prohibition, by some states, of holding two nationalities, however.[267]) Conversely, even the accommodation of plural nationality continues to rely on this logic of 'sacredness', albeit in reverse: holding two nationalities is meant to be a sign of belonging to two national projects, rather than an indication that the status of national has lost its identity function.

In either case, giving away control over a group or possibly the entire population of the state on a collective basis is something that may be done only by express declaration. A declaration of this kind was made by Member States on the occasion of the Maastricht Treaty, for example, when European citizenship was introduced, despite the fact that the control functions of the Community as they relate to individuals are still developing. As discussed, the concept of

---

266. *See also* Magyar Nemzet (Miklós Bakk), *Két nemzetkoncepcó európai versenye zajlik* (7 July 2001).
267. *See* Sec. IV.A.1.

European citizenship as yet poses only an indirect risk to the national identities of Member States, since the European Union is at present simply too different from a state to be perceived as competition. However, a horizontal transfer of control, or the creation of links with another state through kinship laws (as well as plural nationality), may constitute a direct threat to the national project, as well as to sovereignty.

The role of the national – who no longer views her citizenship as sacred – becomes especially problematic in the context of status laws, where minority-protection is intertwined with the politics of nationalism. Thus, only if the individuals targeted by the kin-state form a substantial group in the home-state, and especially if their rights comprise a contentious area of domestic politics, will status laws even register on the radar. This explains why older kinship laws in other European states garnered attention only in the context of the uproar surrounding the Hungarian law. If Romania and Slovakia had not seen the status law in any form as threatening, there would not have been any political problem and, in turn, no identifiable legal problem. Hence, the arguments on both sides – that status laws are an infringement of state sovereignty or that they are a form of minority protection – are not really about either of these points. The real issues are (1) the extent to which a state can influence the collective identity of a group circumscribed by specified criteria, whether they are nationals or not, and (2) a determination of the bases on which these criteria may rely.

Let us be clear then: no actor in this situation has acted without an agenda on what citizenship and nationality (should) mean. Hungary trusts in the (re)creation of a Hungarian space in the Carpathian basin – notwithstanding the state borders it has given up changing – on the basis of officially recognized membership the Hungarian cultural nation. This membership has overtones of membership in the Hungarian political nation through the implication of Hungary, however. It is at this point, then, that we arrive at the cleavage of citizenship and nationality. To be more precise, we are talking about a dissociation of the identity function of traditional citizenship from its rights/duties function, while leaving nationality intact. The home-states, on the other hand, wish to continue their own nation and national-identity building strategies unimpeded, in the hope of reaching the holy grail of the nation-state. Hence, they rely on traditional notions of a unified nationality/citizenship. Meanwhile, the Hungarian minorities hope for both the opportunity to maintain their identity and concrete benefits; for the moment, their home-state is unwilling to provide either of these things, while Hungary, to a limited extent, provides both. Even if it did not, however, the existence of distinct cultural and political nations means that the identity function of citizenship remains – to varying degrees – separate from its other half even in a best-case scenario. Accordingly, the minorities hope for rights from both the cultural and the political nation. Whether these are granted through nationality or quasi-citizenship depends on the politics of the states involved. Finally, the international community simply dreams of the whole mess going away, without contributing more than existing standards.

c.   **The Nation as Legal Entity**

These standards unfortunately do not address one of the underlying assumptions of all status (and kinship) laws: the existence of a cultural or ethnic nation across borders. Through the laws in question, the nation assumes legal existence. In the case of status laws, this occurs through direct references to individuals who are to be supported in their kinship identity with the aim of allowing them to be full members of the given nation. The nation thus exists as an actor separate from the individuals who constitute it, and separate from the state that claims it as a national culture.[268] A number of commentators have argued that this is in fact one of the main novelties of the Hungarian law.[269] The novelty also extends to the interaction of individual and group: the minority individual is more likely to maintain her identity within the minority group if she feels she is part of a larger nation. If she maintains her identity, the minority group will remain strong within its historic region and the nation large enough to reinforce a minority identity outside of the territory in which it sustains the majority culture. It is difficult to determine where the cycle starts, however. This explains why the stated aims of the status law link belonging to the nation with individual identity and general well-being.[270] Better to iterate the connection of everything, as in the first version of the Hungarian law, and leave the rest to time, the drafters seem to have thought.

It is important to distinguish whether one's goal is to maintain a strong nation or to support minority individuals, however. In other words, is the well-being of individuals a means or an end? If the latter, the law in question is not only morally questionable, but also bases its existence on a presumed right that does not exist. There is no such thing as the 'right' of a nation to exist, and no right for an individual to belong to a nation, as such. This remains the status quo despite reliance on the assumed right by, *inter alia*, the Ibarretxe Plan approved by the Basque Parliament in December 2004 – and rejected by the Spanish one in February 2005 – as well as the recently-approved overhaul of Catalonia's autonomy status.[271] However, if the focus of the law is the individual, it is based on

---

268. Stack recognized quite early the possibility that the nation (or, in his terminology, the 'ethnic group') could function as a transnational actor, albeit not a legally recognized one, in the face of declining state nationalism. Stack (1999) [1981], pp. 645–646.
269. Kántor (2002); and Provincia (Zsolt Attila Borbély), *A státustörvény mint a magyar (re)integráció eszköze* (2001/5).
270. In this sense, individual choices will determine how much salience the status law actually has. As we have noted, culture is not a static concept. *See also* Hann (2002), p. 273; and Faist (1999), p. 32. Similarly, identity is ever-changing and may be expressed in varying ways. *See* Kennedy and Roudometof (2002), p. 15. For example, one young Hungarian minority woman noted in an interview that her identity as a liberal is more important to her than her Hungarianness, and that, conversely, she believed she could help the Hungarian minority by working in the National Liberal Party in Romania. *See* Népszabadság, *Magyar fiatalok erősítenek román pártokat* (31 October 2002).
271. The direct context in the Basque and Catalan cases is, obviously, reliance on a right to self-determination; the demand for recognition of the existence of the Basque/Catalan nation is, however, the basis for such a right. *See* Preamble, Rec. 1 of the Propuesta de Estatuto Político

rights that already exist: the right to enjoy one's own culture and the right to identity. A difficult still remains. Even if one accepts that individuals have a right to be part of a group – the cultural nation – that nation is linked to a state, the kin-state, through its institutions.

And this is the main problem. Even if the cultural nation exists without borders – as the ongoing interactions of individuals, groups and organizations – the physical manifestation of this unity is, at present, channelled through a state. It is the state that funds and furnishes the infrastructure of identity. This being so, membership in the cultural nation implicates some degree of membership or at least a presence in the political nation. Hence the symbolic importance of the Hungarian Certificates, for example. In fact, from the minority's point of view, the more threatened the group feels, the more important links with the kin-state and Certificates become, as a concrete device of cohesiveness.[272] It is exactly this symbolism that is threatening to the majority, however, and may spur actions or measures that cause the minority to feel even less secure in its home-state. Conversely, if the minority group feels strong enough in the home-state and has an acknowledged place in the given ethnic or cultural nation, it may feel little or no need for an official link with the kin-state.

This state of affairs is more probable in the case of diaspora communities, both because of distance and because their numbers are generally not perceived as threatening to the home-state. Regardless, here too the nation assumes legal form through reliance on a 'special affinity with people'[273] of the same ethnic background or cultural heritage, as expressed in the constitutional clauses discussed. This 'affinity' supposedly accounts for why individuals claiming membership in the nation have the right to special treatment within the state that claims to house the collective identity. There is no assumption that the community is threatened in its identity by the action (or inaction) of another state in these cases; rather, there is a presumption that individuals may request or require aid

---

de la Comunidad de Euskadi (2003), as well as, *inter alia*, Arts 2(1) and 3(1). *See also* BBC News, 'Basque Independence Plan Rejected' (2 February 2005). For Catalonia, *see also* 'Voters in Catalonia Approve a Plan for Greater Autonomy'. *The New York Times*, 19 June 2006; and BBC News, 'Catalonia endorses autonomy plan' (19 June 2006).

272. The symbolic aspects of power play as important a role in this context as public policy. For example, acknowledging the existence of minorities as equal members of the political community in the home-state is crucial. Many constitutions in Central Europe fail to take this step, however. In addition to the provisions of the Romanian Constitution discussed above at note III.9, *see* the Preamble of the Slovak Constitution, which states: 'We, the Slovak nation, mindful of the political and cultural heritage of our forebears, and of the centuries of experience from the struggle for national existence and our own statehood'. Compare the Preamble of the Croatian Constitution, which states 'the Republic of Croatia is hereby established as the national state of the Croatian nation and the state of members of other nations and minorities who are its citizens: Serbs, Moslems, Slovenes, Czechs, Slovaks, Italians, Hungarians, Jews, and others, who are guaranteed equality with citizens of Croatian nationality'. Compare also the Constitutions of Hungary, Slovenia and the Czech Republic, among others. *See also* Schöpflin (2000), p. 131 for a discussion.

273. Irish Constitution, Art. 2.

from the homeland to help keep their collective identity relevant. As the Slovene law states, 'the goal is the preservation and growth of Slovene identity, language and culture'.[274]

Whatever the particular context, legal reliance on 'affinity' with the nation as the basis for individual-state ties is distinctly novel. As the CoE Report on the Hungarian law noted, in the context of competing conceptions of the 'nation' in Europe, claims-making of this kind generates political tension; it may also clash with existing rules of public international law. For this reason, the CoE Report pointed out the distinct need to formulate new principles to govern emerging kin-state relationships,[275] including 'the possibility of trying to incorporate a positive concept of "nation" into the traditional concepts of public international law ... by accepting – under strict conditions of sovereignty and statehood – the formulation of a sort of part-citizenship'.[276] Clearly, a development of this kind would constitute a fundamental change of legal approach to individual-state ties for the purposes of international law. On this basis, it would seem an unlikely direction for evolution at the present time. That said, analogous suggestions have been proposed in the context of state ties with individuals in diasporas.

In a revealing sentence, the Report of the Council of Europe on Links between Europeans living abroad and their countries of origin (1999)[277] (hereinafter, CoE Report on Europeans abroad or CoE Report) states:

> [W]hat is important is that dialogue may be established, that effective co-operation links can be developed between, on the one hand, the state (government or even parliament and local, regional and professional bodies) and, on the other hand, those who represent expatriates, be they citizens [nationals] registered with consulates or members of firmly rooted communities who have lived abroad for generations.[278]

Unfortunately, as even the section above shows, the CoE Report on Europeans abroad is very sloppy in its language. Expatriates seem to be both nationals and 'families who have lived in a country for two, three or even four generations, while preserving emotional, family and maternal ties to their country of origin',[279] and thus individuals who likely no longer hold nationality.[280] However, the underlying concern seems to be with granting individuals (who are linked to the country of origin either by nationality or through ethnic/cultural ties) certain benefits both within the country of origin and in their own state. The CoE Report bluntly states that the suggested 'law of expatriates', 'entails going beyond the bounds of

---

274. Resolution on Relations with Slovenes Abroad (2002), Art. 1(1).
275. CoE Report on the Hungarian law, para. 26.
276. *Ibid.*, para. 46.
277. Council of Europe, Parliamentary Assembly Committee on Migration, Refugees and Demography, Report on Links between Europeans living abroad and their countries of origin (1999).
278. *Ibid.*, para. 73.
279. *Ibid.*, paras 13 and 24. One example cited are Irish-Americans.
280. *Ibid.*, para. 95. In fact, the CoE Report discusses making it easier for expatriates to recover their nationality of origin.

traditional international law, in so far as it is concerned with and aimed at individuals and not just states'.[281]

The focus on individuals here is crucial, but may, in the case of some members of a diaspora, lead one to miss the interaction of individual and state ties that underlie the initial concern. If such individuals do not hold the nationality of their country of origin then what, besides ethnic or cultural ties, is the basis for the states to have anything to do with them? Let us assume that the CoE Report on Europeans abroad in fact refers to persons who do have citizenship rights in the country of origin, however; the basis for links with their country of origin must be examined. Immigrants and even members of the first generation often maintain ongoing familial and social ties in the states of origin, so that legal ties can at least plausibly be argued for. But what about members of the second or third generation? Leaving aside possible ethnic explanations, which could in any case be discriminatory in the same way status laws may be, the basis for actual and emotional ties to the country of origin is (and can only be) identity-based and cultural, since the persons in question have never lived there. In other words, individuals are, for example, 'Irish' (or more correctly, 'Irish-American') by affiliation, not because they grew up and have memories of or friends in Ireland.

Culture is, by nature, a collective enterprise and impossible without organization. Above the local level, it is civil society and the state that gives infrastructure to culture: people, customs, language, history, all are framed by the state. As Dubois notes in the context of French cultural policy, 'the establishment, then institutionalization of culture as a category of public intervention ... relaunche[s] battles for the definition of culture and for the [state's] proper relationship to culture'.[282] In other words, the state itself constitutes 'a place for the definition of culture'[283] by continuously re-establishing its boundaries. This role seems almost natural today – few would attack the idea of state subsidies for museums, for example – but is actually an important element of the maintenance of national identity. That the state generally has the means to act on the nexus between infrastructure and culture, while civil society often does not – e.g., by maintaining a counter-discourse – means that the former has considerable power in helping to confirm the place of the individual in the 'nation' by whatever means it chooses: through documents, benefits or simply organization (of sponsored language courses, diaspora entities, etc.). Moreover, the notion of 'nation-state', as perpetuated to this day in both political and legal discourse – exemplified by the invitation of Recommendation 1410 for states to 'introduc[e] support measures in the cultural, educational, political and social spheres based on the criterion of nationality rather than territoriality'[284] – only adds to individuals' association

---

281. *Ibid.*, para. 20.
282. '*La formation puis l'institutionnalisation de la culture comme catégorie d'intervention publique n'en ont pas moins relancé les luttes pour la définition de la culture et du rapport légitime à la culture*'. Dubois (1999), p. 302.
283. *Un lieu de définition de la culture*. *Ibid.*, p. 16.
284. Council of Europe, Recommendation 1410, Sec. 5.v.a.

of, for example, 'Irish culture' with Ireland.[285] It is then only one small step to citizenship rights as a means to confirming expat membership in the cultural group for those who have never lived in the country of origin.

Ironically, this connection may be least pertinent for migrants who belonged to national minorities in their countries of origin, since their very identity in that country had involved a struggle with the state.[286] It is also not relevant for minority individuals, including members of the Hungarian minorities in Central Europe, since they have a link to a cultural nation, without any confirmation in the manner the CoE Report suggests for diasporas (at least until recently). The idea behind the revised Hungarian status law (though arguably not its first version) was, among others, to provide such a link, as already discussed. In fact, the end of the CoE Report, arguing for a radical reconfiguration of what it means to be a citizen of a state or a member of a nation, reads like something a proponent of status laws could have written:

> Although in the ... European Convention on Nationality, the terms 'citizenship' and 'nationality' are used to denote the same thing – the legal connection which exists between a person and a state – there are countries where 'state' and 'nation' are not the same thing ... Many problems could be solved by making a clear *distinction between two sets of rights*, those linked with residence in a given geographical area (*citizenship rights* and those linked with possession of a given cultural, civic and *national identity* and *disregarding the traditional definition of the sovereign state*, based on the concept of territory ... This *distinction could also help to solve the problem of minorities*, which has become crucial, following the collapse of the communist system *in eastern and central Europe*.[287]

The Venice Commission seems not to have considered the possibilities raised above, or even acknowledged the existence of the Report. This is puzzling, since the CoE Report on Europeans abroad makes suggestions that are particularly relevant for status laws, most prominently the delinkage of nationality and citizenship rights.[288] While a delinkage of this kind could take a variety of forms, and could grant various types of rights, the underlying idea remains broadly uniform. It suggests that certain rights accrue to an individual through residence in a certain

---

285. The growth of the 'heritage' or 'culture' niche in tourism is but one sign of this phenomenon. See 'Seeking Roots, Finding Them'. *The New York Times*, 5 October 2003.
286. This is strictly true only for national minorities without kin-states or with strong regional identities; when a kin-state exists, the identification of one's cultural identity with a state may simply shift states. Thus, for example, a Hungarian minority individual resident abroad may look to Budapest rather than Belgrade when nostalgic for her roots.
287. CoE Report, paras 107–110 (emphasis added).
288. This division would in essence echo the difference between those theorists who see states and those who see nations 'when they look at a map' (*see* Kántor (2001)), but, unlike present theories of nationalism, would not see the two as mutually exclusive. (*See* Nairn (1997) for a discussion of the views of the two camps).

state, while others are granted through national/cultural affiliation; the two do not necessarily overlap.

The Second Report of the Council of Europe on Links between Europeans living abroad and their countries of origin (2004)[289] (hereinafter, Second CoE Report on Europeans abroad or Second CoE Report) draws out the connection between diaspora and status laws more pointedly, in noting that the Hungarian status law 'aims to create a link between the state and its non-citizen nationals [sic!], thereby establishing a form of transnational or transborder citizenship'.[290] The 'tenor' of the law is accordingly compared by the Second CoE Report to laws 'protecting the rights of expatriates abroad', 'whether or not they have retained their nationality'.[291] Unfortunately, this report is as confusing in its terminology as its predecessor,[292] so that it is difficult to tell what the exact legal status of the Hungarian 'non-citizen nationals' referred to is believed to be. The report also blurs the significant contextual distinctions between minority protection laws and diaspora policies noted above. The contention that both status laws and diaspora laws aim to prod 'the development of a national community with no territorial roots'[293] circumscribed by the geographical borders of the sovereign state holds true, however.

In effect, both visions spell the death of the 'nation-state' in the obvious sense. However, since most states actively support one culture – that which they have helped construct in the past – the idea of nation-state is not, and cannot, be dead in another. The delinkage of cultural affiliation and residence would, however, mean the end of the idea of the multicultural state, since each state would maintain a majority culture, and would in fact work to maintain that culture. At the same time, certain rights of identity would be granted to minority individuals to allow them to preserve their own 'national' identity, while remaining nationals of the states they are resident in.[294] Considering that multiculturalism has rarely, if ever, truly denoted the equal co-existence of various cultural, ethnic or other groups within a state, this outcome is perhaps only realistic. Any delinkage of cultural affiliation and residence could only go so far, in any case, since the state must maintain enough control over the likes of education to ensure enough cohesion to keep the country from falling apart.[295] This outcome would nonetheless require the state to recognise

---

289. Council of Europe, Parliamentary Assembly Committee on Migration, Refugees and Demography, Report on Links between Europeans living abroad and their countries of origin (2004) (hereinafter, Second CoE Report).
290. *Ibid.*, para. 54.
291. Para. 53.
292. In particular, the terms 'migrants', 'expatriates', 'emigrants', 'citizens' and 'nationals' are used interchangeably in the Second CoE Report, without consideration for their varying connotations or legal meanings.
293. *Ibid.*, para. 7.
294. In the region, the ideal of a multicultural (or multinational) state is already near-impossible, since many of the bases on which such a model would rely for unity – such as core values and a common feeling of belonging – do not exist.
295. *See* Kymlicka (2001), pp. 293–316 for a discussion of the difficulties surrounding education, national identity and loyalty. I could also imagine more radical developments, such as a truly

that it does not have a singular role to play in the development of its nationals' collective identities.

The division discussed above in fact mirrors Schöpflin's view that, while ethnicity has a legitimate function in defining identity, it has nothing to do with the civic dimension of states.[296] Or, as he argues in another context, 'all citizens have an equal right to cultural reproduction'. On this basis, 'groups ... [may] have agreed to differ on some aspects of what constitutes loyalty to the state and they do not take these differences as vital to their existence'.[297] The difficulty, however, is that many states continue to measure loyalty on the basis of the unified nationality-citizenship theory, dismissing the possibility of a split between identity and rights. If we take Schöpflin's view far enough, however, we arrive at a potential situation in which the state has no role at all to play in cultural regulation – in other words, we would be dealing with a truly multicultural (and multinational) state, kept together in reality, and not only in theory, by civic values. Sounds quite enlightened, granted, but how sound?

2. THE POSSIBILITIES OF RESOLUTION THROUGH EXISTING STATUSES

Despite the novelty of status laws – and kinship laws in general – the context in which they have emerged is not new. Cultural ties that extend across state borders can be considered the norm in Europe, rather than an exception. What is unique is the attempt of states to give such ties a legal frame more or less within the bounds of international law. Considering the debate status laws have provoked, however, it is worth considering whether existing legal statuses could not accomplish similar objectives without the political and legal fallout.

a. **European Citizenship**

Perhaps European citizenship could be an answer, as certain authors argue[298] and as the CoE Report hints? Unfortunately, the fact of EU citizenship will not necessarily make national/cultural or any other distinctions less problematic. Yes, as Laitin discusses, certain minority groups in the EU, like the Catalans, already conceive of Europe as 'a compound of regions and nations without a state'.[299] The author even argues for a distinct possibility of more fluid relations between

---

borderless EU, in which only cultural/educational matters were left to regional regulation, with EU control over most other policy areas. However, this scenario is likely to stay in the realm of the imaginary and would, in any case, bring its own dilemmas (like the situation of minorities within minorities).
296. Schöpflin (2000), p. 278.
297. *Ibid.*, p. 47. *See also* Kymlicka (2000), pp. 21, 32–33, and 39–42.
298. *See* Murphy (1999).
299. Laitin (2001), p. 101. *See also* Mitchell and Cavanagh (2001), p. 261; but *see* Laible (2001), p. 242, for an argument that if the state becomes too weak an actor within the EU, minorities may begin questioning the legitimacy of the EU as such.

states and groups, as the assurance of the Maastricht treaty that 'decisions are taken at greatest proximity to the people' becomes reality. If there is truly greater subsidiarity, the argument goes, minority language communities have more possibilities to express and maintain their identity. This may lead to a change in the 'institutional locus of autonomy politics',[300] as Brussels becomes as much a focus of minority politics as national capitals, with an attendant diminution in cultural conflict.

In financial terms, some have shown that minorities with links across borders are specially placed to take direct advantage of European funding for cultural (a.k.a. diversity-maintaining) programmes; and indirectly, of structural funds (such as INTERREG).[301] The basis for such funding is precarious, however, to the extent that it relies on cross-border bonds – on the premise, apparently, that anything involving more than one state is 'European' – rather than on a recognition of special affinity. Accordingly, the approach serves to strengthen the (legal) importance of the very borders whose diminution is hoped for. In fact, the regional trend seems to be flagging, as movement toward a re-trenchment of the central role of states gains in momentum.

As we saw, the role of the European Union in cultural regulation is problematic at best; and in any case, does not override Member State action. The emerging European identity, in turn, upholds existing identities rather than dismantles them. On a structural level, moreover, it is still Member States that determine minority access to the EU, since the choice as to the status of minority regions is wholly determined by the internal order of each Member State.[302] Thus, without autonomy and a separate voice, minorities have no institutional voice in the EU.

In reality, a transfer of power to the EU may not bring the hoped for advantages in any case; instead it could result in reduced democratic accountability and, ultimately, a loss of legitimacy, as minority issues of utmost importance on the domestic agenda morph into a mere blip in politics at the European level. In this manner, transnational government could actually result in diminished leverage for the minority, leading to aggravation of the feeling of powerlessness.[303] Another possibility, discussed by Kis, is that of cross-state administrative structures within the EU, 'so as to facilitate the development of regions across state borders'.[304] While it is true that the initiatives grouped under regional (and cohesion) policy have resulted in increased cross-border co-operation – and even specific developments advantageous to minorities, as in the case of Austria and Italy – European (and international) law continues to function with the 'state' as its basic unit. This

---

300. Laitin, *ibid.*, p. 109.
301. INTERREG, adopted in 1990 and now in its third incarnation (for the period 2000–2006), is an initiative guaranteeing financial support and co-ordination for cross-border co-operation between regions. For a discussion of the possibilities this and other regional programs present for minorities *see*, e.g., Bauer and Rainer (2004); and, in the Hungarian context, Horváth and Ríz (2004).
302. de Witte (1993), p. 172.
303. *See* Kymlicka (2001), p. 326 for a similar argument on the EU Member State level.
304. Kis (2001), p. 239.

simple fact means that any innovation, including transnational administration, which involves regional *political* integration, rather than just economic or other co-ordination, is at present highly unlikely. Finally, in the case of kin-minorities, the final factor of the kin-state must also be considered in any equation. The problem of interference in the affairs of the home-state would not lessen, for example, and may lead to more political problems once any bilateral solution is couched in a multinational framework, such as the EU.

Thus, neither from the point of view of 'effective participation' nor on a cultural level is European integration likely to change the interaction of minorities with their state; the problems raised by the status laws, as well as questions regarding citizenship and nationality, will not go away. Indeed, in a Europe with increased migration within and from without – a Europe that hopes for a greater sense of unity through culture – cultural nationalism, whether stated or unstated, stands to gain ground.[305] In the same manner, so may kinship laws of various kinds.

But the suspicion remains: is law the right tool to regulate identity?[306] Or even recognize it?[307] As one young man asked about his Hungarian Certificate remarked, 'an emotional attachment either exists or doesn't; the Hungarian Certificate doesn't change this ....'[308] State attempts to do so may lead to incomprehensible, or in any case bewildering, classifications. The combination of Hungarian nationality and minority law, the status law, EU law and international law has, for example, created (at least) the following legal groupings of Hungarians: (1) nationals of Hungary who are members of the majority; (2) nationals of Hungary who are members of a minority; (3) nationals of Hungary who reside in a Schengen state; (4) nationals of Hungary who reside in a non-Schengen state; (5) Hungarian minority individuals who are nationals of a neighbouring Schengen state and hold a Hungarian Certificate; (6) Hungarian minority individuals who are nationals of a neighbouring Schengen state and do not hold a Hungarian Certificate; (7) Hungarian minority individuals who are nationals of a neighbouring non-Schengen state and hold a Hungarian Certificate; (8) Hungarian minority individuals who are nationals of a neighbouring non-Schengen state and do not hold a Hungarian Certificate; (9) Hungarian diaspora individuals who are nationals of Schengen states; (10) Hungarian diaspora individuals who are nationals of non-Schengen states; (11) Hungarian diaspora individuals who are nationals of a non-Schengen state, reside in one of the

---

305. See Kymlicka (2001b), p. 72 for an argument that both majority and minority nationalisms in the West are moving away from ethnic conceptions to a focus on 'linguistic and institutional integration'.
306. 'Law generally, and laws in particular, are not adapted to determine anyone's national belonging'. ('*A jog általában, illetve a jogszabályok nem alkalmasak arra, hogy meghatározzák bárkinek is a nemzeti hovatartozását*'.) Varga (2002) [2000], p. 223.
307. See Borbély (2000), who argues that nationality is the legal expression of belonging to the national community; in a twist on the usual nation-state paradigm, he does not seem to view nationality exclusively, however. All kin should be included, but others may be too.
308. '*Érzelmi kötődés vagy van, vagy nincs, azon nem változtat a magyarigazolvány*'. Népszabadság, *A magyarigazolvány jó a háznál* (13 May 2004).

neighbouring states and have a Hungarian Certificate; (12) Hungarian diaspora individuals who are nationals of a Schengen state, reside in one of the neighbouring states and have a Hungarian Certificate; (13) nationals of Hungary who also hold the nationality of another state; (14) individuals with permanent residence permits in Hungary who are waiting for Hungarian nationality. So who is Hungarian, exactly?

b.   **Plural Nationality**

Any response to this question has been further complicated since 5 December 2004, when voters in Hungary were asked to answer two questions in a national referendum.[309] The second question read as follows:

> Do you want the National Assembly to draft a law offering Hungarian nationality – with preferential naturalization – upon request to non-Hungarian nationals who reside outside Hungary, declare themselves to be Hungarian and attest to their Hungarianness with a 'Hungarian Certificate' pursuant to Art. 19 of Act 62/2001 or by other means, as stipulated in the law to be prepared?[310]

51.57 per cent of those who cast a ballot answered 'yes' to the question – however, only 37.49 per cent of those eligible to vote did so, so that the referendum was declared without effect (after a tortuous round of court decisions).[311] As one daily commented, the outcome can best be explained by 'distraught perplexity'.[312] No wonder, perhaps, considering the – emotional and decidedly ugly – campaign in the weeks leading up to the vote: opposition parties and some kin-minority politicians divided Hungarian nationals into groups of 'good' and 'evil', in an attempt at prompting a guilt-ridden 'yes' vote; the government resorted to social

---

309. The Hungarian Constitutional Court determined in March 2004 that the wording of the question formulated by the World Federation of Hungarians did not contravene the Constitution or electoral laws, so the signature campaign was allowed to proceed. (*See 5/2004. Alkotmánybírósági határozat*, Hungarian Constitutional Court (2004)). Since the organizers succeeded in collecting the number of signatures required by law, the referendum was held in December 2004.
310. '*Akarja-e, hogy az Országgyűlés törvényt alkosson arról, hogy kedvezményes honosítással – kérelmére – magyar állampolgárságot kapjon az a magát magyar nemzetiségűnek valló, nem Magyarországon lakó, nem magyar állampolgár, aki magyar nemzetiségét a 2001. évi LXII. törvény 19. §-a szerinti 'Magyar igazolvánnyal' vagy a megalkotandó törvényben meghatározott egyéb módon igazolja?*' The other question concerned agreement with the privatization of health care (and was answered with no, though the outcome was, again, without effect).
311. The National Election Office (OVB) declared the referendum (i.e., the answers to both questions) ineffectual on the basis of inadequate participation. *See 196/2004. (XII. 11.) OVB határozat*. Appeals for a re-count on behalf of the World Federation of Hungarians (MVSz), as well as a private individual were, however, granted by the Supreme Court on 14 December (*Kvk. III. 37. 316/2004/2 and Kvk. IV. 37. 315/2004/2*). On 4 January, the OVB declared that the re-count had not produced a substantially different result. (*2/2005. (I. 4.) OVB határozat*), a result accepted by the Supreme Court on 7 January (*Kvk. III. 37. 013/2005/2 and Kvk. III. 37. 011/2005/2*). With that, the lack of effect became final.
312. '*Kétségbeesett tanácstalanság*'. Népszabadság, *A népszavazás kudarca* (6 December 2004).

demagoguery bordering on xenophobia, including the spectre of hordes of new nationals sapping the welfare system, in its call for a 'no' (while both sides attempted to turn the referendum into a party popularity contest); leading intellectuals quarrelled about whether to boycott the referendum or not, and;[313] kin-minority groups plastered the country with sentimental posters.[314] Meanwhile, neighbouring states made intermittent appearances with varied and novel threats: Romania vowed to strip individuals of their Romanian nationality, despite the fact that dual nationality is allowed by the law of the country,[315] while Slovakia declared it would turn to the European Union to hinder the grant of Hungarian nationality to its nationals. The European Union, in turn, announced that the matter was an internal one, in line with the present legal stance whereby nationality matters remain within Member State competence. No wonder the international press had a field day, as the referendum presented a further example of how nationalist 'Eastern' Europeans were causing (or in a rare instance, belatedly avoiding) trouble.[316]

And the individual voter? She was left pondering not only whether to vote (and if so, how) but also how she ended up having to make such a decision in the first place.[317] In fact, the referendum cannot be seen apart from the status law saga already described. Certain individuals within the minorities saw international reactions and the Hungarian government's subsequent amendment of the status law as a sign that any law of this kind could be watered down to the point of being useless. The result has been a return to the more radical demand for dual nationality; a

---

313. See Népszabadság, *Tartózkodunk a szavazástól* (13 November 2004); and Népszabadság, *Miért megyek el szavazni* (20 November 2004).
314. Posters included the following slogans: '*Összefogás a nemzetért*'! (Solidarity for the nation!); '*Újra együtt*'! (Together again!); '*Ne mondj le rólunk*'! (Don't give us up!); '*Nyújts feléje védő kart*' (Lend him/her a protective hand) (quoting the national anthem); '*Soha nem hagynám el a szülőföldömet . . de magyar vagyok*'! (I would never leave my homeland ... but I am Hungarian!); '*ők magyarok? Ma nem lehetnének magyar állampolgárok*' (Are they Hungarian? They could not be Hungarian nationals today) (with pictures of famous writers, composers and politicians who were born in territories that are no longer part of Hungary).
315. In a bizarre instance of legal show-and-tell, Romania relied on a bilateral treaty from 1979 (excluding dual nationality) that Hungary, in turn, claimed to have terminated in 1992. See Ordinance 2 on the Proclamation of the Accord signed on 13 June 1979 between the People's Republic of Hungary and the Romanian Socialist Republic on the Prevention and Solution of Cases of Dual Nationality (1980); and Law VII on the abrogation of Ordinance 2 on the Proclamation of the Accord signed on 13 June 1979 between the People's Republic of Hungary and the Romanian Socialist Republic on the Prevention and Solution of Cases of Dual Nationality (1992).
316. *Inter alia*, Der Spiegel, *Teures Ja* (29 November 2004); BBC News, 'Hungary Vote Angers Romania' (4 December 2004); BBC News, 'Low Turnout Scuppers Hungary Vote' (6 December 2004); International Herald Tribune, 'Uneasy Echo in Hungary' (6 December 2004); Le Monde, *Hongrie: Deux Referendums Invalidés Faute de Participation* (6 December 2004); Die Presse, *Emotionales Referendum* (6 December 2004); Frankfurter Allgemeine Zeitung, *Parteipolitik besiegt Nationalpolitik: Ungarisches Referendum Gescheitert* (7 December 2004).
317. For a thorough overview of the events leading up to the referendum, *see* Küpper (2004). For a general analysis, *see* Kovács (2006) and Horváth (2006).

demand that is, incongruously, less prone to attack from the point of view of international law. In final consideration, no one came away happy from the debacle, however. Voters felt disappointed or ashamed, government and opposition appeared confused as to who had 'won', and Hungarian minorities declared themselves betrayed.[318] In the days following the referendum, however, an increasing number of people declared that a new era had begun in Hungarian-Hungarian relations.[319]

In essence, the outcome signified the public implosion of a kin-minority approach rooted in the peaceful re-establishment, in some form or another, of what had once been; a focus on the past is no longer possible. The arrival of the European Union as a daily reality, rather than an external factor, has meant that regional differences ignored so far are now impossible to overlook. This certainty also holds true for status laws. A policy aimed at the minority in Serbia can no longer be claimed to fit the situation in Slovakia, for example, not only because the needs of the two groups may differ, nor because of diverse home-state policies – these have generally been considered insufficient or ignored, in any case – but because one is a fellow Member State, while the other is unlikely to be one in the near future. Nor does it make sense to speak of hindrances to cultural exchange in Slovenia anymore, for example – the positive effects of diminished borders is apparent – but the question cannot be ignored in the case of Ukraine. This is not to say that events related to one kin-minority may not affect thoughts on another. (The possibility of cultural (and possibly administrative) autonomy in Romania – in the context of the minority draft law presented to Parliament by the government elected in 2004 – led, at least temporarily, to the re-emergence of the topic in the context of Slovakia, for example, and resulted in increased tension between Bratislava and Budapest.) But it does mean that Hungary, like other kin-states in the region, must reconsider the future of its kin-minority policy.

In fact, some of the possibilities now discussed in Hungary – such as the status of 'citizen of the nation' (*nemzetpolgár*) or 'national from outside Hungary' (*külhoni állampolgár*)[320] – are a clear sign of continued experimentation, and confusion. As a theoretical matter, the new statuses considered garble the concepts of membership, citizenship and nationality even more than the status law had. As a practical one, they demonstrate that states with an interest in their kin minorities may have further legal surprises in store for the international community. The profile of the issue in Hungary remains high, in any case, as President Sólyom,

---

318. Accounts and images of crying people, black-ribbonned Hungarian flags, refusals to sing the Hungarian anthem and 'No Hungarian nationals' signs in the windows of stores in Hungarian-minority areas were reported by media in the days following the referendum.
319. The World Federation of Hungarians has nonetheless been authorized by the OVB to organize a new referendum on the issue. At present no party in Hungary supports the initiative, although a number continue to favour of the idea of dual nationality. *See* Népszabadság, *Újra szavaztatna a kettős állampolgárságról az MVSZ* (22 March 2007); and *ibid., Kettős állampolgárság: OVB-igen az MVSZ aláírásgyűjtő ívére* (26 March 2007).
320. *See* Népszabadság, *Európai szakértők vizsgálják a kettős állampolgárság verzióit* (29 July 2005); and HVG, *Ötletvadászat* (19 January 2005).

elected in 2005, has made 'strengthening the unity of the nation' (*nemzeti összetartozás erősítése*) one of his main points of interest; as it is, he refers to Hungarians beyond the borders in speeches (on the occasion of national holidays and even New Year's) and has initiated a round of conferences to stimulate new approaches.[321] In fact, with Romania's entry into the EU, rhetorical (if not yet practical) focus is increasingly shifting to the future of the 'Hungarian nation' – not just Hungary – in the European Union.[322]

With regard to concrete steps taken, these have included a draft amendment to the RSL providing for automatic renewal of the validity of Hungarian Certificates,[323] as well as an amendment to the law on nationality allowing for simplified naturalization for kin-Hungarians,[324] as well as a comprehensive funding system put in place through the Homeland Fund (or *Szülőföld Alap*),[325] to be complemented by EU regional funds. Most interesting, however, is the introduction since January 2006[326] of a 'national visa' (*nemzeti vízum*), which allows for unimpeded travel in and out of Hungary, as well as the right to stay in the country for a period of between 3 months and 5 years – a clear response to some kin-minorities' fear of being cut off from Hungary post-Schengen. Finally, an amendment of Article 6(3) of the Constitution, which today declares 'responsibility for the fate' of Hungarian kin-minorities is in the works. Though its exact scope is still debated, any new language will include a more detailed enunciation of Hungary's role, including the promotion of identity-maintenance and increased ties, as well as a reference to special rights in the territory of the state and benefits/support outside it. The amended clause will also likely declare the existence of a Hungarian

---

321. *See* Communiqué from the Office of the President of the Republic of Hungary (28 April 2006).
322. *See* President László Sólyom's speech at the Hungarian National Opera of Cluj-Napoca (Romania) on the occasion of the anniversary of the 1848–49 revolution and war of idependence (14 March 2007).
323. *See* Népszabadság, *Magyar-igazolvány korlátlan időre* (6 April 2007) and *ibid., Módosul a státustörvény* (9 May 2007).
324. To be more precise, the simplified procedure of application applies to individuals who declare themselves to be Hungarian (*magát magyar nemzetiségűnek valló*), reside in Hungary and have an ancestor with Hungarian nationality. In addition, individuals who have graduated from Hungarian-language schools and universities are exempt from the generally mandatory test on constitutional principles. *See* Arts 1 and 2 of *2005. évi XLVI. törvény a magyar állampolgárságról szóló 1993. évi. LV. törvény és a külföldiek beutazásáról és tartózkodásáról szóló 2001. évi XXXIX. törvény módosításáról*, respectively (Law XLVI amending Law LV on Hungarian Nationality and Law XXXIX on the Entry and Stay of Foreigners) (2005).
325. *See 2005. évi II. törvény a Szülőföld Alapról* (Law II on the Homeland Fund) (2005) and the modifications introduced by *2005. évi XVI. törvény a Szülőföld Alapról szóló 2005. évi II. törvény módosításáról* (Law XVI amending Law II on the Homeland Fund) (2005).
326. *See* Art. 12 of Law XLVI, *supra* note III.324. *See also* Proposal for a Regulation of the European Parliament and of the Council laying down rules on local border traffic at the external land borders of the Member States and amending the Schengen Convention and the Common Consular Instructions (2005), for a Community response to the concerns of new Member States regarding the impenetrability of Schengen borders.

national community bound together by common language, traditions and history, and may even refer to Hungary's protective role.[327]

In light of such developments, the provisions of the status law can be viewed as just one phase in an ongoing debate on the relationship between Hungary and its kin-minorities. The initial question remains, however: who belongs? And how? This question has also been asked in a number of states dealing with large-scale immigration, particularly in the context of measures aimed at integrating long-term residents. The concern of states of immigration in this context is thus not with maintaining existing cultural and other ties, but with developing them in the first place. Specifically, interest has centred on the possibility of allowing plural nationality as a marker of ties to multiple states, albeit with certain conditions. In the process, many countries have determined that nationality laws left relatively unchanged for decades are no longer adequate. It is to this transformation that we now turn.

---

327. *See also* Népszabadság, *Nem változik a közjogi státus* (3 March 2006).

Chapter IV
Plural Nationality

> *So I assumed a double part, and cried*
> *And heard another's voice cry: 'What! are you here?'*
> *Although we were not. I was still the same,*
> *Knowing myself yet being someone other –*
> *And he a face still forming; yet the words sufficed*
> *To compel the recognition they preceded.*
>
> T.S. Eliot, 'Little Gidding', 1942

Plural nationality, or the simultaneous possession of two or more nationalities[1] by the same individual,[2] is effectively the result of legal disorder. The phenomenon arises from states' near-unfettered discretion in matters of nationality (particularly its attribution) and concomitant differences in regulation: variations on *jus soli* and *jus sanguinis*, as well as diverse attitudes toward naturalization. In other words, plural nationality results from the meeting of autonomous legal systems with distinct bases of membership. When individuals move, they export one particular system of legal membership to another. Barring the complete absence of migration, then, cases of multiple or plural nationality are unavoidable.[3]

Traditionally, plural nationality has been viewed as a threat to the unity of the nation state; as such, it was a phenomenon to be restricted by both international instruments and national legislation. Only in the recent past have

---

1. As de Castro y Bravo has discussed, numerous situations can fall under the umbrella of 'plural nationality'; we limit ourselves only those he labelled '*deux nationalités de même valeur ou de portée dissemblable*'. de Castro y Bravo (1961), p. 600.
2. *See* Art. 2(b) of the European Convention on Nationality.
3. *See* Council of Europe, Report on Multiple Nationality (2000), p. 4.

concrete signs of a turn-around materialized, as many European states have modified laws on nationality to permit multiple membership, albeit with significant provisos. We will present the content and context of this change of approach here, using the example of Germany's reform of provisions on nationality in 1999 to show how public debate on the acceptability of plural nationality is increasingly couched in a general discussion of the meaning and salience of national identity and the ties that flow from it. The first section of this chapter surveys how the traditionally hostile approach of international law and domestic legislation to plural nationality has evolved in recent years. In part one, we highlight how the traditional preference for state interests over those of individuals has shaped the evolution of international law. Part two, in turn, charts how mechanisms for dealing with the side effects of multiple membership have slowly taken centre-stage in Europe. We then turn to the role immigration has played in the emergence of such new approaches in part three, with particular emphasis on the case law of the E.Ct.H.R. on Article 8 matters and on the growing importance of individual choice in matters of nationality. Part four looks at how the concrete measures devised to manage the side-effects of plural nationality function in practice. Finally, part five presents the extent of change in the European legal landscape.

In the second section of this chapter, we examine the large-scale reform of nationality legislation in Germany in 1999. We begin in part one with a presentation of the provisions in force for much of the twentieth century, as well as of initial attempts at modification. Part two analyses the reform eventually undertaken, in the wake of which plural nationality has snuck into a regulation previously strongly resistant to it. In part three, we inspect the debate on integration that accompanied this change of norms, with particular attention to the role understandings of German identity played and the manner in which attitudes toward one category of immigrants, the *Statusdeutsche*, have been transformed.

The third section of our chapter will demonstrate how similar debates in other European states have played out. In the first part of this section, we will use the German example to appraise political theories on integration, assimilation and other approaches to the adaptation usually expected of migrants in states of residence. In the second part, we will contrast these expectations with recent conceptions of an individual rights approach to nationality, which aim to harness the identity function of the status for the benefit of persons, rather than states. Our focus in part three will be on transnationalism, or the creation and maintenance of bonding mechanisms with states of origin. In particular, we will examine the content and political and legal implications of diaspora ties. Finally, the last section of this chapter will present the advantages and pitfalls of the two main tendencies of development in Europe on approaches to nationality – that of accepting plural nationality with preconditions, especially proof of integration, and that of framing nationality, in one form or another, as a confirmation of identity.

A. THE TRADITIONAL APPROACH AND RECENT LEGAL EVOLUTION

1. BALANCING STATE AND INDIVIDUAL INTERESTS

Because of the importance attached to the legal status of nationality – its identity function, as already discussed – as well as with an eye to possible conflicts of law – plural nationality has generally been regarded by states as an evil to be avoided or prohibited.[4] Politicians, in particular, have been generous in condemnation: Theodore Roosevelt, in a much-quoted quip, called plural nationality 'a self-evident absurdity'.[5] Critique has generally come in two guises: one approach focused on the (rights and duties of the) individual, the other on the (interests of the) state. With regard to the individual, the main points of contention have been assumed conflicting loyalties and the impossibility of fulfilling civic duties in more than one state. Such fears stem from an obvious blurring of the concepts of nationality and citizenship – and a merger of their separate functions – in the manner already discussed above, however. Nationals, as such, don't necessarily have civic duties after all, but citizens do; conversely, a status for the purposes of international law need not have any connotations of 'loyalty'. State interest, in turn, has centred on asserting sovereignty and minimizing the encroachment of foreign law into the domestic regime.

At times, individual and state interests coincide; but in most instances they diverge, so that plural nationals have generally been left to confront, as best they could, the lacunae or inconsistencies of disparate state practice and nominal international regulation. As discussed, the regulation of nationality remains – if to a lesser extent than in past eras – an almost exclusively state pursuit. Thus, whatever limited international practice on prevention and management of plural nationality exists is rooted in national developments.

In fact, customary international law has not actually formulated a particular approach to plural nationality: it remains, as one scholar states, 'neutral', neither supportive nor critical of the phenomenon.[6] This is not to say that there have not, in practice, been trends during particular periods, however. While states put a great deal of effort into preventing the phenomenon in the first (and in certain cases into the second) half of the 20th century, focus increasingly shifted to managing the side-effects of the phenomenon after the first World War. Problems relating to diplomatic protection, especially as regards the principle of effectivity;[7] military

---

4. This view has also been held by a number of theorists. *See* ILC Report on Multiple Nationality (1953), p. 43 and pp. 48–49; Report of the ILC on the Work of its Sixth Session, 252nd meeting (1954), p. 52; Griffin (1967). For more recent opinions, *see* discussion in Kammann (1984), p. 206 *et seq.* and p. 227 *et seq.*; and Verwilghen (1999), p. 291 *et seq.*
5. Theodore Roosevelt in an article for the *Metropolitan* (1915) as quoted by Martin (2004).
6. '*Neutre: elle n'entend ni les condamner ni les favoriser*'. Verwilghen (1999), p. 170 (emphasis removed).
7. *See*, in this context, *Soering v. the United Kingdom*, E.Ct.H.R. (1989), para. 110.

service;[8] relevant nationality in a given circumstance, especially in private international law;[9] the existence of rights and duties in multiple states; and, finally, integration[10] have all been discussed. It is rather in this second, managerial context that some evidence of emerging custom could be found, if not for the appearance of new approaches that have undermined the status quo, including the rise of the concept of 'habitual residence' as an alternative or complementary status to nationality in possible conflict of law cases.

In the context of prevention, the possibility of interacting *jus sanguinis* regimes – which result in two nationalities for individuals with parents of differing nationalities – was closed until the early 20th century by means of the generally accepted requirement that any woman marrying a foreign national give up her original nationality; her husband's state of nationality, in turn, offered its own nationality. Though the roots of this rule were in domestic law – *not* in international law strictly speaking – it was accepted and even encouraged by all states. The basis for provisions of this kind was the generally recognized principle of dependent nationality, with the goal of unity of nationality within the family. This was a useful aim, perhaps, but one with highly discriminative effects on women, not only by reason of their lost membership and political rights, but also due to the possible loss of property, inheritance and other secondary advantages of nationality.

In fact, numerous problems appeared in practice, particularly upon the death of a woman's spouse or in case of divorce,[11] while domestically, particular provisions came under heavy attack from women's movements.[12] With the Convention on the Nationality of Married Women (1957), the first international step toward equality of the sexes in such questions was taken.[13] Article 1 determines that 'neither the celebration nor the dissolution of a marriage between one of its nationals and an alien, nor the change of nationality by the husband during marriage, shall automatically affect the nationality of the wife'. The Treaty

---

8. *See* Chapter II of the Convention on the Reduction of Cases of Multiple Nationality and Military Obligations in Cases of Multiple Nationality (1963); and Chapter VII of the European Convention on Nationality. For a general discussion, *see* Legomsky (2003), p. 79.

    Many states with particular historical connections have also concluded bilateral treaties on this issue, in addition to international conventions, e.g., *Accord relatif aux obligations du service national*, between France and Algeria (1983). Incidentally, this particular Agreement has been much criticized for breaking with the practice of requiring that plural nationals perform military service in the state of (habitual) residence.
9. *See* Arts 9–15 of the Bustamante Code (adopted at the Sixth International Conference of American States, in 1928).
10. *See also* discussion in Medved (2001), esp. p. 30 *et seq.*
11. In certain cases, women were allowed to keep the nationality of their former husbands; in others, they were automatically re-attributed their previous nationality. *See* Kammann (1984), p. 255.
12. The United States, for example, repealed a law making expatriation obligatory upon marriage to a foreign national fifteen years after it was passed – and a mere five years after the Supreme Court had found it acceptable. *See Mackenzie v. Hare*, US (1915).
13. For an earlier attempt at changing the norm, *see* the Montevideo Convention on the Nationality of Women (1933).

remains of limited utility, however, given the comparatively low number of state parties.[14] The UN Convention on the Elimination of All Forms of Discrimination Against Women (1979), which also has a provision on equal rights in nationality matters, including the right to pass on nationality to children (both in Article 9), has had a much larger impact, given that 185 states are at present party to it; but its effect is tempered by the reservation of numerous states to the article in question.[15] Despite hurdles, however, the indirect result of this – and equivalent domestic law – provision(s) has been a marked increase in the number of individuals with plural nationality, as mothers now pass on their nationality to their children in ever more cases.

The other possible source of plural nationality at birth – a combination of *jus sanguinis* and *jus soli* regimes[16] – has been (even) more vexing to states wary of plural nationality. In the context of individuals whose parents are present in the territory of a state other than their own for diplomatic reasons, states have agreed that *jus soli* remains without effect.[17] No international agreement was ever found for the general case,[18] however, nor has any custom emerged to help prevent such situations due to fundamental differences of approach.[19] In effect, *jus soli* and

---

14. The Treaty has also been attacked for violating the principles of non-discrimination and equality, since Art. 3(1) grants only alien wives, but not husbands, preferential naturalization. *See also In Re Aumeeruddy-Cziffra v. Mauritius*, UN H.R. Comm. (1981) and the Inter-American Court's *Costa Rica* Opinion.
15. E.g., Algeria, Bahrain, Cyprus, Egypt, Iraq, Jordan, Malaysia, Tunisia. (Most reservations concern the provision on the nationality of children.) Cases have also arisen before domestic courts from differences in the nationality rights granted to the children of men and women. *See, inter alia, Benner v. the Secretary of State of Canada* (Supr. Ct. Can.) (1997) and *Dawood v. Minister of Home Affairs* (Const. Ct. South Africa) (2000).
16. Thus, a child born in the United States (where *jus soli* applies) to Hungarian parents (where *jus sanguinis* is the rule) will have both American and Hungarian nationality. If her parents hold the nationality of different states, she may even be born with three nationalities.

    Clearly, there is no possibility for a combination of *jus soli* regimes, since an individual can only be born in one place. That said, the allocation of certain places – such as ships and airplanes – to particular states has needed regulation. The generally accepted rule is that birth on a vessel is deemed to have occurred in the territory of the state whose flag the vessel flies; while birth on a plane is considered to have taken place in the state in which the aircraft is registered. *See* Art. 3 of the Statelessness Reduction Convention.
17. *See* Art. 2 of the Optional Protocol to the Vienna Convention on Consular Relations Concerning Acquisition of Nationality (1963); and discussion in Verwilghen (1999), p. 142.
18. However, there have been continued efforts to deal with statelessness, which may arise in the context of the reverse combination of *jus soli/jus sanguinis* regimes discussed. Beginning with the Convention Relating to the Status of Stateless Persons and that on the Reduction of Statelessness, numerous international instruments have attempted harmonization. In practice, most states guarantee their nationality to children born in their territory if they would otherwise become stateless. *See also* Arts 2 and 4 of the Statelessness Reduction Convention, Arts 6(1)(b) and 6(2) of the European Convention on Nationality; Art. 20(2) of the ACHR; and Art. 6(4) of the African Charter on the Rights and Welfare of the Child (1990).
19. This failure has not been for lack of trying, however. The ILC Report on Multiple Nationality, for example, suggested subordinating *jus sanguinis* regimes to those of *jus soli* in cases of possible multiple nationality (*supra* note IV.4, pp. 46–47); but *see* paras 341 *et seq*. of the ILC Survey presented in the same year, *supra* note I.20.

jus sanguinis states have been unable to reconcile underlying understandings of membership.

Rather, the issue has been – and from the late 19th to the early 20th centuries was almost exclusively – submerged into the general question of the relationship between migration/naturalization and *jus sanguinis* regimes. The principles suggested by the *Institut de Droit International* to states in 1896 summarize the general approach of the time:

> No one may be allowed to obtain naturalization in a foreign country, except upon proving that his country of origin has released him from his allegiance, or at the very least that he has made his intention known to the government of his country of origin and has satisfied [the requirements of] military law during the period of active service in accordance with the laws of this country.[20]

A few decades later, the Hague Convention's attempt to codify certain common provisions on nationality – particularly as regards its attribution and withdrawal – and to reproduce 'prior solutions of a customary nature'[21] started with the underlying aim of the 'abolition' of 'dual nationality', as set out in the Preamble.[22] Neither the regulations nor the idea of harmonized domestic laws ever gained much support, however. Accordingly, no treaty at the universal level was ever concluded on this question.

2. CHANGING VIEWS IN EUROPE

In Europe, multilateral attempts at co-ordinating matters of nationality have had greater legal prominence, as evidenced by the earliest instrument with significant support: the Convention on the Reduction of Cases of Multiple Nationality and Military Obligations in Cases of Multiple Nationality (hereinafter, Multiple Nationality Reduction Convention) (1963).[23] As the title of the Convention illustrates, the primary approach still consisted of avoidance; or, given that this was not feasible, of minimizing the effects of the 'problem'. Rec. 2 of the Preamble sets out both the reasoning and the aims of the Convention: 'cases of multiple nationality

---

20. '*Nul ne peut être admis à obtenir une naturalisation en pays étranger qu'á la charge de prouver que son pays d'origine le tient quitte de son allégeance, out tout au moins qu'il a fait connaître sa volonté au gouvernement de son pays d'origine et qu'il a satisfait à la loi militaire, pendant la période du service actif, conformément aux lois de ce pays*'. Art. 5 of the *Résolutions relatives aux conflits de lois en matière de nationalité (naturalisation et expatriation)*, adopted in Venice (1896).
21. *Des solutions antérieures de nature coutumière*. Verwilghen (1999), p. 401.
22. The Harvard Research project that preceded drafting efforts also aimed to prevent plural nationality (as well as statelessness). *See also* the Montevideo Convention on Nationality, which stipulated that naturalization by the national of one state party in another state party meant automatic loss of the original nationality.
23. The Convention has 15 signatories and 13 ratifications. *See also* Council of Europe, Parliamentary Recommendation 164 on the Reduction of the Number of Cases of Multiple Nationality (1958).

are liable to cause difficulties and ... joint action to reduce as far as possible the number of cases of multiple nationality, as between Member States, corresponds to the aims of the Council of Europe'. The Convention relies on two strategies to limit plural nationality. In the first place, naturalization in another state party automatically leads to loss of the previous nationality.[24] Second, individuals who already possess more than one nationality (on the basis of a combination of *jus sanguinis* and *jus soli*) have the option of renouncing one or more nationalities without state interference (Article 2) or onerous requirements (Article 3). Still, cracks in this dual-pronged approach were evident from the outset. The Annex provides for state reservations allowing for exceptions for married women,[25] as well as for the option of keeping one's previous nationality if the state of naturalization agrees;[26] of which many states took advantage.[27]

The Protocols amending the Convention (adopted in 1977 and 1993) evinced further signs of strain on the underlying structure of the Convention; and were complemented by a number of initiatives in particularly troublesome matters.[28] The first Protocol (1977),[29] for example, introduced the concept of 'ordinary residence' into the framework of the instrument,[30] ostensibly in an attempt to make renunciation of nationality easier.[31] However, the Explanatory Report notes that 'national legislation has instituted many more cases of automatic multiple nationality' since the Convention came into force. It goes on to state that, '[p]ublic law is gradually losing its overriding importance and more attention is being paid to the individual's desire to choose freely'. Increased reliance on free choice was also clear in the greater latitude left to individuals in matters of military obligations[32] and the abolition of reservations 2 and 4 relating to married women.[33] The Second Protocol (1993),[34] in turn, was concerned with the social integration of immigrants, as well as with the legal effects of mixed-nationality marriages. Article 1 essentially lifts all limitations on plural nationality for spouses and children of mixed-marriages,

---

24. Multiple Nationality Reduction Convention, Arts 1 and 7.
25. *Ibid.*, Annex Res. 2 and 4.
26. *Ibid.*, Annex Res. 3.
27. For a list of state reservations, see: <conventions.coe.int/Treaty/Commun/ListeDeclarations.asp?NT=043&CM=1&DF=4/28/05&CL=ENG&VL=1>.
28. *See, inter alia*, Council of Europe, Committee of Ministers Resolution 77(12) on the Nationality of Spouses of Different Nationalities (1977); *ibid.*, Committee of Ministers Resolution 77(13) on the Nationality of Children Born in Wedlock (1977); *ibid.*, Parliamentary Recommendation 1081 on Problems of Nationality in Mixed Marriages (1988).
29. Signed and ratified by eight states; signed by a further three as of March 2007. The Additional Protocol (1977), in turn, attempted to tackle the lack of communication between states regarding nationality status.
30. *See also* paras 7–11 of Council of Europe, Committee of Ministers Resolution 72(1) on the Standardisation of the Concepts of the Legal Concepts of 'Domicile' and of 'Residence' (1972).
31. *See* Art. 1 of the 1977 Protocol.
32. *Ibid.*, Art. 2.
33. *Ibid.*, Art. 4.
34. Signed and ratified only by France, Italy and the Netherlands as of March 2007.

while immigrants are entitled to keep their original nationality upon naturalization in the state of 'ordinary residence'. By the mid-1990s, then, not much was left of the original Convention.

In 1996, the *Projet de convention européenne sur la nationalité* even took the existence of plural nationality as a given and attempted merely to manage its consequences. As was noted in a report giving an opinion on the draft European Convention on Nationality, the 1963 Convention was now considered 'ill-designed to take into account the new situation facing western societies and the democratic changes that have come about in Central and Eastern Europe'.[35] In particular, 'some relaxation of the 1963 convention was needed to provide for the integration of populations permanently resident in European countries'. For states, naturalization was to be considered a 'decisive factor in the integration of immigrant populations';[36] while for individuals 'the need ... to have the possibility of conserving their nationality of origin in certain cases'[37] was acknowledged.

Accordingly, the European Convention on Nationality finally superseded the previous approach to questions of plural nationality.[38] In fact, the instrument attempts to regulate nationality matters comprehensively by including provisions aimed at developing specific areas of law (such as state succession in Sec. VI). Plural nationality is treated here as a legal phenomenon like any other, to be coordinated but not necessarily avoided. With regard to this question, the Convention notes the 'varied approach of States to the question of multiple nationality and recognis[es] that each State is free to decide which consequences it attaches in its internal law to the fact that a national acquires or possesses another nationality',[39] since the 'legitimate interests' of both states and individuals are to be taken into account in matters of nationality.[40]

In a first attempt at international harmonization, Article 6 sets out a number of rules on the acquisition of nationality with the aim of taking individual links into consideration. For example, provision is to be made by domestic law for the acquisition of nationality for individuals 'lawfully and habitually' resident in the state for a maximum of ten years.[41] In turn, Article 7 limits the possible grounds for withdrawing nationality to those enumerated, and makes reference to plural nationality in secs (a) (withdrawal in case of voluntary acquisition of another nationality) and (e) (withdrawal in case of lack of a 'genuine link' with a national

---

35. Council of Europe, Parliamentary Assembly, Report giving an opinion on the draft European Convention on Nationality (1997), para. 2. In fact, no representative opposed the changes during preparatory works; more characteristic were the remarks of one representative, who noted in reference to the 1963 Convention that it '*a abouti à des règles rigides appliquées par des administrations aveugles*'. Council of Europe, Parliamentary Assembly Debates (31 January 1997), p. 294.
36. Report, *Ibid.*, at para. 8.
37. *Ibid.*
38. 'Article 14 of the latest draft establishes that dual nationality is acceptable'. *Ibid.*, at para. 17.
39. European Nationality Convention, Rec. 7.
40. *Ibid.*, Rec. 3.
41. *Ibid.*, Art. 6(3).

habitually resident abroad), while allowing for the recovery of nationality.[42] As a secondary effect, these rules are likely to increase the frequency of plural nationality.

Problems remain however, and are complemented by new ones. The combined effect of Articles 7(a) and 6(3) is noteworthy for the new kind of inequality it creates, for example: while states are required by the latter to grant resident immigrants nationality, they may nonetheless continue to strip nationals of nationality in case they, in turn, accept an additional nationality. The reliance of Article 7(e) on the notion of a 'genuine link' – set out in the *Nottebohm* decision already discussed – is also questionable. One, because it extends an idea formulated in a limited context (diplomatic protection upon naturalization) to all nationality matters. Two, because it leaves states with significant leeway in determining the closeness of particular connections. The Explanatory Report notes that this article must be interpreted in light of other provisions in the Conventions – most of which function as safety mechanisms to individuals[43] – but also states that one of the 'main aims of this provision is to allow a state, which so wishes, to prevent its nationals habitually living abroad to retain its nationality generation after generation'.[44] But if a state allowed for the acquisition of the given nationality in such circumstances, what is the logic of allowing it to withdraw that nationality, unless those circumstances have changed? In light of Parliamentary Recommendations 1410 and 1650, discussed in the previous chapter, this paragraph is all the more puzzling.

A number of articles mention plural nationality specifically, but do so only to reaffirm the traditional rule of state discretion.[45] Article 14 does, however, mention certain groups of people – essentially those in the 1993 Protocol – for whom different nationalities are to be allowed. The Convention follows general international law in other regards,[46] and mirrors the increased flexibility exhibited by states concerning the fulfilment of military obligations.[47] All in all, the Convention represents a complete abandonment of the earlier strategy aimed at elimination and limitation of plural nationality. However, a side-effect of the new, comprehensive approach to questions of nationality – and a sign of their abiding sensitivity – is the freedom granted in Article 29 to states with regard to reservations, which many states have made use of. As of March 2007, the Convention had been ratified by 16 states and signed by another 11, so that it is already more influential than its predecessor; the latter, does, however, remain in force for those signatory states that have not ratified the new Convention.

Finally, a number of states have gone the bilateral route in seeking agreement on matters of nationality; unsurprisingly, with situation-specific results. The most famous – and earliest – series of such agreements are the Bancroft Treaties,

---

42. *Ibid.*, Art. 9.
43. *See* para. 72 of the Explanatory Report.
44. *Ibid.*, para. 69.
45. *See* Art. 15 of the European Nationality Convention.
46. *Ibid., see* Art. 17.
47. *Ibid.*, Chap. VII.

concluded between 1868 and 1937, between the United States and states from Europe, Latin America and the Caribbean. Given their provenance from a period of mass migration,[48] they dealt exclusively with the effects of immigration on nationality regulation and aimed at both preventing plural nationality and regulating the duties (particularly military service) of relevant individuals. Typically, the treaties stipulated that naturalization by an individual in the state of residence (e.g., the United States) would be recognized by the state of origin (e.g., Prussia) after five years of uninterrupted residence in the former. However, if the individual returned to Prussia and resided there for two years, she was presumed to have given up the nationality of the United States and resumed that of Prussia, thereby losing the possibility of diplomatic protection by the US and re-assuming all the rights and duties of a Prussian national. This presumption was disprovable by means of evidence of an intent to return to the United States.[49] (The provision bears a clear resemblance to the domestic provisions of a number of states (then and now) providing for loss of nationality in case of protracted residence abroad, particularly for naturalized nationals, as discussed below).[50] Though the Treaties were renounced by the United States in the late 1970s and despite a subsequent policy turn-around, US naturalization law still contains vestiges of this prohibitive approach. The Oath of Allegiance required of all new nationals,[51] for example, runs, in part, as follows: 'I hereby declare, on oath, that I absolutely and entirely renounce and abjure all allegiance and fidelity to any foreign prince, potentate, state or sovereignty, of whom or which I have heretofore been a subject or citizen'.[52]

Certain treaties from the same period took a different approach, stipulating that emigration would have no effect on nationality[53] or that any naturalization in

---

48. In total, 26 such treaties were concluded. In Europe: Albania, Austria-Hungary, Belgium, Bulgaria, Czechoslovakia, Denmark, certain predecessor states of the German *Reich* (Baden, Bavaria, Hessen, the North German Confederation and Württemberg), Lithuania, Sweden and Norway (then joined in a Union under the Swedish Monarchy), Portugal, and Great Britain. The Inter-American Convention (1906) covered Argentina, Bolivia, Brazil, Cuba, Colombia, Costa Rica, the Dominican Republic, Guatemala, Ecuador, El Salvador, Honduras, Mexico, Nicaragua, Paraguay, Peru, Panama, and Uruguay. A Treaty was also concluded with Haiti.
49. *See, inter alia, Ex parte Gilroy*, S.D.N.Y. (1919), p. 117; and *Anderson v. Howe*, D.C.N.Y. (1916), p. 548.
50. In the United States in particular, it took until 1980 for the US Supreme Court to declare that 'an expatriating act and an intent to relinquish citizenship must be proved by a preponderance of the evidence'. *Vance v. Terrazas*, US (1980), p. 270. (*See* 8 U.S.C. 1481(a) (2000)). In an earlier case, the Court had invalidated an INA provision (8 U.S.C. 1484(a)(1) (1952)) providing for naturalized nationals' automatic loss of nationality after three years of residence in the state of origin. *See Schneider v. Rusk*, US (1964). Compare para. (a)(2) of the same section, providing for loss of nationality after five years of residence in any state other than the US, which was never before the Court, but was likely as unacceptable on equal treatment grounds.
51. 8 U.S.C. 1448(a) (2000).
52. US Citizenship and Immigration Services (2004), p. 28.
53. *See, inter alia*, Art. 10(1) of the Treaty between the German *Reich* and Honduras (12 December 1887); Art. 5 of the Treaty between Belgium and Bolivia (18 April 1912). For a more recent example, *see* Art. 8 of the Treaty between Romania and Bulgaria (24 September 1959). As reproduced in Flournoy, Jr. and Hudson (1929) and Kammann (1984), p. 245.

the state of residence could occur only with the explicit consent of the state of origin, which could refuse to release the individual from her original nationality.[54] In turn, the peace treaties concluded in the wake of the first World War (Versailles, Trianon, etc.) required that individuals choose a particular nationality, making it impossible for anyone to become a plural national. As the Prague Treaty between Germany and Czechoslovakia stated, '[t]he two contracting Parties mutually guarantee that they will not admit nationals of the other State to nationality in their State, except where such admission is based upon the provisions of the Treaty of Peace of Versailles, until the other State has released the person to be thus admitted from its nationality'.[55]

While a significant number of more recent treaties also aimed to exclude the possibility of plural nationality,[56] certain states have created systems not only allowing and managing, but even encouraging dual nationality on the basis of historical, cultural and social ties between the two societies. Accordingly, Spain has concluded twelve bilateral treaties on nationality with states in South America and with the Philippines; Italy and Argentina agreed on a convention in 1971; and Russia concluded a number of treaties with CIS states during the 1990s.[57] In addition, countless treaties have been concluded through the years to regulate the particular rights and duties of plural nationals – especially their military and tax obligations.

Whatever a given state's approach to this question may be then, to the extent states ordinarily have an interest in particular regimes of nationality, this interest is magnified in the context of individuals with legal, cultural or social ties to more than one state, whether these ties are formally recognized by means of plural nationality or not. Exactly because of conflicting state interests, international courts have also been quite active in this context, despite the traditional view that nationality matters are generally domestic in character. The number of cases dealing with questions of dominant nationality or discussing related choice of law issues is accordingly high.

In addition to such discrete inquiries, the possibility of a discrepancy between legal status and social link is increasingly recognized by courts, and has raised the prospect of alternative bases for individual-state attachment. In a case from 1997, the E.Ct.H.R., for example, observed in the context of an applicant fighting a

---

54. *See* Treaty between the *German Reich* and Persia (17 February 1929); compare Art. 30 of the Treaty between Bulgaria and Greece (27 November 1919). *Ibid.*
55. Prague Treaty between Germany and Czechoslovakia (29 June 1920), Art. 13. *See also* the Brunn Treaty between Austria and Czechoslovakia (7 June 1920). *Ibid.*
56. This was certainly the case for all bilateral treaties concluded between the states of the former Soviet bloc. *See, inter alia,* Treaty between Hungary and Bulgaria (27 June 1958); Treaty between Hungary and Czechoslovakia (11 April 1960); Treaty between the German Democratic Republic and the USSR (11 April 1963). *See also* Treaty between China and Indonesia (22 April 1955). *Ibid.*
57. The treaties concluded between Portugal and a number of its former colonies, in turn, do not concern dual nationality, although they allow for equal treatment in nearly all rights and duties. *See* Rezek (1986), p. 382.

permanent exclusion order on the basis of ECHR Article 8 that the individual 'was completely integrated into French society and *had no link whatsoever with Algeria other than his nationality*, which was a *particularly artificial link* in his case because, having been born in France ... to parents of special civil status of Algerian origin, he had French nationality until [1963]'.[58] The Court found a breach of Article 8 in this case, in part on the basis of 'the strength of [applicant's] links with France'.[59] There is thus a distinct possibility of the bond of nationality being undermined in its function as the only legal status fully recognized for the purposes of international law – and with it, the claimed sovereignty of states over particular individuals, generally speaking.[60]

3.   THE QUESTION OF IMMIGRATION

In this vein, even if the regulation of nationality itself remains for the most part free of international (and regional) judicial scrutiny, this is not the case for immigration.[61] The two certainly constitute separate areas of law: nationality law is focused on legal status associated with membership, while immigration law governs entry into, exit from and residence in the territory of the state. But naturalization – as process and as a concrete step toward a change of legal status – forms a bridge between the two. In a sentimental moment, the American Court of Human Rights even characterized the act of naturalization as a 'voluntary act aimed at establishing a relationship with any given political, society, its culture, its way of life and its values'.[62] Similarly, the French Commission on Nationality, mentioned above, argued in its report that 'immigrants who remain in France are themselves candidates for naturalization or [are] the parents of the French of tomorrow'.[63]

While such individuals may be 'candidates' for naturalization, many in fact choose not to become nationals. Accordingly, in a purely legal sense, 'it is more accurate to speak of foreigners than of immigrants'.[64] But few commentators or politicians actually view migrants, especially those with permanent residence, in this manner. Almost exclusively, they are approached as future nationals, although there is often disagreement on conditions of membership. In fact, when it comes to naturalization, the identity function of nationality is highlighted in a manner not

---

58. *Mehemi v. France*, E.Ct.H.R. (1997), para. 31 (emphasis added).
59. *Ibid.*, at para. 37.
60. That said, courts have repeatedly refused to grant 'nationality' a meaning autonomous from that given to the term in the domestic law of the given state in question. *See* Mole (2001), p. 143 for a call to establish new criteria for entitlement to a specific nationality.
61. *See* discussion at p. 19 *et seq.* above.
62. Para. 35 of the Inter-American Court's *Costa Rica* Opinion.
63. '*Les immigrés demeurés en France sont eux-mêmes des candidats à la naturalisation ou les parents des Français de demain*'. Rapport Long, Tome II, *supra* note Intro.7, p. 83.
64. '*[I]l est ... plus correct de parler d'étrangers que d'immigrés*'. Carlier (1992), p. 237.

even possible for nationality attributed at birth, as explained below. Questions of immigration and legal membership are thus so closely entwined in practice that they cannot be artificially separated in policy or legal discussion.[65] In other words, while discrete paths of regulation may be devised for nationality and immigration matters, the two should be considered together when evaluating actual effects.

a.   **Expulsion Measures before the European Court of Human Rights**

To the extent that decisions on entry and exit are ever more readily adjudicated, while nationality has only recently been framed as a matter for rights discourse, questions of membership are increasingly, albeit indirectly, funnelled through immigration cases. In rare instances, the two are directly connected, as in *Slivenko v. Latvia*, where the legality of expulsing certain 'ex-USSR citizens' with no right to Latvian nationality was examined by the E.Ct.H.R. for compatibility with ECHR Article 8.[66] Clearly, a decision on entry, exit and residence rights impacts on the rights traditionally associated with nationality in this context. In a more general manner, however, domestic policies on immigration – circumscribed by international standards – may transform understandings of membership, with mid- or long-term consequences for nationality law.

For this reason, the E.Ct.H.R.'s case law on immigration matters – specifically expulsion or deportation measures examined in light of Article 8 on respect for 'private and family life' – play a discernable role in larger questions of membership. One theorist has gone so far as to claim that the wide scope of interpretation formulated by the Court has led to the creation of a '*quasi-nationalité*'.[67] The beginnings of the approach reach back to 1985, when the Court announced that 'although some aspects of the right to enter a country are governed by Protocol No. 4 as regards States bound by that instrument, it is not to be excluded that measures taken in the field of immigration may affect the right to respect for family life under Article 8'.[68] Thus, although immigration questions – specifically

---

65. This is also true for European integration and minority rights – in fact, any area of law that deals with identity. In addition, politicization and judicialization are closely linked in all matters of membership, since 'national governments who want to restrict the rights of foreigners [or who want to grant rights to kin-minorities] and have realized that national and international courts impede their actions explore new policy venues'. Guiraudon (2003), p. 302.
66. *Slivenko v. Latvia*, E.Ct.H.R. (2003). The Court reached the controversial conclusion that state authorities had 'failed to strike a fair balance between the legitimate aim of the protection of national security and the interest of the protection of applicants' rights under Article 8' (para. 128) in expulsing a former USSR military officer's family after Latvia regained independence. *See also Abdulaziz, Cabales and Balkandali v. the United Kingdom*, E.Ct.H.R. (1985), esp. paras 87–89; and *Ahmut v. the Netherlands*, E.Ct.H.R. (1996), paras 70–73.
67. Verwilghen (1999), p. 112. *See also* the dissenting opinion of Judge Pettiti in *Beldjoudi v. France*, E.Ct.H.R. (1992), where he stated that the Court had considered applicant 'a quasi-Frenchman, a concept which is unknown in international law'.
68. *Abdulaziz*, at para. 60.

decisions on entry and exit rights – remain primarily for states to regulate, the latter are no longer fully sovereign in this capacity.[69] (Co-ordination of such matters at the EU level also impacts on domestic policies, but is obviously of a different quality than monitoring on the basis of human rights concerns). Since that decision, the E.Ct.H.R. has developed a wide-ranging balancing test to deal with such cases, with consideration of all elements of the individual's personal situation, from social integration to life history, as well of as state interests.[70] In *Boughanemi*, for example, the Court found no violation of Article 8, determining that:

> [A]pplicant had failed to show either that he had particularly *close ties with his family living in France* or that he was in any *way integrated in the society of that country*, where he had never really worked. Furthermore, on attaining his majority he had *not sought French nationality*. At the same time he had *retained ties with Tunisia* that went *beyond mere nationality*. His *parents were Tunisian*; he had spent his *infancy* there and in France he *moved in Tunisian circles*. Mr Boughanemi could *speak Arabic* or at least had an adequate command of everyday language. Moreover, having *lived in Tunisia* up to the age of 8, the *two years of schooling* that he had received there had laid the *foundations of his education*. In addition, the applicant did not claim that he had never returned there or that he had cut all ties with that country. Finally, he *maintained active relations with the Tunisian community* so that his *life was not confined to the French dimension*.[71]

In a number of cases, individuals have gained the right to remain in states of which they are not nationals, but to which they are deemed to have social ties on the basis of such veritable psychological surveys.[72] One judge has even declared that 'mere nationality does not constitute an objective and reasonable justification for the existence of a difference as regards the admissibility of expelling someone from what, in both cases, may be called his "own country"'.[73] That said, the Court, like the UN Human Rights Committee, continues to consider a 'desire to acquire ... nationality at the time when [the individual is] entitled to do so' a decisive factor in judging attachment to a given country.[74]

---

69. *See also* the string of cases brought under ECHR Art. 3. E.g., *Hilal v. the United Kingdom*, E.Ct.H.R. (2001); *Venkadajalasarma v. the Netherlands*, E.Ct.H.R. (2004). (*See also* ECHR Art. 5(1)(f) and Protocol Nos 4 and 7).
70. *See Gül v. Switzerland*, E.Ct.H.R. (1996), esp. para. 38. *See* also, *inter alia*, *Berrehab v. the Netherlands*, E.Ct.H.R. (1988).
71. *Boughanemi v. France*, E.Ct.H.R. (1996), para. 39 (emphasis added).
72. *See, inter alia, Moustaquim v. Belgium*, E.Ct.H.R. (1991); and *Beldjoudi*.
73. Concurring opinion of Judge Martens in *Beldjoudi. See also* the determination of the European Commission of Human Rights that '[A]ltough legally an alien, applicant has his family and social ties in France, and the nationality which links him to Algeria, though a legal reality, does not reflect his actual position in human terms'. *Djeroud v. France*, E.Comm.H.R. (1991). (14 Eur.H.R.Rep. 68 [1992], pp. 78–79). Compare *Dalia v. France*, E.Ct.H.R. (1998), para. 53 ('her Algerian nationality is not merely a legal fact but reflects certain social and emotional links'.)
74. *Boujlifa v. France*, E.Ct.H.R. (1997), para. 44; and *El Boujaïdi v. France*, E.Ct.H.R. (1997), para. 40.

State courts seem more reluctant to break down the distinction between national and non-national. In a 2004 case, for example, the German Constitutional Court refused applicant's request to be treated as a 'factual *Inländer*' or non-alien[75] in order to prevent expulsion to Turkey, his state of nationality, despite the fact that he was born and had grown up in Germany and was in possession of an unlimited *Aufenthaltserlaubnis*. After having determined that reliance on a claimed 'rootedness in living conditions in Germany'[76] was not sufficient, on balance, to save him from expulsion under the *Grundgesetz*, the Court proceeded to a lengthy examination of the case at issue from the point of view of the ECHR; the result, in light of the crimes committed by applicant, his knowledge of the Turkish language and his lack of a children or wife in Germany, was unchanged.[77]

It is also noteworthy that E.Ct.H.R. scrutiny of expulsion measures and entry rights has not resulted in any decision on the specific situation of plural nationals – exactly because such individuals are not, in theory, to have immigration issues in 'their' states.[78] In fact, Article 3 of Protocol Four to the ECHR[79] – the only place in the ECHR framework where nationality is addressed directly – has not been used to stop states from expelling (*de jure* or *de facto*) plural nationals from the territory of one of their states of nationality. Though it is rare for a state to legislate directly on the issue of expelling plural nationals – recent legislation in the Netherlands is an exception – *de facto* removal is not rare, especially in the case of children. For example, the Irish Supreme Court determined in 2003 that Irish national minors do not have absolute family rights. Their (third country) non-national parents could thus be deported without infringing on the rights of the children. This was the case even though the parents' deportation resulted in *de facto*, effective exile for the children.[80]

The E.Ct.H.R. settled this question years ago, when it held in *Jaramillo v. the United Kingdom*[81] and in *Sarajbee v. the United Kingdom*[82] that the effective exile of children with British nationality that resulted from their mother's deportation

---

75. *Faktischer Inländer*. BVerfG, 2 BvR 1570/03 (2004), para. 6.
76. *Verwurzelung in den Lebensverhältnissen in Deutschland*. *Ibid.*, para.10.
77. *Ibid.*, paras 20 *et seq.*
78. But *see* the decision of the Supreme Court of Morocco in the *Abraham Serfaty* Case, in which it refused to examine the question of the individual's Moroccan nationality (in light of his Brazilian one), citing lack of competence. The court was to determine whether an order of expulsion (from 1991) had been legal. *Arrêt no. 735 du 16 juillet*, Moroccan Supr. Ct. (1998). *See also* Libération, *L'opposant Abraham Serfaty de retour au Maroc* (1 October 1999).
79. '(1) No one shall be expelled, by means either of an individual or of a collective measure, from the territory of the State of which he is a national. (2) No one shall be deprived of the right to enter the territory of the State of which he is a national'. (The Protocol was adopted in 1963 and is in force since 1968.)
80. *Lobe and Osayande v. the Minister for Justice, Equality and Law Reform*, Irish Supr. Ct. (2003); but *see also Fajujonu v. the Minister for Justice,* Irish Supr. Ct. (1990).
81. *Jaramillo v. the United Kingdom* (Admissibility), E.Ct.H.R. (1995).
82. *Sorajbee v. the United Kingdom* (Admissibility), E.Ct.H.R. (1995).

did not constitute a violation of ECHR Article 8.[83] In practice, children in these situations are deprived of numerous rights linked to a particular nationality (and citizenship), despite continuing to hold the legal status in question.[84]

A case from the United States on the same question is also worth mentioning, since it highlights the importance often attached to conscious choice in adopting a particular nationality, especially in the context of plural nationals. The federal court in the case at hand determined that deporting the parents of a US national child did not deprive the child of a constitutional right. It added that 'a minor child who is fortuitously born here due to his parents' has not exercised *a deliberate decision* to make this country his home, and Congress did not give such a child the ability to confer immigration benefits on his parents. This is a reasonable distinction and contains no constitutional infirmity'.[85] This manner of distinguishing between individuals who became nationals through naturalization – thereby expressing a deliberate wish to reside in the country – and those granted US nationality on the basis of *jus soli* is a rare inversion of the usual partiality for the native-born.

b. The Importance of Individual Choice

In fact, conscious choice seems to play a constant, if inconsistent, role in the nationality regulation of a number of states. In Europe, some states continue to mandate that any national who acquires an additional nationality loses her original one.[86] This practice is generally explained in the following manner: 'the intervention of will in the acquisition of a new nationality permits one to explain the loss of [original] nationality in the light of a presumed wish on the part of the individual to

---

83. But *see Mehemi*, para. 36, where the Court took into consideration the 'radical upheaval' a move to another country would mean for applicant's children in determining that his permanent exclusion constituted a violation of Art. 8. Also compare discussion and outcome in *Winata v. Australia*, UN H.R. Comm. (2001).
84. A number of domestic courts have also considered claims under constitutional provisions or the UN Convention on the Rights of the Child (1989). *See, inter alia*, BVerfG, 2BvR 2108/00 (2003); *Minister of State for Immigration and Ethnic Affairs v. Ah Hin Teoh*, Australian High Ct. (1995) and *Beharry v. Reno*, E.D.N.Y. (2002).
85. *Perdido v. Immigration and Naturalization Service*, 5th Cir. (1969), p. 1181 (emphasis added). Despite the Court's declaration, no explanation was given in the decision as to why such a distinction should warrant differential treatment as regards the right to sponsor family members immigrating to the United States. *See also Aalund v. Marshall*, 5th Cir. (1972); and *Cervantes v. Immigration and Naturalization Service*, 10th Cir. (1975).
86. *See, inter alia*, Art. 27(1) of the Austrian StAG; Arts 17(2) and 25(1) of the German StAG; Art. 7(1) of the Consolidated Nationality Act of Denmark; Art. 22(1)(1) of the Belgian *Code de la Nationalité*; Art. 24(1) of the Spanish *Código Civil*; Arts 25(1) and (7) of the *Loi sur la nationalité* of Luxemburg; Art. 15(a) of the Netherlands Nationality Act (exceptions in case of marriage or protracted residence in the country of other nationality, since amendments in 2000); Art. 17(1) of the Czech Act on Citizenship; and Art. 22(3) of the Estonian Act on Citizenship (as amended in 1998).

detach himself from his original nationality'.[87] But then why do many states allow individuals who acquired their nationality at birth to keep that nationality if they declare their will to continue in the legal status and/or if they maintain links to the state (family, business contacts, property)?[88] Is it that the assumption of detachment can be trumped by a statement to the contrary? If so, why is this option limited to nationals from birth only?

Many states also provide for 'special circumstances', in which an individual wishing to naturalize may keep her previous nationality: these include cases of *de facto* or legal impossibility, as well as exceptions for refugees or the nationals of certain states with historical or cultural ties to the state of naturalization.[89] These exceptions are understandable in the context of impossibility and for refugees, to the extent that the individual's choice regarding her original nationality is not respected by the state in question or is not, in fact, voluntary. But what does holding the nationality of a state with similar traditions have to do with individual choice? The individual's choice for or against membership remains unchanged, regardless of the history or culture of the state of origin. In turn, a number of states stipulating loss of nationality upon naturalization elsewhere contain provisions allowing for its recovery in case of continuous residence (usually for a minimum of twelve months) in the state of origin.[90] In effect, then, the assumption of a choice to give up ties to a particular state can be trumped by proof to the contrary in many cases, as evidenced by residence.

Still other regulations seem to confirm the importance of such choice. For example, children who are attributed more than one nationality at birth through a combination of *jus sanguinis* and *jus soli* may almost always keep these – in some states permanently, in others until the age of majority, when they must choose one.[91] But if states are really concerned with a confirmation of ties, then why are children from mixed-nationality marriages not forced to choose?[92] Still other states

---

Certain states also include provisions on loss of nationality for naturalized nationals only. *See, inter alia*, Art. 25 of the Spanish *Código Civil*; and Art. 28(1) in combination with Art. 28(5)(3) of the Estonian Act on Citizenship.

87. '*L'intervention de la volonté dans l'acquisition de la nouvelle nationalité permet d'expliquer la perte de la nationalité à la lumière d'un présumé souhait de l'individu pour se détacher de sa nationalité originaire*'. Pérez Vera (1996), p. 308.
88. *See* Art. 28(2) of the Austrian StAG. Other states make no distinction between native and naturalized nationals in this respect. *See* Art. 25(2) of the German StAG. Still others allow plural nationality for naturalized nationals only, since loss of the previous nationality is not required. *See* Arts 18–21 of the Belgian *Code de la Nationalité*.
89. Examples of the latter can be found in the regulations in force in Denmark (for other Nordic countries) and Spain (for states in Latin America, the Philippines, Andorra, Portugal and Equatorial Guinea).
90. *See* Art. 24 of the Belgian *Code de la Nationalité*; art. 26 of the Spanish *Código Civil*; and Arts 16 and 23 of the Croatian Act on Nationality.
91. *See* discussion of German practice at Sec. IV.B. *See also* Art. 3 of the Citizenship Act of Estonia (1995).
92. But *see* Art. 3 of the Citizenship Act of Estonia, where it is unclear whether the reference to acquisition of citizenship [sic] 'by birth' extends to *jus sanguinis* and *jus soli* alike.

provide that nationals born or resident abroad for a significant period of time must signal their intention to maintain their nationality; it is otherwise lost (statelessness notwithstanding).[93] Again, the underlying reasoning relies on confirming continued links. But the appearance of European citizenship has transformed the logic of such provisions, since residence in another Member State doesn't generally count as residence 'abroad' for the purposes of such provisions.[94] Thus, the need for proof of attachment to the given state is rendered unnecessary within the European Union.

In final consideration then, individual choice enters into decisions on nationality only when doubts arise as to whether an individual's legal status accords with some sort of attachment to a particular state;[95] or, as one commentator put it, when individuals are suspected of having 'a "real" nationality and an additional legal nationality, which do not correspond'.[96] Questions of this kind do not generally arise in the context of individuals with a sole nationality; and even if they do, states have little room to manoeuvre without rendering persons stateless. However, in the case of (potential) plural nationals, the source of possible doubt, however unfounded, is obvious. Additional nationalities are a sign of concrete ties to other states. Thus, even for plural nationals who have acquired a given nationality at birth – on the basis of *jus sanguinis* or *jus soli* – the presumed existence of some connection may require confirmation. Immigrants, in turn, must take active steps to create such ties. But similar considerations may arise in the context of individuals with some special status based on kinship, as in the context of the Hungarian Certificates already discussed. This suspicion explains why some extremist voices in home-states have called for stripping individuals of their nationality if they applied for such documents.

Given that the majority of persons hold only one nationality, however – the one acquired at birth – individual choice 'appears only as a contributory factor, a supplementary element when it is necessary';[97] in other words, when the 'bonds

---

93. *See, inter alia*, Art. 8(1) of the Danish Nationality Act (before 22 years of age); Art. 24(3) of the Spanish *Código Civil* (within three years of age of majority, for second generation born abroad); and Art. 22(1)(5) of the Belgian *Code de la nationalité*.
94. *See* Dutch provisions, effective April 2003, whereby plural nationals resident outside the Netherlands or another Member State of the European Union lose their nationality after ten years, unless they take clear steps toward its confirmation. (And compare with Art. 22(1)(5)(a) of the Belgian *Code de la nationalité*). Pursuant to amendments to the Netherlands Nationality Act in 2000, former nationals who lost their Dutch nationality on the basis of (unamended) Art. 15(c) of the Act were given a window in which to re-apply.
95. The fact of integration and ties has thus historically – though no longer – been assumed when nationality was acquired at birth. *See* ILC Report on Multiple Nationality, *supra* note IV.4, p. 16.
96. '*Une nationalité 'réelle', et puis une nationalité juridique qui ne correspond[ent] pas*'. *Rapport Long, Tome I*, *supra* note Intro.7, p. 403. Comments by R.P. Delorme. *See also* comments by Djida Tazdait in the same section, in the context of North-African immigrants France.
97. '*N'apparait que comme un élément d'appoint, un élément supplémentaire lorsqu'elle est nécessaire*'. *Ibid.*, at 115–116. Comments by Paul Lagarde.

that link an individual to his people'[98] 'are real, but are not strong enough'.[99] In effect, it is only the suspect who have the right of choice. In reality, such possibility of choice has the potential to become a trap. Exactly because nationals had little say about this legal status in the past,[100] increased respect for individual freedom has led to a strengthened assumption (still disprovable) that certain actions, including naturalization or protracted residence abroad, are a sign of wanting to be freed from the nationality of a particular state. For example, a proposition before the Belgian Senate in 2003 argued in the following terms for the abolishment of Article 22 of the *Code de la Nationalité*, prohibiting plural nationality, for Belgian nationals who naturalize in their spouse's state of nationality:

> Respect for the individuality of each person should be at the centre of concerns in a society in which different cultures inter-mingle ever more often. The fact of voluntarily acquiring the nationality of one's spouse accordingly cannot automatically mean that it is necessary to cut the bonds one has with the community one grew up in. In other words, the acquisition of a new nationality does not necessarily signify that the spouse in question now belongs only to the cultural community of the other spouse.[101]

This should be an obvious point, but is actually one that must be made over and over in many states. Conversely – and somewhat perversely – it is also on the basis of the increased importance attached to individual choice that most recent calls for requiring naturalizing immigrants to give proof that they have (attempted to) give up their previous nationality and/or that they have 'integrated' into society have been couched.[102] In other words, if individual choice is to play a central role in the attribution and withdrawal of nationality, then states can require more explicit signs of commitment from those who wish to acquire (or maintain) a particular nationality, especially at naturalization.

---

98. '*Liens qui unissent un individu à sa population*'. *Ibid.*, p. 115.
99. '*Sont réels, mais ne sont pas suffisamment forts*'. *Ibid.*
100. But *see* proposal for an automatic rule of loss of all nationalities except that of the state of domicile for plural nationals at the age of majority, by Flournoy, Jr. (1921), p. 708 *et seq*. The author argued that this rule would entail 'letting [the individual's] actions speak for him'. The assumption was thus of an indirect expression of will. *See also* p. 709, n. 100.
101. '*Le respect de l'individualité de tout un chacun doit être au centre des préoccupations d'une societé dans laquelle, de plus en plus souvent, les différentes cultures sont mélangées. Le fait d'acquérir volontairement la nationalité de son conjoint ne peut dès lors signifier automatiquement qu'il faille rompre les liens qu'on a avec la communauté dans laquelle on a grandi. En d'autres termes, l'acquisition d'une nouvelle nationalité ne signifie pas nécessairement que le conjoint en question n'appartient plus qu'à la communauté culturelle de l'autre conjoint*'. *Proposition de loi modificant l'article 22 du Code de la nationalité belge* (2003), p. 2.
102. *See* discussion at Secs IV.B.2. and IV.D.1.

4. MANAGING THE SIDE-EFFECTS OF PLURAL NATIONALITY

Given the problems encountered by international efforts to prevent plural nationality, a second strand – that of managing its side-effects – has been of considerable, and in recent years increasing, importance in international law. As a matter of custom, the vast majority of states have traditionally adhered in their jurisdiction to the general principle of disregarding any other nationalities a national may hold. This practice, an attempt both at creating order and asserting sovereignty over one's 'own' national, continues today,[103] despite the fact that it doesn't actually solve conflicts, but only neutralizes them within domestic systems.

In case of a live conflict in front of an international tribunal, in which two or more states invoke their jurisdiction over a national,[104] including by means of diplomatic protection,[105] or in the context of recognition of a judgment from the other state of nationality, for example, the principle cannot function.[106] Clearly, the principle also cannot function before the courts of a third state. For this reason, it has come under increasing attack from international and domestic courts, which have gradually begun to take individual attachment into account. Most often, the individual's nationalities are compared; and one is chosen as the only 'active' nationality, while the other is disregarded.

The birth of this strategy of choice for a particular nationality can be dated back to 1834, when the British Privy Council first determined that applicant, 'technically a British subject, but in substance, a French subject, domiciled ... in France, with all the marks and attributes of French character',[107] could not rely on his British nationality in a claim against the French government. The dominant practice that has emerged since that time constitutes a step forward, at least considering that the accepted doctrine until early in the 20th century consisted

---

103. *See* discussion of general opinion in Kammann (1984), p. 49 *et seq. See also* Art. 3 of the Hague Convention and discussion in ILC Survey (vol. II), *supra* note I.20. For domestic legislation, *see, inter alia*, Germany, Art. 5(1) *Einführungsgesetz zum Bürgerlichen Gesetzbuche* (1896, as amended); and Italy, Art. 19(2) of *Legge no. 218*, *supra* note I.109. The classic approach to diplomatic protection by one state of nationality against another, already discussed, was the external equivalent of this rule.
104. Clearly, the tribunal would need to be seized of the matter through at least one of the states to have jurisdiction.
105. *See*, e.g., the famous *Canevaro* Case (*Italy v. Peru*), decided by the Permanent Court of Arbitration (1912). The Court determined that, of Mr. Canevaro's nationalities, his Peruvian one was the dominant or effective one, since he had acted as a Peruvian citizen in a number of situations (e.g., by running for the Senate). Thus, Italy was not entitled to provide him with diplomatic protection against Peru. The ILC Draft Articles on Diplomatic Protection, *supra* note I.70, also chose to rely on the existence of a 'predominant nationality' in such cases (in Art. 7). *See also* the cases discussed in Kammann, at 64–71 (1984); and general discussion in Hailbronner (2003), p. 22.
106. *See* Lagarde (1988), p. 35; and Mayer (5th ed., 1994), p. 554.
107. *Case of James Louis Drummond*, British Privy Council (1834), as quoted in Rode (1959), p. 140.

of denying the possibility of any state claim on behalf of a national who was also the national of a respondent state.[108]

A decision of this kind is not one courts and tribunals take lightly, in any case, since the selected nationality will determine which law is applicable to the individual in all aspects of her personal status. In the context of a family law matter, for example, it could determine the validity of a marriage, the possibility of divorce, child custody, alimony and the division of assets, not to mention property and inheritance rights. Since this practice provides a great deal of latitude to courts and tribunals in determining which of the nationalities in question to declare primary, numerous approaches have emerged.[109] The two main approaches consist of establishing either 'habitual residence' or 'dominant nationality'.[110] Although these concepts are closely related, they should be distinguished.

The former is relatively straightforward, since it involves only an examination of where the individual habitually lives. The country in which the person's property is located; where she works and pays her taxes; and where her spouse and children are located is generally deemed to be the place of 'habitual residence'. In the case of the latter, focus is on the general principle of effectivity (in the context of establishing an 'effective link', already discussed), but involves a determination of 'the *most effective* attachment: the nationality to favour is the one of the state to which the individual is *most* attached in point of fact'.[111] Considerations in addition to 'habitual residence' are usually taken into account by this approach, including where the individual was educated, where she has lived in her lifetime, which languages she speaks and which culture she feels closer to. Individual choice – as evidenced by decisions taken – is thus central to any final judgment,[112] and is considered in addition to the objective outcomes (residence, property, taxes paid)[113] of such decisions.[114]

Both approaches entail the same danger, however. There is no guarantee that the 'active' nationality chosen by the given court or tribunal will be the one the

---

108. *See, inter alia*, Art. 16(a) of the Draft of the Law of Responsibility for Damages Done in Their Territory to the Persons or Property of Foreigners (Harvard Draft) (1929).
109. *See* discussion in ILC Survey (vol. II), *supra* note I.20, pp. 88–90.
110. *See* Art. 5 of the Hague Convention.
111. *[Le] rattachement le plus effectif: la nationalité à préférer est celle de l'Etat avec lequel [l'individu] se rattache le plus en fait.* Verwilghen (1999), p. 418 (emphasis in original).
112. *See* discussion of the role of individual volition in all three concepts in Carlier (1992), pp. 201–205.
113. The International Law Commission, for example, has listed present residence, past or habitual residence (in case of present residence in a third state), fulfilment of military service, exercise of civil and political rights, language spoken, previous requests for diplomatic protection and ownership of immovable property as factors to be taken into account. ILC Report on Multiple Nationality, *supra* note IV.4, Basis 3.
114. Certain states make a clear reference to individual choice. As Art. 9(9) of the Spanish *Código Civil* states: 'A los efectos de este capítulo será preferida la nacionalidad coincidente con la última residencia habitual y, en su defecto, la última adquirida'.

individual also feels is foremost, assuming that she even views her nationalities in competition with each other. As one author has warned:

> This is making much of the presumed will of the interested [person], who may show himself greatly surprised to learn that, in relying on his presumed nationality, judges have decided to classify his countries as if these could be reduced to the condition of athletes receiving gold, silver or bronze medals.[115]

a. The Factor of European Citizenship

In the context of the European Union, a ranking of this kind would also run afoul of the rights of European citizenship, since the freedom of Member State courts to choose a particular nationality has been restricted to the extent that a right of European citizenship is thereby affected. A good example is the *Micheletti* case, which arose from the refusal of Spain to recognize the Italian nationality of an Italian-Argentinean dual-national (on the basis of Article 9(9) of the *Código Civil* article already referred to). The E.C.J. refused to agree that 'where a national of a Member state is also a national of a non-member country, the other Member States may make recognition of the status of Community national subject to a condition such as the habitual residence of the person concerned in the territory of the first Member State'[116] – on the basis that a grant of nationality by one Member State must be accepted by all others. In the European Union context then, we can speak of one self-contained legal order for the purposes of recognizing nationality. There can be no examination of social or other ties, since Member State nationality, qua legal status, must be automatically recognized in all other Member States. Otherwise, Community-granted rights would be lost.[117]

In a comparable manner, plural nationals holding the nationality of two (or more) Member States are to be treated as a distinct group on the basis of their special connection to more than one state. As *García Avello* demonstrated, Member States may not ignore the additional Member State nationalities of their nationals, as they could theoretically do on the basis of international practice.[118] In addition, despite the E.C.J.'s assertion that 'the rules of private law and family law applying in the Member States ... fall within the competence of those Member States'[119], the decision in *García Avello* effectively disapplied, for plural nationals, the national conflict of law rules that constitute a cornerstone of these laws. Since these conflict rules determine the applicable law in many other circumstances in addition to names – marriage and divorce to name just two – this

---

115. *'C'est faire grand cas de la volonté présumée de l'intéressé, qui pourrait se montrer fort surpris d'apprendre qu'en se fondant sur sa nationalité présumée des juristes ont décidé de classer ses patries comme si elles se réduisaient à la condition de champions sportifs recevant la médaille d'or, d'argent ou de bronze'*. Verwilghen (1999), p. 427.
116. Case 369/90 *Micheletti*, at para. 11.
117. *See* also, *ibid.,* at para. 12.
118. *See* discussion at Sec. II.C.2.f.
119. Case 430/97 *Johannes*, E.C.J. [1999], para. 18.

decision made significant inroads into what has heretofore been considered an important state competence.

The Opinion of Advocate General Jacobs in the *Standesamt Stadt Niebüll* case took a further step in this regard. The Advocate General argued that Germany had violated its nationals' right to free movement when it refused to recognize the name given to a German child by his parents and validly attested to under Danish law, where the family resided. In other words, Germany had attempted to apply its law on personal names to nationals resident in (but not nationals of) Denmark, which was willing to apply its own law on the basis of its own conflict of laws rules.[120] In his reasoning, the Advocate General drew practical parallels to the situation in *García Avello* (and *Konstantinidis*), and even referred to identity concerns, despite the fact that the child in question was not a plural national. Although the Court eventually determined that it lacked jurisdiction to answer the request for a preliminary ruling,[121] a judgment along the lines of the Advocate General's opinion could have sidelined a central tenet of private international law within the legal space of the European Union.

Though the E.C.J. established the necessity of positive discrimination on behalf of dual nationals in *García Avello* – while *Niebüll* introduced the possibility of extending the scope of beneficiaries – an earlier decision had already noted that individuals with the nationality of more than one Member State could not, for that reason, be limited in their Community rights.[122] The basis for this reasoning was not purely the existence of links to multiple states, however, as can be seen when comparing the situation of this group with that of plural nationals whose additional nationality is that of a non-Member State.

In *Mesbah*, a case involving a Belgian-Moroccan dual national, the Court held that:

> [I]t is ... for the national court alone, in the exercise of its exclusive power to interpret and apply its domestic law in the proceedings before it, to determine the nationality of [a plural national] in accordance with the Belgian law,

---

120. *See* Opinion of Advocate General Jacobs in Case C-96/04 (30 June 2005), para. 54. ('Leonard Matthias is however from a practical point of view in a position closely comparable to that of the Garcia Avello children if in the Member State of his nationality a different surname must be registered from that which he bears in the Member State of his birth. While the practical difficulties which he is likely to encounter may not stem from discrimination on grounds of nationality, they constitute a clear obstacle to his right as a citizen to move and reside freely within the territory of the Member States. Although such difficulties may be of a similar kind to those encountered by Mr Konstantinidis, the combined effects of Articles 17 and 18(1) EC mean that it is now unnecessary to establish any economic link in order to demonstrate an infringement of the right to freedom of movement'.) *See also* para. 55.
121. Case C-96/04 *Standesamt Stadt Niebüll*, E.C.J. [2006].
122. *See* Case 292/86 *Claude Gullung v. Conseil de l'ordre des avocats du barreau de Colmar et de Saverne*, E.C.J. [1988], para. 12. *See also* Case 115/78 *Knoors v. Secretary of State for Economic Affairs*, E.C.J. [1979].

in particular the nationality legislation and private international law, applicable.[123]

In other words, the Member State could continue to treat this group of plural nationals as if they held only the nationality of the given state for certain purposes. In the case at issue, Belgium's decision to treat Ms. Mesbah as a Belgian national effectively denied her family a benefit, despite the fact that this treatment resulted in the effective disapplication of a binding EC Treaty that had made no exception for plural nationals. (The outcome of the case is also noteworthy because it reverses the usual status quo, in which treatment as a Member State national, rather than as a third-state national, is advantageous. Here, in light of the denial of social benefits otherwise due, treatment equal to those of other [uni]nationals thus had detrimental effects for the individual.)[124]

This difference in approach to Member State-Member State plural nationals and Member State-third state plural nationals can only be explained by the special place of European citizenship in the Community legal order. As the primary status of individuals for the purposes of European law, it serves to import not just the four freedoms into the domestic spheres of Member States, but also the domestic legal effects of other Member State nationalities.

b.   Applicable Law and Respect for 'Cultural Identity'

Even disregarding EC law, decisions on the 'active' nationality of plural nationals are rendered especially complicated in family law matters.[125] In the first place, even if nationality has lost ground to 'domicile' and 'habitual residence'[126] in a

---

123. Case C-179/98 *Belgian State v. Fatna Mesbah*, E.C.J. [1999], para. 40. *See also* paras 35, 37, and 41.
124. As we saw, a significant portion of human rights discourse aims to place individuals in the situation of nationals exactly because this treatment results in a 'better' outcome for the individual. On the basis of such a 'best of both worlds' approach, perhaps courts could consider applying a rule of 'most favourable nationality' for plural nationals; i.e., they would consider which law provides for the best possible outcome for the individual in the given circumstance. While there may be practical difficulties, a rule of this kind would, in any case, fit squarely in the individual rights approach to nationality discussed below.
125. A similar question arises when the existence of plural nationality affects the applicability of an international instrument signed by the state of the court seized with the decision regarding 'active' nationality ('state A') and one of the individual's states of nationality ('state B'), to the extent that state A is no longer 'neutral' in the decision at hand. State A is, in fact, obliged to extend any rights agreed to in the convention to all nationals of state B, regardless of whether they may be the nationals of any other states. *See* Rigaux (1987), p. 89.
126. *See* Carlier (1992), p. 181 and p. 216 *et seq.* for an overview of possible factors of attachment for the purposes of private international law. In general terms, *'[L]a recherche du facteur rattachant la personne à une loi tourne autour d'une idée centrale: l'appartenance à une communauté'*. *Ibid*. For a general discussion of the individual interest in being judged by the legal system to which one has the closest ties and an evaluation of the role of nationality and domicile, *see* Mankowski (2004), p. 283 *et seq.*; but *see* Mansel (2003), p. 136 for an argument on the principle of democratic legitimacy.

number of traditional functions, including determining court access and applicable law, it nonetheless remains crucial not only because of its greater stability and predictability, but also on account of its supposed identity function. The assumption that an individual is more closely linked to the legal system of the state of her nationality than to any other thus retains considerable influence.[127] A 1981 Convention between France and Morocco on family law matters, for example, set out in its Preamble 'the necessity of preserving, for individuals, the principles of their national identity'.[128] (In the context of Muslim states with legal systems based on or influenced by *shari'a*, religious identity is subsumed here into the rubric of nationality). As one scholar remarked in the mid-1990s:

> [C]ultural identity has reinforced the principle of nationality in the sense that this [latter] principle is considered more suitable for taking into account an individual's cultural link with a particular law [or legal system] than local attachment. If all parties possess the same nationality, application of their national law seems more appropriate for the protection of their cultural identity.[129]

The assumption of a necessary link between culture and nationality[130] is obviously debatable, especially in the context of *jus sanguinis* coupled with migration.[131] For this reason, many states in Europe walk a fine line in relying on both nationality and domicile in family law matters. In France, for example, numerous conventions stipulating the application of the law of the state of nationality co-exist with *Code*

Although the pros and cons of using one basis of attachment rather than another is beyond the scope of this work, it should be noted that the diverse interests of states and individuals should be taken into account in addition to practical considerations of functionality (e.g., nationality is the more stable of the two bases, since it is generally more permanent than domicile). In the first place, it should be recognized that adherence to the principle of habitual residence or domicile is also a preference for the principle of territorial sovereignty, rather than that of personal sovereignty (and vice versa). Second, a choice for one or the other is also a decision for a particular model of social cohesion, circumscribed either by territory or by a trans-state cultural community. Third, from the point of view of the individual, we are faced with a question of timing: to the extent that any legal system can respect the *sentiment d'identité* of an individual, is this better done by recognition of origin or of present-day presence in (and possible future integration into) a given society? *See* Gutmann (2000), p. 381 *et seq.* for an extended discussion.

127. *See* Institut de droit international, *Resolution sur la dualité des principes de nationalité et de domicile en droit international privé* (1987). For a critique of this assumption, *see* de Winter (1969).
128. '*La nécessité de conserver aux personnes les principes de leur identité nationale. Convention entre le Gouvernement de la République française et le Gouvernement du Royaume du Maroc relative au statut des personnes et de la famille et à la coopération judiciaire*' (1981, in force since 1983).
129. '*L'identité culturelle a renforcé le principe de la nationalité dans le sens que ce principe est considéré comme plus apte à tenir compte du lien culturel d'une personne avec un certain droit qu'un rattachement local. Si toutes les parties possèdent la même nationalité, l'application de leur loi nationale semble plus appropriée pour la sauvegarde de leur identité culturelle*'. Jayme (1995), p. 253. *See also* Gaudemet-Tallon (1991), p. 219–220.
130. *See, inter alia*, Gutmann (2000), p. 405.
131. *See* Le Monde, *Les Repudiées de la Republique* (11 June 2004).

Civil Article 3(3), stipulating that French law be applied to French nationals, but also with Article 310, allowing for the application of French law in divorce cases involving non-national residents. The state is thus inconsistent in its supposedly exclusive reliance on the nationality principle in an area of law strongly influenced by religious and other beliefs.

To the extent that interest is increasingly directed not just at the juridical links or nationality of individuals, but at a general concept of attachment – in the context of which 'simply with a view to the principle of justice, no factor can lay claim to supremacy or exclusivity in the concretization of this bond'[132] – the scholar above is somewhat optimistic regarding the strengthened role of nationality. In the opposite vein, one writer has suggested that – to preserve an individual's cultural identity and, more directly, her autonomy of choice in deciding which legal order best reflects that identity – persons should, *professio juris*, have the right to choose the law applicable to them from among those systems to which they have a certain degree of attachment, whether through nationality or habitual residence.[133] (In fact, some states already provide for the possibility of option in cases of divorce; while the Institut de Droit International advanced this approach back in 1987).[134]

In this understanding, nationality is but one means of attachment – now stripped of state concerns regarding the overlap of membership and belonging – which has, moreover, lost its primary function as an expression of state sovereignty. In short, if a plural national may opt for the law of one of her states of nationality (or habitual residence) in the context of 'personal status' only, so that such a choice 'has no impact on nationality, properly called',[135] the control function exercised by the state over the individual – personal sovereignty – is lost. The approach is thus quite radical, begetting a new understanding of what nationality signifies for both legal and identity purposes. As its author discusses, the approach would also require a thorough re-consideration of practices relating to plural nationality.[136] States could no longer ignore the other nationalities of their own nationals, since the individuals in question could choose to request the application of laws on the basis of these additional statuses.

While the proposal is an interesting one, echoing the trend toward increased respect for individual choice, the realities of (some) migration undermine its very foundations. This writer, for example, holds one nationality (that of state A) but has lived in that state only 10 years of her life (during childhood); she has resided in another state (B) for ten years; in a third state (C) for three; a fourth (D) for one; and

---

132. *'Aucun facteur ne peut, pas plus qu'au regard du principe de justice, prétendre à la suprématie ou à l'exclusivité dans la concretisation de ce lien'.* Carlier (1992), p. 249.
133. *Ibid.*, p. 259 *et seq.* (especially to 267). *See also* Gutmann (2000), p. 392 *et seq.*
134. *See* 62(I) Annuaire de l'Institut de Droit International, at 156 (1987). *See also* Art. 1 of *Ley 11/ 1990, de 15 de octubre, sobre reforma del Código Civil, en aplicación del principio de no discriminación por razón de sexo* (1990) in the context of Spain.
135. *'Statut personnel n'a pas d'incidence sur la nationalité proprement dite'.* Carlier (1992), p. 298.
136. *Ibid.*

a fifth (E) – where she now lives – for over three years (and counting). Does it really make sense to speak of a state of 'habitual residence' in such a case? Or of a real connection with any of the states above? If so, who is to say that this connection is not to (the society of) a state of past residence (e.g., B) rather than that of nationality or of residence at the present moment?

5. REVISING APPROACHES IN DOMESTIC LEGISLATION

Independent of international efforts, most attempts to limit plural nationality have taken place at the national level, and have been expressed in some requirement of the given law on nationality. Thus, it is overwhelmingly to domestic laws that we should look to ascertain attitudes and tendencies of development. Traditionally, states have taken two, somewhat contradictory, approaches to plural nationality in domestic legislation. As the foundation of the international practice already discussed, many have simply refused to acknowledge the existence of another nationality:[137] either by ruling out the possibility or by reference to domestic treatment of persons as if they held only the nationality of the state. Thus, states in effect ignored the existence of any other legal ties within the domestic system. Certain states – today a minority – still refuse to release individuals from their original nationality under any circumstances (e.g., Iran). As a result, these states continue to assert jurisdiction even when individuals have lived abroad for decades and hold another nationality. In lieu of ignoring other legal ties within the domestic system, then, this approach simply denies reality. At the other extreme, a large number of states have in the past indicated that voluntary acquisition of other nationalities will result in the loss of the (old) nationality in question, special permission notwithstanding.[138] In this case, the establishment of legal ties elsewhere results in the automatic suspension of membership ties to the original state.

Finally, in a case of exceptions to prove the rule, it should be noted that a small minority of states have simply never had trouble with the fact of their own nationals holding other nationalities. The United Kingdom would be an obvious example in this regard. Plural nationality has never been a point of contention, despite repeated and contentious overhauls to nationality regulation in the 20th century. Even as questions are now raised about the relation between naturalization and the integration of immigrants, the phenomenon of plural nationality is still not a focal point of public debate. Whether the ready acceptance of multiple allegiances in the UK is a remnant of Empire or an expression of confidence is a matter for sociologists;[139] but it is apparent that we deal here with a unique situation.

---

137. *See* Art. 10 of the Citizenship Law of the Ukraine; Art. 9 of the Law on Citizenship of Latvia; and Art. 1(2) of the Citizenship Law of Estonia for recent examples of this approach.
138. *See, inter alia*, Art. 12 of Law No. 391 (on Citizenship) of Egypt (1956) (abrogated in 1958 by Law No. 82).
139. *See* Hansen (2001), p. 74 for a discussion of the British tradition of allegiance.

Generally speaking, 'it is only in the course of recent years that a veritable, rather general turn-around has begun to manifest itself. In a short period of time we have passed from rejection of plural nationality to its cautious acceptance and, in some countries, even to more enthusiastic support'.[140] Though certain authors saw signs of a changing attitude decades ago,[141] a writer in 1984 could still note that 'laws on nationality that specifically and explicitly favour the existence and emergence of plural nationality are only relatively rarely encountered'.[142] At the time, besides the UK, only Ireland (since 1956),[143] Cyprus (since 1967), France (since 1973), Portugal and Turkey (both since 1981) clearly allowed for plural nationality, while Spain allowed for dual nationality with a limited group of states. It is only in the last 15 years that the domestic legislation of many European states has undergone noteworthy evolution, as the table below demonstrates.[144]

Table 1. State Regulation of Plural Nationality in Europe
(On the basis of Nationality Laws)

Prohibit	Allow in Limited Cases Only	Generally Allow
* Almost all states allow dual nationality in the context of dual *jus sanguinis*		
Andorra	Austria (Only at naturalization, very limited)	Albania (since 1998)
Estonia		Armenia (since 2007)
Georgia (reconfirmed in 2004)	Belarus (Only by international treaty)	Bulgarian (since 1998)
		Cyprus (since 1967)
	Belgium (Only at naturalization)	Finland (since 2003)
Monaco	Bosnia-Herzegovina (Through bilateral conventions)	France (since 1973)
San Marino		Hungary (since 1993)
Ukraine	Croatia (Not in context of naturalization)	Iceland (since 2003)
		Ireland (since 1956)
	Czech Republic (Only at marriage/ birth of child and for those who lost nationality between 1948 and 1990)	Italy (since 1992)
		Malta (since 2000)
		Moldova (since 2003)

---

140. '*C'est au cours des dernières années seulement qu'un véritable revirement, assez généralisé, a commencé à se manifester. En peu de temps, on est passé du reject de la plurinationalité à l'acceptation prudente et même, dans quelques pays, à une adhésion plus enthusiaste de cette situation*'. Verwilghen (1999), pp. 316–317.
141. See de Castro y Bravo (1961), p. 588.
142. '*Staatsangehörigkeitsgesetze, die gezielt und ausdrücklich das Be- und Entstehen von Mehrstaatigkeit begünstigen, [sind] nur noch relativ selten anzutreffen*'. Kammann (1984), p. 218.
143. Ireland allowed for plural nationality to allow for maintenance of ties with Irish emigrants.
144. This chart was prepared by the author, on the basis of available laws on nationality. It makes no claims to rigorous comparative analysis, but serves rather to give a general impression of development.

Table 1. (Continued)

Prohibit	Allow in Limited Cases Only	Generally Allow
* Almost all states allow dual nationality in the context of dual *jus sanguinis*		
	Denmark (Only at naturalization, very limited)	Montenegro (since independence)
	Germany (Only at naturalization, limited)	Poland (since 1998)
	Greece (On basis of *jus sanguinis*)	Portugal (since 1981)
	Latvia (Only for refugees/deportees between 1940 and 1990, or their descendants)	Romania (since 1991)
		Russia (since 2002)
		Slovakia (since 1993)
	Liechtenstein (Not in context of naturalization)	Sweden (since 2001)
		Switzerland (since 1992)
	Lithuania (Limited cases on basis of *jus sanguinis*)	Turkey (since 1981)
	Luxembourg (Only at naturalization, very limited)	United Kingdom
	FYRO Macedonia (Not in context of naturalization)	
	Netherlands (Spouses of Dutch nationals and certain immigrants)	
	Norway (Only at naturalization, very limited)	
	Serbia-Montenegro (Not in context of naturalization, unless married to a national)	
	Slovenia (Not in context of naturalization)	
	Spain (For nationals of certain states only)	

The 1990s in particular saw a large number of states (mainly those recently liberated from the Socialist bloc) change position on the issue;[145] while a steady trickle continues to do so since that time. Even states that allow for plural nationality in limited contexts only, like Germany, have extended the scope of cases in which it is allowed.[146] As a general matter, it is increasingly only states that fear

---
145. *See* Liebich (2000).
146. Also worth noting is the tendency of states in Central Europe to limit plural nationality at naturalization, and the opposite trend in Western Europe of allowing it in exactly this context. A possible explanation can be sought in the vastly different rates of immigration to the two groups of states, and related questions of integration.

foreign political interference (like Ukraine, Georgia or Estonia) or which are so small as to protect their (remaining) sovereignty especially fiercely (like Andorra, San Marino or Monaco) that continue to prohibit plural nationality, without much success.

The process of accepting plural nationality plays out in diverse ways, however, in line with national particularities. Questions of integration and plural membership thus did not figure prominently in Belgian debates on nationality before 1984, when important legal changes were introduced, even though the new Code had significant effects on both phenomena. In contrast, one of the main questions raised during the major transformation of German nationality law in 1999 – as well as in Sweden before 2001 – was exactly that of the interaction between integration and plural nationality, as will be discussed. In turn, debate in Italy prior to the 1992 reforms focused on dual nationality only as a means to maintain (legal) ties to emigrants.[147] In a comparable manner, many of the states outside Europe that can be cited as further evidence of a shift toward acceptance of plural nationality have been motivated by an interest in maintaining links with (and control over) their own emigrants. Mexico was one of the last states in Latin America to allow nationals naturalized elsewhere to retain their original nationality, in 1998;[148] the Philippines and India followed suit in 2003 and 2004, respectively.

The possible reasons behind the change of approach are thus manifold: higher rates of migration, resulting in higher numbers of plural nationals (despite laws to the contrary);[149] changed political circumstances (both domestic and international, as will be seen in the German case); the rise of other legal statuses (resulting in new views on the identity function of nationality), and; at least in Europe, a more substantial legal framework to deal with the secondary effects of plural nationality.

That said, plural nationality has not yet become the norm; rather, it remains a matter of special justification for individuals with undeniable links to more than one state. Its acceptance is thus an instance of states reacting to phenomena they can no longer overlook: 'wisdom led to acceptance [of the fact] that [a] bi-national in the sociological sense of the term could also become a dual national in the legal sense'.[150] Let us take a look at the German case to understand how such practicality resulted in a significant instance of reform.

B.   TRANSFORMATION IN GERMANY

1.   Legal Stasis and Initial Steps toward Reform

The nationality law of Germany has long been criticized by theorists as one particularly ill-suited to contemporary realities. In particular, a number of writers

---

147. *See* Pastore (2001), pp. 101–103.
148. *See* Art. 37(a) of the Mexican Constitution.
149. *See also* de Groot (1989), pp. 320–321, who argued over 15 years ago for acceptance of plural nationality in the context of naturalization.
150. '[L]a sagesse conduisait à accepter que le binational au sens sociologique du terme puisse devenir également double national au sens juridique'. Verwilghen (1999), p. 326.

have pointed to its 'ethnocultural'[151] character. As a recent study by Nathans has shown, the importance of ethnic considerations has in reality ebbed and flowed, as concerns of short-term utility, economic advantage, external policy and state organization gained or lost in significance.[152] For example, the Prussian citizenship law of 1842 (the *Untertanengesetz*), the foundation for all later regulation, echoed power struggles between local and central administration, a concern with conscription and fear of the effects national movements in neighbouring Poland and Bohemia could have on German unification.

As Weil notes, 'nationality law is foremost a complex law, most often produced by specialized lawyers to whom the political or administrative leadership has contracted out or delegated the drafting of the law'.[153] The concerns of a given moment in time are often reflected in any resulting legislation. It is true, however, that the two pillars of German nationality law – avoidance of plural nationality, especially in the context of a difficult process of naturalization, and reliance on the principle of *jus sanguinis* – have remained unchanged for decades, despite wide-ranging social transformation. Thus, despite a number of nominal amendments throughout the second half of the 20th century,[154] it was a law from 1913, the *Reichs- und Staatsangehörigkeitsgesetz* (hereinafter, RuStAG),[155] that regulated

---

151. Brubaker (1992), p. 14. *See* also, *inter alia*, Räthzel (1991), p. 41; Kramer (1996), p. xxi; and Giesen (2001). *See also* discussion in Neuman (1998), pp. 250–251.
152. *See* account of the emergence of a unified regulation of German nationality in Chaps 1–7 of Nathans (2004).
153. '*Le droit de la nationalité est d'abord un droit complexe, le plus souvent fabriqué par les juristes spécialisés, à qui le dirigeant politique ou administratif sous-traite voir délègue la rédaction de la loi*'. Weil (2002), p. 194.
154. In particular, to equate women with men in nationality matters (in line with amendments in 1957, 1969 and 1974). Also worth noting is the *Gesetz zur Regelung von Fragen der Staatsangehörigkeit* (1955), which granted German nationality to all individuals resident outside the 1937 borders of the state and placed in the top three categories of the *Volksliste* by Nazi authorities (Arts 1 and 28), since it complemented GG Art. 116(1).
155. The history of the 1913 law is worth recalling in order to understand its significance. The first attempt at regulating nationality in what would later become Germany was that of the North German Federation, by means of the *Gesetz zur Erwerbung und den Verlust der Bundes- und Staatsangehörigkeit* (1870), extended to the entire *Deutsches Reich* upon its inception (on 1 January 1871). This law relied on *Landeszugehörigkeit*, however. In other words, nationality in the German *Reich* was derivative of citizenship in one of its Member States – much like the situation in the United States at the time. Despite continuous efforts by the federal government in Berlin to centralize decisions on naturalization, states (and local governments) continued to conduct their own, wildly varied, policies.

    The 1913 law rendered nationality the primary status of individuals (above *Land* citizenship) and established the authority of the *Bundesrat* over naturalization. The law remained basically unchanged until National Socialism – even as the importance of nationality, *qua* legal status and as a marker of belonging, increased in the wake of World War I – when discriminatory provisions on the basis of ethnicity and religion were introduced into the text. (*See* Hokema (2002), pp. 86–87). These notorious additions were cut from the legislation in 1945 by Kontrollratsgesetz Nr. 1 and, in 1949, definitively repudiated with the country's new Constitution (*see* GG Arts 1, 3, and 16), which simultaneously re-instated the provisions of the 1913 law (*see* GG Arts 123 and 124).

matters of nationality in Germany until 1 January 2000, when significant changes, including a change of designation, came into effect. The 1999 reforms – 'a revolution in German citizenship policies' by one estimation[156] – are accordingly considered by some the final step of a process in which 'Germany gave up one of the instruments it and predecessor regimes had employed to mould society, an instrument used for much of this century to promote the ethnic homogeneity of the nation'.[157]

The simple explanation for legal stasis in the second half of the 20th century is the post World War II division of the country; West Germany insisted on the existence of one unified German nationality, as expressed in GG Article 116.[158] A law proclaimed by one of the two German states and valid only in its territory would, therefore, have been unacceptable politically. There is a more complex explanation, however. As Nathans argues, nationality was seen by most public actors until the late 1970s as 'one of the few remaining legal bulwarks against the full integration of resident aliens into German society'.[159] This was especially the case given the general and wilful refusal of society to acknowledge reality.

As the first federal *Einbürgerungsrichtlinien*, or Guidelines on Naturalization, from 1977 – a year when 6.4 per cent of the population was foreign – clearly stated: *Deutschland ist kein Einwanderungsland.*[160] Despite this announcement, the guidelines nonetheless marked an important shift in emphasis. Although they set a (high) standard of integration, naturalization was at least now officially, if not always practically, possible. In fact, these first guidelines set the benchmark for all later discussion, as the normative value of German identity – already the mainspring of legislation on kin-Germans – had now been extended to the context of immigration. Henceforth, the general question was not to be whether one could become German, but the manner in which this was to be accomplished. The link between integration and naturalization had been forged.[161]

This evolution was not yet reflected in policy, however, and naturalization remained the exception. Nonetheless, the judicial branch begged to differ from the general hostility to immigration, and played an important role in extending the scope of foreigners' rights during the 1970s and '80s.[162] As a result, certain legal developments, which informed the nature of subsequent nationality regulation, did

---

156. Nathans (2004), p. 5.
157. *Ibid.*, p. 269.
158. Incidentally, the first Constitution of East Germany (from 1949) also noted, '*Es gibt nur eine deutsche Staatsangehörigkeit*' (Art. 1). In the Constitution of 1968, however, reference is made to the *Staatsbürgerschaft der DDR* (Art. 19).
159. Nathans (2004), p. 245.
160. 'Germany is not a country of immigration'. *Einbürgerungsrichtlinien*, No. 2.3.
161. The Kühn memorandum was also an important sign in this regard. *See* Heinz Kühn, *Stand und Weiterentwicklung der Integration der ausländischen Arbeitnehmer und ihrer Familien in der Bundesrepublik Deutschland* (1979). *See also* the draft law proposals from the early 1980s, discussed below.
162. Joppke (1999), p. 69 *et seq.* (Both international human rights discourse and constitutional tradition played a significant role in this development.)

occur. In fact, as the scope of the rights due to permanent residents expanded, the legal status of nationality lost much of its urgency as a source of rights;[163] simultaneously, however, its identity function gained in salience. In other words, since most rights could be gained through residence in Germany – voting rights were an important exception and eventually formed the basis for democratic legitimacy-focused arguments during debate in the 1990s – only the symbolic role of acquiring German nationality remained. The public discussion that surrounded reform efforts, when they finally arrived, must be understood through this lens.

With reunification,[164] the nationality law of the *Bundesrepublik* then in force – the 1913 law – was extended to the new *Bundesländer*. Thus, the basic principles of the law – avoidance of plural nationality and reliance on *jus sanguinis* – survived to guide the regulation of nationality in the unified state. The population of Germany in the 1990s was rather different from that of the state in 1913, however. In particular, the West German policy of inviting *Gastarbeiter* (guest workers) from Southern Europe (mainly Italy, Yugoslavia and Turkey) to fill gaps in the workforce between the early 1960s and 1973 had produced an ever-larger population of foreigners, and, with the passage of time, their German-born children. In addition, (pre and post-unification) Germany's comparatively lenient asylum policy – eventually restricted in 1993 – resulted in a flood of (mostly former-Yugoslav) applicants from the mid 1980s onwards.[165] By 1998, 7.3 million (or about 8.9 per cent of the population) were foreigners; of these, 70 per cent had been residing in Germany for over ten years.[166]

Given such demographic changes, as well as the age and structure of the law in force, few doubted the necessity of new regulations on nationality after reunification;[167] but no agreement could be reached on what its outlines should be. This lack of consensus was perhaps un-surprising, given the varied reasons for which change was thought to be necessary.[168] The Christian Democrats (CDU/

---

163. In this context, *see* the *Bundesverfassungsgericht*'s 1978 decision determining that an Indian national legally resident in Germany for over a decade had developed a *Vertrauensschutz* (or reliance interest) in continued residence in the state. 1 BvR 525/77 (1978).
164. Specifically, as a result of Chap. 3, Art. 8 of the *Vertrag zwischen der Bundesrepublik Deutschland und der Deutschen Demokratischen Republik über die Herstellung der Einheit Deutschlands* (1990).
165. In 1992, at its peak, the flood of applicants reached 438,191. From Bundesministerium des Innern, Statistics, *Migration, Asyl*. *See* the web-site of the Ministry of the Interior, at: <www.bmi.bund.de>.
166. *Ibid.*, *Zahl der Ausländer in der Bundesrepublik Deutschland* 16; and as quoted in Gnielinski (1999), p. 46.
167. In fact, the first draft law, prepared by the state of Nordrhein-Westfalen with the goal of integrating the so-called 'Ausländergeneration' (generation of foreigners) was presented to the Bundesrat in 1980; and included a right to naturalization for all individuals who had been permanent residents in Germany since the age of twelve and had been present in the state for a minimum of two years before that time. Application was to be made before the age of 21 and included loss of previous nationality. (*See Viertes Gesetz zur regelung von Fragen der Staatsangehörigheit, Gesetzentwurf* (BR-Dr. 52/80), at 7). A draft from 1982, prepared by the West German government, covered similar ground, but was rejected. *See Viertes Gesetz zur regelung von Fragen der Staatsangehörigheit, Empfehlungen zum Gesetzentwurf* (BR-Dr. 3/1/82).
168. For a general overview of approaches until 1994, *see* Murray (1994), p. 23.

CSU), for example, focused mainly on the need for a clearer and more consolidated nationality law[169] – since a number of sources besides the RuStAG and the Constitution governed particular situations – as well as on the need for better avoidance of plural nationality. In turn, the Socialists (SPD), the Liberals (FDP) and the Greens saw a need for reform due to the age and historical burden of the law, as well as because of the need for better integration of foreigners. Not least, the necessity of a law more in line with European trends and developments in the EU was also pointed out.[170] In addition to such explicit legal reasons – and surely more importantly – a number of social issues were thought to require change. At various points in time, the CDU/CSU and the SPD both referred to the importance of social peace;[171] in a closely-related point, the Greens, the FDP and, again, the SPD noted the need for better integration of foreigners. In effect, such comments were a belated and public recognition of the permanence of migration.[172]

Another, perhaps even greater hindrance to agreement, was the diametrically opposed approach of the main parties to what nationality should signify, particularly in the context of naturalization. The right wing considered the conferral of nationality the final step in a process of integration[173] – in effect, its official recognition – so that acceptance of continued ties to another state, especially the maintenance of one's previous nationality, and hence plural nationality, was deemed undesirable. Left wing circles, on the other hand, saw the attribution of nationality as a necessary element of the integration process[174] – not only a source of legal equality but also a means to 'certify' immigrants as permanent members of German society – by which social acceptance was to be furthered. In turn, plural nationality was viewed as an expression of the multiple ties of new nationals; as such, it was rather an asset to social inclusion than an obstacle thereto.

In 1989, left-wing parties presented several draft laws on nationality to the Bundestag, all of which broke with the principle of pure *jus sanguinis*, allowed for

---

169. *See* parliamentary remarks by Seiters (CDU/CSU), Plenarprotokoll des Deutschen Bundestages 12/155, 13205.
170. *See* parliamentary remarks by Weiß (Bündnis 90/Die Grünen), Plenarprotokoll des Deutschen Bundestages 12/155, 13203; by Özdemir (Bündnis 90/Die Grünen), Plenarprotokoll des Deutschen Bundestages 13/225, 20631; and by Sonntag-Wolgast (SPD), Plenarprotokoll des Deutschen Bundestages 12/155, 13208.
171. *See* parliamentary remarks by Schäuble (CDU/CSU), Plenarprotokoll des Deutschen Bundestages 11/207, 16281 and 16284; and by Schily (SPD), Plenarprotokoll des Deutschen Bundestages 14/40, 3417.
172. *See* remarks by Chancellor Schröder (SPD) on the occasion of the first meeting of the newly constituted Parliament, Plenarprotokoll des deutschen Bundestages 14/3, 47 *et seq*.
173. *See* parliamentary remarks by Marchewski (CDU), Plenarprotokoll des Deutschen Bundestages 12/255, 19407.
174. *See* parliamentary remarks by Sonntag-Wolgast (SPD), Plenarprotokoll des Deutschen Bundestages 12/225, 19405; *Entwurf eines Gesetzes zur Erleichterung der Einbürgerung und Hinnahme der Doppelstaatsangehörigkeit* (BT-Dr. 12/4533), at 6. This point of view resultant from a gradual change of opinion in these circles, given that the 1980 draft nationality law prepared by the SPD government of Nordrhein-Westfalen still held on to the nationality after integration principle. *See* BR-Dr. 52/80.

easier naturalization and accepted plural nationality.[175] Although none of the drafts garnered significant support, debate had begun. In fact, the outlines of future discussion were already established: focus would remain on questions of participation, integration and loyalty. By 1990, as part of a general overhaul of the legal situation of foreigners in the *Gesetz zur Neuregelung des Ausländerrechts* (Law to Newly Regulate the Law Relating to Foreigners) relating to a small, albeit indirect crack appeared in the logic of the 1913 nationality law.

In order to understand the nature of this first opening, we must take a snapshot of the regulation then in force. Pursuant to RuStAG Article 8, an immigrant could naturalize in Germany unless a reason for expulsion under a provision of the *Ausländergesetz* (Law Relating to Foreigners) existed, and so long as the individual had a residence and adequate finances to support herself – a seemingly liberal policy, then. Detailed guidelines to naturalization were (and continue to be) set out in the federal *Einbürgerungsrichtlinien*, however; though these rules were not binding, they did attempt to provide some degree of uniformity to substantially varied *Land* practice.[176] The applicable guidelines (in force since 1977, as amended in 1987) declared that naturalization could be approved only if it was in the public interest. The applicant's financial and even personal circumstances were of no consequence in determining whether this was the case.[177] Rather, public interest required knowledge of German and of the *Grundordnung* of the state, as well as signs of adjustment to German society[178] and ten years of continuous residence.[179] In addition, plural nationality was declared 'undesirable',[180] so that individuals were expected to give up their previous nationality, with certain exceptions. The list of exceptions was actually quite long in practice: if the state of origin refused to free the individual from her previous nationality; for asylum seekers; if the individual had resided in Germany, rather than the other state, for 15 years (for spouses) or 20 years (in all other cases); if naturalization was

---

175. *See Entwurf eines Vierten Gesetzes zur Regelung von Fragen der Staatsangehörigkeit* (BT-Dr. 11/4268) prepared by the SPD (presenting a mixed *jus sanguinis/jus soli* model that allowed for attribution of nationality at birth to the child of parents also born in Germany, but prohibiting plural nationality with the second generation); *Entwurf eines Gesetzes zur rechtlichen Gleichstellung der ausländischen Wohnbevölkerung durch Einbürgerung und Geburt* (BT-Dr. 11/4464) prepared by Bündnis 90/Die Grünen (allowing for a right to naturalization after five years of residence, as well as double *jus soli* nationality at-birth, without limitation on plural nationality); *Entwurf eines Gesetzes zur Regelung der Rechte von Niederlassungsberechtigten, Einwanderinnen und Einwanderern* (BT-Dr. 12/1714) also prepared by the Greens (right to naturalization after five years and unlimited *jus soli*, in the frame of a general reform of foreigners' rights).
176. *See* discussion in Green (2001), p. 37 *et seq.*
177. *Einbürgerungsrichtlinien*, No. 2.1.
178. *Ibid.*, No. 3.1.
179. *Ibid.*, No. 3.2. In the context of the 1999 reform, certain commentators attacked these provisions as '*antiquierte Bestimmungen einer den Realitäten Europas und Deutschlands nicht mehr angemessenen Vorstellung einer ethnokulturellen Nation*'. Kürsat-Ahlers and Waldhoff (1999), p. 48. Given the importance attributed to such requirements after the reform, some are likely to see a continuation of the ethno-cultural state, then.
180. *Unerwünscht. Einbürgerungsrichtlinien*, No. 5.3.

of particular public interest, etc. – so that about a quarter of all naturalizations actually occurred with acceptance of plural nationality.

Given the direct reliance of the 1913 law on the *Ausländergesetz* in matters of naturalization, change to the former arrived in the form of a Trojan horse introduced into the latter. Individuals with residence permits who had grown up and been educated in Germany (and had no criminal record), as well as persons resident in the state for 15 consecutive years acquired the presumption of a right to naturalize.[181] Administrative discretion in granting nationality was thus greatly reduced, while a new category of naturalization – the *Anspruchseinbürgerung* (naturalization by right) – was introduced.[182] The right of 15-year residents to German nationality still depended on proof of ability to support themselves financially, however. In addition, as a final prerequisite to naturalization, both groups of immigrants were required to relinquish their previous nationality.[183] As the Explanatory Comments to the new regulation noted, surrendering one's previous nationality – and supposedly loyalty – was considered by public authorities as a sign of loyalty to Germany.[184] That said, a statutory recognition of exceptions was allowed in practice for a number of years.[185]

In 1993, a new wave of drafts appeared on the political horizon in the wake of a series of attacks on asylum-seekers' residences.[186] Though none of the proposed changes to nationality law would have had any effect on the situation of this particular group, many politicians hoped to use heightened public attention to gain support for a more liberal approach. The SPD, for example, presented a draft[187] focused on the integration of resident foreigners; naturalization was to be one means to such integration, with legal equality stimulating greater social acceptance.[188] The explanatory notes to the draft presented the principle of

---

181. AusIG Arts 85 and 86, as expressed by the words *in der Regel*.
182. Since 1991, German law thus differentiates between *Anspruchseinbürgerung* (now in StAG Arts 10–11) and the traditional, so-called *Ermessenseinbürgerung* (discretionary naturalization) (Art. 8). Since it is now the norm, all references in this paper to naturalization designate the former, unless otherwise noted. (It should be remembered, however, that the principle of avoiding plural nationality applies to both kinds of naturalization; though this is not indicated in the law itself, the federal guidelines do include provisions on the matter).
183. *See* Sec. 1 of AusIG Arts 85 and 86.
184. *Das Neue Ausländerrecht der Bundesrepublik Deutschland* 29 (1990).
185. *See* AusIG. 16 Art. 87.
186. 1993 also brought a further – and still indirect – liberalization of policy, as a new law amending the *Ausländergesetz* (among others) removed administrative discretion completely from the decision on granting nationality under Arts 85 and 86. Individuals who fulfilled the criteria listed now had a full-fledged right to German nationality (AusIG Art. 2(12) and (13)).
187. BT-Dr. 12/4533, *supra* note IV.174.
188. Accordingly, amendment to RuStAG Art. 8 was foreseen to allow for a right to naturalize after five years of continuous (legal) residence for individuals with an adequate financial background and no criminal record. In addition, children born to foreign parents with a right to permanent residence in the country – as proven by an unlimited *Aufenthaltserlaubnis* or *Aufenthaltsberechtigung* – were to be attributed German nationality at birth. In a nod to free choice, the legal custodian of the child in question could refuse the attribution of German

avoiding plural nationality as the main obstacle to naturalization and pointed out the increasing array of exceptions to the rule – including for children from mixed nationality marriages, *Aussiedler* according to GG Article 116(1) and individuals whose states refused to free them of their previous nationality. As a supplemental argument, the notes also highlighted the danger of a democratic deficit if a large category of individuals under the jurisdiction of the state did not have political rights;[189] i.e., the lack of overlap between permanent residents and nationals with citizenship rights was considered a crucial point.[190]

The FDP also presented a draft in 1997,[191] some elements of which were taken up in later discussion; namely, the idea that individuals would be required to give proof of having relinquished any additional nationality (or of having attempted to do so) by the age of 23, without which German nationality would be lost (the *Optionsmodell*). The suggestion of granting a conditional or temporary nationality had been made before, without much success;[192] but this related notion, of requiring a conscious choice for German nationality by plural nationals, now became a fixture of all approaches. Meanwhile, the SPD's 1995 draft law,[193] though little different in content from earlier proposals, had also added a new consideration to public discussion – that of European integration. As Gnielinksi discusses, 'the fact that EU-foreigners resident in Germany for only a short time enjoyed full freedom of movement and could take part in local elections, while other foreigners who had

---

nationality, however. (For the difference between various statuses of residence, *see* AusIG Arts 5 and 15–27. As part of the 2004 revision of the *Gesetz über den Aufenthalt, die Erwerbstätigkeit und die Integration von Ausländern im Bundesgebiet* (*Aufenthaltsgesetz*) (hereinafter, AufenthG), contained in the ZuWG, these two main residence statuses have in any case undergone change. See AufenthG Arts 101 and 3–12.)

189. In an ironic twist, the *Bundesverfassungsgericht* decision BVerfG, BVerfGE 83, 37 (*Ausländerwahlrecht I*) (1990), which found *Land* legislation that allowed for voting by permanent residents in municipal elections unconstitutional, is referred to by the explanatory note as a sign of the importance of such overlap and, indirectly, of plural nationality.

190. A similar argument of equality, seen internationally, was used by the detractors of plural nationality. In essence, plural nationality was considered a violation of the principle since individuals with more than one nationality also had citizenship rights in another state, but could flee from its possible obligations or responsibilities. See Löwer (1993), p. 158.

191. See the 1999 *Entwurf eines Gesetzes zur Förderung der Integration von Kindern dauerhaft in Deutschland lebender Ausländer* (BT-Dr. 14/296), which repeated the ideas already presented in 1997.

192. The *Koalitionsvereinbarung* between the CDU/CDU and the FDP from the year 1994 had contained the idea of a *Kinderstaatszugehörigkeit* (or children's nationality), which would have become active by age 12 and would have required individuals to give up any nationality other than the German one by the age of majority.

The issue of birthright nationality was also the subject of numerous self-standing drafts prepared in the course of 1998. See *Entwurf eines Gesetzes zur Erleichterung des Erwerbs der deutschen Staatsangehörigkeit durch Kinder ausländischer Eltern* (BT-Dr. 13/8157), prepared by the federal state of Hessen in the *Bundesrat*; and *Antrag zur Erleichterung des Erwerbs der deutschen Staatsangehörigkeit für Kinder ausländischer Eltern* (SPD, rejected by the Bundestag in February 1998. See Plenarprotokoll des Deutschen Bundestages 13/225, 20645 *et seq.*).

193. *Entwurf eines Gesetzes zur Änderung des Staatsangehörigkeitsrechts* (BT-Dr. 13/423).

lived here a long time were excluded, meant a threat to internal peace'.[194] The legal and political effects of EU citizenship had thus begun to weigh on discussions of German nationality law.

2. NEW PROVISIONS ON PLURAL NATIONALITY

After general elections in the autumn of 1998, the newly formed SPD/Green coalition presented a fundamentally new, comprehensive law – the *Erstes Gesetz zur Reform des deutschen Staatsangehörigkeitsrechts* (First Law to Reform German Nationality Law)[195] – for public discussion in January 1999. The working draft, which incorporated ideas from earlier drafts across the political spectrum, would henceforth serve as the blueprint for reform with some modifications. Its guiding principles were the acceptance of plural nationality and the conditional attribution of birthright nationality to the children of certain foreigners. Pure *jus soli* – never seriously suggested by any party except the Greens – was thus definitively rejected by this point, in favour of a form of mixed *jus soli* and *jus sanguinis* already present in previous SPD drafts.[196] According to a new RuStAG Article 4(3), a child born to a non-national parent also born in Germany or resident there since the age of 14, in possession of an *Aufenthaltsberechtigung* or – *erlaubnis*, was to be attributed German nationality at birth. No significant change from earlier approaches, then.

The other central issue for reform – naturalization – was resolved in a surprising manner, however. In addition to fulfilling existing (now five-year) residence and financial requirements, any successful candidate for naturalization would now be expected to provide written testimony of her adherence to the principles of the German Constitution and would be asked to give proof of adaptation to German society, including by means of a language test. Although AuslG Article 15 already mandated knowledge of German as a prerequisite to an *Aufenthaltsberechtigung*, while the guidelines on naturalization required proof of a voluntary and lasting 'turn toward' Germany and 'adjustment to German living conditions',[197] as well as democratic convictions, this was the first time such a requirement had been articulated in the context of nationality law by a left-wing party or, for that matter, the national government. In exchange, plural nationality would be tolerated in the context of naturalization.[198] In another novel provision,

---

194. '*Die Tatsache, daß nur kurz in Deutschland befindliche EU-Ausländer volle Freizügigkeit genössen und an Kommunalwahlen teilnehmen könnten, während lange hier lebende sonstige Ausländer davon ausgeschlossen seien, bedeute eine Gefährdung des inneren Friedens*'. Gnielinksi (1999), p. 60.
195. Copy on file with author.
196. Though one form of this mixed system looks a great deal like the French concept of double *jus soli*, it is not the place of birth that matters in the German context, but a presumed level of social and cultural adaptation, as shown by the need for descent from an individual effectively assumed to have integrated into German society.
197. '*Hinwendung*' and '*Einordnung in die deutschen Lebensverhältnisse*'.
198. Other new elements included the possibility of naturalization for special public interest, even without residence in the country; regulation of the nationality of *Statusdeutsche* (as defined in

RuStAG Articles 17(2) and 25, mandating loss of German nationality upon voluntary acquisition of an additional one, were to be struck out from the legislation. Thus, plural nationality was to be fully accepted, in a sharp turnaround from tradition.

In fact, the CDU/CSU was outraged by the perceived radicalness of the changes proposed. In particular, continued adherence to the principles of *jus sanguinis* and avoidance of plural nationality were demanded – not only because they were seen as fundamental to the character of German nationality law, but also in the claimed interest of integration. Most criticism centred on exactly this point; more proof of not only adaptation to and acceptance of German society, but also loyalty to the German state were deemed necessary. In other words, plural nationality had to go. The suggestions made, such as the recondite *Einbürgerungszusicherung*[199] – essentially an i.o.u. of German nationality for certain categories of persons born in Germany, to be validated into full national status upon loss of previous nationality – reflected the right-wing circles' view that membership should be the last point of the integration process. This view was widely publicized during a national signature campaign against plural nationality organized by the CDU/CSU in January 1999 (and signed by over five million individuals) and in the course of crucial regional elections in the state of Hessen in February 1999.

After a surprise CDU/CSU victory many attributed to the plural nationality issue,[200] the national government was forced to present a revised draft of the law to the *Bundestag* in March 1999. The main points of the legislation proposed[201] for our purposes were:

- additional paragraphs to (now) StAG Article 4, entitling a child born to foreigners in Germany to birthright nationality if one parent had been habitually resident in the country for the last eight years and was in possession of an *Aufenthaltsberechtigung* or, for the last three years, of an unlimited *Aufenthaltserlaubnis*.[202] The provision allows for plural nationality indirectly, since the parents will also have passed on their own nationality via *jus sanguinis*.
- revised provisions on German nationals resident abroad. A child born to a German national outside the country is attributed German nationality only

---

GG Art. 116(1)); and removal of the provision mandating that acquisition of another nationality results in the loss of the German one.

199. Translated literally: 'warranty or assurance of naturalization'. *See* description given by Stoiber (CDU/CSU), Bundesrat Plenarprotokoll 738 (21 May 1999), p. 183.
200. *See, inter alia*, remarks by Schäuble (CDU/CSU), Plenarprotokoll Bundesrat 738 (21 May 1999), p. 186. For a general discussion of the debate on plural nationality, including the role of the Hessen elections, *see* Uçar (2003).
201. *Entwurf eines Gesetzes zur Reform der Staatsangehörigkeitsrechts* (BT-Dr. 14/533). Other provisions included a change of designation, so that the amended legislation would now be termed the *Staatsangehörigkeitsgesetz* (Art. 1(1)); and new regulation on attributing nationality to individuals considered Germans in GG Art. 116(1) (Art. 1(4) and (11)).
202. *Ibid.*, Art. 1(3).

if one parent was born in Germany or if she would otherwise be rendered stateless.[203] In other words, concern now centred on the existence of a real link to Germany for any attribution of birthright nationality. This same concern results in the possibility of plural nationality for those who apply for an additional nationality while resident abroad, however.[204]
- amendment to (now) StAG Article 29 to introduce, for naturalized nationals (pursuant to StAG Article 40(a)) and for children of foreigners conferred German nationality at birth (persuant to newly-added StAG Article 4(3)), the requirement of a written declaration of choice between German and any other additional nationality at the age of majority.[205] If the individual in question opts for German nationality, proof of loss of any additional nationality must be supplied to public authorities before the age of 23, unless a *Beibehaltungsgenehmigung*, or authorization of retention, is granted by the latter. (If no choice is expressed by the age of 23, German nationality is automatically lost). An authorization is granted by authorities only if the additional nationalities cannot be relinquished or if the individual has been naturalized in accordance with AusIG Article 87, with acceptance of plural nationality.
- removal of the *Inlandsklausel* (national clause) of RuStAG Article 25, allowing for maintenance of German nationality upon acquisition of an additional one for persons resident in Germany; and
- amendment to AusIG Articles 85–87, on naturalization.[206] According to Article 85, foreigners gain the right to German nationality after eight years of habitual residence if they:
  - affirm their adherence to the principles of the German Constitution and declare that they do not (and have not) supported any efforts aimed at undermining these principles, or the integrity or security of the state;
  - are in possession of an *Aufenthaltsberechtigung* or-*erlaubnis*;
  - have adequate financial resources to support themselves and their family, unless they can give proof that a situation to the contrary is due to circumstances beyond their control;
  - have relinquished or lost their previous nationality; and
  - have not been convicted of any crime.

However, Article 86 listed a number of criteria as grounds to refuse naturalization:

- inadequate knowledge of the German language;

---

203. *Ibid.*, Art. 1(3)(4).
204. *Ibid.*, Art. 1(7)(b). In this context, even the acceptance of an oath of allegiance to another state is not to be considered a ground to refuse permission to retain German nationality, so long as the state of naturalization has a *staatliche und gesellschaftliche Ordnung* (a governmental and social order) comparable to that of Germany. (The United States is given as an example). BT-Dr. 14/533, *supra* note IV.201, p. 18.
205. *Ibid.*, Art. 1(8).
206. *Ibid.*, Art. 2(1).

- discovery of factual indications to reinforce the suspicion that the individual does support (or has supported) efforts aimed at undermining the Constitution or the state; and
- as a discretionary matter, the existence of a ground for expulsion under Article 46(1).

Finally, Article 87 foresaw a number of situations – 'when the foreigner cannot renounce his former nationality or can do so only under particularly difficult conditions'[207] – in which the applicant may retain her previous nationality. These situations comprise:

- when the possibility of renunciation does not exist under the law of the state in question;
- when the applicant has asked to be freed of her nationality and the state in question regularly refuses such requests;
- when the state in question has refused to free applicant on grounds she cannot control or that are linked to unreasonable demands; or when no decision has been made within an appropriate time frame;
- for elderly applicants, when plural nationality is the only obstacle to naturalization, when relinquishment of previous nationality would result in an onerous burden and when refusal of naturalization would constitute a particular difficulty;
- when the relinquishment of previous nationality would result in considerable (economic or financial) disadvantage, beyond that of losing citizenship rights, or;
- when applicant is considered a political refugee or an asylum-seeker pursuant to relevant laws; and
- provision for the nationals of EU Member States to retain their additional nationalities on the basis of reciprocity.[208] As the explanatory note sets out, for the states in question 'the principle of avoidance of plural nationality does not apply when reciprocity exists'.[209]

---

207. *'Wenn der Ausländer seine bisherige Staatsangehörigkeit nicht oder nur unter besonders schwierigen Bedingungen aufgeben kann'.*
208. *Ibid.*, Art. 2(2).
209. *'Der Grundsatz der Vermeidung vom Mehrstaatigkeit [gilt] nicht, wenn Gegenseitigkeit besteht'.* BT-Dr. 14/533, *supra* note IV.201, p. 25. In practice, attempts by certain *Bundesländer* (e.g., Bayern) to limit the scope of this provision have failed. As a 2004 decision of the *Bundesverwaltungsgericht* determined, *'Gegenseitigkeit im Sinne von § 87 Abs. 2 AusIG besteht, wenn und soweit nach dem Einbürgerungsrecht und der Einbürgerungspraxis eines Mitgliedstaats der Europäischen Union bei der Einbürgerung eines deutschen Staatsangehörigen Mehrstaatigkeit generell oder in Bezug auf bestimmte Personengruppen hingenommen wird'* (para. 11). The reasoning of the court is also worth noting; *'die Vorschrift [soll] nämlich für Ausländer, die Staatsangehörige eines anderen Mitgliedstaats der Europäischen Union sind, im Hinblick auf das Ziel der europäischen Integration einen verstärkten Anreiz zum Erwerb der deutschen Staatsangehörigkeit schaffen Dieser Anreiz wurde deshalb als notwendig angesehen, weil das Interesse am Erwerb der deutschen Staatsangehörigkeit bei dem genannten Personenkreis wegen der bereits bestehenden Inländergleichbehandlung gering sei. Der Gesetzgeber wollte mithin Unionsbürger bei der Einbürgerung gegenüber anderen*

On a number of points, then, the law finally presented to the *Bundestag* differed from the working draft first made public by the coalition government. Most prominently, the 'state interest in curtailing cases of plural nationality'[210] had found its way back and – despite the number of listed exceptions – now comprised one of the underlying principles of the law. (This was the case even if the CDU/CSU continued to attack the proposals for allowing a 'double passport through the back door'.)[211] Not only had the general acceptance of plural nationality at naturalization been discarded, but the *Optionsmodell* had been appropriated from the FDP in the context of birthright nationality. Also, the suggestion of removing existing restrictions on acquiring additional nationalities had been replaced by a new limitation. With regard to the listed exceptions foreseen for AusIG Article 87, many already existed in practice,[212] so that the suggested amendments in this area cannot be called revolutionary. In essence, the general rejection of plural nationality for those attributed German nationality at birth – notwithstanding the temporary acceptance period – coupled with the new domestic restrictions signified a definitive end to discussion on the possibility of a more liberal approach to multiple membership.

In addition, the new naturalization requirements – unchanged from the working draft – could no longer be framed as an element of compromise to make plural nationality appear less threatening. Rather, they appeared as a response to CDU/CSU concerns with support for national identity.[213] In effect, since the revision of nationality law was to be 'a case-study for the reform capability of ... society', it was exactly the core of this national identity that was at stake.[214] There seemed to be just one problem. As an editorial from March 1999 put it: 'We don't know who belongs to us; in other words, we don't know who we are'.[215] The right and left wing gave widely divergent responses to the unstated

---

Ausländern privilegieren' (para. 13). In effect, the Court noted that European integration warrants privileged treatment for the nationals of other Member States. The argument that this practice results in the general acceptance of plural nationality for this group of individuals – which is, in fact, the case – was not seen as problematic by the court. BVerwG 1 C 13.03 (2004).

210. *'Staatliches Interesse, die Fälle mehrfacher Staatsangehörigkeit einzuschränken'*. BT-Dr. 14/533, *supra* note IV.201, p. 11.
211. *Doppelpaß durch die Hintertür*. See, *inter alia*, parliamentary remarks of Stoiber (CDU/CSU), Bundesrat Plenarprotokoll 738 (21 May 1999), p. 183 (internal quotation marks removed); Beckstein (CDU/CSU), Bundesrat Plenarprotokoll 737 (30 April 1999), p. 132; Zeitlmann (CDU/CSU), Plenarprotokoll des Deutschen Bundestages 14/28, 2285.
212. Parliamentary remarks of Bürsch (SPD), Plenarprotokoll des Deutschen Bundestages 14/28, 2283.
213. This is not to say that questions of integration were not present in earlier drafts. They were, rather, *the* central concern since the earliest drafts. *See* BT-Dr. 11/4268, p. 1; BT-Dr. 12/5684, p. 9; BT-Dr. 13/8157, at 3; BR-Dr. 52/80, p. 1 and 4; and BR-Dr. 3/82, p. 1.
214. *'Ein Modellprojekt für die Reformfähigkeit unserer Gesellschaft'*. Parliamentary remarks of Bürsch (SPD), Plenarprotokoll des Deutschen Bundestages 14/28, 2283.
215. *'Wir wissen nicht, wer zu uns gehört, oder, anders formuliert, wir wissen nicht, wer wir sind'*. Reinhard Kreissl, in an article published in the Süddeutsche Zeitung (March 1999), as quoted by Minister Schily (SPD), Plenarprotokoll des Deutschen Bundestages 14/28, 2318.

question during parliamentary discussion. One CDU speaker attacked the draft on the basis that foreigners 'would then have German nationality without having gone to school in Germany [which] can't be right'.[216] Nationality was thus not just a question of legal status here – in fact, it seemed not to be one of law at all – but rather a social issue. Party Chairman Stoiber, in turn, spoke of the '*protection of German identity*' and 'common history, culture and cohesion in nation and homeland' as the basis for '*cohesion in the community of law and norms of the nation and the nation state*'; 'citizenship', in turn, was an 'expression of this belonging'.[217] It seems the right wing simply could not decide whether the elements of ethnicity and culture it harked back to could make way for a true community of values.

The left wing, in turn, gave a seemingly simple response. In the words of Minister of the Interior Schily:

> Whoever respects the Constitution and its basic values, and observes our laws belongs to us. Whoever is capable of speaking the language belongs to us. Whoever wishes to take part in social life in Germany on his own terms, without a guiding culture, belongs to us. We recognize who we are in the dignity of each individual person, which we are called on to respect and protect by article 1 of the Constitution.[218]

On inspection, however, this answer is not so clear-cut. Certainly, it is the same approach reflected in the draft legislation; knowledge of the German language coupled with respect for the fundamental laws of the state are the requirements of membership. But what about the reference to the will to take part in social life in Germany – in the claimed absence of a *Leitkultur*, or guiding culture? Though the term has a special significance in Germany – capable of constituting the centre of ongoing, emotional polemics[219] – it would be simply wrong to deny the existence of certain dominant strands to German culture, of which any individual who wishes to belong must partake. Although society is pluralistic enough to manage the

---

216. '*Hätten dann die deutsche Staatsangehörigkeit, ohne in eine deutsche Schule gegangen zu sein. Das kann doch nicht richtig sein*'. Parliamentary remarks of Beckstein (CDU/CSU), Bundesrat Plenarprotokoll 737 (30 April 1999), p. 132.
217. '*Wahrung der deutschen Identität*, '*Gemeinsame Geschichte, Kultur und der Zusammenhalt in Nation und Heimat*', '*Zusammenhalt in der Rechts- und Wertegemeinschaft von Nation und Nationalstaat*', '*Staatsbürgerschaft*' and '*Ausdruck dieser Zusammengehörigkeit*''. Parliamentary remarks of Stoiber (CDU/CSU), Bundesrat Plenarprotokoll 738 (21 May 1999), pp. 183–184 (emphasis in original).
218. '*Zu uns gehört, wer die Verfassung und deren Grundwerte achtet und unsere Gesetze einhält. Zu uns gehört, wer sprachfähig ist. Zu uns gehört wer sich mit dem gesellschaftlichen Leben in Deutschland auf seine eigene Weise ohne Leitkultur verbinden will. Wer wir sind erkennen wir an der Würde jedes einzelnen Menschen, die zu achten und zu schützen uns durch Art. 1 des Grundgesetzes aufgegeben ist*'. Parliamentary remarks of Schily (SPD), Plenarprotokoll des Deutschen Bundestages 14/28, 2318.
219. For example, the use of the term in remarks by Friedrich Menz (CDU/CSU) in October 2000, in the context of the reforms discussed here, set off a storm of discussion on what the integration of immigrants really meant: everything from complete assimilation to minimal adaptation was suggested by commentators.

existence of a great variety of lifestyles – and in this sense there is no one hegemonic culture – all of them function squarely in a larger, consciously German milieu.

In the explanatory note accompanying the draft legislation, the aim of reform was summarized as 'improvement of the integration of foreigners permanently resident in ... Germany and of their children born here, through facilitation of the acquisition of German nationality'[220] – and through greater acceptance of plural nationality, one could add. In fact, considering the frequent appearance of the concept on the note, 'integration' could be considered the motto of the law; in their exuberance, the drafters even foresaw the *staatsangehörigkeitsrechtliche Integration*[221] of foreigners. What this particular form of (nonsensical) integration would consist of – and who was to be integrated, into which group – remained unexplained. Likewise, 'integratory political goals'[222] were the only listed orientation points of the legislation.

Comparable absorption with the concept was manifest during all rounds of parliamentary discussion. While CDU/CSU representatives spoke repeatedly of how the law was inadequate to spur integration,[223] advocates from all parties involved in drafting defended its integration credentials.[224] The *Optionspflicht*, for example, was presented as a conscious choice for membership, not least because of constitutional concerns in light of GG Article 16. As the explanatory

---

220. '*Verbesserung der Integration der dauerhaft in der Bundesrepublik Deutschland lebenden Ausländer und ihrer hier geborenen Kinder durch Erleichterung des Erwerbs der deutschen Staatsangehörigkeit*'. BT-Dr. 14/533, *supra* note IV.201, p. 2. See also p. 16.
221. *Ibid.*, p. 11. (The phrase is particularly difficult to translate, but can be summed up as 'integration by nationality law'.)
222. '*Integrationspolitische Ziele*'. *Ibid.* In fact, the goal of integration appeared for the first time in German political parlance as far back as 1978, with the creation of the position of *Beauftragte der Bundesregierung für die Integration ausländischer Arbeitnehmer und ihre Familienangehöriger* (Commissioner of the Federal Government for the Integration of Foreign Workers and their Family Members). A sign of its actual role: the first two individuals to hold the post (between 1978 and 1991) resigned. For discussion of the development of federal integration policy, *see* Klopp (2002), p. 46.

    Since entry into force of the general overhaul of the Law Relating to Foreigners in 2005, the specifics of the post, now designated *Beauftragte der Bundesregierung für Migration, Flüchtlinge und Integration* (Commissioner of the Federal Government for Migration, Refugees and Integration), are set out in law (*See* AufenthG Arts 92–94. In addition, an entire section of the Federal Office for Migration and Refugees now deals with integration matters.
223. *See* parliamentary remarks of Rüttgers (CDU/CSU), *Plenarprotokoll des Deutschen Bundestages* 14/28, 2310 and 14/40, 3419; Beckstein (CDU/CSU) *Bundesrat Plenarprotokoll* 737 (30 April 1999), 132. *See also Antrag des Freistaates Bayern*, presented in the Bundesrat (BR-Dr. 188/2/99) for a list of critiques. In addition, *see* the CDU draft law, *Entwurf eines Gesetzes zur Reform des Staatsangehörigkeitsrechts* (BT-Dr. 14/535), as well as the papers *Modernes Ausländerrecht* (BT-Dr. 14/532) and *Integration und Toleranz* (BT-Dr. 14/534) for right wing proposals.
224. *See, inter alia*, parliamentary remarks of Bürsch (SPD), *Plenarprotokoll des Deutschen Bundestages* 14/28, 2283; parliamentary remarks of Westerwelle (FDP), *Plenarprotokoll des Deutschen Bundestages* 14/40, 3438; Wienholtz (SPD), *Bundesrat Plenarprotokoll* 737 (30 April 1999), p. 133.

note to the draft law declared, 'it is in the hands of the [individual] concerned whether to retain German nationality'.[225] The choice for German nationality was supposedly even 'an *active decision for integration*'[226] – in other words a decision with ramifications beyond the legal. As the same speaker argued, 'the German passport is ... not some paper one willingly receives in addition, but rather presupposes a conscious turn toward the German state'.[227] On this basis, a decision to opt for German nationality or to naturalize was supposedly lived as a 'break with one's own culture and a disengagement from previous human and informal attachments'.[228] It was to constitute a step in the larger process of adaptation to German society.

But what does such adaptation to consist of? And what does it have to do with the regulation of nationality? Although one speaker spoke of a wider change of consciousness to be initiated by the new regulations, no one seemed to question the existence of a link between the concepts of 'integration' and 'nationality' during discussion. Minister of the Interior Schily even relied openly on their interaction. As the government saw it, 'reform is the core of an encompassing concept of integration, because integration can succeed only when, through the acquisition of German nationality, *equal participation in social life* ... is made possible for citizens of foreign origin'.[229] To some extent, integration was to be a matter of equal rights then; this nod to democratic sovereignty also appeared in the explanatory note to the draft law.[230] But the process of integration seems to stretch beyond the legal, to encompass the 'social, linguistic and cultural fields'; it is to be considered 'a permanent social task'.[231] In other words, integration is to encompass all aspects of life and involve everyone – not a particularly precise basis for a government policy, one would think.[232]

---

225. 'Der Betroffene es selbst in der Hand hat, die deutsche Staatsangehörigkeit zu behalten'. BT-Dr 14/533, *supra* note IV.201, p. 12.
226. '*Eine aktive Integrationsentscheidung*'. Parliamentary remarks of Westerwelle (FDP), *Plenarprotokoll des Deutschen Bundestages* 14/40, 3436 (emphasis in original).
227. '*Der deutsche Paß ist nämlich nicht irgendein Papier, das man gerne zusätzlich in Empfang nimmt, sondern setzt eine bewußte Hinwendung zum deutschen Staat voraus*'. Ibid.
228. '*Bruch mit der eigenen Kultur [und] Lösung von früheren menschlichen und familiären Bindungen*'. Parliamentary remarks of Bürsch (SPD), *Plenarprotokoll des Deutschen Bundestages* 14/28, 2283.
229. '*Die Reform ist der kern eines umfassenden Integrationkonzeptes, weil Integration nur gelingen kann, wenn den Bürgerinnen und Bürgern ausländischer Herkunft über den Erwerb der deutschen Staatsangehörigkeit die gleichberechtigte Teilhabe am gesellschaftlichen Leben in Deutschland ermöglicht wird*'. Parliamentary remarks of Schily (SPD), *Plenarprotokoll des Deutschen Bundestages* 14/28, 2318 (emphasis in original).
230. BT-Dr. 14/533, *supra* note IV.201, p. 11. In fact, even the German language requirement was couched in terms of a prerequisite to participation. *Ibid.*, p. 12.
231. '*Rechtliche[r], soziale[r], sprachliche[r] und kulturelle[r] Bereich*' and '*eine gesellschaftliche Daueraufgabe*'. Parliamentary remarks of Bürsch (SPD), *Plenarprotokoll des Deutschen Bundestages* 14/28, 2283–2284.
232. The integration courses developed by the federal government and offered to (and in many cases required of) foreigners give some idea of the policy in force. *See Verordnung über die*

Exactly this fuzziness explains the concept's political popularity, however. Each party could use the term without clarifying its meaning or its causal link to a particular legal practice. Hence, acceptance of plural nationality (now only in limited cases) could be presented as both a benefit and a hindrance to integration. Only one speaker came close to questioning this connection, when he noted that 'the new Serb, Turkish or Kurdish emotionality doesn't emerge through citizenship after all, but rather exists; and we're working on making a common identity for this Republic from such a split emotionality. You don't change any of this through the refusal of nationality'.[233] In other words, feelings of belonging to a particular group don't necessarily emanate from a legal status; but an offer of membership may help the development of affinity to a collective identity. This view was also expressed repeatedly at a meeting of the *Innenausschuss* (or Committee of the Interior) in April 1999, when it convened to examine the government draft. Besides a lively discussion on the constitutionality of the *Optionspflicht* as the main mechanism for limiting cases of plural nationality[234] – especially whether the revocation of German nationality in this context would constitute a loss against the will of the individual, in contravention of GG Article 16(1) – such identity issues were again the main point on the agenda.

3. THE QUESTION OF INTEGRATION

All experts agreed that nationality was linked to German (collective) identity. Isensee, for example, considered that this status constitutes the identity of the German people on the basis of GG Article 116;[235] as such, it is also the foundation of a particular democratic community. The question of who may be a member of this community is thus partially a legal one – in the German case, a matter to be considered under GG Articles 16(1), 116 and 20(2).[236] However, the constitutional inquiry involved in any amendment of nationality law cannot go beyond procedural and rights-focused questions, by the very terms of these articles. There is no fixed category, so that any definition of 'German' contained in the *Grundgesetz* must be capable of accommodating social change. As the head of the Committee of the Interior put it, 'the question is whether constitutional law can

---

Durchführung von Integrationskursen für Ausländer und Spätaussiedler (Integrationskursverordnung) (hereinafter, IntV) (2004). *See also* AufenthG Arts 43–45 and 104(2), in the context of grants of permanent residence.

233. '*Die neue serbische, türkische oder kurdische Emotionalität entsteht ja nicht durch das Staatsbürgerschaft, sondern sie existiert, und wir arbeiten daran, aus so einer gespaltenen Emotionalität eine gemeinsame Identität für diese Republik zu machen. Durch Verweigerung der Staatsbürgerschaft ändern Sie daran überhaupt nichts*'. Maier (GAL), Bundesrat Plenarprotokoll 737 (30 April 1999), p. 140.
234. *See* comments by Prof. Isensee in *Protokoll über die 12. Sitzung des Innenausschusses* (hereinafter, *12. Sitzung des Innenausschusses*) (13 April 1999).
235. *Ibid.*
236. *Ibid.*, p. 47.

accept that its underlying foundations can also change through a strengthened integration policy between nations and peoples'.[237]

a.   **Identifying the Elusive 'German'**

Although any legal definition must accommodate social change, modification is circumscribed by the existing structure of law; amendment is acceptable, but not a wholesale transformation of the regulation of nationality. For example, the reference in GG Article 116(1) to '*Volkszugehörigkeit*' (*Volk*-belonging) injects the language of ethnic and cultural belonging – to be confirmed by legal membership – into a category ('German') otherwise devoid of such connotations. (In this sense, GG Article 116(1) is a symptom of the split nature of German identity.) Despite a general focus on legal status then, whereby all those who are nationals are 'German', an element of cultural (and ethnic) identity cannot (as yet) be fully exorcised from nationality legislation, exactly because not all Germans on the basis of GG Article 116(1) are nationals.

Badura's view – generally more accepting of the proposed regulation than Isensee – also agreed that 'the "people" exist as a community of law with a cultural dimension and history which is not newly constituted every day'.[238] At a legal level, as much as a social one, the question then becomes the extent to which the introduction of a modified form of *jus soli* or greater acceptance of plural nationality can be considered a systematic transformation that undermines the constitutional understanding of Germanness.

It is perhaps with this consideration in mind that that obsession with integration can be understood. By means of integration (a.k.a. adaptation, assimilation and everything in between) the cultural strand can be woven into the civic one. Yes, individuals not ethnically or culturally 'German' may be German as a matter of legal status, but they are also to become German in at least a nominal cultural sense. As Badura noted during the Committee meeting, 'one should understand *jus soli* rather as a *jus socialisationis* than as a law that approaches [the individual] on the basis of his readiness to incorporate himself into the conditions of the host-state and to desire its nationality'. With regard to integration, then, 'one can imagine different things ... ; what is apparently meant, however, is that whoever, as a German, has corresponding rights and obligations also possesses a closer relationship to this people and this community of law than to another; this, we want to assume'.[239] The assumption is indeed a basic one on which all participants can

---

237. '*Es geht um die Frage, ob das Verfassungsrecht akzeptieren kann, daß sich die ihm zugrunde gelegten Grundlagen auch durch eine verstärkte Integrationspolitik zwischen Nationen und Völkern verändern kann*'. Prof. Penner in *12. Sitzung des Innenausschusses*, p. 47.
238. '*Das Staatsvolk als eine Rechtsgemeinschaft mit einer kulturellen Dimension und Geschichte existiert, die nicht jeden Tag neu konstituiert wird*'. Badura, *ibid.*, p. 42.
239. '*[M]an sollte vielmehr das [j]us soli als ein [j]us socialisationis verstehen, als ein Recht, das einem auf Grund seiner Bereitschaft, sich in die Bedingungen des Gastlandes einzufügen und dessen Staatsangehörigkeit zu begehren, zukommt*' and '*[d]arunter kann mann sich zwar*

likely agree. Beyond this point, however, the area of life in which integration is expected – social, economic, political or cultural – and the level of adaptation required are up for grabs.[240] A minimum requirement seems to be that listed in the draft law.[241]

In practice, integration is not so clear cut an issue, in any case, as a decision by the *Bundesverfassungsgericht*[242] on the eve of the autumn 2005 general elections demonstrated. The applicant in the case was a naturalized German national who had applied to regain her previous (Turkish) nationality before entry into force of the new StAG (on 1 January 2000), but who was granted the additional nationality after that date. Pursuant to Article 25(1) of the new StAG, which forbids this practice, the woman's German nationality was withdrawn, so that she could not vote in the upcoming national elections. Pending the outcome of her case on the issue of nationality, she requested an interim measure to allow her to vote. The Court – having balanced the possibility that her application for a determination of German nationality would be refused against her right, as a national, to vote – found that a denial of this right did not constitute a greater harm than the danger of participation in national elections without nationality, so that the application was rejected.

Curiously, the principle of democratic sovereignty at issue here can cut both ways.[243] One can argue for the denial of an individual's right to vote as an infringement of the principle; or, at the group level, as a protection of the same, since only persons who are undoubtedly members of the polity can exercise their right to participate. In effect, it is the second approach that the Court took, without much concerning itself with the first.[244] Whether one agrees with the outcome or not, the case highlights how the integration arguments of politicians with regard to plural nationality ring hollow. What greater affinity to Germany can a naturalized (plural) national show, after all, than repeated legal attempts at securing her right to participate in general elections? In end effect then, a law meant to aid integration has thus, in this instance at least, served as a clear barrier to that very goal.

A final decision on the constitutionality of withdrawing German nationality in such circumstances was handed down in late 2006. The Court noted that the

---

Verschiedenes vorstellen; gemeint ist aber offenbar, daß derjenige, der als Deutscher entsprechende Rechte und Pflichten hat, auch eine nähere Beziehung zu diesem Staatsvolk, zu dieser Rechtsgemeinschaft besitzt. Dies wollen wir voraussetzen'. Prof. Badura in *12. Sitzung des Innenausschusses*, p. 42.

240. See discussion by Profs. Schmid and Weinacht, and Dr. Kürsat-Ahlers in *12. Sitzung des Innenausschusses*, p. 60 *et seq*.
241. In fact, certain states have had a propensity to interpret federal provisions extremely narrowly; and have demanded e.g., dubiously high levels of linguistic ability in German. See, e.g., Meireis (2003) for a discussion of one such, court-sanctified, instance.
242. BVerfG, 2 BvQ 25/05 (2005).
243. See discussion in Spiro (2003).
244. The short reference made in the decision to the irrelevance of the number of individuals concerned was a sign that the judges were all too aware of the tens of thousands of potential voters in comparable situations.

national stipulations at issue were (and are) clear and foreseeable, so that any loss of nationality resulted from an 'autonomous and free determination' by the individual concerned not just to apply for, but actually to accept another nationality. The reasoning of the Court thus hinged on timing: even if the individual had taken steps that could have resulted in such a loss before the new StAG entered into force, if she was granted the foreign nationality after 1 January 2000, she did so with knowledge of the new prohibition, so that the loss of German nationality was essentially her fault.[245] According to the Court, then, individuals in this situation were no longer German nationals, and rightly so.

b.   **The *Spätaussiedler* v. Other Immigrants**

A comparison of political discussion on the extent to which *Statusdeutsche* – or *Spätaussiedler* – are and, as a legal category, are to continue being German with deliberations on the status of permanent residents reveals a great deal about the role of culture in (at least this) national identity. Indeed, the former had largely taken place in the early 1990s, without too much public fanfare, and resulted in moves toward the gradual disappearance of the category.[246] The latter, on the other hand, resulted in – admittedly reluctant and conditioned – acceptance, amid general and very public self-conscious reflection. In neither case did the most prominent arguments centre on the legal aspects of modification.

For example, it was not much commented upon that *Spätaussiedler* were generally allowed to keep their previous nationalities, thereby becoming plural nationals. The focal point of discussion was rather the nature of the hurdles to be passed before immigration to Germany would be possible. In particular, the introduction of a quota (1993) and language tests (1996) was meant to stem the flow of individuals German by status, but not necessarily by culture. (The automatic grant of German nationality introduced by the draft law for such individuals was accordingly only an administrative simplification and not a new privilege.) In line with the 1992 law, the *Statusdeutsche* will cease to exist as a category as of 2010 – 65 years after the war that ostensibly made their unique treatment necessary.[247]

---

245. '*Selbstverantwortliche[r] und freie[r] Willensentschluss*'. BVerfG, 2 BvR 1339/06 (2006), para. 13. Earlier, narrowly-construed decisions by the Court on the right to vote provided a hint as to the likely outcome. See BVerfG, BVerfGE 83, 37, para. 53 *et seq.*
246. See the *Kriegsfolgenbereinigungsgesetz* (1992). *See also Bekanntmachung der Neufassung des Bundesvertriebenengesetzes* (1993). In addition, numerous court decisions have given strict interpretations of who may be considered German for the purposes of this law. *See, inter alia*, BVerwG 1 C 35.02 (2003). On the other hand, a proposal to amend GG Art. 116(1) to remove the category of *Volksdeustche* was defeated in 1992 and has not been raised since; a radical change of policy has thus been consciously rejected.
247. The presumption of discrimination against those with *deutsche Volkszugehörigkeit* was an important element of the law. In fact, *Vertreibungsdruck* was generally taken for granted until the 1970s. By the time bilateral treaties were signed after 1989, this pressure was no longer recognized in the context of some states and made the changed regulations discussed above possible. *See* Klekowski von Koppenfels (2002), p. 102.

In the context of other immigrants, legal arguments – like the unconstitutionality of particular solutions[248] – tended to appear only as the last line of defence against proposals deemed out of character with whatever particular parties claimed to be for: a 'German' nationality regulation, in line with tradition or a 'European' one, in tune with modernity. As discussed above, there could in fact be few or – after Germany's withdrawal from the 1963 Nationality Convention in 2001[249] – no legal obstacles to plural nationality under international law. On the other hand, the (future) practice of withdrawing German nationality under the *Optionspflicht*[250] could – as of 2008, when the first persons affected reach majority – run into problems under European law, since the loss of German nationality would also automatically result in the loss of European citizenship for individuals whose remaining nationality is that of a third country. Although the E.C.J. has not stated outright that the loss of these rights could result in a finding that the withdrawal of Member State nationality contravenes European law, it is not a far stretch to assume that this could, in fact, be the case. The reference in *Kaur* to the 'effect of depriving any person who did not satisfy the definition of a national ... of rights to which that person might be entitled under Community law'[251] – though not found to be the case there – can certainly be taken as a warning to Member States.[252] Strangely enough, this potential legal problem was not heard at all during public discussion.

Concern in both sets of public discussion was rather with identity; more concretely, the question of what German identity actually consists of. On the one hand, deliberation on the legal status of the *Statusdeutsche* reflected a focus on the past – 'this is who we were' – and coincided with a static view of (German) culture. The very idea that the individuals in question were German in a manner recognizable as such in Germany relied on the existence of some remnant of

---

248. *See* discussion in Hellwig (2001), p. 83 *et seq.*
249. Arguably, the general allowance of plural nationality for EU citizens could have run afoul of Art. 1 of the 1963 Convention; however, given the reciprocity requirement contained in the provision and the developments discussed above, a live legal problem was unlikely to emerge in the first place. Germany proceeded to sign the European Convention on Nationality in 2002, and appended declarations regarding Art. 10 (on *Spätaussiedler*) and Art. 29 (on *Optionspflicht*), among others, at the time of ratification.
250. In fact, the idea of an *Optionsmodell* has been discussed in international circles for some time. An 'election requirement' was suggested by Harvard researchers during drafting stage of the Hague Convention, for example. Art. 12 of the Harvard Draft also suggested that a plural national (from birth) should, at the age of 23, automatically lose the nationality of the state in which she was not a habitual resident. Also, Art. 4 would have limited application of *jus sanguinis* to the second generation born outside the state and habitually resident there. *See also* discussion in the ILC Survey, *supra* note I.20, pp. 107–108. A number of bilateral treaties have also foreseen such an option: Treaty on Dual Nationality between Great Britain and Brazil (29 July 1922); Treaty between France and Switzerland (Art. 1) (23 July 1879); and Art. 6(3) of the Treaty between Germany and Bolivia (22 July 1908).
251. Case C-192/99 *Kaur*, para. 25.
252. For a general discussion of the interaction between specific Member State provisions on nationality and Union citizenship, *see* de Groot (2004), especially p. 14 *et seq.* (for possible Community limitations on loss of Member State nationality).

traditional Germanness supposedly handed down through generations, rather than on a living culture, which changes by definition. Because in many instances the imagined pattern of elements attributed to this 'Germanness' no longer exists, we are essentially dealing with an ethnic category here, realistically leached of all concerns beyond that of descent.[253]

However, the fact that this category is also a legal one spawns the same kinds of court (or administration)-assembled conclusions on identity commentators warned of in the Hungarian case. After a determination of descent, then, *Spütaussiedler* are required to pass further bars before they may immigrate to Germany; they must prove their Germanness, in essence 'imitating' a German as sketched by law. In a case from 1995, for example, the Federal Administrative Court looked at the applicant's family history, social practices (including holidays celebrated), language skills and 'group-consciousness' to determine whether her claim to be German – rejected by authorities – was valid.[254] Thus, even as people are expected to 'live' a specific identity, its content is legally predetermined. In a comparable manner, the post-1991 encouragement of Jewish immigration from Eastern Europe[255] – newly regulated as of 1 January 2005 – was infused with an understanding of culture as object.

On the other hand, a decision on the future place of permanent residents in Germany – or *Inländer* in legal parlance – required a focus on the future – 'who will we be?' – as well as an understanding of culture as process. It required acceptance of the idea that German culture can evolve with time to encompass new elements, while leaving others behind, and accordingly, that the idea of what it means to be German (in more than a legal sense) can also undergo transformation.[256] Exactly because a view of culture-as-flux is difficult to pin down, let alone interpret – and for certain people to accept – public discussion on the subject is bound to be confrontational. The numerous cross-cutting national 'others' in Germany: east and west, *Aussiedler*, permanent residents, immigrants, EU citizens and

---

253. For many *Aussiedler* 'while being German is a part of their social identity, it is largely constructed through descent and fragmentary knowledge of German language and culture. Russian language and culture were the background of their socialization' (Roll, 2003), p. 286.
254. *Gruppenbewußtsein*. BVerwG 9 C 392.94 (1995). See also BVerwG 9 C 8.96 (1996), discussing the meaning of the 'mediation of German culture' required under BVFG Art. 6(2)(1).
255. Strangely enough, the practice of a liberal immigration policy for Jews from Eastern Europe was inherited from East-Germany and, through the quiet re-interpretation by *Land* Prime Ministers of an existing law (the *Kontingentflüchtlingsgesetz* of 1980) in 1991, continued after reunification. Since 1991, over 200,000 individuals have immigrated to Germany under the provisions. See Der Spiegel, *Bund will Zuzug von osteuropäischen Juden begrenzen* (18 December 2004); and Der Spiegel, *Tuerer Exodus* (21 February 2005). For a general discussion, *see* Weizsäcker (2004).
256. The less-than smooth 'integration' of the new *Länder*, and the ongoing discussion of the *kulturelle Differenzen* ('cultural differences') between *Ossies* and *Wessies* – both German – had already led to a sense of crisis in the 1990s (*See* Sabrow (2001), p. 21). The differences were assumed to be reconcilable with time, however. *See also* Gensicke (2001), p. 23. *See also* the essays by Brunssen, Schödel and Kolinsky in Stuart Taberner and Frank Finlay, eds, *Recasting German Identity: Culture, Politics, and Literature in the Berlin Republic*, (2002).

third-country nationals, to name a few, means that the core of what constitutes 'us' is particularly hard to concretize.

This is not to say that the formulation of an approach to one group of immigrants is easier or harder than to another – nor more or less progressive, despite the views of certain post-modernists – but that the number of unknowns is simply greater in the case of any future-oriented dilemma. Plainly put, it is generally easier for societies to agree on who they are (and were) than on who they will (or wish to) be. In an admittedly oversimplified image: folk costumes (especially when worn only once a year, in commemoration of some historical event) are more clearly and for many more innocuously categorized as German than *Berliner Dönerbuden-Quartett* playing cards.

As Senders discusses in the case of *Statusdeutsche*, it was not even actual descent in a genealogical sense that was at issue in discussions on their right to immigration, but an attribution thereof. Descent was simply a 'narrative strategy for designating a degree of likeness, of similarity, seen as necessary for full membership'.[257] Thus, individuals who were 'like' enough were allowed to immigrate and acquire nationality. Others, deemed too dissimilar, were not. When the assumed common cultural, national or ethnic identity – the legitimizing force for repatriation – did not always materialize for *Spätaussiedler,* the lack of acculturation was doubly painful.[258] These persons were assumed to be 'German' on arrival, after all. In reality, given that the *Spätaussiedler* face the same economic and social disadvantages as other immigrants, the policies they need may not be any different either. But an admission of this truth was slow in arriving.

As for other immigrants to Germany, many were already in the country as permanent residents, so that the pick-and-choose entrance strategy utilized for *Spätaussiedler* could not work in this context. Rather, their degree of likeness – and with the requirement of a conscious choice for German nationality, of loyalty – was to be examined at naturalization. The final decision to retain the principle of avoiding plural nationality (albeit with new exceptions), as well as the heightened focus on integration demonstrate how this likeness retains socio-cultural elements even for legal purposes.

Another attribute of the approach to national membership in Germany can be gleaned from a comparison of the two discussions. Both sets of discourse highlighted the increased importance of territoriality and the parallel forfeiture of an expansive approach to personal supremacy. The introduction of the principle of *jus soli*, in particular, is an obvious sign of a concern with individual attachment within the borders of the state. The imminent abolishment of a right to immigrate for *Statusdeutsche* is another. But the appearance of territoriality in German nationality law will not necessarily result in a turn toward this principle in other areas of law. For the purposes of private international law, for example, Germany continues to adhere to the nationality (i.e., personal supremacy) principle. Thus, permanent residents who have decided not to naturalize will be treated in accordance with the

---

257. Senders (2002), p. 89.
258. *See* Tsoukala (1999), p. 120 (in the context of Greece).

law of their state of nationality in certain areas of law (like family law), on the assumption, discussed above, that the original nationality – especially if it has been chosen over the German one – reflects continuing links with the country of nationality, even if the individual has never lived there.[259] It remains to be seen how many individuals will choose to relinquish German nationality in favour of another; but in the unlikely case that many do while remaining resident in the country, Germany may well choose to change its approach to choice of law also.

In May 1999, the draft law on nationality was finally accepted by the Bundestag, with 365 votes for, 182 against and 38 abstentions. With the public announcement of the law,[260] an important chapter in German nationality regulation had been closed. The government at the time also seemed to envisage the beginning of a new era. As a Ministry of the Interior Publication explaining the new regulation put it: 'the hitherto outmoded law has been modernized and adjusted to the European standard'.[261] This European standard – and the European credentials of the new legislation – had in fact been a measuring stick utilized at various points in the debate.[262] When compared to other nationality laws in Europe then, the German law in effect since January 2000 cannot be considered either particularly revolutionary or especially conservative. In light of earlier provisions on nationality, however, it does represent a significant departure from tradition.

As for the actual effects of the new law, these have been mixed. On the one hand, the introduction of *jus soli* has resulted in a noticeable decrease in the number of children born in Germany as foreigners.[263] On the other, the hoped-for spike in naturalization never arrived. Though the year 2000 saw a high of 186,688 naturalizations – after 106,790 in 1998 and 14,267 in 1999 – the tendency has been toward decreasing numbers: in 2004, 127,153 individuals became German nationals.[264] With regard to the greater acceptance of plural nationality, this does seem to have had the expected effect: while in 1997, 21.9 per cent of all naturalizations took place with acceptance of plural nationality, the ratio in 2000 was 44 per cent.[265]

c.   **Further Revision of German Nationality Law**

In 2004, as part of a general revision of laws applicable to foreigners, the StAG underwent a further, minor revision. In particular, Article 1 was modified to

---

259. See Hellwig (2001), p. 181 *et seq.*
260. *Gesetz zur Reform des Staatsangehörigkeitsrechts* (hereinafter, StAGReformgesetz) (1999).
261. *'Das bisherige veraltete Gesetz [wurde] modernisiert und an den europäischen Standard angepasst'. Das neue Staatsangehörigkeitsrecht* (1999), p. 7. *See also* p. 9.
262. *See* parliamentary remarks of Schily (SPD), *Plenarprokoll des deutschen Bundestages* 14/40, pp. 3418–3419; and of Beck (Greens) *ibid.,* p. 3449. *See also* parliamentary remarks of Chancellor Schröder (SPD), *Plenarprotokoll des deutschen Bundestages* 14/3, p. 61.
263. *See* discussion in Renner (2002), p. 266.
264. *See* Ministry of the Interior web-site, *Einbürgerungen in Deutschland*, p. 86, *supra* note IV.165.
265. As quoted in Göbel-Zimmermann (2003), p. 66. The article is a good overview, with discussion of the problems encountered in practice.

confirm the role of German nationality. Thus, 'under the terms of this law whoever possesses German nationality is German'.[266] German nationality (as opposed to *Land* citizenship) has thereby become the primary status for individuals. This change was also underlined elsewhere in the new text, as all references to the *Bundesländer* had been removed.[267] More importantly, the nationality law now contains a clear statement of what the term 'German' means for its purposes. Still, despite this new formulation, StAG Articles 7 and 40(a), with their reference to 'German under the terms of Article 116(1) of the Constitution', remain.[268] Thus, a clear two-pronged *legal* meaning of the status of 'German' exists in the legal system: one according to the terms of the StAG, the other under the *Grundgesetz*. The resulting legal inconsistency – even if not necessarily a source of interpretative problems in daily life – is remarkable, and now mirrors that of social reality.

A number of other minor changes were also made,[269] particularly as regards the *Spätaussiedler*.[270] Belatedly, official policy seems to have determined that all individuals not born German nationals must be acculturated to German society. *Spätaussiedler* are thus privileged in the range and kinds of (free) courses offered, but – in light of the factual reality that few are 'German enough' in linguistic proficiency and socialization[271] – are increasingly treated as another category of immigrant.[272] This change of approach was already evident after passage of the *Gesetz zur Klarstellung des Spätaussiedlerstatus* (Law on the Clarification of the Status of *Spätaussiedler*), (2001), which redefined knowledge of the German language as a general prerequisite for immigration, rather than (just) a characteristic helpful to proving *Volksdeutschtum* (*Volk*-Germanness). In effect, then, the perceived difference of these Germans has allowed for a change of public discourse, from one focused on ethnicity – and a static view of culture – to one focused on

---

266. *Deutscher im Sinne dieses Gesetzes ist, wer die deutsche Staatsangehörigkeit besitzt.* See ZuWG Art. 5(2).
267. *See* revised Art. 8.
268. *Deutscher im Sinne des Artikels 116 Abs. 1 des Grundgesetzes.* The articles were added in 1999 by Arts 1(4) and 1(11) of the *StAGReformgesetz*, respectively.
269. E.g., new StAG Art. 10(3), by which permanent residents who have completed government-run integration courses – and who otherwise fulfil the criteria set out – may apply for naturalization after seven years of residence (rather than eight).
270. E.g., a newly added provision of the *Bundesvertriebenengesetz*, which sets out the circumstances under which *Spätaussiedler* and their family members may take advantage of free integration courses (ZuWG Art.Art. 6(3)(a)). *See also* Art. 6(3)(d) for further integration measures. In addition, newly amended Art. 27 now requires that the spouse of any *Spätaussiedler* also have a basic knowledge of the German language to be allowed to immigrate. *See* ZuWG Art. 6(6)(b).
271. *See* discussion in Roll (2003). For an exhaustive look at the situation of *Aussiedler* – their history and present circumstances – in Germany, *see* Ingenhorst (1997).
272. This fact is also highlighted by the provisions of the *Wohnortzuweisungsgesetz* (1989, as amended to 1996) restricting the provision of social services to the particular *Land* to which the *Aussiedler* and her family have been assigned. *See* Art. 3 of the *Gesetz über die Festlegung eines vorläufigen Wohnortes für Aussiedler und Übersiedler* (1989), as amended by the *Zweites Gesetz zur Änderung des Gesetzes über die Festlegung eines vorläufigen Wohnortes für Spätaussiedler* (1996).

social and cultural integration – and a dynamic understanding of culture. Belonging is now a matter of daily life, not assumed characteristics.

Some assumptions about integration remain unchanged, however, the *Optionspflicht*, for example, has retained its original form even in the wake of the 2004 amendments. Its durability is noteworthy not only because of lingering doubts about constitutionality,[273] but also in light of its possible social effects. As a commission on immigration noted in 2001, there is a distinct possibility that a choice for or against a particular nationality will create conflict in migrant families.[274] In a step forward, however, the 2004 revision did eventually place the (slightly amended) 1999 provisions on naturalization, heretofore contained in the AusIG, into the actual law on nationality.[275] If nothing else, this move represents a general acceptance of provisions once deemed controversial as a rightful part of nationality regulation. It is worth noting that the new *Zuwanderungsgesetz*, through which this was done, is a comprehensive and systematic regulation of all the legal rights and duties of foreigners in Germany. It is also, as Minister of the Interior Schily noted nine months after entry into force, a sign of 'paradigm change: for the first time in the history of Federal Germany, integration has been systematically regulated'.[276] One could add that integration has also moved to the heart of approaches to nationality.

With the 2004 amendments, the provisions discussed above now constitute Germany's new approach to nationality, including plural nationality and naturalization.[277] Given that a spate of new drafts to amend the StAG have since been tabled in both the *Bundestag* and the *Bundesrat*, discussion looks set to continue.[278]

In effect, *Statusdeutsche* are now treated like (in fact somewhat worse than) other immigrants for the purposes of welfare, rather than as German nationals. A constitutional complaint against the practice (on the basis of GG Art. 11(1) on freedom of movement and Art. 3 on equality before the law) failed in 2004. See BVerfG, 1 BvR 1266/00 (2004). For a critique of the decision, *see* Klekowski von Koppenfels (2004).

273. Hailbronner and Renner, p. 6 *et seq.*, p. 30 *et seq.*, and p. 79 *et seq.* (3rd ed., 2001).
274. *Bericht der Unabhängigen Kommission 'Zuwanderung'* 249 (2001). *See also* the March 2003 decision of the Court of Appeals of the State of Baden-Württemberg, refusing the parents' wish to release their child from his German nationality, granted on the basis of the new provisions discussed above, because it was not in the child's best interest to do so.
275. In other words, the movement of former AusIG Arts 85–87 to new StAG Arts 10–12.
276. 'Einen Paradigmenwechsel Erstmals in der Geschichte der Bundesrepublik ist die Integration systematisch geregelt worden'. *See* Press Release of the Ministry of the Interior, *Neun Monate Zuwanderungsgesetz – Qualitätssprung in der Integrationsförderung* (23 September 2005).
277. *See Plenarprotokoll des deutschen Bundestages* 14/40, p. 3473 (*Zusatztagesordnungspunkt* 5). *See also Gesetzesbeschluß des Bundesrates* (21 May 1999) (BR-Dr. 296/99).
278. See *Entwurf eines Gesetzes zur Änderung des Staatsangehörigkeitsrechtes* (BT-Dr 16/265), prepared by Bündnis 90/Die Grünen and presented to the *Bundestag* (with provisions for fully allowing plural nationality and abolishing the *Optionspflicht*, among other measures); and *Entwurf eines Gesetzes zur Änderung des Staatsangehörigkeitsrechtes (StAG)* (BR-Dr 137/07), presented by several federal states to the *Bundesrat* and adopted by the latter in March 2007. The draft, which requires stronger integration measures and suggests the introduction of a citizenship ceremony and oath, is now also before the *Bundestag*.

C. VARIATIONS ON THE THEME OF ADAPTATION

As shown above, discussion on the future of plural nationality in Germany was embedded in a larger public discourse on the kind of adaptation to be expected of new members. By extension, at issue was what it means to be 'German' not only in the legal sense, but also in a more diffuse social one. The underlying concern can thus be summed up in the question: 'who belongs to "us"?' If this question was already in the spotlight because of the influx of *Spätaussiedler* – were they 'really' German? – the case of resident foreigners brought the conundrum into sharper relief.

As the divergent approaches of the right- and left-wing parties in Germany to naturalization demonstrated, the issue of timing is especially important for the membership/belonging dichotomy: should perception of belonging or membership come first? If the latter, it is on the assumption that a change of legal status will also engender a transformation of consciousness, either through the instrument of equality and common norms and values, if one is a constitutional patriot, or, for a proponent of the symbolic role of nationality, by means of an emotional connection. If belonging is to come before membership, however, naturalization serves as a sign of recognition for something that has already occurred.

States in Europe have developed varied, but largely comparable approaches to this question, as rules on plural nationality in the context of naturalization demonstrate. While most states now accept plural nationality in at least some instances – and some in all cases – they also require a period of residence and some level of integration before applicants can naturalize. The benchmarks of adaptation set out in this context are the clearest statement of social expectations, since they provide a minimum level that must be met by any immigrant who wishes to gain membership. In turn, the benchmarks agreed upon reflect legal tradition and public representations of what constitutes the community.

1. INTEGRATION, ASSIMILATION, ACCULTURATION AND OTHER RESPONSES TO MIGRATION

As demonstrated above, 'integration' had become the buzzword in relation to all groups of immigrants to Germany by the late 1990s. This also holds true for other European states. The popularity of the term among politicians and commentators alike can be explained both by dint of its obliqueness and the fact 'there is no alternative expression [like assimilation] which is not open to even greater objections'.[279] Despite the variety of meanings attributed to 'integration', especially in political discourse, it generally encompasses a process of adjustment in which individuals and groups become involved and participate in the social, institutional and cultural structure of a given society, eventually constituting an integral

---

279. Banton (2001), p. 152.

part thereof. The recently created *Bundesamt für Migration und Flüchtlinge* (Federal Office for Migration and Refugees) considers it 'equal participation in social life with respect for cultural diversity (combined with) the readiness of the immigrant to familiarize himself with the language, as well as the norms and values of the receiving community on his own initiative'.[280]

This definition is more nuanced than those usually found in public discussion, but still does not differentiate between spheres of life, as most contemporary sociological approaches do. When speaking of integration then, distinctions are generally made between its various sub-types: structural (membership with rights and duties in the main social institutions, of which nationality is the legal expression); cultural (acquiring the language, norms, beliefs and behaviour of the receiving society); social (private and ongoing interaction with individuals and entities from the receiving society and/or membership in minority organizations) and identificatory (belief of belonging to the receiving society).[281] Thus, even if the acquisition of nationality is an element of structural integration – with possible secondary effects on other kinds of integration – it cannot be seen as the end-all (and be-all) of the process.[282]

The degree to which the integration is reciprocal – i.e., whether the state of residence and society at large accommodate new members – differs from context to context. Certain states are more accommodating of newcomers than others. In all cases, however, integration reflects the social reality of migration better than assumptions of either assimilation or multiculturalism.[283] In the first instance, the self-representation (and identities) of migrants, like migrant groups, is certainly

---

280. '*Eine gleichberechtigte Teilhabe am gesellschaftlichen Leben unter Respektierung kultureller Vielfalt Zugleich setzt erfolgreiche Integration die Bereitschaft der Zuwanderer voraus, sich auch eigeninitiativ mit der Sprache sowie den Normen und Werten der Aufnahmegesellschaft vertraut zu machen*'. See the flyer of the Federal Office for Migration and Refugees, *Welche Ziele hat Integration?* (2005).
281. Political science and legal literature, in turn, generally focuses only on structural and cultural/identificatory integration. See Die Zeit (Jürgen Habermas), '*Die festung Europa und das neue Deutschland*' (28 May 1993) ('*[Es gibt] zwei Stufen der Assimilation Die erste verlangt Zustimmung zu den Prinzipien der Verfassung – eine Assimilation also an die Art und Weise, wie in der aufnehmenden Gesellschaft die Autonomie der Bürger verstanden und wie der "öffentliche Gebrauch der Vernunft" (Rawls) praktiziert wird. Die zweite Stufe erfordert Bereitschaft zu einer weitgehenden Akkulturation, und zwar zur Einübung in die Lebensweise, in die Praktiken und Gewohnheiten der einheimischen Mehrheitskultur. Das bedeutet eine Assimilation, die auf der Ebene ethnisch-kulturelle Integration durchschlägt*'.) See also Fehér and Heller's distinction between 'naturalization' and 'culturization'. Fehér and Heller (1994).
282. *See also* Bauböck (1996).
283. The traditional assimilation theory discussed above (a.k.a. Gordon's melting pot) was recognized – at least as regards its assumption of linearity and the reasons for its maintenance – as false decades ago. See Gans (1979) and Yancey (1976).

    In any case, even when a state policy is officially guided by assimilation or multiculturalism, particular developments tend to be ad hoc. As the first commissioner of the Federal Office of Multicultural Affairs put it in a moment of honesty, 'I have no theory of multiculturalism The art of muddling through is called for'. (This could also be said of assimilative policies, albeit to a lesser extent). Cohn-Bendit (1994), as quoted in Bauböck. (1998), p. 25.

transformed, but is rarely discarded completely. In turn, '[t]he insertion of new elements, previously classified as belonging to an external environment, will not leave existing structures unaffected. Whether insertion takes place as a relatively continuous process or as a singular but massive event, it requires adaptation by the system in order to maintain its internal cohesion'.[284] Thus, the self-images of individuals and groups in the state of residence are also transformed by immigration.

With regard to individual motivation for structural integration through naturalization, cultural factors seem to play a more important role than economic ones.[285] On the other hand, structural and other integration can occur without 'acculturation', or cultural integration.[286] A study prepared for the German Committee of the Interior in 1999, for example, showed that no identificatory or cultural integration had occurred among many immigrants to the country. Rather, 'legal equality with Germans', 'permanent right to residence' and 'the exercise of all political rights' were the top three reasons given in the same survey for why respondents intended to naturalize.[287] (Four out of five youths also reported fear and lack of certainty as to their legal and abode status.[288]) Thus, the cited reasons for naturalization were all practical in nature; they had nothing to do with feeling German. As the authors note, structural integration is often viewed as a prerequisite for identificatory integration by sociologists,[289] so that the latter cannot occur without the former. The lack of identificatory or cultural integration should not come as a surprise then. This presents a paradox, however, since even when naturalization occurs purely out of concern for equal treatment (or even instrumental considerations), it may be viewed by others as a sign of identification.[290] It is thus often difficult to untangle the cause-and-effect relationships involved in various types of integration.

Nonetheless, a degree of attachment to the state of nationality is viewed as necessary by even liberal political theorists.[291] In fact, even assimilation is considered acceptable by some, depending on one's conception of national identity.[292] To the extent assimilation is understood as the complete disappearance of a given collective identity as reference point for the members of the group, it presumes a high degree of (if not complete) acculturation. But, as Bauböck has discussed, 'assimilation is different from acculturation in that the former requires some ratification by the (receiving) group'.[293] Thus, even if acculturation is a matter for migrants, assimilation and indeed, integration, cannot occur without the consent of

---

284. Bauböck (1996), p. 113.
285. Yang (1994), p. 472.
286. The Russian-speaking minority in Israel could be cited as an example. Despite increasingly high rates of social and political (as well as economic) integration, many immigrants choose to move in an exclusively Russian milieu.
287. Kürsat-Ahlers and Waldhoff (1999), p. 23. The survey quoted was carried out in 1995 by the *Bundesministerium für Arbeit und Sozialforschung*.
288. *Ibid.*, p. 30.
289. *Ibid.*
290. *See* Rittstieg (2002), p. 15.
291. Barry (2001), p. 77.
292. *Ibid.*, p. 73.
293. Bauböck (1998), p. 42.

the majority society. In this sense, the official recognition of membership implied by nationality is as important a step as many politicians have claimed, since it implies consent.

The concept of acculturation in fact nearly as controversial as the now debunked, but related, concept of assimilation. Taking the example of requirements to relinquish any previous nationality by states that adhere to the principle of avoiding plural nationality, we see that acculturation is generally viewed in one of two ways. According to the multicultural approach, adhered to, *inter alia*, by the Greens in Germany:

> [L]anguage, religion, and historical, cultural and political consciousness mould individuals in the family home, school and social environment. Such elements of life and personality do not allow themselves to be simply erased, least of all through coerced statements on paper. Nationality law – the last, still admissible form of discrimination – should, already on account of human dignity, not be permitted to lead to ... denial of the self, to loss of personal and human identity.[294]

On this basis, 'foreigners who naturalize execute a first, important step toward integration. To expect them to break with their old homeland, to relinquish return, means crossing the boundary of sacrifice'.[295] In the logic of the opposite approach, supported *inter alia* by the CDU/CSU in Germany, such past-focused argumentation is counterproductive. 'In contrast to a future-oriented immigration mentality, the immigrant is fixed in his past. Since no new identity is offered to him, he must inevitably define himself by what he once was. Reminiscence about the past shapes his self-understanding'.[296] Thus, acculturation is a necessary result of immigration, and naturalization is to be seen 'as a reward'[297] for its successful termination. In this sense, a migrant's 'disinclination to give up his old nationality is at least an indication that the individual has not yet accepted his newly-chosen place of residence as a real homeland'.[298] We are thus back to the question of timing already alluded to.

---

294. *'Sprache, Religion, historisches, kulturelles und politisches Bewußtsein prägen den Menschen im Elternhaus, Schule und sozialer Umwelt. Solche Lebens- und Persönlichkeitselemente lassen sich nicht einfach auslöschen, am wenigsten durch papierene Erklärungen, die abgenötigt sind. Das Staatsangehörigkeitsrecht – die letzte noch zulässige Form von Diskriminierung – darf – schon der menschlichen Würde wegen – zu einem nicht führen, zur Verleugnung des eigenen Ichs, zum Verlust persönlicher und menschlicher Identität'.* Sturm (1999), p. 232.
295. *'Ausländer, die sich einbürgern lassen, vollziehen einen ersten wichtigen Schritt zu voller Integration. Von ihnen zu verlangen, daß sie ganz mit ihrer alten Heimat brechen, ja auf Rückkehr verzichten, heißt die Opfergrenze überschreiten'.* Ibid., p. 231.
296. *'Im Gegensatz zu einer Einwanderungsmentalität, die zukunfbezogen ist, wird der Zuwanderer auf seine Vergangenheit festgelegt. Da ihm keine neue Identität angeboten wird, muß er sich zwangsläufig durch das definieren, was er einmal gewesen ist. Rückschauende Erinnerung prägt sein Selbstverständnis'.* Klein (1996), p. 204.
297. *'Als Belohnung'.* Ibid., p. 205.
298. *'[D]ie mangelnde Bereitschaft zur Aufgabe seiner alten Staatsangehörigkeit ist zumindest ein Indiz dafür, daß das Individuum seinen neu gewählten Aufenthaltsort noch nicht als wirkliche Heimat für sich akzeptiert hat'.* Kamman (1984), p. 229.

In truth, both approaches are caught in their particular catch-22. In the case of the former, there seems to be an 'idealization of foreigner status and the "cultural identity" of immigrants' that denies 'the independence and developmental capacity of the person and especially the migrant, and attests to a fixation on ethnic categories'.[299] The identity of migrants is thus treated as essentially fixed and unchangeable. This phenomenon was clearly visible in the government surveys of immigrants in France and Britain already discussed, for example: they succeeded in perpetuating the same essentialist discourse they claimed to be against.

Like much of the multiculturalist literature that inspires it, denial of the necessity of some acculturation deals in fixed categories: once a Hungarian, always a Hungarian, by any criteria. Aside from the simple inaccuracy of this approach, it also has a logical flaw. Those who argue for plural nationality by saying that it is a means to grant equal status without any secondary consequences – while maintaining the necessity of allowing immigrants to keep their previous nationality as a recognition of existing social and cultural ties[300] – are denying the identity function of the legal status in one case, while maintaining it in another. They forget that any praxis of this kind necessarily affects all nationals' view of what their nationality signifies – and that individuals in the state of residence may view it as a devalorization of their own links to their state of nationality.

On the other hand, the traditional approach to acculturation denies reality: multiple ties exist, irrespective of legal status. For this reason:

> [T]he state of migration that believes the link between it and the emigrant persists through maintenance of nationality overlooks [the fact] that emigration itself and the relocation of the focus of daily life abroad, but especially desired naturalization there show how weak this bond now is. Whereas the state of immigration that naturalizes the immigrant primarily to integrate him into the 'people' and to be able to expect loyalty should rather be interested in having the immigrant manifest attachment explicitly.[301]

Certainly, some immigrants do envisage naturalization as a conscious commitment to their newly chosen state of nationality.[302] Others, however, continue to consider themselves nationals of their country of origin, even if they have the passport of the

---

299. '[I]dealisierung des Ausländerstatus und der "kulturellen Identität" von Einwanderern' and 'Die Eigenständigkeit und Entwicklungsfähigkeit der Person und insbesondere des Migranten und zeugen so von der Fixierung auf ethnische Kategorien. Rittstieg (2002), p. 20.
300. Besides discussion above, *see also* Kürsat-Ahlers and Waldhoff (1999), p. 46, in conjunction with p. 44 ('*Auswirkungen der Sozialisation und der Zugehörigkeit zu einem Kulturkreis können nicht einfach per Dekret oder per Dokument wegradiert werden*').
301. '[D]er Auswanderungstaat, der glaubt, das Band zwichen ihm und dem Emigraten bleibe durch Aufrechterhaltung der Nationalität bestehen, übersieht, daß schon die Emigration selbst und die Verlagerung des Lebensmittelpunkts ins Ausland, besonders aber die dort begehrte Einbürgerung, zeigen, wie schwach dieses Band nur noch ist. Der Einwanderungstaat hingegen, der den Einwanderer in erster Linie einbürgert, um ihn in sein Staatsvolk zu integrieren und Loyalität erwarten zu können, müßte eigentlich daran interessiert sein, daß der Immigrant seine Verbundenheit mit ihm deutlich manifestiert'. Kamman (1984), p. 229.
302. *See* Marger (2006) in the context of Canada.

state of residence. In a discussion with migrants to the Netherlands, for example, 'many respondents perceive[d] their nationality in the historical-biological sense. The acquisition of Dutch nationality in that sense [wa]s considered a formality, often only acquired in order to obtain a Dutch passport'.[303] Consequently, 'the feeling of being "Dutch" [wa]s not common among naturalized citizens [and] a change of nationality d[id] not affect the community to which they fe[lt] they belong[ed]'.[304]

The range of factors that influence a decision to naturalize is extremely wide. It includes, but is not limited to: distance from and general situation in the country of origin; age; sex; cultural similarity of the state of residence with that of the state of origin; the size of the given (national or ethnic) community in the state of residence; legal status at entry (e.g., asylum seeker, refugee, economic or illegal migrant); class; and education.[305] In general terms, the per centage of naturalized immigrants is highest when access to nationality is relatively easy, with short waiting periods, a high certainty of being granted the status (i.e., no discretionary decision), objective and easy requirements and – in this Dutch study – toleration of dual nationality. The states with such regimes – Australia, Canada, the United States and, in Europe, Sweden and (until recent changes) the Netherlands – have the highest rates of naturalization; in general terms, these states also see the easy availability of nationality as a measure to facilitate integration.[306] In a further factor, geographical proximity and historical ties go a long way in explaining the presence of particular groups in particular states; and also influence naturalization rates. For example, the main groups who naturalized in the UK in 2000 were Irish, Indians, and Pakistanis (in that order); in France in 1999, Algerians, Moroccans and Portuguese.[307]

With regard to the idea that acceptance of plural nationality increases the rate of naturalization, it has had mixed confirmation in studies. For example, in the German Committee of the Interior study mentioned above, 70.9 per cent of respondents declined to naturalize primarily because they wanted to remain Turkish, Italian, Greek, etc.; 28.4 per cent answered that they wished to return to their state of origin, in any case; while only 18.0 per cent stated that their decision was also due to the impossibility of retaining their previous nationality.[308] Thus, two of the top three reasons mentioned in this study for refusing to naturalize

---

303. Van den Bedem (1994), p. 102. *See also* Heitmeyer, Müller and Schröder (1997), p. 188.
304. *Ibid.*, p. 103. *See also* Costa-Lascoux (1987), p. 107.
305. Inadequate knowledge of legal rules is also an important factor in (low) rates of naturalization. *See* van den Bedem (1994), pp. 107–108.
306. Çinar (1994), pp. 64–65.
307. Eurostat, Population and Social Conditions, Theme 3, Acquisition of Citizenship (2004), p. 7.
308. On the other hand, the authors note that rates of naturalization have been higher among immigrants who have been allowed to keep their original nationality (under one of the existing exceptions): in 1996, 23.2 per cent of all naturalizations occurred under such conditions. Kürsat-Ahlers and Waldhoff (1999), p. 25.
    For another study showing a negative correlation (when the state of emigration allows plural nationality), *see* Yang (1994), pp. 473–474.

were linked to conserving the nationality of the state of origin, especially in its rights function (in the second and third answers). But the first answer given – by the vast majority of respondents – focused on the identity function of changing legal status. The general assumption that a voluntary decision to relinquish one's original nationality is an emotional decision with ramifications beyond the legal is thus correct.[309]

2.   AN INDIVIDUAL RIGHTS APPROACH TO NATIONALITY

It is no wonder then that, despite distinct arguments for and against plural nationality in various states, integration seems to be a returning theme in all of them; in particular, the debate takes the form of concern with political participation (i.e., rights) and with identity.[310] Of late, it is the latter that has received more attention not only in Germany, but also in other European states. During discussion of the pros and cons of plural nationality in Sweden (in 2000–2001), for example, concern with the identity function of this status revealed changing attitudes. Proponents of plural nationality claimed that 'dual citizenship would facilitate the identity work of migrants'[311] either because the nationality of the state of origin would represent 'emotions, roots, origin and identity' while that of the country of residence was to be a mere legal status, or because it is possible for individuals to have 'multiple roots and identities'.[312] Clearly, the two arguments are at odds with each other – and view integration in opposite ways. What both reveal, however, is a focus on the individual, rather than on the national community. As Gustafson notes, many proponents of plural nationality even saw the issue as one of 'a human *right* to choose freely between different ethnic, cultural and national identities'.[313]

The importance of individual choice was also highlighted in the German context.[314] But approaching nationality matters in the language of rights

---

309. *See also* Kartal (2002), p. 233 for a discussion of the psychological and political reasons for refusing to renounce Turkish nationality, as articulated by one interest group of the Turkish community in Germany.
    In the context of the United States, *see* Jones-Correa (2003), p. 322 *et seq.*
310. *See* discussion in Gustafson (2002), pp. 471–473.
311. Gustafson, *ibid.,* pp. 474–475.
312. *Ibid.*, p. 475.
313. *Ibid.* (emphasis in original).
314. Compare with the French approach, in which a positive declaration is considered crucial for those whose links to French society are not considered strong enough. As a general matter, the conception of nationality rooted in a social contract based on voluntary choice, suggested by the *Rapport Long, Tome II, supra* note Intro.7, is the farthest a state has gone in highlighting individual will; but the idea did not have staying power, even in France.
    Since the actual reforms that followed the report – in May 1993 – resulted in heightened barriers to naturalization, the necessity for the children of foreigners born in France to apply for nationality (between the ages of 16 and 21) was perceived as a restriction, rather than a sign of respect for individual choice.

camouflages the trap of greater individual freedom, as already alluded to. In the German legislation, for example, the claimed respect for individual choice resulted in exactly the kind of loyalty discourse cautioned against above. By the logic of the law, the possibility of choice means that anyone who decides against German nationality does so out of a lack of connection to the society and state. This is why the only individuals not forced to make the choice are those whose decision is not assumed to be free: refugees, individuals who cannot relinquish their additional nationality (by the law of another state),[315] the elderly (who are thought to have too many existing links) and those who can prove that their choice would result in serious disadvantages in their other state of nationality. All others must give a public sign of preference.

Paradoxically, then, the identity function of nationality takes centre stage in this approach; that of rights is but secondary. The legal status is viewed firstly as 'a freely chosen personal attribute to be used for the individual construction of identity and meaning'.[316] This conception is not far removed from that espoused by the proponents of status laws; in the Hungarian context, it likely rings surprisingly familiar to advocates of dual nationality for members of kin-minorities. In all of these cases, a legal status granted by the state is seen as recognition of a particular cultural identity. Naturally, the fact that the status is granted by the state again raises the problem of the nation state. If the nationality of a given state becomes associated with the national identity managed by that state, the nation state (project) is legitimized, at least in the eyes of those who value their nationality for its identity function. To the extent that no state is a nation state, however, this approach is likely to lead to tension both in the state and among states, especially when plural nationality is framed as an issue of concern to both immigrants and emigrants of the state.

While the idea of a right to a particular nationality espoused, inter alia, in Swedish public discussion is quite radical, the concern with identity should not come as a surprise. To the extent there are few genuine legal obstacles to plural nationality – specifically under international law, while constitutional limitations can be overcome – arguments about identity, belonging and diversity are likely to be outcome-determinative. Hence, 'multicultural claims that dual citizenship might represent a "new Swedishness", the explicit inclusion of immigrants as well as expatriates in arguments in favour of dual citizenship, the framing of migrants' choice of citizenship as an individual right, and the association between formal citizenship(s) and the construction of self-identity'.[317]

This approach makes an important assumption, however: that identity decisions are conscious ones. Surely the management of national identities by means of laws and policies that require clear assumptions and goals is a calculated enterprise, but query whether individuals (or families) consciously determine to 'be'

---

315. It would indeed be strange if, by default, another state could make the final determination of who may become a German national.
316. Gustafson (2002), p. 477.
317. *Ibid.*, p. 479.

German or Turkish after a legal or social prototype. Admittedly, this may happen in a minority of cases, but generally it is the sum of small individual decisions that add up to specific identities, which adhere, to a greater or lesser degree, to something identifiable as 'Turkish'. It is simply not (just) a decision for or against a particular nationality that renders someone American or Mexican. In addition, the possibility of superordinate identification – or multiple ties of belonging – should not be dismissed. The burgeoning social psychology literature on biculturalism in individuals who have internalized more than one culture has repeatedly noted that the construction and negotiation of multiple cultural identities is possible.[318] In other words, identity-formation is not necessarily a 'constant-sum game'.[319]

In any case, the question of belonging – of acceptance by the social group, as opposed to official membership – rarely depends wholly on official legal status, whatever its prerequisites. As regards naturalization, the comments of a member of the German Committee of the Interior are worth considering: 'one should not speculate at all about whether the timely allocation of a passport constitutes a help to integration, because the question of integration is determined not so much by the facilitation of naturalization as by other criteria'.[320] Thus, it is not legal status itself that makes the difference, but *recognition in daily life*'.[321] As Habermas has noted, 'the legal status of the citizen is constituted through a net of egalitarian relations [made up] of reciprocal recognition',[322] which depend on factors additional to the possession of a passport. In this sense, politicians (and certain academics) are likely somewhat too optimistic about the role official recognition of membership plays in solving social conflicts. We deal rather with sociological boundaries of belonging[323] that depend on a whole host of factors, many beyond the control of any state.

---

318. *See* discussion in Benet-Martínez and Haritatos (2005). *See also* Berry (1990) for a general discussion and Benet-Martínez *et al.* (2002) for a discussion of cultural frame-switching.
319. Zolberg (1997), p. 151.
320. '*Man sollte überhaupt keine Mutmaßungen dahin geltend anstellen, ob eine rechtzeitige Paßvergabe eine Integrationshilfe darstellt, weil sich die Frage der Integration an anderen Kriterien und nicht so sehr an solchen Einbürgerungsleichterung entscheidet*'. Prof. Weinacht in *12. Sitzung des Innenausschusses*, p. 62.
321. '*Anerkennung im alltäglichen Leben*'. Heitmeyer, Müller and Schröder (1997), p. 111 (emphasis in original). *See also* Kartal (2002), p. 229.
322. '*Die Rechtsstellung des Staatsbürgers konstituiert sich durch ein Netz egalitärer Beziehungen reziproker Anerkennung*'. Habermas (1992) [1990], p. 641. The author's observation was made in the context of active citizenship – and essentially acknowledged that the praxis of participation is impossible alone – but can be extended, as a general matter, to citizenship as membership.

   While I certainly agree that legal recognition does not reproduce itself, but must be complemented by some degree of identification, the author's differentiation between '*gemeinsame ethnische, sprachliche und kulturelle Herkunft*' (p. 642) and a '*gemeinsame politische Kultur*' (p. 643) is not so obvious as it may first seem. The latter is predicated on, coded by and, in most instances, builds on the foundation of the former, so that the particular culture, history and language of a society influence the practice of political culture. Thus, while common origin is not necessary, some degree of shared culture, lived daily, is indeed necessary for a likeminded approach to even citizenship.
323. *See* Bleich (1999), p. 61 *et seq.*

For instance, social norms on what is 'private' or 'public' play a central role in this regard. In the context of the *Statusdeutsche*, the fact that the 'Germanness' of minority individuals was noted in all identity documents in the Soviet Union made this identity publicly relevant, for example, especially in the framework of Soviet minority politics. The public nature of this identity, in turn, had secondary effects. If this minority identity had not been continuously reinforced in official discourse – if it had been merely a matter of personal biography – its relevance to individuals would certainly have decreased. In the same manner, the fact that nationality status is not generally noted in daily life renders it a largely private matter in contemporary European states – only to be replaced by other means of judging belonging.[324] Thus, while a child's nationality may not be known at her school, a decision to attend Turkish or Islam classes will certainly be noted in Germany;[325] in France, a refusal to remove a headscarf is bound to have public implications beyond the legal. In the same manner, whether a student recites the Pledge of Allegiance or not (and whether this is done with or without reference to God) is likely to be noticed in the United States.

The social, cultural, political and other dynamics of integration thus play out at the local level – not at the national one, where general policy is made. With regard to political activism in Germany, for example, one author has claimed that 'resident aliens are in fact actively engaged in struggles to become politically incorporated in their new places of residence and in their new homes, and this activity is partially driven for local equality and justice'.[326] The comments of certain members of foreigners' organizations active at the local level, as quoted by the same writer, show the nature of the problem, however. The 'German citizenship but not Germanness'[327] demanded by one permanent resident, for example, is not necessarily achievable while the identity function of this legal status remains intertwined with that of rights.

Naturally, a conception of national identity less focused on cultural traits (and descent) is more likely to be acceptable to immigrants than one with clear prerequisites of assimilation, or even integration – but, as discussed, some degree of 'Germanness' is sure to remain a requirement of nationality for some time;[328] this legal status, in turn, remains a prerequisite for certain rights, including voting,

---

324. It should be remembered that 'the very reification of "private" as a sphere distinct from the "public" serves to obscure the extent to which the public impinges on and intrudes into the private and the degree to which this division manages to depoliticize some very critical matters'. Lipschutz (2004), p. 46. Thus, a compromise on what should be viewed as 'private' is itself conditioned by cultural, social and political considerations.
325. For a history of instruction in the mother tongue, *see* Klopp (2002), p. 106 *et seq*.
326. *Ibid.*, p. 18.
327. *Ibid.*, p. 20.
328. As the ruckus around the content of the citizenship test introduced by the federal states of Hessen and Baden-Württemberg showed, this degree remains subject to contention. The new consensus, reached in May 2006, resulted in the formulation of common standards for citizenship tests by the federal government, to be administered with some discretion by the states. *See* Frankfurter Allgemeine Zeitung, *Kompromiß beim Einbürgerungstest* (5 May 2006).

as the Constitutional Court recently re-confirmed. As a result, although the 1999 reform of nationality law may play a role in de-ethnicising conceptions of German identity – especially as integration requirements emphasise language skills as an imperative of participation rather than as a cultural practice to be acquired before acceptance[329] – the popular link of identity and nationality does not seem to be in much danger of disappearance.

Moreover, as discussed in the context of the European Union, the assumption that 'values' and 'norms' are less problematic bases for agreement than more outwardly cultural practices is not as obvious as some claim. While at the EU level, reliance on these concepts simply displaced basic disagreements, placing them at a higher level of abstraction – and allowing for references to 'European values' galore – this approach does not work at the Member State level, because the management of national identity does not allow for such generalization. To give but one example, the EU can declare its respect for freedom of religion; and so may a Member State. But a Member State must also determine whether the accommodation of certain social or religious practices 'might undermine [the] polity's need to promote consensual civic values'.[330] The promotion of one norm could easily undermine another.

On the basis of such concerns, the British Home Office Report Community Cohesion from 2001, for instance, argued for a 'meaningful conception of citizenship' that would recognize 'the contributions of many cultures to this Nation's development throughout its history, but establish a clear primary loyalty to this nation'.[331] In essence, a balancing of interests is required. In the UK, universal acceptance of the English language and a statement of allegiance at naturalization have been deemed necessary to establish such loyalty, and were introduced into nationality law (as of 2002, as amended in 2004). However one may view the outcome of balancing in this instance, it should be remembered that but nationality policy does not exist in a vacuum; nor is it devoid of history.[332] In light of recent legislative history and government policies in other, related areas (such as immigration and asylum), the requirements of the UK law could be perceived as assimilationist (or exclusionist). (Indeed, some commentators have been scathing in their criticism of the law.) If immigrants feel unwanted and excluded, however, no

---

329. The language requirement is strictly construed, however. As the Federal Administrative Court has confirmed, applicants must be capable of both speaking and writing German to be naturalized. (However, *Spätaussiedler* must, by the terms of the *Bundesvertriebenengesetz*, only show that they are capable of carrying on a simple conversation in German.) *See* BVerwG (2005), 5 C 8.05 and 5 C 17.05.
330. Klopp (2002), p. 152.
331. British Home Office, Report 'Community Cohesion' (2001), p. 20.
332. It is generally not only the content of a piece of legislation that determines its perception, but also the circumstances surrounding drafting and passage into law. In this way, laws can take on lives of their own, becoming imbued with symbolic significance out of proportion to their actual content. On the other hand, laws ostensibly applicable to all equally may result in practical inequality, due to lack of information or misunderstanding (e.g., in the context of naturalization).

amount of integration policies will result in actual integration. For this reason, despite semantic distinctions by academics, assimilation and integration measures may not be so easy to separate in practice: because there is no fixed category, individual perception determines how a particular policy (and the sum of such policies) will be received by individuals and groups. Given these complexities, approaching nationality matters (and specially claims to a particular nationality) through the prism of identity-linked rights is likely to prove exceedingly difficult.

3.   THE CONSEQUENCES OF TRANSNATIONALISM

In general terms then, 'it is impossible to create objective regulations concerning the acquisition of ... nationality if the core of this nationality is something that is hard to define and contains a number of subjective elements'.[333] While nationality retains its identity function, these subjective elements will remain, so that the likelihood of 'objective regulations' is remote. One can nonetheless accept that the boundary approach sketched by Barth,[334] or any kind of straightforward classificatory thinking – in which categories are 'assumed to be abstract containers, with things either inside or outside'[335] – simply does not apply to collective identities, whether national, religious or other cultural. The in-betweenness of migrants is real, even if it is unacknowledged. Besides, the existence of prototypicality gradients within groups in itself excludes easy pigeonholing, as already discussed.[336] States can thus draw the outer limits of this gradient for membership purposes, but will not succeed in imposing an insular category of 'national' after a model. In this manner, '[T]he objective and general rules, defined by the legislator, mark the borders within which it is left to the applicant to decide which degree there is subjective allegiance to [a given state]'.[337]

The nature of this allegiance is also conditioned by an external factor, however; namely, the active efforts of states of origin to preserve not only ongoing informal, but also legal links between emigrants and the national community – 'bonding mechanisms' in the words of one commentator.[338] In traditional approaches, it was presumed that citizenship would 'act as a "natural barrier" to the continuation of political transnationalism',[339] for a number of reasons. First, it was assumed that loss of nationality in the state of origin – as generally required at naturalization – would impel a shift in political and social (and eventually also

---

333. van den Bedem (1994), p. 99.
334. Barth (1969), p. 14. According to the author, clear boundaries are a means of 'continuing dichotomization between members and outsiders'.
335. Lakoff (1987), p. 6.
336. Hence, the Germanness of *Spätaussiedler* has increasingly been questioned, as their integration seems no easier than that of other immigrants. This evolution is reflected in legislation and practice, as discussed above. *See also* Levy (1999), pp. 102–103.
337. Van den Bedem (1994), p. 99.
338. Chander (2006), p. 69.
339. Guarnizo *et al.* (2003), p. 1216.

cultural) activity in the direction of the state of residence. Second, naturalization was assumed to be a significant step in the one-way process of assimilation already discussed. As recent studies have shown, this is not quite the case.[340]

a. Transnational and Local Ties

In particular, 'many immigrants are no longer individualized or obedient prospective citizens. Instead, they may retain dual citizenship, agitate for special trade deals with their homelands, demand aid in exchange for electoral support and seek to influence social and foreign policy'.[341] Acquisition of the nationality of the state of residence has been shown to have no effect on such transnational activism; while length of residence seems to increase its likelihood.[342] In turn, personal experience, social ties and mobility, as well as the culture and history of the state of origin seem to be determinative factors in the maintenance of transnational ties.[343] What such ties encompass – electoral or more limited political activity, links to local or regional organizations, business activity or just private connections – and what they mean for the individual are also functions of personal history.[344] No matter which of these activities one considers, however, transnational activism is generally considered by commentators 'a constructive phenomenon through which people respond to long-distance social obligations and belonging and seek to transform the political practices in their sending countries'.[345] On a personal level, transnational activism can function as a compensatory mechanism for (especially male) immigrants' status loss in the state of residence, for example.[346] In the

---

340. 'Contrary to the designs of sending and receiving states, the migrant's act of taking on two nationalities may be indicative of neither assimilation nor homeland political identification, but rather of multiple political identities, an ambivalent political identity, or even an apolitical identity'. Koslowski (200), p. 150.
341. Cohen (1997), p. 194.
342. Guarnizo *et al.* (2003), p. 1229.
343. A short note about transnational ties is in order here. As Faist has noted, 'concepts termed "transnational" have become catch-all phrases for sustained cross-border ties'. Faist (1999), p. 3. In our understanding, transnational ties are (formal or informal) social processes that reach across not just state borders, but also societies. Accordingly, '[t]ransnational social spaces are delimited by pentatonic relationships between the government of the immigration state, civil society organizations in the country of immigration, the rulers of the country of emigration (sometimes viewed as an external homeland), civil society groups in the emigration state, and the transnational group – migrants and/or refugee groups, or national, religious and ethnic minorities'. *Ibid.*, p. 4.

    The author distinguishes between three types of transnational social space: transnational kinship groups (which are the main source of remittances), transnational circuits (e.g., trading networks) and transnational communities (e.g., diasporas or border regions). *Ibid.*, p. 8. Though I would not include border regions in the same hat as diasporas, the three-fold distinction is otherwise useful.
344. For a wide-ranging study on transnationalism in the second generation (in the United States) – from who is most involved through the form involvement takes, to its causes and effects – *see* the essays in Levitt and Waters, eds., *The Changing Face of Home: The Transnational Lives of the Second Generation* (2002).
345. Guarnizo *et al.*(2003), p. 1239.
346. Jones-Correa (1998); but *see* discussion in Guarnizo *et al.*, *ibid.*, pp. 1230–1232.

longer run, such activism may even help adaptation in the country of residence by means of social and/or structural integration.

But ties of this kind can also hinder integration. To the extent denizens, or permanent residents without nationality,[347] attempt to influence policies in their state of residence before naturalization, for example, lobbying often takes place in the name of 'the minority formed by Turkish nationals'[348] in Germany, not as immigrants, regardless of the place of origin. For example, demands for dual nationality are voiced because the minority is 'defined by its divided allegiance between the German state and the Turkish state'.[349] Questions that could otherwise be framed as social, political or economic are thereby formulated as matters of identity. In this manner, concepts of identity, culture, religion and ethnicity 'intervene ... to transform an informal local community, constituted de facto by spatial proximity, into a cultural one, from a local community to a transnational one, imagined in terms of common identifications'.[350] By this logic, Chinese-Hungarians ostensibly have more in common with someone in Shanghai or with a Chinese-German than with the other Hungarian they meet every day in the supermarket. This may or may not be the case: actual similarity matters little so long as the perceived or invented one is felt to be the true(r) one.

To the extent the local becomes transnational (and trans-state) in such contexts, the national project of the state of residence may be perceived as being under threat. Matters are also complicated by the fact that political issues are often transferred from one state to another by means of such transnationalization. Thus, the efforts of the Kurdish community in Germany to be recognized as separate from the Turkish one breeds tension at numerous levels. The politicization of this identity in Germany – particularly in a manner impossible to achieve in Turkey itself – raises complex questions of belonging and loyalty, as individual and collective identity claims become entangled in inter-state politics. In other cases, when a given group of (former-) nationals forms a sizable minority in the state of residence – even in the case of diasporas – its clout, *per se*, may generate a perception of interference.[351] Fear of interference or harm to the interests of the state of residence becomes particularly acute when the perceived similarity with members of another national (or other cultural) community also has state recognition – through nationality or some other status, for example.

In the alternative, denizens may gain access to participate in defining the terms of their inclusion in local and state membership before naturalization[352] – i.e., by

---

347. Hammar (1990), p. 14.
348. Kastoryano (2002), p. 135.
349. *Ibid.*
350. *Ibid.*, p. 86.
351. When the state of origin has even recognized a constitutional duty to maintain links (*see* Art. 82 of the Turkish Constitution) and has a host of (educational and cultural) policies in place for this purpose, the insecurity of the state of residence becomes comparable to that of the home-states of national minorities with kin-states in close proximity.
352. Klopp (2002), p. 197. Compare also BVerfG, BVerfGE 83, 60 (*Ausländerwahlrecht II*) (1990).

means of foreigners' associations or organizations such as the *Ausländerbeiräte* in Germany – as 'foreigners', rather than as 'Turks', 'Chinese', etc. While collective identities from the state of origin are less institutionalized in this approach, few states in Europe actually provide for associations of this kind; nor are these organizations likely to eclipse the importance of traditional identifications.[353] However, European citizenship has provided a novel avenue for development in this regard. Through the voting rights available pursuant to ECT Article 19(1), European citizens resident in Member States other than their own have established political parties that cater to issues of special interest to them, including bilingual schooling and property laws; of late, some have had considerable success in local elections in at least one Member State.[354]

European citizenship has also helped to maintain ties to states of origin, however. In the course of 2006, for example, two political parties, the 'Romanian Identity Party' (*Partito Identitatea Romaneasca/ Partito dei Romeni d'Italia*) in Italy and the 'Independent Romanian Party' (*Partido Independiente Rumano*) in Spain were founded to mobilize Romanian migrants in their state of residence. (In addition, numerous Romanian parties have opened local offices in Greece, Italy and Spain to campaign for the votes of these migrants in national elections in the state of origin.)[355] Whether as expats or as Romanians, it is clearly not just integration into existing political entities that is aimed at by migrants in Europe, but also the creation of new forms of affiliation – and the maintenance of existing ones.

b.   Diaspora Policies

Despite such ties, most migrants (and migrant groups) seem to prefer maintaining and developing their identities on their own terms, without interference from any state they may have links to. As Necef shows, immigrant communities themselves debate the 'proper' kind of identity to have, as well as the 'best' kind of approach to take to their state of origin: integrationist and nationalist discourse (as well as Islamist discourse, in the context of Muslim immigration) jostle for

---

353. That said, 'identity politics should not be seen as struggles for the definitive recognition of an authentic, autonomous or self-realizing identity, for no such fixed identity exists. Rather, because the identities in contention are modified in the course of the contests, the aim of identity politics is to ensure that *any* form of public recognition is not a fixed and unchangeable structure of domination, but is open to question, contestation and change over time, as the identities of the participants change. Hence, identity politics is about the freedom of diverse people and peoples to modify the rules of recognition of their political associations as they modify themselves. Consequently, belonging is related to freedom and acknowledgement, more than to recognition'. Tully (2000), p. 232.
354. BBC News, 'Expats a political force in Spain' (12 May 2007); *ibid.*, 'Expats win Spanish council seats' (29 May 2007).
355. *See* El Mundo, *Los Rumanos ya tienen su partido en España* (22 October 2006); Népszabadság, *Eperszedő politikusok* (14 November 2006) and *ibid., Román párt alakult Olaszországban is* (14 November 2006).

dominance.[356] Nonetheless, states of origin attempt to influence migrants on a number of levels: cultural, economic, religious, social or political. In short, the range of options available is wide. Although these policies would warrant a book in and of themselves, a short digression must suffice for our purposes, particularly to highlight their nature as a subset of kinship laws and to draw out their correlation with support for plural nationality.

With regard to cultural policies, these include measures of recognition, like constitutional provisions or official 'diaspora days' or 'months', in India (*Pravasi Bharatiya Divas*) and the Philippines respectively, as well as institutional accommodation (e.g., offices or ministries for diasporas, like the General Secretariat of Greeks Abroad), travel/cultural programmes (e.g., those mentioned above in the context of Israel) and even the organization of language and educational curricula in the state of residence (e.g., Turkey). China, a state with a large population of overseas nationals, even institutionalized a comprehensive programme for 'new migrants' (in 1978) that encompasses overseas newspapers, satellite television and migrant organizations with links in China. The general aim of this programme is to create a 'unified nationalist discourse of belonging', with standardization of state and self-depiction among overseas Chinese.[357]

Economic policies range from diaspora bonds, like the Resurgent India Bonds (1998) or the India Millennium Bonds (2000), guaranteed by the State Bank and available only to members of the diaspora, to policies that encourage channelled remittances, like the *Tres por Uno* programme instituted in Mexico, whereby the federal, state and local governments (especially hometown associations) match every dollar remitted by the migrant,[358] to special measures to encourage direct investment in the state of origin.

Social and political policies are more limited in range, since they require a direct legal relationship between the individual and her state of origin. Still, the maintenance or creation of such a legal relationship – most conventionally through the encouragement of plural nationality for instance – is one of the most widespread means of reincorporating migrants. The status of 'national' opens the door to not only government action on behalf of nationals (e.g., through consular and diplomatic protection), for example, but also the possibility of taxation and social benefits, as well as voting rights. But the nationality status of individuals is not determinative for the purposes of these relationships. In lieu of the traditional approach, in which 'the citizenship [nationality] of emigrants and the ancestral citizenship [nationality] of their descendants'[359] is maintained, the state may also take a more novel track and furnish individuals with alternative statuses, like 'emigrant', 'former national' or even 'person of kin-origin'.

---

356. Necef (2001).
357. *See* Nyíri (2001), p. 648.
358. Hometown localism is especially developed – and supported by the federal state – in the case of Mexican migrants. *See* study by Smith (2003); and discussion in Fitzgerald (2004), p. 237 *et seq.*
359. Fitzgerald (2006), p. 91.

The number of such diaspora statuses has increased noticeably in recent years. For instance, since 1995, Turkish nationals by birth who have relinquished their Turkish nationality (with permission) are entitled to a special legal status, wherever they may now reside. Their special status, which places them on equal footing with nationals in many areas – including inheritance and residence rights, land ownership, education and access to jobs – is confirmed by the so-called 'Pink Card' allotted directly by Turkish authorities. In turn, India introduced the status of 'Person of Indian Origin', complete with a card, in 1999 (with a minor overhaul in 2002). The card entitles its holder to visa-free entry into India, as well as a host of educational, cultural, economic and financial benefits that place her on equal footing with non-resident Indians. Former nationals and individuals whose descendants up to the fourth generation were nationals or whose spouse is a national of India or of Indian origin are eligible for the status.[360] Lebanon has also considered the introduction of a so-called 'emigrants' card' (*carte des émigrés*), which would grant entry rights, as well as social and economic benefits to former nationals and their descendants.[361] As in Hungary, the idea of this card was closely linked to an ongoing and contentious debate on granting (dual-)nationality – in this case to Lebanese migrants – especially given the fragile confessional equilibrium between religious groups in the country.

Clearly, such 'former-national' status can be understood either as a simple nod to the ongoing ties of individuals, irrespective of changes to nationality, or as a subset of the kinship laws already presented in a previous chapter. In either case, many of the issues raised by status laws – territorial sovereignty and discrimination most clearly – must also be considered when discussing diaspora policies. As noted above, it is at times difficult to make a distinction between the content of the two, in any case.[362]

c.   The Political Issues Raised by Diaspora Ties

Barry has referred to the maintenance of such bundles of ongoing cultural, economic, social and political relationships as 'external citizenship', encompassing both legal status, with attendant rights and benefits, and a practiced identity.[363] The interests of the state of origin and the individual in external citizenship are thus two-fold and correspond to the identity/rights duality already discussed in the context of European citizenship and status laws. In the first place, these policies serve to affirm and instrumentalize identity, usually for the benefit of the state of origin. Mexico, which was one of the first states to cultivate and expand relations with migrants in the United States, has openly admitted to this goal, in light of the

---

360. *See* Extra Ordinary Gazette of India, No. 213, Ministry of Home Affairs Notification on PIO Card Scheme (2002).
361. *See* L'Orient-Le Jour, *La mouture finale du projet de loi sur la carte des émigrés est terminée* (12 May 2006).
362. *See* discussion at Sec. III.A.2 above.
363. Barry (2006), pp. 26–31.

fact that the 'Mexican Nation extends beyond the territory contained by its borders'.[364]

In reality, immigrants rarely serve the function their states of origin encourage, as circumstances in the receiving country serve to modify goals, expectations and even identities.[365] This does not change the hope of utility, however. Fitzgerald's differentiation between long-distance nationalism and dual nationalism becomes important in this regard. While neither is actually an instance of transnationalism in the sense of nations transcended – rather, state borders are crossed, while that of that of the nation is considered to extend above these borders – only dual nationalism encompasses membership in two distinct political (and cultural) communities.[366] In the case of long-distance nationalism, we deal rather with an understanding of national identity that stretches beyond borders, (albeit in a manner distinguishable from national minorities).[367] In both instances, however, the politics of identity in the state of origin – and, in case of legal recognition, also its law – may play an important role in the state of residence.

For example, Turkey's regulation of nationality – particularly its practice of re-granting nationality to individuals who had renounced it in order to apply for a German one – was clearly behind the removal of the *Inlandsklausel*, the clause allowing nationals resident in Germany to keep their German nationality upon acquisition of another one, from the German law on nationality in 1999.[368] In an instance of reverse influence, some argue that the Pink Cards mentioned above were introduced in Turkey as an alternative status in response to German pressure on the issue of plural nationality.

When, in addition, nationality is seen as a foreign policy tool by the state of origin – in a manner comparable to the kin-minority context of Russia and Romania – the probability of international tension rises further. Fitzgerald, for example, has noted that Mexican politicians saw the need for a turnaround on the policy of prohibiting plural nationality (in 1998) because of the comparative disadvantage this created for Mexicans, as compared to other minorities in the United States; this disadvantage, in turn, limited their opportunity to lobby for Mexico. Thus, '[n]ational law was to be a tool of Mexican foreign policy in its relationships with the United States in a competition with other states hoping dual nationality would promote emigrant US lobbies'.[369] The message to emigrants was

---

364. *See* González Gutiérrez (1999), para. 2.
365. The influence of social factors in the state of residence often reaches back even to the state of origin. Levitt's idea of social remittances (i.e., normative structures, systems of practice, social capital) to sending states are an example of such impact; to the extent such remittances are generally based on personal transmission (completely or almost wholly uncontrolled by states, unlike their economic kin) they tend to be less obvious, but no less important. Levitt (1998).
366. Fitzgerald (2004), p. 243 *et seq.*
367. *See also* Fitzgerald (2003), p. 35.
368. *See* Art. 8 of the Turkish law on nationality. *See also* discussion in Kiliç (2002), pp. 38–39; and Faist (1999), p. 16. Given the stigma of such 'pink certificates', there have not (yet) been all that many applicants.
369. Fitzgerald (2003), p. 36.

effectively that 'those who are eligible to naturalize fulfil a duty *to Mexico* by becoming Mexican and American, not merely Mexican-Americans'.[370]

In this manner, all diaspora policies, but especially policies on plural nationality can be used to increase geo-political clout. Armenia's recent amendment of its nationality law, which now allows not only for dual nationality but also for voting rights abroad,[371] was motivated in no small part by the wish to activate a large and influential Armenian diaspora, while also increasing the official population of the state. In turn, plural nationality can also be used as a bargaining chip in bilateral relations between particular countries, as has been the case between Russia and many CIS states.[372]

Notions of identity and international clout aside, the question of benefits and resources also looms large in any discussion of diaspora policies. For individuals, the maintenance of legal ties to multiple states doubles (or triples, etc.) the opportunity for favourable citizenship rights and social benefits, with the additional advantage of a ready exit option.[373] For the states of origin, strong ties with emigrants have tremendous economic advantages,[374] mainly in the form of remittances (e.g., Mexico, the Philippines, Armenia or Albania) and investment (e.g., India), but also of taxes (e.g., South Korea and Eritrea) and knowledge networks (e.g., India and China). For the states of residence, in turn, particular regimes of membership are a resource to attract particular categories of (e.g., young or highly skilled) migrants deemed more valuable additions to the national community than others (e.g., refugees). As Shachar notes, there is ever-increasing competition among states, as 'each [state] seeks to extract a share of the welfare-enhancing contributions generated by the highly skilled in an era of increased cross-border mobility, even if this requires a reconception of the nation's membership boundaries'.[375]

d. The Legal Issues Raised by Diaspora Ties

The endorsement of legal ties between individuals and their states of origin – in other words the social and political branch of diaspora policies – raises novel questions, however. For example, do 'former nationals' or 'persons of kin-origin' gain social and political rights of membership, in addition to the benefits

---

370. Barry (2006), p. 49 (emphasis in original).
371. *See* EurasiaNet, 'Armenia allows dual nationality amid controversy' (26 February 2007); BBC News, 'Armenia seeks to boost population' (21 February 2007).
372. In addition to the discussions above, *see* EurasiaNet, 'Turkmenistan's move to eliminate dual citizenship creates political problems for Russian president' (4 June 2003); and *ibid.*, 'Emigration from Kyrgyzstan is surging' (21 March 2006).
373. Obviously, such exit options can become especially valuable during economic crises or war. In a recent example, tens of thousands of Argentinians claimed Italian, Spanish or Israeli nationality in the wake of Argentina's economic collapse. *See* 'Argentines Line Up to Escape to the Old World'. *The New York Times*, 16 January 2002.
374. *See* discussion in Trebilcock and Sudak (2006), p. 255 *et seq.*
375. *See* Shachar (2006), p. 202.

mentioned above? Are 'emigrant citizens' fully recognized citizens in the state of origin or merely nationals, without the full range of citizenship rights? Does either group have voting rights, for example? Do 'persons of kin origin' have at least a consultative role in the state of origin in decisions that impact on them? Clearly, the new statuses now devised by states also require the construction of a legal framework in which these statuses have an ascertainable place. At present, the individuals concerned may have a firm place in the national imagination, but their exact legal position – in-between foreigners and nationals – is distinctly hazy.

The state of legal flux also extends to certain groups of nationals, however. Of late, public and academic debate has focused on the issue of voting rights, for example, with special consideration for the situation of plural nationals.[376] Should nationals resident abroad have the right to vote in national elections in the state of origin? If not, aren't the individuals concerned stripped of a basic citizenship right? If so, how should plural nationals be dealt with, in light of the fact that they may have the right to vote in two different states? In turn, if nationals can vote abroad, is separate representation provided for (as in Italy, Portugal, France, Croatia or Algeria) or are the relevant persons subsumed into existing districts based, e.g., on their last place of residence in the country (as in most other states)? These questions loom especially large in states like Armenia, with diaspora populations that outnumber the entire population of the state; but the issue may be of import to any state. As the Italian example demonstrated in 2006, even a relatively small number of voters abroad can determine the outcome of national elections.[377]

Nonetheless, numerous states, including Italy (2001), Belgium (2003), the Philippines (2004), the Dominican Republic (2004), Mexico (2006) and Armenia (2007), have enabled nationals to vote abroad in recent years, regardless of the size of their diaspora. The Mexican context gives one explanation for why: the right to vote abroad in national elections has been framed in public discussion as a means to 'honour the dignity of that part of our nation which lives and works outside [the] borders'[378] – in other words, as another means to strengthen ties. As a practical matter, the changing tide of opinion may have more to do with financial considerations, since more and more nationals abroad complain of their lack of political representation, despite remittances and taxes.

Conversely, should plural nationals be fully recognized citizens of their state of residence? Should the existence of plural legal ties – of any kind – exclude individuals from holding office, for example? While this issue has not yet gained

---

376. For the views of some commentators, *see* Martin (1999) (critiquing the idea); López-Guerra (2005) (critiquing the idea) and Spiro (2006) (for a positive evaluation).
377. In this instance, the majority gained by the left coalition in the Senate hinged on the votes of 'Italians abroad'. See La Repubblica, *Senato, gli italiani all'estero danno la maggioranza all'Unione* (11 April 2006); and *Legge 27 dicembre 2001, no. 459, Norme per l'esercizio del diritto di voto dei cittadini italiani residenti all'estero* (2001).
378. *The New York Times*, 'Fox Seeks to Allow Mexicans Living Abroad to Vote in 2006' (16 June 2004). In the context of Armenia, *see* Institute for War and Peace Reporting/Caucasus, 'Armenia: Dual Citizenship Debate' (13 October 2004); and Asbarez Online, 'Officials List Conditions for Dual Citizenship in Armenia' (1 November 2005).

public attention in most countries, the fact of public officials with dual nationality has of late stirred up controversy in numerous states, including Mexico, Turkey, and the Netherlands. In Turkey, for example, a parliamentary deputy whose dual Turkish-American nationality came to light after her election was stripped of her Turkish nationality and eventually her parliament seat.[379] In the Netherlands, it was the dual Dutch-Moroccan and Dutch-Turkish nationality of two state secretaries that created a ruckus.[380] In turn, the present Governor General of Canada renounced her French nationality to avoid controversy before taking up office in 2005.[381] On the basis of these examples it is safe to assume that the concession of plural nationality for public officials is one few societies are at present likely to accept.

One overarching question emerges from the political and legal issues introduced above: what becomes of popular sovereignty when the members of the community are scattered in any number of states? On the one hand, the attempted reconceptualizations of the national community discussed here try to keep the state of origin relevant – and extend institutional power beyond its territory; on the other, the efficacy of these policies is conditioned on the parallel efforts of the states of residence to socialize migrants. As the Council of Europe noted in 2004, 'it is no longer really possible to speak of countries of emigration or immigration without immediately qualifying our use of these expressions',[382] however – migration is a two way street these days. Each state, after all, is involved in simultaneous attempts to both socialize the persons within its borders and to extend its influence over individuals abroad. In light of such developments, Schmitter Heisler's recognition (back in 1985) of the necessity of co-operation between states of origin and states of residence in migration and minority matters[383] was notably prescient. Nearly twenty years later the Council of Europe came to a similar conclusion: '[i]t is

---

379. See *Affaire Kavakçi c. Turquie*, E.Ct.H.R. 71907/01 (2007), E.Ct.H.R. (2007) for a description of the circumstances that led to the withdrawal of both nationality and parliamentary mandate.
    See also The Los Angeles Times, 'Pledging Multiple Allegiances' (6 April 1998) for an example of popular mistrust.
    Suspicion of individuals with multiple ties is also reflected in many domestic provisions. In France, naturalized nationals (with or without plural nationality) were excluded from public office until 1983. In the United States (and many other countries), only the native-born may become president. In Belgium, the legal difference between '*naturalisation ordinaire*' and '*grande naturalisation*' persisted until 1993 – only the latter came with political rights, including the right to vote; in Greece, naturalized citizens lost their nationality more easily than the native-born until 1998.
    Finally, in some states today, different bases for loss of nationality are still attributed to the two groups of nationals; compare Arts 24 and 25 of the Spanish *Código Civil* and see Arts 25 and 25-1 of the French *Code Civil*.
380. BBC News, 'Row over Dutch Muslim ministers' (22 February 2007).
381. CBC News, 'New governor general to give up French citizenship' (25 September 2005).
382. Second CoE Report, *supra* note III.289, para. 15.
383. Schmitter Heisler (1999) [1985], p. 481–482. *See also* references to the need for international co-operation between states in Koslowski (2003).
    The Council of Europe also foresaw the necessity of co-operation (on a surprisingly large scale) between states of residence and origin on issues of employment and education.

essential for all parties concerned that the right balance between the process of integration in the host country and the links with the country of origin is defined and maintained'.[384] The nationality and diaspora policies of one state often influence those of another, even as a number of interconnected factors – including categories of initial gate-keeping,[385] the role and scope of particular statuses and the new environment created by a rights-based conception of nationality – guide determinations on the flexibility of provisions on nationality.[386]

D.   TENDENCIES OF DEVELOPMENT

The framing of plural nationality in the language of rights in an increasing number of contexts and the introduction of human rights norms into matters of nationality, discussed above, are the clearest sign that it is no longer just state interests or international management concerns that influence the outcome of debates on the regulation of nationality. In certain domestic contexts, as in Germany, it is the value of naturalization and plural nationality for integration that is focused on. Meanwhile, international norms are moving toward greater acceptance of plural nationality in the name of the 'interests' of individuals: the 1997 Convention on Nationality explicitly defends the retention of plural nationality (in certain contexts) on this basis.

This practical change of approach – from one focused on the international order to one concerned with individual autonomy – has not been widely recognized, although it is significant.[387] Spiro, one of the few commentators to see the transformation, has argued that the emerging framework increasingly identifies a particular (state) addressee for the right to nationality; in other words, the individual right to nationality is transformed into a right to a particular nationality.[388] The reasoning behind this approach can rest on arguments of democratic self-governance, since participation in the political process of the place of residence is considered crucial, or of respect for individual ties, as seen above. In any case, the old approach, in which nationality was considered necessary to provide the individual with a link to international law, is nowhere to be seen.

       See Council of Europe, Committee of Ministers Recommendation No. R 84(9) on Second-Generation Migrants (1984).

384. Council of Europe, Parliamentary Recommendation 1650 on Links between Europeans Living Abroad and their Countries of Origin (2004), Sec. 7.
385. Hammar (1994), p. 189.
386. '*Frage, unter welchen Voraussetzungen die Mehrfachangehörigkeit ihre existentiellen Schrecken verliert, und ab welcher Assozationsintensität und – art Staatenverbindungen den Kollisionsproblemen die Spitze nehmen*'. Grawert (1973), pp. 242–243.
387. That said, scholarship has discussed the justifications for nationality for some time. *See* Neuman (1994).
388. Spiro (2004), p. 99.

1. THE TREND TOWARD PLURAL NATIONALITY, WITH STRINGS ATTACHED

A large number of states have moved toward acceptance of plural nationality in the last few years, motivated both by changing circumstances and, at least in part, the new approach. Whether this trend amounts to a 'collective redefinition of sovereignty',[389] as one writer has claimed, remains to be seen, however, especially in light of the reluctance of most states to give effect to any additional nationalities a national may hold. If this reluctance should lessen or if reliance on habitual residence (or domicile) for choice of law purposes should increase, we could indeed speak of a move away from unitary toward shared (and possibly even overlapping) ongoing authority over persons.

That most European states temper their acceptance of plural nationality with a big – and increasingly important – 'if' should also be taken into account, however. At the moment, 'independent of the conception of nationality that inspires [particular laws], it is common enough to require proof of assimilation into the national community'.[390] Thus, even as states accept the possibility of multiple legal ties in the name of respect for individual autonomy, they require proof of attachment to their state and society, especially in the context of naturalization.[391] In light of this, shared authority is perhaps not as likely a path for evolution as it may otherwise seem.

The logic of the two developments is actually quite similar: if individuals are free to maintain membership in multiple state-focused communities, they are also capable of being functioning members of a number of societies (and cultures), if need be through integration. It is perhaps no coincidence, then, that the number of nationality laws with integration requirements of some sort – from language or civic tests to history and 'culture' courses – has increased significantly in the last ten years, in parallel with the growing acceptance of plural nationality.[392] Nor is it

---

389. Waever (1995), pp. 417–418.
390. '*Indépendamment de la conception de nationalité qui les inspire, il est assez habituel d'exiger une preuve d'assimilation à la communauté nationale*'. Pérez Vera (1996), p. 283. If this was true in 1996, it is even more accurate today.
391. In the context of the Netherlands, *see* Entzinger (2003), p. 75 *et seq.*
392. Most European states now have or are in the process of introducing requirements for linguistic proficiency at naruralization. *Inter alia*, Hungary requires a test of constitutional values and norms in Hungarian since 1993; Austria introduced a language test in 1998; Norway will require language training for applicants from September 2008.

However, a new wave of integration tests go further, aiming to determine the extent to which new candidates for national citizenship know and accept the 'national' culture. *See The New York Times*, 'Refining the Tests that Confer Citizenship' (23 January 2006). Besides the new German test already discussed, these include the United Kingdom, on the basis of Sec. 1 of the Nationality, Immigration and Asylum Act (2002) (BBC News Online, 'New UK Citizenship Testing Starts' (1 November 2005)); Denmark (Le Monde, *Le Danemark dresse de nouvelles barrières face aux candidats à la naturalisation* (11 December 2005)); and the Netherlands, where the new test is to be administered before potential immigrants even leave their country (BBC News Online, 'Dutch Set Immigrants Culture Test' (22 December

an accident that there have been pointed efforts in numerous states to make nationality more meaningful. The United Kingdom, for example, introduced so-called 'citizenship ceremonies' in 2004 – with an oath or affirmation of allegiance to the Queen and a citizenship pledge to the state – as part of a general overhaul of the regulation of nationality;[393] Germany is at present considering a similar option. The hope is that such rituals of entry will strengthen the meaning of membership.[394]

In turn, France, which accepts plural nationality without restriction, has recently introduced the most explicit of legal expectations for integration. In 2006, a law was approved that, in addition to instituting a citizenship ceremony,[395] also requires – rather than, as in the past, offers – future immigrants to sign a 'reception and integration contract' with the French state, in which they promise to attend civic courses (comprised of a presentation of French history, institutions, as well as the 'values of the Republic, notably equality between men and women and laicity') and, if necessary, also language instruction.[396] While a decree sets out the exact form (duration, renewal, content) and role of this contract,[397] the law notes that 'disregard, manifested by blatant will, for the stipulations of the welcome and integration contract by the foreigner'[398] will be taken into account when decisions on the renewal of residence permits are made.

Such contractualization of expectations for integration patently reconceptualizes the individual-state relationship in a manner citizenship ceremonies do not: duties are now clearly spelled out and monitored, with clear consequences for non-compliance. This in itself is unusual. However, the assumptions and likely results of this law are even more peculiar. In the first place, the law openly relies on the assumption that immigrants are, in some form, a threat to 'French' society; the reference to the equality of sexes and to *laïcité* is a thinly veiled nod to Muslim immigrants in particular. This leads us to the second point. Given that the law

---

2005)). For a description of integration requirements in the Netherlands, *see* Vrinds (2004), p. 5 *et seq.*; for the importance of integration in the context of Belgium, *see* Liénard-Ligny (2001), p. 204 *et seq.* For a discussion of the general trend toward integration, *see* Joppke and Morawska (2003).

393. Introduced by the Nationality, Immigration and Asylum Act (2002). Denmark also now requires a 'loyalty oath' of all new nationals, in addition to language classes and knowledge of Danish society. DR Nyheder, 'Oath of Allegiance Comes to Denmark' (4 November 2005).
394. *See also* Benhabib (2004), p. 1.
395. Art. 86 of *Loi no. 2006-911 du 24 juillet 2006 relative à l'immigration et à l'intégration* (2006). The law, which incidentally touches on a number of other elements of immigration, including family reunification and special residence permits, and includes the transposition of Directive 2004/58/EC, entered into force in July 2006.
396. *Contrat d'accueil et d'intégration* and *valeurs de la République, notamment l'égalité entre les hommes et les femmes et la laïcité. Ibid.*, Art. 5(1).
397. *Décret no. 2006-1791 du 23 décembre 2006 relatif au contrat d'accueil et d'intégration et au contrôle des connaissances en français d'un étranger souhaitant durablement s'installer en France et modifiant le code de l'entrée et du séjour des étrangers et du droit d'asile (partie réglementaire)* (2006).
398. '*Non-respect, manifesté par une volonté caractérisée, par l'étranger, des stipulations du contrat d'accueil et d'intégration*'. Art. 5(1) of the *Loi relative à l'immigration et à l'intégration, supra* note IV.395.

obviously applies to non-nationals only, immigrants will now be expected to 'integrate' linguistically and socially – and, to some extent, culturally – into society before they may even be considered for membership.[399] As one of the materials prepared for use in the mandatory civic course notes, 'a nation has a history – one must know it and accept its rules to be its citizen'[400]

To the extent someone considered to have breached the integration contract is, for example, denied a residence permit – thereby closing off the road to nationality – the debate on whether nationality is a means to or the last step in integration, already discussed in the context of Germany, has clearly been decided here. It is certainly viewed as the final element of that process. The expectation of conduct demonstrating a conscious choice 'for' the state – a will to integrate[401] – is also comparable to the expectation of an *aktive Integrationsentscheidung* (active decision for integration) already noted in the German context. But questions of identity are linked here to the status of nationality in a more conspicuous manner than is usually done in the context of immigration, since the future membership of immigrants hinges, at least in part, on their conduct actually being deemed 'French' enough by authorities.[402] Finally, in light of the importance attached to 'French' identity in the law, it is also worth noting that the law will apply only to immigrants from outside the European Union. European citizens will not be required to sign any integration contract, no matter how long they intend to reside in the country. The increasingly differentiated social and legal approach of Member States to European citizens, already discussed, thus finds further confirmation here.

One could raise a number of further questions with regard to the law – including its compatibility with the E.Ct.H.R. jurisprudence on ECHR Article 8 discussed above – but let us emphasize only how its content displays the state-specificity of the context (and content) of integration. The presence of the principle of laicity among the values of the Republic every immigrant must learn about shows as much, since it would not feature in any civic course in Germany or Italy, for example. The existence of such specificity should be obvious, in a sense, since no society perceives difference or diversity in the same manner. Thus, a central

---

399. The integration and Dutch language courses now required of potential immigrants to the Netherlands – already mentioned – are a more radical implementation of the same principle.
400. *'Une nation a une histoire, il faut la cônnaitre et accepter ses règles pour en être citoyen'*. Slide 87 in the Presentation *Contrat d'accueil et de'intégration: Formation civique* (2006) prepared by the Ministry for Employment, Cohesion and Housing (*Ministère de l'emploi, de la cohésion et du logement*) for use during the mandatory civic courses.
401. In fact, exactly this language (*'volonté d'intégration'*) was utilized in the draft of the law presented to the National Assembly in May 2006. *See* Art. 5(1) of the *Projet de Loi relatif à l'immigration et à l'intégration* (No. 576) (2006).
402. Art. 7(1) of the *Loi relative à l'immigration et à l'intégration*, *supra* note IV.395 stipulates that the mayor of the town in which the immigrant is resident give her opinion on the integration of the person in question. It is the National Agency for the Reception of Foreigners and Migrations (*l'Agence nationale de l'accueil des étrangers et des migrations*) that is responsible for monitoring that integration, however. *See* Art. R. 311-29 of Decree 2006-1791, *supra* note IV.397.

criterion of difference in one state may not even be considered worthy of note in another.[403] This is why categories – especially for legal purposes – are society-specific rather than inherent, as already indicated. That said, '[s]tates tend to differ more in regard to the degree of self-ascribed and properly institutionalized meaning, than to the degree of cultural diversity'.[404] Some states simply acknowledge the reality of diversity more readily than others.

Whatever the relevant bases of distinction, however, efforts to maintain the 'identity' of majority society despite changing boundaries of membership are undertaken everywhere. Hence the increasing preoccupation with 'national values' in all European states.[405] Even the focus of the emerging European migration policy[406] on integration matters is also example of this practice – with the

---

403. Thus, the term 'ethnic group' in the UK Race Relations Act (1976) has been interpreted in a very specific manner, on the basis of cultural and racial criteria. (*See Mandla v. Lee*, UK House of Lords (1983)).

   In the United States, however, ethnicity is understood in terms of the geographical place (generally state) one's ancestors immigrated from. See Kibria (2002), p. 300–303. As the author notes, the states of origin concerned take an active role in strengthening feelings of attachment through a number of programs, including 'homeland trips'. In effect, classification in a given ethnic group is today purely a matter of choice, (often) devoid of cultural connotations; but *see* Louie (2002), p. 326 *et seq*. ('Under US multiculturalism, specific racial backgrounds become associated with sets of essentialized cultural traits'.) *ibid.*, p. 329.

   The constellation of identity politics in the United States results in curious classifications, in any case. The census of 2000, for example, included, under 'race', the following possibilities: White; Black; American Indian; Asian Indian; Chinese; Filipino; Japanese; Korean; Vietnamese; Native Hawaiian; Guamanian; Samoan; Other Pacific Islander; Other Race. (The existence of a Vietnamese or Chinese race is likely a surprise to any anthropologists that still apply this category of classification).

   In addition, the same census also included a question on Hispanic origin, with the following possibilities: Not Spanish; Hispanic or Latino; Mexican, Mexican-American or Chicano; Other Spanish, Hispanic or Latino; Puerto Rican; Cuban; Other. Clearly, this classification is also the result of a context-specific development in identities.

   In a literary vein:

   "It's just that you, for example, are one-quarter Russian, one-quarter Hungarian, one-quarter Polish, and one-quarter German". I didn't say anything "Actually", she said, "you could say you're three-quarters Polish and one-quarter Hungarian, since Bubbe's parents were from Poland before they moved to Nuremberg, and Grandma Sasha's town was originally in Belarus, or White Russia, before it became part of Poland". I turned to go. "Now that I'm thinking about it", she said, "I suppose you could also say you're three-quarters Polish and one-quarter Czech, because the town Zeyde came from was in Hungary before 1918, and in Czechoslovakia after, although the Hungarians continued to consider themselves Hungarian, and briefly even became Hungarian again during the Second World War. Of course, [y]ou could actually make sixteen different pie charts, each of them accurate"! I looked at the paper. "Then again, you could always just stick with half English and half Israeli, since–" "I'M AMERICAN"! I shouted. My mother blinked. "Suit yourself", she said and went to put the kettle on to boil. From the corner of the room where he was looking at the pictures in a magazine, Bird muttered: "No, you're not. You're Jewish". Krauss (2005), p. 95–97.

404. Tishkov (200), p. 642.
405. *See* BBC News, 'Schools "must teach Britishness"' (25 January 2007).
406. *See* discussion at Sec.II.C.1.a.

minor difference of an additional adjective, since 'European' values are now referred to. In a recent communication, for example, the Commission spoke of the need for programmes 'for newly arrived third-country nationals with the view of ensuring that immigrants understand, respect and benefit from common European and national values'.[407] While the nature of these values is distinctly hazy, as already discussed, the development of Common Basic Principles on Integration (in 2004) and the publication of the first Handbook on Integration (in November 2004) is certainly a sign that an 'EU approach to integration'[408] is being nursed. Given the express call for programmes that help migrants gain a 'basic knowledge about [the] language, history, institutions, socio-economic features, cultural life and fundamental values'[409] of the Member State in question at admission, it is nonetheless existing Member State integration policies that are to form the basis of any understanding of European integration.[410] That such integration is to be aimed at extra-EU (and not intra-EU) migrants is, moreover, a clear indication that the idea of a European 'us' and an outside 'Other' is present in the context of migration.[411]

With developments like these in mind, the propositions of some scholars with regard to integration are somewhat puzzling; in particular, then seem to overlook that changing boundaries of membership result in altered perceptions of collective identity. According to one recommendation, for example, 'in addition to all the rights foreigners have already been granted in different countries, they ought to enjoy the *full franchise as soon as they satisfy the general conditions of residence*'. Granted, this suggestion is quite unusual, but it is not outside the realm of (remote) possibility. However, the author then claims the following: 'This *total equalization of rights* need not deprive the *status of nominal citizenship* of any attraction and meaning. It would retain its *symbolic value* as a formal expression of membership in the polity, whereas others would be only informal members. Immigrants could choose this status as an expression of their commitment to their society of residence'.[412]

A transformation of this kind has not (yet) occurred even in a European Union increasingly involved in re-drawing the boundaries of membership, with a parallel identity project to boot. So how would a much more radical re-structuring of 'ins' and 'outs', as suggested by the author, occur without changing perceptions of membership? As a general matter, '[p]olitical socialization via transmission also

---

407. Sec. 2(2) of Commission Communication, 'A Common Agenda for Integration: Framework for the Integration of Third-Country Nationals in the European Union' (2005).
408. *Ibid.*, at Sec. 3.
409. Commission Communication on Integration, *supra* note IV.407, at Sec. 2(4).
410. It is worth noting that intra-Community policy on migrants has evolved from favouring passive assimilation in the state of residence to concern with the fundamental rights of citizens, including respect for cultural identity. *See* Nic Shuibhne (2002), p. 22.
411. *See also* discussion at Sec. II C.3.b.
412. Bauböck (1994a), p. 227 (emphasis added). For a more nuanced discussion of immigrant citizenship rights by the same author, *see ibid.* (1994b).
413. Faist (2001), p. 22.

means that ties towards [a] state are intrinsically tied to feelings towards members of such political communities. This implies that there is a close correlation between specific reciprocity and focused solidarity, on the one hand, and generalized reciprocity and diffuse solidarity, on the other hand'.[413] In other words, perceived modification of the bounds of membership results in altered understandings of what the consequences of such membership are. In the case of nationality in particular, granting all the rights of national citizenship to non-nationals means that the identity and rights functions of nationality are to be divvied up by legal status: permanent residence is to be the basis of rights, nationality that of identity. Consequently, only the identity function of nationality remains meaningful, while that of rights is necessarily reassessed.[414]

This is naturally a choice a state may make; but it is one that comes with consequences. Ordinarily, despite the 'relative mutability' of regulations governing the modes of acquiring nationality, two inter-related considerations are outcome-determinative for states: 1) 'the function that these norms play in the incorporation of foreigners into the population', as expressed in 2) particular 'modes of acquisition that will rarely assume a fundamental modification of the conception established by the legal order of a state of its own nationality'.[415] In the German case discussed, for example, the function of norms on acquiring nationality was integration; in turn, the suggested amendments to modes of acquisition were evaluated for their consistency with conceptions of what German nationality signifies.

A change as radical that suggested by the scholar above is far removed from the concept of nationality (or citizenship) as understood by any legal order and would indeed require modification of conceptions of membership. For example, the idea of having 'formal' and 'informal' members with the same rights is unusual – although it does mirror the reality of both European citizenship and status laws in many respects, even without full franchise. As previous chapters have demonstrated, both of these processes of legal evolution have affected understandings of membership and belonging in the relevant states. In the same way, the proposal above would necessarily transform the function that norms of membership play in the incorporation of foreigners – and would engender a new understanding of what nationality connotes.

Aside from this development, however, the near-exclusive focus of the proposal on the 'symbolic value' of nationality would likely be problematic.

---

414. Thus, increasing the (precarious) rights of foreigners while making nationality more difficult to attain may result in nationality becoming that much more valued as a sign of membership, based only on identity. *See* Rozakis (2001), p. 190 in the context of Greece. Bauböck in any case overestimates the importance of voting for the sake of civic participation and underestimates the symbolic role of national citizenship (and voting) as a sign of inclusion. *See* Shklar (1991), p. 3.
415. '*Relative mutabilité*', '*la fonction que ces normes jouent dans l'incorporation des étrangers à la population des Etats*' and '*modes d'acquisition qui rarement supposeront une profonde modification du concept consacré par l'ordre juridique d'un Etat de sa propre nationalité*'. Pérez Vera (1996), p. 300.
416. Spiro (2004), p. 101.

Exactly because of its prominence as a sign of 'commitment', the status of national would essentially serve only as a sign of identity. But it is exactly this, nationality's identity function that gains importance in situations of 'suspect' membership, as 'informal' membership is sure to be. As it is, suspicions crop up quite clearly in the context of non-nationals – e.g., legal permanent residents – and plural nationals, but may also surface in connection with nationals resident abroad for extended periods. In lieu of integration then, the unintended secondary effect of such a basic reconception of nationality status could be both irrelevance as a source of rights and excessive significance as a source (or confirmation) of identity.

2.   NATIONALITY AS CONFIRMATION OF IDENTITY

If nationality is to serve primarily as a confirmation of identity, however, – since all rights come through permanent residence – its identity function could develop in two parallel directions. On the one hand, the national identity it is hitched to may itself become suspect, or devalued. As Spiro warns, 'mandated inclusion may diminish state-based solidarities, as a legal definition of community replaces an organic one'.[416] Without the bundle of citizenship rights that flow from it, the legal status of 'nationality' could well become meaningless, since it entails few civic, social or political advantages. In turn, if few such bases of attachment to the state subsist, the linked identity function of the status also withers. This would be an especially acute danger in states that claim to found their national identities on civic norms and values. For example, if the vast majority of UK nationals are also nationals of other states – as a sign of respect for their ties to (the societies of) Greece, China or India, for example – the content of what it means to be 'British' becomes indistinct – and possibly increasingly meaningless. The 'British' thereby become a grouping of individuals with a particular legal status – no more and no less. In the long term this transformation could well blur the very distinctions between national identities it seeks to maintain.

On the other hand, as nationality's identity function disengages from the edifice of rights, it could also mutate into a purely cultural (or ethnic) category. Since the only difference between residents and nationals would be in the nature of their attachment to the state, it is not inconceivable that the boundary of membership should be re-drawn on the basis of intangible cultural or social ties like language, religion, descent, etc., for example. Nationality would then become but one status in competition with other, alternative frameworks, like status laws and diaspora statuses, that aim to give recognition to cultural and social ties. Indirectly, this evolution could even entail the danger of a turn-around on the general principle that nationality does not indicate a person's (ethnic) origins, since nationality would thereby be rendered an enduring personal attribute.[417]

---

417. *See* Art. 2 of the European Convention on Nationality.

Generally speaking then, although certain collective identities may be strengthened by the recognition of their legitimacy through legal ties, others weaken; depending on the individual, the same nationality could even be a central confirmation of belonging or a meaningless category of membership it is not even worth applying for. In either case, an explicit importation of identity recognition into legal categories transforms the function of nationality – and refashions concepts of attachment to the national community.

In a related concern, if we are to have a territorially-defined citizenship norm, requiring that permanent residents acquire membership, while nationality or an alternative status is to be a sign of a deeper (and in many cases necessarily non-territorial) sense of community, it is difficult to see how the state, as the locus of a given political community – responsible for distribution of resources and the protection of order and rights – is to maintain enough authority to function. If French citizens are not necessarily French nationals, because French nationality is a sign of a sense of membership that goes beyond 'just' rights, who is the French state then responsible for – citizens or nationals? And in what manner? Residence and common local interests are not necessarily enough of a tie to allow for agreement on (or even commitment to) questions of government beyond daily practice-solving:[418] common norms to underlie structures or the redistribution of resources, in particular, may be lacking.

Perhaps the concept of nationality ought to be scrapped altogether? Kostakopoulou has perhaps gone the farthest on this road to repudiation in recommending a 'system of automatic civic registration, thereby transcending the nationality model of citizenship'.[419] In this approach, all individual registered in a given jurisdiction would be entitled to the same rights; and could move freely from state to state, only to be re-registered each time. The author articulated this proposal in the context of a general critique of the UK's recent review of migration policy for disregarding the everyday processes that construct a sense of belonging; in the process, she herself forgot about the importance of perception, however.

For example, her assertion that '[b]y making knowledge of language and society prerequisites to naturalization, the government does not only symbolically reassert its traditional sovereign prerogative of determining who will be included as a formal member, but it also uses the borrowed vocabulary of national communitarianism in order to promote its vision of integration and membership'[420] is difficult to grasp. In the first place, the UK government's constant concern with integration – in a manner comparable to the German one, albeit with greater focus

---

418. But *see* Parekh (1995), p. 139 *et seq.* for an assertion that the state is the only necessary source of unity, in addition to criss-crossing and overlapping patterns of support by nationals; in other words, the only foundation for the community is to be political.

   Unfortunately, to the extent that the 'political' is itself partly culturally determined, the problem of interest and consensus has only been moved to a higher (albeit admittedly possibly less contentious) level of abstraction.
419. Kostakopoulou (2003), p. 93.
420. *Ibid.*, p. 108.

on social cohesion in tandem with diversity – should not be surprising in light of state interest in some kind of collective identity. And if it is not norms set by the state that determine membership in a state-focused community, it is difficult to know what should. The international community certainly cannot without infringing on the right to (or at least the logic of) self-determination, to the extent state X remains an agent expressing the will of people X. While basic principles, like the prohibition of racial discrimination, set a minimum standard, then, the capacity to define who the 'people' are remains a central state function.[421] (To the extent a group of states may decide to set common standards – as may be the case in the EU at some point in the future – the outcome is itself the result of sovereign action). With regard to Kostakopoulou's second assertion, the need for knowledge of English and social norms is not necessarily symptomatic of identity status quo maintenance (or of cultural assimilation), but a matter of basic civic necessity. It is a minimum standard of assent to a particular membership, of which residence is already an important indicator, while the extent of subjective allegiance is left up to applicant. If cultural and identificatory integration develops then, it does so independent of or only indirectly through naturalization.

Thus, while residence certainly creates entitlements – simply by the fact that the individual in question lives her daily life in the given milieu – and while concern for democratic legitimacy dictates that any individual affected by policies should have a say in their development, especially when she already holds partial rights of membership by virtue of residence, her suggestion for a system of civic registration simply goes too far. Simply put, it is difficult to imagine how a collectivity of individuals who do not speak the language of the majority society, who do not know much of its history or organizing principles and who are not necessarily accepted by that society, whatever their legal status, will ever be able to participate in either political or social life as equals, as demanded by the principles of modern democracies.

On the basis of exactly this reality, some commentators have suggested alternative forms of citizenship, such as the 'creat[ion of] transitional phases in which new residents can adjust to a new society and a new nationality'.[422] Conversely, external citizenship can also be seen as an 'intermediate membership tier[423]', distinct from resident citizenship in the country of origin. Such multi-level

---

421. *Inter alia*, Michael Walzer has repeatedly argued for the right of particular democratic, cultural communities to exist and govern themselves – in part by limiting immigration – on the basis of self-determination. Walzer (1994), p. 67 *et seq*. Other theorists have argued against this approach. *See* Benhabib (2004), p. 122. *See also ibid.* (2001) and Walzer's response in the same issue of the journal.

    As a general matter, issues of moral justice in the context of membership (and the rights that come with it) have been outside the scope of this study, not because their importance is not recognized, but because our focus has rather been on what states do – and why – with and within legal frameworks. For an excellent overview of philosophical arguments for and against open borders, *see* Bader (2005).
422. Van den Bedem (1994), p. 106.
423. Barry, p. 50.

or layered citizenship, with various statuses of partial belonging and rights on different scales – while possibly a 'short-term alternative' and a 'relief to second-class citizens of strong states'[424] does not amount to full membership, however; and may be perceived as exactly the second-class status one is trying to avoid. In a worst-case scenario, migrants may not be conceived of as full citizens in any political community, regardless of nationality status. For these reasons, the interaction of nationality and such 'intermediate' citizenships would need to be clearly enunciated in both states of origin and states of residence; particularly if the individuals are to be nationals, but not full citizens of given states, questions of equality are certain to arise. In any case, the identity function of nationality will again be altered through the introduction of such graded citizenships.

Alternatively, there is the possibility of segmented or fragmented citizenship, 'selectively available to different identity groups that match regimes'.[425] In substance, this version of citizenship would amount to the (re)introduction of separate legal statuses in place of national citizenship on the basis of religious or another cultural identities. Whether group-differentiated rights based on membership in cultural groups were introduced or an existing status (with or without attendant rights) were justified by cultural underpinnings, this possibility would inject identity matters into determinations of legal status in the most direct manner of all the alternatives discussed here.

Clearly, both functions of nationality would be undermined domestically by such a development, since the alternative statuses would guide both rights and identity. To the extent that various communities of rights would emerge in this scenario, the role of the state in 'national identity' maintenance would also be altered, since it would need to accommodate the additional, nested cultural statuses. A development of this kind would also serve to heighten the importance of both the state and the rights function of nationality internationally, however, since each state is likely to have its own, unique constellation of group-differentiated rights.

In a variant of this argument, some commentators have urged the creation of separate legal spheres or 'multicultural jurisdictions' within states.[426] Others have even foreseen a transformation of the international order, so as to re-adjust the existing territorially delineated system to accommodate overlapping authority and dual loyalties through international recognition of non-territorial political associations, like nations.[427] In this model, states would be complemented by a host of other communities in the international order. The reliance of certain Hungarian politicians on the nation as international actor in the context of the status law is also worth remembering here, since the suggested models are broadly comparable.

A larger question emerges from all of these proposals: 'can societal groups claim a certain kind of legal status, such as dual nationality or dual citizenship because this is conducive to uphold a certain way of life in transnational social

---

424. Brysk and Shafir (2004), p. 214.
425. *Ibid.*, p. 213.
426. *See* Schachar (2001). *See also* discussion in Scheinin (2004) and Gutmann (200), p. 431.
427. *See* Gottlieb (1993), p. 35 *et seq.*

spaces?'[428] As discussed, they already do. But how far must a state go in recognizing the diversity of the population within its borders when the state container has been pierced? For example, should a claim that 'the ultimate reason for granting expatriates a *right* to retain their nationality of origin is the fact that most people feel significantly attached to their national societies and cultures'[429] be given legal approval? This is, in fact, the same issue being negotiated in the context of European citizenship and status laws. Given that nationality is the only legal status of the three with a firm place in international law, as well as a long history, any state reply given with regard to nationality stands apart, however; the answer must negotiate both accepted ideas about the significance of this status and an existing legal frameworks.

So far, state reactions to demands for recognition of trans-state ties have been surprisingly uniform: while plural nationality is increasingly accepted, proof of links and, in the context of immigration, integration is required. Meanwhile, states rely more and more on habitual residence in family and personal law matters to narrow the influence of (non-EU member-) foreign state law, when permanent residents are not (yet) nationals.[430] In turn, the proposals made by numerous scholars for civic registration, intermediate or segmented citizenships point to a range of possible directions for nationality to evolve. Despite such developments, there has not yet been a general recognition that 'there can be no definitive general law that determines who belongs and who does not, because the criteria and standards are subject to change and redefinition as the composition of society and the citizenry changes over time'.[431]

As our Conclusion will show, the three processes of legal evolution discussed here are instead attempts by European states to manage the fluidity of belonging – and the inadequacy of law in dealing with the lack of fixed categories – as multicultural claims spread across borders.

---

428. Faist (1999), p. 18.
429. Rubio-Marín (2006), p. 142 (emphasis in original).
430. *See* general discussion in Mansel (2003).
431. Klopp (2002), p. 185.

Conclusion

> *We here and that man, this man, and that other in-between, and that woman,*
> *this woman, and that other, whoever,*
>
> *those people, and these, and these others in-between, this thing, that thing,*
> *and this other in-between, whichever...*
>
> Nammalwar, 'The Paradigm', ca. 850

In 1997, a scholar claimed that 'nation states are adapting to ... new pressures by changing their functions. For example, ... the nation state no longer crystallizes and organizes domestic capital, but ... continues to police inward labour flows and seeks to galvanize, although with diminishing capacity, a single identity around a national leadership, common citizenship and social exclusion of outsiders'.[1] The meaning of many of these terms – 'nation state', 'single identity' and 'outsiders' may be in flux, but the message of adaptation holds true. States are indeed reacting to changing circumstances – including the evolving interdependence of rights and identities and the institutions and cultural communities that maintain them – in part by negotiating new norms of membership, as reflected by new legal statuses.

The necessity of membership remains unchanged, then. In fact, if it is generally true that '[t]he central focus of collective identities is the combination of the definition of distinctiveness of any collectivity, with the specification of the criteria of membership in it; and of the attributes of the similarity of the members of these collectivities',[2] then this holds doubly true for contemporary states. The emphasis on clearly delineated borders – whether real or imagined, exemplified by fences or passport control – and the reliance of all modern democracies on legal

---

1. Cohen (1997), p. 156.
2. Eisenstadt (2003), p. 78.

classification means that '[t]erritory and membership are closely related. Indeed political territory as we know it today.... *presupposes* membership'.[3]

The predominant (ideal) form of membership in the 20th century, national citizenship, is no longer the only, nor even the main, game in town, however. The fusion of its two components – citizenship and nationality – is increasingly coming undone, as distinctive functions (re-)surface. Nationality, in particular, seems to be undergoing significant transformation. Heretofore the sole individual-state link recognized for international law purposes, it has traditionally been the principal legal status not only for its rights function – as the basis for claims of diplomatic protection or as a gateway to citizenship rights – but also for that of identity. The assumed existence of a special bond (of loyalty or at least attachment) between national and state – of a nationality that constitutes a relevant component of individual identity – has thus been central to the discussion and practice of nationality regulation.

The three processes of legal evolution examined here, each in its own way, deconstruct the individual-state link and reconstruct it on the basis of new (or retooled) statuses. The possibilities for variation include kinship laws, which rely on the existence of an ethereal nation, embodied in a particular state, as the keystone for a status that binds individual and kin-state not only symbolically but also through special rights and benefits. As the Hungarian case showed, it is this development that is considered most dangerous and unwelcome, at least in the short-term. Given that kinship laws neither aspire to replace nationality nor to undermine it in any particular manner, this may be surprising. For the state whose nationals are targeted, however, such laws represent legal bonds that interfere with the identity function of their own nationality regulation.

Another modulation of the theme of new statuses is European Union citizenship, which, though a corollary to Member State nationality, is an ever-more obvious candidate (or victim) for Commission-led efforts at nursing a European (cultural) identity, not to mention the E.C.J.-steered depreciation of the relevance of nationality for rights purposes. Though we saw the nebulous nature of both processes, it is ever more apparent that nationality is no longer the fundamental status of individuals from EU Member States, at least; and that whatever identity function is finally attributed to Union citizenship, it will influence how Swedish or Portuguese nationality is viewed by those who hold it.

Finally, the emergence of plural nationality as an acceptable and even welcome phenomenon, rather than an 'evil', demonstrates a reversal of the fundamental assumption that the status of nationality is the link between one individual and one state only. It seems that individuals may now be members of numerous state-centred communities, even if the exact scope of this membership and its attendant rights varies when the relevant persons are not in the territory of a

---

3. Brubaker (1992), p. 22. In fact, the 'state', as a way of thinking about the world and, more conceretely, of approaching political and social membership, can likely be considered a cultural idiom (or, in the terminology of Theda Skocpol, a built-in interest). Theorizing its demise is thus premature.

state of nationality. As the German case showed, however, integration – especially in the context of immigration – is often considered a counterpart to any accommodation of multiple membership. For this reason, the foreseeable effects of accepting a plurality of memberships on the identity function of nationality may not be as comprehensive as would otherwise be the case.

In substance then, such debates on nationality, like all the legal statuses discussed here, are part of a larger negotiation of identities. By engaging in such negotiation, states can 'remain a structuring force of [the] collectivity, defining the limits of recognition'.[4] Bases of solidarity, social bonds, equality, internal peace and obviously membership – all are reconsidered and reinvented in the process. Such negotiation also allows states to remain – or, in the case of the EU, to become – relevant, as the basis of their legitimacy is reinforced both in- and outside their borders. The social and political processes of identity negotiation in various states may interact and clash, however, as particular points of consensus (at a given point in time) are eventually fixed in legislation and policies. When these have external effects – as the legal statuses discussed here all do – both other states and the international system are affected.

In fact, the developments discussed here raise larger questions for legal and political theory, since existing approaches do not provide much guidance on supplementary forms of membership. Are any new statuses to be recognized as equivalent to, or in a limited area, comparable to – as yet unique – nationality, for example? Should membership in culturally defined communities unbounded by a given state even be available? And how is international law to deal with them? The emergence of EU citizenship, kinship laws and plural nationality all compel us to consider an abundance of novel issues and tendencies.

In the first place, all three statuses demonstrate that traditional state borders no longer signify the limits of membership, nor of control. Above all, the principles of personal and territorial sovereignty, still crucial props in shoring up the international system, are reconstituted in distinct ways by each. As discussed above, the territory of the state has traditionally been sacrosanct, at least for (most) other states; while authority over nationals was questioned only in exceptional circumstances, including when the state had submitted to the jurisdiction of particular courts. But individuals who are European citizens, plural nationals or members of a kin-minority increasingly tote the dominion of other states (and entities) into the territory of their states of residence directly, regardless of nationality status. Thus, Slovenia accepts the benefits granted by Hungary to kin-minority individuals; Belgium takes into account the naming practices of Spain for certain European citizens, who also happen to be its nationals; and the UK accepts the multitude of diaspora ties maintained by its residents. While the principle of territoriality has certainly maintained or even gained in influence in

---

4. Kastoryano (2002), p. 6.
5. As evidenced by the UNESCO Convention on the Diversity of Cultural Expressions, discussed above, in the context of public international law; or, in private international law, as seen in Art. 11 of the Rome Convention on the Law Applicable to Contractual Obligations (1980).

some areas of law then,[5] it has also been undermined by the emergence of such legal statuses.[6] That said, it remains an important factor in attenuating the parallel erosion of singular personal sovereignty.

This erosion has occurred in a multitude of ways. The acceptance of plural nationality certainly challenges the indivisibility of state control over nationals, for example, even if it does so on the basis of a status firmly embedded in the international order. Still, states can rely on equally established rules favouring the state of residence to manage particular challenges to their authority, as discussed above. Social, cultural and other diaspora policies, in turn, rely either on nationality or, more ambiguously when statuses like 'former-national' are created, on 'transnational' claims in encouraging practices that weaken the unity of personal sovereignty. To the extent states of residence (and sometimes nationality) do not object to the maintenance of such ties, they are accepted practice with potential benefits for all parties involved; but they change the status quo of control nonetheless. Consent, implied or direct, is also what underpins the encroachment of EC/EU law into policy areas – including culture, education and welfare – that are traditionally associated only with the state, with the caveats discussed above.

Finally, in targeting individuals who are neither nationals nor residents, status laws challenge states both in their personal and territorial sovereignty. More threatening still, they do so in the name of 'minority protection' – a politically sensitive issue – in direct geographic proximity to the home-states. On a normative level then, they are the most disruptive of developments in the name of identity. To defend them, one could reason on the basis of variants on principles of minority protection (for individuals); or draw parallels to the right to self-determination (at least in cultural matters) for particular groups; or – in light of the growing reliance in both EC/EU law and international instruments on the 'right of cultures' *qua* cultures to exist – to the legitimate interest of states in fostering 'their' culture in regions where persons express an interest. But any attempt to balance normative arguments finally comes down to the question of whether one believes that certain cultural identities should be legalized. The answer given to this question also guides one's understanding of membership.

In essence, we are dealing with overlapping possibilities of membership, then: personal or territorial. Benhabib is thus quite right when she states that the 'new politics of membership is about negotiating [the] complex relationship between the rights of full membership, democratic voice, and territorial residence'.[7] Each of the three processes presented here plots a different course. But there are inherent limits to the constellation of possible answers. The logic of democratic legitimacy

---

6. Most clearly, this is the case in human rights, but also EC/EU law. The original draft of the Services Directive (Proposal for a Directive of the European Parliament and of the Council on Services in the Internal Market) from 2004, for example, foresaw the importation (or at least acceptance) of the standards and legislation of other Member States within the territory of a particular Member State (see, especially Arts 16 to 19); the well-established 'state of origin' principle would thus have been extended to services. After a hefty backlash, the Directive was considerably watered down.
7. Benhabib (2004), p. 20.

demands that the deterritorialization of community only go so far, for instance: law is to bind those individuals who authorized their making and whose chosen representatives are held accountable through the electoral process. Clear demarcation through membership thus remains necessary and retains a territorial component – but there are now new issues in setting borders.

To the extent that globalization has rendered state boundaries increasingly permeable – as social rights give way to market mechanisms and political and judicial authority shifts to the supra-national – the content of national citizenship has already been subverted to a considerable degree.[8] But clear borders retain an important function nonetheless: they 'remain significant not so much for keeping sovereignty and citizenship tightly bounded in political space, but because they are remaking domains of value'.[9] In other words, even when they do not structure particularized sets of rights and duties, borders serve to separate 'ins' and 'outs'.

In turn, the demarcation of borders continues to rely on claims of distinctiveness in all three of the processes presented here and constitutes our second theme. The kind of particularity – language? values? traditions? – asserted by a given community is less important in this regard than the fact of simultaneous reliance on some degree of commonality among members, whether nationals, citizens or kin, as the case may be.[10] It is ultimately the boundaries themselves that help maintain any collective identity, rather than particular content:[11] while being French may mean different things to different people (at different points in time), the affirmation and re-affirmation of laws on membership helps delineate and sustain the existence of the 'French'. Thus, '[p]rovided that assimilation to a common identity is not ruled out by descent-based criteria, the core of common national identity is a common commitment to the welfare of the larger society ... and mutual trust in others to abide by that commitment even when it entails sacrifices'.[12] This recognition of solidarity as the core of a shared collective identity goes far in explaining why the E.C.J. has extended European citizenship rights to the realm of social benefits, as noted above; in turn, the critique heaped on this course of action demonstrates that,

---

8. Regardless of legal status then, those with certain backgrounds (especially the upper classes) live the transnational lives written of by many commentators, while those with inadequate education (but especially the poor) find themselves increasingly unable to practice even their most basic citizenship rights. In this sense, class continues to matter more than nationality for most individuals.
9. Ong (2004), p. 56.
10. In other words, whether the state has clear cultural requirements for membership or whether these are 'civic' in nature makes a difference, obviously; but, as discussed, it is more of degree than kind. The need for self-perpetuation means that even universal principles are tinted by history and the particularities of the society that interprets them.

    For example, the questions raised by Muslim immigration to Western Europe – the role of religion in public life, in particular – has crystallized around different issues in each state. 'The issue at the forefront of debate in Britain, State aid to separate Islamic schools, is not even on the political agenda in France. On the other hand, a very controversial issue in France, students' wearing of the *hijāb* in public schools, has been settled in Britain and Germany with little fanfare'. Fetzer and Soper (2005), p. 132.
11. Compare Barth (1994) [1969], pp. 14–15.
12. Barry (2001), p. 88.

contrary to the Court's assumption, a common European identity is not yet salient enough to shoulder such commitment. Solidarily also underlies the logic of kinship laws and the bonding mechanisms formulated by states of origin in the context of migration.

References to the role of 'culture' and 'cultural identity' in domestic discussions of membership thus have more to do with trust – with some representation of a commonly-held, if not universal view of who we can 'trust' for the purposes of maintaining the community – than with particular cultural practices.[13] The real issue is thus not whether someone celebrates Divali or St Stephen's Day, but whether they are similar enough to members of the community to be accepted into it. The borders of acceptance – of belonging – fluctuate with time. Still, the development and maintenance of a collective identity is more likely to succeed when individuals have relatively clear means of identifying members of the 'in-group', as our presentation of social identity theory showed: this is why language, dress and customs play such an important role as markers of belonging in many societies.

And this is the crux of the problem: the markers of commonality must be publicly established and enforced to be maintained. If the underlying assumption of the identity claims discussed above is that certain collective identities should be publicly recognized – in other words officially sanctioned in some manner, rather than sublimated, or, in the European context, simply noticed – there comes a turning point when identity maintenance and preservation become (in perception if not in fact) a matter for positive action and even legalization. This is why all the legal statuses discussed here make reference to clear hallmarks, whether shared language, history, traditions, norms or just the 'common culture' of the national or European identity they lay claim to. On the basis of delineated criteria then, membership is circumscribed. In the context of national identity, it is laws on nationality that serve this function; but other collective identities have had only limited official recognition until recently.

As a component of this boundary-setting process, nationality comes with a great deal of luggage: legal history, widely accepted functional roles, present-day political and social understandings, psychological value – all of which inform its further development. The need for effective sociological connection[14] that appeared for the first time in the French Law on Nationality of 1889 has in any case become a permanent element of practically all laws on nationality since that time. The perception of nationality, as an ever-evolving concept in which the attachment traditionally required can be understood in minimal or maximal terms, is conditioned by circumstances, however. With regard to its identity function, in particular, while numerous factors account for the traditional

---

13. *See also ibid.* (2001), p. 86. Durkheim's early description of solidarity as 'collective representation' – or shared beliefs, evaluations and symbols – was an expression of this same idea in slightly different terms. Durkheim (1965) [1912], p. 471. Whether such representation coheres into a collective identity and becomes institutionalized (in norms on nationality, for example) depends on a number of factors.
14. Weil (2001a), p. 59 (emphasis in original).

assumption that nationality has a constitutive role to play in individual identity, it is increasingly a discourse of respect for identity – especially for migrants or national minorities – as something to be publicly acknowledged that has endowed the question of legal status with emotional content. Previously, debate on this status centred on the importance of granting citizenship rights instead. Considering this turn toward identity, there is a distinct danger of nationality becoming a 'cultural manifestation', one of an increasing number of legal statuses with primary identity functions.

While ongoing discourse on and changes to laws on membership are part and parcel of collective identity maintenance then, the ever-increasing number of claims for public recognition in diverse identities threaten the monopoly of the very statuses that serve as examples to be emulated. If individuals are simultaneously European citizens, kin, external citizens and nationals, which legal tie is pre-eminent, for example? For the moment it is nationality, although European citizenship comes a close second. To the extent individuals, in particular, nurture and promote cultural identities – which divide and exclude by definition – the public sphere becomes infused with particularities that serve to undermine the commonality that is the basis for community distinction. As one scholar has noted, '[r]egarding citizenship as an identity, the investment of one's emotive allegiances and loyalties in the subnational, deterritorialized categories of ethnicity and race revoke the abstractions from one's communal and natural ties that have historically underpinned "civic" life, thus cutting off the ties that bind the members of that state'.[15]

Competing national identities have the longest history of being perceived as a threat to such distinction, for obvious reasons;[16] but the rise of 'neo-national' groups is a new twist on an old dilemma.[17] Membership in such groups may cross borders or encompass only some of the state's nationals, but nonetheless relies on traditions of citizenship and nationalist sources. In the process, the claims-making of migrant and autochthonous minority communities across borders – like those of the Hungarian minorities or of immigrants who wish to keep and institutionalize ties to their old homeland – forces the emergence of new legal frameworks.[18] The legal interaction of such cultural – especially religious – communities and national ones is becoming increasingly fraught, however, not only because of the depth of emotions aroused, but also because the necessarily non-territorial nature of the former is seen as a threat to the territorial sovereignty and claimed cultural distinctness of the nation state.[19]

---

15. Joppke (1998), p. 24.
16. Compare Theiler (2003), p. 264.
17. Feldblum (2003), p. 241.
18. In the context of religious communities, *see* Riad, who has advocated the drafting of a European Code of Muslim law, based entirely on a contemporary interpretation of *shari'a* in line with universal principles of human rights (Riad 1992).
19. When a given cultural community is state-focused, 'culture' easily becomes reified as something 'belonging' to the particular state; it becomes an object of protection, like land or the intangible power of sovereignty, especially in its incarnation as heritage or tradition.

What to make of Mexican politicians who regularly visit communities in Texas and California to lobby for Mexican (financial or political) state interests, for example? (These states in particular could incidentally ring bells in the context of the Mexican-American War of 1846–48.) And the foundation of the Romanian party in Italy or 'expat' parties in Spain, discussed above? Or the regular meetings between Hungarian kin-minority politicians with members of the Hungarian government? Are these positive developments that advance personal liberty? Or are they rather dangerous tendencies that undermine the international order?

To the extent the legal statuses discussed here are a *'legalized' in-betweenness* – one in which (some of) the individual's myriad attachments are given official acknowledgement – the difference between belonging and membership in state-centred societies, already referred to, becomes crucial. This is the third notable theme of the processes of legal evolution discussed here. While belonging is, as discussed, an intangible matter of individual-group dynamics, of social ties and interactions the state has no control over – and could not regulate in any case – membership presents an opportunity for clear boundary-drawing, traditionally through the mechanism of nationality. Accordingly, individuals with the nationality of the given state are clearly members of the specific community, with official, state-administered documents to prove their status. It is with the interaction of the two – belonging, as social process, and membership, as rigid formula – that real difficulties arise, however, to the extent that the fluidity of the former and the rigidity of the latter lead to incongruities. (Thus, an individual perceived as one who 'belongs' may not be a national, and vice versa.) These gaps are what kinship laws, plural nationality and even European citizenship step into. Each has a different take with regard to the cause-effect relationship of belonging and membership, however. Status laws, for example, are an attempt to give legal recognition – including in the form of physically tangible certificates or other documents – to assumed, existing ties of belonging.[20] In the case of European citizenship, however,

---

The recently adopted UNESCO Convention on the Diversity of Cultural Expressions is, as noted, the first instrument to sanction this approach at the international level – so that the trend seems to be on the upswing. Even when the community is not (principally) state-focused, however, or when focus is not on the state in which members of the community are resident, existing social (and legal) frameworks constrain claims and expressions of cultural identity. *See, inter alia,* the balancing of individual and public interests in a case before the German Constitutional Court on the right of a public school teacher to wear a headscarf. BVerfG (2003), 2 BvR 1436/02, esp. para. 47.

For this reason, contested situations are framed in terms that fit existing categories in given states. As Barry discusses, in the context of the UK Race Relations Act (1976), there is an incentive to code wearing a headscarf as an ethnic cultural practice to bring it within scope of legal protection. In the French context, there is an incentive to code the same practice as religious. *See* Barry (2001), pp. 57–59.

20. In this context, *see also* the idea of a *'citoyenneté de la francophonie'*, discussed by the Commission on Nationality in France in 1987–1988, in light of *'les implications que peut avoir l'appartenance commune au même ensemble culturel'*. *Rapport Long, Tome II, supra* note Intro.7, pp. 59–60. The Report goes on to note that settling on a definition for this *'ensemble'* is likely to pose difficulties.

membership is a given (as a corollary of Member State nationality), while belonging is, as yet, in the process of formation.

It is perhaps the phenomenon of plural nationality that brings such considerations most clearly to the fore, as states set requirements for the acquisition of nationality (in the context of naturalization) or for its maintenance (in the context of birthright nationality) at varied points of an imagined spectrum between belonging, as a matter of purely subjective feeling, and membership, with objective criteria. Thus, language and civic or history tests, as well as, of late, integration courses may be required of individuals before or after naturalization, in addition to possible demands to relinguish previous nationality. Others, hoping to maintain more than one nationality, may be required to make clear declarations of intent or give evidence of attachment to a particular state before being allowed to continue as plural nationals. Such prerequisites – and, more publicly, debates on the subject – are palpable signs of attempts to set identifiable minimum standards for belonging, such as speaking the official or dominant language of the state, before the status of 'member' may be assumed. Given diverse understandings of the 'nation' or 'people', particular states set the bar for official recognition at different points on the continuum.

Officially recognized membership is not simply a legal formula, then. It is an increasingly salient social and cultural fact. The stronger the identity function of a given legal status and the more legal statuses created to give recognition to claimed cultural distinction, however, the more sociological questions of recognition by self and others enter into law; and the more complex psychological and emotional elements of belonging are embedded in a practice ill-equipped to deal with it. Simply put, '[i]t is difficult for the law to deal with feelings and evaluations of this kind: it is one thing to say "I am French", which usually means "I feel French", quite another to be legally so, and yet a third, recognized by the law of some countries, to be recognised as such by the state'.[21]

The fourth issue raised in the context of all these legal statuses is thus whether to confer 'a *legal effect to individual belonging*'[22] – and if so, which community the individual is to be a member of. (And on which basis)? Even if nationality is to maintain its privileged position – and events in the last few years certainly point to an ever-central role – what is to happen to individuals with plural nationality? The idea that nationality is a sign of cultural attachment (*à la* Mancini) is dangerous, if not new. But the introduction of rights discourse also adds a new dimension to demands for recognition of particular identities via legal status.

Through claims of a 'right' to plural nationality or kinship status – though not European citizenship, for now – identity becomes not only the proclaimed basis for law, but itself an object of legal regulation. A given collective identity is thereby codified, in language or integration requirements, and firmly anchored in particularized criteria of membership for individuals, as in the context of

---

21. Casuto (2001), p. 45.
22. '*Un effet juridique à l'appartenance de l'individu*'. Gutmann (2000), p. 374.

German nationality or Hungarian kinship. Or, vice versa, the existence of prescribed commonalities, such as shared values, norms and heritage, is claimed to constitute a (European) identity that, in turn, serves to legitimize particular policies.

The proliferation of statuses discussed above results directly from such processes of legalization: they constitute attempts at state adaptation through the reconstitution of membership and belonging in the face of pre-existing constellations of facts. In this sense, European states are merely reacting to social processes (and identities) individuals – subjects of law – demand legal recognition of. Thus, politicians and scholars (but, in a telling sign, few citizens) argue about what constitutes the 'European citizen'; members of Hungarian minorities demand some legal status to reflect recognition of their ties to Hungary; while migrants and, more generally, individuals with ties to multiple states demand that states make provision for the plural membership they believe should come with such links. The danger here is clear: the very injection of identity issues – the need for 'convergence between the feeling of one [person] and the perception of another'[23] before the form (and content) of recognition can be agreed on – creates a new dilemma of control.

Questions of control are raised not only by the challenge to borders, pointed out above, but also, in the fifth issue of note, by *the interaction of law and identity*. All of the legal statuses discussed here – each part-and-parcel of a general negotiation of what defines 'us' as Hungarians, Germans or European citizens – attempt discreetly or quite overtly to mandate identity. Most transparently, as we saw in the context of the Hungarian status law or the *Statusdeutsche* – and as the new French law on integration confirmed – they require that individuals conform to the characteristics of the 'German' or 'Hungarian' set out in legislation to be recognized as such by the states in question.[24] But the prescription works in more covert ways too. As Bourdieu noted, 'we create the categories by which we construct the social world; and these categories produce the world, within the limits of their correspondence with pre-existing structures'.[25] Thus, any act of nomination or classification defines our perception of reality. In an example from a very different discipline, the consignment of the former-planet Pluto to 'dwarf planet' status resulted in

---

23. '*Convergence entre le sens de l'un et le perçu de l'autre*'. Gutmann (2000), p. 213.
24. *See also* Guenancia (1995), p. 570 ('*La constitution de l'identité n'est pas seulement la tâche de nombreux savoirs, peut-être même de toute connaissance, c'est aussi un acte éminemment social; exister socialement c'est recevoir une identité, être inscrit sous cette identité dans des registres et, en droit tout au moins, être susceptible d'être reconnu partout et tout au long de son existence come le même individu. Il y a une fonction sociale, pratique de l'identité même si cette fonction d'ordre et de classement ne fait pas toute la signification, ni la signification essentielle, de la notion d'identité.*')
25. '*[N]ous produisons les catégories selon lesquelles nous construisons le monde sociale et ces catégories produisent le monde ... dans les limites de leur correspondance avec des structures préexistantes*'. Bourdieu (1986), p. 13.

quite a bit of controversy (and sympathy) in some corners for exactly this reason[26] – a 'dwarf planet' just does not have the same cachet as its larger cousins.

Legal categorization, in particular, can create social reality, due to the prescriptive role of law in modern societies. Thus, 'a new order of legal classification results in a new mode of organizing what is real'.[27] As we observed, the existence of the category of 'European citizen', as well as of 'third-country national' have affected a new division of 'us' and 'them', even without measures from 'Brussels' aimed at generating identification, for example. On this basis, the multiplicity of legal statuses discussed here simultaneously expand and constrict the range of publicly recognized cultural identities available. On the one hand, they allow for officially recognized memberships in cultural communities in ways not heretofore available – and are in that sense a new source of freedom in identity matters. On the other hand, these laws and policies also set out expectations, including, but not limited to language skills, origins, proper values and encouraged activities to demarcate those same identities. Of course, no individual is forced to seek confirmation of a given identity or to reap the benefits that may flow from official membership. In that sense, there is no compulsion.

But there is a further concern. While questions of this kind are not generally for states to care about in so familiar a manner, the linkage of legal status with cultural identities results in an unusual interaction. In effect, the functions of socialization discussed above – including the internalization of a group prototype – are institutionalized.[28] We see a concrete instance of what Bourdieu has called the 'dialectic of the internalization of externality and the externalization of internality',[29] as the requirements of law are incorporated into collective expectations and vice versa. In this manner, legal authority continues to be a unique form of power, especially when it is used to establish categories that are essential to the maintenance of public order. For the individual in particular, legal personality comprises more than a state controlled, permanent characteristic. In essence, 'after having proceeded for its own needs to simplify the concrete person, [law] in turn influences the *sense* of the concrete person of remaining the same through time and [changing] situations'.[30] The real problem is one of process and classification,

---

26. *See*, 'Debate Lingers Over Definition for a Planet'. *The New York Times* 1 September 2006 and 'Resolution 6A: Definition of Pluto-class Objects' of the International Astronomical Union (passed 24 August 2006).
27. *'[D]u nouvel ordre de classement juridique résultera un autre mode d'organization du réel'.* Caillosse (2004), p. 33. *See also* Roussel (2004), pp. 50–51.
28. Since sentiments of belonging are at once private (to the extent they are an element of self-fulfilment and an expression of identity-maintenance) and public (since they depend on recognition by others in the community), public perceptions become crucial when such legalization occurs.
29. Bourdieu (1977) [1972], p. 72 (emphasis removed). *See also ibid.* (1980), p. 1.
30. *'Après avoir procédé pour ses besoins propres à une réduction de la personne concrète, influe en retour sur le sentiment de la personne concrète de demeurer la même au travers du temps et des situations'.* Gutmann (2000), p. 13 (emphasis in original). A parallel process is also present

however, since any link of law and identity assumes 'a veritable philosophy of personal identity, centred on the idea that, at least from the legal point of view, an immutability of the essential characteristics of the person exists'.[31] The potential for mischief in this approach is, perhaps, evident.

This potential is all the greater today, in light of the processes presented above. To the extent that cultural rights remain an underdeveloped category – and in any case one whose promotion remains firmly in state hands – and given near unfettered state discretion in managing legal statuses, the linkage of identity issues with particular legal statuses, at least at the level of rhetoric, is unlikely to disappear in the near future. The characteristic fluidity of belonging, *qua* sociological process, does not allow for fixed membership, however. It does not belong in law; and results only in statuses of partial membership. This is why, as multicultural claims spread across borders and the impossibility of creating a bounded group of members becomes manifest, the two traditional state-linked forms of membership take on new forms: citizenship is taken apart, its rights and identity functions redistributed among newly created statuses, while nationality becomes, simultaneously, more than a legal status and a mere piece of paper.

Once the rights function of a given status (such as citizenship) has been lost or transformed beyond recognition, however, its identity-function also evolves. This is the sixth point to remember. Joppke's perception of parallel de- and re-ethnicization in the migration policies of a number of states is especially pertinent in this regard,[32] since the increased mobility of individuals, coupled with an ever louder call for respect of individual identity has resulted not only in a more flexible approach to singular loyalty and unique membership, but also greater emphasis on community, generally defined in the fuzziest of terms. Hence the constant references to identification with and attachment to a given community, whether European, national or kin: the individual need for belonging is increasingly couched in the right of the community to demand a degree of commitment, so that proof of a common sense of identity is required and affirmed.[33]

Certainly, this strain of 'individual in communal' thinking is new to public discussion on norms of membership. As such, the attempted legalization of modes of belonging – essentially their fixation in norms of membership – has resulted in 'jurisgenerative politics',[34] as the content of the identities themselves are debated.

---

in the law itself. In the realm of human rights, for example, individuals are considered abstract and universal 'persons' for the purposes of applying general principles, while their distinctiveness (race, culture, religion, language, nationality, etc.) is recognized in practical application.

31. *'Une véritable philosophie de l'identité personelle, centré sur cette idée qu'il existe, au moins du point de vue juridique, une immutabilité des caractéristiques essentielles de la personne'*. *Ibid.*, p. 376.
32. Joppke (2005).
33. But, for a recent instance of a purely liberal approach, *see* Benhabib, who argues for a 'human right to membership', including an entitlement to all civil and political rights, after first admission. Benhabib (2004), p. 136 *et seq*. Thus, even if admission does not imply automatic membership, it does mean a cascade of rights that, in time, are to result in it.
34. Michelman (1988), p. 1495.

Naturally, all legal development serves as a catalyst for social transformation in some manner, since 'symbols like law not only refer to or express something, but themselves exercise structuring and constituting power in day-to-day, political and other spheres, by penetrating these in a subtle and diffuse manner'.[35] But questions of membership are singular in their perceived significance not only because they mandate (or at least inform) perceptions and identities, but also because they determine access to rights and benefits.

Though this second basic function of nationality and citizenship, not to mention of our three new legal developments, has received less attention in this discussion than identity matters, the theme of rights and benefits has nonetheless interlaced our discussion, as well it should. The continued practical importance of such rights and benefits is thus the seventh point to recall. The derivate rights of European citizenship are what have an effect on the daily lives of individuals, after all; and it is simultaneously on the basis and through further extension of these rights that the profile and meaning of the status is hoped to be raised. These same individual rights and benefits – not the rhetoric of European citizenship – are also which may upset the content and meaning of national identities, at least for now. In a similar fashion, it was the character of the benefits granted by the (first) Hungarian status law that elicited consternation and claims of interference, even if identity issues accounted for both the benefits and the hostility of some home-states. And it was at least in part (some would say wholly) the benefits of the (first) law that help explain the high number of applications. In turn, it is (hoped-for) financial, political, social and other benefits that drive states of emigration to develop diaspora policies; the advantages of which individuals accept not only for sentimental reasons, but also for convenience. Finally, plural nationality offers a double set of rights to its holders, while attendant responsibilities are in most cases muted by geographical distance from at least one of the states. For states, the acceptance of the phenomenon offers the advantage of either maintaining or developing official ties with persons who wish to belong to the given national communities.

Accordingly, if nationality is truly a distributable resource,[36] a prize unevenly distributed among individuals by fate of birth and bargained for by migrants, then the legal statuses discussed above transform calculations. For some, holding on to the nationality of the state of origin may matter less if they have the option of remaining 'former nationals', with attendant rights, especially if their state of residence still discourages plural nationality. For members of kin-minorities, the educational and cultural benefits provided by status laws may make the difference between sending their children to a majority-language school and a minority-language one, with foreseeable effects on degrees of assimilation/integration. For the person who realises that her right to be treated equal to the nationals of

---

35. *'Symbole wie Recht verweisen nicht nur auf etwas oder sind der Ausdruck von etwas, sondern üben selbst strukturiende und konstituierende Kraft in alltäglichen, politischen usw. Bereichen aus, indem sie diese in subtiler und oft diffuser Weise durchdringen'*. Haltern (2003), p. 23. *See also* Horváth (forthcoming).
36. Shachar (2003).

the Member State in which she is an expat stems from European citizenship, the recognition may make the difference between support and rejection of the European project; it may also factor in her decision not to apply for nationality in that Member State since she does not 'need' it. A 'realist' may even go so far as to say that identity matters are but a gloss to camouflage the selective extension or curtailment of membership – and a corresponding manipulation of collective identity – to fit the consequences of decisions governed, in large part, by economics. Though I would not go so far as to agree completely with such a view, it contains a kernel of truth. But it does not change the importance of identity as a framing mechanism, which organizes our perspective of reality.

In addition to engendering new approaches to matters of membership and belonging, the processes of legal evolution presented have also woven a fresh web of legal relationships. The nature of some of these liaisons, like the one between European citizenship and Member State nationality, has already been discussed. But the newfangled relationships also raise new legal issues, which constitute our final point of discussion. We will mention only a few here, relating especially to the European Convention on Nationality.

As a general matter, the phenomenon of plural nationality raises the most prominent questions for now, exactly because the status of 'national' (still) retains its special role for the purposes of international law. As the long history of attempts to deal with the conflicting rights and duties of multiple nationalities canvassed above demonstrated, this particular legal problem is not new; states have tried to balance the multiplicity of individual-state ties maintained by plural nationals for decades. Still, the changed approach to plural nationality has also generated new questions for resolution both domestically and internationally, as we will see below.

Conversely, despite the important role they play in domestic and regional systems, the supplementary forms of membership presented here have no legal effect under international law. For this reason, they do not raise comparable questions of conflict at present. The fact that a Hungarian minority individual is a 'status Hungarian', for example, means nothing for international law purposes, despite the fact that it is a new form of horizontal link to another state. In a more obvious manner, European citizenship is no threat to the status of nationality, not only because it is a quantitatively different, vertical link between state and individual, but also because it has clearly and repeatedly been subordinated to Member State nationalities. This does not mean that other legal questions may not arise, however. With regard to European citizenship, for example, giving practical application to the right to protection by the diplomatic or consular authorities of any Member State, guaranteed in ECT Article 20,[37] requires the co-operation of third states, both because only action by the state of nationality is recognized automatically under international law and because the third state is not a party to the ECT (on the basis of

---

37. *See* Green Paper on diplomatic and consular protection of Union citizens in third countries (2006). *See also* proposals 7–11 of the Barnier Report, prepared by Michel Barnier at the request of the Commission and the Council (2006).

the principle of *pacta tertii nec nocent nec prosunt*). Thus, Member States (and the EU) must obtain the consent of the relevant third countries to be able to exercise their duty of protection.

The legal issues raised by kinship ties are more complex. For example, Article 5(1) of the European Convention on Nationality establishes that the rules of state parties on nationality may not be discriminatory in nature, including on the basis of 'national or ethnic origin'. This is fully in line with the generally accepted view that nationality is not a sign of ethnic origin. The Explanatory Report to the Convention, however, explains that 'facilitated acquisition of nationality due to descent or place of birth' is a 'justified ground of distinction' (i.e., preferential treatment) rather than discrimination.[38] Kinship laws that provide for nationality (e.g., that of Slovakia, which has ratified the Convention) would probably also draw a line between 'distinction' and 'discrimination'; as would the proponents of preferential provisions in the nationality regulations of many European states.

Consistent separation of the two is not quite so simple a matter, however. Legal status is not a multifaceted process, like minority protection, in which one can make a plausible argument that preferential treatment for members of the minority does not constitute discrimination against members of the majority; it is rather, by nature, a simple question of ins and outs. Preferential treatment of persons with particular roots necessarily lowers the membership chances of those without these same roots. Moreover, ethnic origin is not something applicants can control, like language capabilities. It is given and unchanging; and incidentally increasingly rejected as the basis for any kind of differential treatment in both practice and theory. Some signatories of the Convention have in fact not taken the reassurance of the Explanatory Report at face value. Certain states with 'distinctive' provisions, including Greece and Italy, have signed but not ratified the Convention – no wonder, perhaps, since no reservation may be made to Article 5(1).

Germany, however, ratified this instrument in 2005, while lodging a noteworthy declaration. The declaration states that 'the admission of late expatriates (*Spätaussiedler* ...) is not aimed at acquiring German nationality and that it is not part of any procedures relating to nationality'.[39] Technically, this is true; their admission is a matter of immigration. However, in light of the fact that German nationality is attributed to *Spätaussiedler* automatically, this kind of argumentation is facetious. The note that 'the admission procedures may involve waiting periods of several years' since quotas have been introduced – while Article 10 of the Convention requires that applications be processed 'within a reasonable time' – seems to serve as an additional argument to support the German rationale, but instead betrays the dubious nature of the initial distinction made. If nonetheless accepted, the German argument would also apply to other, much commented-upon of state practices in which facilitated kin-migration is intertwined with the

---

38. *See* Explanatory Report on the European Convention on Nationality (1997), paras 39–42.
39. Declaration contained in the instrument of ratification, completed by a letter from the Permanent Representative of Germany, deposited on 11 May 2005 (2005).

attribution of nationality, including that of Greece, Israel and Spain (with regard to Sephardic Jews) – none of which are bound by the provisions of the European Convention of Nationality, however.

Another issue raised in light of the growing acceptance of plural nationality is whether the Convention – at present neutral with regard to the practice – should adopt a protocol expressly recognizing it. Given recent trends in Europe, this step would only mirror the evolution already underway in domestic legislation; but it would also take a clear stance on a much-debated practice for the purposes of (regional) international law. More intriguingly, if the Council of Europe does take this route, should it do so as a manifestation of respect for the identity rights of individuals? Given the frequency with which identity matters are now formulated in the language of rights – as discussed, both in the guise of 'cultural rights' and a right to a specific nationality – the idea is not particularly outlandish.

If this is done, however, some thought needs to be given to the new legal statuses presented here. What justification – besides the historical pre-eminence of nationality – can be given for recognizing that particular expression of 'social ties of attachment' (to use the words of *Nottebohm*) but not kinship laws or even European citizenship? Although neither is likely to displace nationality as the pre-eminent legal status for the purposes of international law in the near future, some concrete accommodation (or even recognition) of such developments in regional and international norms should be considered. Otherwise, the rights and benefits that flow from them – not to mention their identity function *per se* – could create considerable political tension among the states concerned. Whether or not the processes of legal evolution presented here will, in fact, influence regional and general international legal norms, as new forms of individual–state ties are acknowledged, they have already altered understandings of (the function of) nationality and citizenship, as well as the role of identity matters in norms of membership.

References

E. PRIMARY MATERIALS

1. LEGAL INSTRUMENTS

a. **International (Conventions, Treaties, Recommendations and Resolutions)**

i. *Bilateral Conventions and Treaties*

Austria and Czechoslovakia, Brunn Treaty (7 June 1920)
Austria and Italy, Paris Agreement (Gruber-Degasperi Agreement) (1946)
Austria and Italy, South Tyrol Package (1969)
Belgium and Bolivia, Treaty between Belgium and Bolivia (18 April 1912)
Bulgaria and Greece, Treaty between Bulgaria and Greece (27 November 1919)
Bulgaria and Romania, Treaty between Bulgaria and Romania (24 September 1959)
China and Indonesia, Treaty between China and Indonesia (22 April 1955)
France and Algeria, *Accord relatif aux obligations du service national* (1983)
France and Switzerland, Treaty between France and Switzerland (23 July 1879)
Germany and Bolivia, Treaty between the German *Reich* and Bolivia (22 July 1908)
Germany and Honduras, Treaty between the German *Reich* and Honduras (12 December 1887)
Germany and Persia, Treaty between the Germany and Persia (17 February 1929)
Germany (DDR) and USSR, Treaty between the German Democratic Republic and the USSR (11 April 1963)
Hungary and Allied Powers, Treaty of Trianon (4 June 1920)

Hungary and Bulgaria, Treaty between Hungary and Bulgaria (27 June 1958)
Hungary and Croatia, *Szerződés a Magyar Köztársaság és a Horvát Köztársaság között a baráti kapcsolatokról és együttmûködésrõl* (Convention between the Republic of Hungary and the Republic of Croatia on friendly relations and co-operation) (1992)
Hungary and Croatia, Convention between the Republic of Hungary and the Republic of Croatia on the protection of the Hungarian minority in the republic of Croatia and the Croatian minority in the Republic of Hungary (1995)
Hungary and Czechoslovakia, Treaty between Hungary and Czechoslovakia (11 April 1960)
Hungary and Romania, Treaty between the Republic of Hungary and Romania on Understanding, Co-operation and Good Neighborhood (1996)
Hungary and Romania, Memorandum of Understanding between Romania and Hungary (22 December 2001)
Hungary and Romania, *Megállapodás a szomszédos államokban élõ magyarokról szóló törvény romániai alkalmazásáról* (Agreement between the Government of Romania and the Government of the Republic of Hungary on Implementation of the Amended Benefit Law in Romania) (2003)
Hungary and Slovakia, Treaty on Good-Neighbourly Relations and Friendly Cooperation between the Republic of Hungary and the Slovak Republic (1995)
Hungary and Slovakia, *Megállapodás a Magyar Köztársaság Kormánya és a Szlovák Köztársaság Kormánya között a nemzeti kisebbségek kölcsönös oktatási és kulturális támogatásáról* (Agreement between the Government of the Republic of Hungary and the Government of the Slovak Republic on Mutual Educational and Cultural Support of National Minorities) (2003)
Hungary and Slovenia, Convention on providing special rights for the Slovenian minority living in the Republic of Hungary and for the Hungarian minority living in the Republic of Slovenia (1992)
Hungary and Slovenia, *Barátsági és együttmûködési szerzõdés a Magyar Köztársaság és a Szlovén Köztársaság között* (Convention on friendship and co-operation between the Republic of Hungary and the Republic of Slovenia) (1992)
Hungary and Ukraine, Declaration on the principles of co-operation between the Republic of Hungary and the Ukrainian Soviet Socialist Republic in guaranteeing the rights of national minorities (1991)
Hungary and Ukraine, Declaration of the Prime-Ministers of Hungary and Ukraine (2 August 2001)
Portugal and Brazil, Convention of Brasilia (1971)
Hungary and Ukraine, *Szerzõdés a jószomszédság és az együttmûködés alapjairól a Magyar Köztársaság és Ukrajna között* (Convention on good-neighbourliness and the bases of co-operation between the Republic of Hungary and Ukraine) (1991)
United Kingdom (Great Britain) and Brazil, Treaty on Dual Nationality between Great Britain and Brazil (29 July 1922)

United States and Iran, Claims Settlement Declaration of the Democratic and Popular Republic of Algeria concerning the Settlement of Claims by the Government of the United States and the Government of the Islamic Republic of Iran (1981)

*ii.	Multilateral Instruments*

Council of Europe, European Convention for the Protection of Human Rights and Fundamental Freedoms (1950) (CETS No. 5)
Council of Europe, European Convention on Extradition (1957) (CETS No. 24) and subsequent Protocols (1975, 1978) (CETS Nos. 86 and 98)
Council of Europe, Parliamentary Recommendation 164 on the Reduction of the Number of Cases of Multiple Nationality (1958)
Council of Europe, Convention on the Reduction of Cases of Multiple Nationality and Military Obligations in Cases of Multiple Nationality (1963) (CETS No. 43) and attendant Additional Protocol (1977) (CETS No. 95) and Second Protocol (1993) (CETS No. 149)
Council of Europe, Committee of Ministers Resolution 72(1) on the Standardisation of the Legal Concepts of 'Domicile' and of 'Residence' (1972)
Council of Europe, Additional Protocol to the Convention on the Reduction of Cases of Multiple Nationality and Military Obligations in Cases of Multiple Nationality (1977) (CETS No. 96)
Council of Europe, Committee of Ministers Resolution 77(12) on the Nationality of Spouses of Different Nationalities (1977)
Council of Europe, Committee of Ministers Resolution 77(13) on the Nationality of Children Born in Wedlock (1977)
Council of Europe, European Declaration on Cultural Objectives (1984)
Council of Europe, Committee of Ministers Recommendation R 84(9) on Second-Generation Migrants (1984)
Council of Europe, Parliamentary Recommendation 1081 on Problems of Nationality in Mixed Marriages (1988)
Council of Europe, Parliamentary Recommendation 1201 on an Additional Protocol on the Rights of Minorities to the European Convention on Human Rights (1993)
Council of Europe, Framework Convention on the Rights of National Minorities (1994) (CETS No. 157)
Council of Europe, Helsinki Declaration on the Political Dimension of Cultural Heritage Conservation in Europe, adopted at the 4th European Conference of Ministers Responsible for the Cultural Heritage (1996)
Council of Europe, Resolution No. 1, The Cultural Heritage as a Factor in Building Europe, adopted at the 4th European Conference of Ministers Responsible for the Cultural Heritage (1996)

Council of Europe, European Convention on Nationality (1997) (CETS No. 166)
Council of Europe, Parliamentary Recommendation 1410 on Links between Europeans Living Abroad and their Countries of Origin (1999)
Council of Europe, Protocol No. 12 to the Convention for the Protection of Human Rights and Fundamental Freedoms (2000) (CETS No. 177)
Council of Europe, Conclusions of the Fifth European Conference of Ministers Responsible for the Cultural Heritage (2001)
Council of Europe, Parliamentary Resolution 1314 on the Contribution of the Council of Europe to the Constitution-Making Process of the European Union (2003)
Council of Europe, Parliamentary Resolution 1335 on the Preferential Treatment of National Minorities by the Kin-state: the Case of the Hungarian Law on Hungarians Living in Neighbouring Countries ('Magyars') of 19 June 2001 (2003)
Council of Europe, Parliamentary Recommendation 1650 on Links between Europeans Living Abroad and their Countries of Origin (2004)
Council of Europe, Convention on the Avoidance of Statelessness in Relation to State Succession (2006) (CETS No. 200)
International Labour Organization, Convention No. 169 concerning Indigenous and Tribal Peoples in Independent Countries (1991)
League of Nations, Hague Convention on Certain Questions relating to the Conflict of Nationality Laws (1930)
Organization of African Unity, African (Banjul) Charter on Human and Peoples' Rights (1981)
Organization of African Unity, African Charter on the Rights and Welfare of the Child (1990)
Organization of American States, Bustamante Code (adopted at the Sixth International Conference of American States) (1928)
Organization of American States, (Montevideo) Convention on Nationality (1933)
Organization of American States, (Montevideo) Convention on the Nationality of Women (1933)
Organization of American States, American Convention on Human Rights (1969)
Organization of American States, Additional Protocol to the American Convention on Human Rights in the Area of Economic, Social and Cultural Rights (1988)
OSCE/CSCE, Helsinki Final Act (1975)
OSCE/CSCE, Document of the Copenhagen Meeting of the Conference of the Human Dimension of the CSCE (1990)
UNESCO, Convention Concerning the Protection of the World Cultural and Natural Heritage (1972)
UNESCO, Recommendation on Participation by the People at Large in Cultural Life and their Contribution to it (1976)
UNESCO, Draft Declaration on Cultural Rights prepared by the UNESCO Project Concerning a Declaration of Cultural Rights (11th version, 1996)
UNESCO, Convention for the Safeguarding of the Intangible Cultural Heritage (2003)

UNESCO, Convention on the Protection and Promotion of the Diversity of Cultural Expressions (2005)
United Nations, Charter of the United Nations (1945)
United Nations, Statute of the International Court of Justice (1945)
United Nations, Universal Declaration of Human Rights (1948)
United Nations, Convention Relating to the Status of Stateless Persons (1954)
United Nations, Convention on the Nationality of Married Women (1957)
United Nations, General Assembly Resolution 1497 (XV) on The Status of the German-speaking Element in the Province of Bolzano (Bozen); Implementation of the Paris Agreement, of 31 October 1960 (1960)
United Nations, Convention on the Reduction of Statelessness (1961)
United Nations, General Assembly Resolution 1661 (XVI) on The Status of the German-speaking Element in the Province of Bolzano (Bozen), of 28 November 1961 (1961)
United Nations, Vienna Convention on Diplomatic Relations (1961)
United Nations, Vienna Convention on Consular Relations (1963)
United Nations, Optional Protocol to the Vienna Convention on Consular Relations Concerning Acquisition of Nationality (1963)
United Nations, Declaration on the Elimination of All Forms of Racial Discrimination (1963)
United Nations, International Covenant on Civil and Political Rights (1966)
United Nations, International Covenant on Economic, Social and Cultural Rights (1966)
United Nations, Optional Protocol to the International Covenant on Civil and Political Rights (1966)
United Nations, Declaration on the Elimination of Discrimination Against Women (1967)
United Nations, Vienna Convention on the Law of Treaties (1969)
United Nations, Convention for the Reduction of Cases of Statelessness (1973, not in force)
United Nations, General Assembly Resolution 3274 (XXIX) on the Question of the Establishment, in Accordance with the Convention on the Reduction of Statelessness, of a Body to which Persons Claiming the Benefit of the Convention May Apply, of 10 December 1974 (1974)
United Nations, Convention on the Elimination of All Forms of Discrimination against Women (1979)
United Nations, Declaration on the Human Rights of Individuals Who are not Nationals of the Country in which They Live, UN Doc. No. A/40/53 (1985)
United Nations, Convention on the Rights of the Child (1989)
United Nations, Declaration on the Rights of Persons Belonging to National or Ethnic, Religious and Linguistic Minorities (1992)
United Nations, Resolution 1995/24 on the Rights of Persons Belonging to National or Ethnic, Religious and Linguistic Minorities (1995) (See UN Doc. E/CN.4/1995 L.32 for draft)

b.   European Union

Treaty Establishing the European Community (Consolidated) (OJ 1997 C 340/3) (1997) [1957]
Council Directive 64/221/EEC of 25 February 1964 on the coordination of special measures concerning the movement and residence of foreign nationals which are justified on grounds of public policy, public security or public health (OJ 1964 L 56/850)
Communiqué for the Conference of Heads of Government in Paris on 9 and 10 December 1974, EC Bulletin 12/7 (1974)
Council Directive 76/207/EEC of 9 February 1976 on the implementation of the principle of equal treatment for men and women as regards access to employment, vocational training and promotion, and working conditions (OJ 1976 L 39/40)
Rome Convention on the Law Applicable to Contractual Obligations (OJ 1980 L 266/1) (1980)
Council Directive 90/364/EEC of 28 June 1990 on the right of residence (OJ 1990 L 180/26)
Council Directive 90/365/EEC of 28 June 1990 on the right of residence for employees and self-employed persons who have ceased their occupational activity (OJ 1990 L 180/28)
Conclusions of the Ministers of Culture meeting within the Council of 12 November 1992 on guidelines for Community cultural action (OJ 1992 C 336/1)
Treaty on European Union (Maastricht Treaty) (OJ 1992 C 191/1) (1992)
Parliament Resolution on the Commission communication entitled 'New Prospects for Community cultural action' (OJ 1993 C 42/173) (1992)
Agreement on the European Economic Area (OJ 1994 L 1/3) (1992)
Council Directive 93/96/EEC of 29 October 1993 on the right of residence for students (OJ 1993 L 317/59)
Parliament Resolution on Linguistic and Cultural Minorities in the European Community (OJ 1994 C 61/110) (1994)
Concluding Document of the Inaugural Conference for a Pact on Stability in Europe *as found in* Council Decision of 14 June 1994 on the continuation of the joint action adopted by the Council on the basis of Article J.3 of the Treaty on European Union on the inaugural conference on the Stability Pact (94/367/CFSP) (Annex) (OJ 1994 L 165/2) (1994)
Convention of 10 March 1995 on simplified extradition procedure between the Member States of the European Union (OJ 1995 C 78/2)
Decision of the Representatives of the Governments of the Member States meeting within the Council of 19 December 1995 regarding protection for citizens of the European Union by diplomatic and consular representations (OJ 1995 L 314/75)

Convention Implementing the Schengen Agreement (1990) as incorporated by the Schengen Protocol to the Treaty of Amsterdam (1997)

Convention of 27 September 1996 relating to extradition between the Member States of the European Union (OJ 1996 C 313/12)

Decision No. 716/96/EC of the European Parliament and of the Council of 29 March 1996 establishing a programme to support artistic and cultural activities having a European dimension (OJ 1996 L 99/20)

Council Decision 96/664/EC of 2 November 1996 on the adoption of a multiannual programme to promote the linguistic diversity of the Community in the information society (OJ 1996 L 306/40)

Treaty of Amsterdam amending the Treaty on European Union, the Treaties Establishing the European Communities and Related Acts (OJ 1997 C 340/2) (1997)

Stability Pact for South-Eastern Europe, Cologne Document (1999)

Charter of Fundamental Rights of the European Union (OJ 2000 C 364/1) (2000)

Decision No. 508/2000/EC of the European Parliament and of the Council of 14 February 2000 on establishing the Culture 2000 programme (OJ 2000 L 63/1)

Council Directive 2000/43/EC of 29 June 2000 implementing the principle of equal treatment between persons irrespective of racial or ethnic origin (OJ 2000 L 180/22)

Council Directive 2000/78/EC of 27 November 2000 establishing a general framework for equal treatment in employment and occupation (OJ 2000 L 303/16)

Council Regulation 44/2001 of 22 December 2000 on jurisdiction and the recognition and enforcement of judgments in civil and commercial matters (OJ 2001 L 12/1)

Council Regulation 539/2001/EC of 15 March 2001 listing the third countries whose nationals must be in possession of visas when crossing the external borders and those whose nationals are exempt from that requirement (OJ 2001 L 81/1)

Council Resolution of 21 January 2002 on the Role of Culture in the Development of the European Union (OJ 2002 C 32/2)

Council Framework Decision 2002/584/JHA of 13 June 2002 on the European arrest warrant and the surrender procedures between Member States (OJ 2002 L 190/1)

Council Regulation (EC) No. 859/2003 of 14 May 2003 extending the provisions of Regulation (EEC) No. 1408/71 and Regulation (EEC) No. 574/72 to nationals of third countries who are not already covered by those provisions solely on the ground of their nationality (OJ 2003 L 124/1)

Council Directive 2003/86/EC of 22 September 2003 on the right to family reunification (OJ 2003 L 251/12)

Council Regulation 2201/2003 of 27 November 2003 concerning jurisdiction and the recognition and enforcement of judgments in matrimonial matters and the matters of parental responsibility, repealing Regulation 1347/2000 (OJ 2003 L 338/1)

Regulation 2004/2003 of the European Parliament and of the Council of 4 November 2003 on the regulations governing political parties at European level and the rules regarding their funding (OJ 2003 L 297/1)

Treaty Establishing a Constitution for Europe (OJ 2004 C 310/1) (2004)

Council Directive 2003/109/EC of 25 November 2003 concerning the status of third-country nationals who are long-term residents (OJ 2004 L 16/44)

General budget of the European Union for the financial year 2004/ Education and Culture (OJ 2004 L 53 II/789)

Decision No. 626/2004/EC of the European Parliament and of the Council of 31 March 2004 amending Decision No. 508/2000/EC establishing the Culture 2000 programme (OJ 2004 L 99/3)

Decision No. 792/2004/EC of the European Parliament and of the Council of 21 April 2004 establishing a Community action programme to promote bodies active at the European level in the field of culture (OJ 2004 L 138)

Council and Parliament Directive 2004/58/EC of 29 April 2004 on the right of citizens of the Union and their family members to move and reside freely within the territory of the Member States (OJ 2004 L 229/35)

Council Decision No. 2004/849/EC of 25 October 2004 on the signing, on behalf of the European Union, and on the provisional application of certain provisions of the Agreement between the European Union, the European Community and the Swiss Confederation concerning the Swiss Confederation's association with the implementation, application and development of the Schengen acquis (OJ 2004 L 368/26)

Council Decision of 22 December 2004 providing for certain areas covered by Title IV of Part Three of the Treaty establishing the European Community to be governed by the procedure laid down in Article 251 of that Treaty (OJ 2004 L 396/45)

Regulation (EC) No. 562/2006 of the European Parliament and of the Council of 15 March 2006 establishing a Community Code on the rules governing the movement of persons across borders (Schengen Borders Code) (OJ 2006 L 105/1)

Decision No. 1718/2006/EC of the European Parliament and of the Council of 15 November 2006 concerning the implementation of a programme of support for the European audiovisual sector (MEDIA 2007) (OJ 2006 L 327/12)

Decision No. 1855/2006/EC of the European Parliament and of the Council of 12 December 2006 establishing the Culture Programme (2007 to 2013) (OJ 2006 L 378/22)

Decision No. 1904/2006/EC of the European Parliament and of the Council of 12 December 2006 establishing for the period 2007 to 2013 the programme Europe for Citizens to promote active European citizenship (OJ 2006 L 378/32)

Council Regulation (EC) No. 168/2007 of 15 February 2007 establishing a European Union Agency for Fundamental Rights (OJ 2007 L 53/01)

c. National

Argentina, Constitution (as amended to 2006) (1853)*
Armenia, Constitution (as amended to 2006) (1995)
Austria, *Bundesgesetz über die Gleichstellung von Südtirolern mit österreichischen Staatsbürgern auf bestimmten Verwaltungsgebieten* (BGBl. 57/1979) (1979)
Austria, *Bundesgesetz über die österreichische Staatsbürgerschaft* (StbG) (BGBl. 311/1985) (as amended) (1985)
Austria, *Tiroler Landesordnung* (Constitution) (1989)
Austria, *Entschliessung des Tiroler Tandtages vom 23. November 1994* (1994)
Austria, *Verordnung des Bundesministers für Wissenschaft und Verkehr über die Festlegung von Personengruppen bei der Zulassung zu ordentlichen Studien (Personengruppenverordnung)* (BGBl. II, 211/1997) (1997)
Austro-Hungarian Empire, *Allgemeinen Bürgerlichen Gesetzbuch für die gesamten Deutschen Erbländer der Österreichischen Monarchie* (AGBG) (1812)
Austro-Hungarian Empire, *Reichsverfassung für das Kaisertum Österreich vom 4. März 1849* (1849)
Belgium, *Code de la Nationalité* (as amended) (1984)
Bulgaria, Constitution (as amended to 2006) (1991)
Bulgaria, Law for the Bulgarians living outside the Republic of Bulgaria (2000)
Croatia, Constitution (as amended to 2006) (1990)
Croatia, Act on Nationality (as amended) (1991)
Czech Republic, Act on Citizenship (1993)
Denmark, Nationality Act (Consolidated) (1999)
Dominican Republic, Constitution of the Dominican Republic (2002)
Egypt, Law No. 391 (on Citizenship) (1956) (abrogated in 1958)
Egypt, Constitution of the Arab Republic of Egypt (as amended to 2006) (1971)
Estonia, Citizenship Act (as amended in 1998) (1995)
France, *Code Civil* (as amended to 2006)
France, Constitution (1946, no longer in force)
France, Constitution (as amended to 2006) (1958)
France, *Loi No. 98-170 relative à la nationalité*. Published in the *Journal Officiel* 17 March 1998
France, *Loi No. 2003-1119 du 26 novembre 2003 relative à la maîtrise de l'immigration, au séjour des étrangers en France et à la nationalité*. Published in the *Journal Officiel* 27 November 2003
France, *Projet de loi de finances pour 2004, adopté par l'Assemblée nationale, Tome I, Culture, La Progression des Dotations* (2004). At: <www.senat.fr/leg/index.html>.*

---

* All Constitutional texts are those found at 'Constitutions of the Countries of the World', unless otherwise indicated.
* All sites last visited on 15 March 2007.

France, *Loi No. 2004-228 du 15 mars 2004 encadrant, en application du principe de laïcité, le port de signes ou de tenues manifestant une appartenance religieuse dans les écoles, collèges et lycées publics*. Published in the *Journal Officiel* 17 March 2004

France, *Loi No. 2006-911 du 24 juillet 2006 relative à l'immigration et à l'intégration*. Published in the *Journal Officiel* 25 July 2006

France, *Décret no. 2006-1791 du 23 décembre 2006 relatif au contrat d'accueil et d'intégration et au contrôle des connaissances en français d'un étranger souhaitant durablement s'installer en France et modifiant le code de l'entrée et du séjour des étrangers et du droit d'asile (partie réglementaire)*. Published in the *Journal Officiel* 31 December 2006

Georgia, Constitution (as amended to 2006) (1995)

Germany (North German Federation), Constitution (1867)

Germany (North German Federation), *Gesetz zur Erwerbung und den Verlust der Bundes- und Staatsangehörigkeit* (BGBl. 1870, 355) (1870)

Germany (*Deutsches Reich*), Constitution (1871)

Germany (*Deutsches Reich*), *Einführungsgesetz zum Bürgerlichen Gesetzbuche* (EGBGB)(RGBl. 604) (as amended to 2006 and re-published in BGBl. I, 2494) (1896)

Germany, *Staatsangehörigkeitsgesetz* (StAG) (RGBl., 583) (as amended to 2006) (1913)

Germany, *Kontrollratsgesetz Nr. 1 betreffend die Aufhebung von NS-Recht* (ABl. 6) (20 September 1945)

Germany, *Grundgesetz* (as amended to 2006) (1949)

Germany (DDR), Constitution (1949, no longer in force)

Germany, *Gesetz über die Angelegenheiten der Vertriebenen und Flüchtlinge* (BVFG) (BGBl. I, 203) (1953)

Germany, *Gesetz zur Regelung von Fragen der Staatsangehörigkeit* (BGBl. I, 65) (1955)

Germany (DDR), Constitution (1968, no longer in force)

Germany, *Gesetz über Maßnahmen für im Rahmen humanitärer Hilfsaktionen aufgenommene Flüchtlinge* (Kontingentflüchtlingsgesetz) (BGBl. I, 1057) (1980)

Germany, *Gesetz über die Festlegung eines vorläufigen Wohnortes für Aussiedler und Übersiedler* (BGBl. I, 1378) (1989)

Germany, *Vertrag zwischen der Bundesrepublik Deutschland und der Deutschen Demokratischen Republik über die Herstellung der Einheit Deutschlands* (BGBl. 1990 II, 889) (1990)

Germany, *Gesetz über die Einreise und den Aufenthalt von Ausländern im Bundesgebiet* (AuslG) (BGBl. I, 1354) (1990) (since 2005 covered by the AufenthG)

Germany, *Gesetz zur Neuregelung des Ausländerrechts* (BGBl. I, 1354) (1990)

Germany, *Gesetz zur Bereinigung von Kriegsfolgengesetzen* (KfbG) (BGBl. I, 2094) (1992)

Germany, *Bekanntmachung der Neufassung des Bundesvertriebenengesetzes* (BGBl. I, 829) (1993)
Germany, *Verwaltungsvorschrift des Innenministeriums über die Aufnahme und die ausländerrechtliche Behandlung jüdischer Emigrantinnen und Emigranten aus der ehemaligen Sowjetunion* (VwV-jüdEmigr) (4-13-GUS/6) (1996)
Germany, *Zweites Gesetz zur Änderung des Gesetzes über die Festlegung eines vorläufigen Wohnortes für Spätaussiedler* (BGBl. I, 223) (1996)
Germany, Bundesrat, *Gesetzesbeschluß des Bundesrates* (21 May 1999) (BR-Dr. 296/99)
Germany, *Gesetz zur Reform des Staatsangehörigkeitsrechts* (StAGReformgesetz) (BGBl. I, 1618) (1999)
Germany, *Gesetz zur Klarstellung des Spätaussiedlerstatus* (BGBl. I, 2266) (2001)
Germany, *Gesetz zur Steuerung und Begrenzung der Zuwanderung und zur Regelung des Aufenthalts und der Integration von Unionsbürgern und Ausländern* (ZuWG) (BGBl. I, 1950) (2004)
Germany, *Gesetz über den Aufenthalt, die Erwerbstätigkeit und die Integration von Ausländern im Bundesgebiet* (AufenthG) (published as ZuWG Art. 1, BGBl. I, 1950) (2004)
Germany, *Verordnung über die Durchführung von Integrationskursen für Ausländer und Spätaussiedler* (IntV) (BGBl. 2004, I, 3370) (2004)
Germany, Declaration contained in the instrument of ratification of the European Convention on Nationality, completed by a letter from the Permanent Representative of Germany, deposited on 11 May 2005 (2005)
Greece, Legislative Decree 3370/1955 on the ratification of the Code of Greek Nationality (as amended) (1955)
Greece, Law 1975/1991 on the Acquisition of Greek nationality by Aliens of Greek Origin (1991)
Greece, Law 2130/1993 on the supporting documents required for the acquisition of Greek nationality by aliens of Greek origin (1993)
Greece, *Décision ministérielle commune No. 4000/3/10/e des Ministres de l'Interieur, de la Défense, des Affaires étrangères, du Travail et de l'Ordre public du 15.4.1998 sur les conditions, la durée et la procédure d'octroi de la carte d'identité spéciale aux ressortissants albanais d'origine grecque* (1998)
Greece, Law 2790/2000 on the Reinstatement of the returning people of Greek origin from the former Soviet Union and other stipulations (2000)
Greece, Law 2910/2001 on the Entry and residence of foreign persons in Greek Territory, Acquisition of Greek nationality by naturalization and other stipulations (as amended by Law 3013/2002) (2001)
Hungary, *1879. évi L. törvény* (1879)
Hungary, Constitution (as amended to 2006) (1949)
Hungary, *1980. évi 2. Törvényerejű rendelet a Magyar Népköztársaság és a Román Szocialista Köztársaság között a kettős állampolgárság eseteinek megoldásáról és megelőzéséről Bukarestben, 1979. július 13-án aláírt Egyezmény kihirdetéséről* (Ordinance 2 on the Proclamation of the Accord signed on 13 June 1979 between the People's Republic of Hungary and the Romanian

Socialist Republic on the Prevention and Solution of Cases of Dual Nationality) (1980)

Hungary, *1992. évi VII. törvény a Magyar Népköztársaság és a Román Szocialista Köztársaság között a kettős állampolgárság eseteinek megoldásáról és megelőzéséről Bukarestben, 1979. július 13-án aláírt Egyezmény kihirdetéséről szóló 1980. évi 2. törvényerejű rendelet hatályon kívül helyezéséről* (Law VII on the abrogation of Ordinance 2 on the Proclamation of the Accord signed on 13 June 1979 between the People's Republic of Hungary and the Romanian Socialist Republic on the Prevention and Solution of Cases of Dual Nationality) (1992)*

Hungary, *1993. évi LXXVII. törvény a nemzeti és etnikai kisebbségek jogairól* (Law LXXVII on the Rights of National and Ethnic Minorities) (1993)

Hungary, *1993. évi LV. törvény a magyar állampolgárságról* (Law LV on Hungarian Nationality) (1993)

Hungary, *2001. évi XXXIX. törvény a külföldiek beutazásáról és tartózkodásáról* (Law XXXIX on the Entry and Stay of Foreigners) (2001)

Hungary, *2001. évi LXII. törvény a szomszédos államokban élő magyarokról* (Law LXII on the Hungarians Living in Neighbouring States) (2001). An English translation of the Act is available at: <www.kum.hu/Szovivoi/Aktualis/actSTeng.htm>.

Hungary, *2003. évi LVII. törvény a szomszédos államokban élő magyarokról szóló 2001. évi LXII. törvény módosításáról* (Law LVII on the Amendment of Law LXII of 2001 Concerning the Hungarians Living in Neighbouring States) (2003)

Hungary, *A nemzeti kulturális örökség miniszterének 18/2003. (XII. 10.) NKÖM rendelete a szomszédos államokban élő magyarokról szóló 2001. évi LXII. törvény hatálya alá tartozó személyeket megillető kulturális kedvezményekről* (Ordinance 18/2003 of the Minister of National Cultural Heritage on the Benefits Due to Individuals Covered by Law LXII on Hungarians Living in Neighbouring States) (2003)

Hungary, *Az oktatási miniszter 36/2003. (XII. 27.) OM rendelete a szomszédos államokban élő magyarokról szóló 2001. évi LXII. törvény oktatást érintő rendelkezéseinek végrehajtásáról szóló 47/2001. (XII. 29.) OM rendelet módosításáról* (Ordinance 36/2003 of the Minister for Education on the Amendment of Ordinance 47/2001 on the Implementation of the Provisions on Education set forth in Law LXII on Hungarians Living in Neighbouring States) (2003)

Hungary, *198/2003. (XII.10.) Korm.r. a Magyar Köztársaság Kormánya, valamint Szerbia és Montenegró Minisztertanácsa között az állampolgáraik utazásának feltételeiről szóló, Budapesten, 2003. október 21. napján aláírt Megállapodás kihirdetéséről* (Government Ordinance 198/2003 on the Proclamation of the

---

* All Hungarian laws accessed through the web-site of the Parliament, for lack of access to *Magyar Közlöny*, at: <www.complex.hu/kzlcim/kzl90_96>.

Understanding signed on 21 October 2003 between the Government of the Republic of Hungary and the Ministerial Council of Serbia and Montenegro on Citizens' Conditions of Travel) (2003)

Hungary, *199/2003. (XII.10.) Korm.r. a Magyar Köztársaság Kormánya és Ukrajna Miniszteri Kabinetje között az állampolgárok utazásának feltételeiről szóló, Kijevben, 2003. október 9. napján aláírt Megállapodás kihirdetéséről* (Government Ordinance 199/2003 on the Proclamation of the Understanding signed on 9 October 2003 between the Government of the Republic of Hungary and the Ministerial Cabinet of Ukraine on Citizens' Conditions of Travel) (2003)

Hungary, *A Kormány 31/2004. (II. 28.) Korm. rendelete a szomszédos államokban élő magyarokról szóló 2001. évi LXII. törvény alapján nyújtott támogatások rendjéről* (Government Ordinance 31/2004 on the Regulation of the Support Granted on the Basis of Law LXII on Hungarians Living in Neighbouring States) (2004)

Hungary, *2005. évi II. törvény a Szülőföld Alapról* (Law II on the Homeland Fund) (2005)

Hungary, *2005. évi XVI. törvény a Szülőföld Alapról szóló 2005. évi II. törvény módosításáról* (Law XVI amending Law II on the Homeland Fund) (2005)

Hungary, *2005. évi XLVI. törvény a magyar állampolgárságról szóló 1993. évi LV. törvény és a külföldiek beutazásáról és tartózkodásáról szóló 2001. évi XXXIX. törvény módosításáról* (Law XLVI amending Law LV on Hungarian Nationality and Law XXXIX on the Entry and Stay of Foreigners) (2005)

Ireland, Nationality and Citizenship Act (1956, no longer in force)

Israel, Law of Return, 5710-1950 (1950) and subsequent amendments (1954 and 1970)

Italy, Constitution (as amended to 2006) (1947)

Italy, *Legge 27 ottobre 1988, no. 470, sull'iscrizione all'AIRE (Anagrafe Italiana Residenti all'Estero)* (1988). Published in *Gazzetta Ufficiale* no. 261 (November 7, 1988). As amended by *Legge 27 maggio 2002, no. 104* (2002). Published in *Gazzetta Ufficiale* no. 127 (1 June 2002)

Italy, *Legge 9 gennaio 1991, no. 19, Norme per lo sviluppo delle attività economiche e della cooperazione internazionale della regione Friuli-Venezia Giulia, della provincia di Belluno e delle aree limitrofe* (1991). Published in *Gazzetta Ufficiale* no. 17 (January 21, 1991)

Italy, *Legge 31 maggio 1995, no. 218, Riforma del sistema italiano di diritto internazionale privato* (1995). Published in suppl. no. 68 to *Gazzetta Ufficiale* no. 128 (June 3, 1995)

Italy, *Legge 8 aprile 1998, no. 89, Proroga dell'efficacia di disposizioni riguardanti il Ministero degli affari esteri* (1998). Published in *Gazzetta Ufficiale* no. 84 (April 10, 1998)

Italy, *Legge 6 novembre 1989, no. 368, Istitutiva del CGIE (Consiglio Generale degli Italiani all'Estero)*. Published in *Gazzetta Ufficiale* no. 264 (November 11, 1989). As amended by *Legge 18 guignio 1998, no. 198*. Published in

Gazzetta Ufficiale no. 150 (June 30, 1998). And by *Regolamento emanato con D.P.R. 14 settembre 1998, no. 329* (1998). Published in *Gazzetta Ufficiale* no. 221 (September 22, 1998)

Italy, *Legge costituzionale 31 gennaio 2001, no. 2, Disposizioni concernenti l'elezione diretta dei Presidenti delle Regioni a Statuto speciale e delle Province autonome di Trento e di Bolzano* (2001). Published in *Gazzetta Ufficiale* no. 26 (1 February 2001)

Italy, *Legge 21 marzo 2001, no. 73, Interventi a favore della minoranza italiana in Slovenia e in Croazia* (2001). Published in *Gazzetta Ufficiale* no. 73 (21 March 2001)

Italy, *Legge 27 dicembre 2001, no. 459, Norme per l'esercizio del diritto di voto dei cittadini italiani residenti all'estero* (2001). Published in *Gazzetta Ufficiale* no. 4 (5 January 2002)

Italy, *Legge 23 ottobre 2003, no. 286, Norme relative alla disciplina dei Comitati degli italiani all'estero* (2003). Published in *Gazzetta Ufficiale* no. 250 (27 October 2003). (The law abrogated *Legge 8 maggio 1985, no. 205, istitutiva dei COMITES*, as amended by *Legge del 5 luglio 1990, no. 172* and by *Legge del 31 dicembre 1996, no. 668*) (1996))

Latvia, Law on Citizenship (1994)

Luxembourg, *Loi sur la nationalité* (as amended in 2001) (1968)

Mexico, Apatzingán Constitution (1814)

Mexico, Constitution (as amended to 2006) (1917)

The Netherlands, Nationality Act (as amended) (1985)

Portugal, *Lei da Nacionalidade, no. 37/81 de 3 de Outubro (alterado pela Lei 25/94)* (1994)

Portugal, *Ministério dos Negócios Estrangeiros, Regulamento de atribuição de apoio pela Direcção-Geral dos Assuntos Consulares e Comunidades Portuguesas (Despacho no. 6162/99)* (1999)

Portugal, *Lei no. 48/96 de Setembro com a redacção que lhe foi dada pela Lei no. 21/2002 de Agosto (que Estabelece a definição e atribuições do Conselho das Comunidades Portuguesas)* (2002)

Romania, Constitution (as amended to 2006) (1991)

Romania, Law regarding the support granted to the Romanian communities from all over the world (1998)

Russia, Federal Law on the State policy of the Russian Federation in respect of the compatriots abroad (1999)

Slovakia, Constitution (as amended to 2006) (1992)

Slovakia, Law 70/1997 on expatriate Slovaks and changing and complementing some laws (1997)

Slovenia, Resolution on the position of autochthonous Slovene minorities in neighbouring countries and the related tasks of state and other institutions in the Republic of Slovenia (1996)

Slovenia, Resolution on Relations with Slovenes Abroad (2002)

Spain, *Código Civil* (1889, as amended to 2006)

Spain, *Ley 11/1990, de 15 de octubre, sobre reforma del Código Civil, en aplicación del principio de no discriminación por razón de sexo* (1990)
Turkey, Constitution (as amended to 2006) (1982)
Turkey, Law No. 4112 on Nationality (1995)
Ukraine, Law on Citizenship (1991)
United Kingdom (Great Britain), Act of May 5 (1870)
United Kingdom, British Commonwealth Immigrants Act (1962)
United Kingdom, Race Relations Act (1976)
United Kingdom, Nationality, Immigration and Asylum Act (2002)
United States, United States Immigration and Nationality Act (as amended) (1952) (8 U.S.C)
United States, United States Code [U.S.C.] (as amended)
United States, Illegal Immigration Reform and Immigration Responsibility Act (Pub L. 104-208) (1996)
United States, Antiterrorism and Effective Death Penalty Act (Pub. L. No. 104-132) (1996)
United States, USA Patriot Act (Uniting and Strengthening America by Providing Appropriate Tools Required to Intercept and Obstruct Terrorism Act) (Pub. L. No. 107-56) 2001)

2. PROPOSALS/REPORTS/DECLARATIONS/DRAFTS/ETC.

a. International and Non-Governmental Organizations

Amnesty International, Human Rights Assessment of the Tampere Agenda: The European Union – Now More Free, Secure and Just? (2004), at: <www.amnesty-eu.org/static/html/pressrelease.asp?cfid=7&id=187&cat=4>
Amnesty International, Briefing to the UN Committee on Economic, Social and Cultural Rights, 35th Session: Slovenia, AI Index: EUR 68/002/2005 (2005)
Council of Europe, Committee for the Protection of National Minorities, Draft Articles and Alternative Versions for Possible Inclusion in a Protocol Complementing the ECHR in the Cultural Field, CAHMIN(95)17 (1995)
Council of Europe, Explanatory Report on the Framework Convention for the Protection of National Minorities (1995)
Council of Europe, Explanatory Report on the European Convention on Nationality (1997)
Council of Europe, Parliamentary Assembly Committee on Legal Affairs and Human Rights, Report Giving an Opinion on the Draft European Convention on Nationality (Doc. 7718) (1997)
Council of Europe, Comments of Council of Europe Deputy Secretary General Krüger on the Occasion of the First European Conference on Nationality, 'Trends and Developments in National and International Law on Nationality', Proceedings 9 (CONF/NAT (99) Pro 1) (1999)

Council of Europe, Parliamentary Assembly Committee on Migration, Refugees and Demography, Report on Links between Europeans living abroad and their countries of origin (Doc. 8339) (1999)

Council of Europe, Committee of Experts on Nationality, Report on Multiple Nationality (CJ-NA (2000)13) (2000)

Council of Europe, Venice Commission, Report on the Preferential Treatment of National Minorities by their Kin-state (CDL-INF(2001)019) (2001)

Council of Europe, Parliamentary Assembly Committee on Legal Affairs and Human Rights, Report on Preferential Treatment of National Minorities by the Kin-State: the Case of the Hungarian Law of 19 June 2001 on Hungarians Living in Neighbouring Countries ('Magyars') (Doc. 9744 rev) (2003)

Council of Europe, Venice Commission, Opinion on the Draft Law Concerning the Support to Romanians Living Abroad (Opinion No. 299/2004) (2004)

Council of Europe, Parliamentary Assembly Committee on Migration, Refugees and Demography, Report on Links between Europeans living abroad and their countries of origin (Doc. 10072) (2004)

Harvard Group, Nationality, Responsibility of States, Territorial Waters – Draft of Conventions (Harvard Draft on Nationality), 23 American Journal of International Law 21 (1929)

Harvard Group, Draft of the Law of Responsibility for Damages Done in Their Territory to the Persons or Property of Foreigners, 23 American Journal of International Law Special Supplement 131 (1929)

Institut de Droit International, *Résolutions relatives aux conflits de lois en matière de nationalité (naturalisation et expatriation)*, 20 Annuaire de l'Institut de Droit International (1896)

Institut de Droit International, *Resolution sur la dualité des principes de nationalité et de domicile en droit international privé*, 62(I) Annuaire de l'Institut de Droit International (1987)

International Law Association, Committee on Feminism and International Law, Final Report on Women's Equality and Nationality in International Law (2000), at: <www.unhcr.org/cgi-bin/texis/vtx/home/opendoc.pdf?tbl=PROTECTION&id=3dc7cccf4>

International Law Commission, Report on Multiple Nationality, 6 Yearbook of the International Law Commission, Volume II, UN Doc. A/CN.4/83 (1954)

International Law Commission, Survey of the Problem of Multiple Nationality, 6 Yearbook of the International Law Commission, Volume II, UN Doc. A/CN.4/84 (1954)

International Law Commission, Report of the International Law Commission on the Work of its Sixth Session, 252nd meeting, 6 Yearbook of the International Law Commission Yearbook, Volume I, UN Doc. A/CN.4/88 (1954)

International Law Commission, Report of the International Law Commission On the Work of its Forty-Seventh Session, UN GAOR Supp. (No. 10), UN Doc. A/50/10 (1995)

International Law Commission, Preamble of Draft Articles on Nationality of Natural Persons in Relation to the Succession of States, Report of the

International Law Commission On the Work of its Fifty-First Session, UN Doc. A/54/10 (1999)
International Law Commission, Draft Articles on the Responsibility of States for Internationally Wrongful Acts, Report of the International Law Commission on the Work of its Fifty-Third Session, UN Doc. A/56/10 (2001)
International Law Commission, Report of the International Law Commission on the Work of its Fifty-Seventh Session, UN Doc. A/60/10 (2005)
International Law Commission, Draft Articles on Diplomatic Protection, Report of the International Law Commission on the Work of its Fifty-Eighth Session, UN Doc. A/61/10 (2006)
Kojanec, G., 'Report on Multiple Nationality' in *Council of Europe Report on Multiple Nationality* 35 (CJ-NA (2000)13) (2000).
MÁÉRT (Magyar Állandó Értekezlet) (Hungarian Standing Conference), *A Magyar Állandó Értekezlet második ülésének Zárónyilatkozata* (Closing Statement of the Second Meeting of the Hungarian Standing Conference) (November 12, 1999). Included in: Státustörvény: Dokumentumok, Tanulmányok, Publikációk 166 (Zoltán Kántor, ed., Teleki László Alapítvány, Budapest, 2002)
MÁÉRT, *A Magyar Állandó Értekezlet harmadik ülésének Zárónyilatkozata* (Closing Statement of the Third Meeting of the Hungarian Standing Conference) (14 December 2000). Included in: Státustörvény: Dokumentumok, Tanulmányok, Publikációk 170 (Zoltán Kántor, ed., Teleki László Alapítvány, Budapest, 2002)
MÁÉRT, *A Magyar Állandó Értekezlet a Romániában, a Szlovák Köztársaságban, a Jugoszláv Szövetségi Köztársaságban, az Ukrán Köztársaságban, a Horvát Köztársaságban és a Szlovén Köztársaságban parlamenti, illetve tartományi képviselettel rendelkező tagszervezetei képviselőinek nyilatkozata* (Statement of the Representatives of the Member-Organizations of the Hungarian Standing Conference with Parliamentary or Provincial Representation in Romania, the Slovak Republic, the Yugoslav Federal Republic, the Republic of Ukraine, the Republic of Croatia and the Republic of Slovenia) (27 June 2001) (2001a), included in: Státustörvény: Dokumentumok, Tanulmányok, Publikációk 178 (Zoltán Kántor, ed., Teleki László Alapítvány, Budapest, 2002)
MÁÉRT, *A Magyar Állandó Értekezlet negyedik ülésének Zárónyilatkozata* (Closing Statement of the Fourth Meeting of the Hungarian Standing Conference) (26 October 2001) (2001b). Included in: Státustörvény: Dokumentumok, Tanulmányok, Publikációk 175 (Zoltán Kántor, ed., Teleki László Alapítvány, Budapest, 2002)
MÁÉRT, *A határon túli magyar politikai vezetők nyilatkozata a Magyarországgal szomszédos államokban élő magyarokról szóló törvény hatályba lépése alkalmából* (Statement of the Political Leaders of Hungarians Beyond the Borders on the Occasion of the Entry into Force of the Law on Hungarians Living Beyond the Borders) (9 January 2002) (2002a). Included in: Státustörvény: Dokumentumok, Tanulmányok, Publikációk 180 (Zoltán Kántor, ed., Teleki László Alapítvány, Budapest, 2002)

MÁÉRT, *A Magyar Állandó Értekezlet ötödik ülésének Zárónyilatkozata* (Closing Statement of the Fifth Meeting of the Hungarian Standing Conference) (17 July 2002) (2002b), at: <www.htmh.hu>
MÁÉRT, *A Magyar Állandó Értekezlet hatodik ülésének Zárónyilatkozata* (Closing Statement of the Sixth Meeting of the Hungarian Standing Conference) (17 November 2002) (2002c), at: <www.htmh.hu>
OSCE/CSCE, Report of the CSCE Meeting of Experts on National Minorities in Geneva (1991)
United Nations (Türk, Danilo), Final Report of the Special Rapporteur of the Sub-Commission on Prevention of Discrimination and Protection of Minorities on the Realization of Economic, Social and Cultural Rights, UN Doc. E/CN.4/Sub.2/1992/16 (1992)
United Nations (Mikulka, Vaclav), Second Report on State Succession and Its Impact on the Nationality of Natural and Legal Persons, UN Doc. A/CN.4/474 (1996)
United Nations (Deschênes, Jules), Proposal Concerning a Definition of the Term 'Minority', UN Doc. E/CN.4/Sub.2/1985/31 (1985)
United Nations (Gál, Kinga), The Role of Bilateral Treaties in the Protection of National Minorities in Central and Eastern Europe, UN Doc. No. E/CN.4/Sub.2/AC.5/1998 CRP.2 (1998)
United Nations (Weissbrodt, David), Final Report on the Rights of Non-Citizens, UN Doc. E/CN.4/Sub.2/2003/23 (2003)
United Nations (Dugard, John), Seventh Report on Diplomatic Protection, UN Doc. A/CN.4/567 (2006)

b.   European Union

Third General Report on the Activities of the European Union: 1969 (1970)
Copenhagen Declaration on European Identity (1973) (on file with author)
Tindemans Report ('European Union'), EC Bulletin Suppl. 1/76 (1976)
Commission Communication to the Council: Community Action in the Cultural Sector, EC Bulletin Suppl. 6/77 (1977)
Stuttgart Solemn Declaration, EC Bulletin 6/83 (French) (1983)
Draft Treaty Establishing the European Union (Spinelli Treaty) (OJ 1984 C 77/33) (1984)
Adonnino Report ('A People's Europe'), EC Bulletin Suppl. 7/85 (1985)
Commission Communication to the Council: A Fresh Boost for Culture in the European Community, EC Bulletin 4/87 (1987)
A People's Europe: Communication from the Commission to the European Parliament, COM (1988) 331 final (1988)
Union Citizenship, EC Bulletin Suppl. 2/91 (1991)
Proposal of the Spanish Delegation at the Inter-Governmental Conference on Political Union, on European Citizenship (February 21, 1991) (CONF-UP 1731/91) (on file with author)

European Parliament, Report of the Committee of Institutional Affairs on Union Citizenship, PE 153.099/FIN (1991)
Commission Communication to the Council: New Prospects for Community Cultural Action, COM (92) 149 (1992)
Conclusions of the Copenhagen European Council, EC Bulletin 6/93 (1993)
Call for proposals for European Commission backing involving actions in favour of promoting and safeguarding regional or minority languages and cultures (OJ 1995 C 322/34) (1995)
Opinion of the Committee of the Regions on Culture and Cultural Differences and their Significance for the Future of Europe (OJ 1998 C180/63) (1998)
Proposal for a European Parliament and Council Decision establishing a single financing and programming instrument for cultural co-operation (Culture 2000 programme), COM (1998) 266 final (1998)
Action plan of the Council and the Commission on how best to implement the provisions of the Treaty of Amsterdam on an area of freedom, security and justice (OJ 1999 C 19) (1999)
Call for proposals for Support from the European Commission for measures to promote and safeguard regional and minority languages and cultures (OJ 2000 C 266/7) (2000)
Commission Communication to the Council and the European Parliament on a Community Immigration Policy, COM (2000) 757 final (2000)
The Future of the European Union – Laeken Declaration (2001)
European Parliament Resolution on Hungary's application for membership of the European Union and the state of negotiations (COM (2000) 705-C5-0605/2000-1997/2175 (COS)) (2001)
Proposal for a Council Directive on the conditions of entry and residence of third-country nationals for the purpose of paid employment and self-employed economic activities, COM (2001) 386 final (2001)
(Third) Report from the Commission on Citizenship of the Union, COM (2001) 506 final (2001)
Commission Communication: A Project for the European Union, COM (2002) 247 final (2002)
Proposal for a Council Directive on the conditions of admission of third-country nationals for the purpose of studies, pupil exchange, unremunerated training or voluntary service, COM(2002) 548 final (2002)
Communication from the Commission to the Council and the European Parliament on integrating migration issues in the EU's relations with third countries, COM (2002) 703 final (2002)
Proposal for a Framework Decision on certain procedural rights in criminal proceedings throughout the European Union, COM (2004) 328 final (2003)
Communication from the Commission to the Council, the European Parliament, the European Economic and Social Committee and the Committee of the Regions on immigration, integration and employment, COM (2003) 336 final (2003)

Report from the Commission on the implementation of the 'Culture 2000' programme in the years 2000 and 2001, COM (2003)722 final (2003)

Opinion of the European Economic and Social Committee on 'Access to European Union citizenship' (OJ 2003 C 208/76) (2003)

Proposal for a Directive of the European Parliament and of the Council on Services in the Internal Market, COM (2004) 2 final/3 (2004)

Communication from the Commission: Making Citizenship Work: Fostering European Culture and Diversity Through Programmes for Youth, Culture, Audiovisual and Civic Participation, COM (2004) 154 final (2004)

Proposal for a Council Directive on a specific admission procedure for third country researchers, COM(2004) 178 final (2004)

Communication from the Commission: Study on the links between legal and illegal immigration, COM (2004) 412 final (2004)

Proposal for a Decision of the European Parliament and of the Council establishing the Culture 2007 programme (2007-2013), COM (2004) 469 final (2004)

(First) Annual Report on Migration and Integration, COM(2004) 508 final (2004)

(Fourth) Report on Citizenship of the Union, COM (2004) 695 final (2004)

Recommendation from the Commission to the Council to authorize the Commission to participate, on behalf of the Community, in the negotiations within UNESCO on the convention on the protection of the diversity of cultural contents and artistic expressions, SEC (2004) 1062 final (2004)

Brussels European Council Conclusions (4-5 November 2004), Doc. No. 14292/1/04 REV 1

Green Paper on an EU approach to managing economic migration, COM (2004) 811 final (2005)

Proposal for a Regulation of the European Parliament and of the Council laying down rules on local border traffic at the external land borders of the Member States and amending the Schengen Convention and the Common Consular Instructions, COM (2005) 56 final (2005)

Report from the Commission based on Article 34 of the Council framework decision of 13 June 2002 on the European arrest warrant and the surrender procedures between Member States, COM (2005) 63 final (2005)

Proposal for a Decision of the European Parliament and of the Council establishing for the period 2007-2013 the programme 'Citizens for Europe' to promote active European citizenship, COM (2005) 116 final (2005)

Commission Communication to the Council, the European Parliament, the European Economic and Social Committee and the Committee of the Regions: A Common Agenda for Integration: Framework for the Integration of Third-Country Nationals in the European Union, COM (2005) 389 final (2005)

Commission Communication: Policy Plan on Legal Migration, COM (2005) 669 final (2005)

Proposal for a Council Decision on the conclusion of the UNESCO Convention on the Protection and Promotion of the Diversity of Cultural Expressions, COM (2005) 678 final (2005)

(Second) Annual Report on Migration and Integration, SEC (2006) 892 (2006)

Communication from the Commission to the Council and the European Parliament on Implementing the Hague Programme: the way forward, COM (2006) 331 (2006)
Communication from the Commission on Policy priorities in the fight against illegal immigration of third country nationals, COM (2006) 402 final (2006)
Green Paper on diplomatic and consular protection for citizens of the Union in third countries, COM(2006) 712 final (2006)
Communication from the Commission to the Council and the European Parliament, The Global Approach to Migration one year on: Towards a comprehensive European migration policy, COM (2006) 735 final (2006)
Barnier Report ('For a European civil protection force: europe aid') (2006), available at: <ec.europa.eu/commission_barroso/president/pdf/rapport_barnier_en.pdf>
Declaration on the occasion of the 50th anniversary of the signature of the Treaty of Rome (2007)

c. **National**

Austria, *Petition zur Verankerung einer Südtirol-Bestimmung* (Doc. No. 302/AVORL-K) (14 January 2004)
Belgium, *Proposition de loi modificant l'article 22 du Code de la nationalité belge*, Doc. No. 3-146/1 (2003)
Canada, Report of Attorney General Marion Boyd, Dispute Resolution in Family Law: Protecting Choice, Promoting Inclusion (2004), at: <www.attorneygeneral.jus.gov.on.ca/english/about/pubs/boyd/executivesummary.pdf>
France, *Être français aujourd'hui et demain: Rapport de la Commission de la nationalité* (*Rapport Long*) (1988)
France, *Projet de Loi relatif à l'immigration et à l'intégration* (No. 576) (2006) (adopted in the *Assemblée Nationale* on 17 May 2006)
Germany (Prussia), Administrative Treatise on Naturalization (1904)
Germany, *Einbürgerungsrichtlinien* (GMBl. 1978) (1977)
Germany (Kühn, Heinz), *Stand und Weiterentwicklung der Integration der ausländischen Arbeitnehmer und ihrer Familien in der Bundesrepublik Deutschland* (1979)
Germany (Land Nordrhein-Westfalen), *Viertes Gesetz zur Regelung von Fragen der Staatsangehörigkeit, Gesetzentwurf* (BR-Dr. 52/80) (1980)
Germany (Bundesregierung), *Viertes Gesetz zur Regelung von Fragen der Staatsangehörigkeit, Empfehlungen zum Gesetzentwurf* (BR-Dr. 3/1/82) (1982)
Germany (SPD), *Entwurf eines Vierten Gesetzes zur Regelung von Fragen der Staatsangehörigkeit* (BT-Dr. 11/ 4268) (1989)
Germany (Greens), *Entwurf eines Gesetzes zur rechtlichen Gleichstellung der ausländischen Wohnbevölkerung durch Einbürgerung und Geburt* (BT-Dr. 11/4464) (1989)

Germany (Greens), *Entwurf eines Gesetzes zur Regelung der Rechte von Niederlassungsberechtigten, Einwanderinnen und Einwanderern* (BT-Dr. 12/1714) (1991)
Germany (FDP), *Entwurf eines Gesetzes zur Änderung des Reichs- und Staatsangehörigkeitsgesetzes* (Umdruck Nr. 12/204) (April 27, 1993)
Germany (SPD), *Entwurf eines Gesetzes zur Erleichterung der Einbürgerung und Hinnahme der Doppelstaatsangehörigkeit* (BT-Dr. 12/4533) (1993)
Germany (Bundesrat), *Entwurf eines Geseztes zur Änderung und Ergänzung des Staatsangehörigkeitsrechts* (BT-Dr. 12/5684) (1993)
Germany (Greens), *Entwurf eines Gesetzes zur Änderung des Staatsangehörigkeitsrechts* (BT-Dr. 13/423) (1995)
Germany (Bundesrat), *Entwurf eines Gesetzes zur Erleichterung des Erwerbs der deutschen Staatsangehörigkeit durch Kinder ausländischer Eltern* (BT-Dr. 13/8157) (1997)
Germany (SPD), *Antrag zur Erleichterung des Erwerbs der deutschen Staatsangehörigkeit für Kinder ausländischer Eltern* (BT-Dr. 13/9941) (1998)
Germany (FDP), *Entwurf eines Gesetzes zur Förderung der Integration von Kindern dauerhaft in Deutschland lebender Ausländer* (BT-Dr. 14/296) (1999)
Germany (CDU/CSU), *Modernes Ausländerrecht* (BT-Dr. 14/532) (1999)
Germany (Bundesregierung), *Entwurf eines Gesetzes zur Reform der Staatsangehörigkeitsrechts* (BT-Dr. 14/533) (1999)
Germany (CDU/CSU), *Integration und Toleranz* (BT-Dr. 14/534) (1999)
Germany (CDU/CSU), *Entwurf eines Gesetzes zur Reform des Staatsangehörigkeitsrechts* (BT-Dr. 14/535) (1999)
Germany (Freistaat Bayern), *Entwurf eines Gesetzes zur Reform des Staatsangehörigkeitsrechts* (BR-Dr. 188/2/99) (1999)
Germany, Bundesministerium des Innern, *Zuwanderung gestalten – Integration fördern: Bericht der Unabhängigen Kommission 'Zuwanderung'* (2001), at: <www.bmi.bund.de/cln_028/nn_174266/Internet/Content/Broschueren/ 2001/Zuwanderung_gestalten_-_Integration_Id_48169_de.html>
Germany, *Fünftes Bericht der Beauftragten der Bundesregierung für Ausländerfragen über die Lage der Ausländer in der Bundesrepublik Deutschland* (August 2002), at: <www.integrationsbeauftragte.de/download/ lage5.pdf>
Germany (Greens), *Entwurf eines Gesetzes zur Änderung des Staatsangehörigkeitsrechtes* (BT-Dr 16/265) (2006)
Germany (various federal states), *Entwurf eines Gesetzes zur Änderung des Staatsangehörigkeitsrechtes (StAG)* (BR-Dr 137/07) (2007)
Hungary, *T/9126 számú törvényjavaslat a kisebbségi önkormányzati képviselők választásáról, valamint a nemzeti és etnikai kisebbségekre vonatkozó egyes törvények módosításáról* (Proposal T/9126 for a Law on the Election of Minority Government Representatives and the Amendment of some Laws pertaining to National and Ethnic Minorities) (2005)
India, Ministry of Home Affairs Notification on PIO Card Scheme, Extra Ordinary Gazette of India, No. 213 (2002), at: <mha.nic.in/pioscheme.htm>

The Netherlands (R.F.A. van den Bedem), Motives for naturalization (Summary), Report No. K28 (The Netherlands Ministry of Justice, 1993)
Romania, Declaration of the Government of Romania with Regard to the Adoption of the Law Concerning the Hungarians Living in Neighbouring Countries (19 June 2001)
Romania, The Official Position of the Romanian Government on the Law on Hungarians Living in Neighbouring Countries, submitted to the Venice Commission (CDL(2001)081) (2001)
Spain, *Propuesta de Estatuto Político de la Comunidad de Euskadi* (2003), at: <www.el-mundo.es/documentos/2003/10/estatuto_vasco.pdf>
United Kingdom, British Home Office, Community Cohesion: A Report of the Independent Review Team (Chaired by Ted Cantle) (2001)
United States, 7 Foreign Affairs Manual 1111 (Basic Terms and Distinctions) (1995)

3. COMMENTARIES/SPEECHES/ADDITIONAL SOURCES

Council of Europe, Parliamentary Assembly Debates (Eighth Sitting) (January 31, 1997), Official Report of Debates (Ordinary Session), Vol. I, 291 (1997)
Duna TV, Stúdóbeszélgetés a kettős állampolgárság kérdéséről, Heti Hírmondó (3 August 2003)
Esterházy, P., A halacska csodálatos élete (1991)
European Union, Romano Prodi (President of the European Commission), EU Bulletin 9/1999 § 2.2.1 (September 14, 1999)
European Union, European Bureau for Lesser Used Languages, Charte 4237/00, Contrib. 110 (18 April 2000)
European Union, Commission, Standard Eurobarometer 54 (Autumn 2000, Full Report), at: <europa.eu.int/comm /public_opinion>
European Union, Commission, How Europeans See Themselves (2001)
European Union, European Convention Contribution of József Szájer, CONV 580/03 (26 February 2003)
European Union, Commission, Standard Eurobarometer 60 (Autumn 2003, Full Report), at: <europa.eu.int/comm /public_opinion>
European Union, Commission, Candidate Countries Eurobarometer (Autumn 2003, Full Report), at: <europa.eu.int/comm /public_opinion>
European Union, Commission, A Constitution for Europe (2004), at: <europa.eu.int/constitution/why_en.htm>
European Union, Commission Reflection Group, Concluding Remarks: The Spiritual and Cultural Dimension of Europe (2004), at: <europa.eu.int/comm/research/socialsciences/pdf/michalski_281004_ final_report_ en.pdf>
European Union, Viviane Reding (Commissioner for Education and Culture), Speech 04/322 (18 June 2004)

European Union, José Manuel Barroso (President of the European Commission), Speech 04/478 (29 October 2004)
European Union, Romano Prodi, Speech 04/479 (29 October 2004)
European Union, José Manuel Barroso, Speech 04/495 (26 November 2004)
European Union, Eurostat, Population and Social Conditions, Theme 3, Acquisition of Citizenship (2004), at: <epp.eurostat.cec.eu.int>
European Union, Commission, The Future of Europe, Special Eurobarometer 251 (May 2006), at: <ec.europa.eu/public_opinion/archives/ebs/ebs_251_en.pdf>
European Union, Commission, Standard Eurobarometer 65 (Spring 2006, First Results), at: <europa.eu.int/comm /public_opinion>
France, Ministère de l'emploi, de la cohésion et du logement, *Contrat d'accueil et d'intégration: Formation civique* (2006), at: <www.social.gouv.fr/IMG/pdf/formationcivique.pdf>
Germany, Bundesministerium des Innern, *Das neue Ausländerrecht der Bundesrepublik Deutschland* (1990)
Germany, Bundesministerium des Innern, Statistics, *Migration, Asyl* and *Einbürgerungen in Deutschland,* at: <www.bmi.bund.de>
Germany, *Plenarprotokoll des Deutschen Bundestages*, Sessions 11/207, 12/155, 12/255, 13/225, 14/3, 14/20, 14/28 and 14/40 (1990-1999)
Germany, Daniel Cohn-Bendit (Commissioner for the Federal Office of Multicultural Affairs), *Praktische Politik der Anerkennung.* Speech given at the Conference, *Gefahren der Politisierung ethnisch-kultureller und religiöser Differenzen*, held at the Universität Bielefeld (Bielefeld) (November 23–25, 1994)
Germany, *Bundesrat Plenarprotokoll*, Sessions 737 and 738 (1999)
Germany, *Protokoll über die 12. Sitzung des Innenausschusses* (April 13, 1999) (on file with author)
Germany, Bundesministerium des Innern, *Das neue Staatsangehörigkeitsrecht* (1999), at: <www.einbuergerung.de/staatsangehoerigkeit.pdf>
Germany, Bundesministerium des Innern, *Pressemitteilung: Neun Monate Zuwanderungsgesetz – Qualitätssprung in der Integrationsförderung* (23 September 2005), at: <www.bamf.de>
Germany, Bundesamt für Migration und Flüchtlinge, *Welche Ziele hat Integration?* (2005), at: <www.bamf.de>
Hungary, Délvidéki Levél Gyurcsány Ferenchez (Letter from Vojvodina to [the Hungarian Prime Minister]), at: <www.kettosallampolgarsag.hu>
Hungary, Statements of János Martonyi (Minister for Foreign Affairs) on 20 June 2001 and 22 June 2001, at: <www.kum.hu/Archivum/Korabbiszovivoi/2001/MartonyiJ/0620mjstvangol.htm> and <www.kum.hu/Archivum/Korabbiszovivoi/2001/MartonyiJ/0622statemj.htm> respectively
Hungary, Office of the President of Hungary, *Közlemény: Sólyom László köztársasági elnök Határon túli magyarság a XXI. században. Tények és perspektívák – egy új megközelítés igénye címmel konferenciasorozatot kezdeményez* (28 April 2006), at: <www.keh.hu/keh>

Krauss, N., The History of Love (2005)
Judt, T., From the Home of the Dead: On Modern European Memory, 52(15) The New York Review of Books (6 October 2005)
Magyar Rádio, Interview with Miklós Duray, Határok Nélkül (15 November 2004)
Martin, D.A., Dual Nationality: TR's 'Self-Evident Absurdity', Chair Lecture at Virginia University School of Law (27 October 2004), at: <www.law.virginia.edu/home2002/html/alumni/uvalawyer/sp05/martin_lecture.htm>
OSCE, Rolf Ekeus (High Commissioner on National Minorities), Sovereignty, responsibility, and national minorities (Statement issued on 26 October 2001), at: <www.osce.org/hcnm/item_1_6352.html>
OSCE, Rolf Ekeus, High Commissioner warns of Hungarian 'Status Law' precedent (Statement issued on 24 June 2003), at: <www.osce.org/hcnm/item_1_7602.html>
United Kingdom, Remarks of United Kingdom Home Secretary David Blunkett on the occasion of the first citizenship ceremony performed (February 2004), at: <www.ind.homeoffice.gov.uk/british_citizenship/english/homepage/press/first_citizenship.html>
United States, Department of State, International Travel Information: Dual Nationality, at: <travel.state.gov/travel/dualnationality.html>
United States, U.S. Citizenship and Immigration Services, A Guide to Naturalization (2004)
Yezierska, A., *Bread Givers* (1925)
Zangwill, I., *The Melting-Pot*, Drama in Four Acts (1908)

4.   PRESS

168 Óra (Weekly, Hungary)
Asbarez Online (Online Service, Armenia)
BBC News/Monitoring (Online Service, United Kingdom)
Beszélő (Weekly, Hungary)
CBC News/cbc.ca (Online Service, Canada)
Der Spiegel (Weekly, Germany)
Deutsche Welle (Online Service, Germany)
Die Presse (Daily, Austria)
Die Welt (Daily, Germany)
DR Nyheder (Online Service, Denmark)
Enlargement Weekly (Weekly, European Union)
Erdely.ma (Online Service, Romania)
ÉS (Élet és Irodalom) (Weekly, Hungary)
Eurasian Daily Monitor (Online Service, United States)
EurasiaNet (Online Service, United States)
Financial Times (Daily, United Kingdom)
Frankfurter Allgemeine Zeitung (Daily, Germany)

HVG (Heti Világgazdaság) (Weekly, Hungary)
Institute for War and Peace Reporting/Caucasus (Online Service)
International Herald Tribune (Daily, France)
La Repubblica (Daily, Italy)
Le Monde (Daily, France)
L'Orient-Le Jour (Daily, Lebanon)
Magyar Hírlap (Daily, Hungary)
Magyar Narancs (Weekly, Hungary)
Magyar Nemzet (Daily, Hungary)
Magyar Szó (Daily, Serbia)
Mozgó Világ (Monthly, Hungary)
Népszabadság (Daily, Hungary)
Népszava (Daily, Hungary)
Provincia (Bi-Monthly, Romania)
Romániai Magyar Szó (Daily, Romania)
Szabadság (Daily, Romania)
The Economist (Weekly, United Kingdom)
The Los Angeles Times (Daily, United States)
The New York Times (Daily, United States)
The Observer (Weekly, United Kingdom)

F.   CASES

1.   INTERNATIONAL COURTS

a.   **European Court of Human Rights**

Case 'relating to certain aspects of the laws on the use of languages in education in Belgium' (Merits), E.Ct.H.R. 1474/62, 1677/62, 1691/62, 1769/63, 1994/63, 2126/64 (1968)
X v. Germany, E.Comm.H.R. 3745/68 (1970)
Abdulaziz, Cabales and Balkandali v. the United Kingdom, E.Ct.H.R. 9214/80, 9473/81, 9474/81 (1985)
Family K and W v. the Netherlands, E.Ct.H.R. 11278/84 (1985)
Berrehab v. the Netherlands, E.Ct.H.R. 10730/84 (1988)
Soering v. the United Kingdom, E.Ct.H.R. 14038/88 (1989)
Moustaquim v. Belgium, E.Ct.H.R. 12313/86 (1991)
Djeroud v. France, E.Comm.H.R. 13446/87 (1991) (14 Eur.H.R.Rep. 68 (1992))
Beldjoudi v. France, E.Ct.H.R. 12083/86 (1992)
Burghartz v. Switzerland, E.Ct.H.R. 16213/90 (1994)
Sorajbee v. the United Kingdom (Admissibility), E.Ct.H.R. 23938/94 (1995)
Jaramillo v. the United Kingdom (Admissibility), E.Ct.H.R. 24865/94 (1995)
Ahmet Sadik v. Greece, E.Ct.H.R. 18877/91 (1996)

Boughanemi v. France, E.Ct.H.R. 22070/93 (1996)
Ahmut v. the Netherlands, E.Ct.H.R. 21702/93 (1996)
Gül v. Switzerland, E.Ct.H.R. 23218/94 (1996)
Kafkalsi v. Turkey, E.Ct.H.R. 21106/92 (1997)
Mehemi v. France, E.Ct.H.R. 25017/94 (1997)
Boujlifa v. France, E.Ct.H.R. 25404/94 (1997)
El Boujaïdi v. France, E.Ct.H.R. 25613/94 (1997)
Unified Communist Party of Turkey and Others (TBKP) v. Turkey, E.Ct.H.R. 19392/92 (1998)
Petrovic v. Austria, E.Ct.H.R. 20458/92 (1998)
Socialist Party of Turkey and Others v. Turkey, E.Ct.H.R. 21237/93 (1998)
Sidiropoulos and Others v. Greece, E.Ct.H.R. 26695/95 (1998)
Party of Freedom and Democracy (ÖZDEP) v. Turkey, E.Ct.H.R. 23885/94 (1999)
Matthews v. the United Kingdom, E.Ct.H.R. 24833/94 (1999)
Karassev v. Finland (Admissibility), E.Ct.H.R. 31414/94 (1999)
Dalia v. France, E.Ct.H.R. 26102/95 (1998)
Larkos v. Cyprus, E.Ct.H.R. 29515/95 (1999)
Beard v. the United Kingdom, E.Ct.H.R. 24882/94 (2001)
Chapman v. the United Kingdom, E.Ct.H.R. 27238/95 (2001)
Stankov and the United Macedonian Organisation Ilinden v. Bulgaria, E.Ct.H.R. 29221/95 and 29225/95 (2001)
Case of Refah Partisi (The Welfare Party) and Others v. Turkey (Third Section), E.Ct.H.R. 41340/98, 41342/98, 41343/98 and 41344/98 (2001)
Gorzelik and Others v. Poland (Fourth Section), E.Ct.H.R. 44158/98 (2001)
Hilal v. the United Kingdom, E.Ct.H.R. 45276/99 (2001)
Metropolitan Church of Bessarabia and Others v. Moldova, E.Ct.H.R. 45701/99 (2001)
Boultif v. Switzerland, E.Ct.H.R. 54273/00 (2001)
Affaire Dicle pour le Partie de la Democratie (DEP) c. Turquie, E.Ct.H.R. 25141/94 (2002)
Selim Sadak and Others v. Turkey, E.Ct.H.R. 25144/94, 26149/95 to 26154/95, 27100/95 and 27101/95 (2002)
Christine Goodwin v. the United Kingdom (Grand Chamber), E.Ct.H.R. 28957/95 (2002)
Affaire Parti Socialiste de Turquie (STP) et Autres c. Turquie, E.Ct.H.R. 26482/95 (2003)
Case of Refah Partisi (The Welfare Party) and Others v. Turkey (Grand Chamber), E.Ct.H.R. 41340/98, 41342/98, 41343/98 and 41344/98 (2003)
Slivenko v. Latvia, E.Ct.H.R. 48321/99 (2003)
Napijalo v. Croatia, E.Ct.H.R. 66485/01 (2003)
Gorzelik and Others v. Poland (Grand Chamber), E.Ct.H.R. 44158/98 (2004)
Venkadajalasarma v. the Netherlands, E.Ct.H.R. 58150/00 (2004)
Ždanoka c. Lettonie, E.Ct.H.R. 58278/00 (2004)
Bosphorus Hava Yollari Turizm v. Ireland, E.Ct.H.R. 45036/98 (2005)
Kosteski v. (FYRO) Macedonia, E.Ct.H.R. 55170/00 (2006)

Affaire Linkov c. République Tchèque, E.Ct.H.R. 10504/03 (2006)
Affaire Kavakçi c. Turquie, E.Ct.H.R. 71907/01 (2007)
Biserica Adevărat Ortodoxă din Moldova and Others v. Moldova, E.Ct.H.R. 952/03 (2007)

b. **Inter-American Court/Commission of Human Rights**

Juan Raul Ferreira v. Uruguay (Case 2711), Inter-Am.Comm.H.R. Res. 8/53 (1983)
Proposed Amendments to the Naturalization Provisions of the Constitution of Costa Rica (Advisory Opinion OC-4/84) Inter-Am.Ct.H.R. (Ser. A) No. 4 (1984)

c. **International Court of Justice/Permanent Court of International Justice**

Nationality Decrees Issued in Tunis and Morocco (Advisory Opinion), February 7, 1923, PCIJ, Series B, No. 4, 24 (1923)
Acquisition of Polish Nationality (Advisory Opinion), September 15, 1923, PCIJ, Series B, No. 7, 20 (1923)
Mavrommatis Palestine Concessions (Judgment), August 30, 1924, PCIJ, Series A, No. 2, 6 (1924)
Minority Schools in Albania (Advisory Opinion), April 6, 1935, PCIJ, Series A/B, No. 64, 4 (1935)
German settlers in Poland (Advisory Opinion), September 10, 1923, PCIJ, Series B, No. 6 (1923)
Panevezys-Saldutiskis Railway (Judgment), February 28, 1939, PCIJ, Series A/B, No. 76, 4 (1939)
Reparation for Injuries Suffered in the Service of the United Nations (Advisory Opinion), ICJ Reports (1949)
Liechtenstein v. Guatemala (Nottebohm) (Judgment, Second Phase), ICJ Reports (1955)
Belgium v. Spain (Barcelona Traction) (Judgment), ICJ Reports (1970)
Germany v. United States of America (LaGrand) (Judgment), ICJ Reports (2001)
Mexico v. United States of America (Avena and Other Nationals) (Judgment), ICJ Reports (2004)
Democratic Republic of the Congo v. Uganda (Armed Activities on the Territory of the Congo (Judgment), ICJ Reports (2005)

d. **Permanent Court of Arbitration**

Canevaro Case (Italy v. Peru), 11 R.I.A.A. 405 (1912)
Island of Las Palmas (United States v. The Netherlands), 2 R.I.A.A. 829 (1928)

e. United Nations Human Rights Committee

In Re Aumeeruddy-Cziffra v. Mauritius, Communication No. 35/1978 (1981)
Sophie Vidal Martins v. Uruguay, Communication No. 57/1979 (1982)
Stewart v. Canada, Communication No. 538/1993 (1996)
Winata v. Australia, Communication No. 930/2000 (2001)
General Comment No. 23(50) (Article 27), UN Doc. CCPR/C/21/Rev.1/Add.5 (1994)
General Comment No. 27 (Freedom of movement (Art.12)), UN Doc. CCPR/C/21/Rev.1/Add.9 (1999)
Consideration of Reports Submitted by States Parties under Article 40 of the Covenant. Concluding Observations of the Human Rights Committee: Slovenia, UN Doc. CCPR/CO/84/SVN (2005)

f. Other Courts and Tribunals

Mergé Claim (United States v. Italy), 22 International Law Reports 443 (United States-Italian Conciliation Commission) (1955)
Nasser Esphahanian and Bank Tejarat (Case No. 157), 9 Yearbook Commercial Arbitration 273 (Iran-United States Claims Tribunal) (1983)
Case Concerning the Question of Jurisdiction Over Claims of Persons With Dual Nationality (Case No. A-18), 23 International Legal Materials 489 (Iran-United States Claims Tribunal) (1984)

2. EUROPEAN COURT OF JUSTICE/COURT OF FIRST INSTANCE

Case 26/62 *Van Gend en Loos v. Nederlandese Administratie der Belastungen* [1963] ECR 1
Case 6/64 *Costa v. Enel* [1964] ECR 1251
Case 7/68 *Commission v. Italy* [1968] ECR 423
Case 29/69 *Stauder v. City of Ulm* [1969] ECR 419
Case 11/70 *Internationale Handelsgesellschaft* [1970] ECR 1125
Case 4/73 *Nold v. Commission* [1974] ECR 491
Case 36/74 *Walrave and L.J.N. Koch v. Association Union Cycliste Internationale, Koninklijke Nederlandsche Wielren Unie and Federación Española Ciclismo* [1974] ECR 1405
Case 13/76 *Donà v. Mantero* [1976] ECR 1333
Case 115/78 *Knoors v. Secretary of State for Economic Affairs* [1979] ECR 399
Case 120/78 *Rewe-Zentrale v. Bundesmonopolverwaltung für Branntwein (Cassis de Dijon)* [1979] ECR 649
Case 34/79 *Regina v. Henn and Darby* [1980] ECR 3795
Case 149/79 *Commission v. Belgium* (No. 1) [1980] ECR 3881
Cases 60 and 61/84 *Cinéthèque SA and Others v. Federation Nationale des Cinémas Français* [1985] ECR 2605

Case 137/84 *Ministère Public v. Robert Heinrich Maria Mutsch* [1985] ECR 2681
Case 187/84 *Commission v. Germany (Beer)* [1987] ECR 1227
Cases C-281, 283, 284, 285 and 287/85 *Federal Republic of Germany and Others v. Commission* [1987] ECR 3203
Case 407/85 *Drei Glocken and Kritzinger v. USL Centro-Sud and Bolzano* [1988] ECR 4233
Case 292/86 *Claude Gullung v. Conseil de l'ordre des avocats du barreau de Colmar et de Saverne* [1988] ECR 111
Case 302/86 *Commission v. Denmark (Containers)* [1988] ECR 4607
Case 242/87 *Commission v. Council (Erasmus)* [1989] ECR 1425
Case C-379/87 *Groener v. Minister for Education* [1989] ECR 3967
Case C-145/88 *Torfaen Borough Council v. B&Q* [1989] ECR 3851
Case C-154/89 *Commission v. France (Tour Guides)* [1991] ECR I-659
Case C-353/89 *Commission v. Netherlands (Broadcasting)* [1991] ECR I-4069
Case C-159/90 *Society for the Protection of Unborn Children Ireland v. Grogan* [1991] ECR I-4685
Case 369/90 *Mario Vicente Micheletti and others v. Delegación del Gobierno en Cantabria* [1992] ECR I-4239
Case C-288/89 *Stichting Collective Antennevoorziening Gouda and others v. Commissariaat vor de Media* [1993] ECR I-487
Case C-168/91 *Christos Konstantinidis v. Stadt Altensteig Standesamt* [1993] ECR I-1191
Case C-17/92 *Federacíon de Distribuidores Cinematográficos (Fedicine) v. Spanish State* [1993] ECR I-2239
Case C-415/93 *Union Royale Belge des Sociétés de Football Association and Others v. Bosman and Others* [1995] ECR I-4921
Opinion 2/94 *European Convention* [1996] I-1759
Case C-473/93 *Commission v. Luxemburg (Public Sector Posts)* [1996] ECR I-3207
Case C-368/95 *Vereinigte Familia Press v. Heinrich Bauer Verlag* [1997] ECR I-3689
Cases C-51/96 and C-191/97 *Deliège v. LFJ et Disciplines ASBL* [2000] ECR I-2549
Case C-85/96 *Martínez Sala v. Freistaat Bayern* [1998] ECR I-2691
Case C-274/96 *Criminal Proceedings against Bickel and Franz* [1998] ECR I-7637
Case C-350/96 *Clean Car Autoservice v. Landeshauptmann von Wien* [1998] ECR I-2521
Case C-262/96 *Sema Sürül v. Bundesanstalt für Arbeit* ECR [1999] ECR I-2685
Case C-348/96 *Criminal Proceedings against Donatella Calfa* [2000] ECR I-11
Case C-42/97 *European Parliament v. Council of the European Union* [1999] ECR I-869
Case C-224/97 *Ciola v. Land Vorarlberg* [1999] ECR I-2517
Case C-378/97 *Criminal Proceedings against Wijsenbeek* [1999] ECR I-6207
Case C-430/97 *Johannes v. Johannes* [1999] ECR I-3475

Case C-179/98 *Belgian State v. Fatna Mesbah* [1999] ECR I-7955
Case C-281/98 *Angonese v. Cassa di Risparmio di Bolzano SpA* [2000] ECR I-4139
Case C-285/98 *Tanja Kreil v. Germany* [2000] ECR I-69
Case C-54/99 *Association Église de Scientologie de Paris and Scientology International Reserves Trust v. The Prime Minister* [2000] ECR I-1335
Case 184/99 *Rudy Grzelczyk v. le Centre public d'aide sociale d'Ottignies-Louvain-la-Neuve* [2001] ECR 6193
Case C-192/99 *The Queen v. Secretary of State for the Home Department, ex parte Manjit Kaur* [2001] ECR I-1237
Case C-413/99 *Baumbast and R v. Secretary of State for the Home Department* [2001] ECR I-7091
Case T-120/99 *Christina Kik v. Office for Harmonisation in the Internal Market (Trade Marks and Designs)* [2001] ECR II-2235
Case C-224/98 *Marie-Nathalie D'Hoop v. Office National d'Emploi* [2002] ECR I-1691
Case T-54/99 *Maxmobil v. Commission* [2002] ECR II-313
Case C-112/00 *Eugen Schmidberger, Internationale Transporte und Planzüge v. Republic of Austria* [2003] ECR I-5659
Case C-109/01 *Secretary of State for the Home Department v. Hacene Akrich* [2003] ECR I-9607
Case C-186/01 *Alexander Dory v. Federal Republic of Germany* [2003] ECR I-2479
Case C-361/01 P *Christina Kik v. Office for Harmonisation in the Internal Market (Trade Marks and Designs)* [2003] ECR I-8283
Case C-388/01 *Commission v. Italy (Museum Entry)* [2003] ECR I-721
Case C-36/02 *Omega Spielhallen- und Automatenaufstellungs-GmbH v. Oberbürgermeisterin der Bundesstadt Bonn* [2004] ECR I-9609
Case C-148/02 *Carlos García Avello v. État Belge* [2003] ECR I-11613
Case C-200/02 *Zhu and Chen v. Secretary of State for the Home Department* [2004] ECR I-9925
Case C-224/02, *Heikki Antero Pusa v. Osuuspankkien Keskinäinen Vakuutusyhtiö* [2004] ECR I-5763
Case T-313/02 *David Meca-Medina and Igor Majcen v. Commission* [2004] ECR II-3291
Case C-45/03 *Prefetto della Provincia di Catania c. Oxana Dem'Yanenko* [2004] (not reported)
Case C-65/03 *Commission v. Belgium* [2004] ECR I-6427
Case C-147/03 *Commission v. Austria* [2005] ECR I-5969
Case C-209/03 *The Queen on the application of Dany Bidar v. London Borough of Ealing* [2005] ECR I-2119
Case C-403/03 *Egon Schempp v. Finanzamt München* [2005] ECR I-6421
Case C-540/03 *Parliament v. Council (Family Life)* [2006] ECR I-5769
Case C-96/04 *Standesamt Stadt Niebüll* [2006] ECR I-3561
Case C-258/04 *Office national de l'emploi v. Ioannis Ioannidis* [2005] ECR I-8275

Case C-145/04 *Spain v. the United Kingdom* [2006] ECR I-7917
Case C-300/04 *Eman and Sevinger v. College van burgemeester en wethouders van Den Haag* [2006] ECR I-8055
Case C-406/04 *Gérald De Cuyper v. Office national de l'emploi* [2006] ECR I-6947
Case C-192/05 *K. Tas-Hagen and R.A. Tas v. Raadskamer WUBO van de Pensioen- en Uitkeringsraad* [2006] ECR I-10451
Case C-208/05 *ITC Innovative Technology Center GmbH v. Bundesagentur für Arbeit* [2007] (not yet reported)
Case C-346/05 *Monique Chateignier v. Office national de l'emploi (ONEM)* [2006] ECR I-10951
Case C-168/91, Opinion of Advocate General Jacobs (9 December 1992)
Case C-274/96, Opinion of Advocate General Jacobs (19 March 1998)
Case C-42/97, Opinion of Advocate General La Pergola (5 May 1998)
Case C-184/99, Opinion of Advocate General Alber (28 September 2000)
Case C-138/02, Opinion of Advocate General Ruiz-Jarabo Colomer (10 July 2003)
Case C-224/02, Opinion of Advocate General Jacobs (20 November 2003)
Case C-36/02, Opinion of Advocate General Stix-Hackl (18 March 2004)
Case C-209/03, Opinion of Advocate General Geelhoed (11 November 2004)
Case C-96/04, Opinion of Advocate General Jacobs (30 June 2005)
Cases C-145/04 and C-300/04, Opinion of Advocate General Tizzano (6 April 2006)
Case C-303/05, Opinion of Advocate General Colomer (12 September 2006)

3. NATIONAL COURTS

a. **Courts and Tribunals in Germany**

BVerfG, BVerfGE 37, 239 (Constitutional Court) (1974)
BVerfG, 1 BvR 525/77 (Constitutional Court) (1978)
BVerfG, BVerfGE 55, 349 (*Hess Entscheidung*) (Constitutional Court (1980))
BVerfG, BVerfGE 83, 37 (*Ausländerwahlrecht I*) (Constitutional Court) (1990)
BVerfG, BVerfGE 83, 60 (*Ausländerwahlrecht II*) (Constitutional Court) (1990)
BVerfG, 2 BvR 2134/92 (*Maastricht-Urteil*) (Constitutional Court) (1993)
    English: *Brunner and Others v. the European Union Treaty (Maastricht)*, 1 Common Market Law Review 57 (1994)
BVerwG, 9 C 392.94 (Federal Administrative Tribunal) (1995)
BVerwG, 9 C 8.96 (Federal Administrative Tribunal) (1996)
BVerfG, 2BvR 2108/00 (Constitutional Court) (2003)
BVerfG, 2 BvR 1436/02 (Constitutional Court) (2003)
BVerwG, 1 C 35.02 (Federal Administrative Tribunal) (2003)
OLG Stuttgart, 17 UF 259/02 (Beschluss vom 17.3.2003) (State Court of Appeals, Baden-Württemberg) (2003)

BVerfG, 1 BvR 1266/00 (Constitutional Court) (2004)
BVerfG, 2 BvR 1570/03 (Constitutional Court) (2004)
BVerwG, 1 C 13.03 (Federal Administrative Tribunal) (2004)
BVerfG, 2 BvR 2236/04 (Constitutional Court) (2005)
BVerfG, 2 BvQ 25/05 (Constitutional Court) (2005)
BVerwG, 5 C 8.05 and 5 C 17.05 (Federal Administrative Tribunal) (2005)
BVerfG, 2 BvR 1339/06 (Constitutional Court) (2006)

b.   Courts and Tribunals in Hungary

5/2004. Alkotmánybírósági határozat (Constitutional Court) (2004)
196/2004. (XII. 11.) OVB határozat (National Election Office) (2004)
Kvk. III. 37. 316/2004/2 (Supreme Court) (2004)
Kvk. IV. 37. 315/2004/2 (Supreme Court) (2004)
2/2005. (I. 4.) OVB határozat (National Election Office) (2005)
Kvk. III. 37. 013/2005/2 (Supreme Court) (2005)
Kvk. III. 37. 011/2005/2 (Supreme Court) (2005)

c.   Courts in the United States

Dred Scott v. Sandford, 60 U.S. 393 (1857)
Elk v. Wilkins, 112 U.S. 94 (1884)
In re Martonelli, 63 F. 437 (C.C.S.D.N.Y.) (1894)
Mackenzie v. Hare, 239 U.S. 299 (1915)
Anderson v. Howe, 231 F. 546 (D.C.N.Y. 1916)
Ex parte Gilroy, 257 F. 110 (S.D.N.Y. 1919)
United States ex rel. Tisi v. Tod, 264 U.S. 131 (1924)
United States ex rel. Vajtauer v. Commissioner of Immigration, 173 U.S. 103 (1927)
Colgate v. Harvey, 296 U.S. 404 (1935)
Perez v. Brownell, 356 U.S. 44 (1958)
Trop v. Dulles, 356 U.S. 86 (1958)
Kent v. Dulles, 357 U.S. 116 (1958)
Schneider v. Rusk, 377 U.S. 163 (1964)
United States v. Laub, 385 U.S. 475 (1967)
Perdido v. Immigration and Naturalization Service, 420 F.2d 1179 (5th Cir. 1969)
Aalund v. Marshall, 461 F.2d 710 (5th Cir. 1972)
Cervantes v. Immigration and Naturalization Service, 510 F.2d 89 (10th Cir. 1975)
Vance v. Terrazas, 444 U.S. 252 (1980)
Maria v. McElroy, 68 F. Supp. 2d 206 (E.D.N.Y. 1999)
Beharry v. Reno, 183 F. Supp. 2d 584 (E.D.N.Y. 2002)
Hamdan v. Rumsfeld, 548 U.S. (2006)

d. Other Courts and Tribunals

Mandla v. Lee, [1983] I.R.L.R. 209 (UK House of Lords) (1983)
Fajujonu v. the Minister for Justice, [1990] 2 I.R. 151 (Irish Supreme Court) (1990)
R. v. Keegstra, [1990] 3 S.C.R. 697 (Supreme Court of Canada) (1990)
Minister of State for Immigration and Ethnic Affairs v. Ah Hin Teoh, 128 A.L.R. 353 (Australian High Court) (1995)
Benner v. the Secretary of State of Canada, [1997] 1 S.C.R. 358 (Supreme Court of Canada) (1997)
Arrêt no. 735 du 16 juillet 1998 (Abraham Serfaty) (Supreme Court of Morocco) (1998)
Dawood v. Minister of Home Affairs, [2000] 3 S.A. 936 (Constitutional Court of South Africa) (2000)
Abbasi and Another v. Secretary of State for Foreign and Commonwealth Affairs and Secretary of State for the Home Department, [2002] EWCA Civ. 1598 (UK Court of Appeal) (2002)
Lobe and Osayande v. the Minister for Justice, Equality and Law Reform, [2003] IESC 1 (Irish Supreme Court) (2003)
Kaunda & Others v. the President of the RSA and Others, 44 ILM 173 (Constitutional Court of South Africa) (2004)
Arrêt no. 7071 du 14 décembre 2004 (French Cour de Cassation, Chambre Criminelle) (2004)
Case P 1/05 (Application of the European Arrest Warrant to Polish Citizens) (Polish Constitutional Court) (2005)
Case Pl. ÚS 66/04 (European Arrest Warrant Decision) (Czech Constitutional Court) (2006)
Al Rawi and Others v. Secretary of State for Foreign and Commonwealth Affairs and Secretary of State for the Home Department, [2006] EWHC Admin. 972 (UK High Court) (2006)

G. LITERATURE

Alegre, S. and M. Leaf, 'Mutual Recognition in European Judicial Cooperation: A Step Too Far Too Soon? Case Study – the European Arrest Warrant' (2004) 10(2) *European Law Journal*.
Aleinikoff, T. A., 'After Nationality, Then What?' (1999) 2(2) *Research Perspectives on Migration*.
Aleinikoff, T. A. and D. Klusmeyer, *Citizenship Policies in the Age of Migration* (Migration Policy Institute, Washington, DC, 2002).
Aleinikoff, T. A., 'Between National and Post-National: Membership in the United States' in C. Joppke and E. Morawska (eds), *Toward Assimilation and Citizenship in Liberal Nation-States* (Palgrave Macmillan, Basingstroke, 2003).
Anderson, B., *Imagined Communities* (Verso, London, 1983).

Anderson, B., 'Exodus' (1994) 20(2) *Critical Inquiry*.
Andreescu, G., 'Multiculturalism in Central Europe: Cultural Integration and Group Privacy' (Part III) (6 February 2002) 4(3) *East European Perspectives*.
Anwar, M., 'Young Asians Between Two Cultures' (1976) 38 *New Society*.
Arendt, H., *The Origins of Totalitarianism* (Harcourt Brace and Company, London, 1979) [1951].
Arday, L., *Magyarok a szomszédos államokban – külpolitikánk változása* 11 (1990). Manuscript No. 1040/90 at the former Teleki László Alapítvány (TLA), Budapest.
Asad, T., 'Muslims and European Identity: Can Europe Represent Islam?' in A. Pagden (ed.), *The Idea of Europe: From Antiquity to the European Union* 209 (Woodrow Wilson Center Press, Washington, DC, 2002).
Aslam, J., 'Judicial Oversight of Islamic Family Law Arbitration in Ontario: Ensuring Meaningful Consent and Promoting Multicultural Citizenship' (Note) (2006) 38(4) *N.Y.U. Journal of International Law and Politics*.
Autem, M., 'The European Convention on Nationality: Is a European Code of Nationality Possible?' (2000) in *Council of Europe Report on Multiple Nationality* 19 (CJ-NA [2000]13).
Bader, V., 'The Ethics of Immigration' (2005) 12(3) *Constellations*.
Balibar, E., 'The Nation Form: History and Ideology' in E. Balibar and I. Wallerstein (eds), *Race, Nation, Class* (Verso, London, 1991).
Balibar, E., 'Dissonances within *Laïcité*' (2004) 11(3) *Constellations*.
Banton, M., 'National Integration in France and Britain' (2001) 27(1) *Journal of Ethnic and Migration Studies*.
Barber, N.W., 'Citizenship, Nationalism and the European Union' (2002) 27(3) *European Law Review*.
Barnard, C., 'P v. S: Kite Flying or a New Constitutional Approach' in A. Dashwood and S. O'Leary (eds), *The Principle of Equal Treatment in European Community Law* (Sweet & Maxwell, London, 1997).
Barnard, C., 'Article 13: Through the Looking Glass of Union Citizenship' in D. O'Keeffe and P. Twomey (eds), *Legal Issues of the Amsterdam Treaty* (Hart, Oxford, 1999).
Barry, B., *Culture & Equality: An Egalitarian Critique of Multiculturalism* (Harvard University Press, Cambridge, MA, 2001).
Barry, K., 'Home and Away: The Construction of Citizenship in an Emigration Context' (2006) 81 *New York University Law Review*.
Barth, F., 'Introduction; in F. Barth (ed.), *Ethnic Groups and Boundaries: The Social Organization of Culture Difference* (Pensumtjeneste, Oslo, 1994) [1969].
Barthes, R., *Leçon* (Éditions du Seuil, Paris, 1978).
Basch, L. *et al.*, *Nations Unbound: Transnational Projects, Postcolonial Predicaments and Deterritorialized Nation-States* (Gordon & Breach, New York, 1994).
Bauböck, R., 'Changing the Boundaries of Citizenship: The Inclusion of Immigrants in Democratic Polities' in R. Bauböck (ed.), *From Aliens to*

Citizens: Refining the Status of Immigrants in Europe 199 (Avebury, Aldershot, 1994).
Bauböck, R., *Transnational Citizenship: Membership and Rights in International Migration* (Edward Elgar, Aldershot, 1994).
Bauböck, R., 'Social and Cultural Integration in a Civil Society' in R. Bauböck, Á. Heller and A. Zollberg (eds), *The Challenge of Diversity: Integration nd Pluralism in Societies of Immigration* (Avebury, Aldershot, 1996).
Bauböck, R., 'Citizenship and National Identities in the European Union' (1997), Robert Schuman Centre (Florence), Jean Monnet Working Papers 4/97, at: <www.jeanmonnetprogram.org/papers/97/97-04-.html>.
Bauböck, R., 'The Crossing and Blurring of Boundaries in International Migration: Challenges for Social and Political Theory' in R. Bauböck and J. Rundell (eds), *Blurred Boundaries: Migration, Ethnicity, Citizenship* (Ashgate, Aldershot, 1998).
Bauer, W. and K. Rainer, 'Möglichkeiten der Nutzung von EU-Förderprogrammen durch Minderheiten' (2004) 61(1/2) *Europa Ethnica*.
Bauman, Z., *Culture as Praxis* (Sage, London, 1999).
Baumeister, R.F. and M.R.L. Leary, 'The Need to Belong: Desire for Interpersonal Attachments as a Fundamental Human Motivation' (1995) 117 *Psychological Bulletin*.
Bárdi, N., 'Látszat és való – a budapesti kormányzatok támogatáspolitikája' (2003) XIII(30) *Magyar Kisebbség*.
van den Bedem, R., 'Towards a System of Plural Nationality in the Netherlands. Changes in Regulations and Perceptions' in R. Bauböck (ed.) *From Aliens to Citizens: Redefining the Status of Immigrants in Europe* (Avebury, Aldershot 1994).
Beiner, R., 'Why Citizenship Constitutes a Theoretical Problem in the Last Decade of the Twentieth Century' in R. Beiner (ed.), *Theorizing Citizenship* (State University of New York Press, Albany, 1995).
Bell, M., *Anti-Discrimination Law and the European Union* (Oxford University Press, Oxford, 2002).
Bellamy, R., 'Still in Deficit: Rights, Regulation, and Democracy in the EU' (2006) 12(6) *European Law Journal*.
Benet-Martínez, V. and J. Haritatos, 'Bicultural Identity Integration: Components and Psychosocial Antecedents' (2005) 73(4) *Journal of Personality*.
Benet-Martínez, V. et al., 'Negotiating Biculturalism: Cultural Frame-switching in Biculturals with Oppositional vs. Compatible Cultural Identities' (2002) 33 *Journal of Cross-Cultural Psychology*.
Benhabib, S., 'Dismantling the Leviathon: Citizens and State in a Global World' (2001) 11(2) *The Responsive Community* (electronic journal).
Benhabib, S., *The Rights of Others* (Cambridge University Press, Cambridge, 2004).
Bernsdorff, N., *Probleme der Ausländerintegration in Verfassungsrechtlicher Sicht* (Peter Lang, Frankfurt am Main, 1986).

Berry, J.W., 'Acculturation as Varieties of Adaptation' in A.M. Padilla (ed.), *Acculturation: Theory, Models and Some New Findings* (Westview Press, Boulder, CO, 1980).
Berry, J.W., et al., 'Acculturation Strategies in Plural Societies' (1989) 38(2) *Applied Psychology: An International Review*.
Berry, J.W., 'Psychology of Acculturation' in N.R. Goldberger and J.B. Veroff (eds), *The Culture and Psychology Reader* (New York University Press, New York, 1990).
Bhabha, J., ' "Get Back to Where You Once Belonged": Identity, Citizenship and Exclusion in Europe' (1998) 20(3) *Human Rights Quarterly*.
Bibó, I., 'The Distress of the East European Small States' [1946] in K. Nagy (ed.), *Democracy, Revolution, Self-Determination: Selected Writings* (Social Science Monographs, Boulder, CO, 1991).
Blackman, J.L., 'State Successions and Statelessness: The Emerging Right to an Effective Nationality Under International Law' (1998) 19 *Michigan Journal of International Law*.
Bleich, E., 'Re-imagining Communities? Education Policies and National Belonging in Britain and France' in A. Geddes and A. Falwell (eds), *The Politics of Belonging: Migrants and Minorities in Contemporary Europe* (Ashgate, Aldershot, 1999).
von Bogdandy, A., 'Leistungsgrenzen des Verfassungsrechts. Europäische und nationale Identität: Integration durch Verfassungsrecht?' (2002) 62 *Veröffentlichungen der Vereinigung der Deutschen Staatsrechtslehrer*.
Borbély, I., 'Külhoni állampolgárság vagy státustörvény' (2000) 8 *Kapu*.
Borchard, E.M., *The Diplomatic Protection of Citizens Abroad; Or the Law of International Claims* (The Banks Law Publishing Company, New York, 1915).
Bourdieu, P., 'L'identité et la représentation: éléments pour une réflexion critique sur l'idée de region' (1980) 35 *Actes de la recherche en sciences sociales*.
Bourdieu, P., 'La force du droit: éléments pour une sociologie du champ juridique' (1986) 64 *Actes de la recherche en sciences socials*.
Bourdieu, P., *Outline of a Theory of Practice* (Cambridge University Press, Cambridge, 1977) [1972].
Bousakla, M., 'Le fait pour un enfant d'acquerir la nationalité du pays d'immigration lui permet-il de s'intégrer?' (2004) Third European Conference on Nationality, 'Nationality and the Child', Proceedings 1 (CONF/NAT[2004] Rap).
Bowker, G.C., and S. Leigh Star, *Sorting Things Out: Classification and Its Consequences* (MIT Press, Cambridge, MA, 1999).
Böhm, M., 'Das Europäische Haftbefehlsgesetz und seine rechtsstaatlichen Mängel' (2005) 58 *Neue Juristische Wochenschrift*.
Brah, A., *Cartographies of Diaspora: Contesting Identities* (Routledge, London, 1996).
Brötel, D., 'Concepts of Identity in the Teaching of History in Germany' in Gottfried Bräuer et al. (eds), *Nationaliy – Identity – Education* (Kovač, Hamburg, 1999).

Brubaker, R., *Nationalism Reframed: Nationhood and the National Question in the New Europe* (Cambridge University Press, Cambridge, 1996).
Brubaker, R., 'Immigration, Citizenship, and the Nation-State' in G. Shafir (ed.), *The Citizenship Debates: A Reader* (University of Minnesota Press, Minneapolis, MN 1998).
Brubaker, R., *Accidental Diasporas and External 'Homelands' in Central and Eastern Europe: Past and Present* (Institute for Advanced Studies, Vienna, 2000). German: *Zufällige Diasporas und externe Heimatländer in Mittel- und Osteuropa in Staatsbürgerschaft* in C. Conrad and J. Kocka (eds), *Europa: Historische Erfahrungen und aktuelle Debatten* (Körber Stiftung, Hamburg, 2001).
Brubaker, R., *Citizenship and Nationhood in France and Germany* (Harvard University Press, Cambridge, MA, 2002).
Brubaker, R., 'Ethnicity Without Groups' in S. May, T. Modood and J. Squires (eds), *Ethnicity, Nationality and Minority Rights* (Cambridge University Press, New York, 2004).
Bruter, M., 'On What Citizens Mean by Feeling "European": Perceptions of News, Symbols and Borderless-ness' (2004) 30(1) *Journal of Ethnic and Migration Studies*.
Bruter, M., *Citizens of Europe? The Emergence of a Mass European Identity* (Palgrave Macmillan, Basingstoke, 2005).
Brysk, A. and G. Shafir, 'Conclusion: Globalizing Citizenship?' in A. Brysk and G. Shafir (eds), *People Out of Place: Globalization, Human Rights and the Citizenship Gap* (Routledge, New York, 2004).
de Búrca, G., *The EU Constitution: In Search of Europe's International Identity* (26 November 2004) (Fourth) Walter van Gerven Lecture, Leuven Centre for a Common Law of Europe), at: <www.law.kuleuven.ac.be/ccle/pdf/wvg4.pdf>.
Bustamante, J.A., *et al.*, 'The Process of Acquiring Citizenship at Birth in Mexico and the United States' in *Migration between Mexico and the United States – Binational Study*, Vol. II, 695 (US Commission on Immigration Reform, Washington, DC and Mexican Ministry of Foreign Affairs, Mexico City, 1998).
Caillosse, J., 'Pierre Bourdieu, juris lector: anti-juridisme et science du droit' (2004) 56–57 *Droit et Société*.
Calhoun, C., 'Imagining Solidarity: Cosmopolitanism, Constitutional Patriotism, and the Public Sphere' (2002) 14(1) *Public Culture*.
Calhoun, C., 'Is it Time to be Postnational?' in S. May, T. Modood and J. Squires (eds), *Ethnicity, Nationality and Minority Rights* (Cambridge University Press, New York, 2004).
Callan, E., *Creating Citizens: Political Education and Liberal Democracy* (Clarendon Press, Oxford, 1997).
Cameron, J.E., 'A Three-Factor Model of Social Identity' (2004) 3 *Self and Identity*.

Cameron, J.E., et al., 'Perceptions of Self and Group in the Context of a Threatened National Identity: A Field Study' (2005) 8(1) *Group Processes and Intergroup Relations*.
Campani, G., 'L'exemple de la diaspora italienne' in R. Gallissot (ed.), *Pluralisme Culturel en Europe* (L'Harmattan, Paris, 1993).
Canovan, M., 'Patriotism Is Not Enough' in C. McKinnon and I. Hampsher-Monk (eds), *The Demands of Citizenship* (Continuum, New York, 2000).
Carens, J., *Culture, Citizenship and Community* (Oxford University Press, Oxford, 2000).
Carlier, J-Y., *Autonomie de la volonté et statut personnel* (Bruylant, Bruxelles, 1992).
Carter, A., *The Political Theory of Global Citizenship* (Routledge, London, 2001).
Carrera, S., 'What Does Free Movement Mean in Theory and Practice in an Enlarged EU?' (2005) 11(6) *European Law Journal*.
Castles, S. and M.J. Miller, *The Age of Migration: International Population Movements in the Modern World* (1961) Recueil des Cours (Macmillan, Basingstoke, 1993).
de Castro y Bravo, F., 'La nationalité, la double nationalité et la supra-nationalité' (1961) 102 *Recueil des Cours*.
Castro Oliveira, Á., 'The Position of Resident Third-Country Nationals' in M. La Torre (ed.), *European Citizenship: an Institutional Challenge* (Kluwer Law International, The Hague, 1998).
Casuto, T., 'Identity and Nationality, Second European Conference on Nationality, Challenges to the National and International Law on Nationality at the Beginning of the New Millennium', Proceedings 41 (CONF/NAT (2001) Pro) (2001).
Castano, E., *European Identity: A Social-Psychological Perspective* in R.K. Herrmann, T. Risse and M.B. Brewer (eds), *Transnational Identities: Becoming European in the EU0* (Rowman & Littlefield, Lanham, MD, 2004).
Catani, M., 'Les collectivités italiennes à l'étranger et les "Comitati degli Italian all'Estero"' in R. Gallissot (ed.), *Pluralisme Culturel en Europe* (L'Harmattan, Paris, 1993).
Cerulo, K.A., *Identity Designs: The Sights and Sounds of a Nation* (Rutgers University Press, New Brunswick, NJ, 1995).
Chabot, J.-L., *Aux origines intellectuelles de l'Union européenne* (Presses Universitaires de Grenoble, Grenoble, 2005).
Chan, J.M.M., 'The Right to a Nationality as a Human Right: The Current Trend Towards Recognition' (1991) 12 *Human Rights Law Journal*.
Chander, A., 'Homeward Bound' (2006) 81 *New York University Law Review*.
Charlesworth, H. and C. Chinkin, *The Boundaries of International Law: a Feminist Analysis* (Manchester University Press, Manchester, 2000).
Chryssostalis, J.H., 'The Work of Values: Between Global and Local, National and Post-national' in S. Millns and M. Aziz (eds), *Values in the Constitution of Europe* (forthcoming).

Çinar, D., 'From Aliens to Citizens. A Comparative Analysis of Rules of Transition' in R. Bauböck (ed.), *From Aliens to Citizens: Redefining the Status of Immigrants in Europe* (Avebury, Aldershot, 1994).

Citrin, J. and Sides, J., 'More than Nationals: How Identity Choice Matters in the New Europe' in R.K. Herrmann, T. Risse and M.B. Brewer (eds), *Transnational Identities: Becoming European in the EU* (Rowman & Littlefield, Lanham, MD, 2004).

Citron, S. *Le mythe national* (Éditions ouvrières, Paris, 1988).

Clifford, J., 'Diasporas' (1994) 9(3) *Current Anthropology*.

Cohen, R., *Global Diasporas: an Introduction* (UCL Press, London, 1997).

Collins, J. and R.K. Blot, *Literacy and Literacies: Texts, Power and Identity* (Cambridge University Press, Cambridge, 2003).

Connerton, P., *How Societies Remember* (Cambridge University Press, Cambridge, 1989).

Connolly, A., S. Day and J. Shaw, 'The Contested Case of EU Electoral Rights' in R. Bellamy, D. Castiglione and J. Shaw (eds), *Making European Citizens* (Palgrave Macmillan, Basingstoke, 2006).

Connor, W., 'Nationalism and Political Legitimacy' in D. Conversi (ed.),*Ethnonationalism in the Contemporary World: Walker Connor and the Study of Nationalism* (Routledge, London, 2002).

Conversi, D., 'The Smooth Transition: Spain's 1978 Constitution and the Nationalities Question' (2002) 4(3) *National Identities*.

Conversi, D., 'Can Nationalism Studies and Ethnic/Racial Studies be Brought Together?' (2004) 30(4) *Journal of Ethnic and Migration Studies*.

Costa-Lascoux, J., 'L'acquisition de la nationalité française, une condition de l'intégration?' in S. Laacher (ed.), *Questions de Nationalité: Histoire et Enjeux d'un Code* (L'Harmattan, Paris, 1987).

Craufurd Smith, R. (ed.), *Culture and European Union Law* (Oxford University Press, Oxford, 2004).

Craufurd Smith, R., 'Community Intervention in the Cultural Field: Continuity or Change?' in R. Craufurd Smith (ed.), *Culture and European Union Law* (Oxford University Press, Oxford, 2004).

Craufurd Smith, R., 'Introduction' in R. Craufurd Smith (ed.), *Culture and European Union Law* (Oxford University Press, Oxford, 2004).

Craufurd Smith, R., 'From Heritage Conservation to European Identity: Article 151 EC and the Multi-Faceted Nature of Community Cultural Policy' (2007) 32(1) *European Law Review*.

Cross, S.E. and J.S. Gore, 'Cultural Models of the Self' in M.R. Leary and J. P. Tangney (eds), *Handbook of Self and Identity* (Guilford Press, New York, 2003).

Crowley, J., 'The Politics of Belonging: Some Theoretical Considerations' in A. Geddes and A. Favell (eds), *The Politics of Belonging: Migrants and Minorities in Contemporary Europe* (Ashgate, Aldershot, 1999).

Csapó, J., *Észrevételek a státustörvényről* in Z. Kántor (ed.), *Státustörvény: Dokumentumok, Tanulmányok, Publikációk* (Teleki László Alapítvány, Budapest, 2002).

Csergő, Z. and J.M. Goldgeier, 'Pooled and Shared Nationalism in Europe' 3-4, Paper presented at the Annual Meeting of the American Political Science Association (28 August–1 September 2002).

Culic, I., 'Nationhood and Identity: Romanians and Hungarians in Transylvania' in B. Trencsényi *et al.* (eds), *Nation-Building and Contested Identities: Romanian and Hungarian Case Studies* (Régio Books and Iaşi, Polirom, Budapest, 2001).

Cunningham, C.B., 'In Defence of Member State Culture: The Unrealized Potential of Article 151(4) of the EC Treaty and the Consequences for EC Cultural Policy' (2001) 34 *Cornell International Law Journal*.

Curtin, D., *Postnational Democracy: The European Union in Search of a Political Philosophy* (Kluwer Law International, The Hague, 1997).

Davies, G., ' "Any Place I Hang My Hat?" or: Residence is the New Nationality' (2005) 11(1) *European Law Journal*.

Davies, G., 'The Process and Side-Effects of Harmonisation of European Welfare States', Jean Monnet Working Paper 02/06 (2006), at: <www.jeanmonnetprogram.org/papers/06/060201.html>.

Dawes, A., ' "Bonjour Herr Doctor": National Healthcare Systems, the Internal Market and Cross-border Medical Care within the European Union' (2006) 33(2) *Legal Issues of Economic Integration*.

Day, S. and J. Shaw, 'Transnational Political Parties' in R. Bellamy, D. Castiglione and J. Shaw (eds), *Making European Citizens: Strategies for Civic Inclusion* (Palgrave Macmillan, Basingstoke, 2006).

Declet, R.A., Jr., 'The Mandate Under International Law for a Self-Executing Plebiscite on Puerto Rico's Political Status, and the Right of U.S.-Resident Nationals to Participate' (2001) 28 *Syracuse Journal of International Law and Commerce*.

Delanty, G., *Inventing Europe: Idea, Identity, Reality* (St. Martin's Press, New York, 1995).

Derrida, J., *L'Autre Cap* (Éditions de Minuit, Paris, 1991).

Dewey, J., *Democracy and Education* (Free Press, New York, 1966) [1916].

Dhamoon, R., 'Shifting From "Culture" to "Cultural": Critical Theorizing of Identity/Difference Politics' (2006) 13(3) *Constellations*.

Dhawan, N., *et al.*, 'Self-Concepts Across Two Cultures: India and the United States' (1995) 26 *Journal of Cross-Cultural Psychology*.

Dobos, F. and I. Apró, 'Intergrációs esélyek és veszélyek' (2000 ősz/autumn) *Pro Minoritate*.

Donders, Y., 'The Right to Cultural Identity in International Human Rights Law' in Y. Donders *et al.* (eds,) *Law and Cultural Diversity* (SIM, Utrecht, 1999).

Donner, R., *The Regulation of Nationality in International Law* (Finnish Society of Sciences and Letters, Helsinski, 1983).

Dornbusch, S.M., K.L. Glasgow and I.-C. Lin, 'The Social Structure of Schooling' (1996) 47 *American Review of Psychology*.

Dougan, M., 'The Constitutional Dimension to the Case Law on Union Citizenship' (2006) 31(5) *European Law Review*.

Dowty, A., *Closed Borders: the Contemporary Assault on Freedom of Movement* (Yale University Press, New Haven, 1987).
Driedger, L., 'Ethnic Self-Identity: A Comparison of In-group Evaluations' (1976) 39(2) *Sociometry*.
Druckman, D., 'Nationalism, Patriotism, and Group Loyalty: A Social Psychological Perspective' (1994) 38 *Mershon International Studies Review*.
Dubois, V., *La politique culturelle: genèse d'une catégorie d'intervention publique* (Éditions Belin, Paris, 1999).
Dundes Renteln, A., *The Cultural Defence* (Oxford University Press, Oxford, 2004).
Durkheim, É., *The Division of Labor in Society*, Book I (Free Press, New York, 1997) [1893].
Durkheim, É., *The Elementary Forms of Religious Life* (Free Press, New York, 1965) [1912].
Eder, K., 'Integration Through Culture? The Paradox of the Search for a European Identity' in K. Eder and B. Giesen (eds), *European Citizenship* (Oxford University Press, Oxford, 2001).
Editors, 'A magyar közvélemény a státustörvény tervezetéről' (2001 *tavasz/ spring*) *Pro Minoritate*.
Eide, A.E., 'Cultural Rights as Individual Human Rights' in A. Eide, C. Krause and A. Rosas (eds), *Economic, Social and Cultural Rights* (M. Nijhoff, The Hague, 2001).
Eistenstadt, S.N., 'The Construction of Collective Identities and the Continual Reconstruction of Primordiality and Sacrality – Some Analytical and Comparative Indications' in S.N. Eisenstadt (ed.), *Comparative Civilizations and Multiple Modernities*, Vol. I (Brill, Leiden, 2003).
Ellison, C.G., 'Religious Involvement and Self-Perception Among Black Americans' (1993) 71 *Social Forces*.
Emmons, S., 'Russian Jewish Immigration and its Effect on the State of Israel' (1997) 5(1) *Indiana Journal of Global Legal Studies*.
Engelen, E., 'How To Combine Openness and Protection? Citizenship, Migration, and Welfare Regimes' (2003) 31(4) *Politics & Society*.
Entzinger, H., 'The Rise and Fall of Multiculturalism: The Case of the Netherlands' in C. Joppke and E. Morawska (eds),*Toward Assimilation and Citizenship in Liberal Nation-States* (Palgrave Macmillan, Basingstoke, 2003).
Eriksen, E.O. and J.E. Fossum, 'Europe in Search of Legitimacy: Strategies of Legitimation Assessed' (2004) 25(4) *International Political Science Review*.
Eriksen, E.O., 'An Emerging European Public Sphere' (2005) 8(3) *European Journal of Social Theory*.
Evans, A., 'Nationality Law and European Integration' (1991) 16 *European Law Review*.
Faist, T. 'Transnationalization in International Migration: Implications for the Study of Citizenship and Culture' (1999) Economic and Social Research Council (UK), WPTC (1999). Later published with the same title in 23(2)

Ethnic and Migration Studies (2000), at: <www.transcomm.ox.ac.uk/working%20papers/faist.pdf>.

Faist, T., 'Dual Citizenship as Overlapping Membership' (2001) School of International Migration and Ethnic Relations (Sweden) Willy Brandt Series of Working Papers in International Migration and Ethnic Relations 3/01, at: <dspace.mah.se:8080/dspace/bitstream/2043/691/1/Workingpaper301.pdf>.

Falk, R., 'The Making of Global Citizenship' in B. Van Steenbergen (ed.), *The Condition of Citizenship* (Sage, London, 1994)

Falk, R., 'Citizenship and Globalism: Markets, Empire and Terrorism' in A. Brysk and G. Shafir (eds), *People Out of Place: Globalization, Human Rights and the Citizenship Gap* (Routledge, New York, 2004).

Favell, A. and R. Hansen, 'Markets Against Politics: Migration, EU Enlargement and the Idea of Europe' (2002) 28(4) *Journal of Ethnic and Migration Studies*.

Fehér, F. and A. Heller, 'Naturalization or Culturalization?' in R. Bauböck (ed.), *From Aliens to Citizens: Redefining the Status of Immigrants in Europe* (Avebury, Aldershot, 1994).

Feinberg, W., *Common Schools/Uncommon Identities: National Unity and Cultural Difference* (Yale University Press, New Haven, 1998).

Feldblum, M., 'Immigrants and Citizenship Today: A Comparative Perspective' (1999) 2(2) *Research Perspectives on Migration*.

Feldblum, M. 'Reconfiguring Citizenship in Western Europe' in C. Joppke and E. Morawska (eds), *Toward Assimilation and Citizenship in Liberal Nation-States* (Palgrave Macmillan, Basingstoke, 2003).

Feldbrugge, F.J.M., *et al.*, *Encyclopedia of Soviet Law* 528 and 560, respectively (F.J.M. Feldbrugge *et al.* eds, Dordrecht, M. Nijhoff, 2nd ed. 1985). Entries on 'Nationality' and 'Passports'.

Fenton, S., *Ethnicity* (Polity Press, Cambridge, 2003).

Fetzer, J.S. and J.C. Soper, *Muslims and the State in Britain, France and Germany* (Cambridge University Press, Cambridge, 2005).

Fine, R. and W. Smith, 'Jürgen Habermas's Theory of Cosmopolitanism' (2003) 10(4) *Constellations*.

Fitzgerald, D., 'Immigrants and Emigrants: Modern Mexican Nationality Law and the Boundaries of Membership', Paper presented at Centre for Comparative Social Analysis Workshop, UCLA (Los Angeles) (13 February 2003), at: <www.sscnet.ucla.edu/soc/groups/ccsa/fitzgerald.pdf>.

Fitzgerald, D., 'Beyond Transnationalism: Mexican Hometown Politics in an American Labour Union' (2004) 27(2) *Ethnic and Racial Studies*.

Fitzgerald, D., 'Rethinking Emigrant Citizenship' (2006) 91 *New York University Law Review*.

Fletcher, G.P., 'Citizenship and Personhood in the Jurisprudence of War' (2004) 2 *Journal of International Criminal Justice*.

Flournoy, R.W., Jr., 'Dual Nationality and Election' (1921) 30 *Yale Law Journal*.

Flournoy, R.W., Jr. and M.O. Hudson, *A Collection of Nationality Laws of Various Countries as Contained in Constitutions, Statutes and Treaties* (Oxford University Press, New York, 1929).

Flynn, M., 'Returning Home? Approaches to Repatriation and Migrant Resettlement in Post-Soviet Russia' in R. Münz and R. Ohliger (eds), *Diasporas and Ethnic Migrants* (Frank Cass, London, 2003).
Fowler, B., 'Fuzzy Citizenship, Nationalizing Political Space' (2002) Economic and Social Research Council (UK), 'One Europe or Several? Programme', Working Paper 40/02.
Fox, J.E., 'National Identities on the Move: Transylvanian Hungarian Labour Migrants in Hungary' (2003) 29(3) *Journal of Ethnic and Migration Studies*.
Franck, T.M., 'Clan and Superclan: Loyalty, Identity and Community in Law and Practice' (1996) 90 *American Journal of International Law*.
Fuss, D., 'The Meaning of Nationality and European Identity Among Youths from Different Nations', paper presented at the National Political Cultures and European Integration Workshop of the European Consortium for Political Research (Edinburgh) (2003), at: <www.essex.ac.uk/ECPR/events/jointsessions/paperarchive/edinburgh/ws2/Fuss.pdf>.
Gamberale, C., 'European Citizenship and Political Identity' (1997) 1 *Space and Polity*.
Gans, H. J., 'Symbolic Ethnicity: The Future of Ethnic Groups and Cultures in America' (1979) 2(1) *Ethnic and Racial Studies*.
García, S. and H. Wallace, 'Conclusion' in S. García, (ed.), *European Identity and the Search for Legitimacy* (Pinter Publishers, London, 1993).
Gargas, S., 'Die Staatenlosen' in *Bibliotheca Visseriana' VII, 6 (Brill, Leiden, 1928)*.
Garner, J.W., 'Another Triumph of Arbitration' (1926) 20(1) *American Journal of International Law*.
Gaudemet-Tallon, H., 'La désunion du couple en droit international privé' (1991) 226 *Recueil des Cours*.
Gál, G., B. Jarábik and A. Lamacková, *A magyar és a szlovák státustörvény összehasonlító jogi elemzése: Státushatár* in Z. Kántor (ed.), *Státustörvény: Dokumentumok, Tanulmányok, Publikációk* 315 (Teleki László Alapítvány, Budapest, 2002). English at: <kbdesign.sk/cla/projects/project.php?melyik=comparative_statuslaw&nyelv=en>.
Gelazis, N.M., 'The Effects of EU Conditionality on Citizenship Policies and Protection of National Minorities in the Baltic States', Robert Schuman Centre (Florence), RSC No. 2000/68 (2000).
Gellner, E., *Nations and Nationalism* (Blackwell, Oxford, 1983).
Gensicke, T., 'Auf dem Wege der Integration. Die Neuen Bundesländer Heute' in M. Sabrow (ed.), *Die Grenzen der Entgrenzung: Zehn Jahre Deutsche Einheit* (Akademische Verlagsgesellschaft, Leipzig, 2001).
Gerber, C.F., *Über Öffentliche Rechte* (Wissenschaftliche Buchgesellschaft, Darmstadt, 1968) [1852].
von Gierke, O., *Labands Staatsrecht und die Deutsche Rechtswissenschaft* (Wissenschaftliche Buchgesellschaft, Darmstadt, 1961) [1883].
Giesen, B., 'National Identity and Citizenship: The Cases of Germany and France' in K. Eder and B. Giesen (eds.), *European Citizenship Between National Legacies and Postnational Projects* (Oxford University Press, Oxford, 2001).

Gilbert, G., 'The Burgeoning Minority Rights Jurisprudence of the European Court of Human Rights' (2002) 24(3) *Human Rights Quarterly*.

Gilbert, G., Article 5 in M. Weller (ed.), *The Rights of Minorities in Europe: Commentary on the European Framework Convention for the Protection of National Minorities* (Oxford University Press, Oxford, 2005).

Gnielinski, T., *Die Reform des deutschen Staatsangehörigkeitsrechts* (Peter Lang, Frankfurt am Main, 1999).

González Gutiérrez, C., 'Fostering Identities: Mexico's Relations with its Diaspora' (1999) 86(2) *Journal of American History*.

Gordon, M.M., *Assimilation in American Life: The Role of Race, Religion, and National Origins* (Oxford University Press, New York, 1964).

Gottlieb, G., *Nation Against State* (Council on Foreign Relations Press, New York, 1993).

Göbel-Zimmermann, R., *Das Neue Staatsangehörigkeitsrecht – Erfahrungen und Reformvorschläge* (2003) 23(2) *Zeitschrift für Ausländerrecht und Ausländerpolitik*.

Görömbei, S., 'A kisebbségek esélyei az EU-csatlakozás után' (2001 ősz/autumn) *Pro Minoritate'*.

Grawert, R., *Staat und Staatsangehörigkeit: Verfassungsgeschichtliche Untersuchung zur Entstehung der Staatsangehörigkeit* (Duncker & Humblot, Berlin, 1973).

Green, S., 'Citizenship Policy in Germany: The Case of Ethnicity over Residence' in R. Hansen and P. Weil (eds), *Towards a European Nationality: Citizenship, Immigration and Nationality Law in the European Union* (Palgrave Macmillan, Basingstoke, 2001).

Griffin, W.L., 'The Right to a Single Nationality' (1967) 40 *Temple Law Quarterly*.

de Groot, G.-René, *Staatsangehörigkeitsrecht im Wandel* (Carl Heymanns, Köln and T.M.C. Asser Instituut, The Hague, 1989).

de Groot, G.-René, 'Towards a European Nationality Law' (2004) 8(3) *Electronic Journal of Comparative Law* (electronic journal).

Guarnizo, L.E., *et al.*, 'Assimilation and Transnationalism: Determinants of Transnational Political Action Among Contemporary Migrants' (2003) 108(6) *American Journal of Sociology*.

Guenancia, P., 'L'identité' in D. Kambouchner (ed.), *Notions de Philosophie II* (Gallimard, Paris, 1995).

Guild, E., *The Legal Elements of European Identity* (Kluwer Law International, The Hague, 2004).

Guiraudon, V., 'Citizenship Rights for Non-Citizens: France, Germany, and the Netherlands' in C. Joppke and E. Morawska (eds), *Toward Assimilation and Citizenship in Liberal Nation-States* (Palgrave Macmillan, Basingstoke, 2003).

Gustafson, P., 'Globalisation, Multiculturalism and Individualism: the Swedish Debate on Dual Citizenship' (2002) 28(3) *Journal of Ethnic and Migration Studies*.

Gutmann, D., *Le sentiment d'identité: Étude de droit des personnes et de la famille* (LGDJ, Paris, 2000).
Gyertyánfy, A., 'A határon túli németek jogállása a magyar Schengen-probléma tükrében' (2000), 1 *Regio*.
Gyertyánfy, A., 'Migráció, régiók, egységes piac' (2002) 3 *Regio*.
Habermas, J., 'Staatsbürgerschaft und Nationale Identität' [1990] reproduced in R. Beiner (ed.), *Faktizität und Geltung* (1992). In English: 'Citizenship and National Identity: Some Reflections on the Future of Europe' in *Theorizing Citizenship* (State University of New York Press, Albany, 1995).
Habermas, J. and J. Derrida, 'February 15, or What Binds Europeans Together: A Plea for a Common Foreign Policy, Beginning in the Core of Europe' (2003) 10(3) *Constellations*.
Haenel, H. and F. Sicard, *Enraciner l'Europe* (Éditions du Seuil, Paris, 2003).
Hailbronner, K. and G. Renner, *Staatsangehörigkeitsrecht: Kommentar* (C.H. Beck, München, 3rd ed. 2001).
Hailbronner, K., 'Rights and Duties of Dual Nationals: Changing Concepts and Attitudes' in D.A. Martin and K. Hailbronner (eds), *Rights and Duties of Dual Nationals* (Kluwer Law International, The Hague, 2003).
Hailbronner, K, 'Die Unionbürgerschaft und das Ende rationaler Jurisprudenz durch den EuGH?' (2004), 57 *Neue Juristische Wochenschrift*.
Hailbronner, K., 'Union Citizenship and Access to Social Benefits' (2005) 42 *Common Market Law Review*.
Hall, S., 'The European Convention on Nationality and the Right to Have Rights' (1999) 24(6) *European Law Review*.
Hall, S., 'Determining the Scope *ratione personae* of European Citizenship: Customary International Law Prevails for Now' (2001) 28(3) *Legal Issues of Economic Integration*.
Halman, L., R. Luijkx and M. van Zundert, *Atlas of European Values* (Brill and Tilburg University, Leiden, 2005).
Haltern, U., 'Recht als kulturelle Existenz' in E. Jayme (ed.), *Kulturelle Identität und Internationales Privatrecht* (C. F. Müller Verlag, Heidelberg, 2003).
Hammar, T., *Democracy and the Nation State: Aliens, Denizens and Citizens in a World of International Migration* (Avebury, Aldershot, 1990).
Hammar, T., 'Legal Time of Residence and the Status of Immigrants' in R. Bauböck (ed.) *From Aliens to Citizens: Redefining the Status of Immigrants in Europe* (Avebury, Aldershot, 1994).
Hann, C., 'All *Kulturvölker* now? Social Anthropological Reflections on the German-American Tradition' in R.G. Fox and B.J. King, eds., *Anthropology Beyond Culture* (Berg, Oxford, 2002).
Hannum, H., *The Right to Leave and Return in International Law and Practice* (M. Nijhoff, Dordrecht, 1987).
Hansen, R., 'From Subjects to Citizens: Immigration and Nationality Law in the United Kingdom' in R. Hansen and P. Weil (eds), *Towards a European Nationality: Citizenship, Immigration and Nationality Law in the European Union* (Palgrave Macmillan, Basingstoke, 2001).

Hansen, R. and P. Weil, 'Introduction: Citizenship, Immigration and Nationality: Towards a Convergence in Europe?' in R. Hansen and P. Weil (eds), *Towards a European Nationality: Citizenship, Immigration and Nationality Law in the European Union* (Palgrave Macmillan, Basingstoke, 2001).

Heater, D., Citizenship: *The Civic Ideal in World History, Politics, and Education* (Longman, London, 1990).

Heater, D., *What is Citizenship?* (Polity Press, Malden, MA, 1999).

Heintze, H.-J., 'The Status of German Minorities in Bilateral Agreements of the Federal Republic' in S. Wolff (ed.), *German Minorities in Europe: Ethnic Identity and Cultural Belonging* (Berghahn Books, New York and Oxford, 2000).

Heitmeyer, W., J. Müller, and H. Schröder, *Verlockender Fundamentalismus: türkische Jugendliche in Deutschland* (Suhrkamp, Frankfurt am Main, 1997).

Held, D., *Democracy and the Global Order: From the Modern State to Cosmopolitan Governance* (Polity Press, Cambridge, 1995).

Hellwig, H., *Die Staatsangehörigkeit als Anknüpfung im deutschen IPR* (Peter Lang, Frankfurt am Main, 2001).

Henkin, L., 'International Human Rights as "Rights"' in J.R. Pennock and J.W. Chapman (eds), *Nomos XXIII: Human Rights* (New York University Press, New York, 1981).

Henrard, K., 'Devising an Adequate System of Minority Protection' (2000) 62 *International Studies in Human Rights*.

Herzfeld, M., *Cultural Intimacy: Social Poetics in the Nation-State* (Routledge, New York and London, 1997).

Hilpold, P., *Hochschulzugang und Unionbürgerschaft – Das Urteil des EuGH vom 7.7.2005 in der Rechtssache C-147/03, Kommission gegen Österreich* (2005) 16(21) *Europäische Zeitschrift für Wirtschaftsrecht*.

Hilson, C., 'What's in a Right? The Relationship between Community, Fundamental and Citizenship Rights in EU Law' (2004) 29(5) *European Law Review*.

Hinarejos Parga, A., 'Commentary on *Bundesverfassungsgericht* (German Constitutional Court), Decision of 18 July 2005 (2 BvR 2236/04) on the German European Arrest Warrant' (2006) 43 *Common Market Law Review*.

Hjerm, M., 'National Sentiments in Eastern and Western Europe' (2003) 31(4) *Nationalities Papers*.

Hofmann, R., 'Overview of Nationality and Citizenship in International Law' in S. O'Leary and T. Tiilikainen (eds), *Citizenship and Nationality Status in the New Europe* (Institute for Public Policy Research and Sweet & Maxwell, London, 1998).

Hogg, M.A. and D. Abrams, *Social Identifications: A Social Psychology of Intergroup Relations and Group Processes* (Routledge, London, 1988).

Hogg, M.A., D.J. Terry and K.M. White, 'A Tale of Two Theories: A Critical Comparison of Identity Theory with Social Identity Theory' (1995) 58(4) *Social Psychology Quarterly*.

Hogg, M.A., 'Social Identity' in M.R. Leary and J.P. Tangney (eds), *Handbook of Self and Identity* (Guilford Press, New York, 2003).
Hokema, T.O., *Mehrfache Staatsangehörigkeit* (Peter Lang, Frankfurt am Main, 2002).
Horváth, E., *Steady Exit, Stable Voice, Seldom Loyalty: Hungarian Identity and Political Goals in Serbia, Slovakia, and Romania* (2000) (on file at Columbia University, Department of Political Science).
Horváth, E., 'European Entanglements: Minority Matters in Post-Accession Hungary and the EU' in W. Sadurski *et al.*, (eds), *Après Enlargement* (Robert Schuman Centre, Florence, 2006).
Horváth, E., 'Cultural Identity and Legal Status' in F. Francioni and M. Scheinin (eds), *Cultural Rights as Human Rights* (forthcoming).
Horváth, T. and Á. Ríz, 'Kárpát-medencei magyarok támogatásának új lehetőségei az Európai Unióban' (2004) X(34) *Magyar Kisebbség*.
Hutton, W., *The World We're In* (Little, Brown, London, 2002).
Ingenhorst, H., *Die Rußlanddeutschen: Aussiedler zwischen Tradition und Moderne* (Campus, Frankfurt, 1997).
Iordachi, C., *A nemzet újrarajzolt határai: a magyar státustörvény és Románia kettős állampolgárságra vonatkozó politikája a Moldovai Köztársaságban* in Z. Kántor (ed.), *A Státustörvény: Előzmények és Következmények* (Teleki László Alapítvány, Budapest, 2002). In English: 'Dual Citizenship and Policies toward Kin-Minorities in East-Central Europe: A Comparison between Hungary, Romania and the Republic of Moldova' in Z. Kántor *et al.* (eds), *The Hungarian Status Law: Nation Building and/or Minority Protection* (Slavic Research Centre at Hokkaido University, Sapporo, 2004).
Jackson-Preece, J., 'Article 18' in M. Weller (ed.), *The Rights of Minorities in Europe: A Commentary on the European Framework Convention for the Protection of National Minorities* (Oxford University Press, Oxford, 2005).
Jacobson, D., *Rights Across Borders: Immigration and the Decline of Citizenship* (Johns Hopkins University Press, Baltimore, 1996).
Jacqueson, C., 'Union Citizenship and the Court of Justice: Something New Under the Sun?' (2002) 27(3) *European Law Review*.
Jayme, E., 'Identité culturelle et intégration: Le droit international privé postmoderne' (1995) 251 *Recueil des Cours*.
Jayme, E., 'Die Kulturelle Dimension des Rechts – ihre Bedeutung für das Internationale Privatrecht und die Rechtsvergleichung' (2003) 67(2) *Rabels Zeitschrift für Ausländisches und Internationales Recht*.
Jayme, E., 'Kulturelle Identität und Internationales Privatrecht' in E. Jayme (ed.), *Kulturelle Identität und Internationales Privatrecht* (C. F. Müller Verlag, Heidelbreg, 2003).
Jenks, C., *Culture* (Routledge, London, 1993).
Jones, P., 'Toleration, Recognition and Identity' (2006) 14(2) *Journal of Political Philosophy*.

Jones-Correa, M., 'Different Paths: Gender, Immigration and Political Participation' (1998) 32(2) *International Migration Review*.
Jones-Correa, M., 'Under Two Flags: Dual Nationality in Latin America and its Consequences for Naturalization in the United States' in D.A. Martin and K. Hailbronner (eds), *Rights and Duties of Dual Nationals* (Kluwer Law International, The Hague, 2003).
Joppke, C., 'Immigration Challenges the Nation-State' in C. Joppke (ed.), *Challenge to the Nation-State* (Oxford University Press, Oxford, 1998).
Joppke, C., *Immigration and the Nation-State: The United States, Germany, and Great Britain* (Oxford University Press, Oxford, 1999).
Joppke, C. and E. Morawska, 'Integrating Immigrants in Liberal Nation-States: Policies and Practices' in C. Joppke and E. Morawska (eds), *Toward Assimilation and Citizenship in Liberal Nation-States* (Palgrave Macmillan, Basingstoke, 2003).
Joppke, C., *Selecting by Origin: Ethnic Migration in the Liberal State* (Harvard University Press, Cambridge, MA, 2005).
Kadelbach, S., *Union Citizenship*, Jean Monnet Working Papers 9/03 (Robert Schuman Centre, Florence, 2003) at: <www.jeanmonnetprogram.org/papers/03/030901-04.pdf>.
Kalvaitis, R.M., 'Citizenship and National Identity in the Baltic States' (1998) 16 *Boston University International Law Journal*.
Kammann, K., *Probleme mehrfacher Staatsangehörigkeit: Unter Besonderer Berücksichtigung des Völkerrechts* (Peter Lang, Frankfurt am Main, 1984).
Kartal, C., 'Die 'doppelte Staatsbürgerschaft' als Integrationsfaktor in der Bundesrepublik Deutschland' (2002) 15(1/2) *Zeitschrift für Türkeistudien*.
Kasinitz, P. et al., 'Transnationalism and the Children of Immigrants in Contemporary New York' in P. Levitt and M.C. Waters (eds), *The Changing Face of Home: The Transnational Lives of the Second Generation* (Russell Sage Foundation, New York, 2002).
Kastoryano, R., *Negotiating Identities: States and Immigrants in France and Germany* (Princeton University Press, Princeton, 2002).
Kántor, Z., 'Nationalizing Minorities and Homeland Politics: The Case of the Hungarians in Romania' in B. Trencsényi et al. (eds), *Nation-Building and Contested Identities: Romanian and Hungarian Case Studies* (Régio Books and Iași, Polirom, Budapest, 2001).
Kántor, Z., 'A státustörvény: nemzetpolitika vagy a kisebbségvédelem új megközelítése?' (2002) VII(23) *Magyar Kisebbség, Új Sorozat*.
Kennedy, P. and V. Roudometof, 'Transnationalism in a Global Age' in P. Kennedy and V. Roudometof (eds), *Communities Across Borders* (Routledge, London, 2002).
Kertzer, D.I. and D. Arel, *Census and Identity: The Politics of Race, Ethnicity, and Language in National Census* (Cambridge University Press, New York, 2002).

Kibria, N., 'Of Blood, Belonging and Homeland Trips: Transnationalism and Identity Among Second-Generation Chinese and Korean Americans' in P. Levitt and M.C. Waters (eds), *The Changing Face of Home: The Transnational Lives of the Second Generation* (Russell Sage Foundation, New York, 2002).
Kiely, R., *et al.*, 'The Markers and Rules of Scottish National Identity' (2001) 49(1) *The Sociological Review*.
Kiliç, M., 'Öffentlich-rechtliche Folgen der doppelten Staatsangehörigkeit aus türkischer Sicht', in D.-T. Juristenvereinigung (ed.), *Auswirkungen der deutsche Staatsangehörigkeitsreform* (Deutsch-Türkische Juristenvereinigung, Hamburg, 2002).
Kis, J., 'Nation-Building and Beyond' in W. Kymlicka and M. Opalski (eds), *Can Liberal Pluralism Be Exported? Western Political Theory and Ethnic Relations in Eastern Europe* (Oxford University Press, Oxford, 2001).
Kiss, Á., 'Románia határon túli románságpolitikája az 1990–2004 között hatályos jogszabályok tükrében' (2005) IX(35–36) *Magyar Kisebbség*.
Kisteleki, K., 'Magyar állampolgárság a XX. században' (2000) XLI *Állam és Jogtudomány*.
Klein, M.A., *Zu einer reform der deutschen Staatsangehörigkeitsrechts* (Peter Lang, Frankfurt am Main, 1996).
Klekowski von Koppenfels, A., 'The Decline of Privilege: The Legal Background to the Migration of Ethnic Germans' in D. Rock and S. Wolff (eds), *Coming Home to Germany?* (Berghahn Books, New York, 2002).
Klekowski von Koppenfels, A., 'Second-Class Citizens? Restricted Freedom of Movement for *Spätaussiedler* is Constitutional' (2004) 5(7) *German Law Journal*.
Klopp, B., *German Multiculturalism: Immigrant Integration and the Transformation of Citizenship* (Praeger, Westport, CT, 2002).
Knop, K. and C. Chinkin, 'Remembering Chrystal Macmillan: Women's Nationality and Equality in International Law' (2001) 22 *Michigan Law Journal*.
Koessler, M., ' "Subject", "Citizen", "National", and "Permanent Allegiance" ' (1946) 56 *Yale Law Journal*.
Kohn, H., *The Idea of Nationalism* (Macmillan, New York, 1945).
Kondo, A., 'Introduction' in A. Kondo (ed.), *Citizenship in a Global World: Comparing Citizenship Rights for Aliens* (Palgrave Macmillan, Basingstoke, 2001).
Koopmans, R. and P. Statham, 'How National Citizenship Shapes Transnationalism: Migrant and Minority Claims-making in Germany, Great Britain and the Netherlands' in C. Joppke and E. Morawska (eds), *Toward Assimilation and Citizenship in Liberal Nation-States* (Palgrave Macmillan, Basingstoke, 2003).
Korhecz, T., *Otthon legyen Magyar* (2000) 3 *Fundamentum*.

Koslowski, R., *Migrants and Citizens: Demographic Change in the European State System* (Cornell University Press, Ithaca, NY., 2000).
Koslowski, R., 'Challenges of International Cooperation in a World of Increasing Dual Nationality' in D.A. Martin and K. Hailbronner (eds), *Rights and Duties of Dual Nationals* (Kluwer Law International, The Hague, 2003).
Kostakopoulou, D., 'Why Naturalization?' (2003) 4(1) *Perspectives on European Politics and Society*.
Kostakopoulou, D., 'Ideas, Norms and European Citizenship: Explaining Institutional Change' (2005) 68 *The Modern Law Review*.
Kovács, P., *A schengeni kérdés* (Osiris, Budapest, 2000).
Kovács, É., *Etnicitás vagy etnopolitika?* in N. Bárdi and C. Fedinec (eds), *Etnopolitika: A közösségi, magán- és nemzetközi érdekek viszonyrendszere közép-Európában* (Teleki László Alapítvány, Budapest, 2003).
Kovács, M.M., 'The Politics of Dual Citizenship in Hungary' (2006) 10(4) *Citizenship Studies*.
Kramer, J., *The Politics of Memory: Looking for Germany in the New Germany* (Random House, New York, 1996).
Kraus, P.A., 'Von Westfalen nach Kosmopolis? Die Problematik kultureller Identität in der europäischen Politik' (2000) 10(2) *Berliner Journal für Soziologie*.
Krosnick, J.A., 'Attitude Importance in Social Evaluation: A Study of Policy Preferences, Presidential Candidate Evaluation and Voting Behaviour' (1998) 53 *Journal of Personality and Social Psychology*.
Künzli, A., 'Exercising Diplomatic Protection – The Fine Line Between Litigation, Démarches and Consular Assistance' (2006) 66(2) *Zeitschrift für ausländisches öffentliches Recht und Völkerrecht*.
Küpper, H., 'Ungarns umstrittenes Statusgesetz' (2001) 47(5) *Osteuropa Recht*.
Küpper, H., 'Die Volkabstimmung über die doppelte Staatsbürgerschaft für Auslandsungarn vor dem Verfassungsgericht' (2004) 61(3–4) *Europa Ethnica*.
Kürsat-Ahlers, E. and H.-P. Waldhoff, *Auch die Einwanderer sind das Volk: Von ethnischen Enklaven zum vollen Bürgerstatus? Stellungname zur Reform (Bundestagsgutachten zur Reform des Staatsangehörigkeitsrechts)*, presented on 13 April 1999 (on file with author).
Kürti, L., 'Globalisation and the Discourse of Otherness in the 'New' Eastern Europe and Central Europe' in T. Modood and P. Werbner (eds), *The Politics of Multinationalism in the New Europe* (Zed Books, London, 1997).
Kymlicka, W. and W. Norman, 'Return of the Citizen: A Survey of Recent Work on Citizenship Theory' in R. Beiner (ed.), *Theorizing Citizenship* (State University of New York Press, Albany, 1995).
Kymlicka, W., *Multicultural Citizenship: A Liberal Theory of Minority Rights* (Clarendon Press, Oxford, 1995).
Kymlicka, W., 'Multicultural Citizenship' in G. Shafir (ed.), *The Citizenship Debates: A Reader* (University of Minnesota Press, Minneapolis, MN, 1998).

Kymlicka, W., 'Nation-Building and Minority Rights: Comparing West and East' (2000) 26(2) *Journal of Ethnic and Migration Studies*.

Kymlicka, W., *Politics in the Vernacular: Nationalism, Multiculturalism and Citizenship* (Oxford University Press, Oxford, 2001).

Kymlicka, W., 'Immigrant Integration and Minority Nationalism' in M. Keating and J. McGarry (eds), *Minority Nationalism and the Changing International Order* (Oxford University Press, Oxford, 2001).

Kymlicka, W. and M. Opalski (eds), *Can Liberal Pluralism Be Exported? Western Political Theory and Ethnic Relations in Eastern Europe* (Oxford University Press, Oxford, 2001).

Kymlicka, W., 'The Evolving Basis of European Norms of Minority Rights: Rights to Culture, Participation and Autonomy', paper presented at the 'Nations, Minorities and European' Conference held at the European University Institute (Florence) 7–8 May 2004.

Lagarde, P., 'Vers une approche fonctionnelle des conflits positifs de nationalités' (1988) 77 *Revue Critique de Droit International Privé*.

Lagarde, P., 'La nationalité française rétrécie' (1993) 82(4) *Revue Critique de Droit International Privé*.

Laible, J., 'Nationalism and a Critique of European Integration: Questions from the Flemish Parties' in M. Keating and J. McGarry (eds), *Minority Nationalism and the Changing International Order* (Oxford University Press, Oxford, 2001).

Laitin, D.D., 'National Identities in the Emerging European State' in M. Keating and J. McGarry (eds), *Minority Nationalism and the Changing International Order* (Oxford University Press, Oxford, 2001).

Lakoff, G., *Women, Fire and Dangerous Things: What Categories Reveal About the Mind* (University of Chicago Press, Chicago, 1987).

Lauterpacht, H., *The Function of Law in the International Community* (Clarendon Press, Oxford, 1933).

Legomsky, S.H., 'Dual Nationality and Military Service: Strategy Number Two' in D.A. Martin and K. Hailbronner (eds), *Rights and Duties of Dual Nationals* (Kluwer Law International, The Hague, 2003).

Lehning, P.B., 'European Citizenship: Towards a European Identity?' (2001) 20 *Law and Philosophy*.

Leigh, G.I.F., 'Nationality and Diplomatic Protection' (1971) 20 *International and Comparative Law Quarterly*.

Lenaerts, K., 'Fundamental Rights to be Included in a Community Catalogue' (1991) 16(5) *European Law Review*.

Lepsius, M.R., 'The European Union: Economic and Political Integration and Cultural Plurality' in K. Eder and B. Giesen (eds), *European Citizenship* (Oxford University Press, Oxford, 2001).

Levitt, P., 'Social Remittances: Migration Driven Local-Level Forms of Cultural Diffusion' (1998) 32(4) *International Migration Review*.

Levitt, P. and M.C. Waters.(eds), *The Changing Face of Home: The Transnational Lives of the Second Generation* (Russell Sage Foundation, New York, 2002).

Levitt, P., 'Keeping Feet in Both Worlds: Transnational Practices and Immigrant Incorporation in the United States' in C. Joppke and E. Morawska (eds), *Toward Assimilation and Citizenship in Liberal Nation-States* (Palgrave Macmillan, Basingstoke, 2003).

Levy, D., 'Coming Home? Ethnic Germans and the Transformation of National Identity in the Federal Republic of Germany' in A. Geddes and A. Favell (eds), *The Politics of Belonging: Migrants and Minorities in Contemporary Europe* (Ashgate, Aldershot, 1999).

Liebich, A., 'Plural Citizenship in Post-Communist States' (2000) 12(1) *International Journal of Refugee Law*.

Liénard-Ligny, M., 'Nationality Law in Belgium and Luxembourg' in R. Hansen and P. Weil (eds), *Towards a European Nationality: Citizenship, Immigration and Nationality Law in the European Union* (Palgrave Macmillan, Basingstoke, 2001).

Lillich, R.B., *The Human Rights of Aliens in Contemporary International Law* (Manchester University Press, Manchester, 1984).

Linke, U., 'Ethnolinguistic Racism' (2004) 4(2) *Anthropological Theory*.

Linklater, A., 'Cosmopolitan Citizenship' (1998) 1 *Citizenship Studies*.

Linklater, A., 'Cosmopolitan Citizenship' in K. Hutchings and R. Dannreuther (eds), *Cosmopolitan Citizenship* (Macmillan, Basingstoke, 1999).

Lipschutz, R.D., 'Constituting Political Community: Globalization, Citizenship, and Human Rights' in A. Brysk and G. Shafir (eds), *People Out of Place: Globalization, Human Rights and the Citizenship Gap* (Routledge, New York, 2004).

Locke, J., *The Second Treatise of Civil Government* (Blackwell, Oxford, 1966) [1690].

Loman, J.M.E. et al., *Culture and Community Law – Before and After Maastricht* (Kluwer Law and Taxation, Deventer, 1992).

Lombard, A., *Politique culturelle internationale: le modèle français face á la mondialisation* (Actes Sud, Arles and Maison des cultures du monde, Paris, 2003).

Longley, C., *Chosen People: The Big Idea That Shaped England and America* (Hodder & Stoughton, London, 2003).

López-Guerra, C., 'Should Expatriates Vote?' (2005) 13(2) *The Journal of Political Philosophy*.

Louie, A., 'Creating Histories for the Present: Second-Generation (Re)definitions of Chinese American Culture' in P. Levitt and M.C. Waters (eds), *The Changing Face of Home: The Transnational Lives of the Second Generation* (Russell Sage Foundation, New York, 2002).

Lowenthal, D., 'Fabricating Heritage' (1998) 10(1) *History and Memory*.

Löwer, W., 'Abstammungsprinzip und Mehrstaatigkeit' (1993) 13(4) *Zeitschrift für Ausländerrecht und Ausländerpolitik*.

MacCormick, N., 'Democracy, Subsidiarity and Citizenship in the "European Commonwealth"' (1997) 16 *Law and Philosophy*.

Majtényi, B., 'A szomszédos államokban elő magyarokról szóló törvény vitás jogi kérdései' (2002) VII(23) *Magyar Kisebbség, Új Sorozat.*
Makarov, A. *Allgemeine Lehren des Staatsangehörigkeitsrechts* (W. Kohlhammer, Stuttgart, 2nd ed., 1962).
af Malmborg, M. and B. Stråth, *The Meaning of Europe* (Berg, Oxford, 2002).
Mankowski, P., 'Kulturelle Identität und Internationales Privatrecht' (2004) 24(4) *Praxis der Internationalen Privat- und Verfahrenrechts.*
Mannens, W., 'A Structure Called Culture' in Y. Donders *et al.* (eds), *Law and Cultural Diversity* (SIM, Utrecht, 1999).
Mansel, H.-P., 'Das Staatsangehörigkeitsprinzip im deutschen und gemeinschaftlichen Internationalen Privatrecht: Schutz der kulturellen Identität oder Diskriminierung der Person?' in E. Jayme (ed.), *Kulturelle Identität und Internationales Privatrecht* (C. F. Müller Verlag, Heidelberg, 2003).
Manzini, P., 'The Priority of Pre-Existing Treaties of EC Member States within the Framework of International Law' (2001) 12(4) *European Journal of International Law.*
Marger, M.N., 'Transnationalism or assimilation? Patterns of socio-political adapatation among Canadian business immigrants' (2006) 29(5) *Ethnic and Racial Studies.*
Marias, E., 'From Market Citizen to Union Citizen' in E. Marias (ed.), *European Citizenship* (European Institute of Public Administration, Maastricht, 1994).
Marshall, T.H., 'Citizenship and Social Class' in G. Shafir (ed.), *The Citizenship Debates: A Reader* (University of Minnesota Press, Minneapolis, MN, 1998).
Martin, D.A., 'New Rules on Dual Nationality for a Democratizing Globe: Between Rejection and Embrace' (1999) 14 *Georgetown Immigration Law Journal.*
Martin, D., 'Comments on Mazzoleni (*ex parte* Guillaume), Leclere and Grzelczyk' (2002) 4(1) *European Journal of Migration and Law.*
Martin, S., 'The Politics of US Immigration Reform' in S. Spencer (ed.), *The Politics of Migration: Managing Opportunity, Conflict and Change* (Blackwell, Oxford, 2003).
Mayer, F.C. and J. Palmowski, 'European Identities and the EU – The Ties that Bind the Peoples of Europe' (2004) 42(3) *Journal of Common Market Studies.*
Mayer, P., *Droit international privé* (Montchrestien, Paris, 5th ed., 1994).
McMurray, O.K., 'Inter-Citizenship: A Basis for World Peace' (1918) 27(3) *The Yale Law Journal.*
McDougal, M.S., H.D. Lasswell and L. Chen, 'Nationality and Human Rights: The Protection of the Individual in External Areas' (1974) 83 *Yale Law Journal.*
McMahon, J.A., *Education and Culture in European Community Law* (Athlone Press, London, 1995).
McMahon, J., 'Preserving and Promoting Differences? The External Dimension of Cultural Cooperation' in R. Craufurd Smith (ed.), *Culture and European Union Law* (Oxford University Press, Oxford, 2004).

Medved, F., 'Interaction Between Nationality and Integration', Second European Conference on Nationality, 'Challenges to the National and International Law on Nationality at the Beginning of the New Millennium', Proceedings 23 (CONF/NAT (99) Pro 1) (2001).

Meireis, R., 'Ausreichende Kenntnisse der deutschen Sprache als Voraussetzung der Einbürgerung' (2003) 56(1) *Das Standesamt*.

van Meurs, W., 'Social Citizenship and Non-Migration: The Immobility of the Russian Diaspora in the Baltics' in R. Münz and R. Ohliger (eds), *Diasporas and Ethnic Migrants: Germany, Israel and Post-Soviet Successor States in Comparative Perspective* (Frank Cass, London, 2003).

Meyer, T., *Die Identität Europas: der EU eine Seele?* (Suhrkamp, Frankfurt am Main, 2004).

Meyer-Bisch, P., *Les droits culturels: Une catégorie sous-developée de droits de l'homme, Cahiers du Centre Interdisciplinaire d'Ethique et des Droits de l'Homme* (Éditions Universitaires de Fribourg, Fribourg, 1993).

Michelman, F., 'Law's Republic' (1988) 97 *Yale Law Journal*.

Miller, D., 'Community and Citizenship' in S. Avineri and A. de-Shalit (eds), *Communitarianism and Individualism* (Oxford University Press, Oxford, 1992).

Mitchell, J. and M. Cavanagh, 'Context and Contingency: Nationalisms and Europe' in M. Keating and J. McGarry (eds), *Minority Nationalism and the Changing International Order* (Oxford University Press, Oxford, 2001).

Modood, T. et al., *Ethnic Minorities in Britain – Diversity and Disadvantage: The Fourth National Survey of Ethnic Minorities* (Policy Studies Institute, London, 1997).

Mole, N., 'Multiple Nationality and the European Convention on Human Rights', Second European Conference on Nationality, 'Challenges to the National and International Law on Nationality at the Beginning of the New Millennium', Proceedings 129 (CONF/NAT (99) Pro 1) (2001).

Moltmann, G., 'American-German Return Migration in the Nineteenth and Early Twentieth Centuries' (1980) 13(4) *Central European History*.

Morawska, E., 'Immigrant Transnationalism and Assimilation: A Variety of Combinations and the Analytic Strategy it Suggests' in C. Joppke and E. Morawska (eds), *Toward Assimilation and Citizenship in Liberal Nation-States* (Palgrave Macmillan, Basingstoke, 2003).

Moreno Fuentes, F.J., 'Migration and Spanish Nationality Law' in R. Hansen and P. Weil (eds), *Towards a European Nationality: Citizenship, Immigration and Nationality Law in the European Union* (Palgrave Macmillan, Basingstoke, 2001).

Mouton, J.D., *La citoyenneté de l'union: passé, présent et avenir* (Europa-Institut der Universität des Saarlandes, Saarbrücken, 1996).

Mölders, S., 'Case Note – The European Arrest Warrant in the German Federal Constitutional Court' (2006) 7(1) *German Law Journal* (electronic journal).

Mummendey, A. and S. Waldzus, 'National Differences and European Plurality: Discrimination and Tolerance between European Countries' in R.K. Herrmann, T. Risse and M.B. Brewer (eds), *Transnational Identities: Becoming European in the EU* (Rowman & Littlefield, Lanham, MD, 2004).

Murphy, A.B., 'Rethinking the Concept of European Identity' in G.H. Herb and D.H. Kaplan (eds), *Nested Identities: Nationalism, Territory and Scale* (Rowman & Littlefield, Lanham, MD, 1999).
Murray, L.M., 'Einwanderungsland Bundesrepublik Deutschland? Explaining the Evolving Positions of German Political Parties on Citizenship Policy' (1994) 33 *German Politics and Society*.
Münz, R. and R. Ohlinger, 'Long-Distance Citizens: Ethnic Germans and Their Immigration to Germany' in P.H. Schuck and R. Münz (eds), *Paths to Inclusion: The Integration of Migrants in the United States and Germany* (Berghahn Books, New York, 1998).
Nagel, C., 'Constructing Difference and Sameness: the Politics of Assimilation in London's Arab Communities' (2002) 25(2) *Ethnic and Racial Studies*.
Nagy, C.I., 'Státustörvény és EU-csatlakozás, van-e helye a státustörvénynek az EU-ban?' (2004) VIII(30) *Magyar Kisebbség*.
Nairn, T., *The Break-up of Britain: Crisis and Neo-Nationalism* (NLB, London, 1977).
Nairn, T., *Faces of Nationalism: Janus Revisited* (Verso, London, 1997).
Nathans, E., *The Politics of Citizenship in Germany: Ethnicity, Utility and Nationalism* (Berg, Oxford, 2004).
Necef, M.Ü., 'Renegades and the Remote-Controlled: The Turkish Debate on the National Allegiance of the Turkish Immmigrants in Germany' in M.P. Frykman (ed.), *Beyond Integration: Challenges of Belonging in Diaspora and Exile* (Nordic Academic Press, Lund, 2001).
Neff, S.C., 'International Law and the Criticism of Cosmopolitan Citizenship' in K. Hutchings and R. Dannreuther (eds), *Cosmopolitan Citizenship* (Macmillan, Basingstoke, 1998).
Neto, F., 'Acculturation Strategies Among Adolescents from Immigrant Families in Portugal' (2002) 26(1) *International Journal of Intercultural Relations*.
Neuman, G.L., 'Justifying U.S. Naturalization Policies' (1994) 35 *Virginia Journal of International Law*.
Neuman, G.L., 'Nationality Law in the United States and Germany' in P.H. Schuck and R. Münz (eds), *Paths to Inclusion: The Integration of Migrants in the United States and Germany* (Berghahn Books, New York, 1998).
Newby, H., 'Citizenship in a Green World: Global Commons and Human Stewardship' in M. Bulmer and A.M. Rees (eds), *Citizenship Today* (UCL Press, London, 1996).
Newdick, C., 'Citizenship, Free Movement and Health Care: Cementing Individual Rights by Corroding Social Solidarity' (2006) 43 *Common Market Law Review*.
Németh, Z., 'A határokon átívelő nemzeti integráció jegyében' (2002) VII(23) *Magyar Kisebbség, Új Sorozat*.
Nic Shuibhne, N., *EC Law and Minority Language Policy: Culture, Citizenship and Fundamental Rights* (Kluwer Law International, The Hague, 2002).
Niedobitek, M., *The Cultural Dimension in EC Law* (Kluwer Law International, London, 1997).

Nielsen, K., 'Cultural Nationalism, Neither Ethnic Nor Civic' (1996-1997) 28(1-2) *The Philosophical Forum*.

Nyíri, P., 'Expatriating is Patriotic? The Discourse on "New Migrants" in the People's Republic of China and Identity Construction among Recent Migrants from the PRC' (2001) 27(4) *Journal of Ethnic and Migration Studies*.

Offe, C., ' "Homogeneity" and Constitutional Democracy: Coping with Identity Conflicts Through Group Rights' (1998) 6(2) *Journal of Political Philosophy*.

O'Keeffe, D. and A. Bavasso, 'Fundamental Rights and the European Citizen' in M. La Torre (ed.), *European Citizenship: an Institutional Challenge* (Kluwer Law International, The Hague, 1998).

Oksenberg-Rorty, A., 'The Hidden Politics of Cultural Identification' (1994) 22(1) *Political Theory*.

Oldfield, A., 'Citizenship and Community: Civic Republicanism and the Modern World' in G. Shafir (ed.), *The Citizenship Debates: A Reader* (University of Minnesota Press, Minneapolis, MN, 1998).

O'Leary, S., 'The Relationship between Community Citizenship and the Protection of Fundamental Rights in Community Law' (1995) 32 *Common Market Law Review*.

O'Leary, S., *European Union Citizenship: the Options for Reform* (Institute for Public Policy Research, London, 1996).

O'Leary, S., *The Evolving Concept of Community Citizenship* (Kluwer Law International, The Hague, 1996).

d'Oliveira, H.U.J., 'European Citizenship: Its Meaning and Potential' in R. Dehousse (ed.), *Europe After Maastricht: An Ever Closer Union?* (Law Books in Europe, München, 1994).

Ong, A., 'Latitudes if Citizenship: Members, Meaning, and Multiculturalism' in A. Brysk and G. Shafir (eds), *People Out of Place: Globalization, Human Rights and the Citizenship Gap* (Routledge, New York, 2004).

Oppenheim's International Law, Vol. I., 'Peace', H. Lauterpacht (ed.), (Longmans, Green and Co., London, 8th ed., 1955).

Oppenheim's International Law, Vol. I., 'Peace', R. Jennings and A. Watts (eds), (Longman, London, 9th ed., 1992).

Orakhelashvili, A., 'The Position of the Individual in International Law' (2001) 31 *California Western International Law Journal*.

Pagden, A., 'Introduction' in A. Pagden (ed.), *The Idea of Europe: From Antiquity to the European Union* (Woodrow Wilson Center Press, Washington, DC and Cambridge University Press, Cambridge, 2002).

Pan, C., 'Minderheitenschutz in Europa und in der EU: Theorie und Praxis' (2003) 60(1) *Europa Ethnica*.

van Panhuys, H.F., *The Role of Nationality in International Law* (A.W. Sijthoff, Leiden, 1959).

Panzera, A.F., *Limiti internazionali in materia di cittadinanza* (Jovene, Napoli, 1984).

Papi, S., 'La proposition de réforme du code de la nationalité marocaine: les raisons d'un consensus' (2005) 121(4) *Revue du Droit Public*.

Parekh, B., 'Politics of Nationhood' in K. von Benda-Beckmann and M. Verkuyten (eds), *Nationalism, Ethnicity and Cultural Identity in Europe* (European Research Centre on Migration and Ethnic Relations at Utrecht University, Utrecht, 1995).
Pastore, F., 'Nationality Law and International Migration: The Italian Case' in R. Hansen and P. Weil (eds), *Towards a European Nationality: Citizenship, Immigration and Nationality Law in the European Union* (Palgrave Macmillan, Basingstoke, 2001).
Patsch, K.J., 'Individual as Subject of International Law' in R. Bernhardt (ed.), *Encyclopedia of Public International Law*, Volume II, 957 (North-Holland, Amsterdam, 2000).
Peers, S., 'Transforming Decision Making on EC Immigration and Asylum Law' (2005) 30(2) *European Law Review*.
Pentassuglia, G., 'The EU and the Protection of Minorities: The Case of Eastern Europe' (2001) 12(3) *European Law Journal*.
Pérez Vera, E., 'Citoyenneté de l'union européenne, nationalité et condition des étrangers' (1996) 261 *Recueil des Cours*.
Piaget, J. and A.-M. Weil, 'The Development in Children of the Idea of the Homeland and of Relations with Other Countries' (1951) 3 *International Social Science Bulletin*.
Pickard, R., *European Cultural Heritage*, Vol. II (Council of Europe Publishing, Strasbourg, 2002).
Plachta, M. and W. van Ballegooij, 'The Framework Decision on the European Arrest Warrant and Surrender Procedures between Member States of the European Union' in R. Blekxtoon (ed.), *Handbook on the European Arrest Warrant* (T.M.C. Asser Press, The Hague, 2005).
Preuß, U.K., 'Problems of a Concept of European Citizenship' (1995) 1(3) *European Law Journal*.
Preuß, U.K., 'Prospects of a Constitution for Europe' (1995) 3 *Constellations*.
Psychogiopoulou, E., 'EC State Aid Control and Cultural Justifications' (2006) 33(1) *Legal Issues of Economic Integration*.
Randelzhofer, A. 'Nationality' in R. Bernhardt (ed.), *Encyclopedia of Public International Law*, Volume III (North-Holland, Amsterdam, 2000).
Räthzel, N., 'Germany: One Race, One Nation?' (1991) 32(3) *Race and Class*.
Reich, N., 'Union Citizenship – Metaphor or Source of Rights?' (2001) 7(1) *European Law Journal*.
Reich, N., 'The Constitutional Relevance of Citizenship and Free Movement in an Enlarged Union' (2005) 11(6) *European Law Journal*.
Renan, E., 'What is a Nation?' in H. Bhabha (ed.), *Nation and Narration* (Routledge, London, 1990).
Renner, K., *Die Rechtsinstitute des Privatrechts und ihre soziale Funktion: ein Beitrag zur Kritik des bürgerlichen Rechts* (Fischer, Stuttgart, 1965) [1904].
Renner, G., 'Erfahrungen mit dem neuen deutschen Staatsangehörigkeitsrecht' (2002) 8 *Zeitschrift für Ausländerrecht und Ausländerpolitik*.
Rezek, J.F., 'Le droit international de la nationalité' (1986) 198 *Recueil des Cours*.

Riad, F., 'Pour un code européen de droit musulman' in J.-Y. Carlier and M. Verwilghen (eds), *Le Statut Personnel des Musulmans, Droit Comparé et Droit International Privé* (Bruylant, Bruxelles, 1992).

Rigaux, F., *Droit international privé (Tome I)* (Larcier, Bruxelles, 1987).

Rigobello, A., 'Diritti culturali e identità europea' in R. Papini (ed.), *Per una Politica Culturala Europea: la Sfida dei Diritti Culturali* (Massimo, Milano, 1986).

Ringelheim, J., 'Identity Controversies Before the European Court of Human Rights: How to Avoid the Essentialist Trap?' (2002) 3(7) *German Law Journal* (electronic journal).

Risse, T., 'European Institutions and Identity Change: What Have We Learned?' in R.K. Herrmann, T. Risse and M.B. Brewer (eds), *Transnational Identities: Becoming European in the EU* (Rowman & Littlefield, Lanham, MD, 2004).

Rittstieg, H., 'Staatsangehörigkeit, deutsche Leitkultur und die deutsch-türkischen Beziehungen' in D.T. Juristenvereinigung (ed.), *Auswirkungen der deutsche Staatsangehörigkeitsreform* (Deutsch-Türkische Juristenvereinigung, Hamburg, 2002).

Roberts, A.E., 'Traditional and Modern Approaches to Customary International Law: A Reconciliation' (2001) 95 *American Journal of International Law*.

Rode, Z.R., 'Dual Nationals and the Doctrine of Dominant Nationality' (1959) 53 *American Journal of International Law*.

Roll, H., 'Young Ethnic German Immigrants from the Former Soviet Union: German Language Proficiency and its Impact on Integration' in R. Münz and R. Ohliger (eds), *Diasporas and Ethnic Migrants* (Frank Cass, London, 2003).

Romano, S., *L'ordre juridique [L'ordinamento giuridico]* (Dalloz, Paris, 1975) [1915].

Roosens, E., 'Ethnicity as Creation: Some Theoretical Reflections' in K. von Benda-Beckman and M. Verkuyten (eds), *Nationalism, Ethnicity and Cultural Identity in Europe* (European Research Centre on Migration and Ethnic Relations at Utrecht University, Utrecht, 1995).

Ros, M. et al., 'Who Do You Think You Are? Regional, National and European Identities in Interaction', Research Briefing Two (July 2004), at: <www.sociology.ed.ac.uk/youth/docs/Briefing%202.pdf>.

Roussel, V., 'Le droit et ses formes' (2004) 56-57 *Droit et Societé*.

Rozakis, C.L., 'Nationality Law in Greece' in R. Hansen and P. Weil (eds), *Towards a European Nationality: Citizenship, Immigration and Nationality Law in the European Union* (Palgrave Macmillan, Basingstoke, 2001).

Rubenstein, K. and D. Adler, 'International Citizenship: The Future of Nationality in a Globalized World' (2000) 7 *Indiana Journal of Global Legal Studies*.

Rubio-Marín, R., 'Transnational Politics and the Democratic Nation-State: Normative Challenges of Expatriate Voting and Nationality Retention of Emigrants' (2006) 81 *New York University Law Review*.

Rumford, C., 'European Civil Society or Transnational Social Space?' (2003) 6(1) *European Journal of Social Theory*.

Sabrow, M., 'Irritation and Integration: *Deutschland heute – eine geeinte Republik?*' in M. Sabrow (ed.), *Grenzen der Entgrenzung: Zehn Jahre Deutsche Einheit* (Akademische Verlagsgesellschaft, Leipzig, 2001).
Sadurski, W., 'Laundering Values' in S. Millns and M. Aziz (eds), *Values in the Constitution of Europe* (forthcoming).
Sajó, A., *Jogosultságok* (MTA Állam- és Jogtudományi Intézete – Seneca Kiadó, Budapest, 1996).
Salins, P.D., *Assimilation, American Style* (Basic Books, New York, 1997).
Sassatelli, M., 'Imagined Europe: The Shaping of a European Cultural Identity through EU Cultural Policy' (2002) 5(4) *European Journal of Social Theory*.
Sasse, G., 'EU Conditionality and Minority Rights in Central and Eastern Europe', paper presented at the 'Nations, Minorities and European Conference' held at the European University Institute (Florence) 7-8 May 2004.
Sata, K.-K., 'The Idea of the "Nation" in Transylvanism' in B. Trencsényi *et al.* (eds), *Nation-Building and Contested Identities: Romanian and Hungarian Case Studies* (Régio Books and Iaşi, Polirom, Budapest, 2001).
Scheinin, M., 'How to Resolve Conflicts between Individual and Collective Rights?' in M. Scheinin and R. Toivanen (eds), *Rethinking Non-discrimination and Minority Rights* (Institute for Human Rights at Åbo Akademi University, Turku, 2004).
Schindler, D., 'Regional International Law' in R. Bernhardt (ed.), *Encyclopedia of Public International Law*, Volume IV (North-Holland, Amsterdam, 2000).
Schlesinger, P., 'Europeanness: a New Cultural Battlefield?' (1992) 5(2) *Innovation*.
Schmahl, S., *Die kulturkompetenz der Europäischen Gemeinschaft* (Nomos, Baden-Baden, 1996).
Schmitter Heisler, B., 'Sending Countries and the Politics of Emigration and Destination' (1985) 19(3) *International Migration Review,* reproduced in S. Vertovec and R. Cohen (eds), *Migration, Diasporas and Transnationalism* (Edward Elgar, Aldershot, 1999).
Schnapper, D., *La France de l'intégration: Sociologie de la nation en 1990* (Gallimard, Paris, 1991).
Schönberger, C., *Unionsbürger* (Mohr Siebeck, Tübingen, 2005).
Schöpflin, G., *Nations, Identity, Power: The New Politics of Europe* (Hurst & Co., London, 2000).
Schuck, P.H., 'Membership in the Liberal Polity: The Devaluation of American Citizenship' (1989) 3 *Georgetown Immigration Law Journal*.
Schuck, P.H., 'The Re-Evaluation of American Citizenship' in C. Joppke (ed.), *Challenge to the Nation-State* (Oxford University Press, Oxford, 1998).
Schwencke, O., *Das Europa der Kulturen – Kulturpolitik in Europa* (Kulturpolitische Gesellschaft and Essen, Klartext, Bonn, 2001).
Senders, S., '*Jus Sanguinis* or *Jus Mimesis*? Rethinking "Ethnic German" Repatriation' in D. Rock and S. Wolff (eds), *Coming Home to Germany?* (Berghahn Books, New York, 2002).
Shachar, A., 'Group Identity and Women's Rights in Family Law: The Perils of Multicultural Accommodation' (1998) 6 *Journal of Political Philosophy*.

Shachar, A., *Multicultural Jurisdictions: Cultural Differences and Women's Rights* (Cambridge University Press, Cambridge, 2001).

Shachar, A., 'Children of a Lesser State: Sustaining Global Inequality Through Citizenship Laws' in S. Macedo and I.M. Young (eds), *Nomos XLIV: Child, Family and State* (New York University Press, New York, 2003).

Shachar, A., 'The Race for Talent: Highly Skilled Migrants and Competitive Immigration Regimes' (2006) 81 *New York University Law Review*.

Shafir, G., 'Citizenship and Human Rights in an Era of Globalization' in A. Brysk and G. Shafir (eds), *People Out of Place: Globalization, Human Rights and the Citizenship Gap* (Routledge, New York, 2004).

Shaw, J., 'Equality of Treatment for Teachers in European Community Law' (1991) 3(1) *Education and the Law*.

Shaw, M.N., *International Law* (Cambridge University Press, Cambridge, 5th ed., 2003).

Sheffer, G., 'From Diasporas to Migrants – from Migrants to Diasporas' in R. Münz and R. Ohliger (eds), *Diasporas and Ethnic Migrants: Germany, Israel and Post-Soviet Successor States in Comparative Perspective* (Frank Cass, London, 2003).

Shklar, J.N., *American Citizenship: the Quest for Inclusion* (Harvard University Press, Cambridge, MA, 1991).

Shore, C., *Building Europe: The Cultural Politics of European Integration* (Routledge, London, 2000).

Shore, C., 'Whither European Citizenship? Eros and Civilization Revisited' (2004) 7(1) *European Journal of Social Theory*.

Shore, C., ' "Government Without Statehood?" Anthropological Perspectives on Governance and Sovereignty in the European Union' (2006) 12(6) *European Law Journal*.

Singbartl, H., '50 Jahre Bundesvertriebenengesetz' (2003) 60 (3/4) *Europa Ethnica*.

Singer, A. and G. Gilbertson, 'Naturalization in the Wake of Anti-Immigration Legislation: Dominicans in New York City', Carnegie Endowment for International Peace Working Paper No. 10 (International Migration Policy Program) (2002).

Smith, A.D., *National Identity* (Penguin Books, London, 1991).

Smith, A.D., 'National Identity and the Idea of European Unity' (1992) 68 *International Affairs*.

Smith, A.D., 'The Problem of National Identity: Ancient, Medieval and Modern' (1994) 17(3) *Ethnic and Racial Studies*.

Smith, M.P., 'Transnationalism, the State and the Extraterritorial Citizen' (2003) 31(4) *Politics and Society*.

Soysal, Y.N., *Limits of Citizenship: Migrants and Postnational Membership in Europe* (University of Chicago, Chicago, 1994).

Soysal, Y.N., 'Citizenship and Identity: Living in Diasporas in Post-War Europe?' (2000) 23(1) *Ethnic and Racial Studies*.

Soysal, Y.N., 'Changing Boundaries of Participation in European Public Spheres' in K. Eder and B. Giesen (eds), *European Citizenship* (Oxford University Press, Oxford, 2001).
Spiro, P.J., 'Political Rights and Dual Nationality' in D.A. Martin and K.Hailbronner (eds), *Rights and Duties of Dual Nationals: Evolution and Prospects* (Kluwer Law International, The Hague, 2003).
Spiro, P.J., 'Mandated Membership, Diluted Identity: Citizenship, Globalization, and International Law' in A. Brysk and G. Shafir (eds), *People Out of Place: Globalization, Human Rights and the Citizenship Gap* (Routledge, New York, 2004).
Spiro, P.J., 'Perfecting Political Diaspora' (2006) 81 *New York University Law Review*.
Stack, J.F., 'Ethnic Groups as Emerging Transnational Actors' (1981) reproduced in S. Vertovec and R. Cohen (eds), *Migration, Diasporas and Transnationalism* (Edward Elgar, Aldershot, 1999).
Staples, H., *The Legal Status of Third Country Nationals Resident in the EU* (Kluwer Law International, The Hague, 1999).
Stavenhagen, R., 'Cultural Rights: A Social Science Perspective' in A. Eide, C. Krause and A. Rosas (eds), *Economic, Social and Cultural Rights* (M. Nijhoff, The Hague, 2001).
van Steenbergen, B., 'Towards a Global Ecological Citizen' in B. van Steenbergen (ed.), *The Condition of Citizenship* (Sage, London, 1994).
Stets, J.E. and P.J. Burke, 'Identity Theory and Social Identity Theory' (2000) 63(3) *Social Psychology Quarterly*.
Stewart, M., 'The Hungarian Status Law: A New European Form of Transnational Politics, Economic and Social Research Council' (UK), Working Paper WPTC (2002), at: <www.transcomm.ox.ac.uk/working%20papers/WPTC-02-09%20Stewart.pdf>.
St. Korowicz, M., 'The Problem of the International Personality of Individuals' (1956) 50 *American Journal of International Law*.
Stråth, B., 'A European Identity: To the Historical Limits of a Concept' (2002) 5(4) *European Journal of Social Theory*.
Stråth, B., 'Common European Values? Critical Reflections from a Historical Perspective' in S. Millns and M. Aziz (eds), *Values in the Constitution of Europe* (forthcoming).
Streek, W., 'Competitive Solidarity: Rethinking the European Social Model', MPIfG Working Paper 99/8 (1999), at: <www.mpi-fg-koeln.mpg.de/publikation/working_papers/wp99-8/index.html>.
Stryker, S., 'Identity Theory: Developments and Extensions' in T. Honess and K. Yardley (eds), *Self and Identity: Psychosocial Perspectives* (John Wiley and Sons, New York, 1987).
Sturm, F., 'Europa auf dem Weg zur mehrfachen Staatsangehörigkeit' (1999) 52(8) *Das Standesamt*.
Swidler, A., 'Culture in Action: Symbols and Strategies' (1986) 51 *American Sociological Review*.

Symmons, C.R., 'Irish Nationality Law' in R. Hansen and P. Weil (eds), *Towards a European Nationality: Citizenship, Immigration and Nationality Law in the European Union* (Palgrave Macmillan, Basingstoke, 2001).

Szabó, I., *Cultural Rights* (A.W. Sijthoff, Leyden, 1974).

Szarka, L., Table on Hungarian Certificates prepared for 'The Status Law Syndrome: Post-Communist Nation-Building or Post-Modern Citizenship?' (Budapest) 14-16 October 2004 (on file with author).

Szarka, L., 'A magyar kedvezménytörvény identitáspolitikai céljai' in I. Halász, B. Majtényi and L. Szarka (eds), *Ami összeköt? Státustörvények közel s távol* (Gondolat, Budapest, 2004).

Szyszczak, E., 'Making Europe More Relevant to Its Citizens: Effective Judicial Process' (1996) 21 *European Law Review*.

Taberner, S. and F. Finlay (eds), *Recasting German Identity: Culture, Politics, and Literature in the Berlin Republic* (Camden House, Rochester, 2002).

Tajfel, H., *Differentiation Between Social Groups* (Academic Press, London, 1978).

Tassin, É., 'Europe: a Political Community?' in C. Mouffe (ed.), *Dimensions of Radical Democracy: Pluralism, Citizenship, Community* (Verso, London, 1992).

Taylor, C., *Multiculturalism and 'The Politics of Recognition': An Essay* (Princeton University Press, Princeton, 1992).

Teitel, R., 'Human Rights on the Eve of the Next Century: Beyond Vienna and Beijing' (1997) 66 *Fordham Law Review*.

Theiler, T., 'Societal Security and Social Psychology' (2003) 29 *Review of International Studies*.

Theiler, T., *Political Symbolism and European Integration* (Manchester University Press, Manchester, 2005).

Thomas, E.R., 'Who Belongs? Competing Conceptions of Political Membership' (2002) 5(3) *European Journal of Social Theory*.

Tilly, C., *Identities, Boundaries, and Social Ties* (Paradigm Publishers, Boulder, CO, 2005).

Tishkov, V.A., 'Forget the "Nation": Post-nationalist Understanding of Nationalism' (2000) 23(4) *Ethnic and Racial Studies*.

Todd, E., *Le destin des immigrés: Assimilation et ségrégation dans les démocraties occidentals* (Éditions du Seuil, Paris, 1994).

Toggenburg, G.N., 'Minority Protection in a Supranational Context: Limits and Opportunities' in G.N. Toggenburg (ed.), *Minority Protection and the Enlarged European Union: The Way Forward* (OSI/LGI, Budapest, 2004).

Torpey, J., *The Invention of the Passport: Surveillance, Citizenship and the State* (Cambridge University Press, Cambridge, 2000).

Tóth, J., 'A diaszpóra a jogszabályok tükrében' (1999) 3-4 *Regio*.

Trebilcock, M.J. and M. Sudak, 'The Political Economy of Emigration and Immigration' (2006) 81 *New York University Law Review*.

Trivalat, M., *Faire France: Une grande enquéte sur les immignés et leurs enfants* (La Découverte, Paris. 1995).

Tsoukala, A., 'The Perception of the "Other" and the Integration of Immigrants in Greece' in A. Geddes and A. Favell (eds), *The Politics of Belonging: Migrants and Minorities in Contemporary Europe* (Ashgate, Aldershot, 1999).

Tully, J., 'The Challenge of Reimagining Citizenship and Belonging in Multicultural and Multinational Societies' in C. McKinnon and I. Hampsher-Monk (eds), *The Demands of Citizenship* (Continuum, New York, 2000).

Turack, D.C., *The Passport in International Law* (Lexington Books, Lexington, MA, 1972).

Uçar, B., 'Eine retrospektive Nachzeichnung der Debatte um die doppelte Staatsbürgerschaft in Deutschland', (2003) 16(1/2) *Zeitschrift für Türkeistudien*.

Vandenberg, A., 'Cybercitizenship and Digital Democracy' in A. Vandenberg (ed.), *Citizenship and Democracy in a Global Era* (Macmillan, Basingstoke, 2000).

de Varennes, F., 'An Analysis of the "Act on Hungarians Living in Neighbouring Countries" and the Validity of Measures Protecting and Promoting the Culture and Identity of Minorities Outside Hungary' in Z. Kántor et al. (eds), *The Hungarian Status Law: Nation Building and/or Minority Protection* (Sapporo, Slavic Research Center at Hokkaido University, 2004). In Hungarian, 'A magyar kedvezménytörvényről', *Pro Minoritate* (2002 *tavasz*).

Varga, A., 'A jogállástól a kedvezményekig' (2000) 3 *Fundamentum*, as reproduced in Z. Kántor (ed.), *Státustörvény: Dokumentumok, Tanulmányok, Publikációk* (Teleki László Alapítvány, Budapest, 2002).

Veress, L., *Határon túli támogatások – elmélet és gyakorlat* in Z. Kántor (ed.), *Státustörvény: Dokumentumok, Tanulmányok, Publikációk* (Teleki László Alapítvány, Budapest, 2002).

Verkuyten, M. and J. Thijs, 'Multiculturalism Among Minority and Majority Adolescents in the Netherlands' (2002) 26(1) *International Journal of Intercultural Relations*.

Vertovec, S. and R. Cohen (eds), *Migration, Diasporas and Transnationalism* (Edward Elgar, Aldershot, 1999).

Vertovec, S., 'Transnational Challenges to the "New" Multiculturalism. Economic and Social Research Council' (UK), Working Paper WPTC (2001), paper presented to the ASA Conference at the University of Sussex (30 March–2 April 2001), at: <www.transcomm.ox.ac.uk/working%20papers/WPTC-2K-06%20Vertovec.pdf>.

Verwilghen, M., 'Conflits de nationalités: Plurinationalité et apatridie' (1999) 277 *Recueil des Cours*.

Vogel, J., *Europäischer Haftbefehl und deutsches Verfassungsrecht* (2005) 60(17) *Juristen Zeitung*.

Vogel, S., *Kisebbségek és (kulturális) külpolitika Európában* (2002), unpublished study at the Teleki László Intézet, Budapest.

Vrinds, E.P.J., 'Die Reform des niederlänischen Staatsangehörigkeitsrechts' (2004) 57(1) *Das Standesamt.*
Waever, O., 'Identity, Integration and Security: Solving the Sovereignty Puzzle in EU Studies' (1995) 48(2) *Journal of International Affairs.*
Waldron, J., 'Minority Cultures and the Cosmopolitan Alternative' (1992) 25 *University of Michigan Journal of Law Reform.*
Walker, N., *Adding Constitutional Value? The Genealogy of Values in the EU's Constitutional Acquis* in S. Millns and M. Aziz (eds), *Values in the Constitution of Europe* (forthcomig).
Walzer, M., *Thick and Thin: Moral Argument at Home and Abroad* (University of Notre Dame Press, Notre Dame, 1994).
Walzer, M., 'A Response from Michael Walzer' (2001) 11(2) *The Responsive Community* (electronic journal).
Weber, E., *Peasants into Frenchmen: The Modernization of Rural France, 1870–1914* (Stanford University Press, Stanford, 1976).
Weber, M., 'Class, Status, Party' in H.H. Gerth and C. Wright Mills (eds), *From Max Weber: Essays in Sociology* (Routledge & Kegan Paul, London, 1948) [posthumous].
Weber, M., *Wirtschaft und Gesellschaft: Grundriss der verstehenden Soziologie* (Mohr, Tübingen, 5th ed., 1976) [1922].
Weber, R., 'Törvény a határon túli magyarokról' in Z. Kántor (ed.), *Státustörvény: Dokumentumok, Tanulmányok, Publikációk' (Teleki László Alapítvány, Budapest, 2002).*
Weber, R., 'A kisebbségek védelme az európai normák szempontjából' in Z. Kántor (ed.), *Státustörvény: Dokumentumok, Tanulmányok, Publikációk* (Teleki László Alapítvány, Budapest, 2002).
Weil, P., 'The History of French Nationality: A Lesson for Europe' in R. Hansen and P. Weil (eds), *Towards a European Nationality: Citizenship, Immigration and Nationality Law in the European Union* (Palgrave Macmillan, Basingstoke, 2001).
Weil, P., 'Access to Citizenship: A Comparison of Twenty-Five Nationality Laws' in T.A. Aleinikoff and D. Klusmeyer (eds), *Citizenship Today: Global Perspectives and Practices* (Carnegie Endowment for International Peace, Washington, DC, 2001).
Weil, P., *Qu'est-ce qu'un Français? Histoire de la nationalité française depuis la révolution* (Grasset, Paris, 2002).
Weiler, J.H.H., 'European Citizenship: Identity and Differentity' in M. La Torre (ed.), *European Citizenship: an Institutional Challenge* (Kluwer Law International, The Hague, 1998).
Weiler, J.H.H., *The Constitution of Europe* (Cambridge University Press, Cambridge, 1999).
Weis, P., *Nationality and Statelessness in International Law* (Sijthoff & Noordhoff, Alphen aan den Rijn, 2nd ed., 1979).
Weissbrodt, D. and C. Collins, 'The Human Rights of Stateless Persons' (2006) 28 *Human Rights Quarterly.*

Weizsäcker, E., 'Jüdische Migranten im Geltenden Staatsangehörigkeits- und Ausländerrecht' (2004) 24(3) *Zeitschrift für Ausländerrecht und Ausländerpolitik*.

Weller, M. (ed.), *The Rights of Minorities in Europe: Commentary on the European Framework Convention for the Protection of National Minorities* (Oxford University Press, Oxford, 2005).

Widdicombe, S. and R. Wooffitt, *The Language of Youth Subcultures: Social Identity in Action* (Harvester Wheatsheaf, New York, 1995).

Williams, M.S., 'Citizenship as Identity, Citizenship as Shared Fate, and the Functions of Multicultural Education' in K. McDonough and W. Feinberg (eds), *Education and Citizenship in Liberal-Democratic Societies* (Oxford University Press, Oxford, 2003).

Wilson, K. and J. van der Dussen (eds), *The History of the Idea of Europe* (Open University, Milton Keynes and Routledge, London, 1993).

de Winter, L.I., 'Nationality of domicile?: The Present State of Affairs', (1969) 128 *Recueil des Cours*.

de Witte, B., 'Building Europe's Image and Identity' in A. Rijksbaron *et al.* (eds), *Europe from a Cultural Perspective* (Nijgh & Van Ditmar Universitair, The Hague, 1987).

de Witte, B., 'The European Community and its Minorities' in C. Brölmann *et al.* (eds), *Peoples and Minorities in International Law* (M. Nijhoff, Dordrecht, 1993).

de Witte, B., 'The Value of Cultural Diversity', paper for the workshop 'Values in the Constitution of Europe', European University Institute (Florence) December 2003 (on file with author).

de Witte, B., 'The Constitutional Resources for an EU Minority Protection Policy' in G.N. Toggenburg (ed.), *Minority Protection and the Enlarged European Union: The Way Forward* (OSI/LGI, Budapest, 2004).

de Witte, B. and E. Horváth, 'The Many Faces of Minority Policy in the European Union' in K. Henrard and R. Dunbar (eds), *Synergies in Minority Protection* (forthcoming).

Wolff, S., 'Changing Priorities or Changing Opportunities? German External Minority Policy, 1919–1998' in S. Wolff (ed.), *German Minorities in Europe: Ethnic Identity and Cultural Belonging* (Berghahn Books, New York and Oxford, 2000).

Yancey, W.L., E.P. Ericksen and R.N. Juliani, 'Emergent Ethnicity: A Review and Reformulation' (1976) 41 *American Sociological Review*.

Yang, P.Q., 'Explaining Immigrant Naturalization' (1994) 28(3) *International Migration Review*.

Yoshino, K., *Cultural Nationalism in Contemporary Japan: A Sociological Enquiry* (Routledge, London, 1992).

Young, I.M., 'Polity and Group Difference: A Critique of the Ideal of Universal Citizenship' (1989) 99 *Ethics*.

Young, I.M., *Justice and the Politics of Difference* (Princeton University Press, Princeton, NJ, 1990).

Zolberg, A.R., 'Modes of Incorporation: Toward a Comparative Framework' in V. Bader (ed.), *Citizenship and Exclusion* (Macmillan, Houndsmills, 1997).

Index

A

Acculturation 34, 51, 264, 268, 270-2
Aleinikoff 8, 11, 13, 37, 40
Allegiance 8, 9, 12-3, 27, 31, 218, 222, 239, 252, 277-9, 291
Armenia 141-2, 240, 286-7
Assimilation 10-1, 37, 39, 51, 214, 259, 268-71, 277, 279-80, 290, 305
Attachment 6-9, 12-4, 20, 26, 37, 49, 60, 71, 106, 113, 124, 127, 133, 187, 236-8, 296
Aussiedler 249, 263, 266
Austria 82-3, 107, 116, 118, 146, 149, 152-3, 161-2, 164, 173-4, 179, 189, 205, 223, 240, 290

B

Badura 259-60
Barthes 55
Bauböck 35-6, 127, 269-70, 294-5
Belgium 8, 59, 82-3, 101, 109, 146, 179, 222, 226, 236, 240, 287-8, 291, 303
Benhabib 291, 298, 304, 312
Biculturalism 32, 276
Birthright nationality 9
Bourdieu 310-1
Brubaker 8, 9, 46-8, 138, 140, 145, 192, 243, 302

Bruter 126-8, 132-3
Bulgaria 61, 97, 140-2, 148, 150, 155, 222-3

C

Canada 14, 31, 43, 217, 272-3, 288
Charter 6, 21, 33, 57, 91, 117, 120, 189, 217
  of Fundamental Rights 33, 117
CIS States 223, 286
Citizens 3-5, 8, 26-8, 34, 71-2, 86-7, 90, 95-6, 99, 100, 105, 107, 113-5, 195-6, 199, 200, 202-4, 299
Citizens Directive 100, 104-7, 115, 126
Citizenship 2-5, 7-9, 26-30, 33-6, 71-3, 86-7, 97-8, 100-1, 104-7, 113-4, 121-2, 129-30, 195-7, 228-9, 275-6, 297-9
  active 113, 276
  basic 287
  centres 26
  ceremonies 267, 291
  common European 121
  context of European 284
  cosmopolitan 35, 131
  emergence of European 66, 86
  external 284, 298
  identity function of 33, 132-3, 197
Citizenship Act 134
  of Estonia 229

Citizenship-nationality link 98, 102, 133, 135
Citizenship rights 4, 5, 7, 9, 10, 26, 28-30, 35, 54, 91, 97-8, 128, 133, 159, 201-2, 249, 296, 302
  of European 92, 96, 99, 109, 129, 135, 234
  extension of 30, 126
Constitutional Treaty 67, 69, 70, 74-5, 77, 91, 93, 96, 113-5, 118-9, 121-5
Consular protection 21, 95, 97, 135, 314
Conversi 47-8
Council of Europe 3, 8, 14, 18, 38, 57, 59, 76-7, 83, 95, 167-8, 190, 200-1, 203, 218-20, 288-9
Craufurd Smith 71, 81, 84
Croatia 25, 139, 141-2, 145, 148, 154-6, 166, 169, 188, 240, 287
Crowley 52, 54
Cultural
  actions 83, 89
  activities 66, 83-4, 121, 146
  communities 54, 143, 192, 195-6, 231, 237, 298, 301, 307, 311
  development 140, 142-3
  differences 84, 111, 263
  dimension 95, 259
  diversity 55, 57-8, 81, 89, 119, 128, 134, 269, 293
  exchanges 70, 144, 209
  groups 30, 58, 62, 179, 202, 299
  heritage 57, 75, 77, 81, 83, 130, 134, 160, 185, 199
  identity 2, 32, 47, 50-2, 55-61, 63, 65, 73, 77, 117-8, 123-5, 130-1, 144-5, 192-3, 236-7, 306-8
  policy 49, 51, 68, 71-2, 76-8, 81-3, 85, 88, 119, 126, 172, 201, 283
  rights 26, 55-8, 65, 69, 116, 118, 120, 312, 316
  ties 140, 160, 201, 204, 229, 272
  expressions 66, 88, 119-20, 303, 308
Culture 47, 50-2, 56-62, 68-78, 83-9, 119-25, 129-30, 143, 154, 171-2, 179, 185-7, 189-91, 198-201, 203, 261-3
  definition of 201
  2000 84, 120, 130
  2007 85-7, 123
  common 87, 122, 131, 306
  dominant 49, 51

  and education 84, 171
  guiding 255
  national 36, 48, 60, 76, 80, 146, 198, 290
Czech Constitutional Court 111
Czech Republic 109, 174, 199, 240

D

De Varennes 171, 176-7, 183
De Witte 73, 89, 118, 128, 190-1, 205
Diaspora 36-7, 148-51, 154-5, 157, 164, 167, 170, 172-3, 192-3, 196, 199-203, 206-7, 214, 280-4, 286-7, 303-4
  policies 172, 192-3, 203, 282, 284, 286, 289, 304, 313
Diplomatic protection 4, 6, 7, 13, 20-4, 215, 221-2, 232-3, 283
Diversity 33, 39, 57, 73, 75-7, 85-6, 88, 94, 119-20, 130-2, 134-5, 190-1, 275, 292-3, 298, 300
  of Cultural Expressions 66, 88, 303, 308
Domicile 13, 219, 231, 236-7, 290
Dubois 201
Durkheim 42, 122, 306
Dutch 23, 82, 143, 230, 241, 273, 288, 290, 292

E

ECHR 5, 7, 14, 19, 20, 24-5, 38, 59-63, 65, 80, 91, 96, 110, 112, 117, 178-9, 224-8
ECJ 8, 15, 38, 68, 76, 78-82, 89, 91, 94, 96-107, 115-7, 120, 128, 134, 189-90, 234-6
Emigrants 37, 203, 242, 272, 275, 279, 283, 285-6
Emigration 9, 36, 157, 222, 272-3, 280, 286, 288, 313
Equality 10, 19, 23, 25, 30, 57, 91, 96, 117, 122-3, 181, 183, 216-7, 248-9, 267-8, 291
Estonian 228-9
Ethnic
  group 11, 198, 293
  origin 3, 39, 40, 62, 91, 161, 184, 190, 315
Ethno-cultural community 161
European
  arrest warrant 108-9, 111

Index 385

citizenship 29, 68-9, 86-7, 90-3, 95-9, 101-4, 106-9, 115-6, 120-2, 126-30, 132-5, 195-6, 204, 234, 307-9, 313-4
community 7, 70-1, 73-4, 79, 87, 91, 94, 119, 153
convention on human rights 138
court
    of human Rights 60-1, 91, 225
    of justice 8, 68, 78
cultural identity 77
European Nationality Convention 18, 220-1
European union 7, 8, 32-3, 36, 66-75, 77-8, 88-93, 97-8, 107-8, 113-5, 117-9, 123-5, 127, 129-33, 189-91, 208-10, 234-5
European Union Citizenship 54, 68-9, 71, 73, 75, 77, 89, 95, 101, 105, 107, 111, 113, 115, 117, 135
Europeanness 126, 133
Expatriates 138, 200, 203, 275, 300
Expulsion 16, 19, 38, 106, 155, 225, 227, 247, 253
External citizenship 284, 298
Extradition 23, 108-12

F

Family law 31, 234, 236-7, 265
Fowler 183, 192
Framework Convention 59, 60, 159, 169-71, 175, 177-8, 181, 183, 190-1
France 8-10, 12, 38-9, 46, 59, 67, 79, 112, 143-4, 224-6, 237, 240, 272-4, 287-8, 291, 305
Free movement 19, 68, 81, 91, 95-6, 98-100, 102, 105-7, 115, 126, 134, 185, 235
Freedom, fundamental 56, 69, 74, 80, 91, 104-5
Fundamental rights 4, 33, 73, 76-8, 80, 91, 107, 110, 114, 117-8, 120, 294

G

Genuine link 101-2, 106, 113, 220-1
German
    context 250, 274, 292, 309
    culture 255, 263
    identity 214, 244, 255, 259, 262, 278
    language 153, 252, 255, 263, 266

nationality 152, 243, 245, 248-9, 251-2, 255, 257-8, 260-1, 264-7, 275, 285, 295, 315
    acquisition of 256-7
    attributed 248, 250-1, 254
nationality, loss of 261-2
society 244, 246-7, 250-1, 257, 266
German Nationality Law 8, 152, 242-3, 250-1, 264-5
Germany 8-10, 46-7, 102, 150, 152-3, 223, 227, 235, 241-5, 247-8, 250-2, 255-6, 260-8, 271, 277, 281-2
Grawert 3, 9, 11, 14, 16, 19, 27-8, 150, 289
Great Britain 9, 30, 222
Greece 59, 61, 109, 139, 141, 150-3, 155, 158-9, 170, 179, 223, 241, 282, 288, 296, 315-6
Gustafson 274-5
Gutmann 237-8, 299, 309-11

H

Habermas 34-5, 122, 124, 276
Habitual residence 32, 101, 107, 216, 233-4, 236-9, 252, 290, 300
Hague Nationality Convention 15-6, 23
Hailbronner 98, 102-3, 106-7, 232, 267
Hansen 3, 4, 10-1, 93, 239
Hogg and Abrams 43, 45
Home-states 137-8, 142, 148-9, 152, 154-5, 159-60, 162-5, 167-8, 170-2, 174, 176-8, 182-3, 185-7, 191, 193-7, 199
Human rights 5, 7, 9, 16-7, 22, 26, 36, 56-8, 60-1, 65, 91, 98, 117, 122, 168, 224-6
Hungarian
    context 139, 146, 156, 194, 205, 275
    culture 163, 186-8
    diaspora individuals 206-7
    identity 158, 163, 184-5
    kin-minorities 146, 210
    minorities 53, 139, 146, 156-8, 160, 165, 169, 180, 182, 195, 197-8, 202, 209, 307, 310, 314
    minority
        individuals 155, 157, 160, 162, 180, 182, 184, 206
        parties 166, 193-4
    model 154-5

nation 156-7, 159-60, 166, 182, 185, 194, 210
nationalism 159, 162, 177
nationals 53, 139, 155, 160-2, 164-5, 208
state 138, 169, 177, 182, 185-6
Hungarian Certificates 161-3, 166, 184, 186, 188, 195, 199, 206-7, 210, 230
Hungarian Status Law 139, 153, 156, 159, 168, 175, 179, 191-2, 203, 310, 313
Hungary 43, 53, 138-9, 141, 144, 146-9, 155-65, 167-71, 176-8, 180, 182-4, 186-9, 193-5, 197, 207-11, 223

I

Identification 12, 34, 36, 41, 45, 49, 68, 106, 121-2, 125-8, 130, 132, 170, 202, 270, 276
Identity 2, 28-30, 32-3, 35-8, 41-2, 57-61, 68-70, 115-8, 121-5, 127-33, 193-9, 274-7, 281-2, 295-6, 301-4, 309-14
  common 34, 138, 258, 305
    European 72, 306
  function 2, 29, 33, 46, 55, 92, 114, 145-6, 196-7, 214-5, 245, 272, 275, 277, 279, 302
  of nationality 13, 224, 242, 275, 295, 299, 303
  nationality's 296
  individual's 41
  maintenance 154, 210, 306, 311
  politics 2, 37, 124, 280, 282, 285, 293
  religious 52, 62, 140, 237
  shared 29, 121, 129
  single 301
  theory 41-2
  social 2, 41, 54, 71, 128, 306
Immigration 8, 10-1, 14, 38-9, 45, 48, 93-4, 146, 152, 164, 174, 190, 224-5, 266-7, 270-2, 291-2
In-group 43-5, 54, 58, 306
India 154, 242, 283-4, 286, 296
Individual-state link 302
Integration 11, 33-4, 39, 51, 69-72, 94, 113-4, 133-4, 241-2, 244, 246-9, 256-60, 267-71, 273-4, 276-7, 289-97
  requirements 133, 290-1, 309
International Court of Justice 13, 17

International covenant on civil and political rights 5
International Law Commission 5, 15-6, 22, 233
Iordachi 147, 149, 174
Ireland 8, 30, 79, 100, 117, 141, 150, 154, 201-2, 240
Isensee 258-9
Islam 31-2, 71
Israel 24, 31, 54, 154, 172-4, 179, 270, 283, 286, 293, 316
Italy 23, 78, 104, 115, 118, 142, 149-50, 152-5, 159, 173-4, 205, 219, 223, 232, 282, 287

J

Jacobs 35, 99, 100, 117, 235
Jus
  domicilii 11
  sanguinis 9, 10, 12-3, 152, 213, 217, 219, 229-30, 237, 241, 243, 245-6, 250-1, 262
  soli 9, 10, 12, 213, 217, 219, 228-30, 250, 259, 264-5

K

Kin-minority 138, 147, 167-8, 170, 176-7, 196, 207-9, 285, 303, 308
Kin-states 59, 137-8, 140, 142, 144, 146-9, 153-5, 159, 167-8, 170-1, 178, 182-3, 190-1, 193-5, 199, 202
Kinship 46, 113, 139-40, 148, 152, 161-2, 180, 198, 230
Kis 165, 195, 205
Koopmans and Statham 12, 37-8
Kostakopoulou 98, 297-8
Kymlicka 26, 29, 30, 137, 183, 190, 194, 203-6

L

Lagarde 11, 230, 232
Latvia 25, 59, 145, 151, 154, 225, 239, 241
Legal
  personality 6, 311
  status 3, 5, 19, 25-6, 29, 39, 46, 54, 223-4, 228-9, 258-9, 272-7, 295-6, 298-9, 309-12, 315-6

Index

Links 3, 4, 6, 7, 21-2, 32-3, 99, 100, 139-40, 145-6, 148, 179, 185-6, 199-203, 224, 229-31, 272, 280-3, 289
Long-distance nationalism 36, 285

M

Maastricht Treaty 68-9, 73-5, 78, 90, 107-8, 196, 205
Marshall 27-8, 87, 228
Mayer and Palmowski 67, 116, 126
Membership 2, 27-33, 35-7, 41-2, 46, 94, 118, 184, 196-7, 199, 224-5, 268-9, 285-6, 292-9, 301-10, 312-4
Mexico 4, 5, 154, 172, 222, 242, 276, 283-8, 293, 308
Migrants 38-9, 54, 93, 137, 172, 202-3, 214, 224, 269-75, 279-80, 282-4, 286, 294, 299, 307, 310
Migration 10, 12, 35, 54, 93-4, 200, 203, 213, 237-8, 242, 245-6, 256, 268-9, 272, 288, 292
Minorities 50-1, 53, 59-65, 118-9, 122, 137-8, 146-8, 157-9, 161-6, 169-71, 176-8, 180-3, 187-90, 193-5, 199, 204-6
  cultural 51, 63, 65, 119
  ethnic 40, 63-4, 119, 163, 177, 280
  immigrant 30, 183
Minority protection 60, 63, 78, 118-9, 156, 159, 179-80, 183, 190-1, 197, 304, 315
Moldova 13, 62, 149, 174-5, 240
Multiculturalism 49, 51, 53, 203, 269
Multiple membership 214, 254, 303

N

Nathans 243-4
Nation 3, 5, 7, 8, 28-9, 36, 46-9, 52-3, 62, 127, 139, 142-8, 155, 197-202, 255, 285, 292
  ethnic 2, 46-8, 139, 194, 198
Nation-state 28-9, 33-4, 36, 40, 49, 50, 52, 54, 72, 97-8, 122, 128, 130, 132, 203, 275, 301
National
  citizenship 2, 11, 27, 33, 37, 57, 92, 106, 134-5, 290, 295, 299, 302, 305
  community 11-2, 30, 35, 44, 49, 53, 103, 113, 134, 203, 206, 274, 279, 286, 288, 290
  cultural heritage 139, 186
  elections 4, 30, 44, 194, 260, 282, 287

  identities 29, 30, 33-4, 37-8, 46, 48, 50-1, 69, 70, 81-2, 94-5, 130-3, 143, 159-60, 202-3, 254, 274-5, 296
  common 28, 305
  context of 29, 46, 70, 306
  maintenance of 29, 191, 201, 299
identity
  politics 76, 97
  projects 66, 74
minorities 45, 51, 54, 59, 63-5, 118-9, 137-8, 140, 145, 147, 156, 167-70, 187-8, 190, 202, 281
  members of 59
minority 59, 63-5, 118, 140, 143, 147
security 61-2, 98, 225
National-citizen 27, 55
Nationalism 29, 36, 44, 46, 48-9, 144-6, 162, 174, 197, 202
  cultural 48-9, 162, 170, 206
Nationalité 6, 12, 17, 28, 38, 213, 218, 220, 228-31, 233, 237, 243, 290
Nationality 2-20, 22-8, 31-4, 91-5, 196-7, 213-40, 242-6, 248-51, 257-62, 267-75, 277-81, 283-5, 288-92, 295-300, 302-9, 312-6
Naturalization 11, 115, 174-5, 196, 213, 218-22, 224, 228-9, 231, 239-41, 243-5, 247-54, 264-74, 276, 278-81, 297-8
Netherlands 14-6, 23, 51, 59, 67, 125, 219, 225-7, 230, 241, 273, 288, 290-1
Non-discrimination 17-8, 32, 82, 95, 98, 100, 123, 178, 217
Nottebohm decision 221

O

Oppenheim's International Law 5, 7, 15

P

Permanent residence 5, 20, 33, 102, 105-6, 207, 224, 248, 258, 295-6
Personal identity 33, 35, 40, 44, 117, 312
Philippines 154, 223, 229, 283, 286-7
Plural nationality 11-3, 174-5, 192, 196-7, 213-5, 217-21, 231-3, 235-43, 245-7, 249-55, 257-63, 267-9, 271-5, 285-91, 308-9, 313-4
Poland 63-4, 109, 111, 139, 141-3, 148, 150, 154, 174, 241, 293

Polish courts 64, 111
Portugal 5, 109, 139, 141-2, 149-50, 152, 154, 158, 222-3, 240-1, 287
Post-national citizenship 2, 22, 35
Preuß 124, 127
Prototype 44-5, 53-4, 92, 132
Prototypicality gradients 45, 131, 279

R

Reduction of Cases of Multiple Nationality 13, 17, 216, 218
Remittances 154, 280, 285-7
Rights 4-8, 18-9, 25-6, 28-33, 36-40, 55-9, 64, 90-2, 98, 113, 115-6, 129, 188-90, 195-8, 294-9, 312-4
Romania 13, 138-41, 143-5, 147-9, 156-7, 159, 162, 166-8, 174-5, 178, 183-4, 187-9, 194, 197, 208-10, 222
Russia 140, 142, 148, 223, 241, 285-6

S

Schöpflin 34, 199, 204
Self-identification 144, 161-3, 177, 180, 186
Shore 92, 125, 129, 133
Slovakia 53, 141, 145-6, 148, 155-7, 162, 166, 168, 170, 174, 179, 187-8, 194, 197, 208-9, 241
Slovenia 25-6, 140-2, 148-9, 154-6, 159, 166, 169, 188, 199, 209, 241, 303
Social identity 41-3, 54, 263
  theory 2, 41, 54, 71, 128, 306
Sovereignty 14-5, 28, 74, 97-8, 112, 143, 171-2, 175, 178, 188, 196-7, 200, 215, 222, 232, 242
Soysal 30, 35-7, 125
Spain 48, 90, 95-6, 140, 142, 151, 158, 223, 229, 234, 238, 240-1, 282, 303, 308, 316
Spiro 260, 287, 289, 295
State succession 13, 15-6, 18, 220
Stateless person 19, 20, 24, 217
Statelessness 12, 17-9, 217-8, 230
Status laws 54, 138-9, 155, 157-9, 163-6, 168-9, 174, 177, 179-80, 182, 189-98, 201-4, 206, 208-9, 284, 295-6
Statusdeutsche 152, 214, 250, 261-4, 267, 277, 310
Stets and Burke 41-2
Stewart 14, 159, 167, 192

Stråth 71, 123
Supremacy 238
Sweden 30, 150, 222, 241-2, 273-4

T

Tajfel 42
Third-country nationals 29, 91-2, 94-6, 98, 106, 115, 133, 264, 294, 311
Tirol 173-4
Tishkov 46, 293
Torpey 24-5
Trans-nationalism 146
Trans-sovereign nationalism 138, 145-6
Trans-state right 135
Transnational ties 280
Turkey 16, 32, 48, 59, 62, 97, 141-2, 150-1, 154, 171, 227, 240-1, 245, 281, 283, 288

U

Ukraine 139, 141-2, 148, 156-8, 166, 174, 176, 188, 209, 239, 242
UNESCO 87
United Kingdom 4, 22, 60, 96, 183, 215, 225-7, 239, 241, 290-1
United Nations 23, 156
United States 3-5, 8-10, 12, 14-5, 19, 23-4, 29, 30, 46-8, 51, 172, 216-7, 222, 228, 273-4, 284-5, 293
Universal Declaration of Human Rights 5, 56

V

Venice Commission 138-9, 167-8, 179, 187, 189, 202
  report 183
Verwilghen 6, 13, 20, 23, 215, 217-8, 225, 233, 240
Vienna Convention 169, 175
  on
    Consular Relations 21, 176
    Diplomatic Relations 21
Voting rights 3, 30, 33, 150, 245, 282-3, 286-7

W

Weiler 122, 124, 129
Weis 5, 8, 15, 17-9, 21, 24

EUROPEAN MONOGRAPHS

1. Lammy Betten (ed.), *The Future of European Social Policy* (second and revised edition, 1991). ISBN/ISSN 9065445854, ISBN 13: 9789065445858
2. J.M.E. Loman, K.J.M. Mortelmans, H.H.G. Post, J.S. Watson, *Culture and Community Law: Before and after Maastricht* (1992). ISBN/ISSN 9065446389, ISBN 13: 9789065446381
3. Prof. Dr. J.A.E. Vervaele, *Fraud Against the Community: The Need for European Fraud Legislation* (1992). ISBN/ISSN 9065446346, ISBN 13: 9789065446343
4. P. Rawortli, *The Legislative Process in the European Community* (1993). ISBN/ISSN 9065446907, ISBN 13: 9789065446909
5. J. Stuyck, *Financial and Monetary Integration in the European Economic Community* (1993). ISBN 9065447180
6. J.H.V. Stuyck, A.J. Vossestein (eds.), *State Entrepreneurship, National Monopolies and European Community Law* (1993). ISBN/ISSN 9065447733, ISBN 13: 9789065447739
7. J. Stuyck, A. Looijestijn-Clearie (eds.), *The European Area EC-EFTA* (1994). ISBN 9065448152
8. R.B. Bouterse, *Competition and Integration – What Goals Count?* (1994). ISBN/ISSN 9065448160, ISBN 13: 9789065448163
9. R. Barents, *The Agricultural Law of the EC* (1994). ISBN/ISSN 9065448675, ISBN 13: 9789065448675
10. Nicholas Emiliou, *The Principle of Proportionality in European Law: A Comparative Study* (1996). ISBN/ISSN 9041108661, ISBN 13: 9789041108661
11. Eivind Smith, *National Parliaments as Cornerstones of European Integration* (1996). ISBN/ISSN 904110898X, ISBN 13: 9789041108982
12. Jan H. Jans, *European Environmental Law* (1996). ISBN/ISSN 9041108777, ISBN 13: 9789041108777
13. Siofra O'Leary, *The Evolving Concept of Community Citizenship: From the Free Movement of Persons to Union Citizenship* (1996). ISBN/ISSN 9041108785, ISBN 13: 9789041108784
14. Laurence Gormley (ed.), *Current and Future Perspectives on EC Competition Law* (1997). ISBN/ISSN 904110691X, ISBN 13: 9789041106919
15. Simone White, *Protection of the Financial Interests of the European Communities: The Fight against Fraud and Corruption* (1998). ISBN/ISSN 9041196471, ISBN 13: 9789041196477
16. Morten P. Broberg, *The European Commission's Jurisdiction to Scrutinise Mergers,* Third Edition (2006). ISBN/ISSN 9041124748, ISBN 13: 9789041124746
17. Doris Hildebrand, *The Role of Economic Analysis in the EC Competition Rules: The European School,* Second Edition (2002). ISBN/ISSN 9041117067, ISBN 13: 9789041117069

KLUWER LAW INTERNATIONAL

EUROPEAN MONOGRAPHS

18. Christof R.A. Swaak, *European Community Law and the Automobile Industry* (1999). ISBN/ISSN 9041111409, ISBN 13: 9789041111401
19. Dorthe Dahlgaard Dingel, *Public Procurement. A Harmonization of the National Judicial Review of the Application of European Community Law*(1999). ISBN/ISSN 9041111611, ISBN 13: 9789041111616
20. J.A.E. Vervaele (ed.), *Compliance and Enforcement of European Community Law* (1999). ISBN/ISSN 9041111514, ISBN 13: 9789041111517
21. Martin Trybus, *European Defence Procurement Law: International and National Procurement Systems as Models for a Liberalised Defence Procurement Market in Europe* (1999). ISBN/ISSN 9041111670, ISBN 13: 9789041111678
22. Helen Staples, *The Legal Status of Third Country Nationals Resident in the European Union* (1999). ISBN/ISSN 9041112774, ISBN 13: 9789041112774
23. Damien Geradin (ed.), *The Liberalization of State Monopolies in the European Union and Beyond* (2000). ISBN/ISSN 9041112642, ISBN 13: 9789041112644
24. Katja Heede, *European Ombudsman: Redress and Control at Union Level* (2000). ISBN/ISSN 9041114130, ISBN 13: 9789041114136
25. Ulf Bernitz, Joakim Nergelius (eds.), *General Principles of European Community Law* (2000). ISBN/ISSN 9041114025, ISBN 13: 9789041114020
26. Michaela Drahos, *Convergence of Competition Laws and Policies in the European Community* (2001). ISBN/ISSN 9041115625, ISBN 13: 9789041115621
27. Damien Geradin (ed.), *The Liberalization of Electricity and Natural Gas in the European Union* (2001). ISBN/ISSN 9041115609, ISBN 13: 9789041115607
28. Gisella Gori, *Towards an EU Right to Education* (2001). ISBN/ISSN 9041116702, ISBN 13: 9789041116703
29. Brendan Smith, *Constitution Building in the European Union* (2001). ISBN/ISSN 9041116958, ISBN 13: 9789041116956
30. Freidl Weiss and Frank Wooldridge, *Free Movement of Persons within the European Community* (2002). ISBN/ISSN 9041125450, ISBN 13: 9789041125453
31. Ingrid Boccardi, *Europe and Refugees: Towards an EU Asylum Policy* (2002). ISBN/ISSN 9041117091, ISBN 13: 9789041117090
32. John A.E. Vervaele, André Klip (eds.), *European Cooperation Between Tax, Customs and Judicial Authorities* (2001). ISBN/ISSN 9041117474, ISBN 13: 9789041117472
33. Wouter P.J. Wils, *The Optimal Enforcement of EC Antitrust Law: Essays in Law and Economics* (2002). ISBN/ISSN 9041117571, ISBN 13: 9789041117571
34. Damien Geradin (ed.), *The Liberalization of Postal Services in the European Union* (2002). ISBN/ISSN 9041117806, ISBN 13: 9789041117809

EUROPEAN MONOGRAPHS

35. Nick Bernard, *Multilevel Governance in the European Union* (2002). ISBN/ISSN 9041118128, ISBN 13: 9789041118127
36. Jill Wakefield, *Judicial Protection through the Use of Article 288(2) EC* (2002). ISBN/ISSN 9041118233, ISBN 13: 9789041118233
37. Sebastiaan Princen, *EU Regulation and Transatlantic Trade* (2002). ISBN/ISSN 9041118713, ISBN 13: 9789041118714
38. Amaryllis Verhoeven, *The European Union in Search of a Democratic and Constitutional Theory* (2002). ISBN 9041118721
39. Paul Torremans, *Cross Border Insolvencies in EU English and Belgian Law* (2002). ISBN/ISSN 9041118888, ISBN 13: 9789041118882
40. Malcolm Anderson, Joanna Apap (eds.), *Police and Justice Co-operation and the New European Borders* (2002). ISBN/ISSN 9041118934, ISBN 13: 9789041118936
41. Christine M. Forstinger, *Takeover Law in the EU and the USA: A Comparative Analysis* (2002). ISBN/ISSN 9041119191, ISBN 13: 9789041119193
42. Antonio Bavasso, *Communications in EU Antitrust Law: Market Power and Public Interest* (2003). ISBN/ISSN 9041119744, ISBN 13: 9789041119742
43. Fiona Wishlade, *Regional State Aid and Competition Policy* (2003). ISBN/ISSN 9041119752, ISBN 13: 9789041119759
44. Gareth Davies, *Nationality Discrimination in the European Internal Market* (2003). ISBN/ISSN 9041119981, ISBN 13: 9789041119988
45. René Barents, *The Autonomy of Community Law* (2004). ISBN/ISSN 9041122516, ISBN 13: 9789041122513
46. Gerhard Dannecker, Oswald Jansen (eds.), *Competition Law Sanctioning in the European Union. The EU-Law Influence on the National System of Sanctions in the European Area* (2004). ISBN/ISSN 9041121005, ISBN 13: 9789041121004
47. NautaDutilh (ed.), *Dealing with Dominance. The Experience of National Competition Authorities* (2004). ISBN/ISSN 9041122117, ISBN 13: 9789041122117
48. Stefaan Van den Bogaert, *Practical Regulation of the Mobility of Sportsmen in the EU Post Bosman* (2005). ISBN/ISSN 904112327X, ISBN 13: 9789041123275
49. Katalin Judit Cseres, *Competition Law and Consumer Protection* (2005). ISBN/ISSN 9041123806, ISBN 13: 9789041123800
50. Philipp Kiiver, *The National Parliament, in the European Union* (2006). ISBN/ISSN 9041124527, ISBN 13: 9789041124524
51. Alexander Heinrich Türk, *The Concept of Legislation in European Community Law: A Comparative Perspective* (2006). ISBN/ISSN 9041124721, ISBN 13: 9789041124722

KLUWER LAW INTERNATIONAL

EUROPEAN MONOGRAPHS

52. Dimitrios Sinaniotis, *The Interim Protection of Individuals before the European and National Courts* (2006). ISBN/ISSN 9041124985, ISBN 13: 9789041124982
53. Michael Holoubek, Dragana Damjanovic, Matthias Traimer (eds.), *Regulating Content – European Regulatory Framework for the Media and Related Creative Sectors* (2007). ISBN/ISSN 9041125973, ISBN 13: 9789041125972
54. Anneli Albi and Jacques Ziller (eds.), *The European Constitution and National Constitutions: Ratification and Beyond* (2007). ISBN/ISSN 9041125248, ISBN 13: 9789041125248
55. Gustavo E. Luengo Hernández de Madrid, *Regulation of Subsidies and State Aids in WTO and EC Law* (2007). ISBN/ISSN 9041125477, ISBN 13: 9789041125477
56. Enikő Horváth, Mandating Identity: *Citizenship, Kinship Laws and Plural Nationality in the European Union* 2007, ISBN/ISSN 9041126627, ISBN 13: 9789041126627

KLUWER LAW INTERNATIONAL